SUPERGIRL

VOLUME 2 BREAKING THE CHAIN

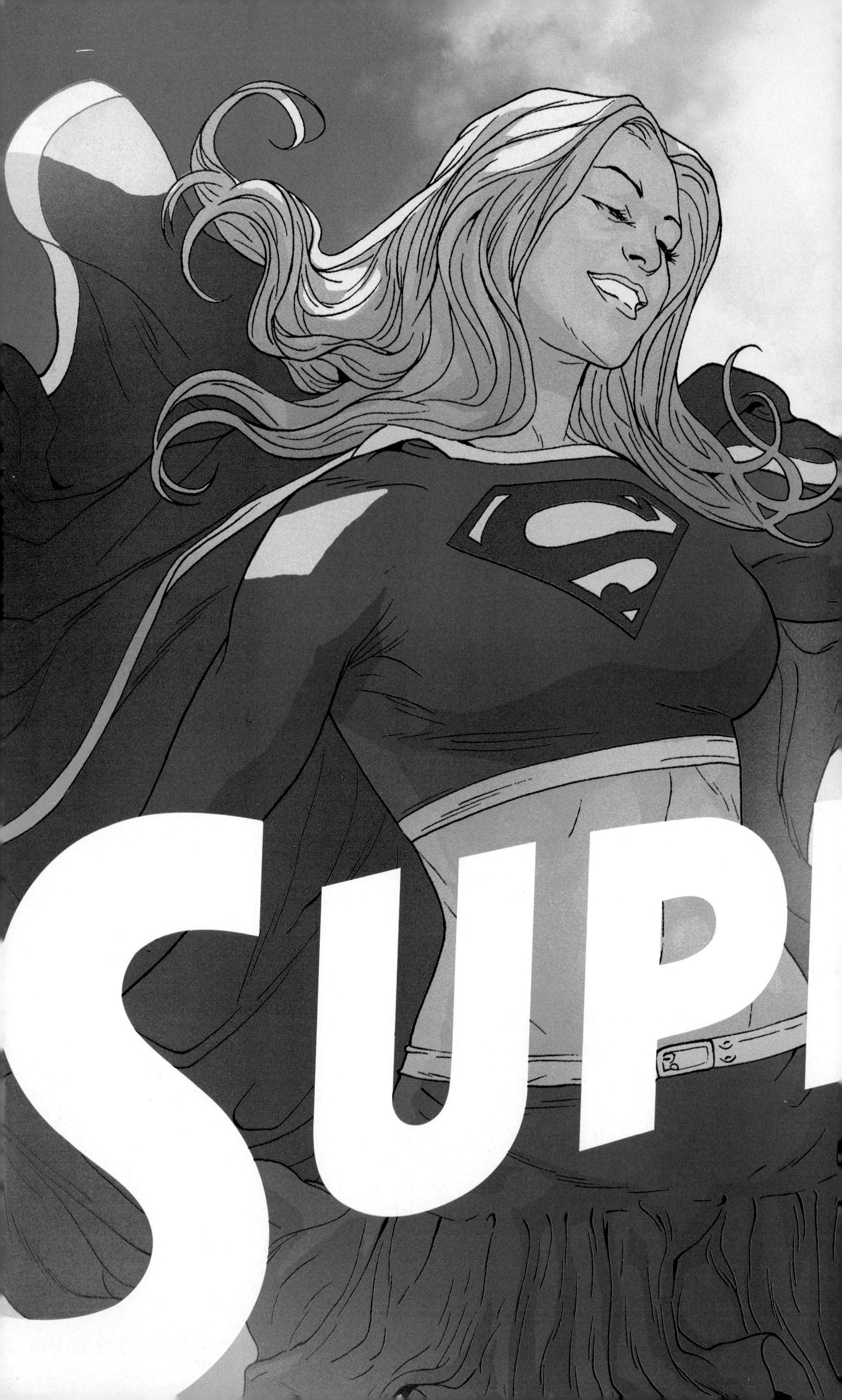
SUP

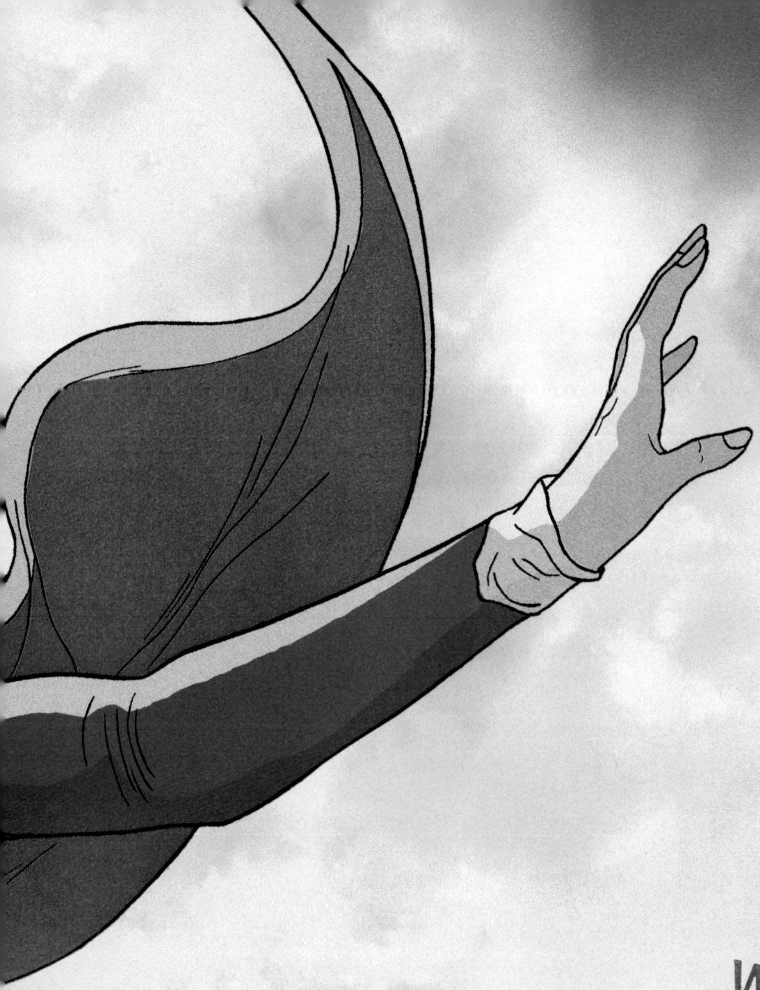

ERGIRL

VOLUME 2 BREAKING THE CHAIN

SUPERGIRL BASED ON CHARACTERS CREATED BY JERRY SIEGEL AND JOE SHUSTER
SUPERMAN CREATED BY JERRY SIEGEL AND JOE SHUSTER
SUPERBOY CREATED BY JERRY SIEGEL
By special arrangement with the Jerry Siegel family
NIGHTWING CREATED BY MARV WOLFMAN AND GEORGE PÉREZ
BATMAN CREATED BY BOB KANE WITH BILL FINGER

Collection cover by Alé Garza,
Richard Friend and Rod Reis

Eddie Berganza
Matt Idelson Editors – Original Series
Nachie Castro
Jeanine Schaefer Associate Editors – Original Series
Adam Schlagman Assistant Editor – Original Series
Jeb Woodard Group Editor – Collected Editions
Liz Erickson Editor – Collected Edition
Steve Cook Design Director – Books
Lori Jackson Publication Design

Bob Harras Senior VP – Editor-In-Chief, DC Comics

Diane Nelson President
Dan Didio and Jim Lee Co-Publishers
Geoff Johns Chief Creative Officer
Amit Desai Senior VP – Marketing & Global Franchise Management
Nairi Gardiner Senior VP – Finance
Sam Ades VP – Digital Marketing
Bobbie Chase VP – Talent Development
Mark Chiarello Senior VP – Art, Design & Collected Editions
John Cunningham VP – Content Strategy
Anne Depies VP – Strategy Planning & Reporting
Don Falletti VP – Manufacturing Operations
Lawrence Ganem VP – Editorial Administration & Talent Relations
Alison Gill Senior VP – Manufacturing & Operations
Hank Kanalz Senior VP – Editorial Strategy & Administration
Jay Kogan VP – Legal Affairs
Derek Maddalena Senior VP – Sales & Business Development
Jack Mahan VP – Business Affairs
Dan Miron VP – Sales Planning & Trade Development
Nick Napolitano VP – Manufacturing Administration
Carol Roeder VP – Marketing
Eddie Scannell VP – Mass Account & Digital Sales
Courtney Simmons Senior VP – Publicity & Communications
Jim (Ski) Sokolowski VP – Comic Book Specialty & Newsstand Sales
Sandy Yi Senior VP – Global Franchise Management

SUPERGIRL VOLUME 2: BREAKING THE CHAIN

DC Comics, 2900 West Alameda Ave., Burbank, CA 91505
Printed by RR Donnelley, Owensville, MO, USA. 7/8/16. First Printing.
ISBN: 978-1-4012-6467-3

Library of Congress Cataloging-in-Publication Data is available.

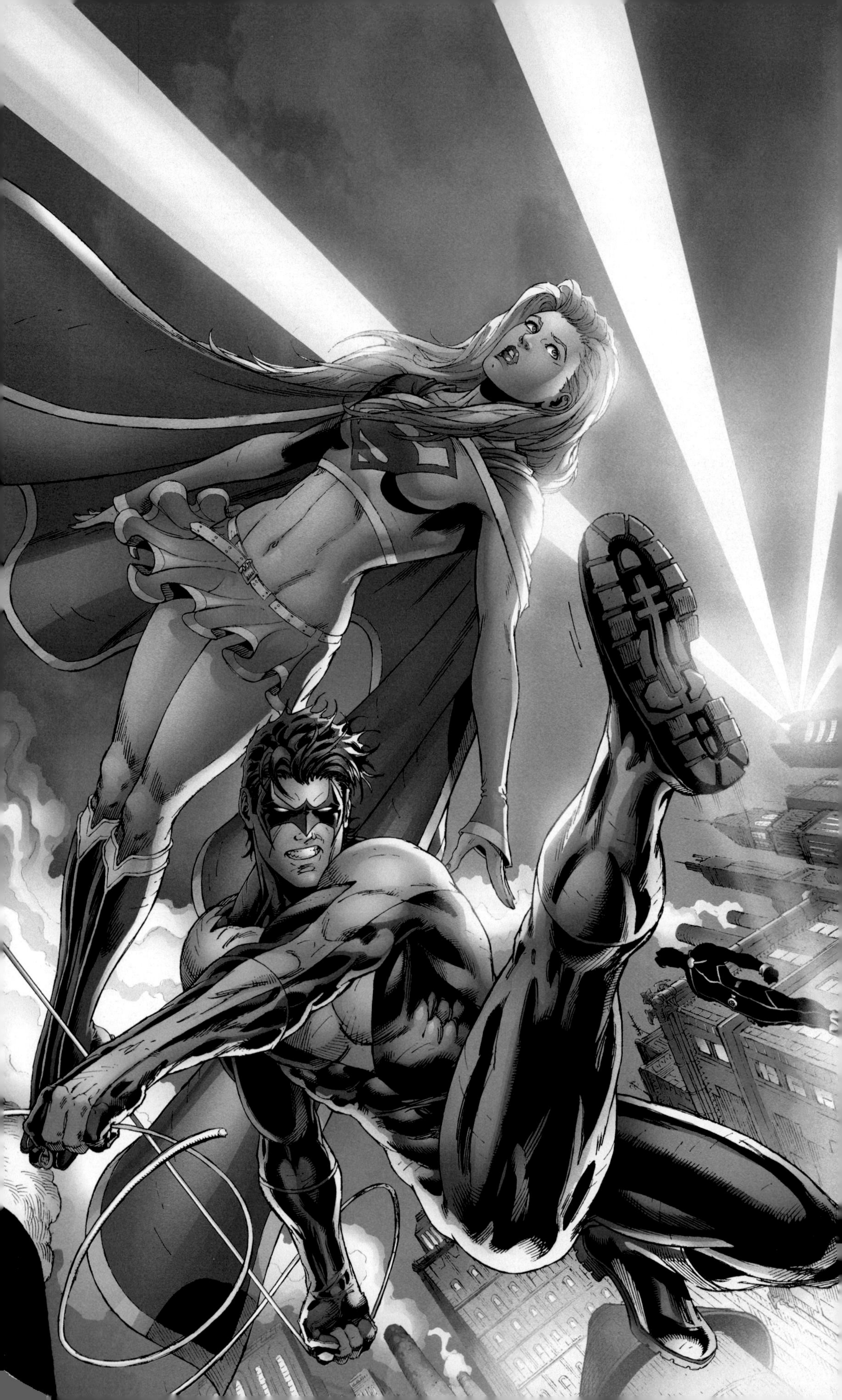

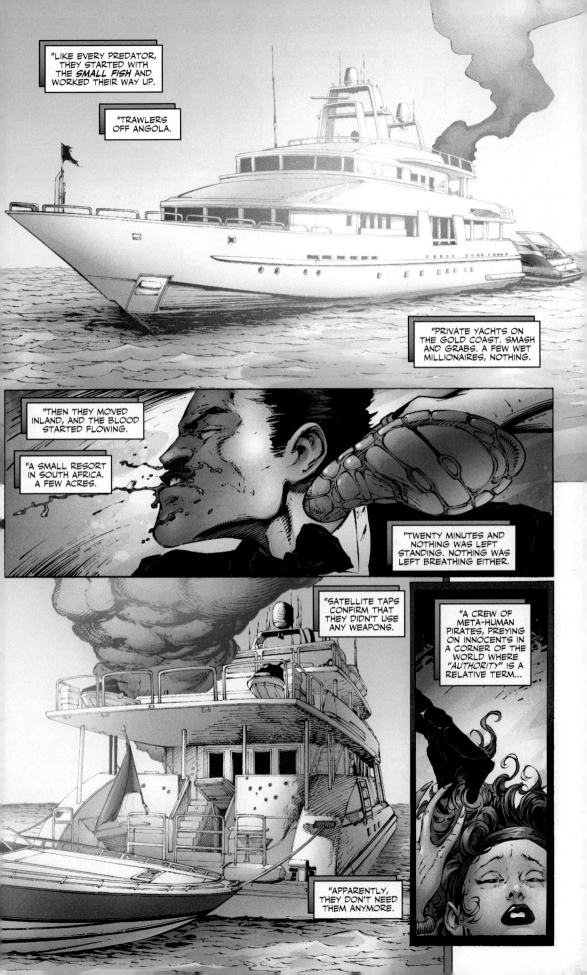

"LIKE EVERY PREDATOR, THEY STARTED WITH THE *SMALL FISH* AND WORKED THEIR WAY UP.

"TRAWLERS OFF ANGOLA.

"PRIVATE YACHTS ON THE GOLD COAST. SMASH AND GRABS. A FEW WET MILLIONAIRES, NOTHING.

"THEN THEY MOVED INLAND, AND THE BLOOD STARTED FLOWING.

"A SMALL RESORT IN SOUTH AFRICA. A FEW ACRES.

"TWENTY MINUTES AND NOTHING WAS LEFT STANDING. NOTHING WAS LEFT BREATHING EITHER.

"SATELLITE TAPS CONFIRM THAT THEY DIDN'T USE ANY WEAPONS.

"A CREW OF META-HUMAN PIRATES, PREYING ON INNOCENTS IN A CORNER OF THE WORLD WHERE "AUTHORITY" IS A RELATIVE TERM...

"APPARENTLY, THEY DON'T NEED THEM ANYMORE.

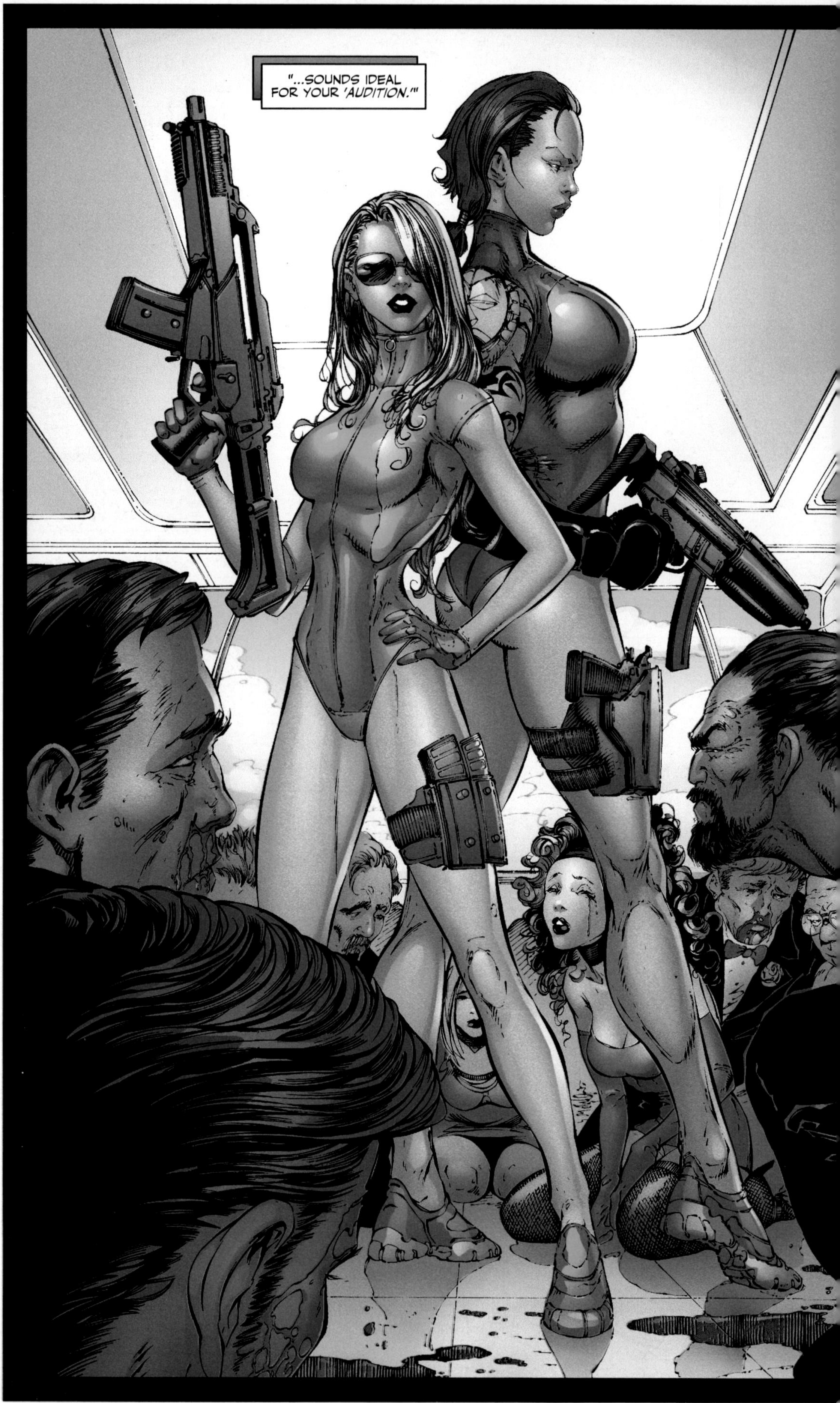
"...SOUNDS IDEAL FOR YOUR 'AUDITION.'"

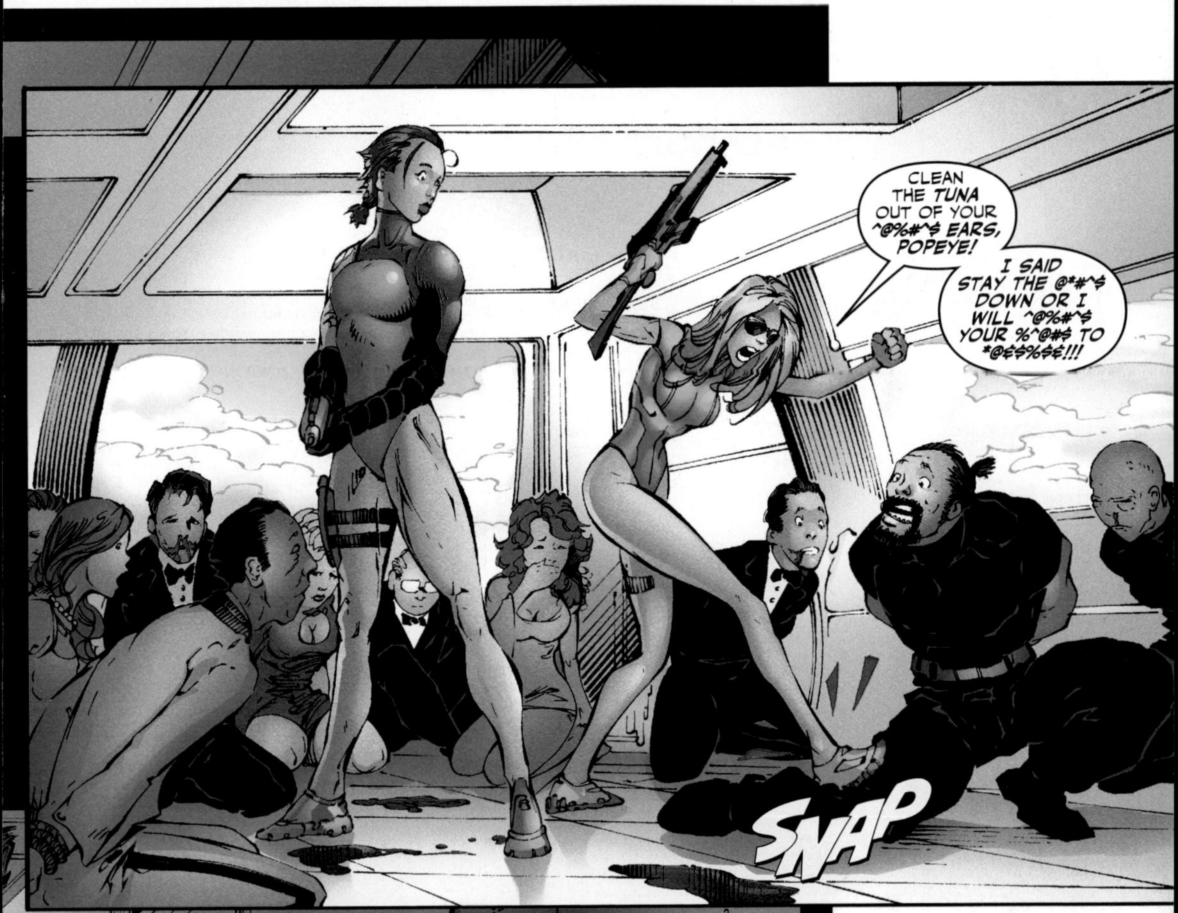
CLEAN THE TUNA OUT OF YOUR ^@%#^$ EARS, POPEYE!
I SAID STAY THE @*#^$ DOWN OR I WILL ^@%#^$ YOUR %^@#$ TO *@€$%$€!!!
SNAP

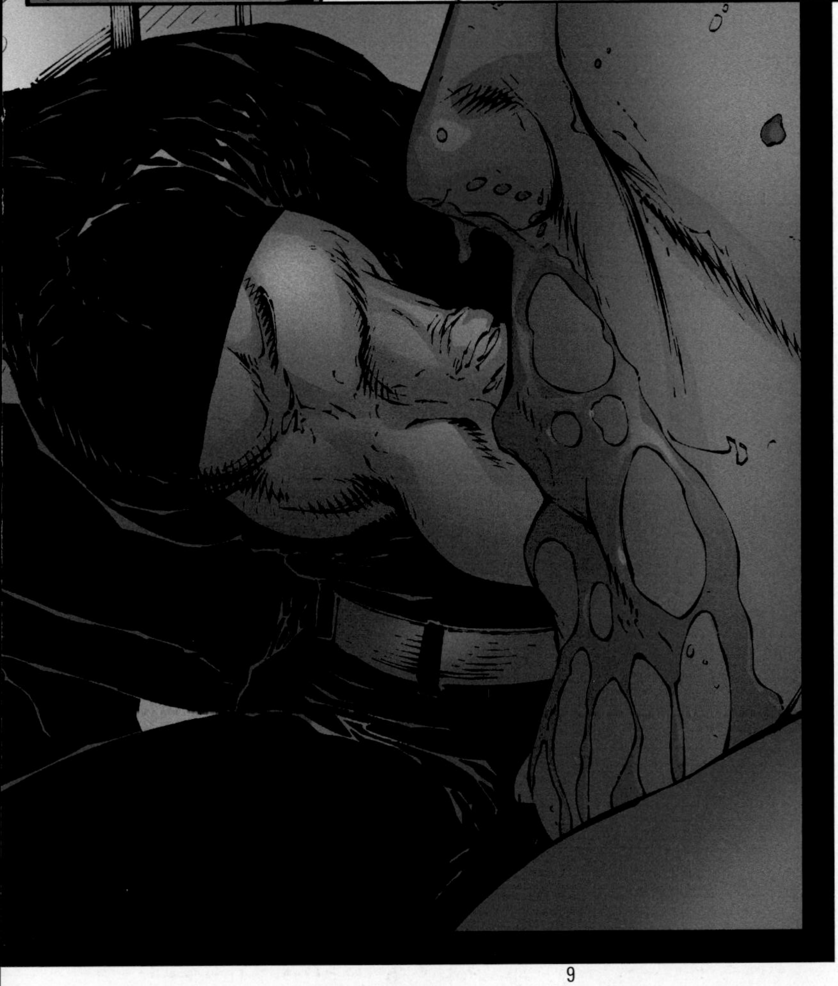

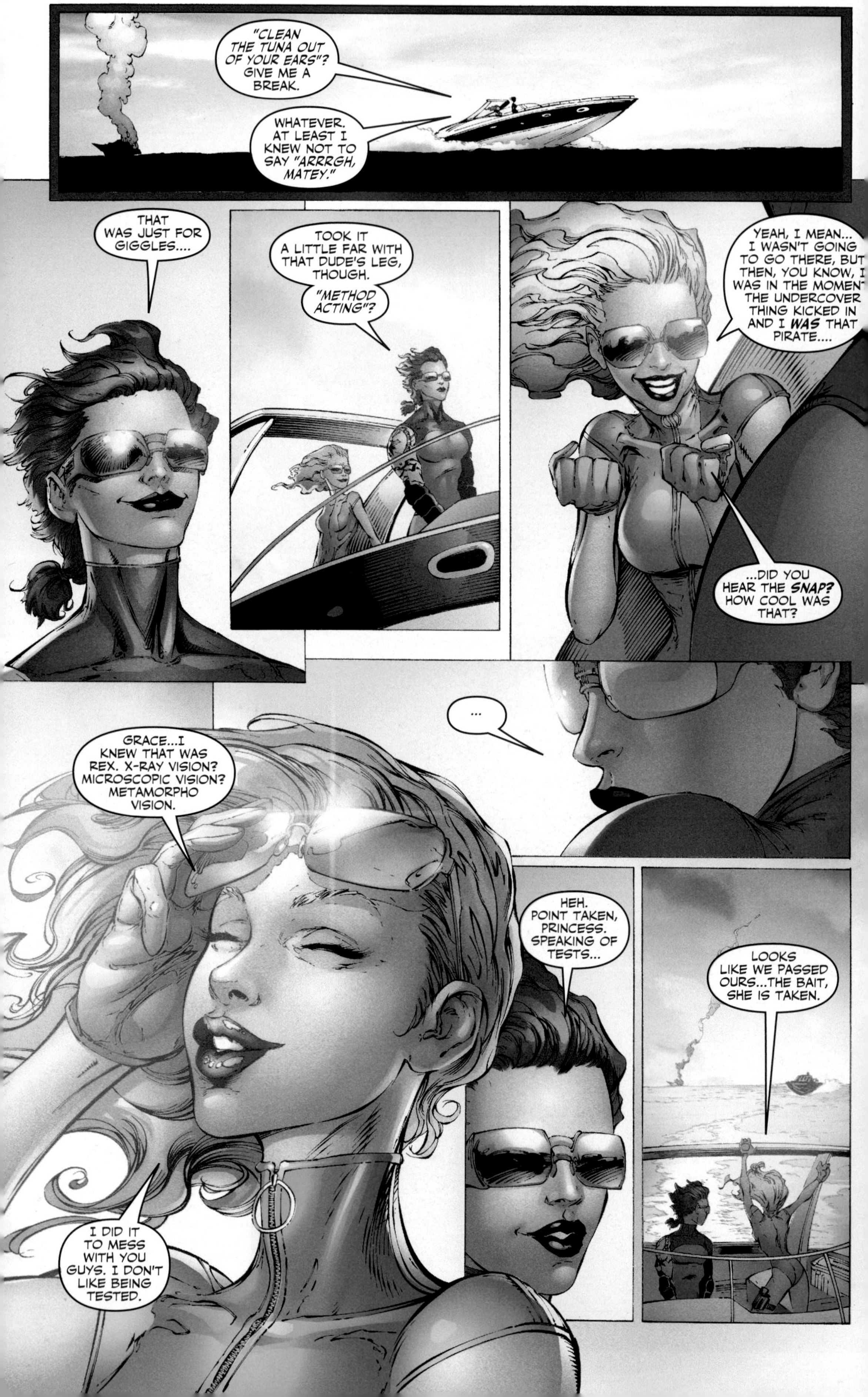
"CLEAN THE TUNA OUT OF YOUR EARS"? GIVE ME A BREAK.
WHATEVER. AT LEAST I KNEW NOT TO SAY "ARRRGH, MATEY."
THAT WAS JUST FOR GIGGLES....
TOOK IT A LITTLE FAR WITH THAT DUDE'S LEG, THOUGH.
"METHOD ACTING"?
YEAH, I MEAN... I WASN'T GOING TO GO THERE, BUT THEN, YOU KNOW, I WAS IN THE MOMENT THE UNDERCOVER THING KICKED IN AND I WAS THAT PIRATE....
...DID YOU HEAR THE SNAP? HOW COOL WAS THAT?
...
GRACE...I KNEW THAT WAS REX. X-RAY VISION? MICROSCOPIC VISION? METAMORPHO VISION.
I DID IT TO MESS WITH YOU GUYS. I DON'T LIKE BEING TESTED.
HEH. POINT TAKEN, PRINCESS. SPEAKING OF TESTS...
LOOKS LIKE WE PASSED OURS...THE BAIT, SHE IS TAKEN.

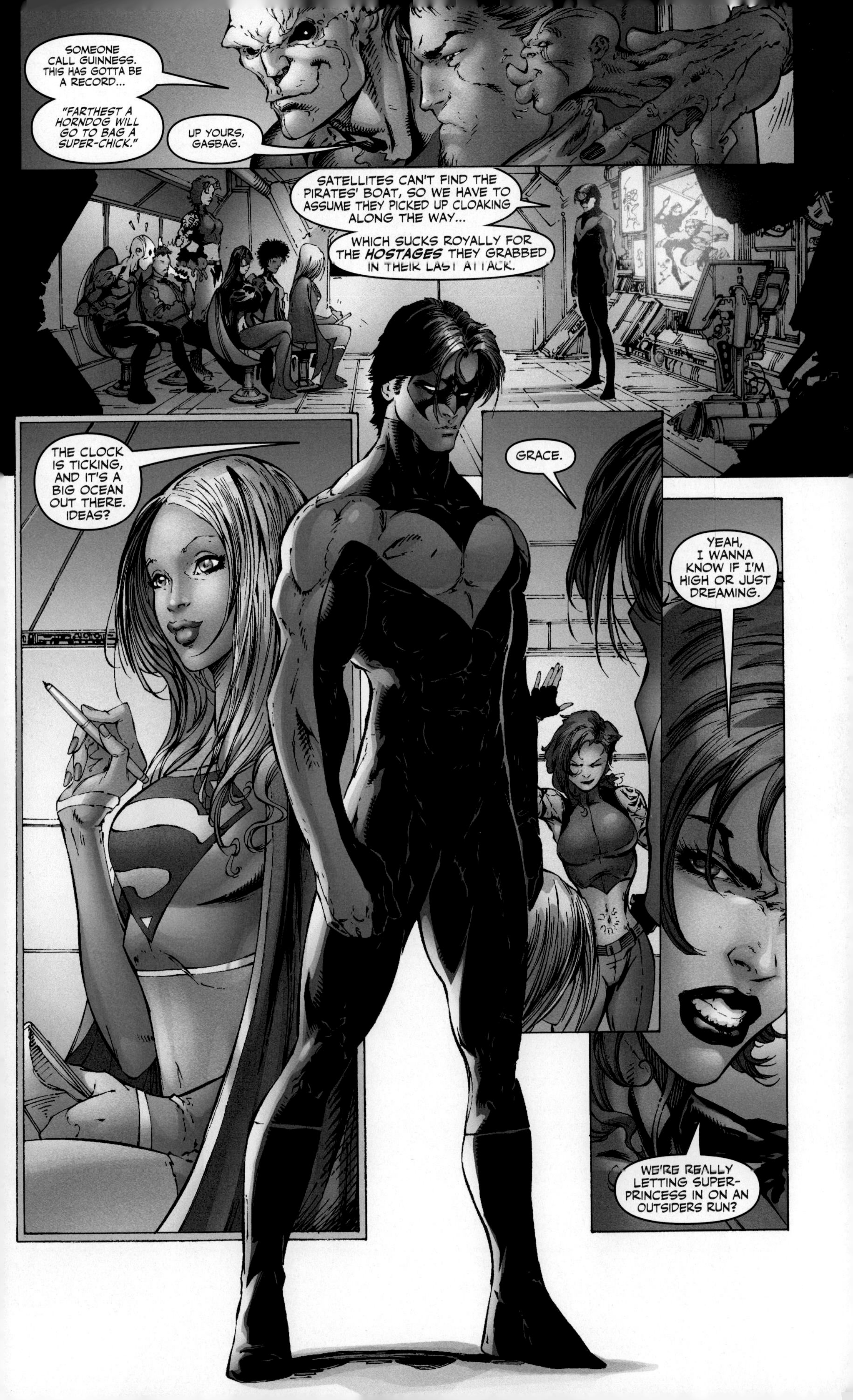
SOMEONE CALL GUINNESS. THIS HAS GOTTA BE A RECORD...
"FARTHEST A HORNDOG WILL GO TO BAG A SUPER-CHICK."
UP YOURS, GASBAG.
SATELLITES CAN'T FIND THE PIRATES' BOAT, SO WE HAVE TO ASSUME THEY PICKED UP CLOAKING ALONG THE WAY...
WHICH SUCKS ROYALLY FOR THE HOSTAGES THEY GRABBED IN THEIR LAST ATTACK.
THE CLOCK IS TICKING, AND IT'S A BIG OCEAN OUT THERE. IDEAS?
GRACE.
YEAH, I WANNA KNOW IF I'M HIGH OR JUST DREAMING.
WE'RE REALLY LETTING SUPER-PRINCESS IN ON AN OUTSIDERS RUN?

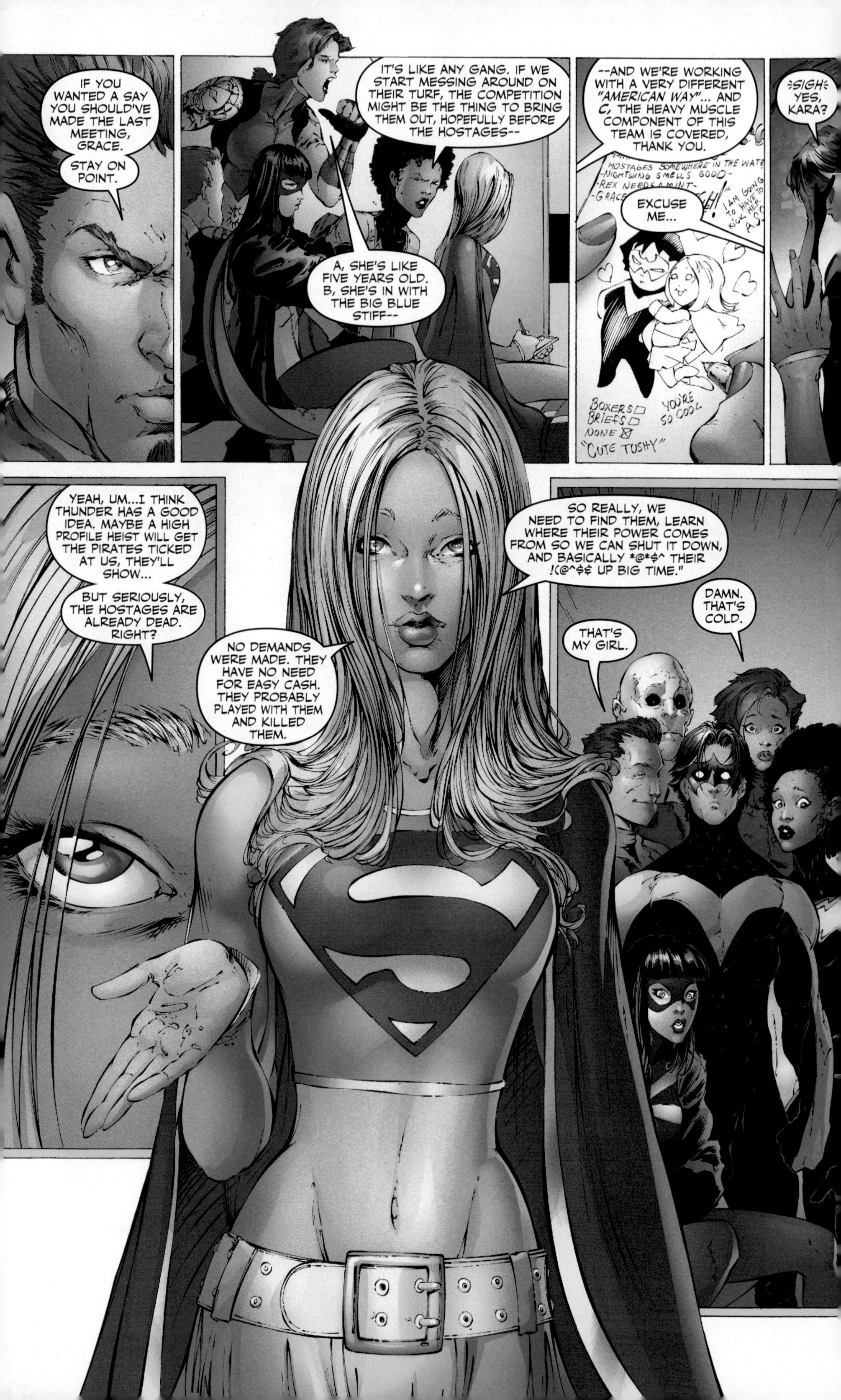
IF YOU WANTED A SAY YOU SHOULD'VE MADE THE LAST MEETING, GRACE.
STAY ON POINT.
IT'S LIKE ANY GANG. IF WE START MESSING AROUND ON THEIR TURF, THE COMPETITION MIGHT BE THE THING TO BRING THEM OUT, HOPEFULLY BEFORE THE HOSTAGES--
A, SHE'S LIKE FIVE YEARS OLD. B, SHE'S IN WITH THE BIG BLUE STIFF--
--AND WE'RE WORKING WITH A VERY DIFFERENT "AMERICAN WAY"... AND C, THE HEAVY MUSCLE COMPONENT OF THIS TEAM IS COVERED, THANK YOU.
HOSTAGES SOMEWHERE IN THE WATE
-NIGHTWING SMELLS GOOD-
-REX NEEDS A MINT-
EXCUSE ME...
I AM GOING TO HAVE TO KICK HER
BOXERS ☐
BRIEFS ☐
NONE ☒
"CUTE TUSHY"
YOU'RE SO COOL
SIGH YES, KARA?
YEAH, UM...I THINK THUNDER HAS A GOOD IDEA. MAYBE A HIGH PROFILE HEIST WILL GET THE PIRATES TICKED AT US, THEY'LL SHOW...
BUT SERIOUSLY, THE HOSTAGES ARE ALREADY DEAD. RIGHT?
NO DEMANDS WERE MADE. THEY HAVE NO NEED FOR EASY CASH. THEY PROBABLY PLAYED WITH THEM AND KILLED THEM.
SO REALLY, WE NEED TO FIND THEM, LEARN WHERE THEIR POWER COMES FROM SO WE CAN SHUT IT DOWN, AND BASICALLY *@*$^ THEIR !(@^$$ UP BIG TIME."
THAT'S MY GIRL.
DAMN. THAT'S COLD.

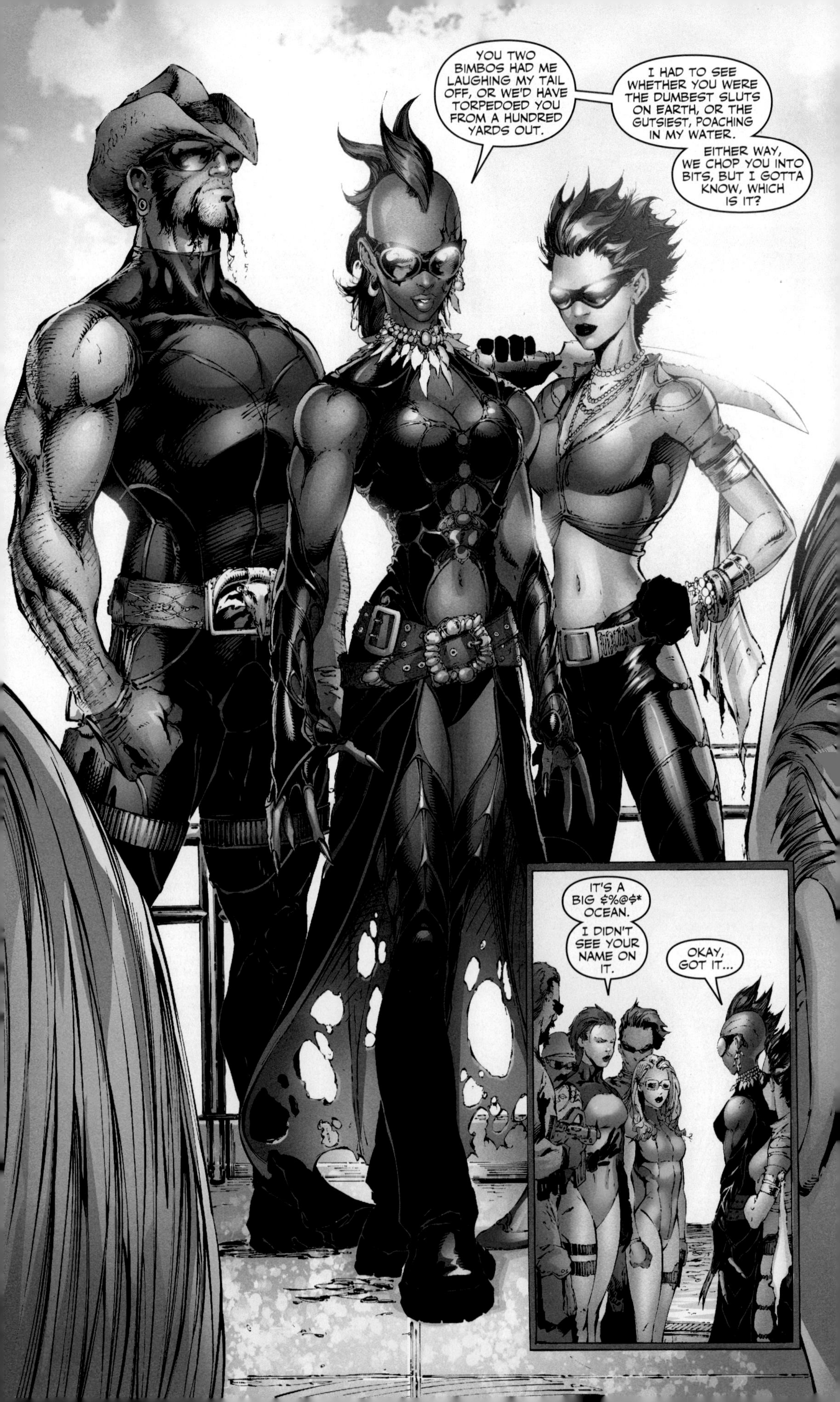
YOU TWO BIMBOS HAD ME LAUGHING MY TAIL OFF, OR WE'D HAVE TORPEDOED YOU FROM A HUNDRED YARDS OUT.
I HAD TO SEE WHETHER YOU WERE THE DUMBEST SLUTS ON EARTH, OR THE GUTSIEST, POACHING IN MY WATER.
EITHER WAY, WE CHOP YOU INTO BITS, BUT I GOTTA KNOW, WHICH IS IT?
IT'S A BIG $%@$* OCEAN.
I DIDN'T SEE YOUR NAME ON IT.
OKAY, GOT IT...

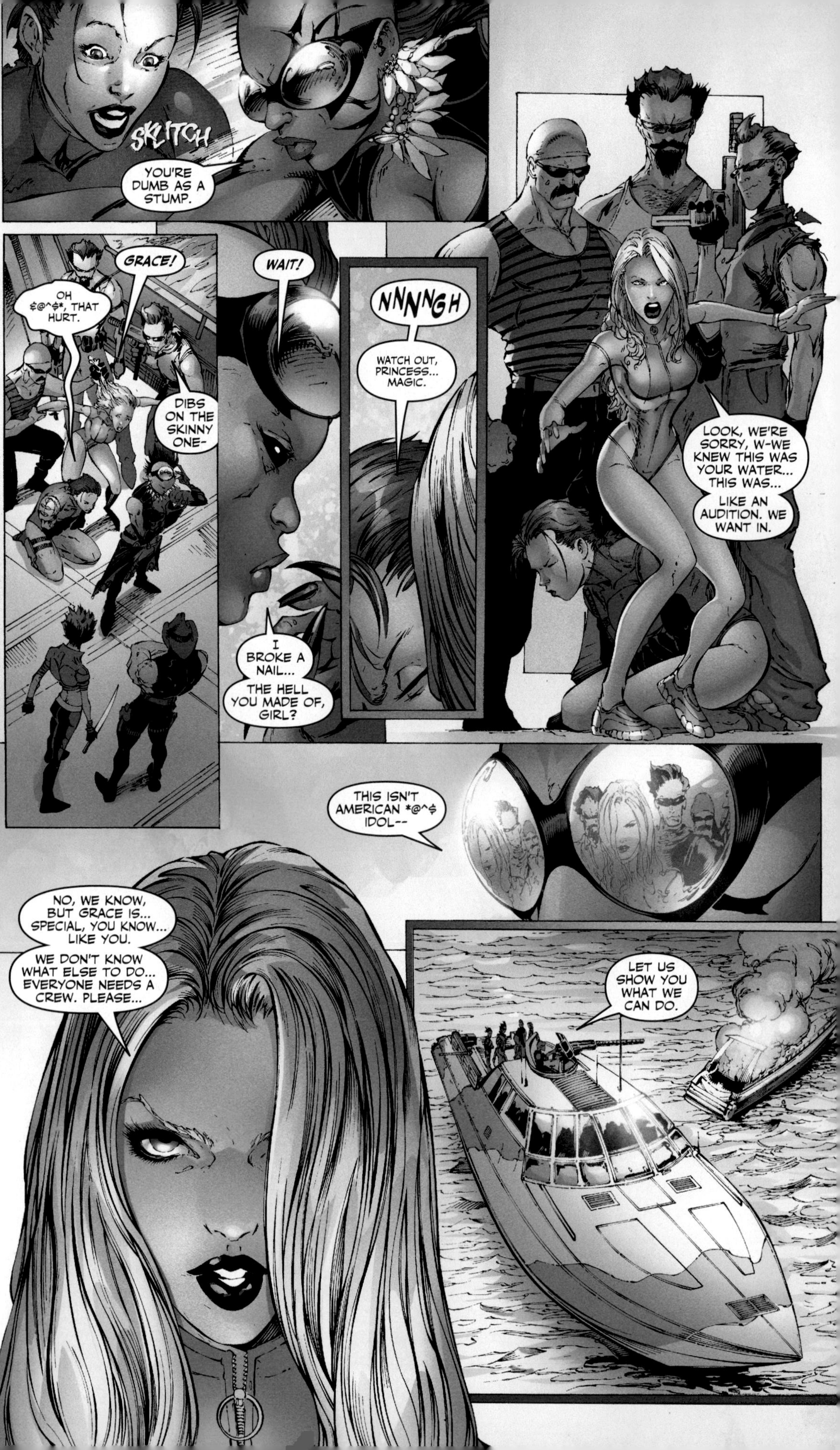
SKLITCH
YOU'RE DUMB AS A STUMP.
GRACE!
OH $@^$*, THAT HURT.
DIBS ON THE SKINNY ONE-
WAIT!
I BROKE A NAIL... THE HELL YOU MADE OF, GIRL?
NNNNGH
WATCH OUT, PRINCESS... MAGIC.
LOOK, WE'RE SORRY, W-WE KNEW THIS WAS YOUR WATER... THIS WAS...
LIKE AN AUDITION. WE WANT IN.
THIS ISN'T AMERICAN *@^$ IDOL--
NO, WE KNOW, BUT GRACE IS... SPECIAL, YOU KNOW... LIKE YOU.
WE DON'T KNOW WHAT ELSE TO DO... EVERYONE NEEDS A CREW. PLEASE...
LET US SHOW YOU WHAT WE CAN DO.

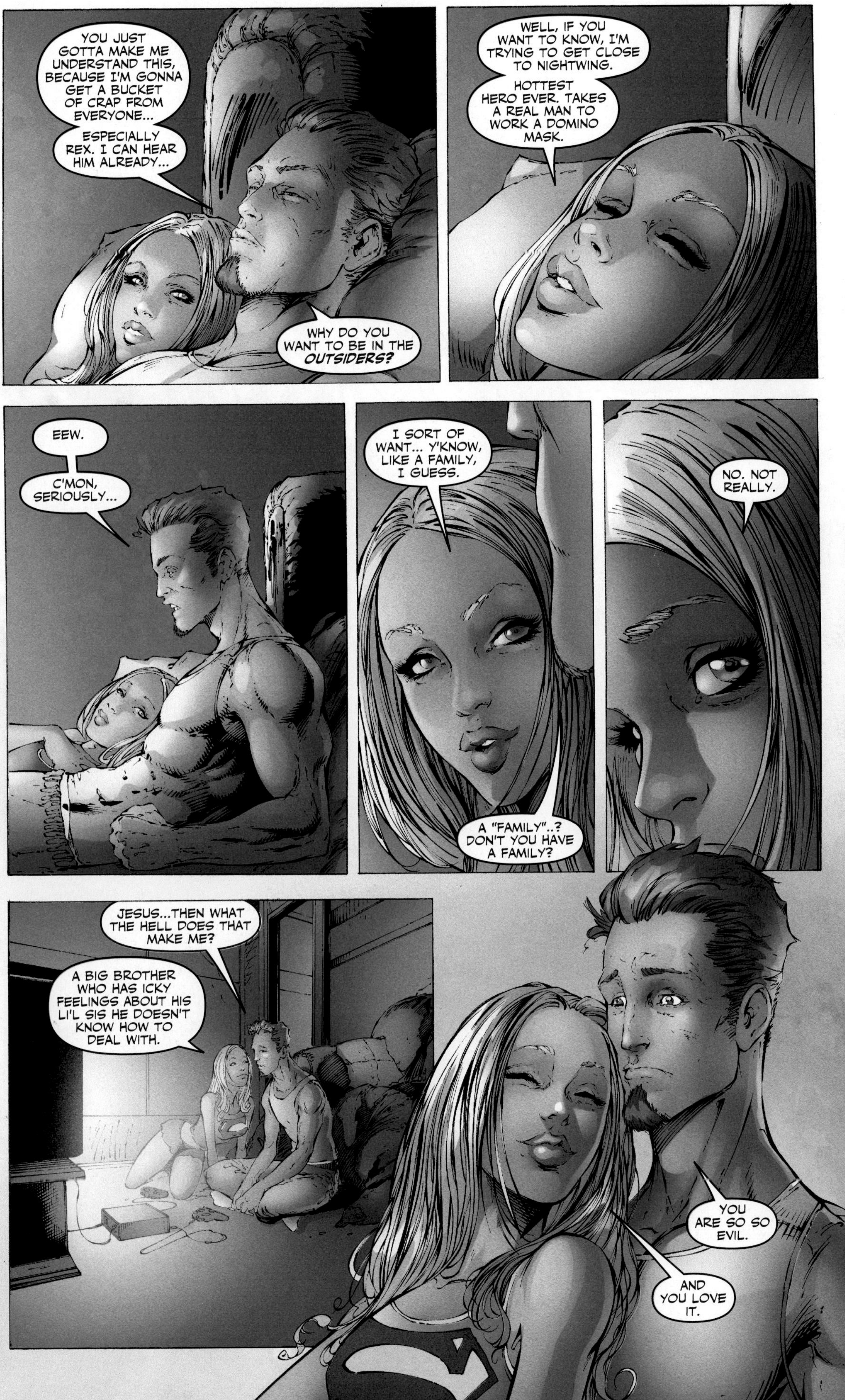
YOU JUST GOTTA MAKE ME UNDERSTAND THIS, BECAUSE I'M GONNA GET A BUCKET OF CRAP FROM EVERYONE...
ESPECIALLY REX. I CAN HEAR HIM ALREADY...
WHY DO YOU WANT TO BE IN THE OUTSIDERS?
WELL, IF YOU WANT TO KNOW, I'M TRYING TO GET CLOSE TO NIGHTWING.
HOTTEST HERO EVER. TAKES A REAL MAN TO WORK A DOMINO MASK.
EEW.
C'MON, SERIOUSLY...
I SORT OF WANT... Y'KNOW, LIKE A FAMILY, I GUESS.
A "FAMILY"..? DON'T YOU HAVE A FAMILY?
NO. NOT REALLY.
JESUS...THEN WHAT THE HELL DOES THAT MAKE ME?
A BIG BROTHER WHO HAS ICKY FEELINGS ABOUT HIS LI'L SIS HE DOESN'T KNOW HOW TO DEAL WITH.
YOU ARE SO SO EVIL.
AND YOU LOVE IT.

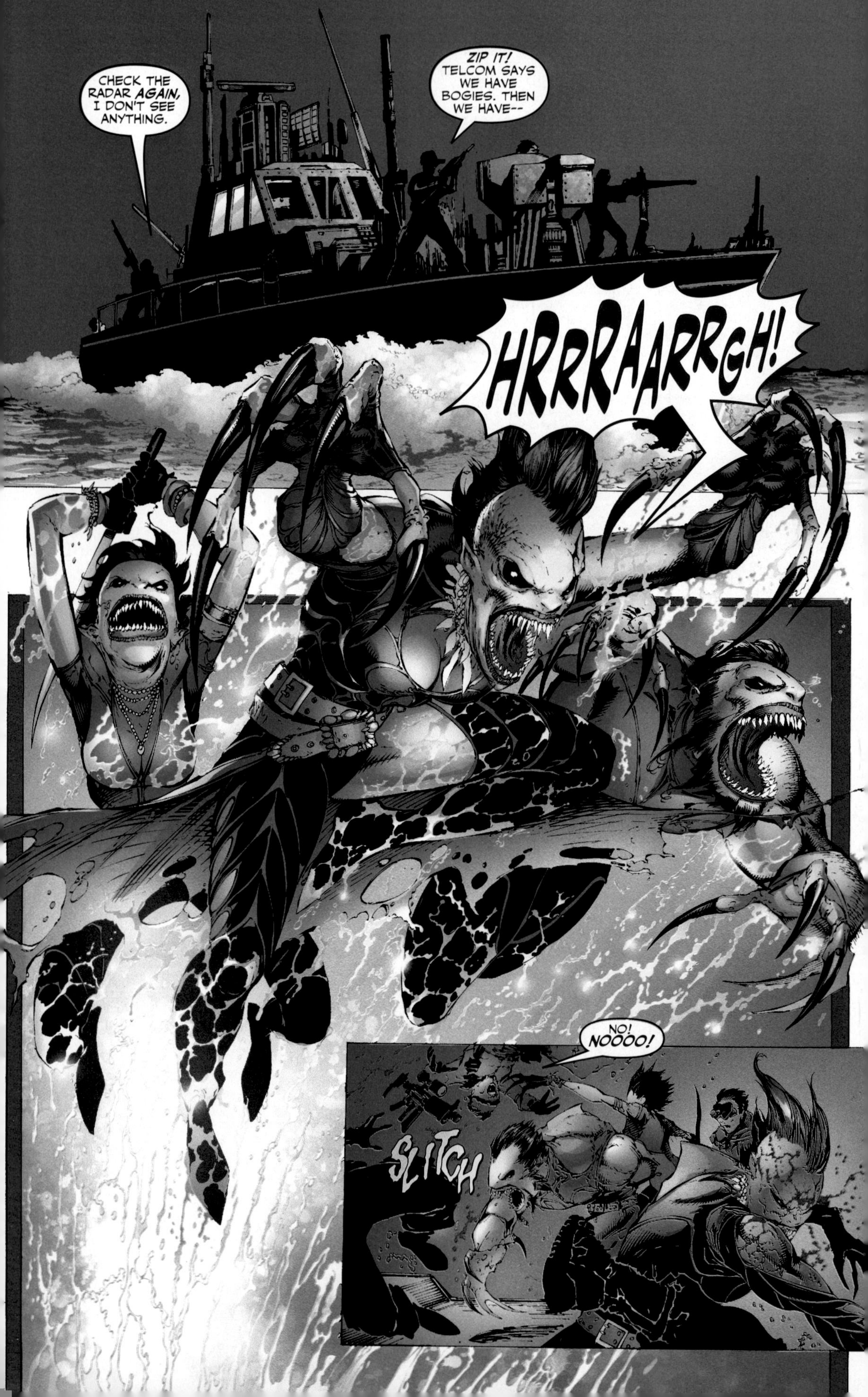
CHECK THE RADAR AGAIN, I DON'T SEE ANYTHING.
ZIP IT! TELCOM SAYS WE HAVE BOGIES. THEN WE HAVE--
HRRRAARRGH!
NO! NOOOO!
SLITCH

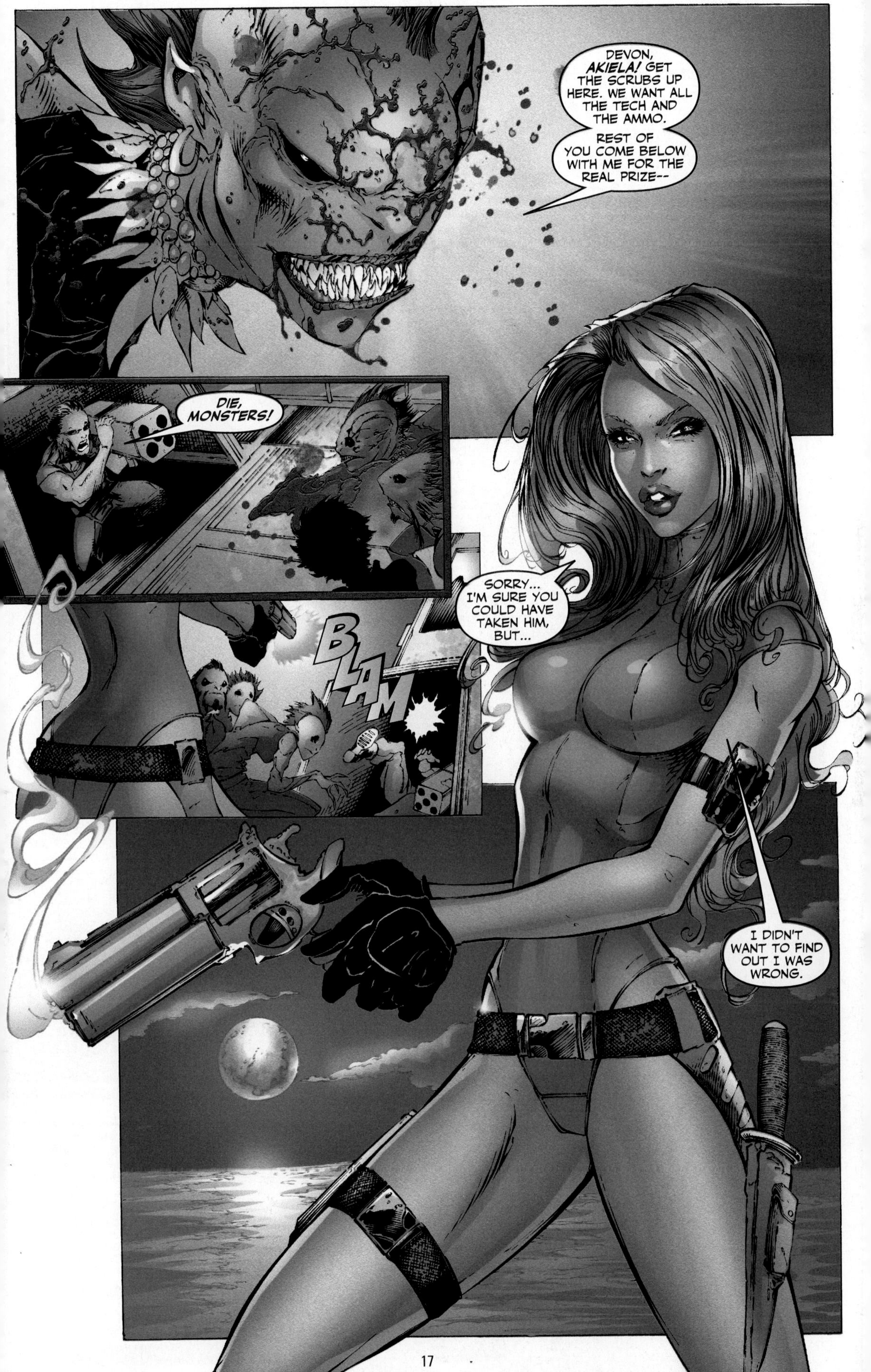
DEVON, *AKIELA!* GET THE SCRUBS UP HERE. WE WANT ALL THE TECH AND THE AMMO.
REST OF YOU COME BELOW WITH ME FOR THE REAL PRIZE--
DIE, MONSTERS!
SORRY... I'M SURE YOU COULD HAVE TAKEN HIM, BUT...
BLAM
I DIDN'T WANT TO FIND OUT I WAS WRONG.

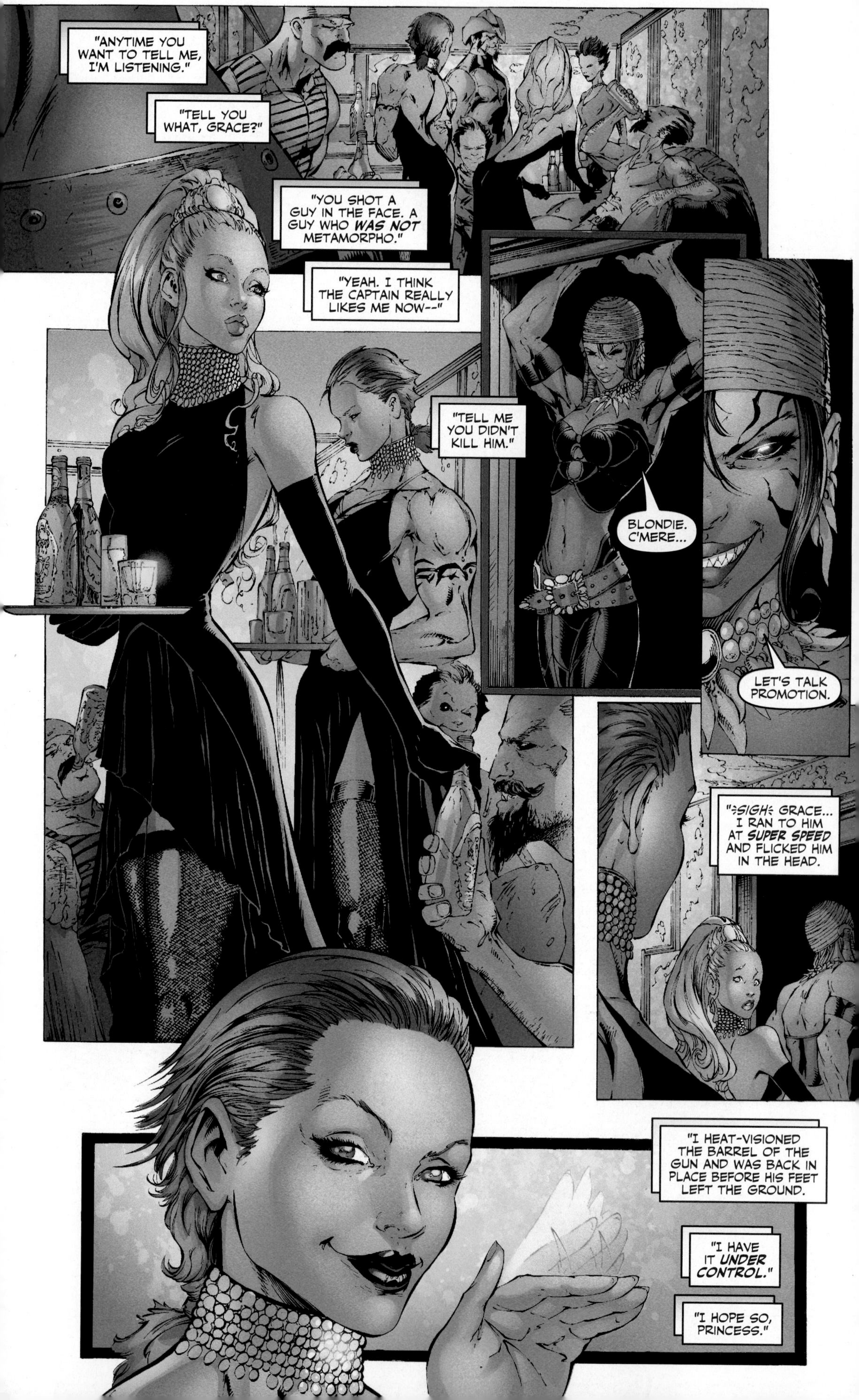
"ANYTIME YOU WANT TO TELL ME, I'M LISTENING."
"TELL YOU WHAT, GRACE?"
"YOU SHOT A GUY IN THE FACE. A GUY WHO WAS NOT METAMORPHO."
"YEAH. I THINK THE CAPTAIN REALLY LIKES ME NOW--"
"TELL ME YOU DIDN'T KILL HIM."
BLONDIE. C'MERE...
LET'S TALK PROMOTION.
"SIGH GRACE... I RAN TO HIM AT SUPER SPEED AND FLICKED HIM IN THE HEAD.
"I HEAT-VISIONED THE BARREL OF THE GUN AND WAS BACK IN PLACE BEFORE HIS FEET LEFT THE GROUND.
"I HAVE IT UNDER CONTROL."
"I HOPE SO, PRINCESS."

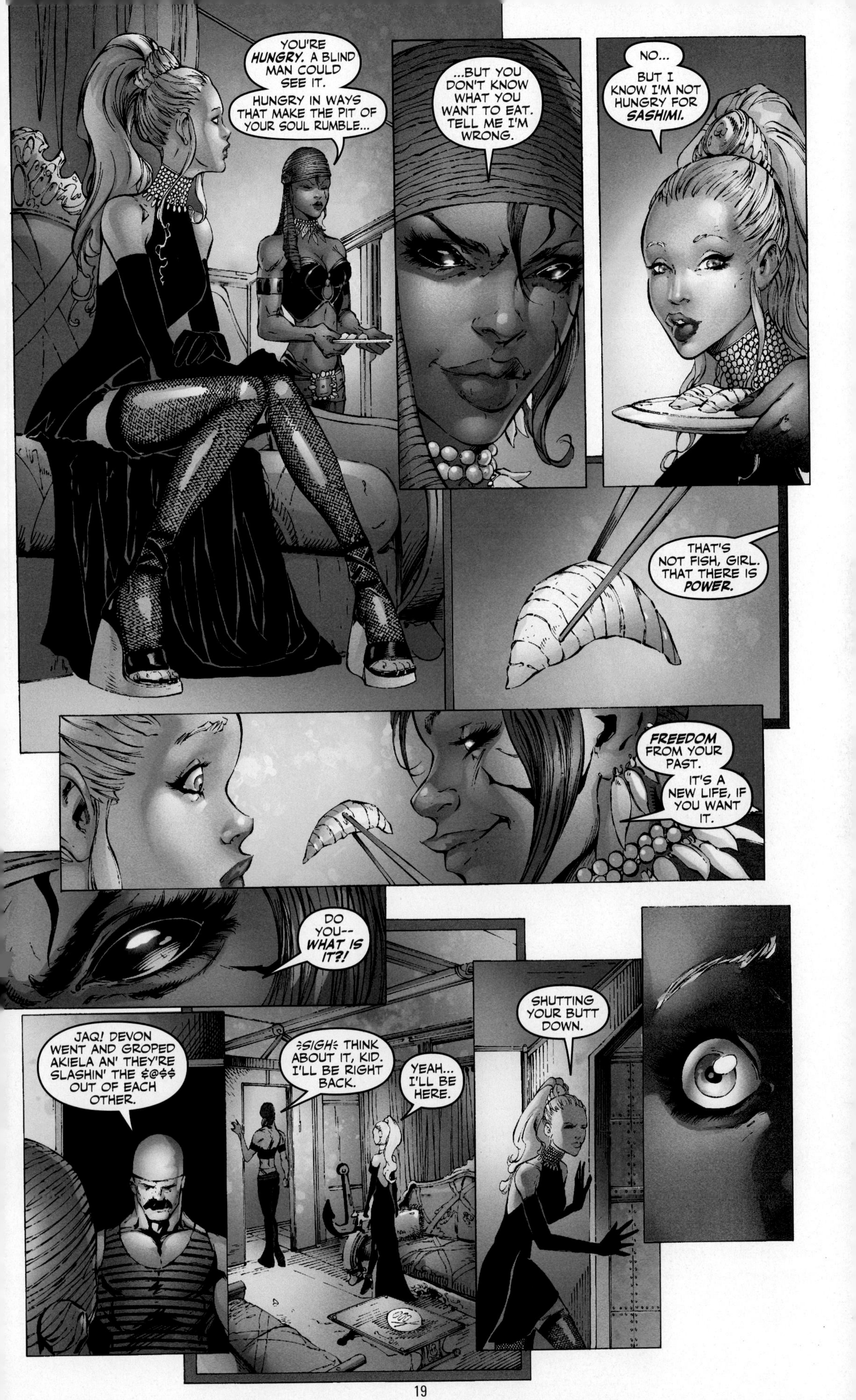
YOU'RE HUNGRY. A BLIND MAN COULD SEE IT.
HUNGRY IN WAYS THAT MAKE THE PIT OF YOUR SOUL RUMBLE...
...BUT YOU DON'T KNOW WHAT YOU WANT TO EAT. TELL ME I'M WRONG.
NO...
BUT I KNOW I'M NOT HUNGRY FOR SASHIMI.
THAT'S NOT FISH, GIRL. THAT THERE IS POWER.
FREEDOM FROM YOUR PAST.
IT'S A NEW LIFE, IF YOU WANT IT.
DO YOU-- WHAT IS IT?!
SHUTTING YOUR BUTT DOWN.
JAQ! DEVON WENT AND GROPED AKIELA AN' THEY'RE SLASHIN' THE $@$$ OUT OF EACH OTHER.
SIGH THINK ABOUT IT, KID. I'LL BE RIGHT BACK.
YEAH... I'LL BE HERE.

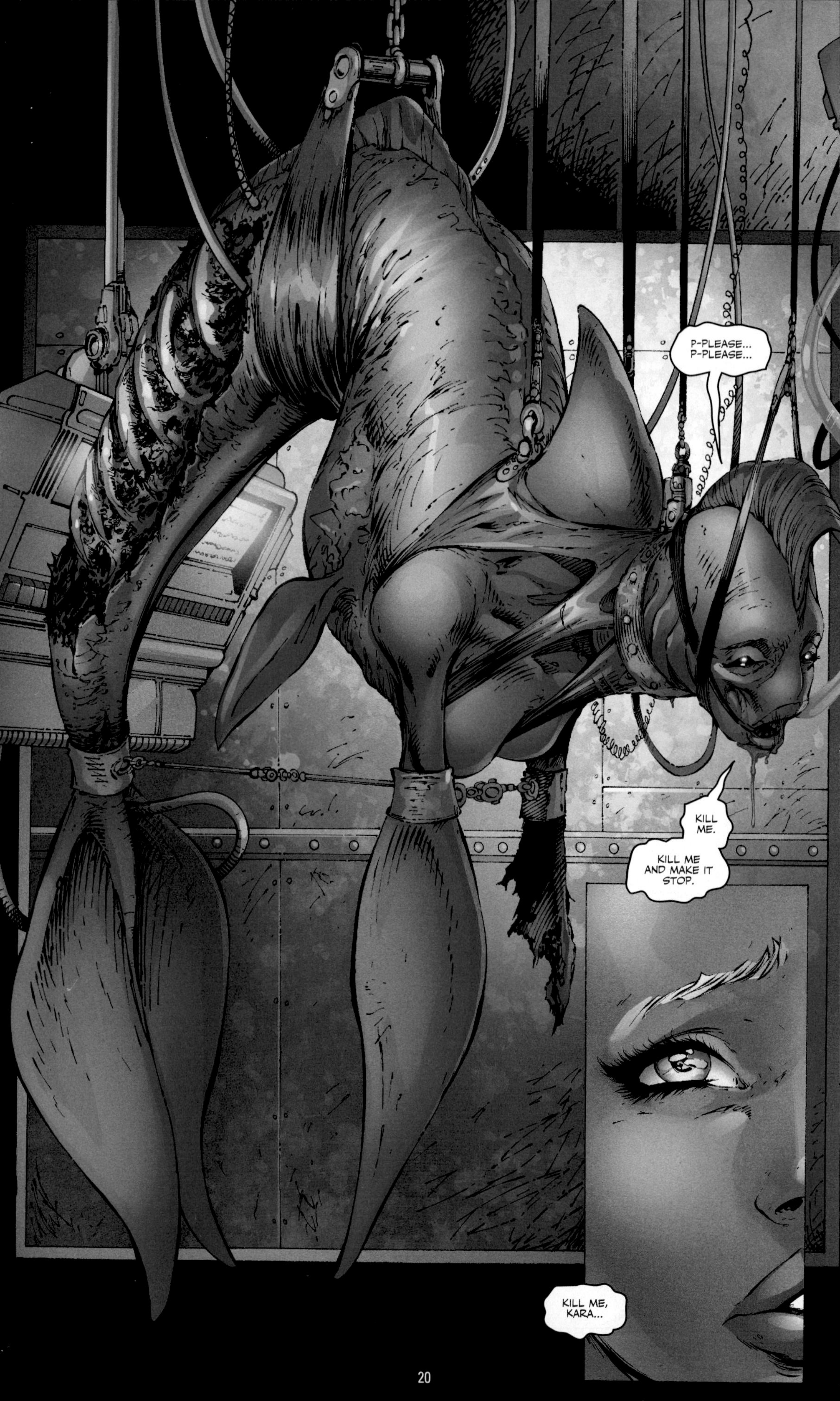
P-PLEASE...
P-PLEASE...
KILL ME.
KILL ME AND MAKE IT STOP.
KILL ME, KARA...

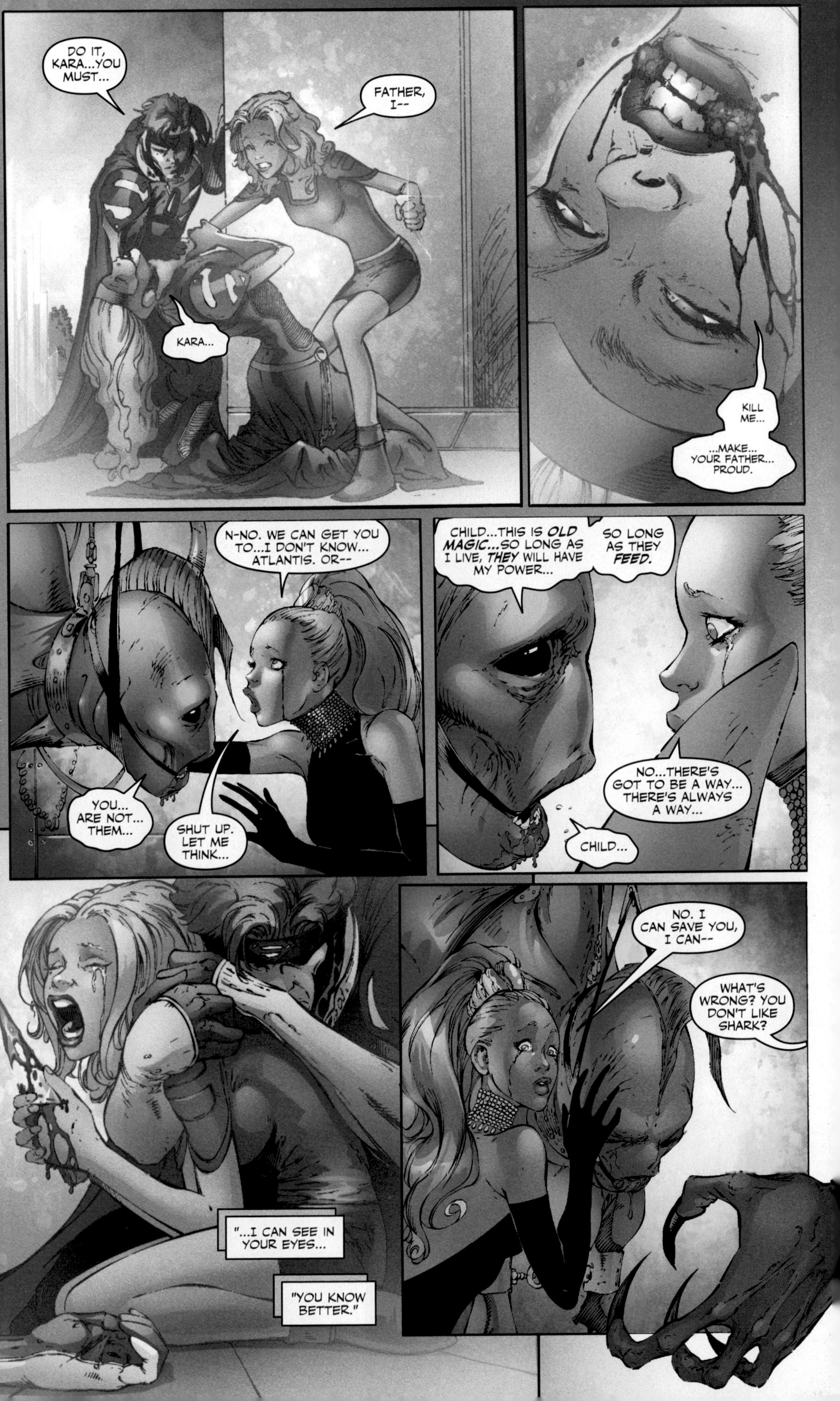

DO IT, KARA...YOU MUST...
FATHER, I--
KARA...
KILL ME...
...MAKE... YOUR FATHER... PROUD.
N-NO. WE CAN GET YOU TO...I DON'T KNOW... ATLANTIS. OR--
YOU... ARE NOT... THEM...
SHUT UP. LET ME THINK...
CHILD...THIS IS *OLD MAGIC*...SO LONG AS I LIVE, *THEY* WILL HAVE MY POWER...
SO LONG AS THEY *FEED.*
NO...THERE'S GOT TO BE A WAY... THERE'S ALWAYS A WAY...
CHILD...
"...I CAN SEE IN YOUR EYES...
"YOU KNOW BETTER."
NO. I CAN SAVE YOU, I CAN--
WHAT'S WRONG? YOU DON'T LIKE SHARK?

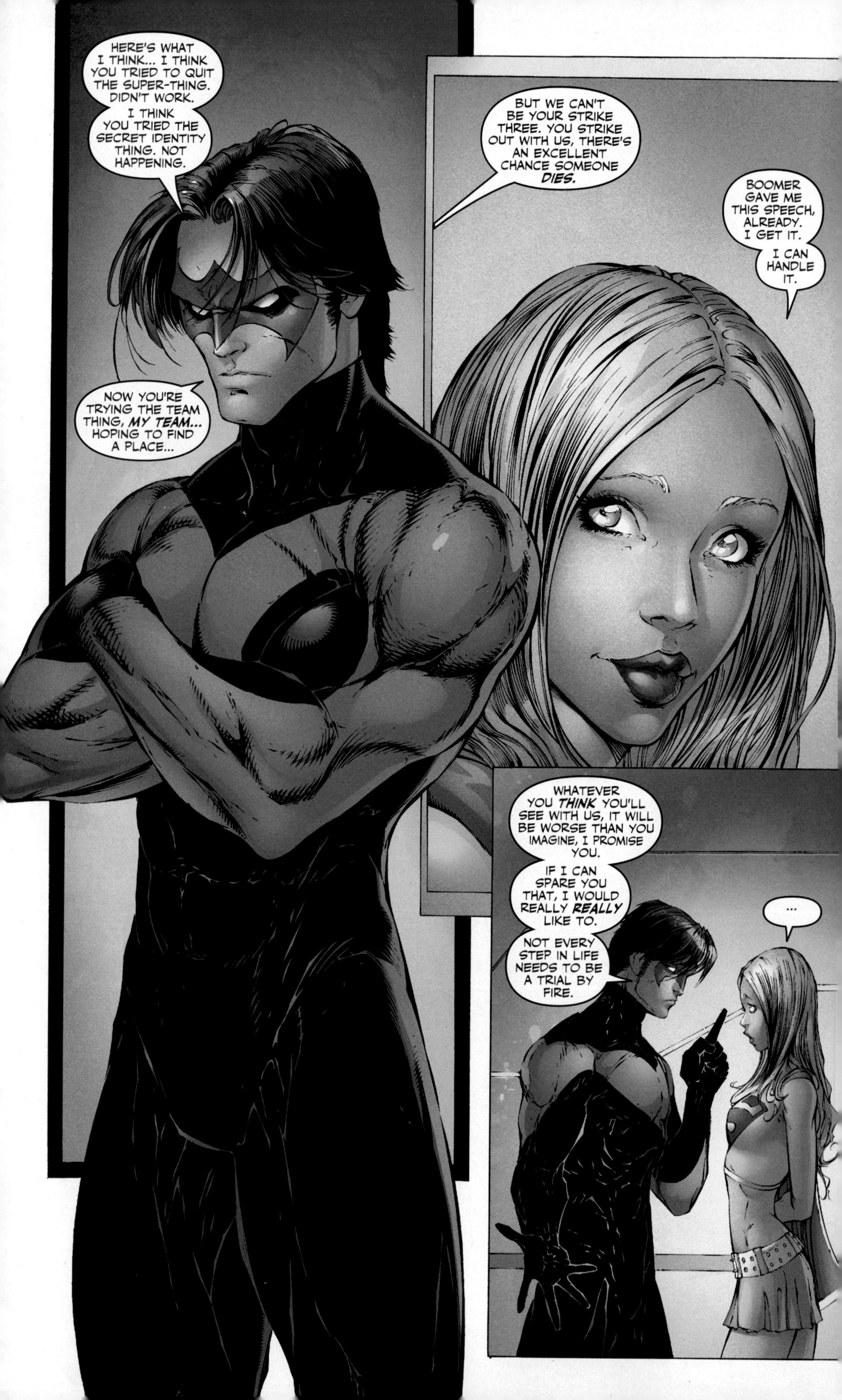
HERE'S WHAT I THINK... I THINK YOU TRIED TO QUIT THE SUPER-THING. DIDN'T WORK.
I THINK YOU TRIED THE SECRET IDENTITY THING. NOT HAPPENING.
NOW YOU'RE TRYING THE TEAM THING, *MY TEAM...* HOPING TO FIND A PLACE...
BUT WE CAN'T BE YOUR STRIKE THREE. YOU STRIKE OUT WITH US, THERE'S AN EXCELLENT CHANCE SOMEONE *DIES.*
BOOMER GAVE ME THIS SPEECH, ALREADY. I GET IT.
I CAN HANDLE IT.
WHATEVER YOU *THINK* YOU'LL SEE WITH US, IT WILL BE WORSE THAN YOU IMAGINE, I PROMISE YOU.
IF I CAN SPARE YOU THAT, I WOULD REALLY *REALLY* LIKE TO.
NOT EVERY STEP IN LIFE NEEDS TO BE A TRIAL BY FIRE.
...

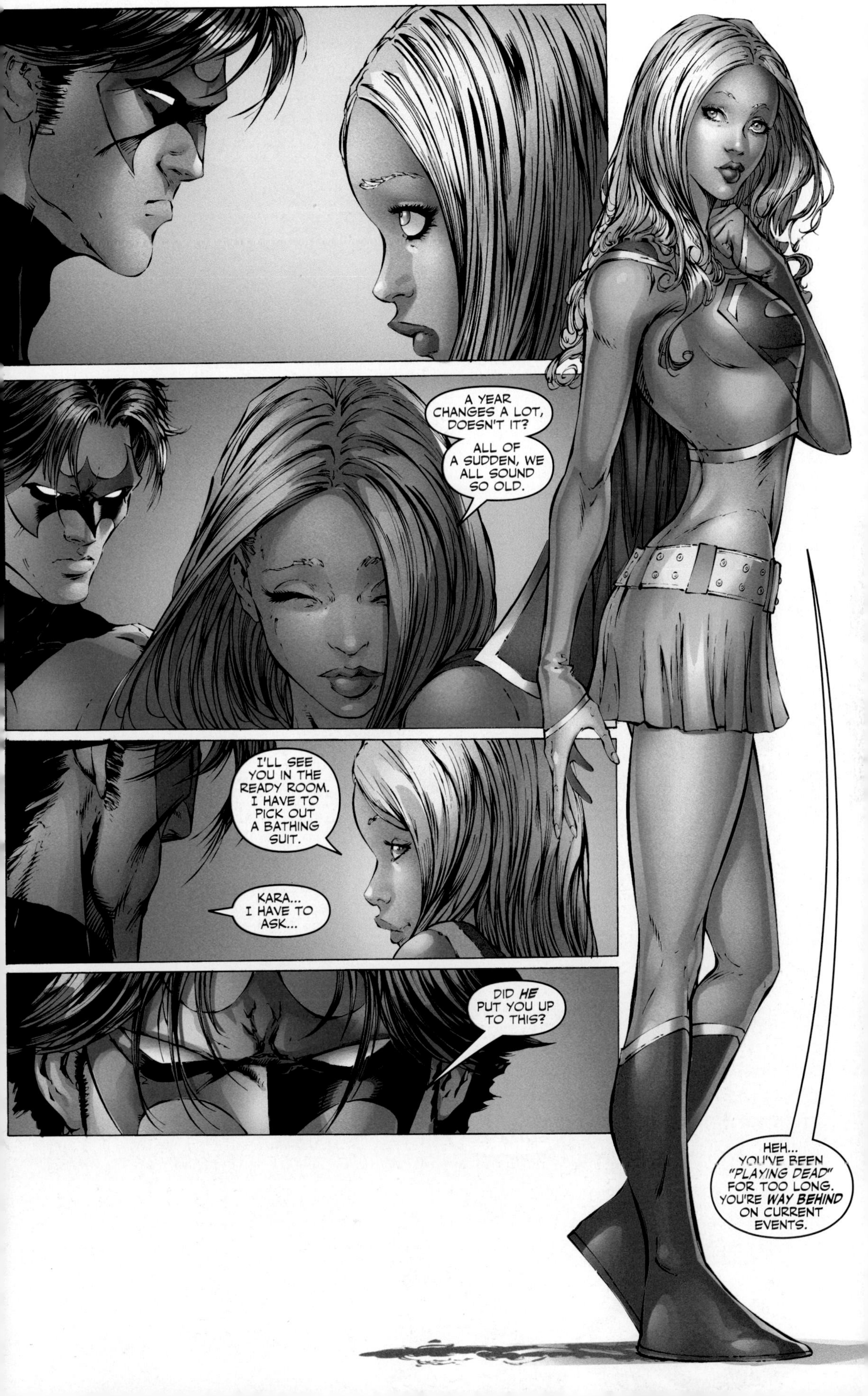
A YEAR CHANGES A LOT, DOESN'T IT?
ALL OF A SUDDEN, WE ALL SOUND SO OLD.
I'LL SEE YOU IN THE READY ROOM. I HAVE TO PICK OUT A BATHING SUIT.
KARA... I HAVE TO ASK...
DID *HE* PUT YOU UP TO THIS?
HEH... YOU'VE BEEN *"PLAYING DEAD"* FOR TOO LONG. YOU'RE *WAY BEHIND* ON CURRENT EVENTS.

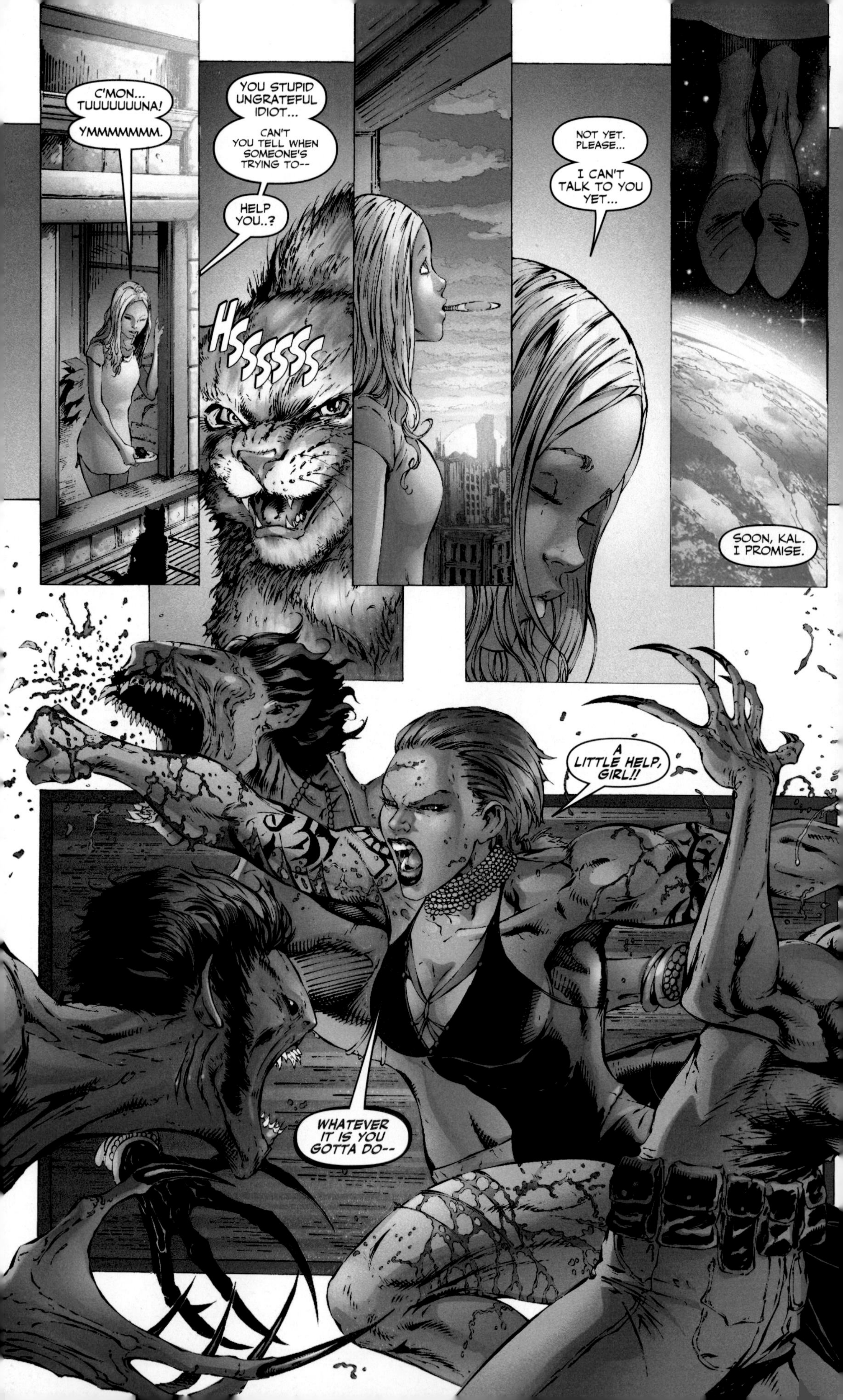
C'MON... TUUUUUUUNA!
YMMMMMMM.
YOU STUPID UNGRATEFUL IDIOT...
CAN'T YOU TELL WHEN SOMEONE'S TRYING TO--
HELP YOU..?
HSSSSSS
NOT YET. PLEASE...
I CAN'T TALK TO YOU YET...
SOON, KAL. I PROMISE.
A LITTLE HELP, GIRL!!
WHATEVER IT IS YOU GOTTA DO--

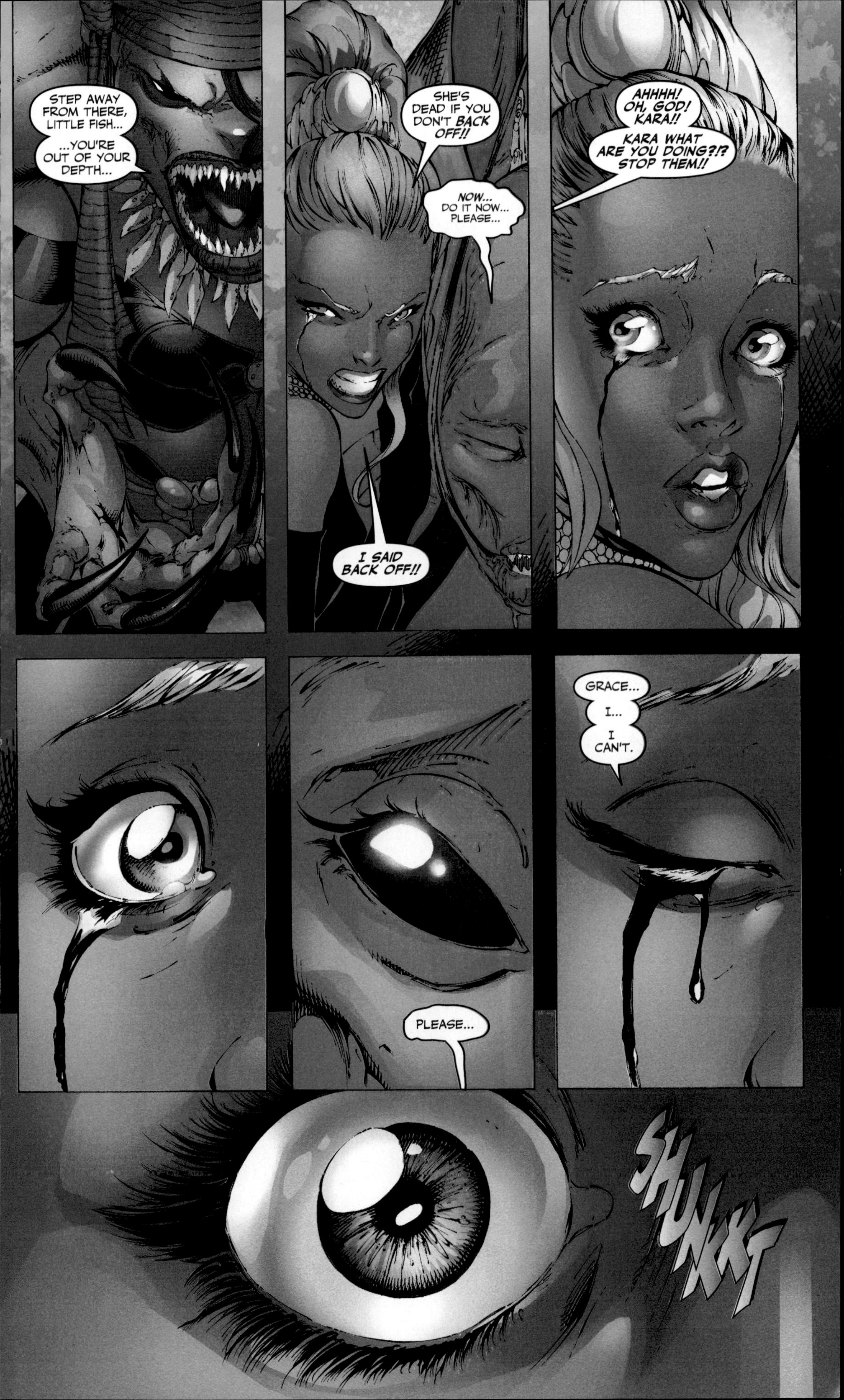
STEP AWAY FROM THERE, LITTLE FISH...
...YOU'RE OUT OF YOUR DEPTH...
SHE'S DEAD IF YOU DON'T BACK OFF!!
NOW... DO IT NOW... PLEASE...
I SAID BACK OFF!!
AHHHH! OH, GOD! KARA!!
KARA WHAT ARE YOU DOING?!? STOP THEM!!
PLEASE...
GRACE...
I...
I CAN'T.
SHUNKKT

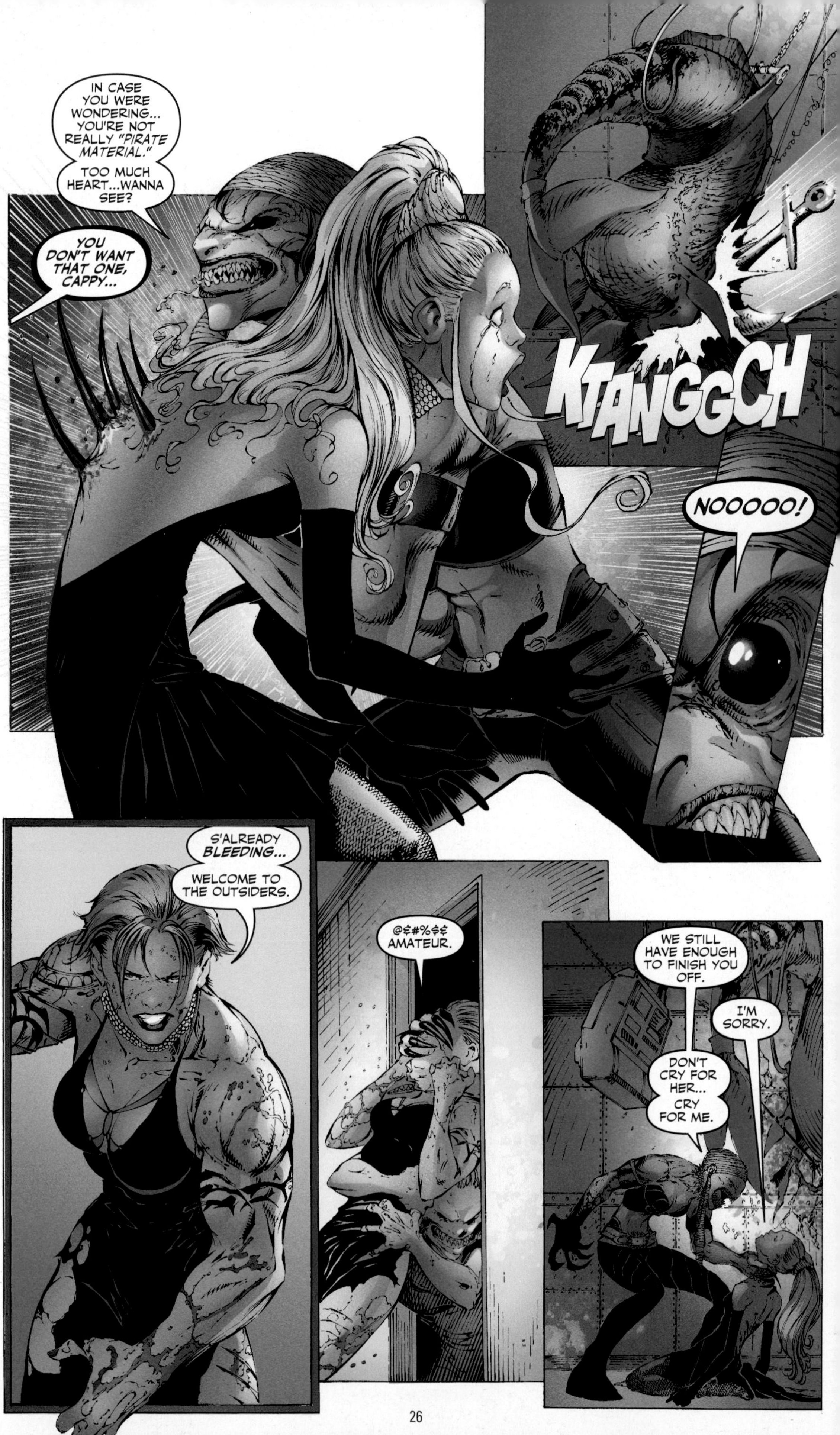
IN CASE YOU WERE WONDERING... YOU'RE NOT REALLY "PIRATE MATERIAL."
TOO MUCH HEART...WANNA SEE?
YOU DON'T WANT THAT ONE, CAPPY...
KTANGGCH
NOOOOO!
S'ALREADY BLEEDING...
WELCOME TO THE OUTSIDERS.
@¢#%$¢ AMATEUR.
WE STILL HAVE ENOUGH TO FINISH YOU OFF.
I'M SORRY.
DON'T CRY FOR HER... CRY FOR ME.

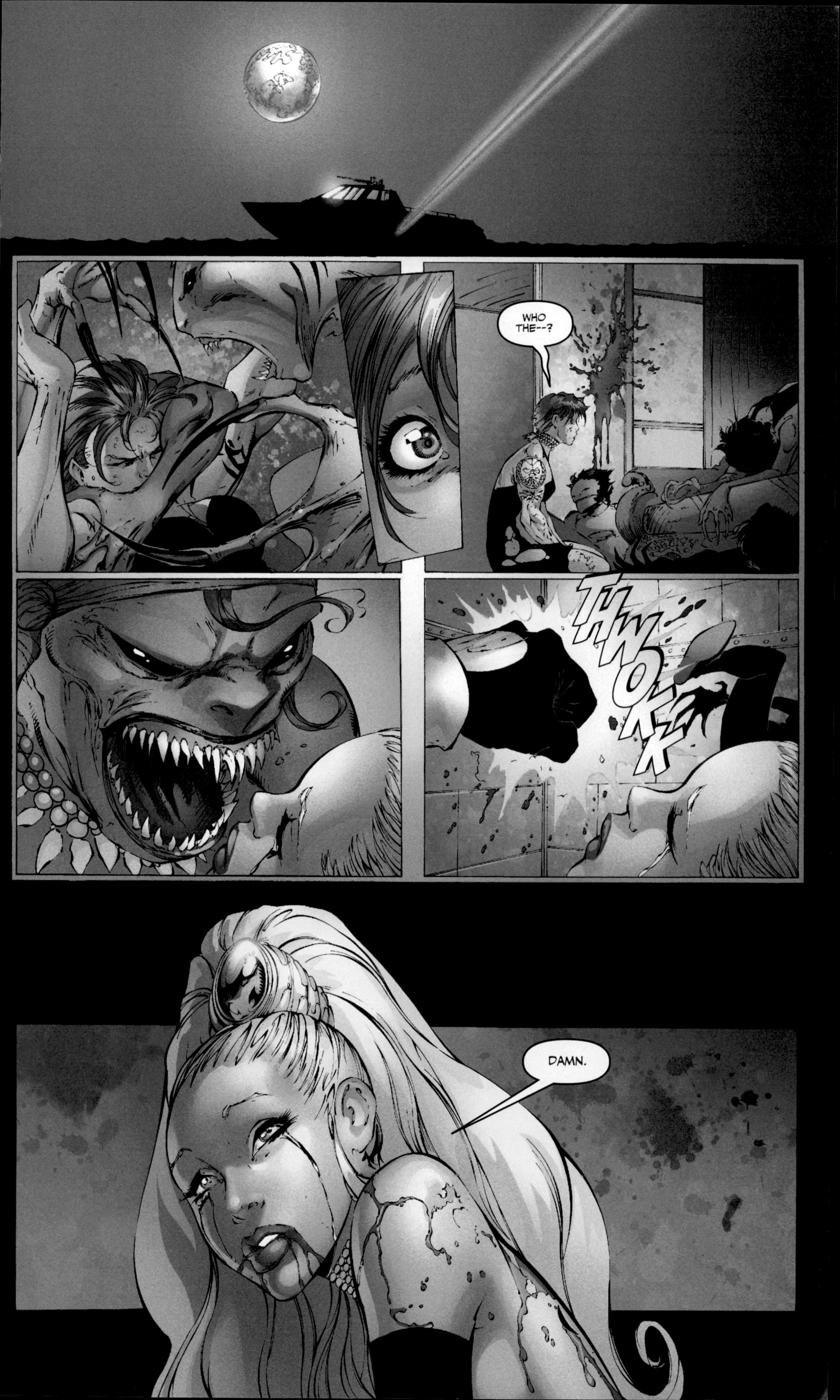
WHO THE--?
THWOKK
DAMN.

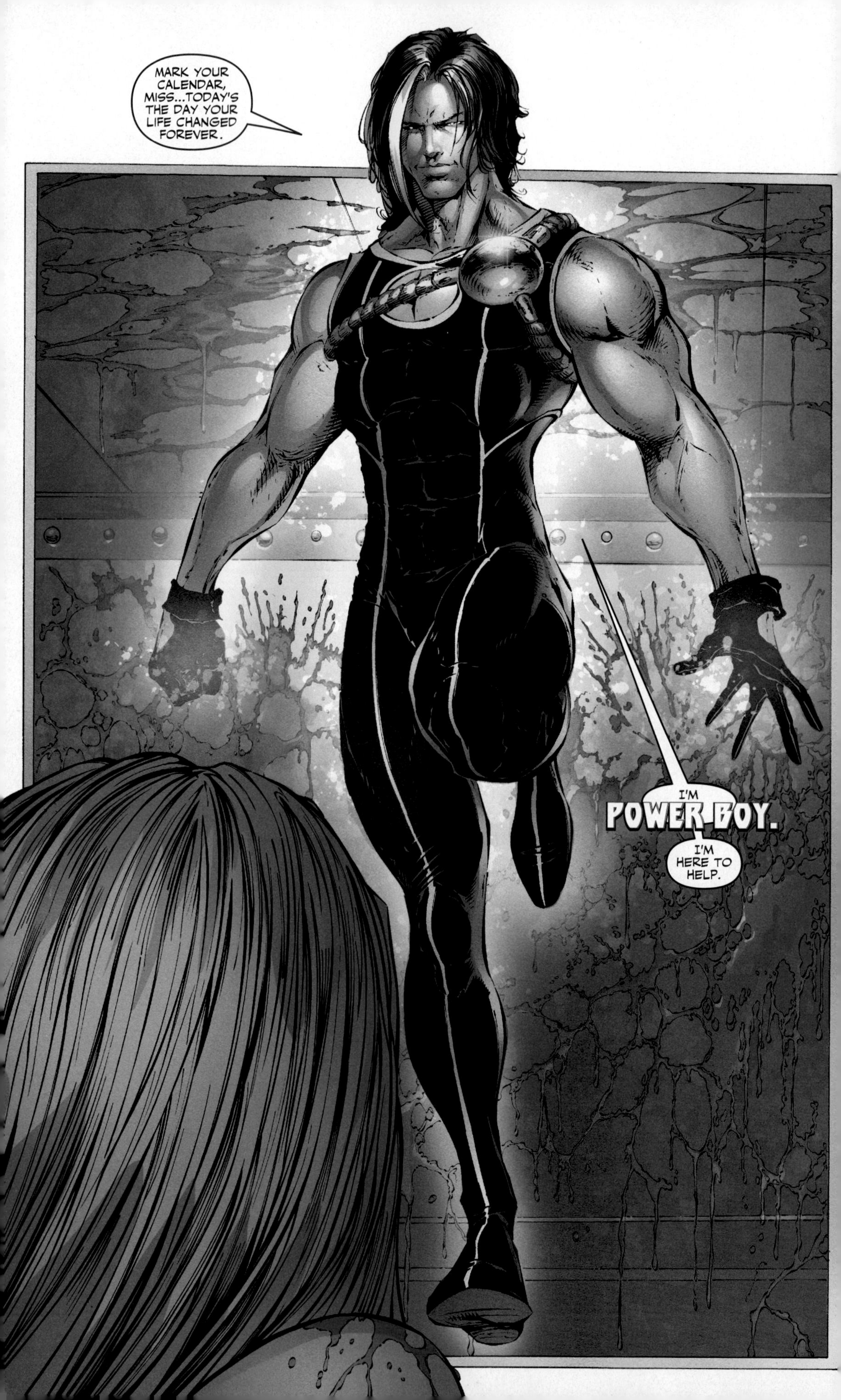
MARK YOUR CALENDAR, MISS...TODAY'S THE DAY YOUR LIFE CHANGED FOREVER.
I'M POWER BOY.
I'M HERE TO HELP.

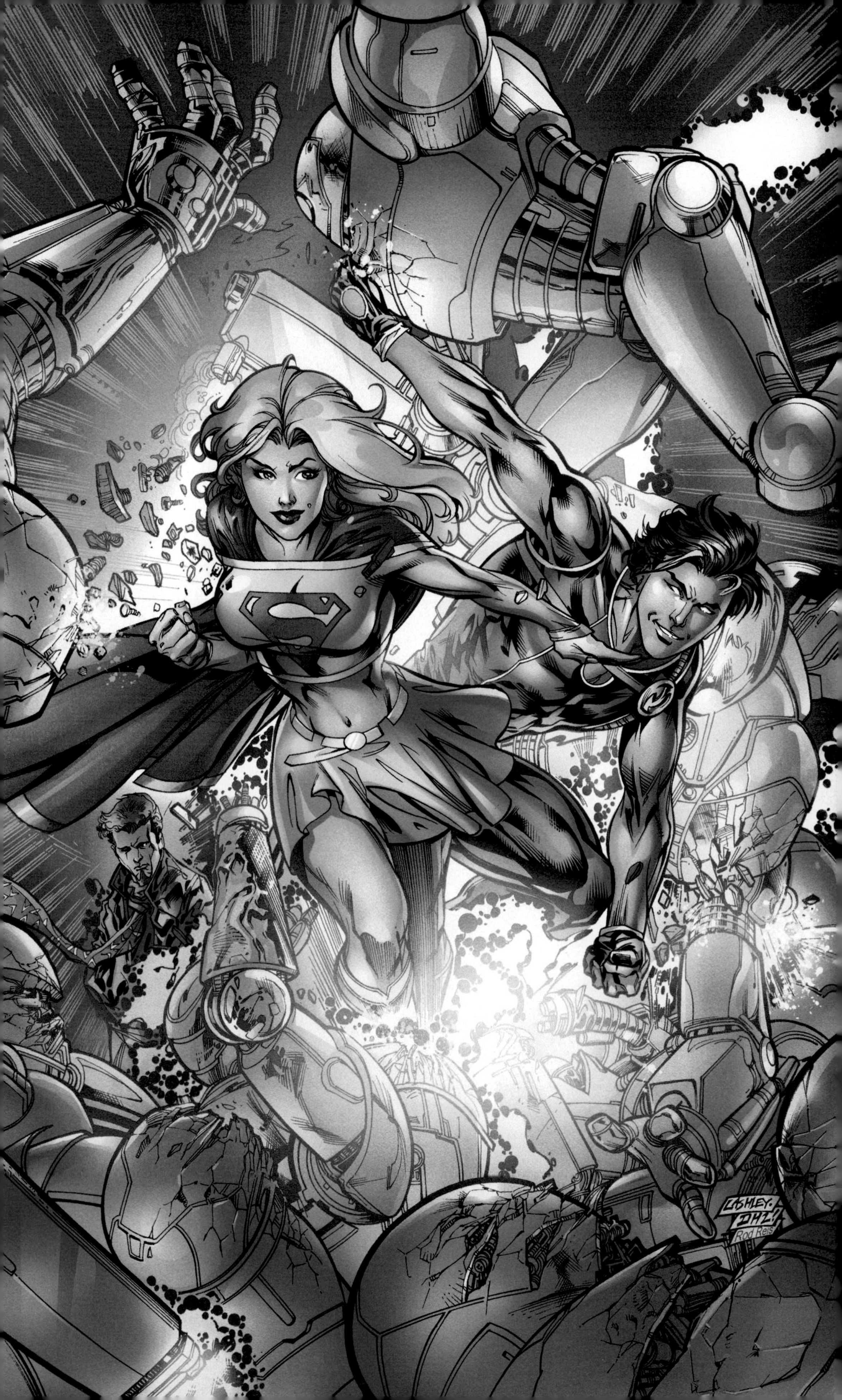
LASHLEY.
DHZ!
Rod Reis

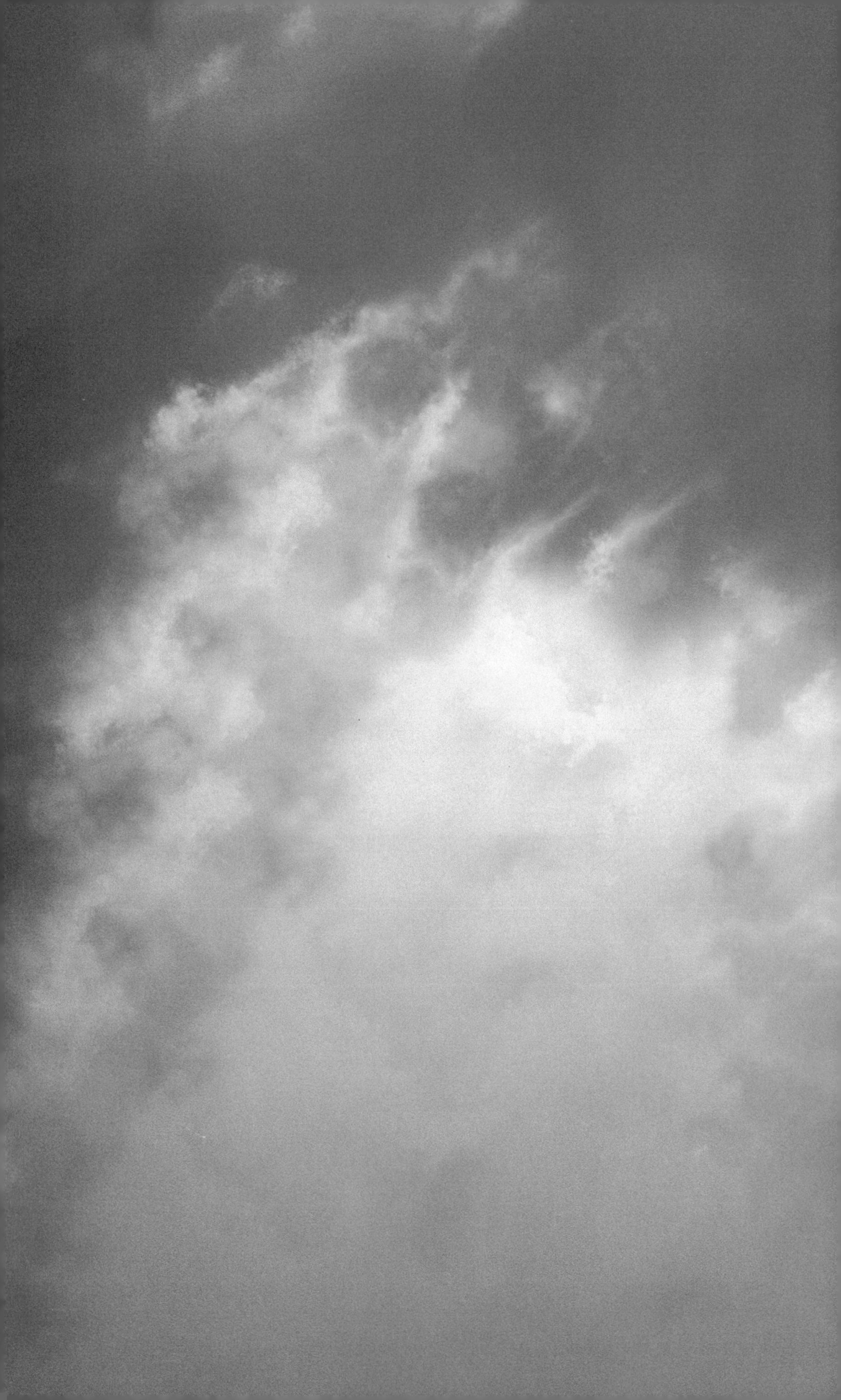

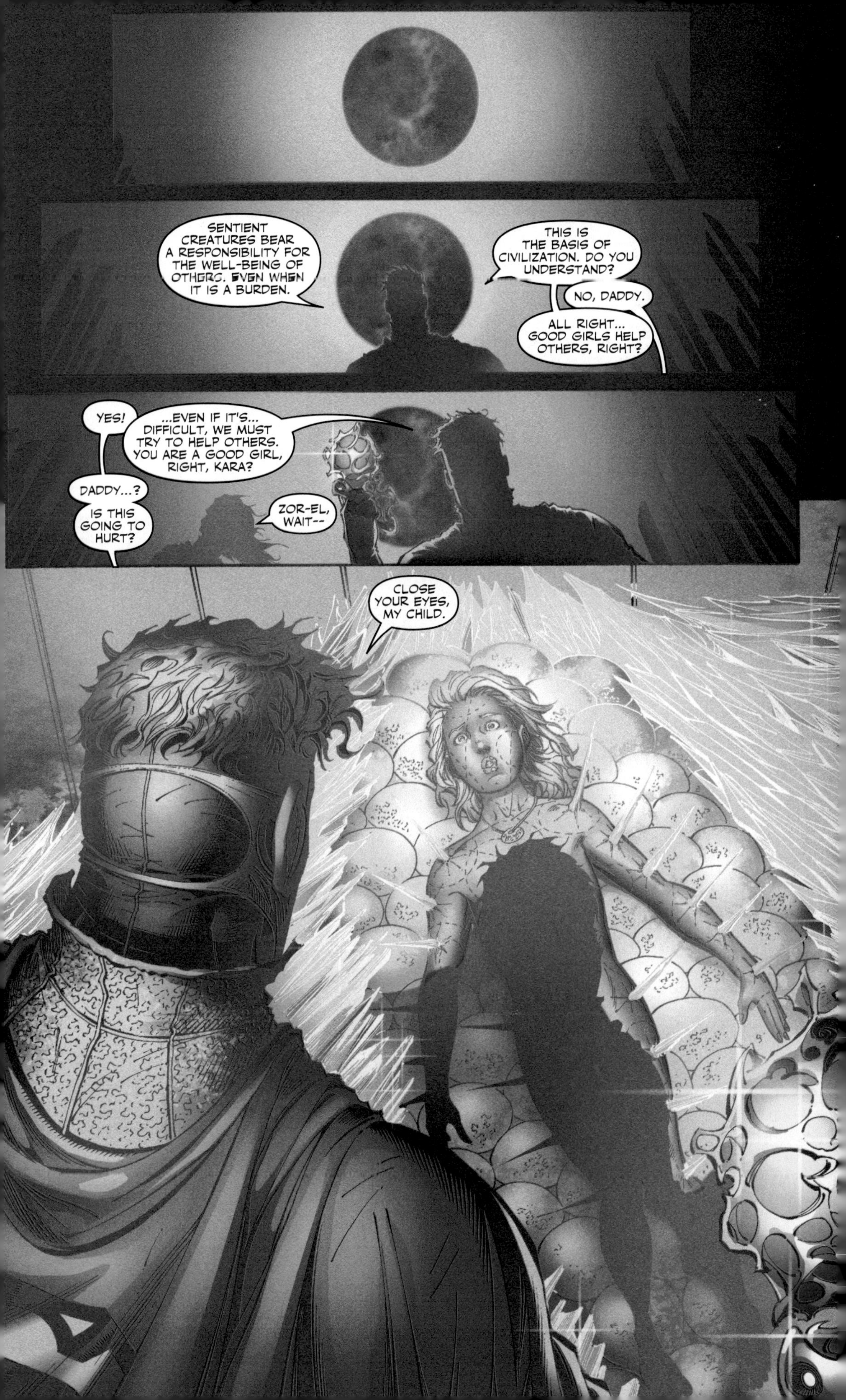
SENTIENT CREATURES BEAR A RESPONSIBILITY FOR THE WELL-BEING OF OTHERS. EVEN WHEN IT IS A BURDEN.
THIS IS THE BASIS OF CIVILIZATION. DO YOU UNDERSTAND?
NO, DADDY.
ALL RIGHT... GOOD GIRLS HELP OTHERS, RIGHT?
YES!
...EVEN IF IT'S... DIFFICULT, WE MUST TRY TO HELP OTHERS. YOU ARE A GOOD GIRL, RIGHT, KARA?
DADDY...?
IS THIS GOING TO HURT?
ZOR-EL, WAIT--
CLOSE YOUR EYES, MY CHILD.

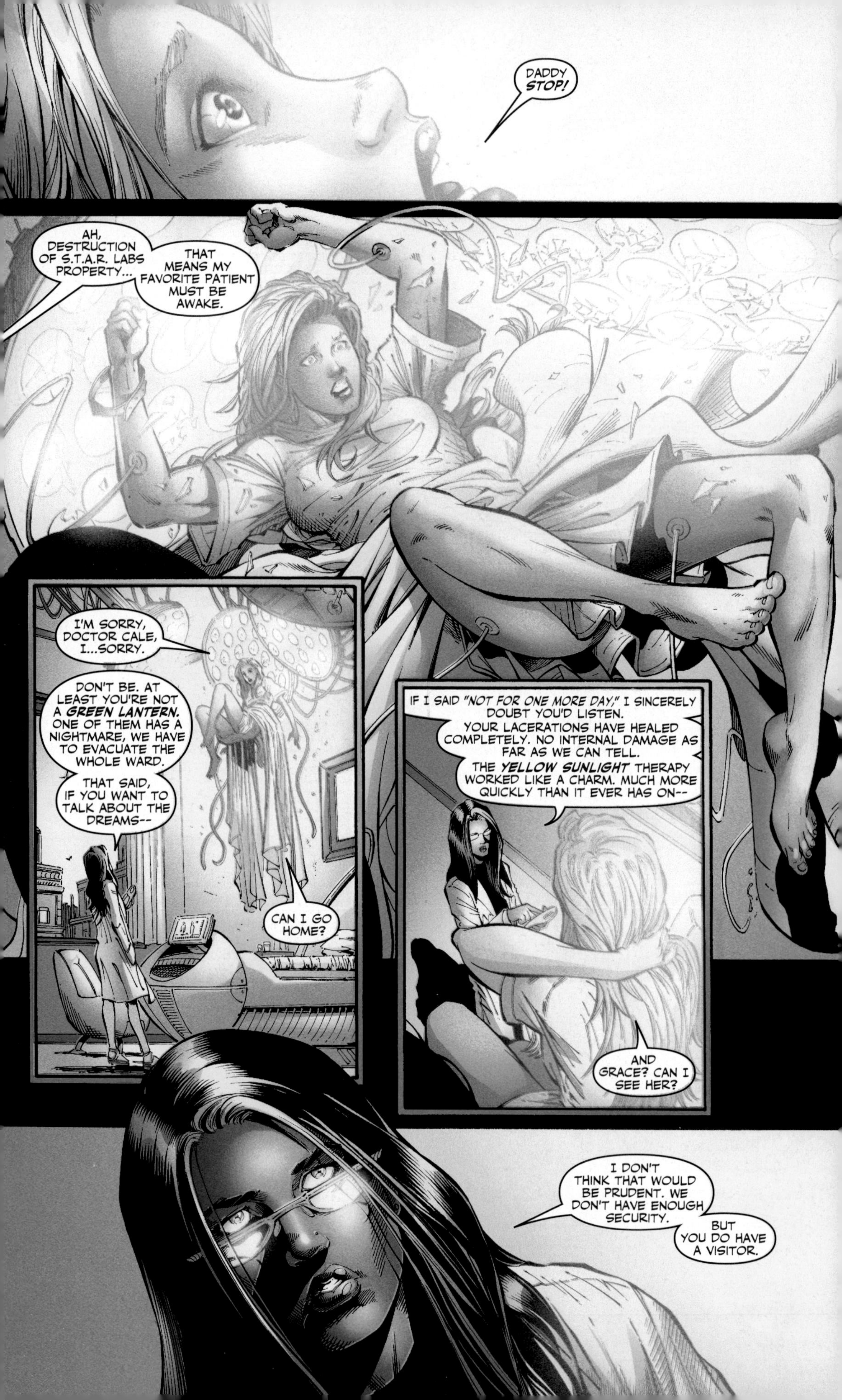

DADDY STOP!
AH, DESTRUCTION OF S.T.A.R. LABS PROPERTY...
THAT MEANS MY FAVORITE PATIENT MUST BE AWAKE.
I'M SORRY, DOCTOR CALE, I...SORRY.
DON'T BE. AT LEAST YOU'RE NOT A GREEN LANTERN. ONE OF THEM HAS A NIGHTMARE, WE HAVE TO EVACUATE THE WHOLE WARD.
THAT SAID, IF YOU WANT TO TALK ABOUT THE DREAMS--
CAN I GO HOME?
IF I SAID "NOT FOR ONE MORE DAY," I SINCERELY DOUBT YOU'D LISTEN.
YOUR LACERATIONS HAVE HEALED COMPLETELY. NO INTERNAL DAMAGE AS FAR AS WE CAN TELL.
THE YELLOW SUNLIGHT THERAPY WORKED LIKE A CHARM. MUCH MORE QUICKLY THAN IT EVER HAS ON--
AND GRACE? CAN I SEE HER?
I DON'T THINK THAT WOULD BE PRUDENT. WE DON'T HAVE ENOUGH SECURITY.
BUT YOU DO HAVE A VISITOR.

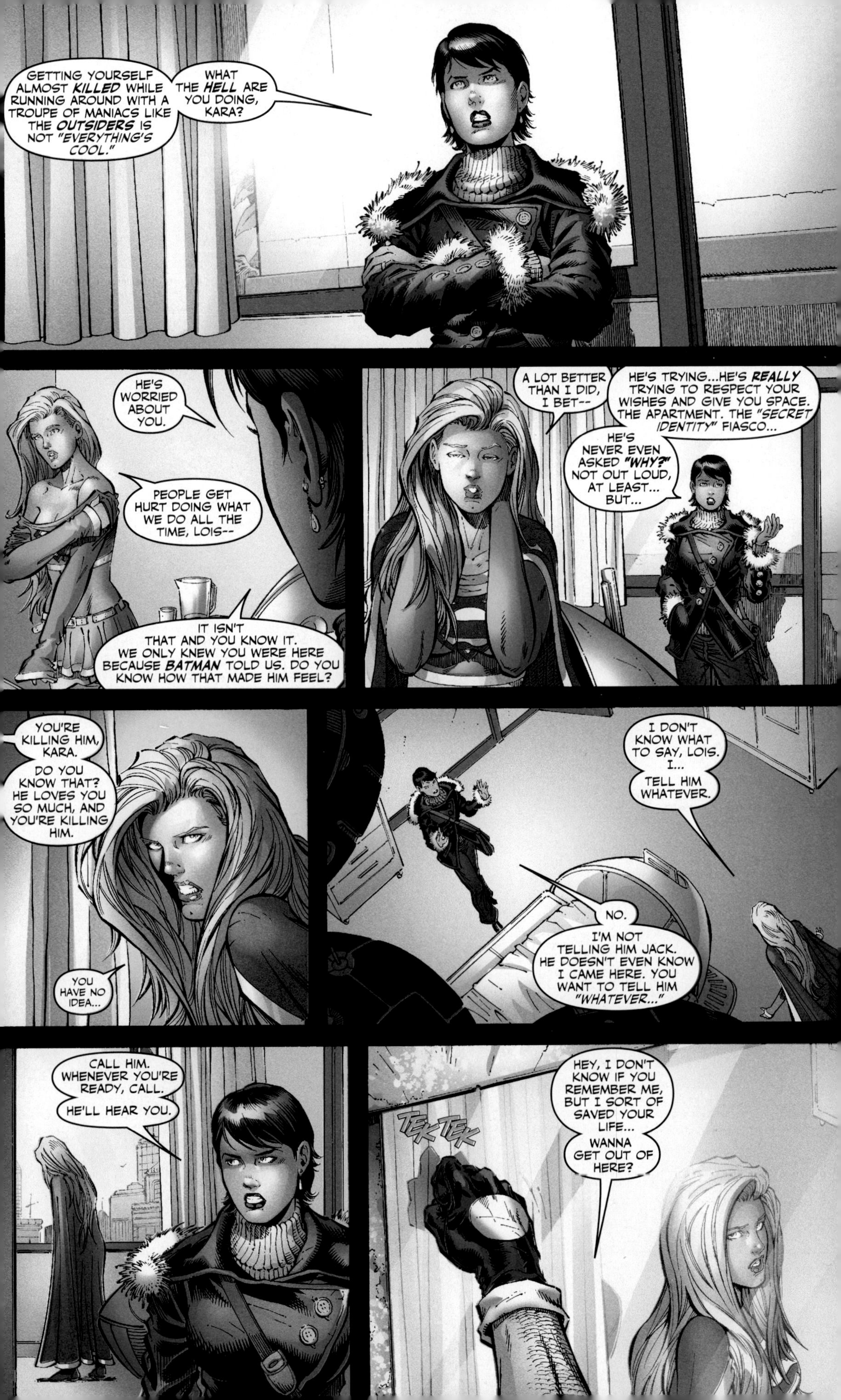

GETTING YOURSELF ALMOST KILLED WHILE RUNNING AROUND WITH A TROUPE OF MANIACS LIKE THE OUTSIDERS IS NOT "EVERYTHING'S COOL."
WHAT THE HELL ARE YOU DOING, KARA?
HE'S WORRIED ABOUT YOU.
PEOPLE GET HURT DOING WHAT WE DO ALL THE TIME, LOIS--
IT ISN'T THAT AND YOU KNOW IT. WE ONLY KNEW YOU WERE HERE BECAUSE BATMAN TOLD US. DO YOU KNOW HOW THAT MADE HIM FEEL?
A LOT BETTER THAN I DID, I BET--
HE'S TRYING...HE'S REALLY TRYING TO RESPECT YOUR WISHES AND GIVE YOU SPACE. THE APARTMENT. THE "SECRET IDENTITY" FIASCO...
HE'S NEVER EVEN ASKED "WHY?" NOT OUT LOUD, AT LEAST... BUT...
YOU'RE KILLING HIM, KARA.
DO YOU KNOW THAT? HE LOVES YOU SO MUCH, AND YOU'RE KILLING HIM.
YOU HAVE NO IDEA...
I DON'T KNOW WHAT TO SAY, LOIS. I...
TELL HIM WHATEVER.
NO.
I'M NOT TELLING HIM JACK. HE DOESN'T EVEN KNOW I CAME HERE. YOU WANT TO TELL HIM "WHATEVER..."
CALL HIM. WHENEVER YOU'RE READY, CALL.
HE'LL HEAR YOU.
TEK TEK
HEY, I DON'T KNOW IF YOU REMEMBER ME, BUT I SORT OF SAVED YOUR LIFE...
WANNA GET OUT OF HERE?

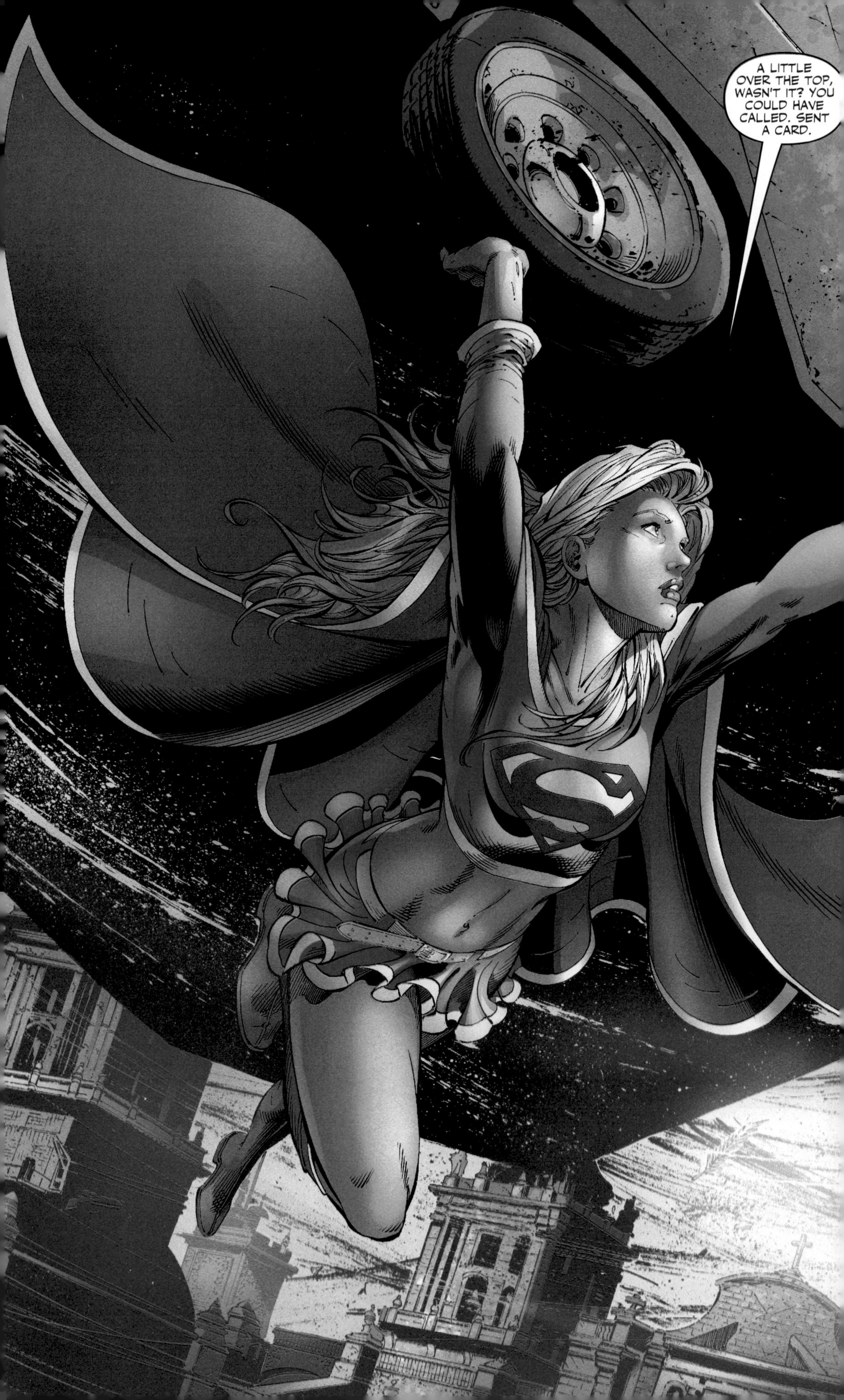
A LITTLE OVER THE TOP, WASN'T IT? YOU COULD HAVE CALLED. SENT A CARD.

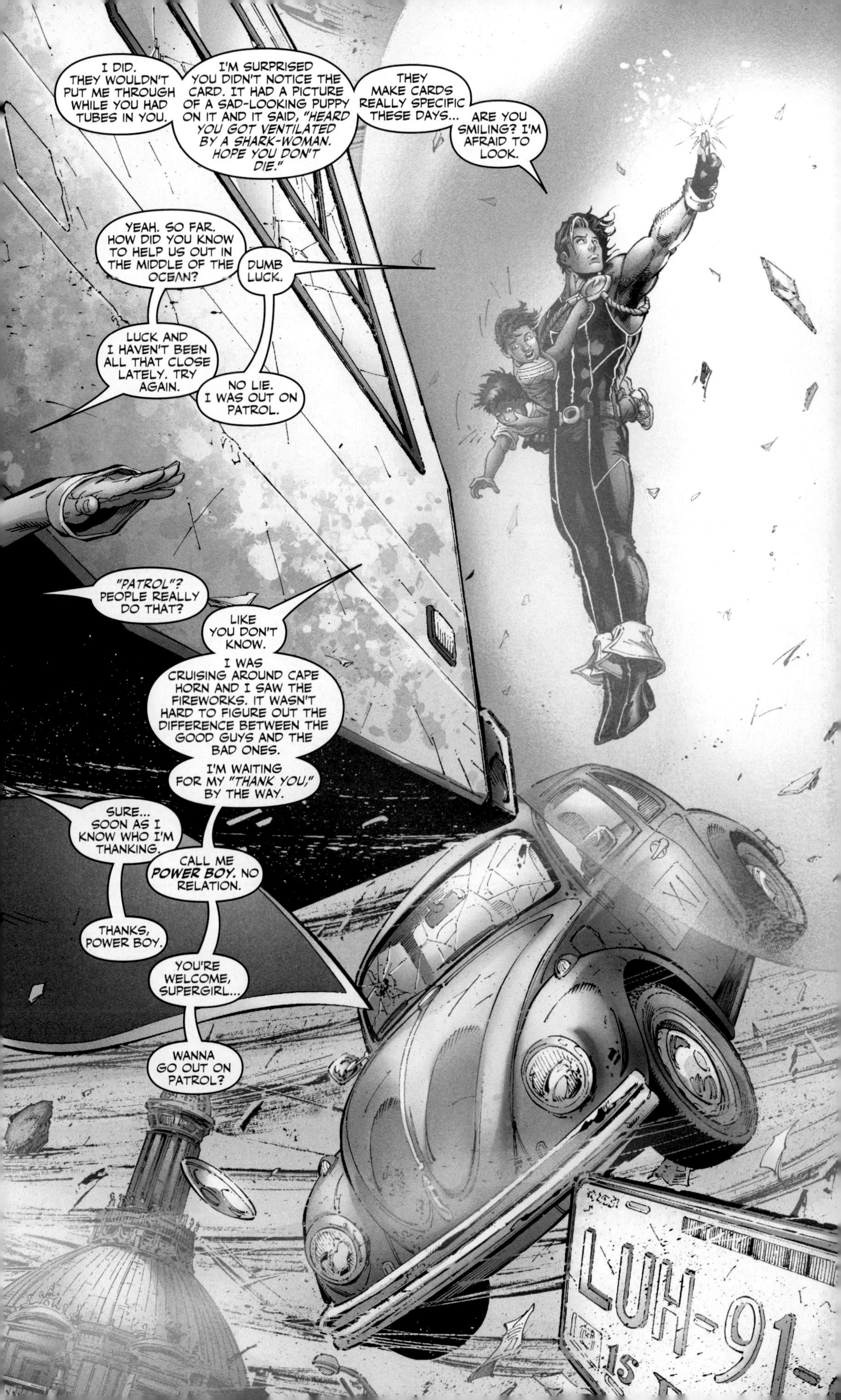

I DID. THEY WOULDN'T PUT ME THROUGH WHILE YOU HAD TUBES IN YOU.
I'M SURPRISED YOU DIDN'T NOTICE THE CARD. IT HAD A PICTURE OF A SAD-LOOKING PUPPY ON IT AND IT SAID, *"HEARD YOU GOT VENTILATED BY A SHARK-WOMAN. HOPE YOU DON'T DIE."*
THEY MAKE CARDS REALLY SPECIFIC THESE DAYS...
ARE YOU SMILING? I'M AFRAID TO LOOK.
YEAH. SO FAR. HOW DID YOU KNOW TO HELP US OUT IN THE MIDDLE OF THE OCEAN?
DUMB LUCK.
LUCK AND I HAVEN'T BEEN ALL THAT CLOSE LATELY. TRY AGAIN.
NO LIE. I WAS OUT ON PATROL.
"PATROL"? PEOPLE REALLY DO THAT?
LIKE YOU DON'T KNOW.
I WAS CRUISING AROUND CAPE HORN AND I SAW THE FIREWORKS. IT WASN'T HARD TO FIGURE OUT THE DIFFERENCE BETWEEN THE GOOD GUYS AND THE BAD ONES.
I'M WAITING FOR MY *"THANK YOU,"* BY THE WAY.
SURE... SOON AS I KNOW WHO I'M THANKING.
CALL ME ***POWER BOY.*** NO RELATION.
THANKS, POWER BOY.
YOU'RE WELCOME, SUPERGIRL...
WANNA GO OUT ON PATROL?
LUH-91-
15

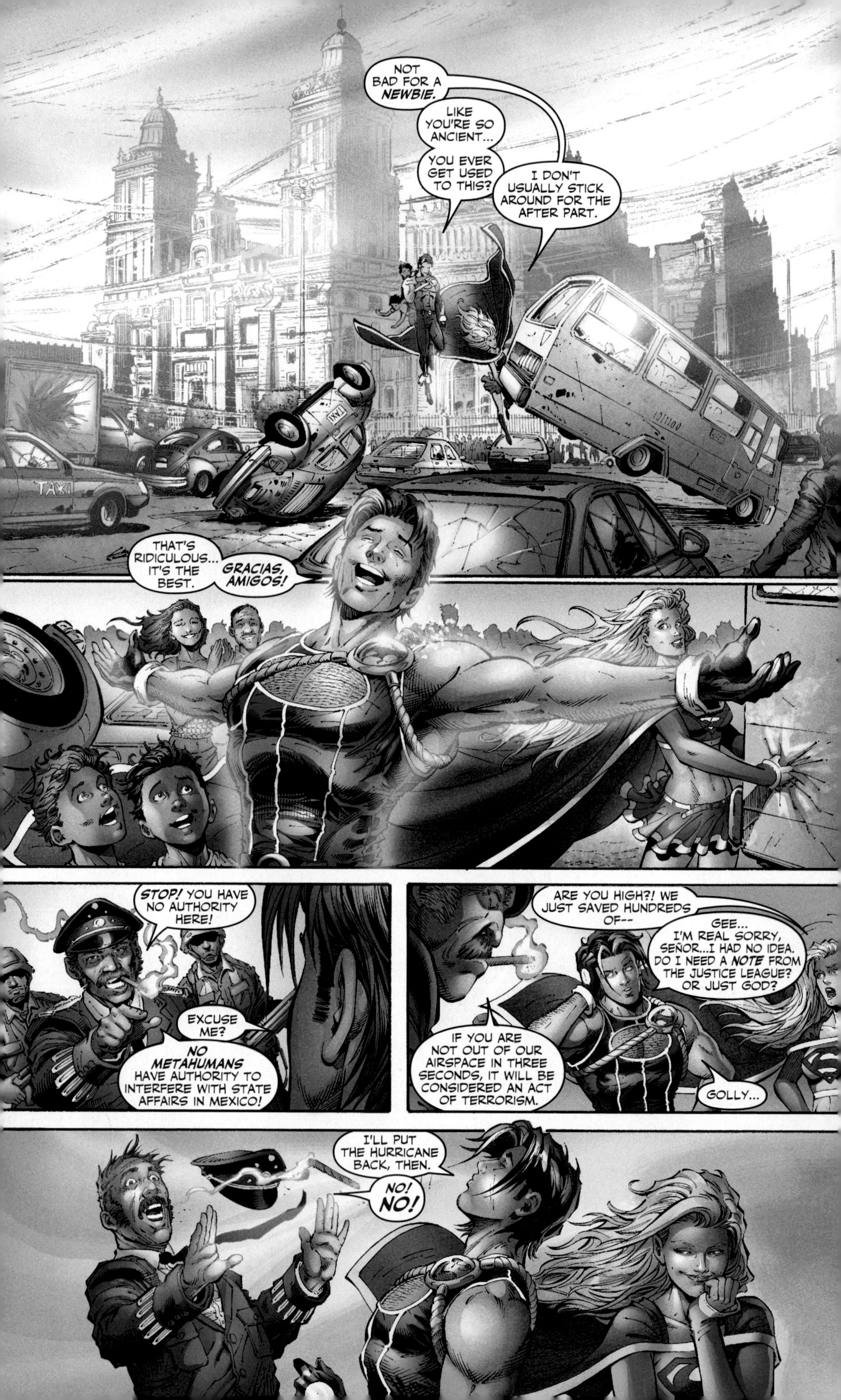

NOT BAD FOR A NEWBIE.
LIKE YOU'RE SO ANCIENT...
YOU EVER GET USED TO THIS?
I DON'T USUALLY STICK AROUND FOR THE AFTER PART.
THAT'S RIDICULOUS... IT'S THE BEST.
GRACIAS, AMIGOS!
STOP! YOU HAVE NO AUTHORITY HERE!
EXCUSE ME?
NO METAHUMANS HAVE AUTHORITY TO INTERFERE WITH STATE AFFAIRS IN MEXICO!
ARE YOU HIGH?! WE JUST SAVED HUNDREDS OF--
GEE... I'M REAL SORRY, SEÑOR...I HAD NO IDEA. DO I NEED A NOTE FROM THE JUSTICE LEAGUE? OR JUST GOD?
IF YOU ARE NOT OUT OF OUR AIRSPACE IN THREE SECONDS, IT WILL BE CONSIDERED AN ACT OF TERRORISM.
GOLLY...
I'LL PUT THE HURRICANE BACK, THEN.
NO! NO!

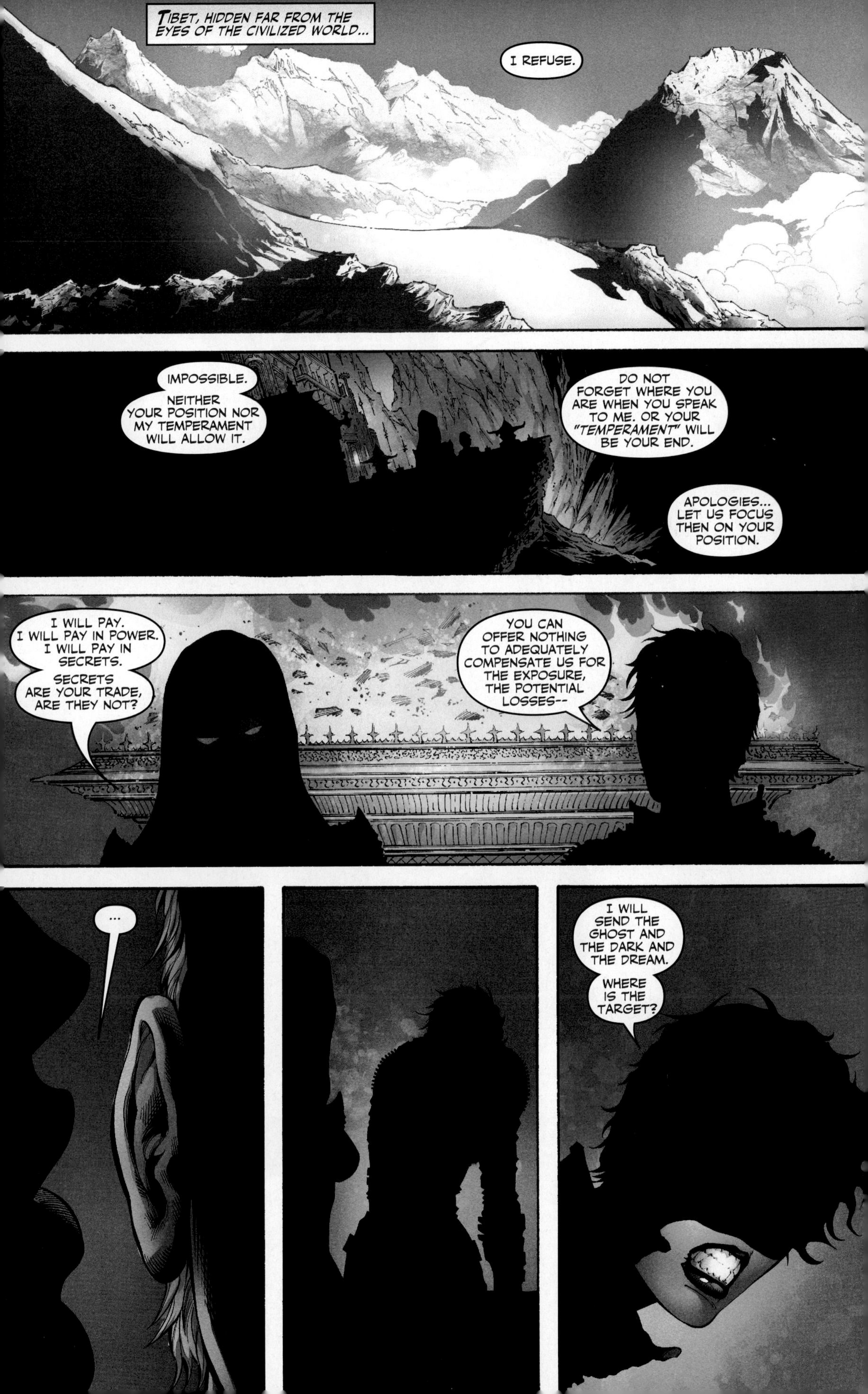
TIBET, HIDDEN FAR FROM THE EYES OF THE CIVILIZED WORLD...
I REFUSE.
IMPOSSIBLE.
NEITHER YOUR POSITION NOR MY TEMPERAMENT WILL ALLOW IT.
DO NOT FORGET WHERE YOU ARE WHEN YOU SPEAK TO ME. OR YOUR "TEMPERAMENT" WILL BE YOUR END.
APOLOGIES... LET US FOCUS THEN ON YOUR POSITION.
I WILL PAY. I WILL PAY IN POWER. I WILL PAY IN SECRETS.
SECRETS ARE YOUR TRADE, ARE THEY NOT?
YOU CAN OFFER NOTHING TO ADEQUATELY COMPENSATE US FOR THE EXPOSURE, THE POTENTIAL LOSSES--
...
I WILL SEND THE GHOST AND THE DARK AND THE DREAM.
WHERE IS THE TARGET?

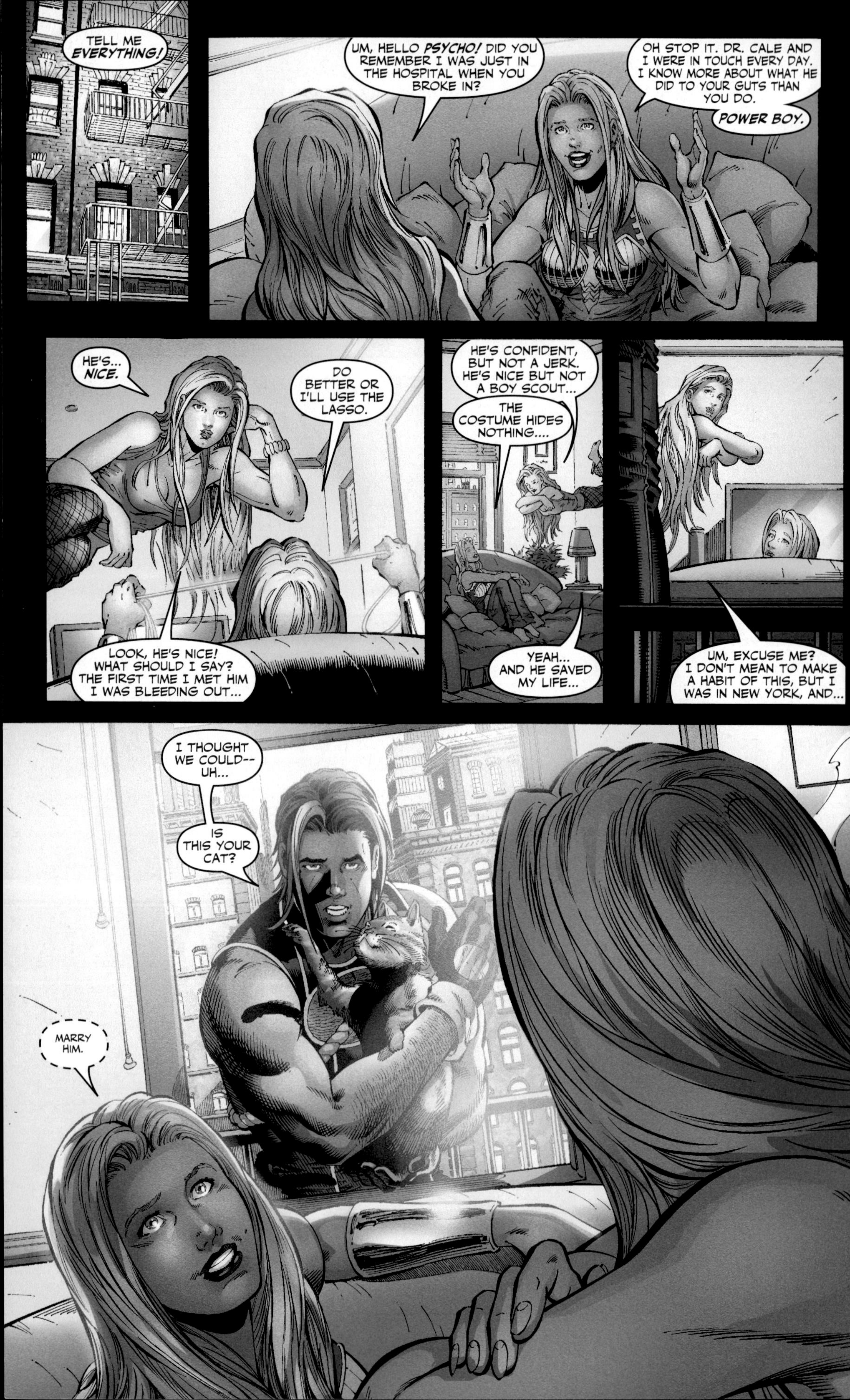
TELL ME *EVERYTHING!*
UM, HELLO *PSYCHO!* DID YOU REMEMBER I WAS JUST IN THE HOSPITAL WHEN YOU BROKE IN?
OH STOP IT. DR. CALE AND I WERE IN TOUCH EVERY DAY. I KNOW MORE ABOUT WHAT HE DID TO YOUR GUTS THAN YOU DO.
POWER BOY.
HE'S... *NICE.*
DO BETTER OR I'LL USE THE LASSO.
LOOK, HE'S NICE! WHAT SHOULD I SAY? THE FIRST TIME I MET HIM I WAS BLEEDING OUT...
HE'S CONFIDENT, BUT NOT A JERK. HE'S NICE BUT NOT A BOY SCOUT...
THE COSTUME HIDES NOTHING....
YEAH... AND HE SAVED MY LIFE...
UM, EXCUSE ME? I DON'T MEAN TO MAKE A HABIT OF THIS, BUT I WAS IN NEW YORK, AND...
I THOUGHT WE COULD-- UH...
IS THIS YOUR CAT?
MARRY HIM.

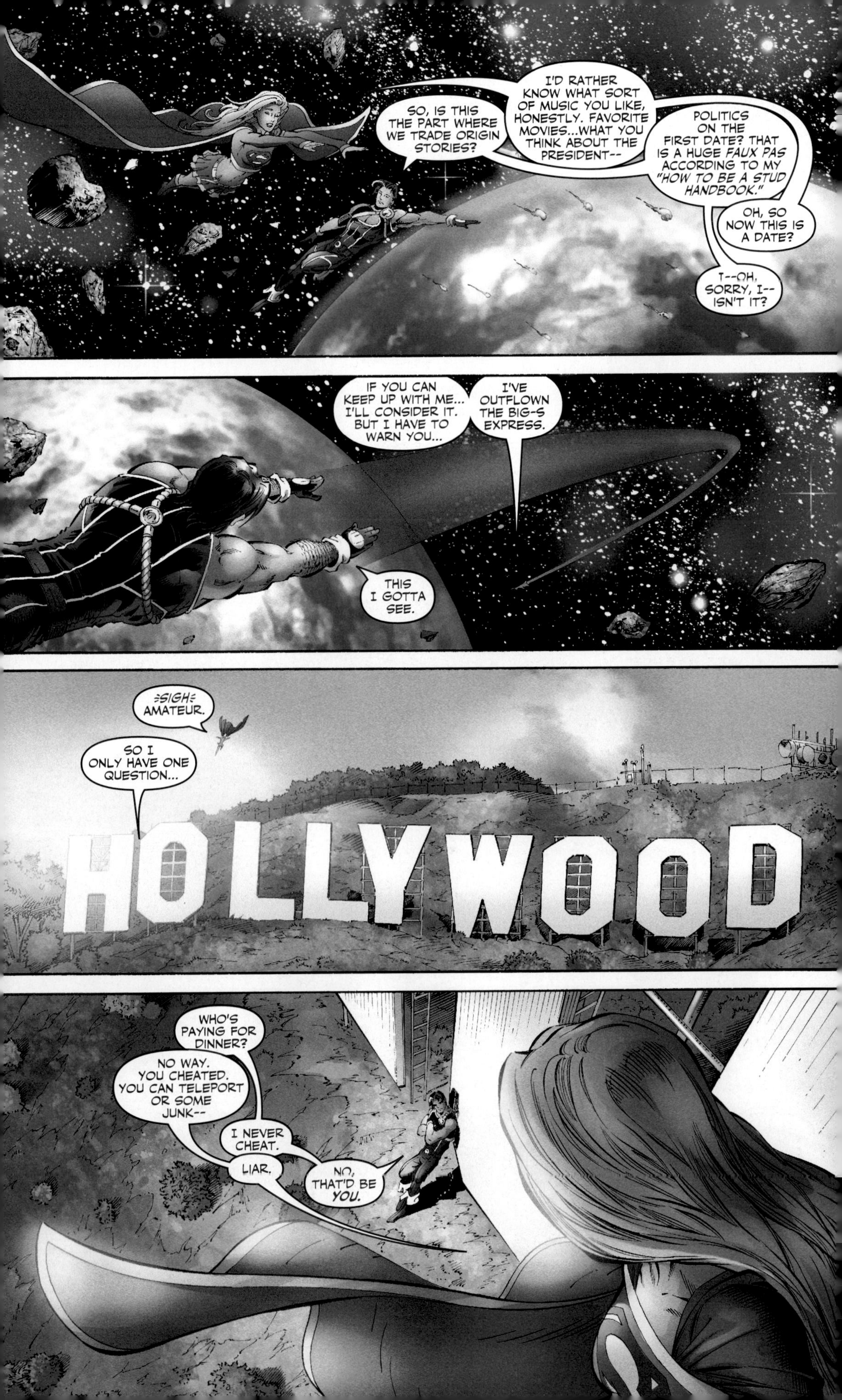

SO, IS THIS THE PART WHERE WE TRADE ORIGIN STORIES?
I'D RATHER KNOW WHAT SORT OF MUSIC YOU LIKE, HONESTLY. FAVORITE MOVIES...WHAT YOU THINK ABOUT THE PRESIDENT--
POLITICS ON THE FIRST DATE? THAT IS A HUGE *FAUX PAS* ACCORDING TO MY *"HOW TO BE A STUD HANDBOOK."*
OH, SO NOW THIS IS A DATE?
I--OH, SORRY, I--ISN'T IT?
IF YOU CAN KEEP UP WITH ME... I'LL CONSIDER IT. BUT I HAVE TO WARN YOU...
I'VE OUTFLOWN THE BIG-S EXPRESS.
THIS I GOTTA SEE.
SIGH AMATEUR.
SO I ONLY HAVE ONE QUESTION...
HOLLYWOOD
WHO'S PAYING FOR DINNER?
NO WAY. YOU CHEATED. YOU CAN TELEPORT OR SOME JUNK--
I NEVER CHEAT.
LIAR.
NO, THAT'D BE *YOU*.

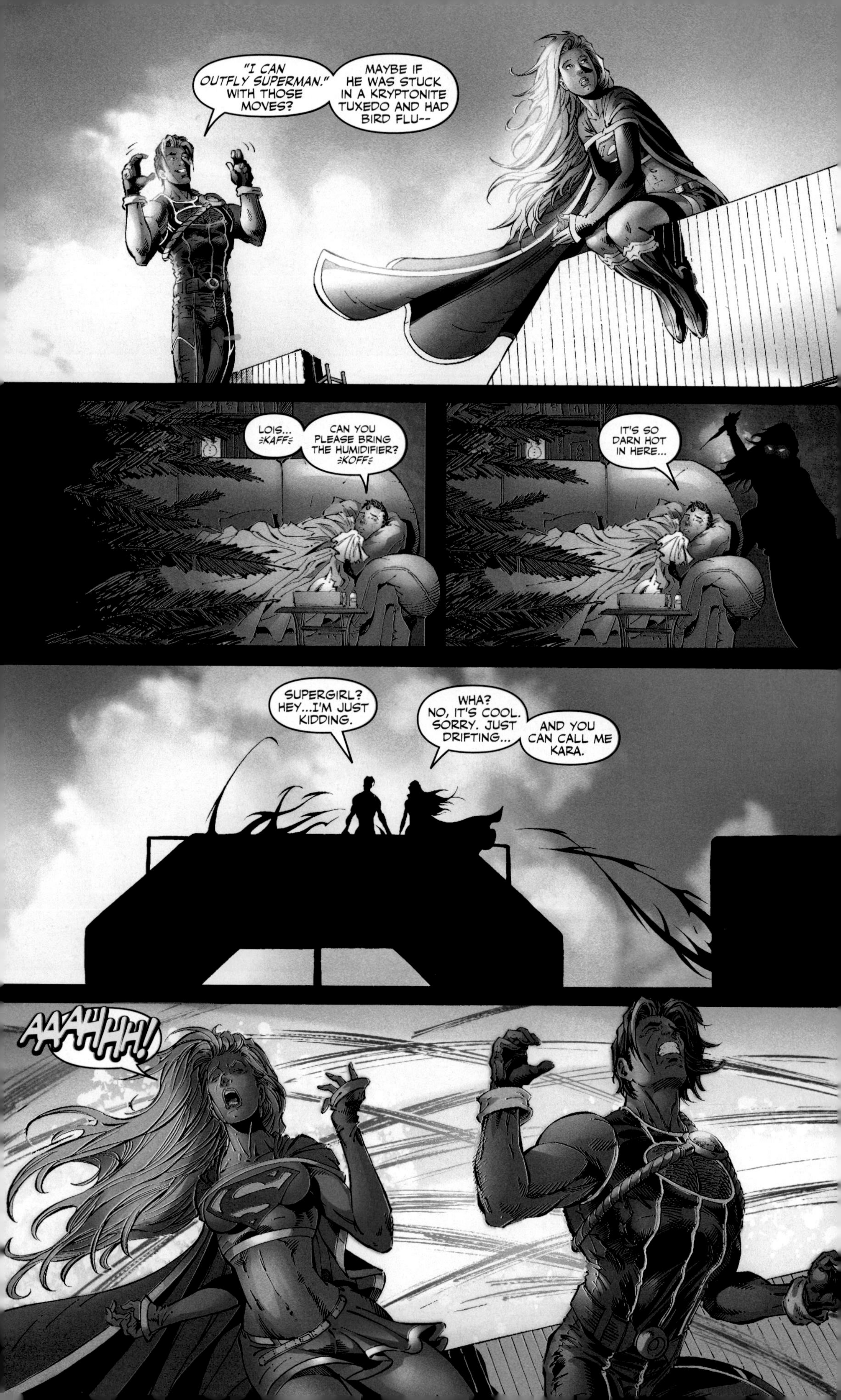
"I CAN OUTFLY SUPERMAN." WITH THOSE MOVES?
MAYBE IF HE WAS STUCK IN A KRYPTONITE TUXEDO AND HAD BIRD FLU--
LOIS... KAFF
CAN YOU PLEASE BRING THE HUMIDIFIER? KOFF
IT'S SO DARN HOT IN HERE...
SUPERGIRL? HEY...I'M JUST KIDDING.
WHA? NO, IT'S COOL. SORRY. JUST DRIFTING...
AND YOU CAN CALL ME KARA.
AAAHHH!

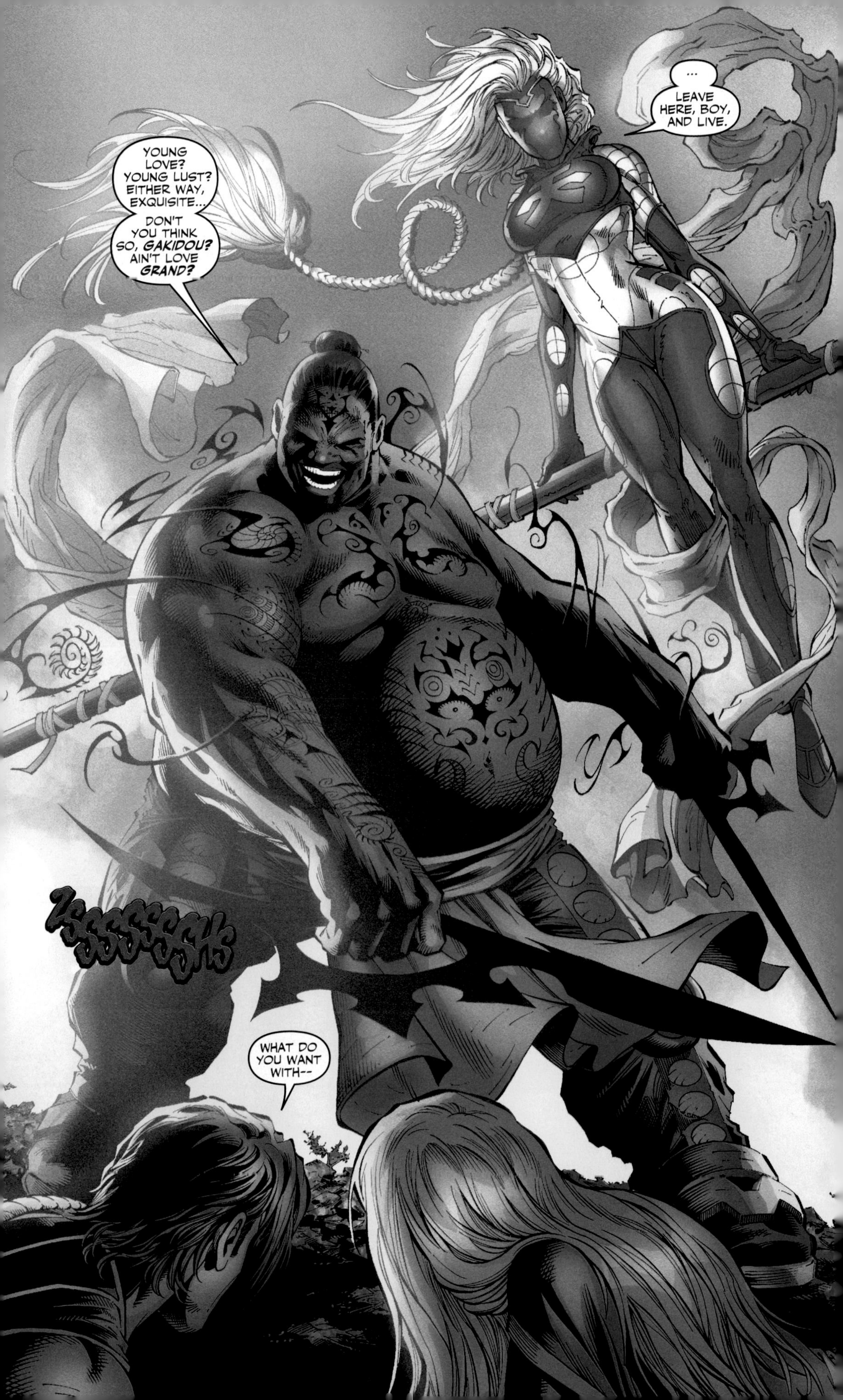
...
LEAVE HERE, BOY, AND LIVE.
YOUNG LOVE? YOUNG LUST? EITHER WAY, EXQUISITE...
DON'T YOU THINK SO, GAKIDOU? AIN'T LOVE GRAND?
ZSSSSSSHS
WHAT DO YOU WANT WITH--

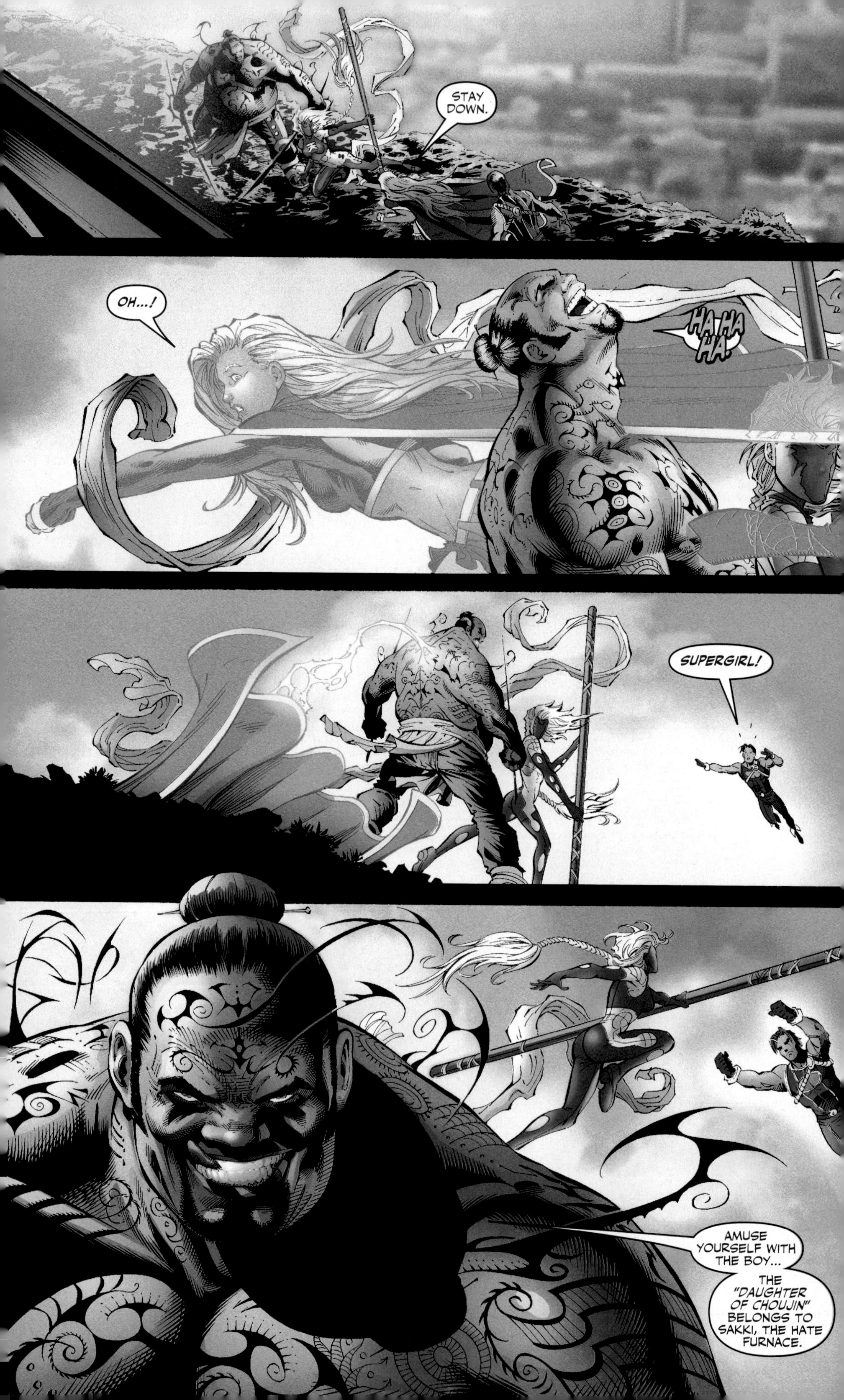
STAY DOWN.
OH...!
HA HA HA HA!
SUPERGIRL!
AMUSE YOURSELF WITH THE BOY...
THE "DAUGHTER OF CHOUJIN" BELONGS TO SAKKI, THE HATE FURNACE.

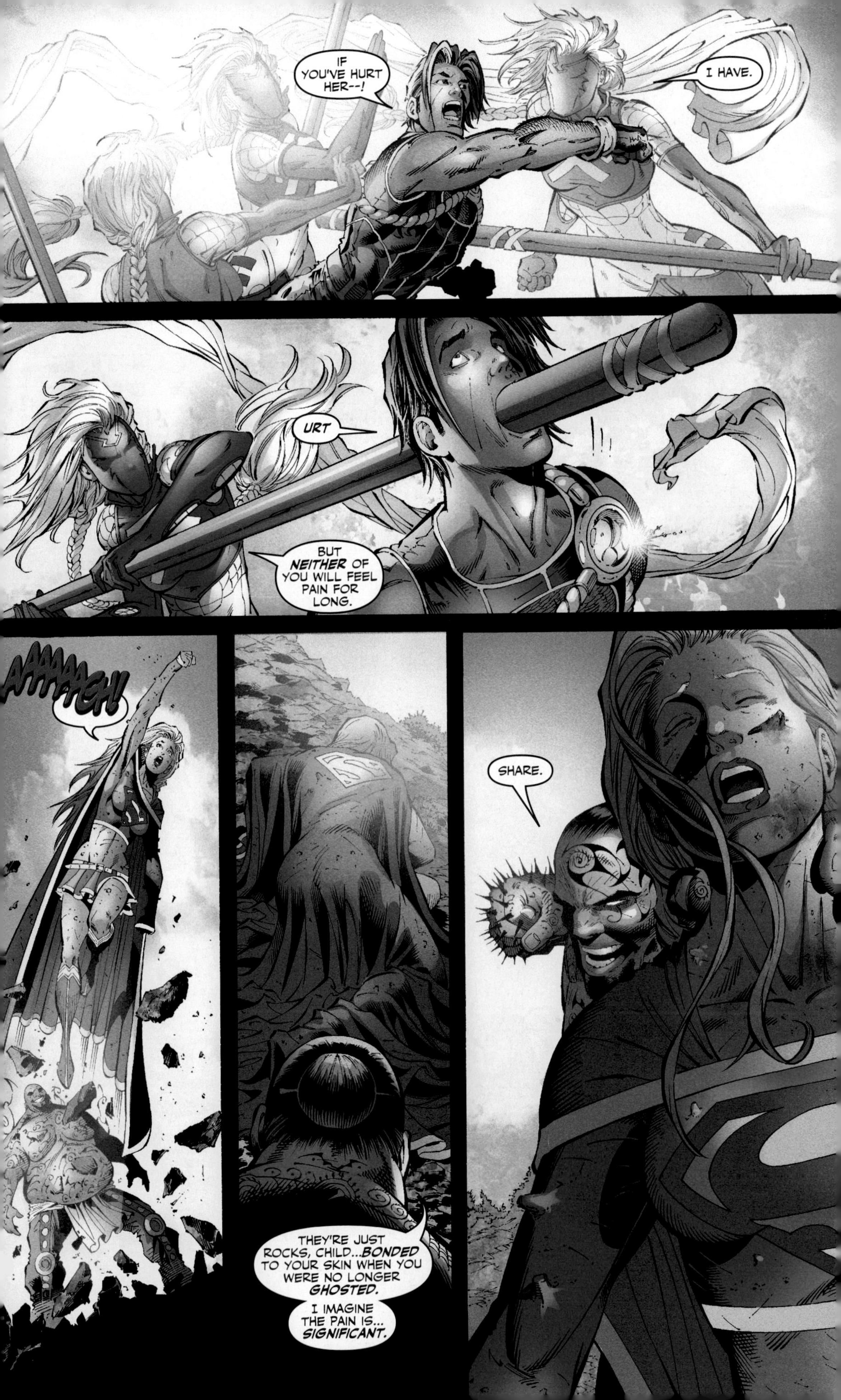
IF YOU'VE HURT HER--!
I HAVE.
URT
BUT NEITHER OF YOU WILL FEEL PAIN FOR LONG.
AAAAAAGH!
THEY'RE JUST ROCKS, CHILD...BONDED TO YOUR SKIN WHEN YOU WERE NO LONGER GHOSTED.
I IMAGINE THE PAIN IS... SIGNIFICANT.
SHARE.

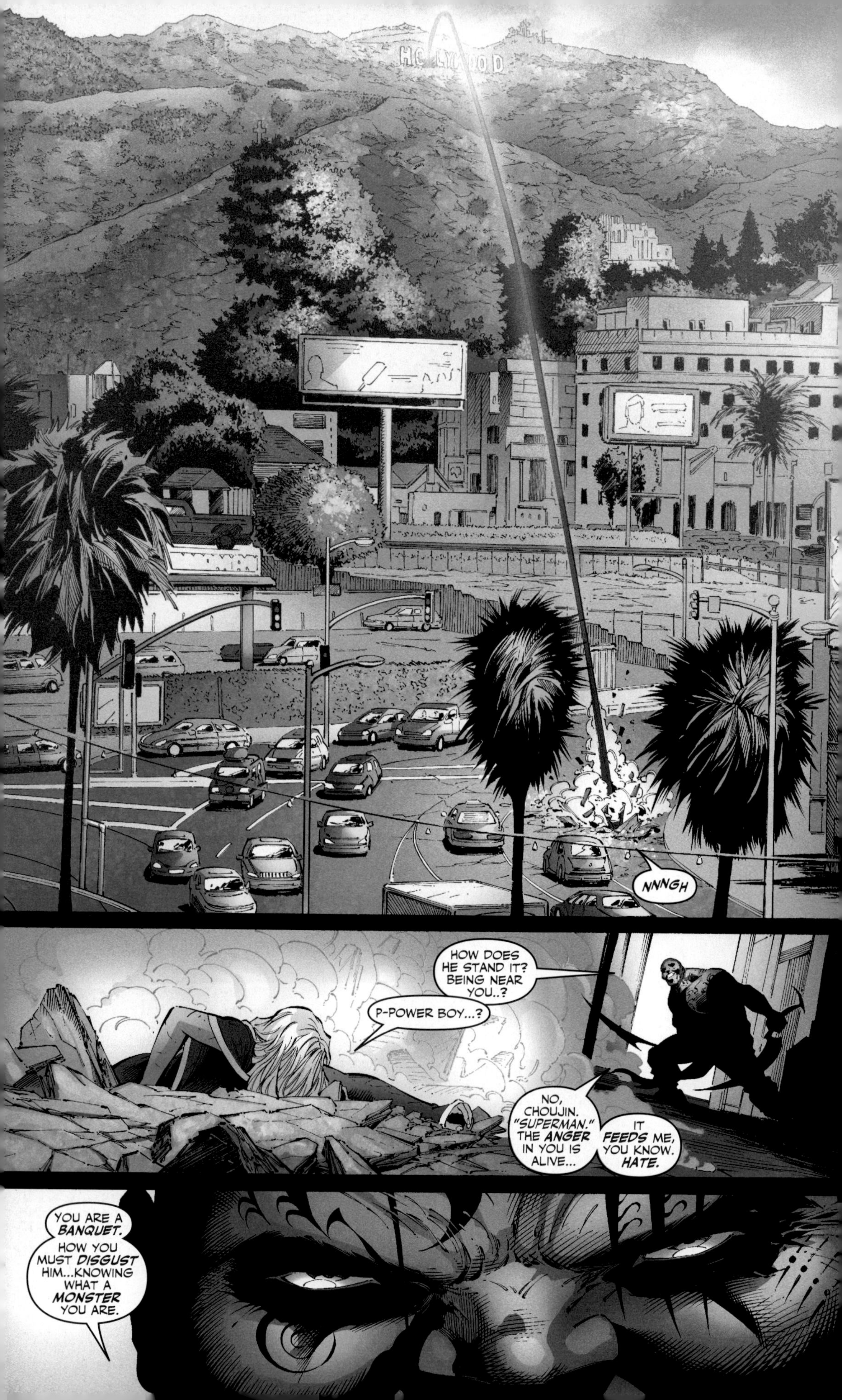
HOLLYWOOD
NNNGH
HOW DOES HE STAND IT? BEING NEAR YOU..?
P-POWER BOY...?
NO, CHOUJIN. "SUPERMAN." THE ANGER IN YOU IS ALIVE...
IT FEEDS ME, YOU KNOW. HATE.
YOU ARE A BANQUET. HOW YOU MUST DISGUST HIM...KNOWING WHAT A MONSTER YOU ARE.

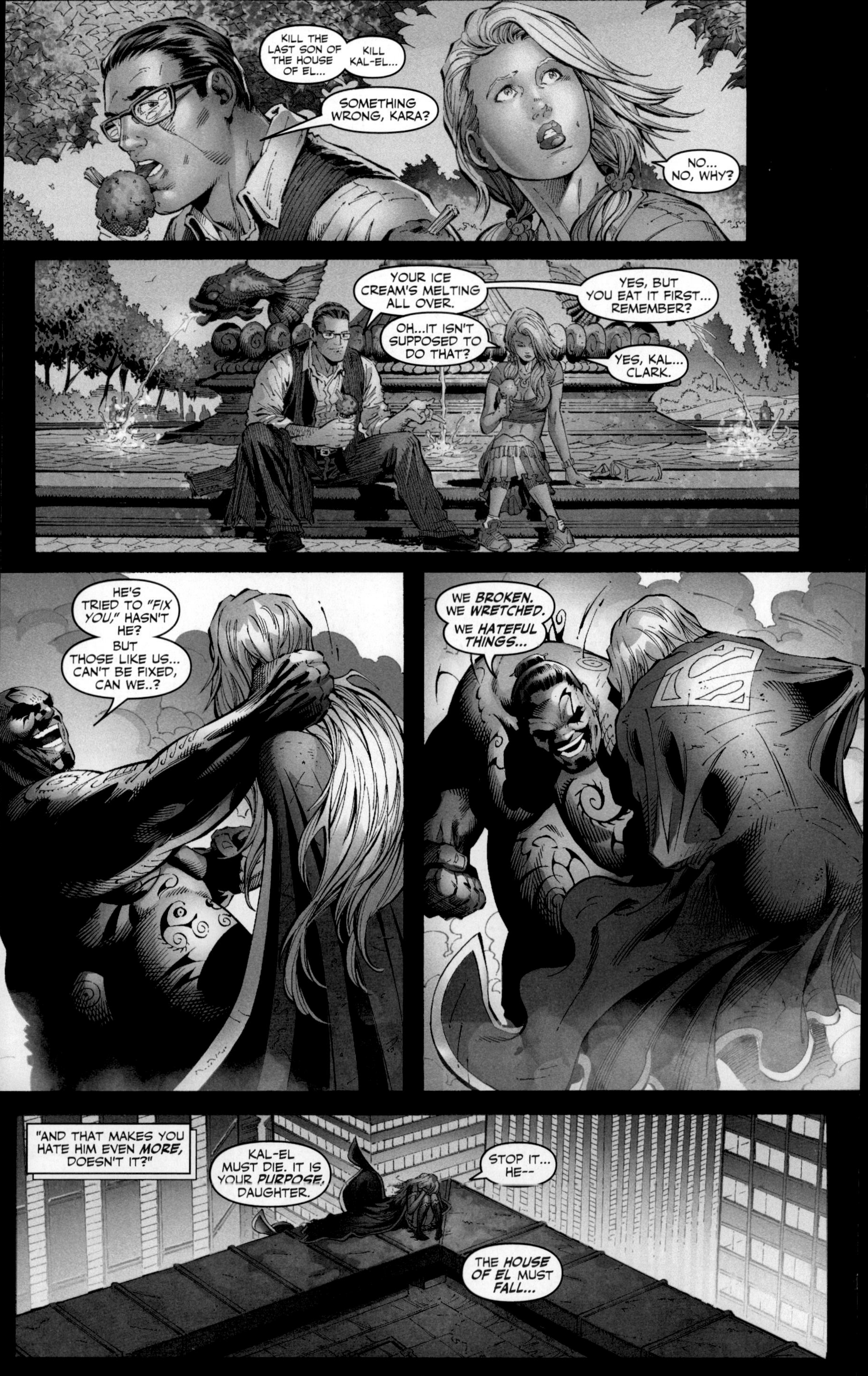
KILL THE LAST SON OF THE HOUSE OF EL...
KILL KAL-EL...
SOMETHING WRONG, KARA?
NO... NO, WHY?
YOUR ICE CREAM'S MELTING ALL OVER.
YES, BUT YOU EAT IT FIRST... REMEMBER?
OH...IT ISN'T SUPPOSED TO DO THAT?
YES, KAL... CLARK.
HE'S TRIED TO "FIX YOU," HASN'T HE?
BUT THOSE LIKE US... CAN'T BE FIXED, CAN WE..?
WE BROKEN. WE WRETCHED. WE HATEFUL THINGS...
"AND THAT MAKES YOU HATE HIM EVEN MORE, DOESN'T IT?"
KAL-EL MUST DIE. IT IS YOUR PURPOSE, DAUGHTER.
STOP IT... HE--
THE HOUSE OF EL MUST FALL...

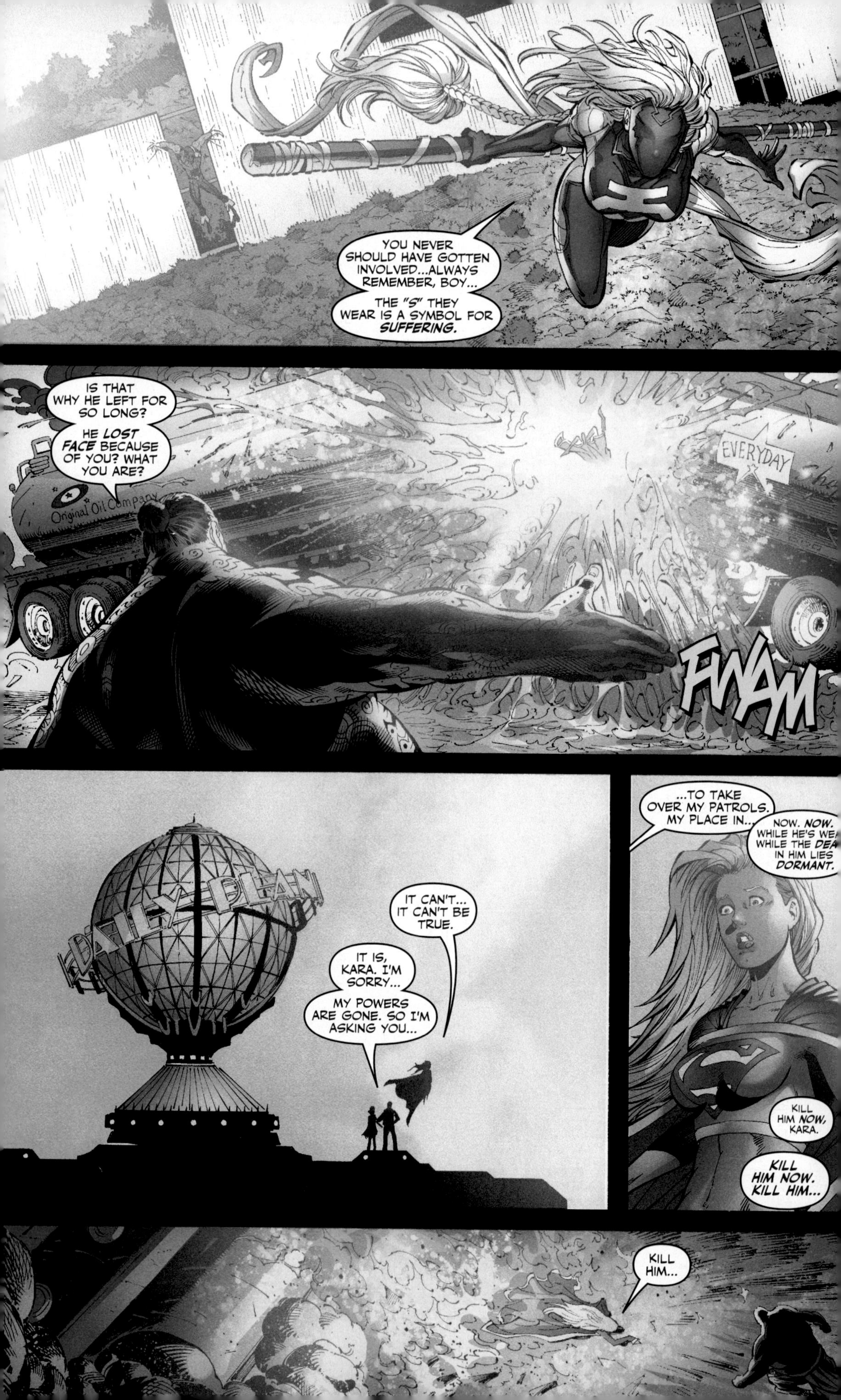

YOU NEVER SHOULD HAVE GOTTEN INVOLVED...ALWAYS REMEMBER, BOY...
THE "S" THEY WEAR IS A SYMBOL FOR *SUFFERING.*
IS THAT WHY HE LEFT FOR SO LONG?
HE *LOST FACE* BECAUSE OF YOU? WHAT YOU ARE?
Original Oil Company
EVERYDAY
FWAM
DAILY PLAN
IT CAN'T... IT CAN'T BE TRUE.
IT IS, KARA. I'M SORRY...
MY POWERS ARE GONE. SO I'M ASKING YOU...
...TO TAKE OVER MY PATROLS. MY PLACE IN...
NOW. *NOW.* WHILE HE'S WE WHILE THE *DEA* IN HIM LIES *DORMANT.*
KILL HIM *NOW,* KARA.
KILL HIM NOW. KILL HIM...
KILL HIM...

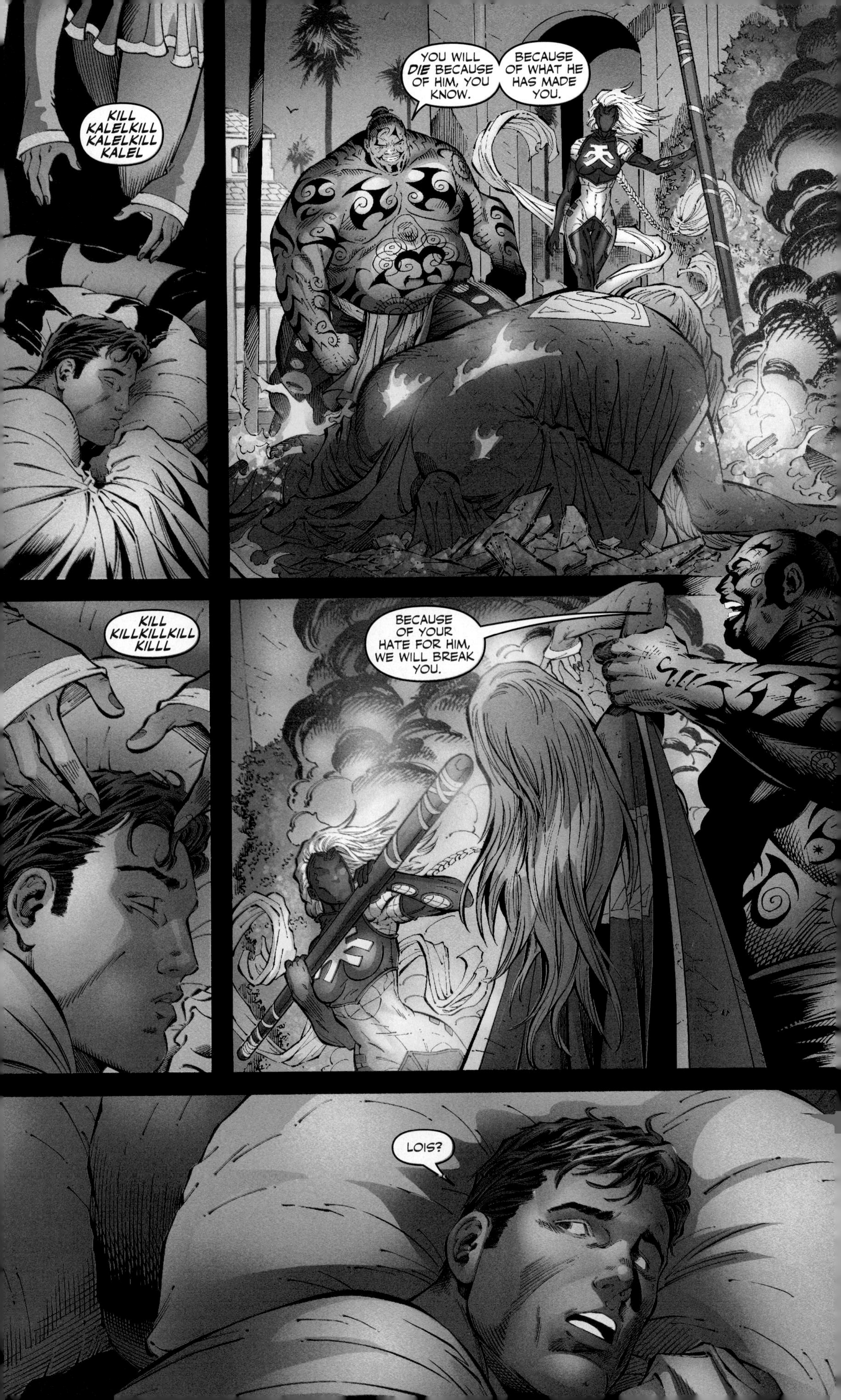
KILL KALELKILL KALELKILL KALEL
YOU WILL DIE BECAUSE OF HIM, YOU KNOW.
BECAUSE OF WHAT HE HAS MADE YOU.
KILL KILLKILLKILL KILLL
BECAUSE OF YOUR HATE FOR HIM, WE WILL BREAK YOU.
LOIS?

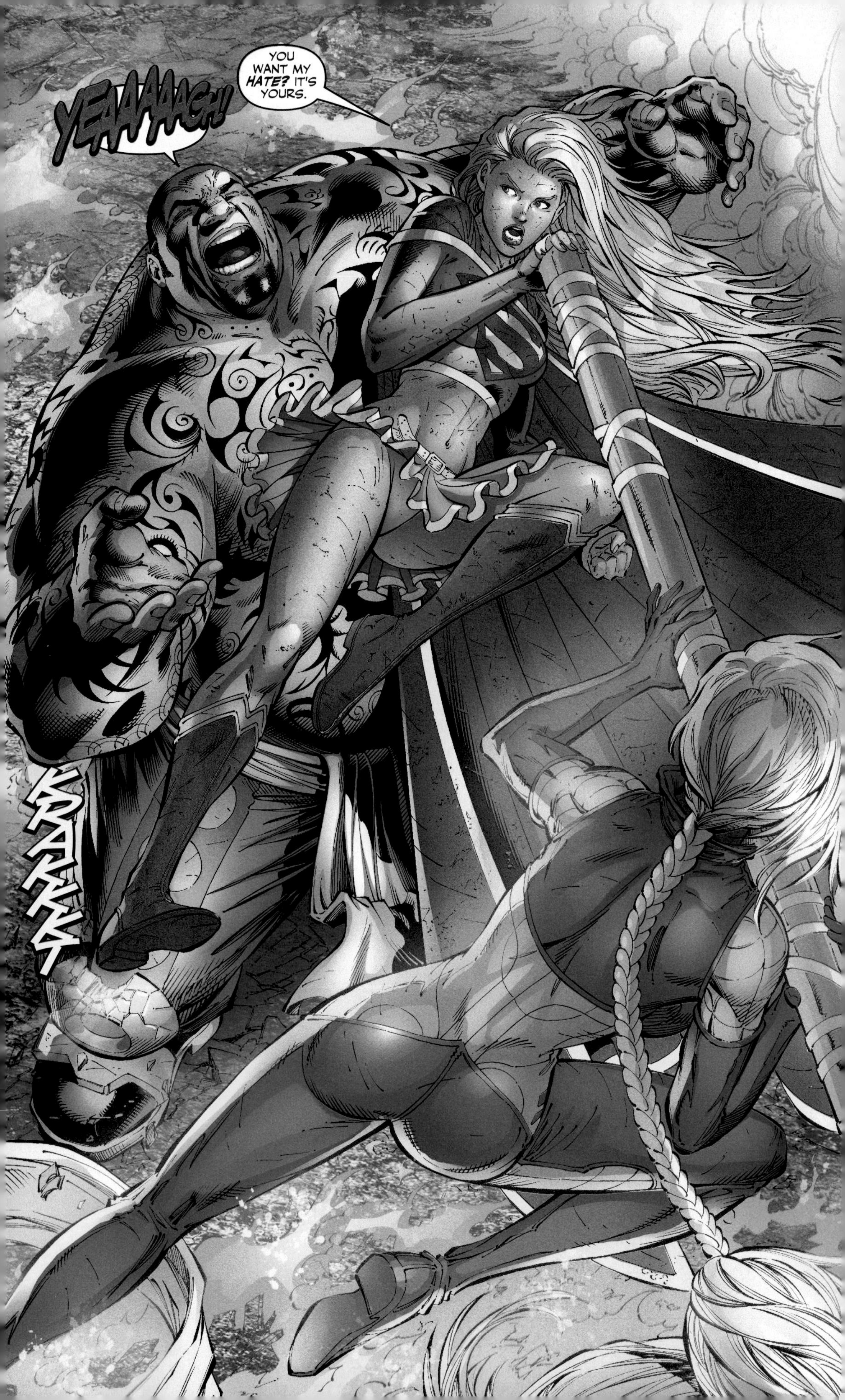
YEAAAAAGH!
YOU WANT MY HATE? IT'S YOURS.
KRAKKA

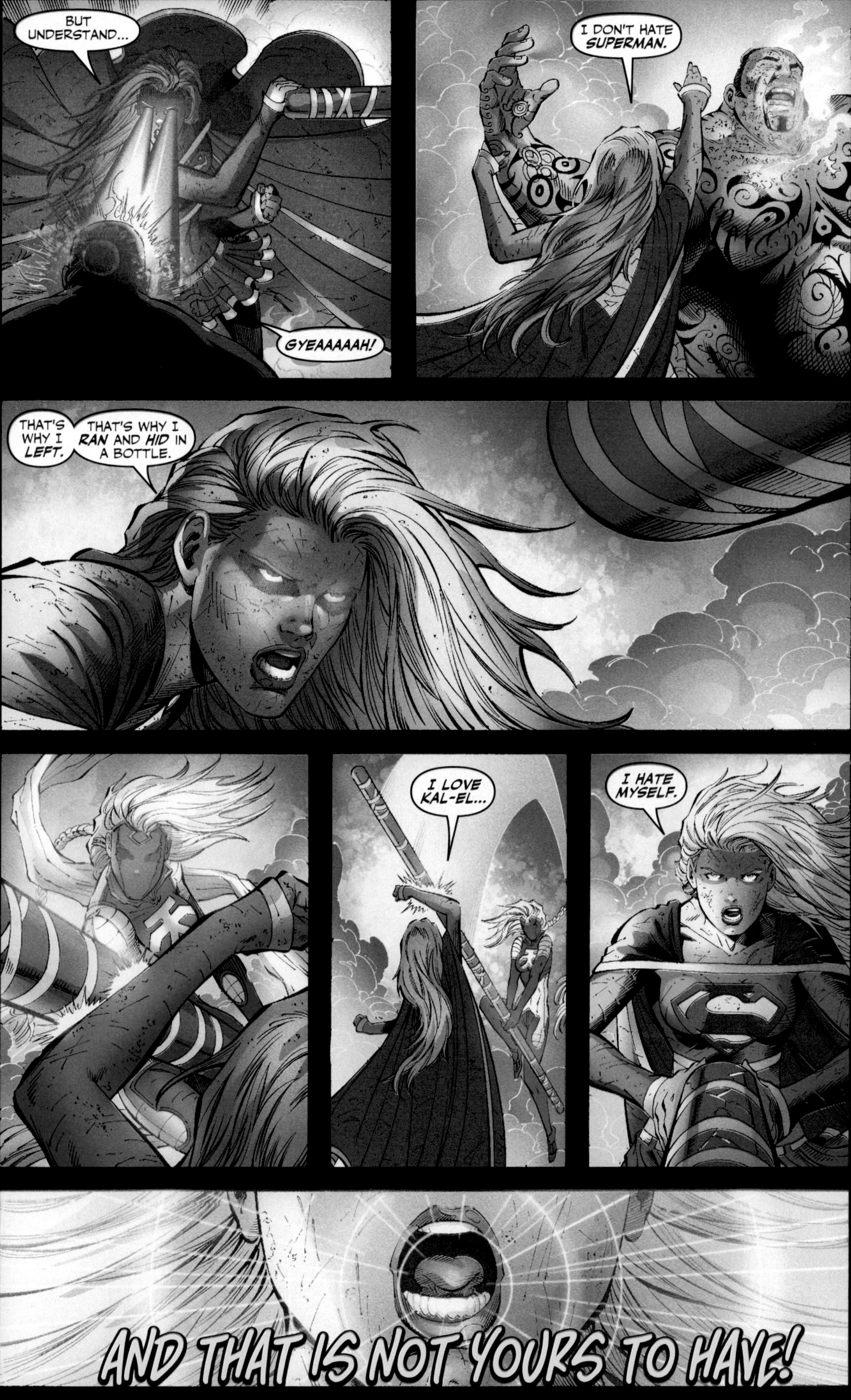
BUT UNDERSTAND...
GYEAAAAAH!
I DON'T HATE SUPERMAN.
THAT'S WHY I LEFT.
THAT'S WHY I RAN AND HID IN A BOTTLE.
I LOVE KAL-EL...
I HATE MYSELF.
AND THAT IS NOT YOURS TO HAVE!

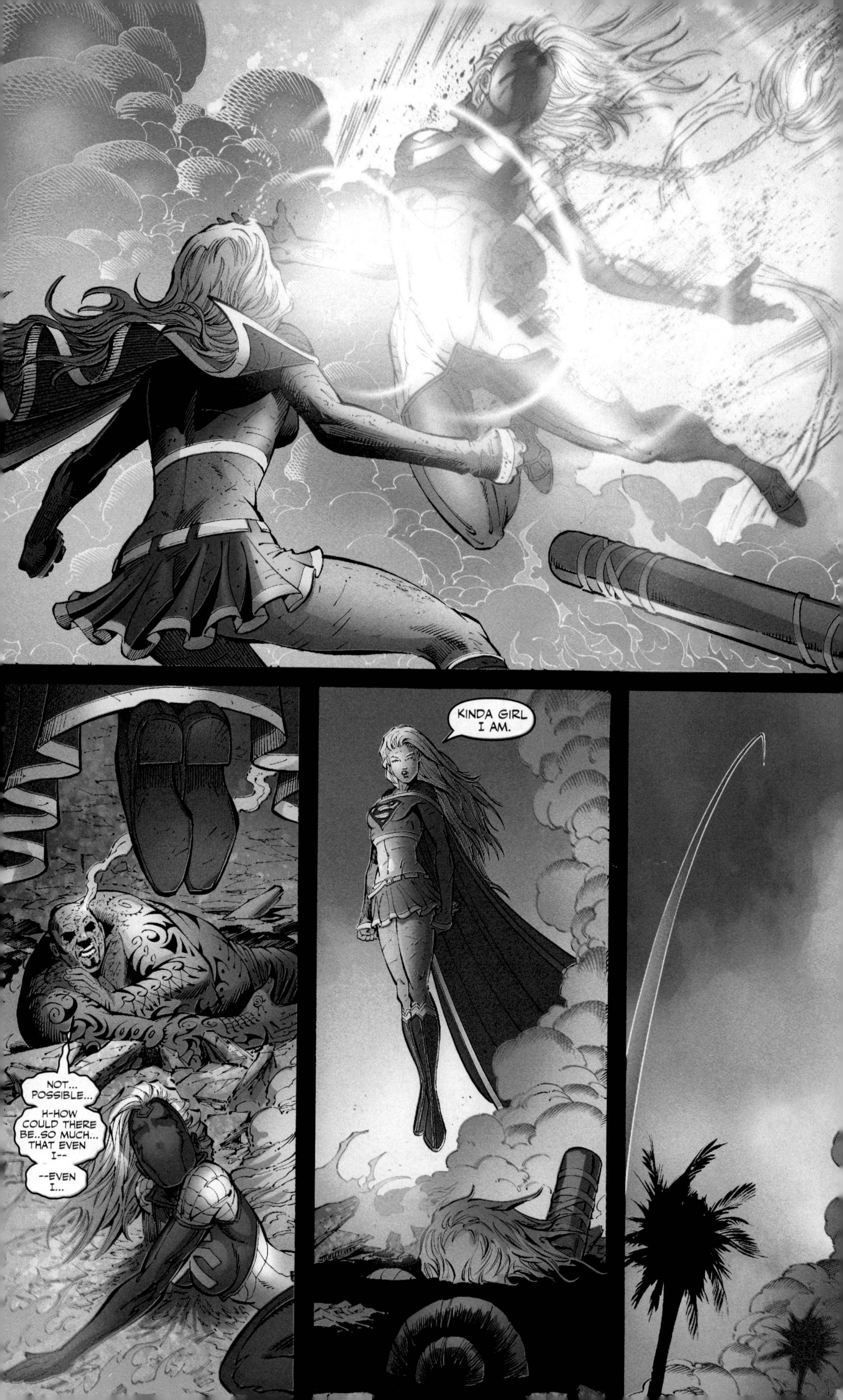
NOT... POSSIBLE...
H-HOW COULD THERE BE..SO MUCH... THAT EVEN I--
--EVEN I...
KINDA GIRL I AM.

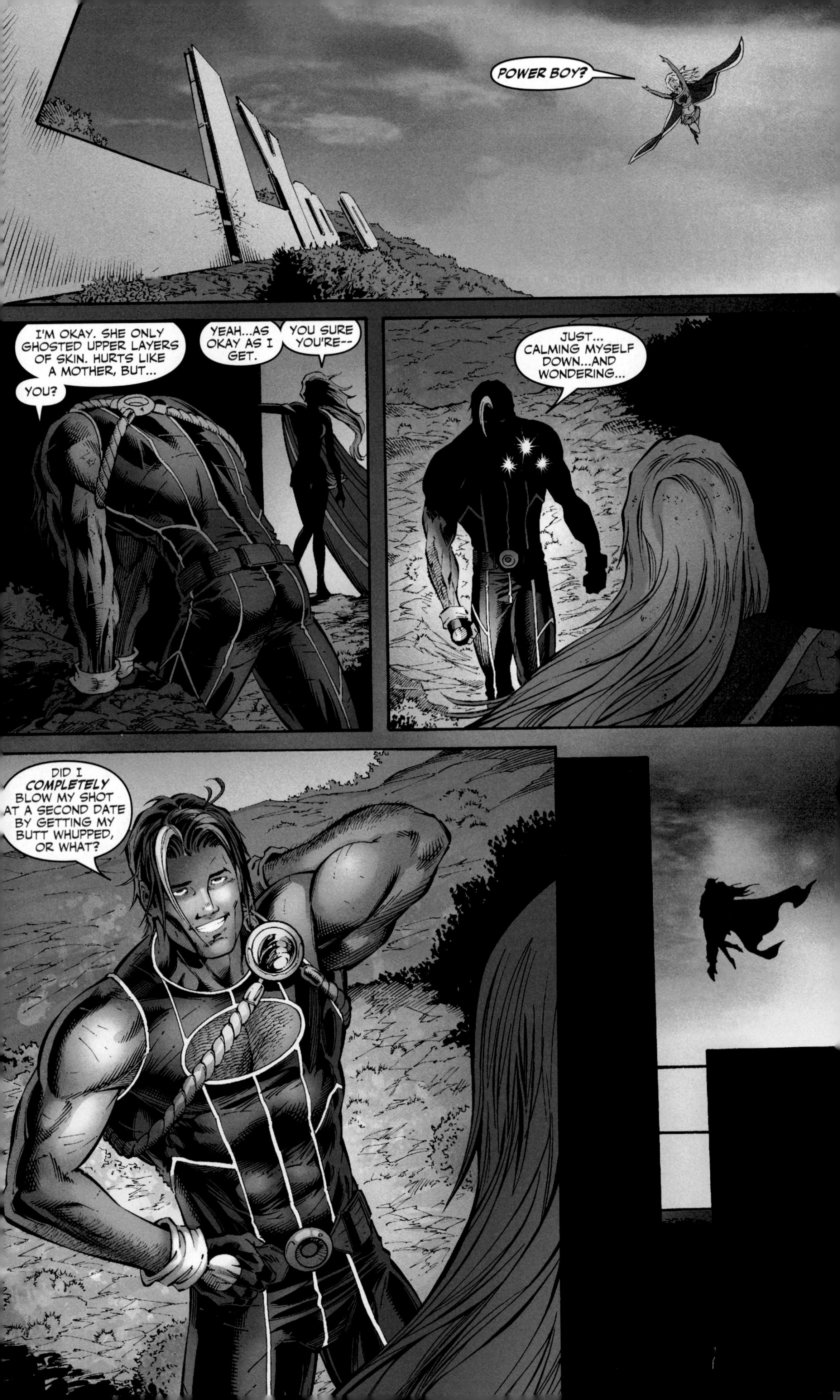
POWER BOY?
I'M OKAY. SHE ONLY GHOSTED UPPER LAYERS OF SKIN. HURTS LIKE A MOTHER, BUT...
YOU?
YEAH...AS OKAY AS I GET.
YOU SURE YOU'RE--
JUST... CALMING MYSELF DOWN...AND WONDERING...
DID I COMPLETELY BLOW MY SHOT AT A SECOND DATE BY GETTING MY BUTT WHUPPED, OR WHAT?

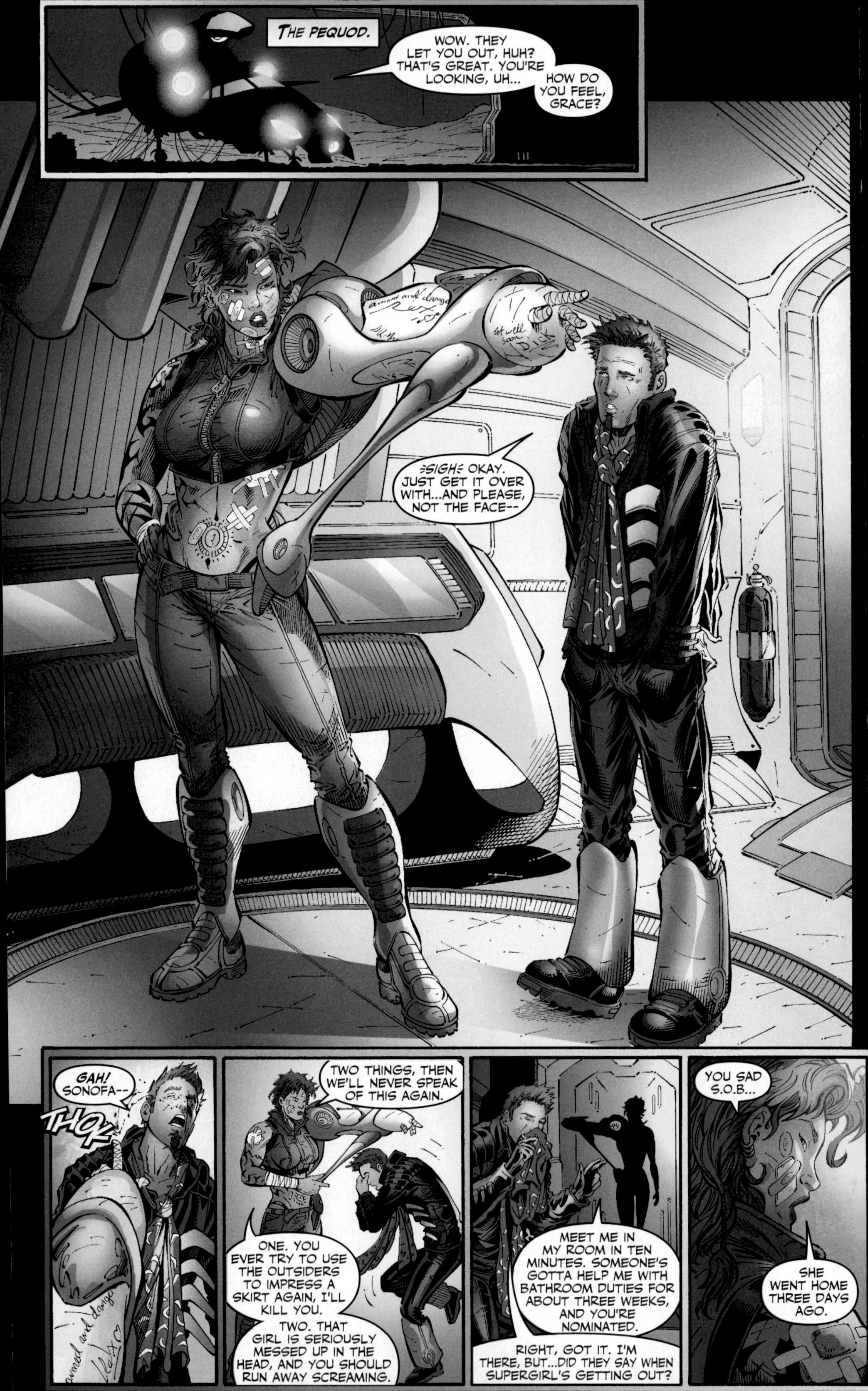
THE PEQUOD.
WOW. THEY LET YOU OUT, HUH? THAT'S GREAT. YOU'RE LOOKING, UH...
HOW DO YOU FEEL, GRACE?
SIGH OKAY. JUST GET IT OVER WITH...AND PLEASE, NOT THE FACE--
GAH! SONOFA--
THOK
TWO THINGS, THEN WE'LL NEVER SPEAK OF THIS AGAIN.
ONE. YOU EVER TRY TO USE THE OUTSIDERS TO IMPRESS A SKIRT AGAIN, I'LL KILL YOU.
TWO. THAT GIRL IS SERIOUSLY MESSED UP IN THE HEAD, AND YOU SHOULD RUN AWAY SCREAMING.
MEET ME IN MY ROOM IN TEN MINUTES. SOMEONE'S GOTTA HELP ME WITH BATHROOM DUTIES FOR ABOUT THREE WEEKS, AND YOU'RE NOMINATED.
RIGHT, GOT IT. I'M THERE, BUT...DID THEY SAY WHEN SUPERGIRL'S GETTING OUT?
YOU SAD S.O.B...
SHE WENT HOME THREE DAYS AGO.

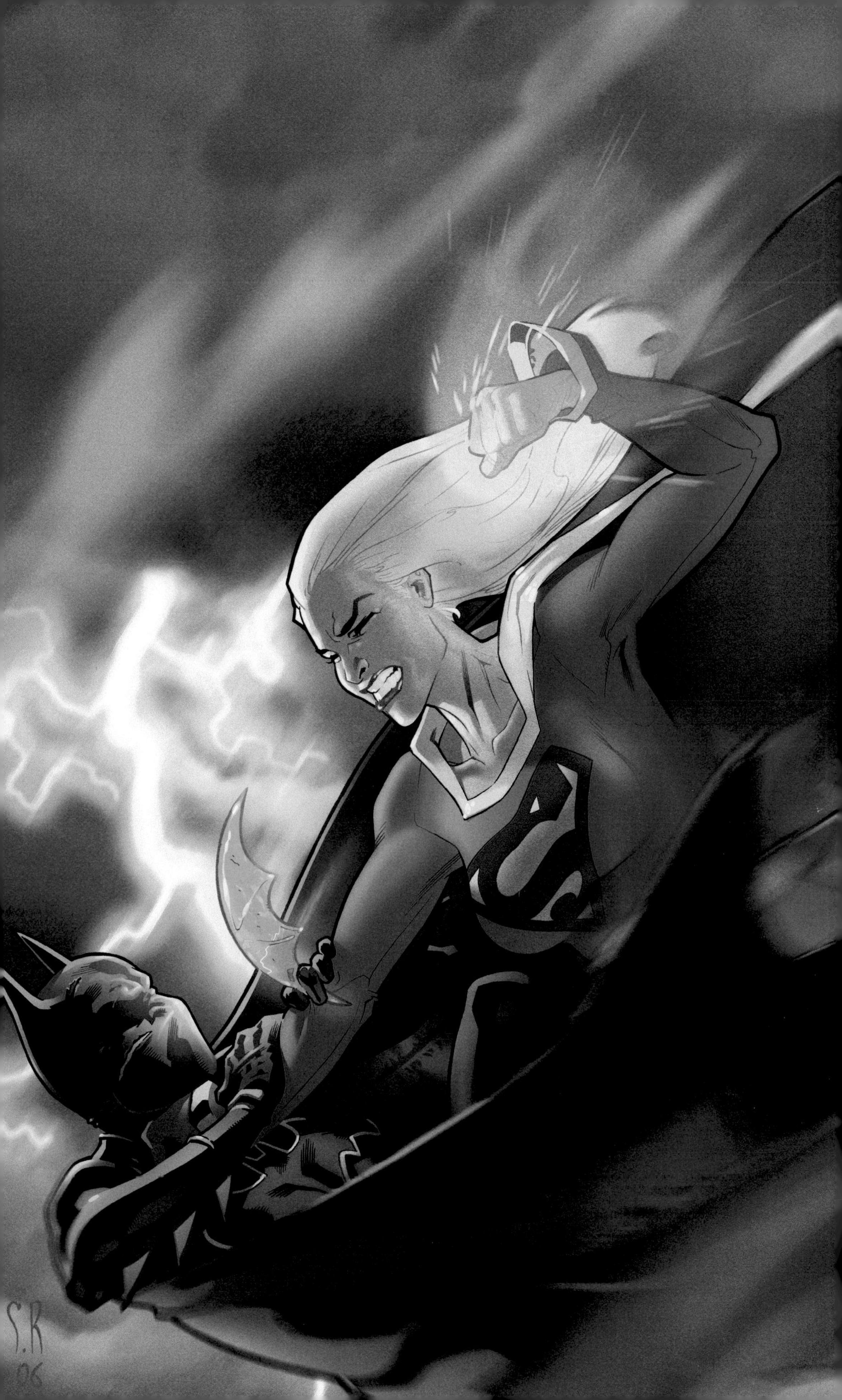

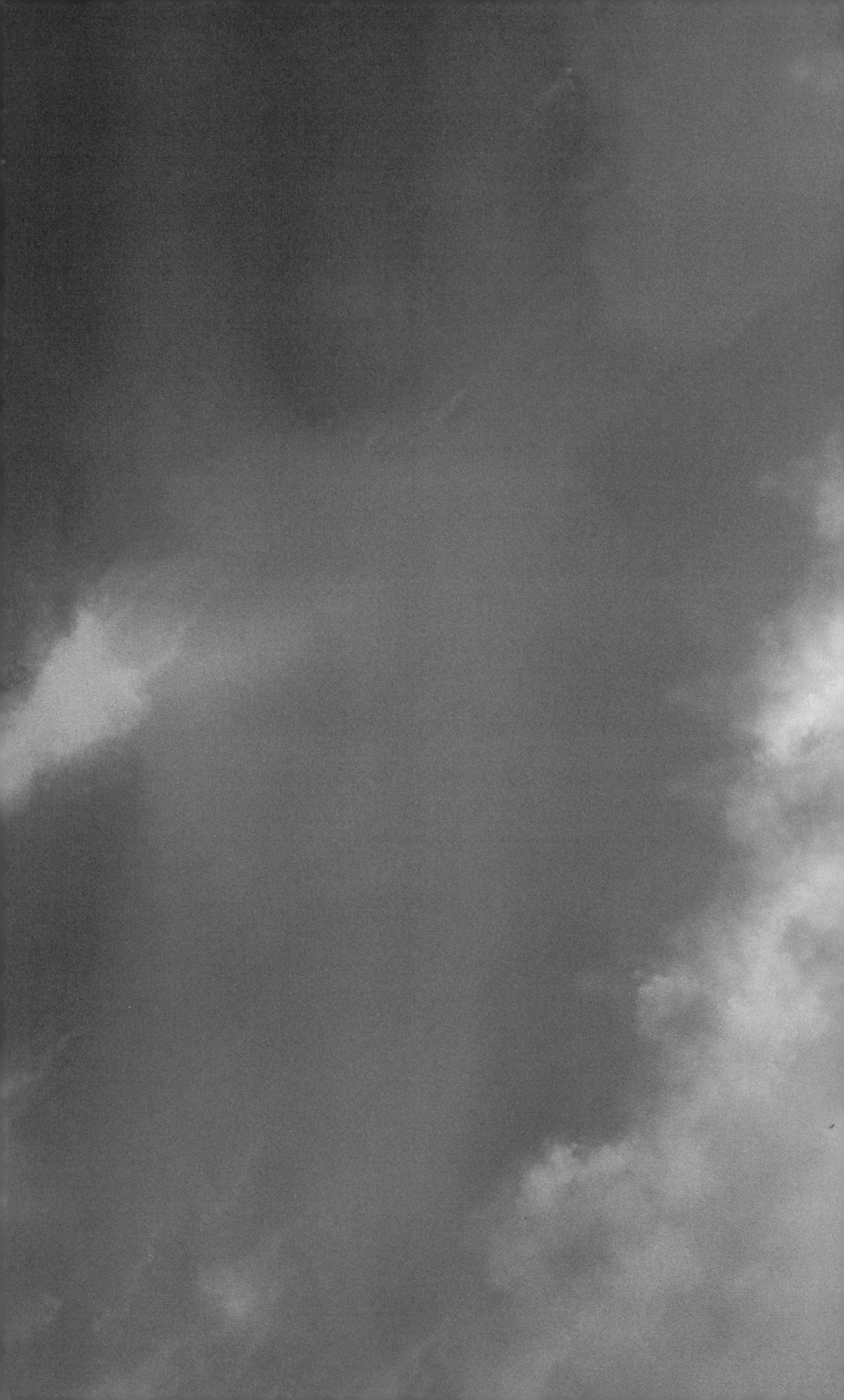

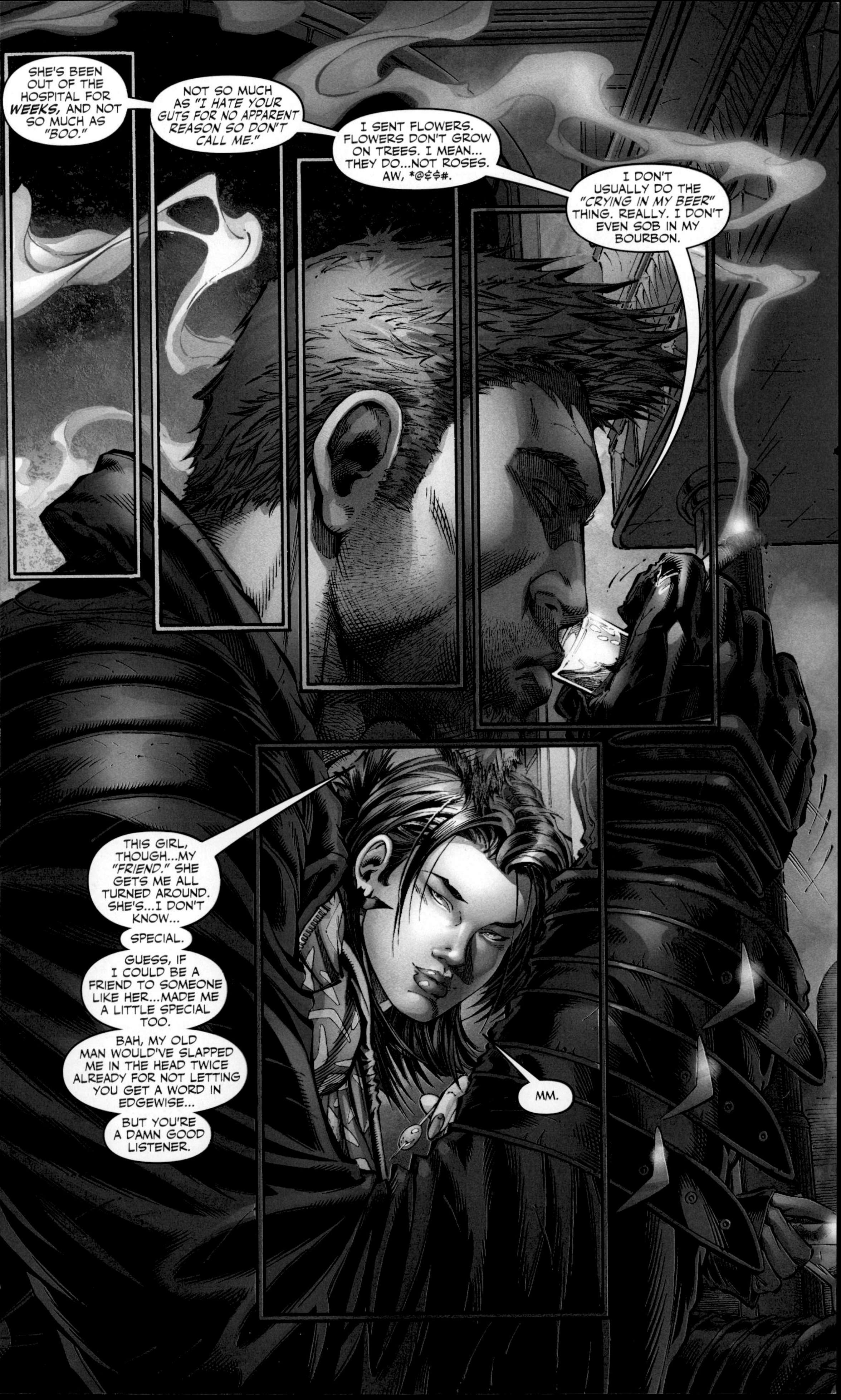
SHE'S BEEN OUT OF THE HOSPITAL FOR WEEKS, AND NOT SO MUCH AS "BOO."
NOT SO MUCH AS "I HATE YOUR GUTS FOR NO APPARENT REASON SO DON'T CALL ME."
I SENT FLOWERS. FLOWERS DON'T GROW ON TREES. I MEAN... THEY DO...NOT ROSES. AW, *@$$#.
I DON'T USUALLY DO THE "CRYING IN MY BEER" THING. REALLY. I DON'T EVEN SOB IN MY BOURBON.
THIS GIRL, THOUGH...MY "FRIEND." SHE GETS ME ALL TURNED AROUND. SHE'S...I DON'T KNOW...
SPECIAL.
GUESS, IF I COULD BE A FRIEND TO SOMEONE LIKE HER...MADE ME A LITTLE SPECIAL TOO.
BAH, MY OLD MAN WOULD'VE SLAPPED ME IN THE HEAD TWICE ALREADY FOR NOT LETTING YOU GET A WORD IN EDGEWISE...
BUT YOU'RE A DAMN GOOD LISTENER.
MM.

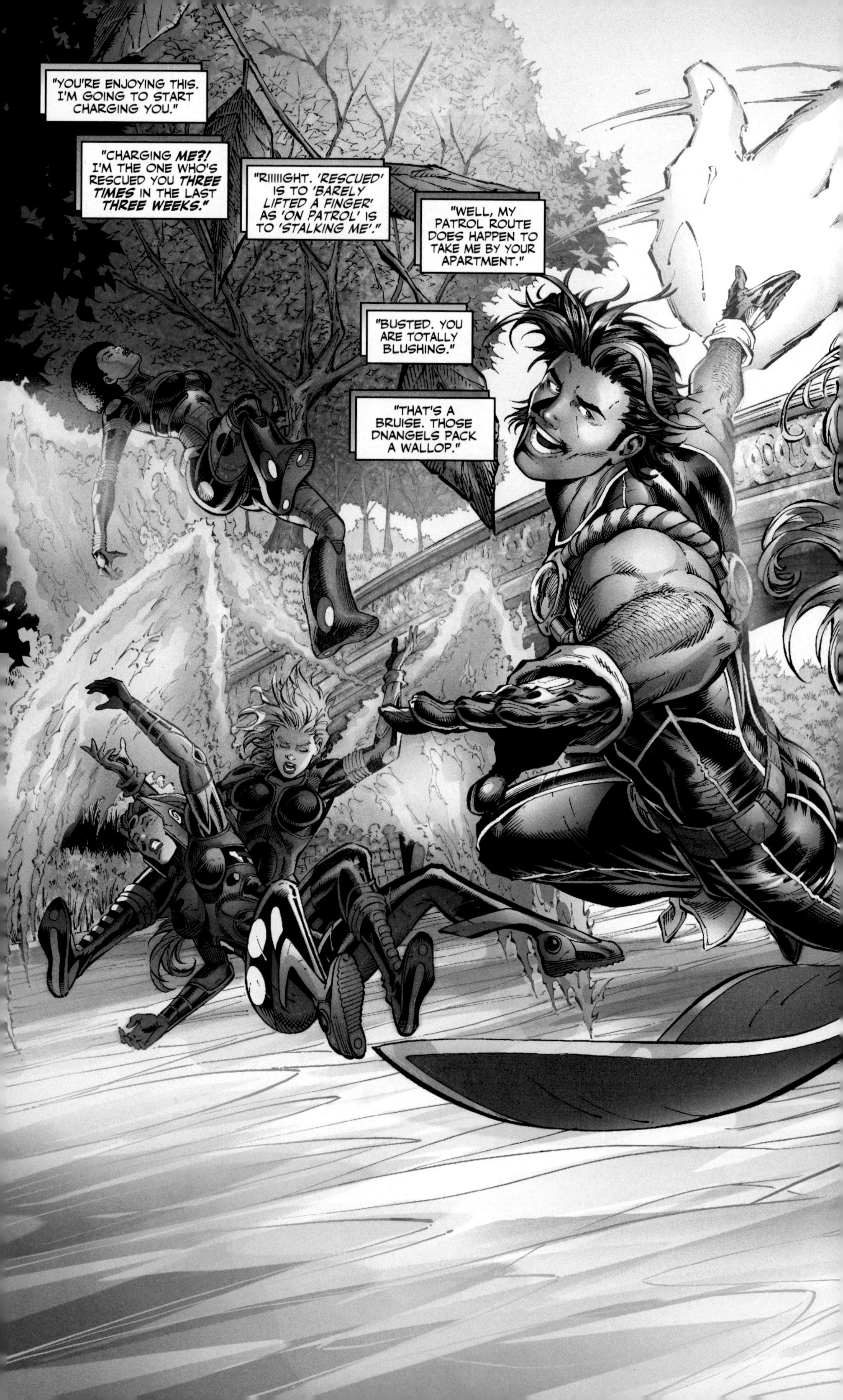
"YOU'RE ENJOYING THIS. I'M GOING TO START CHARGING YOU."
"CHARGING ME?! I'M THE ONE WHO'S RESCUED YOU THREE TIMES IN THE LAST THREE WEEKS."
"RIIIIIGHT. 'RESCUED' IS TO 'BARELY LIFTED A FINGER' AS 'ON PATROL' IS TO 'STALKING ME'."
"WELL, MY PATROL ROUTE DOES HAPPEN TO TAKE ME BY YOUR APARTMENT."
"BUSTED. YOU ARE TOTALLY BLUSHING."
"THAT'S A BRUISE. THOSE DNANGELS PACK A WALLOP."

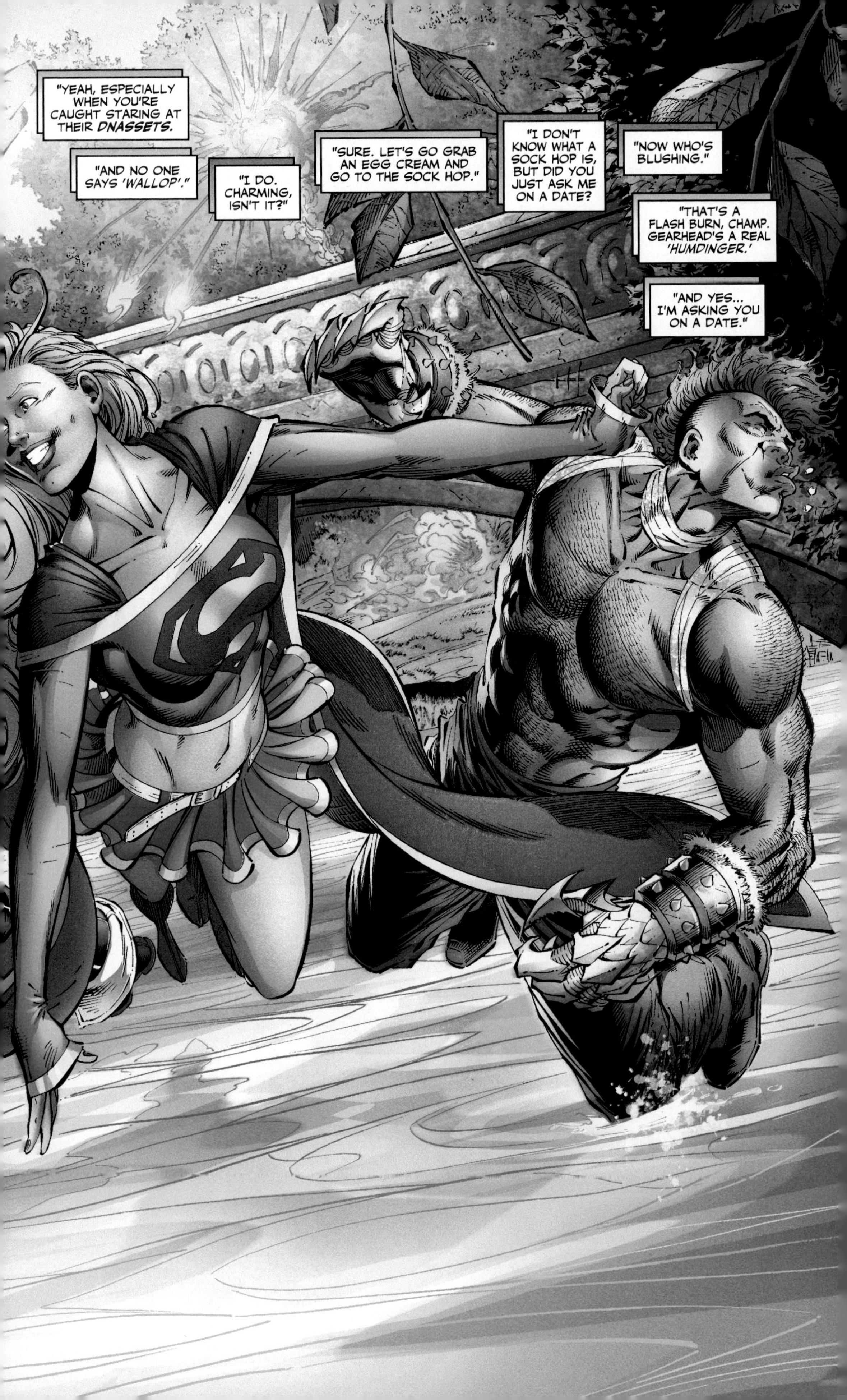
"YEAH, ESPECIALLY WHEN YOU'RE CAUGHT STARING AT THEIR *DNASSETS*.
"AND NO ONE SAYS '*WALLOP*'."
"I DO. CHARMING, ISN'T IT?"
"SURE. LET'S GO GRAB AN EGG CREAM AND GO TO THE SOCK HOP."
"I DON'T KNOW WHAT A SOCK HOP IS, BUT DID YOU JUST ASK ME ON A DATE?
"NOW WHO'S BLUSHING."
"THAT'S A FLASH BURN, CHAMP. GEARHEAD'S A REAL '*HUMDINGER*.'
"AND YES... I'M ASKING YOU ON A DATE."

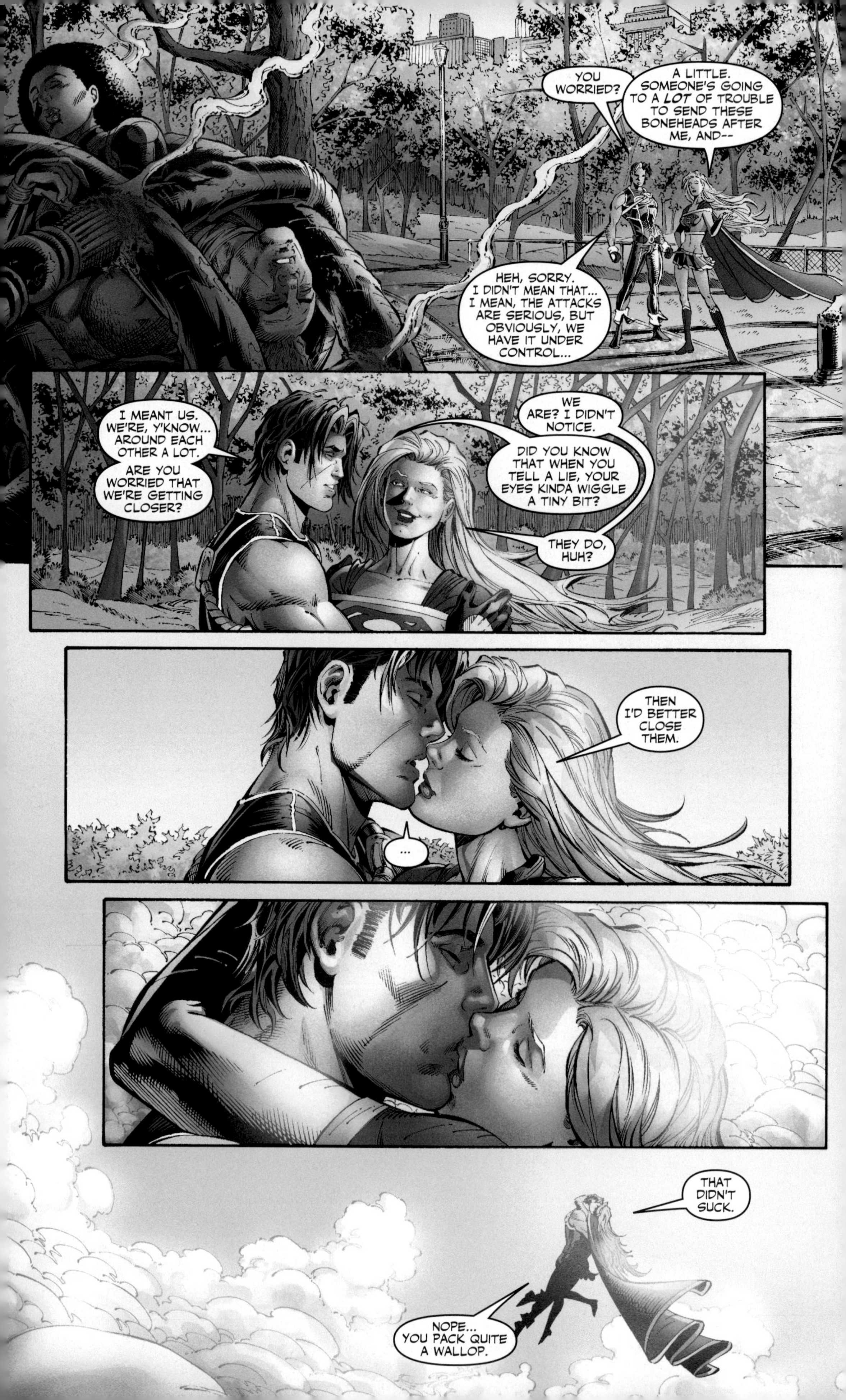
YOU WORRIED?
A LITTLE. SOMEONE'S GOING TO A LOT OF TROUBLE TO SEND THESE BONEHEADS AFTER ME, AND--
HEH, SORRY. I DIDN'T MEAN THAT... I MEAN, THE ATTACKS ARE SERIOUS, BUT OBVIOUSLY, WE HAVE IT UNDER CONTROL...
I MEANT US. WE'RE, Y'KNOW... AROUND EACH OTHER A LOT.
ARE YOU WORRIED THAT WE'RE GETTING CLOSER?
WE ARE? I DIDN'T NOTICE.
DID YOU KNOW THAT WHEN YOU TELL A LIE, YOUR EYES KINDA WIGGLE A TINY BIT?
THEY DO, HUH?
THEN I'D BETTER CLOSE THEM.
...
THAT DIDN'T SUCK.
NOPE... YOU PACK QUITE A WALLOP.

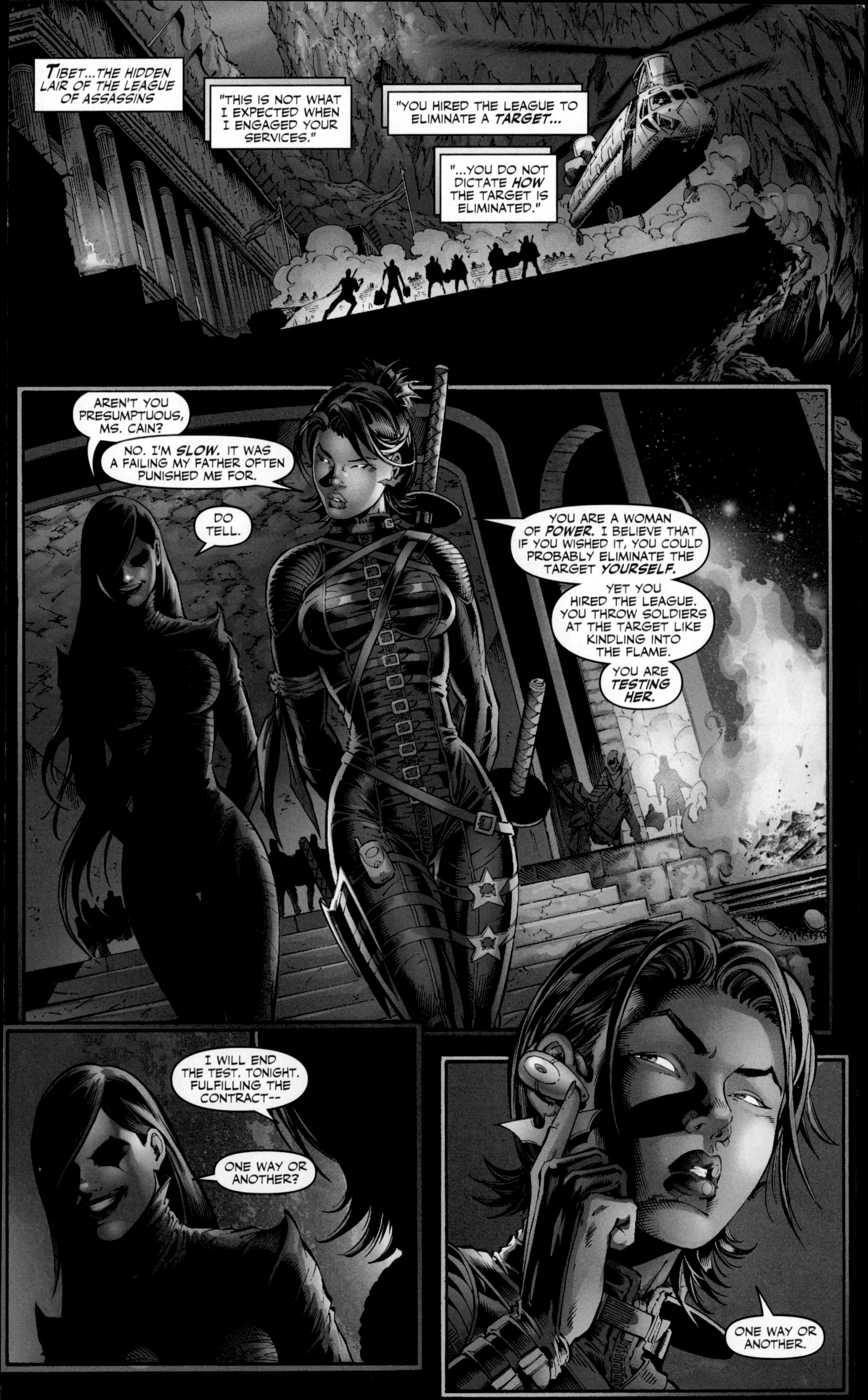
TIBET...THE HIDDEN LAIR OF THE LEAGUE OF ASSASSINS
"THIS IS NOT WHAT I EXPECTED WHEN I ENGAGED YOUR SERVICES."
"YOU HIRED THE LEAGUE TO ELIMINATE A TARGET...
"...YOU DO NOT DICTATE HOW THE TARGET IS ELIMINATED."
AREN'T YOU PRESUMPTUOUS, MS. CAIN?
NO. I'M SLOW. IT WAS A FAILING MY FATHER OFTEN PUNISHED ME FOR.
DO TELL.
YOU ARE A WOMAN OF POWER. I BELIEVE THAT IF YOU WISHED IT, YOU COULD PROBABLY ELIMINATE THE TARGET YOURSELF.
YET YOU HIRED THE LEAGUE. YOU THROW SOLDIERS AT THE TARGET LIKE KINDLING INTO THE FLAME.
YOU ARE TESTING HER.
I WILL END THE TEST. TONIGHT. FULFILLING THE CONTRACT--
ONE WAY OR ANOTHER?
ONE WAY OR ANOTHER.

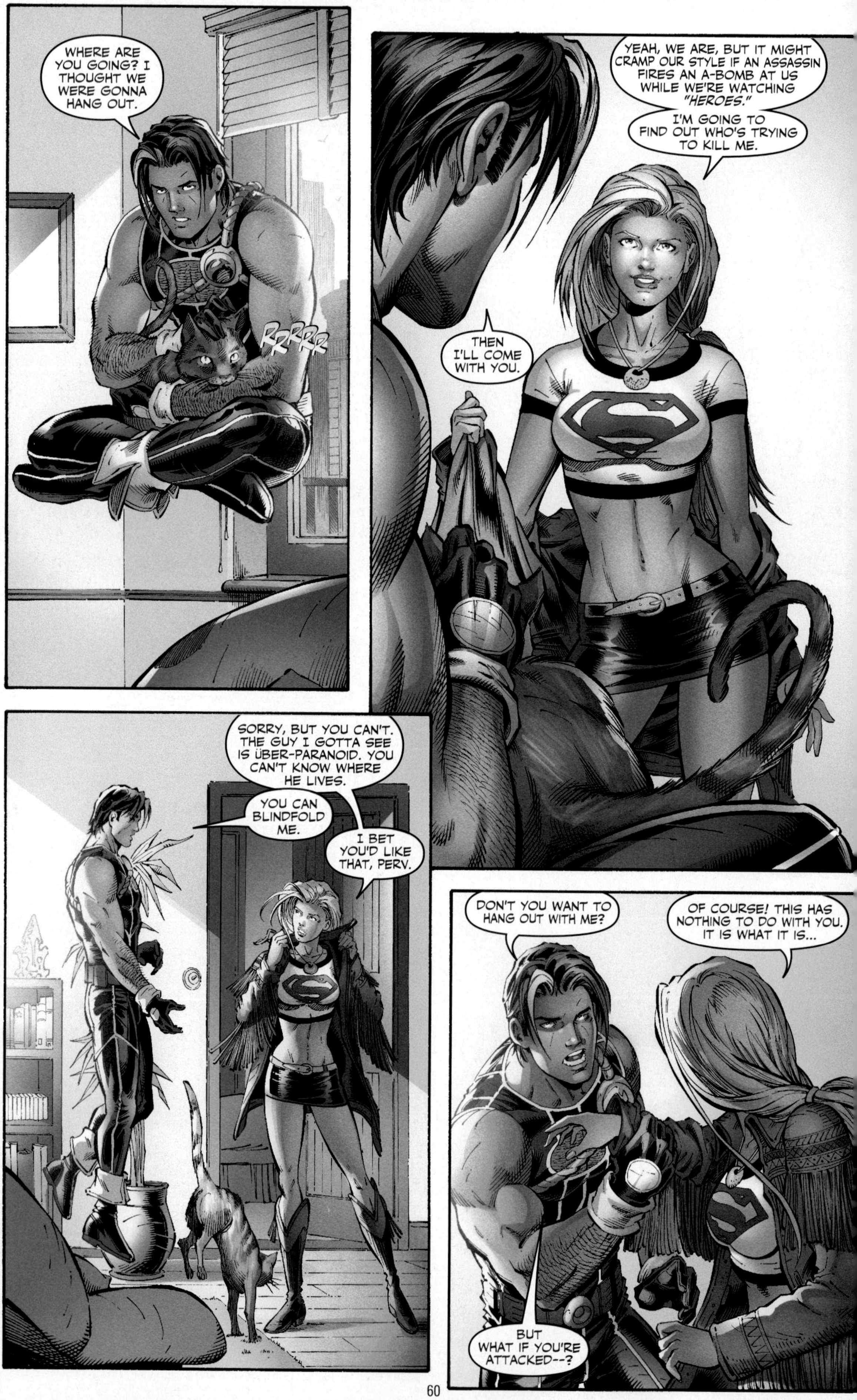
WHERE ARE YOU GOING? I THOUGHT WE WERE GONNA HANG OUT.
RRRRR
YEAH, WE ARE, BUT IT MIGHT CRAMP OUR STYLE IF AN ASSASSIN FIRES AN A-BOMB AT US WHILE WE'RE WATCHING "HEROES."
I'M GOING TO FIND OUT WHO'S TRYING TO KILL ME.
THEN I'LL COME WITH YOU.
SORRY, BUT YOU CAN'T. THE GUY I GOTTA SEE IS ÜBER-PARANOID. YOU CAN'T KNOW WHERE HE LIVES.
YOU CAN BLINDFOLD ME.
I BET YOU'D LIKE THAT, PERV.
DON'T YOU WANT TO HANG OUT WITH ME?
OF COURSE! THIS HAS NOTHING TO DO WITH YOU. IT IS WHAT IT IS...
BUT WHAT IF YOU'RE ATTACKED--?

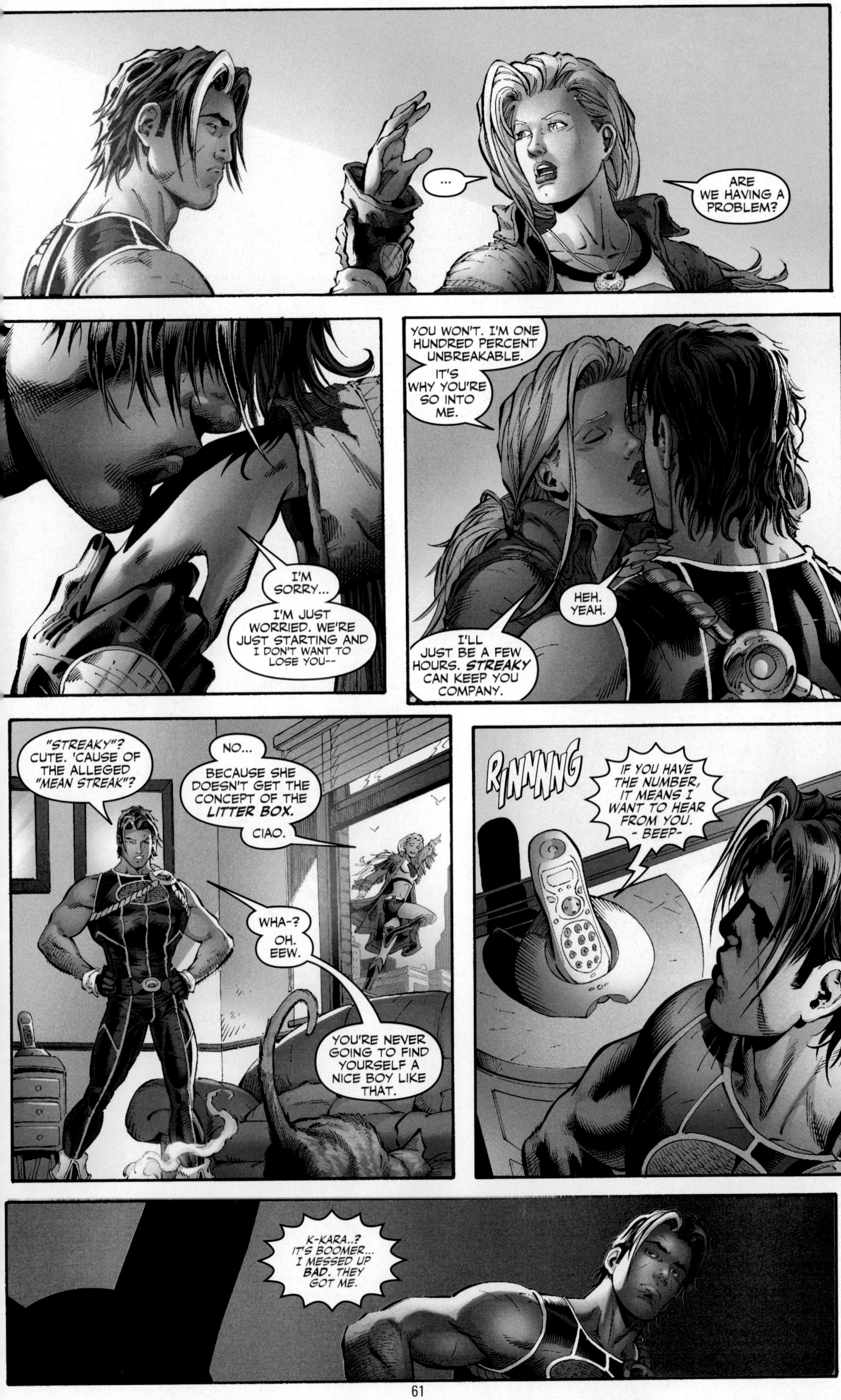
...
ARE WE HAVING A PROBLEM?
I'M SORRY...
I'M JUST WORRIED. WE'RE JUST STARTING AND I DON'T WANT TO LOSE YOU--
YOU WON'T. I'M ONE HUNDRED PERCENT UNBREAKABLE.
IT'S WHY YOU'RE SO INTO ME.
HEH. YEAH.
I'LL JUST BE A FEW HOURS. STREAKY CAN KEEP YOU COMPANY.
"STREAKY"? CUTE. 'CAUSE OF THE ALLEGED "MEAN STREAK"?
NO...
BECAUSE SHE DOESN'T GET THE CONCEPT OF THE LITTER BOX.
CIAO.
WHA-? OH. EEW.
YOU'RE NEVER GOING TO FIND YOURSELF A NICE BOY LIKE THAT.
RINNNNG
IF YOU HAVE THE NUMBER, IT MEANS I WANT TO HEAR FROM YOU. - BEEP-
K-KARA..? IT'S BOOMER... I MESSED UP BAD. THEY GOT ME.

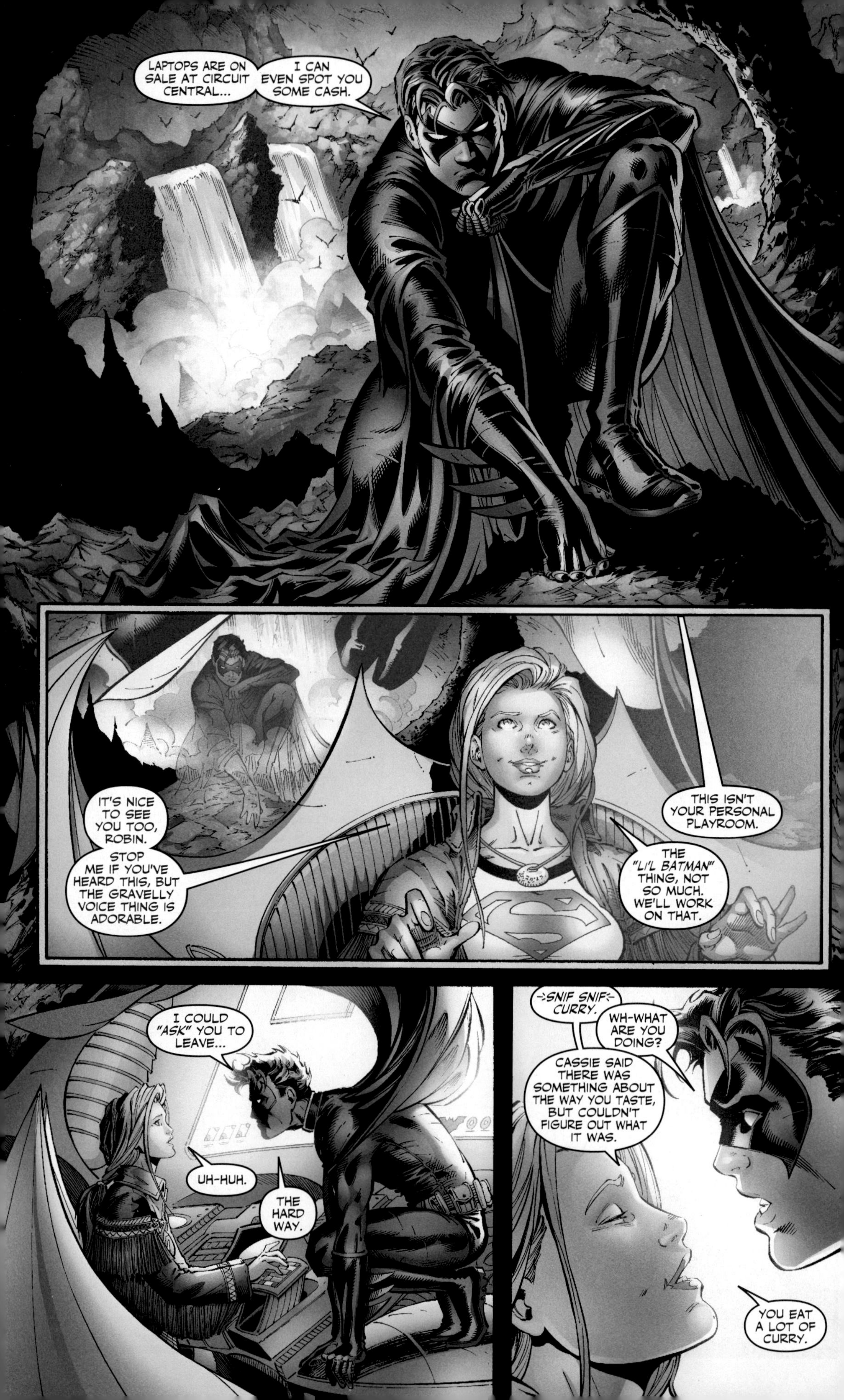
LAPTOPS ARE ON SALE AT CIRCUIT CENTRAL...
I CAN EVEN SPOT YOU SOME CASH.
IT'S NICE TO SEE YOU TOO, ROBIN.
STOP ME IF YOU'VE HEARD THIS, BUT THE GRAVELLY VOICE THING IS ADORABLE.
THE "LI'L BATMAN" THING, NOT SO MUCH. WE'LL WORK ON THAT.
THIS ISN'T YOUR PERSONAL PLAYROOM.
I COULD "ASK" YOU TO LEAVE...
UH-HUH.
THE HARD WAY.
-SNIF SNIF- CURRY.
WH-WHAT ARE YOU DOING?
CASSIE SAID THERE WAS SOMETHING ABOUT THE WAY YOU TASTE, BUT COULDN'T FIGURE OUT WHAT IT WAS.
YOU EAT A LOT OF CURRY.

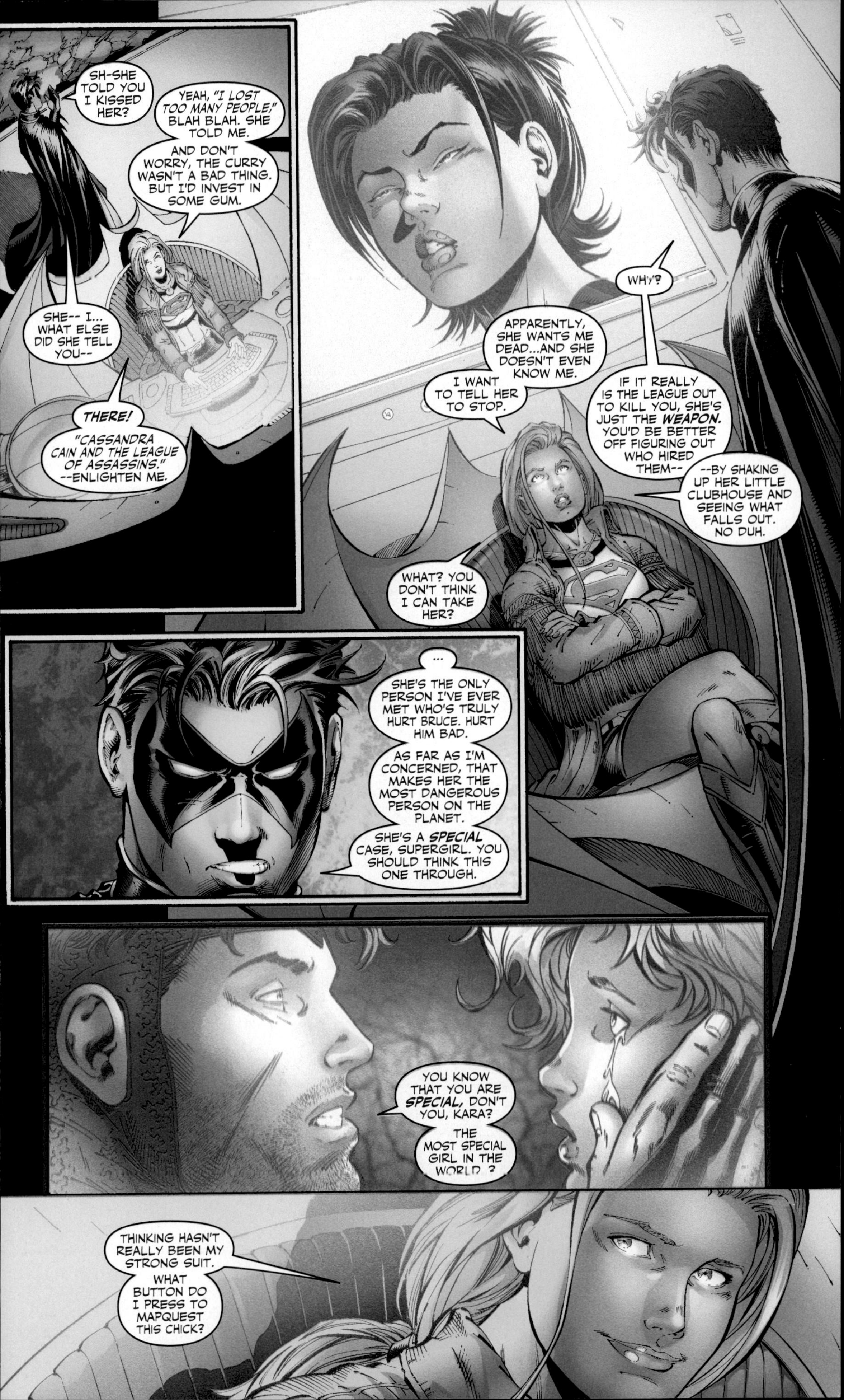
SH-SHE TOLD YOU I KISSED HER?
YEAH, "I LOST TOO MANY PEOPLE," BLAH BLAH. SHE TOLD ME.
AND DON'T WORRY, THE CURRY WASN'T A BAD THING. BUT I'D INVEST IN SOME GUM.
SHE-- I... WHAT ELSE DID SHE TELL YOU--
THERE! "CASSANDRA CAIN AND THE LEAGUE OF ASSASSINS." --ENLIGHTEN ME.
WHY?
APPARENTLY, SHE WANTS ME DEAD...AND SHE DOESN'T EVEN KNOW ME.
I WANT TO TELL HER TO STOP.
IF IT REALLY IS THE LEAGUE OUT TO KILL YOU, SHE'S JUST THE WEAPON. YOU'D BE BETTER OFF FIGURING OUT WHO HIRED THEM--
--BY SHAKING UP HER LITTLE CLUBHOUSE AND SEEING WHAT FALLS OUT. NO DUH.
WHAT? YOU DON'T THINK I CAN TAKE HER?
...
SHE'S THE ONLY PERSON I'VE EVER MET WHO'S TRULY HURT BRUCE. HURT HIM BAD.
AS FAR AS I'M CONCERNED, THAT MAKES HER THE MOST DANGEROUS PERSON ON THE PLANET.
SHE'S A SPECIAL CASE, SUPERGIRL. YOU SHOULD THINK THIS ONE THROUGH.
YOU KNOW THAT YOU ARE SPECIAL, DON'T YOU, KARA?
THE MOST SPECIAL GIRL IN THE WORLD...?
THINKING HASN'T REALLY BEEN MY STRONG SUIT.
WHAT BUTTON DO I PRESS TO MAPQUEST THIS CHICK?

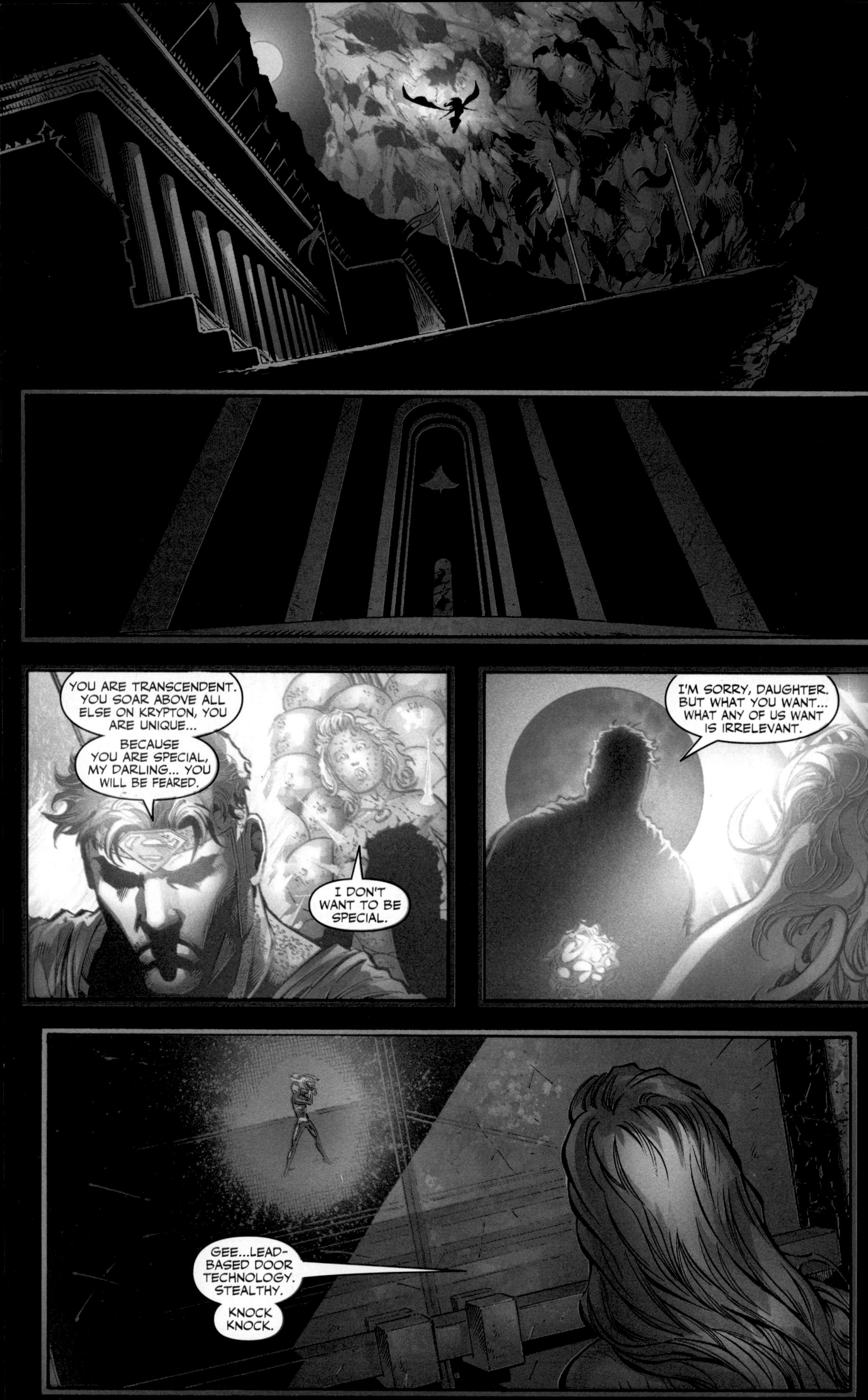
YOU ARE TRANSCENDENT. YOU SOAR ABOVE ALL ELSE ON KRYPTON, YOU ARE UNIQUE...
BECAUSE YOU ARE SPECIAL, MY DARLING... YOU WILL BE FEARED.
I DON'T WANT TO BE SPECIAL.
I'M SORRY, DAUGHTER. BUT WHAT YOU WANT... WHAT ANY OF US WANT IS IRRELEVANT.
GEE...LEAD-BASED DOOR TECHNOLOGY. STEALTHY.
KNOCK KNOCK.

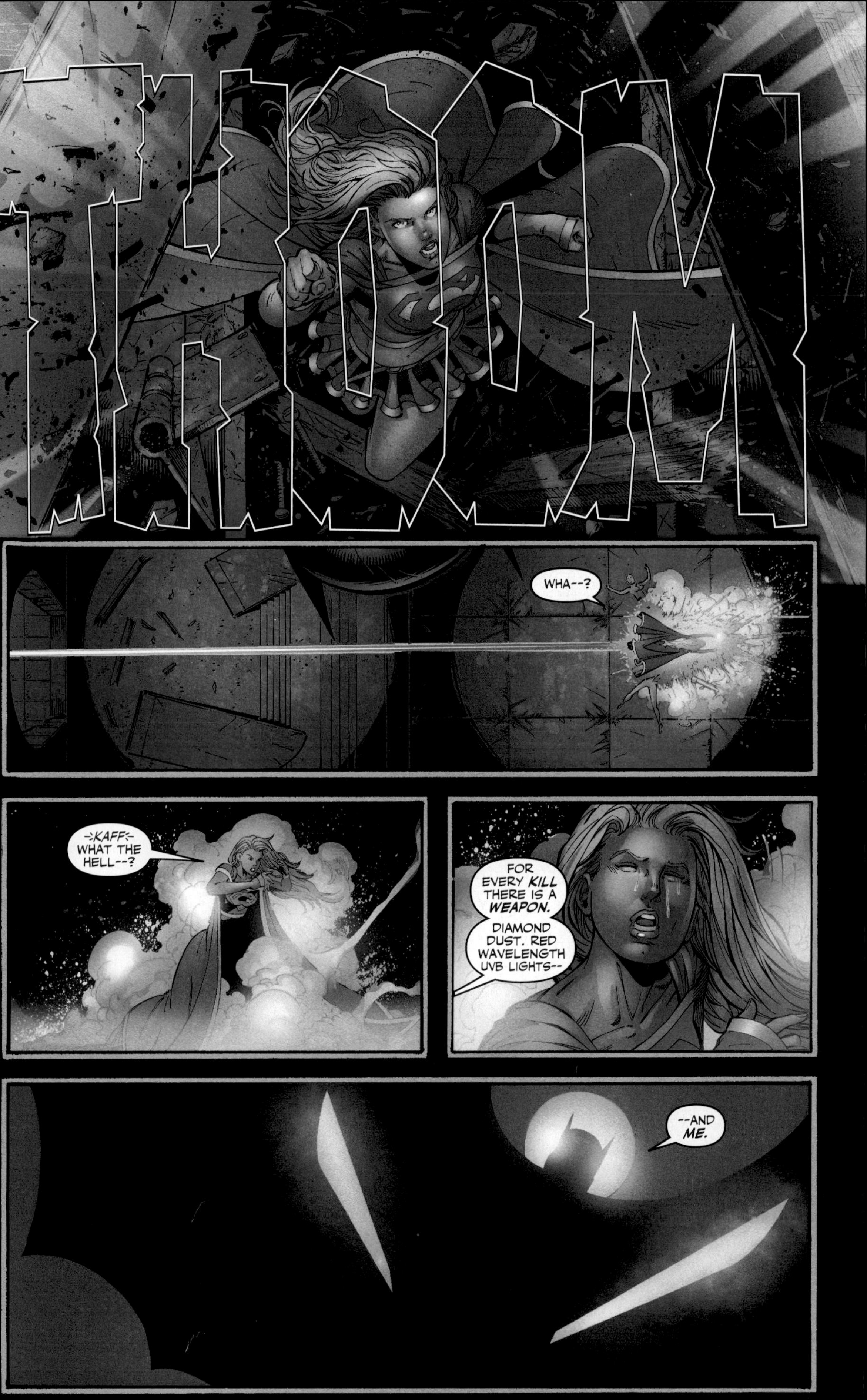
THOOOM
WHA--?
-KAFF- WHAT THE HELL--?
FOR EVERY KILL THERE IS A WEAPON.
DIAMOND DUST. RED WAVELENGTH UVB LIGHTS--
--AND ME.

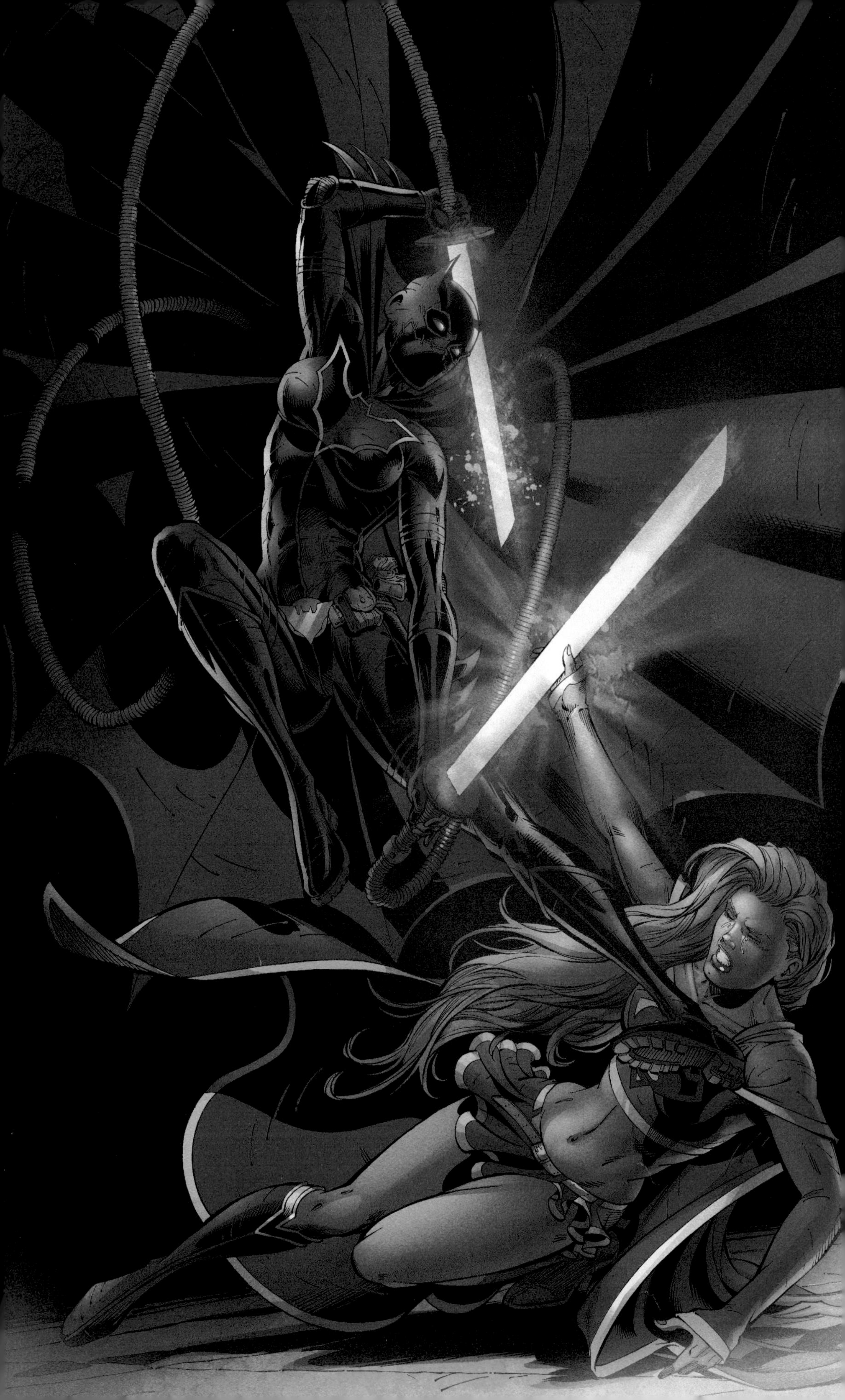

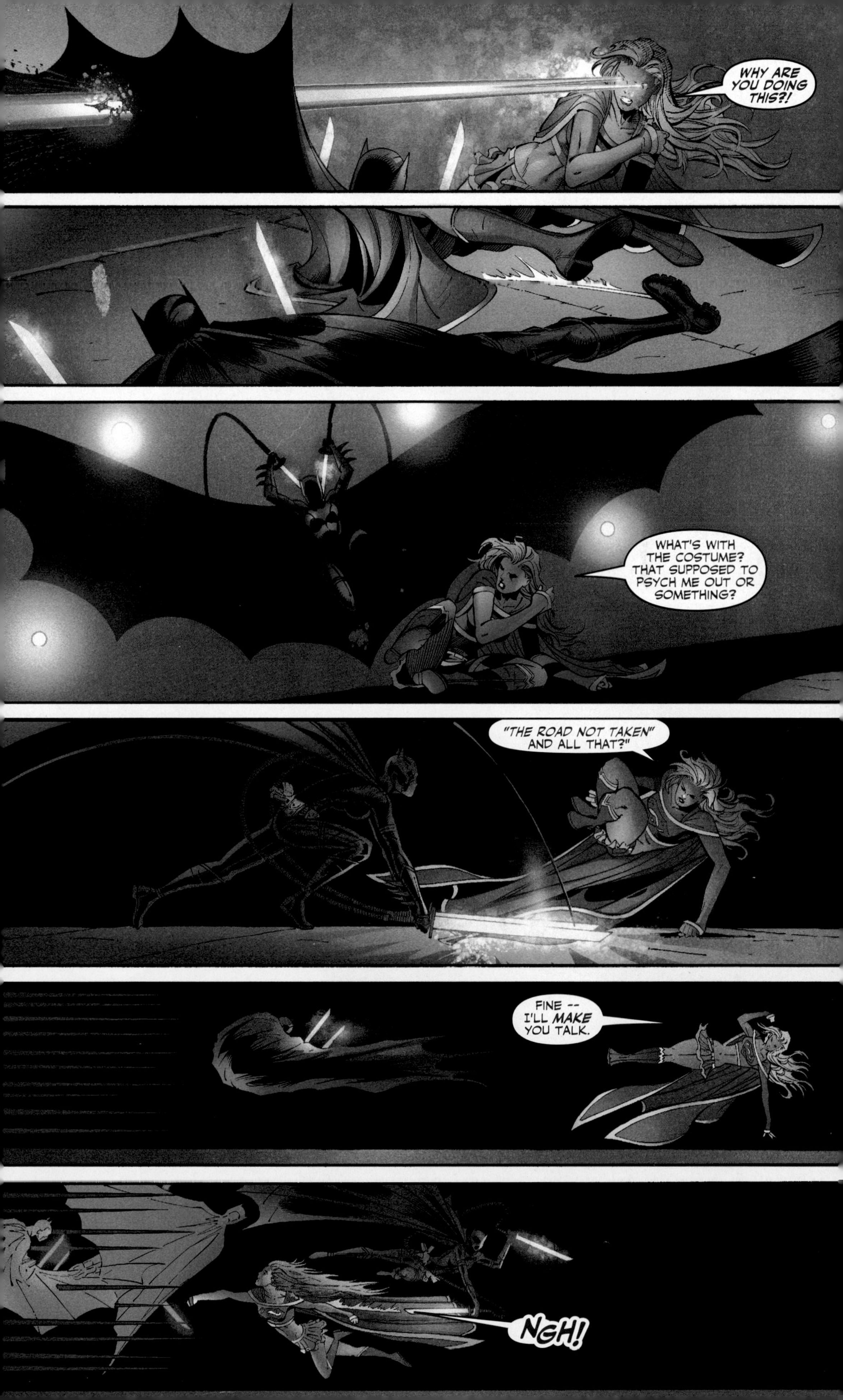
WHY ARE YOU DOING THIS?!
WHAT'S WITH THE COSTUME? THAT SUPPOSED TO PSYCH ME OUT OR SOMETHING?
"THE ROAD NOT TAKEN" AND ALL THAT?"
FINE -- I'LL MAKE YOU TALK.
NGH!

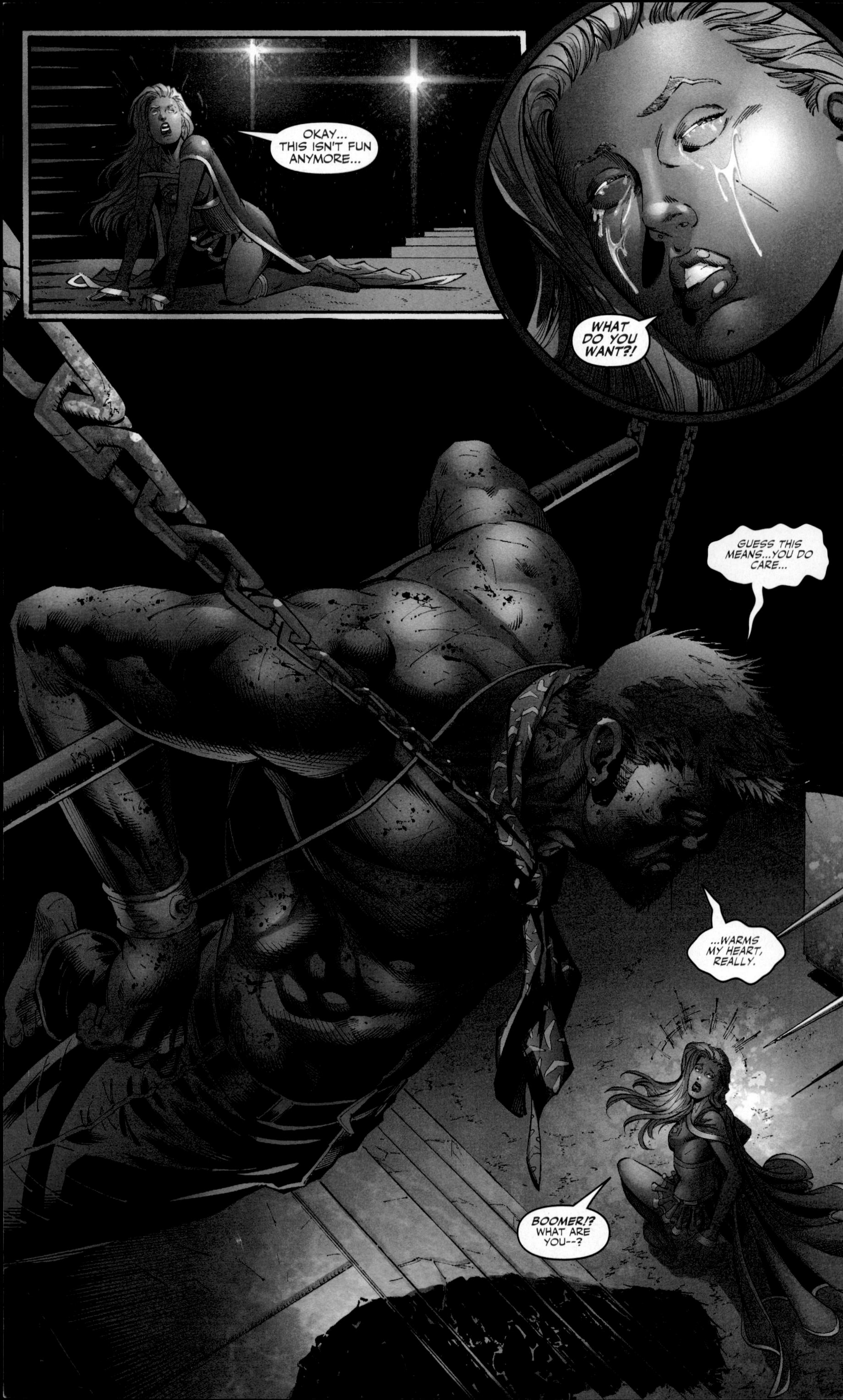
OKAY... THIS ISN'T FUN ANYMORE...
WHAT DO YOU WANT?!
GUESS THIS MEANS...YOU DO CARE...
...WARMS MY HEART, REALLY.
BOOMER!? WHAT ARE YOU--?

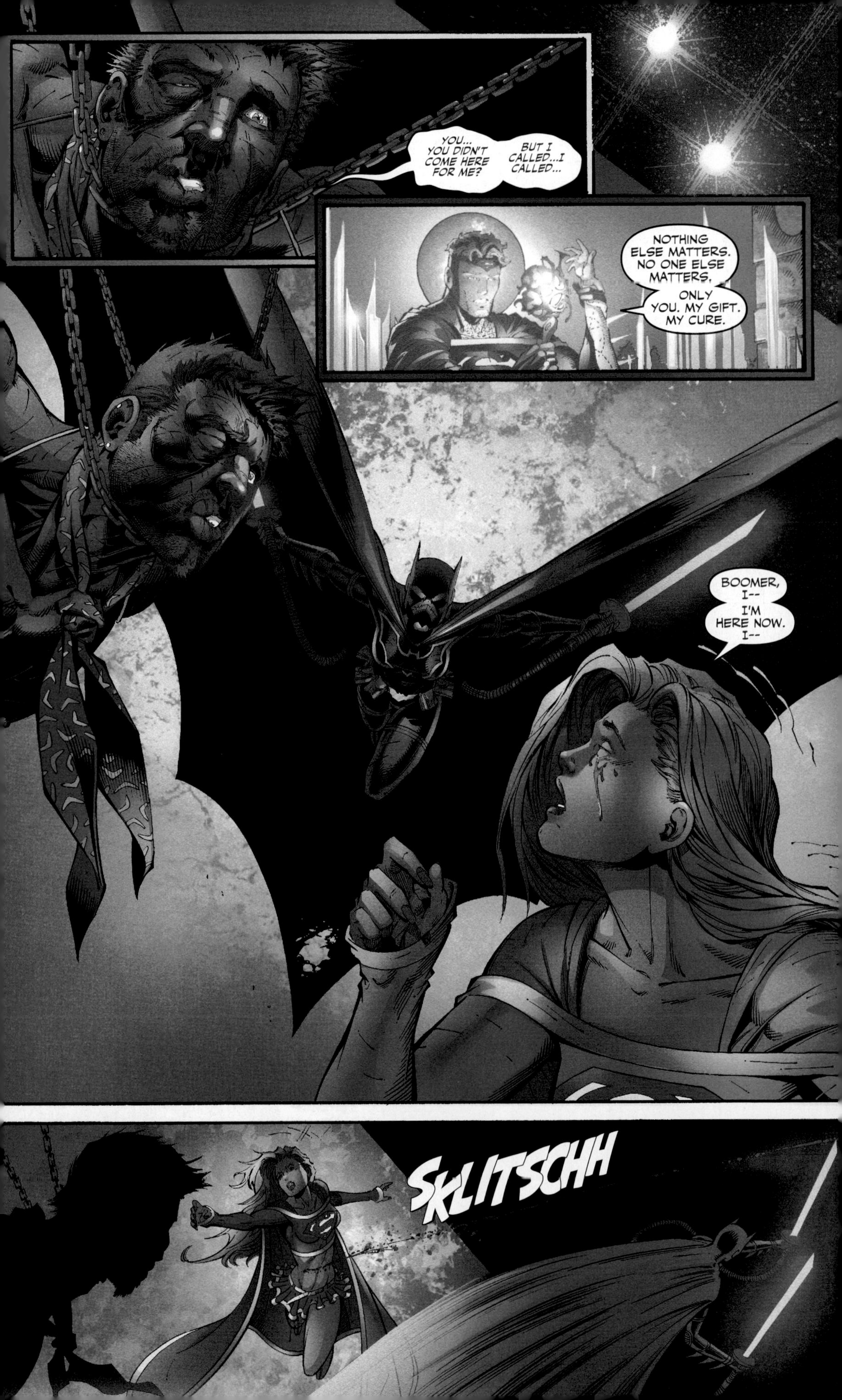

YOU... YOU DIDN'T COME HERE FOR ME?
BUT I CALLED...I CALLED...
NOTHING ELSE MATTERS. NO ONE ELSE MATTERS.
ONLY YOU. MY GIFT. MY CURE.
BOOMER, I--
I'M HERE NOW. I--
SKLITSCHH

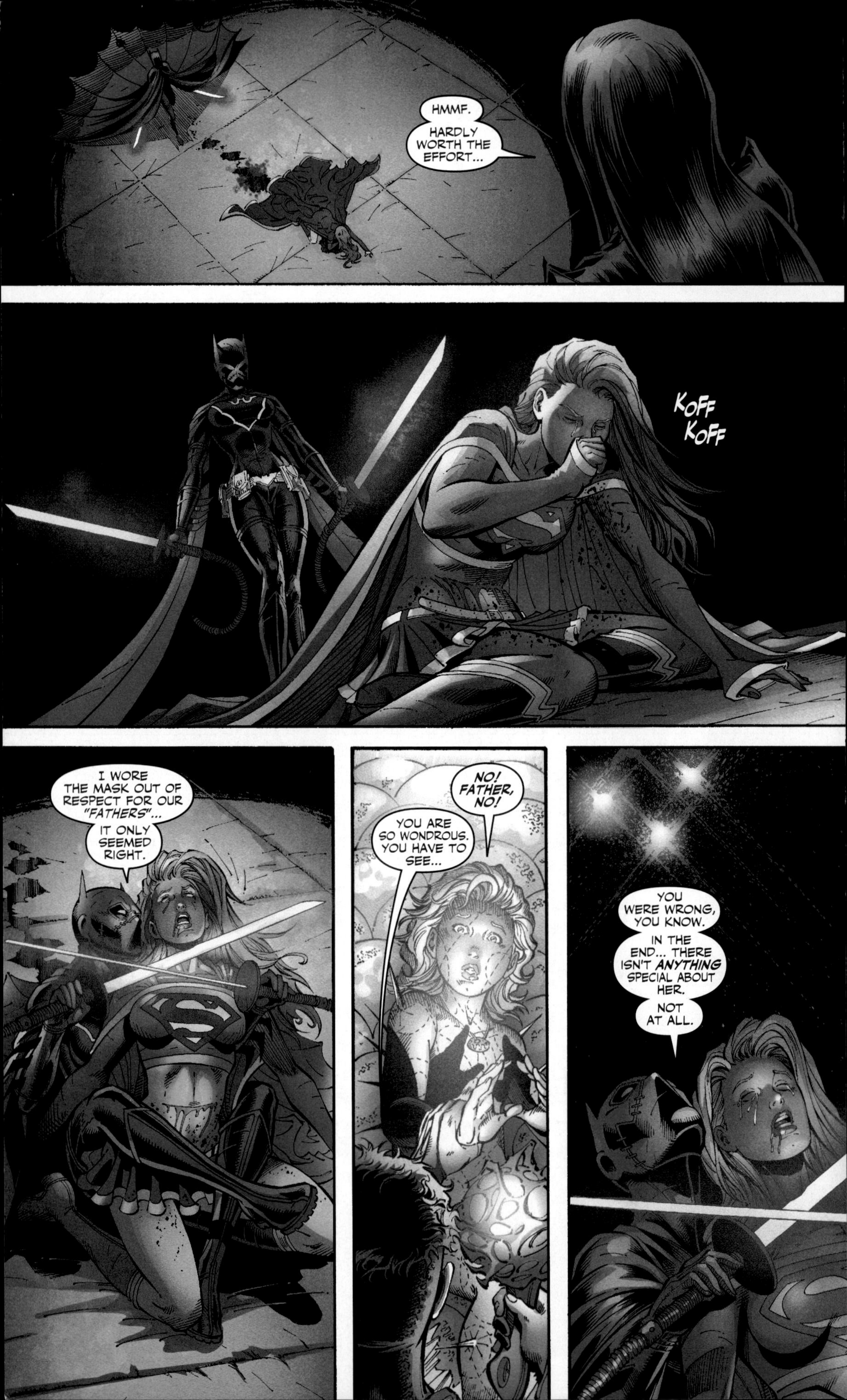
HMMF. HARDLY WORTH THE EFFORT...
KOFF KOFF
I WORE THE MASK OUT OF RESPECT FOR OUR "FATHERS"...
IT ONLY SEEMED RIGHT.
NO! FATHER, NO!
YOU ARE SO WONDROUS. YOU HAVE TO SEE...
YOU WERE WRONG, YOU KNOW.
IN THE END... THERE ISN'T ANYTHING SPECIAL ABOUT HER.
NOT AT ALL.

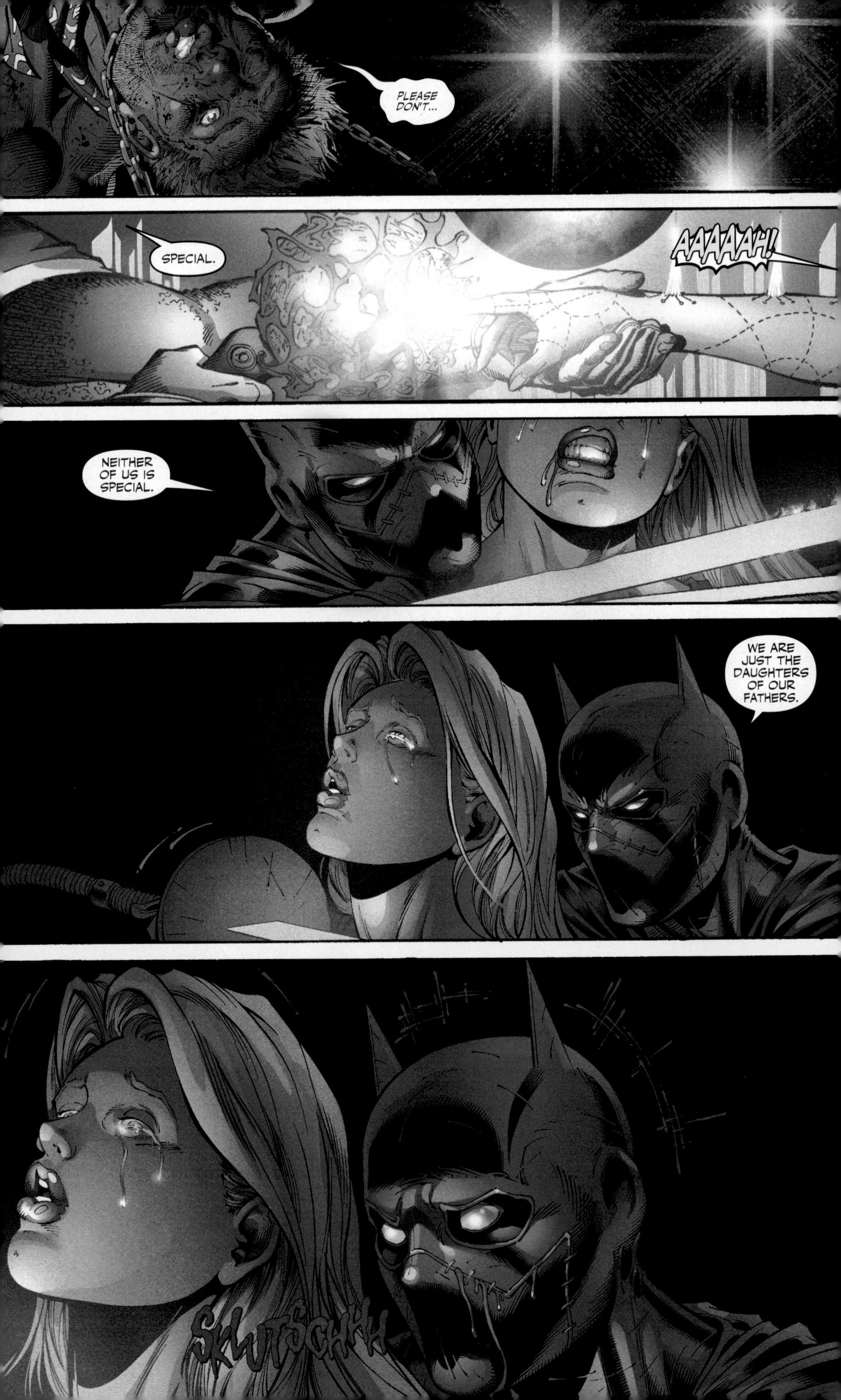
PLEASE DON'T...
SPECIAL.
AAAAAAH!
NEITHER OF US IS SPECIAL.
WE ARE JUST THE DAUGHTERS OF OUR FATHERS.
SKLUTSCHHH

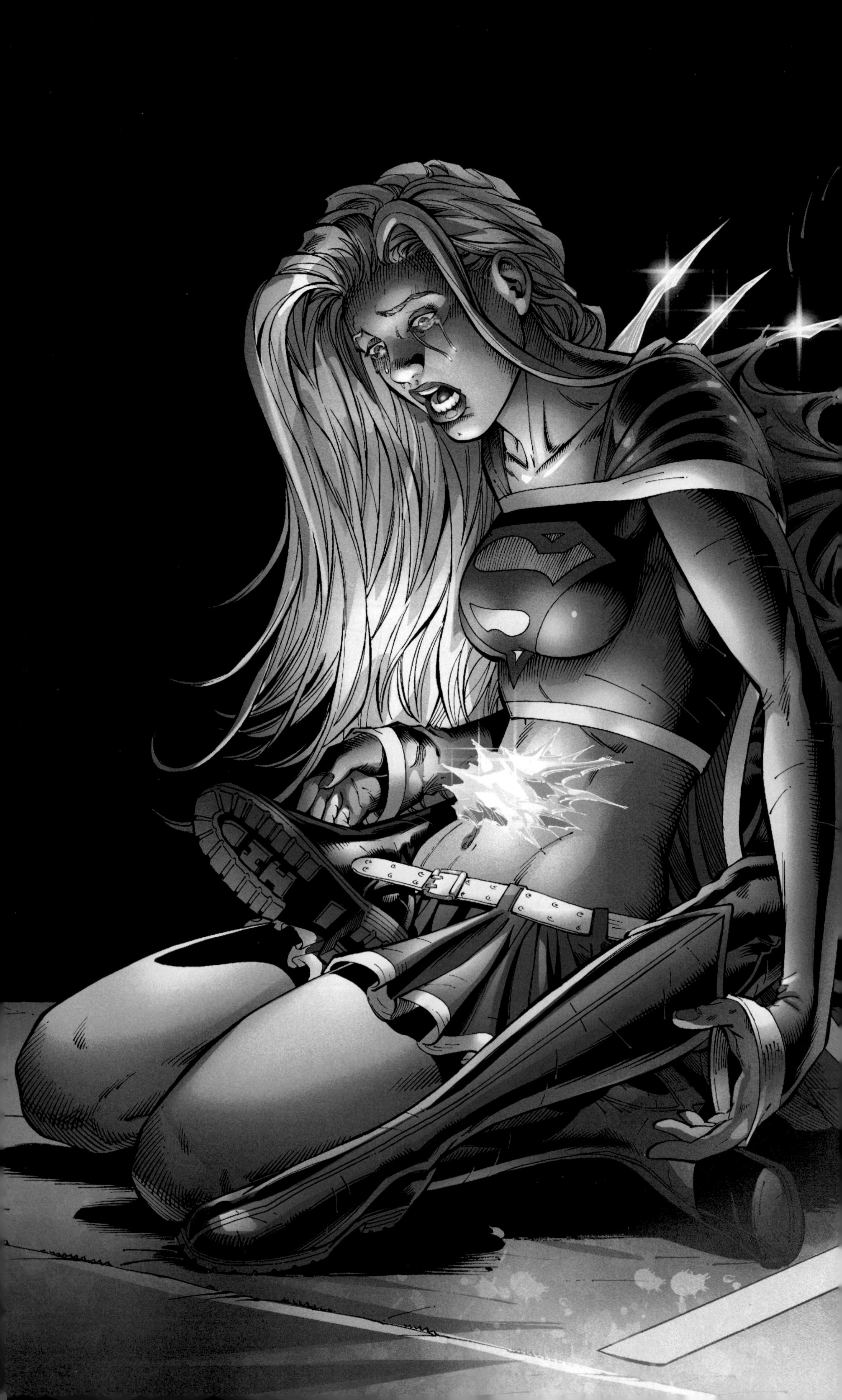

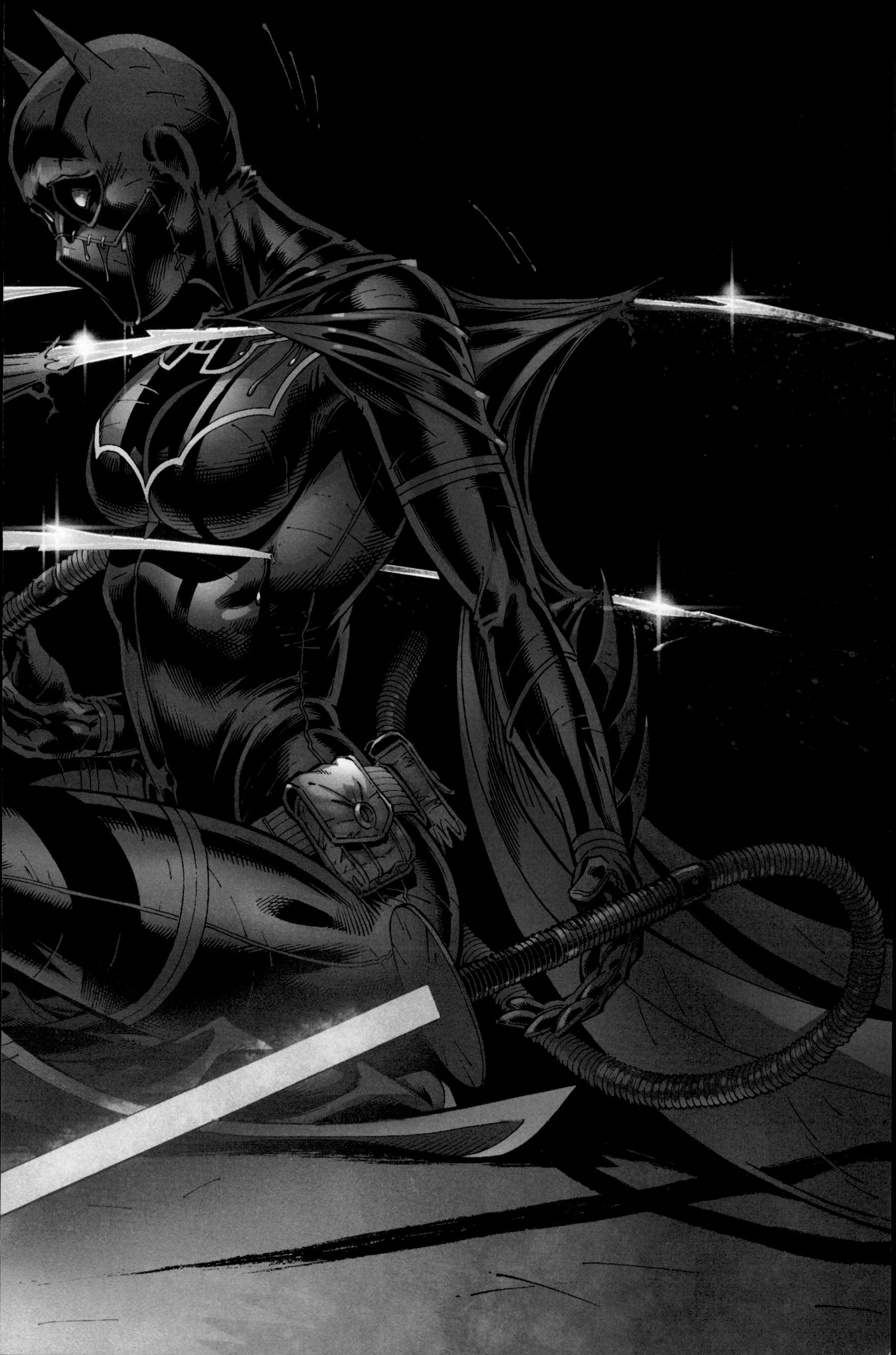

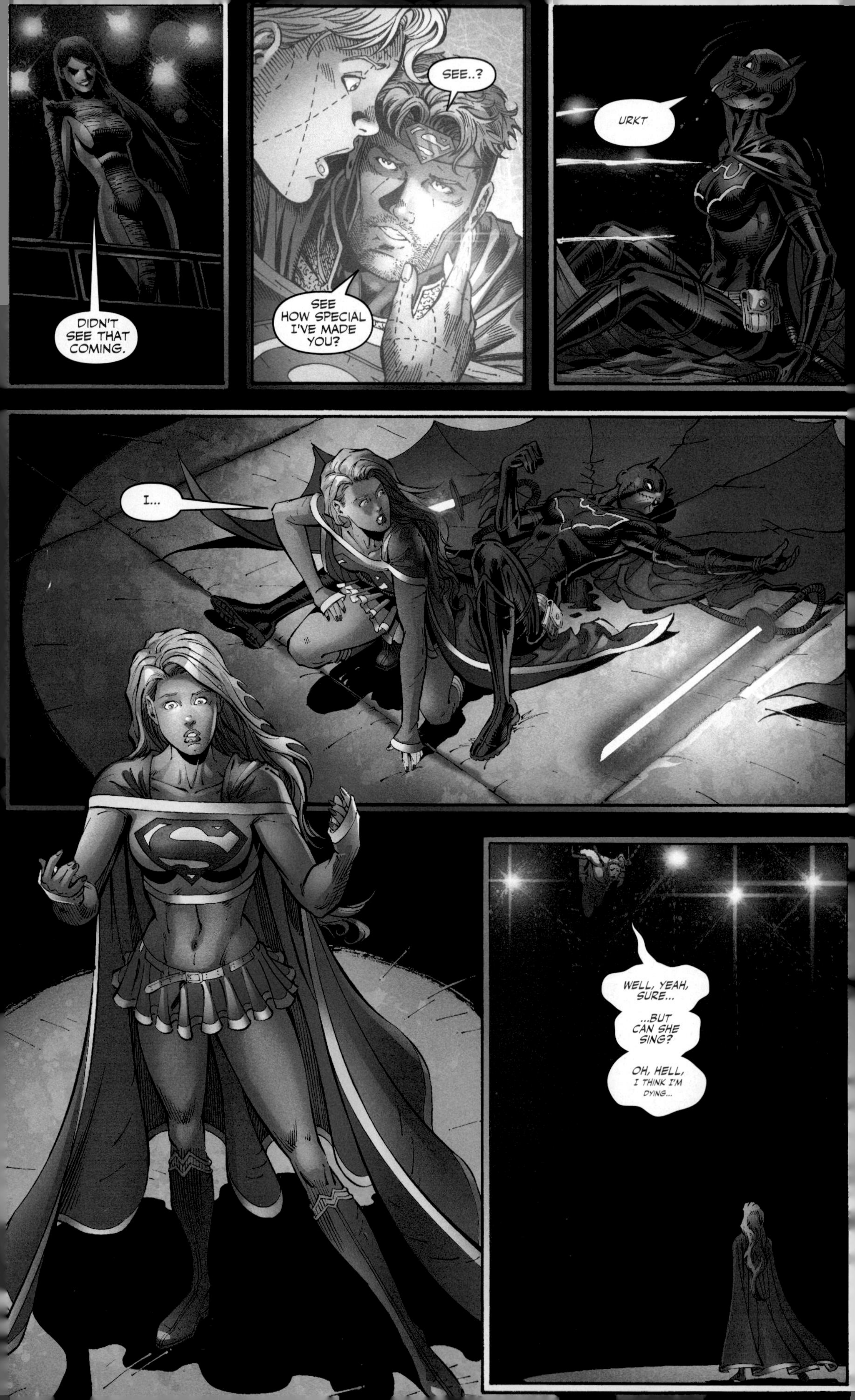
DIDN'T SEE THAT COMING.
SEE..?
SEE HOW SPECIAL I'VE MADE YOU?
URKT
I...
WELL, YEAH, SURE...
...BUT CAN SHE SING?
OH, HELL, I THINK I'M DYING...

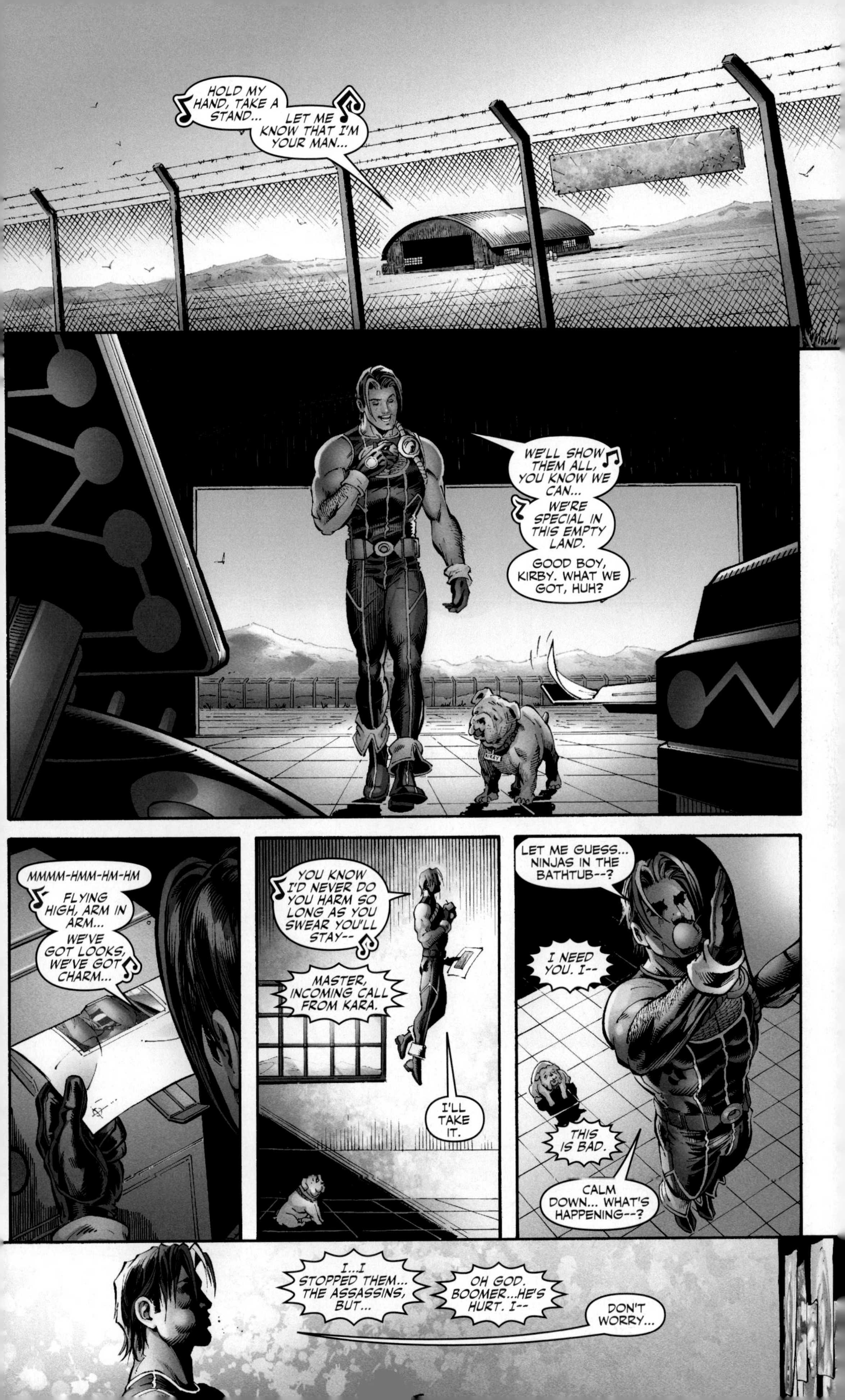
HOLD MY HAND, TAKE A STAND...
LET ME KNOW THAT I'M YOUR MAN...
WE'LL SHOW THEM ALL, YOU KNOW WE CAN...
WE'RE SPECIAL IN THIS EMPTY LAND.
GOOD BOY, KIRBY. WHAT WE GOT, HUH?
KIRBY
MMMM-HMM-HM-HM
FLYING HIGH, ARM IN ARM...
WE'VE GOT LOOKS, WE'VE GOT CHARM...
YOU KNOW I'D NEVER DO YOU HARM SO LONG AS YOU SWEAR YOU'LL STAY--
MASTER, INCOMING CALL FROM KARA.
I'LL TAKE IT.
LET ME GUESS... NINJAS IN THE BATHTUB--?
I NEED YOU. I--
THIS IS BAD.
CALM DOWN... WHAT'S HAPPENING--?
I...I STOPPED THEM... THE ASSASSINS, BUT...
OH GOD. BOOMER...HE'S HURT. I--
DON'T WORRY...

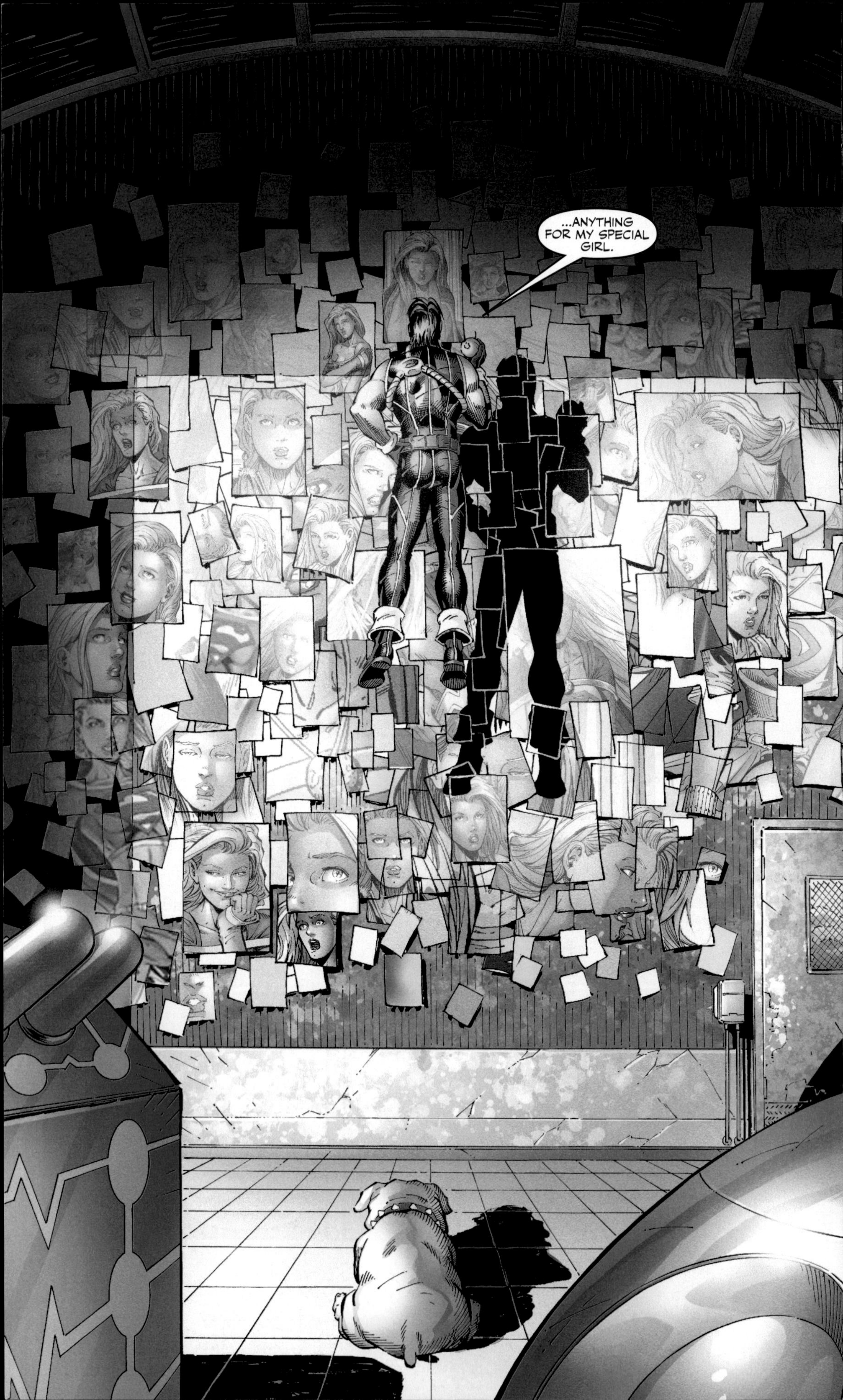
...ANYTHING FOR MY SPECIAL GIRL.

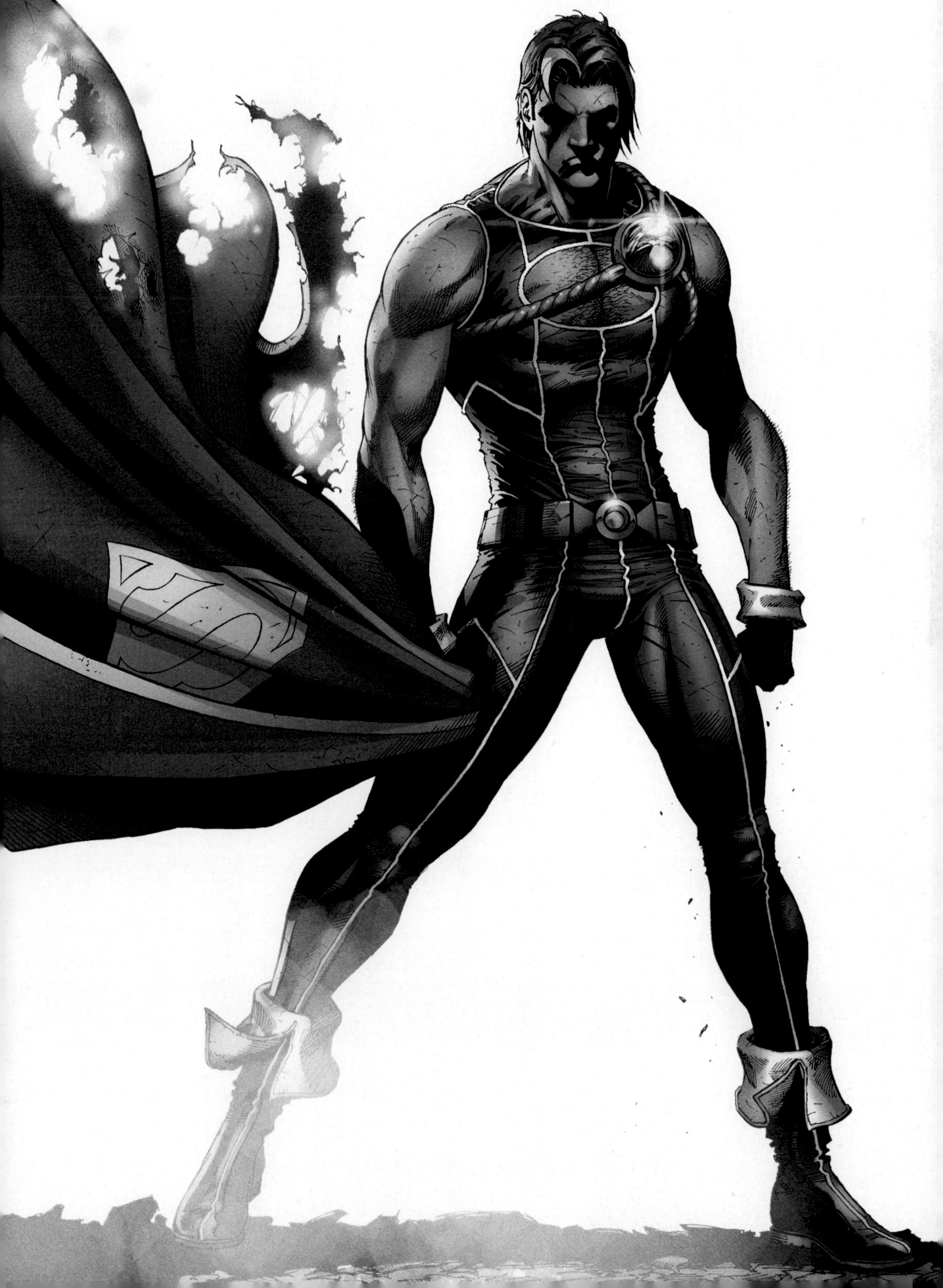

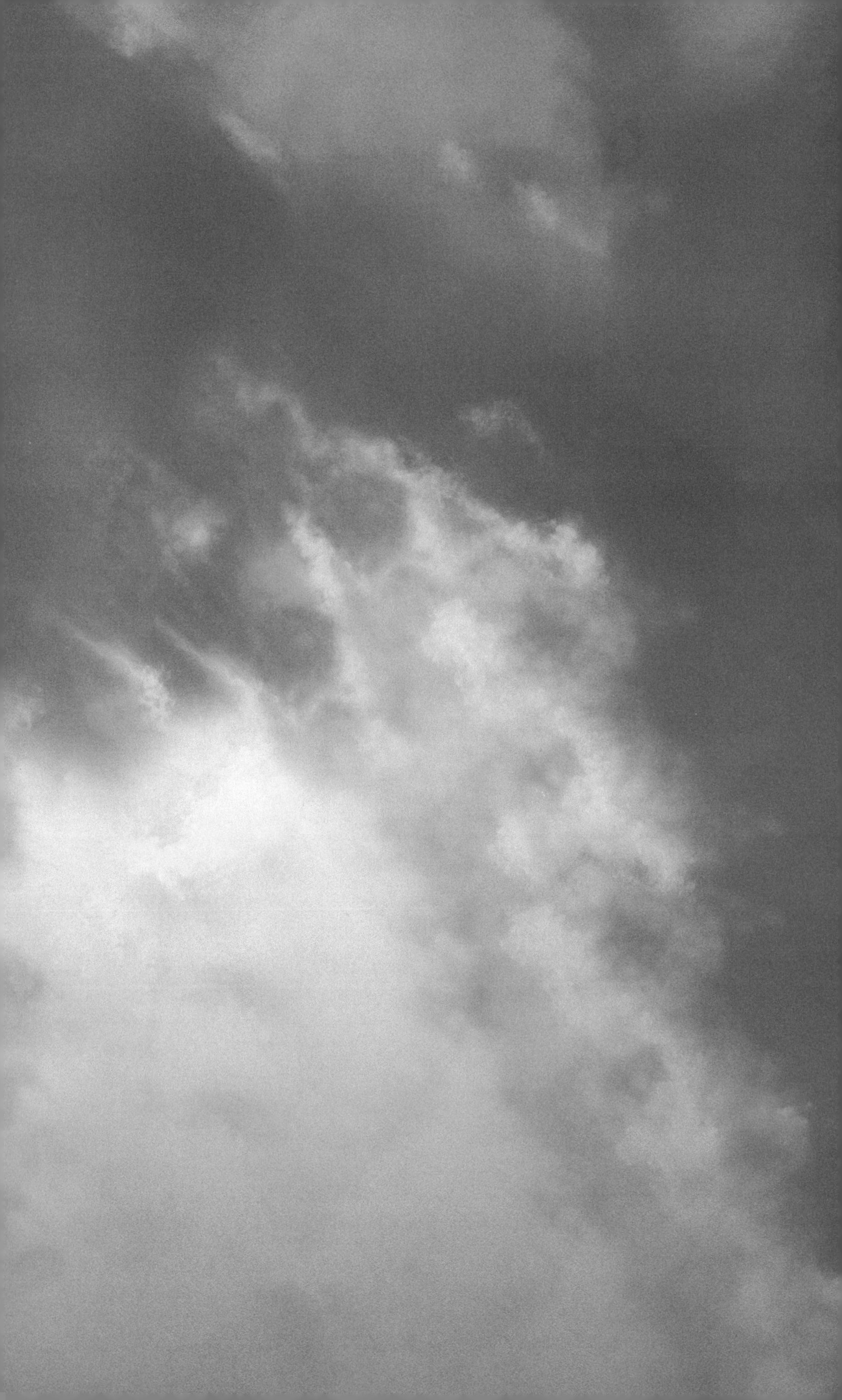

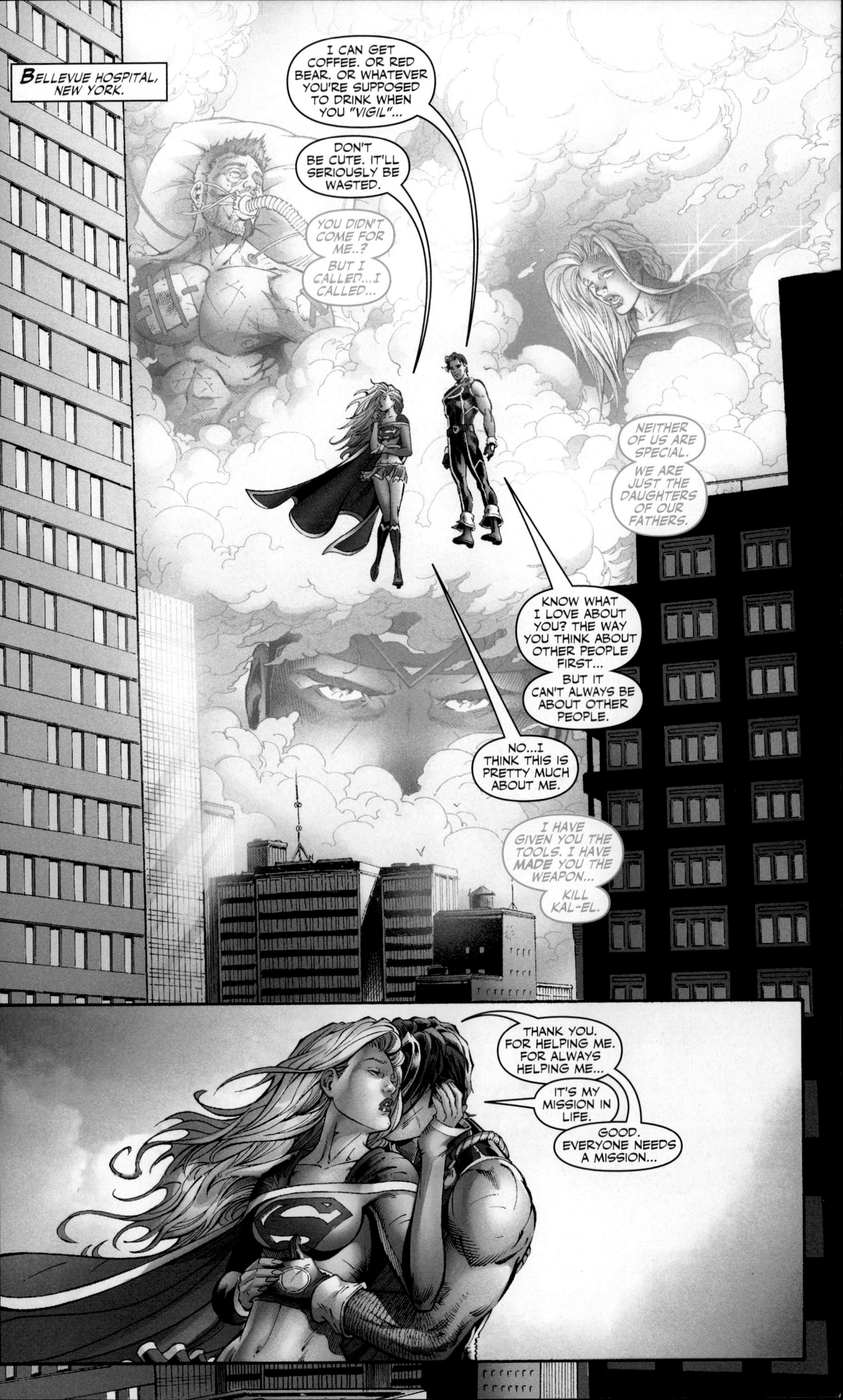
BELLEVUE HOSPITAL, NEW YORK.
I CAN GET COFFEE. OR RED BEAR. OR WHATEVER YOU'RE SUPPOSED TO DRINK WHEN YOU "VIGIL"...
DON'T BE CUTE. IT'LL SERIOUSLY BE WASTED.
YOU DIDN'T COME FOR ME..?
BUT I CALLED...I CALLED...
NEITHER OF US ARE SPECIAL.
WE ARE JUST THE DAUGHTERS OF OUR FATHERS.
KNOW WHAT I LOVE ABOUT YOU? THE WAY YOU THINK ABOUT OTHER PEOPLE FIRST...
BUT IT CAN'T ALWAYS BE ABOUT OTHER PEOPLE.
NO...I THINK THIS IS PRETTY MUCH ABOUT ME.
I HAVE GIVEN YOU THE TOOLS. I HAVE MADE YOU THE WEAPON...
KILL KAL-EL.
THANK YOU. FOR HELPING ME. FOR ALWAYS HELPING ME...
IT'S MY MISSION IN LIFE.
GOOD. EVERYONE NEEDS A MISSION...

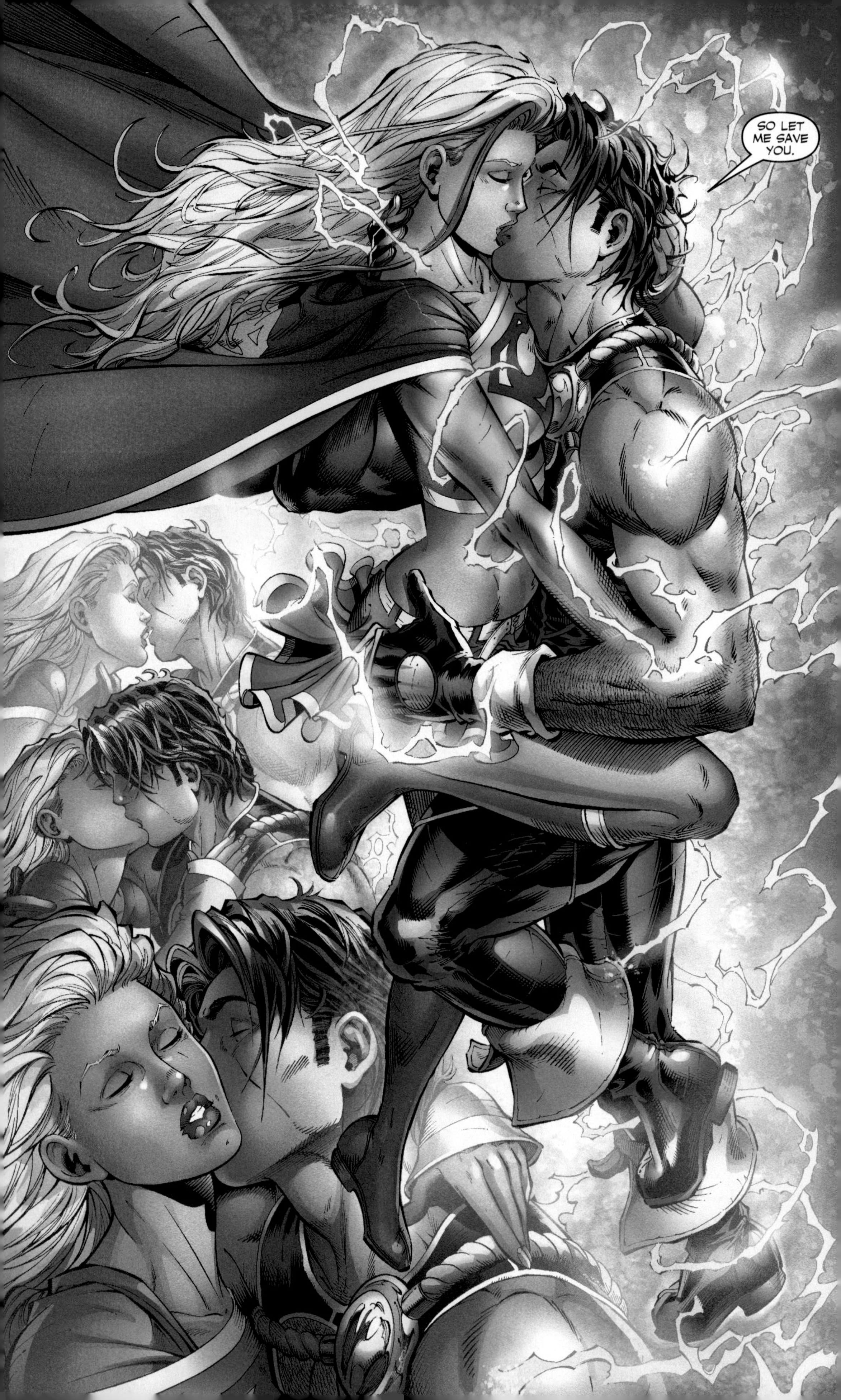
SO LET ME SAVE YOU.

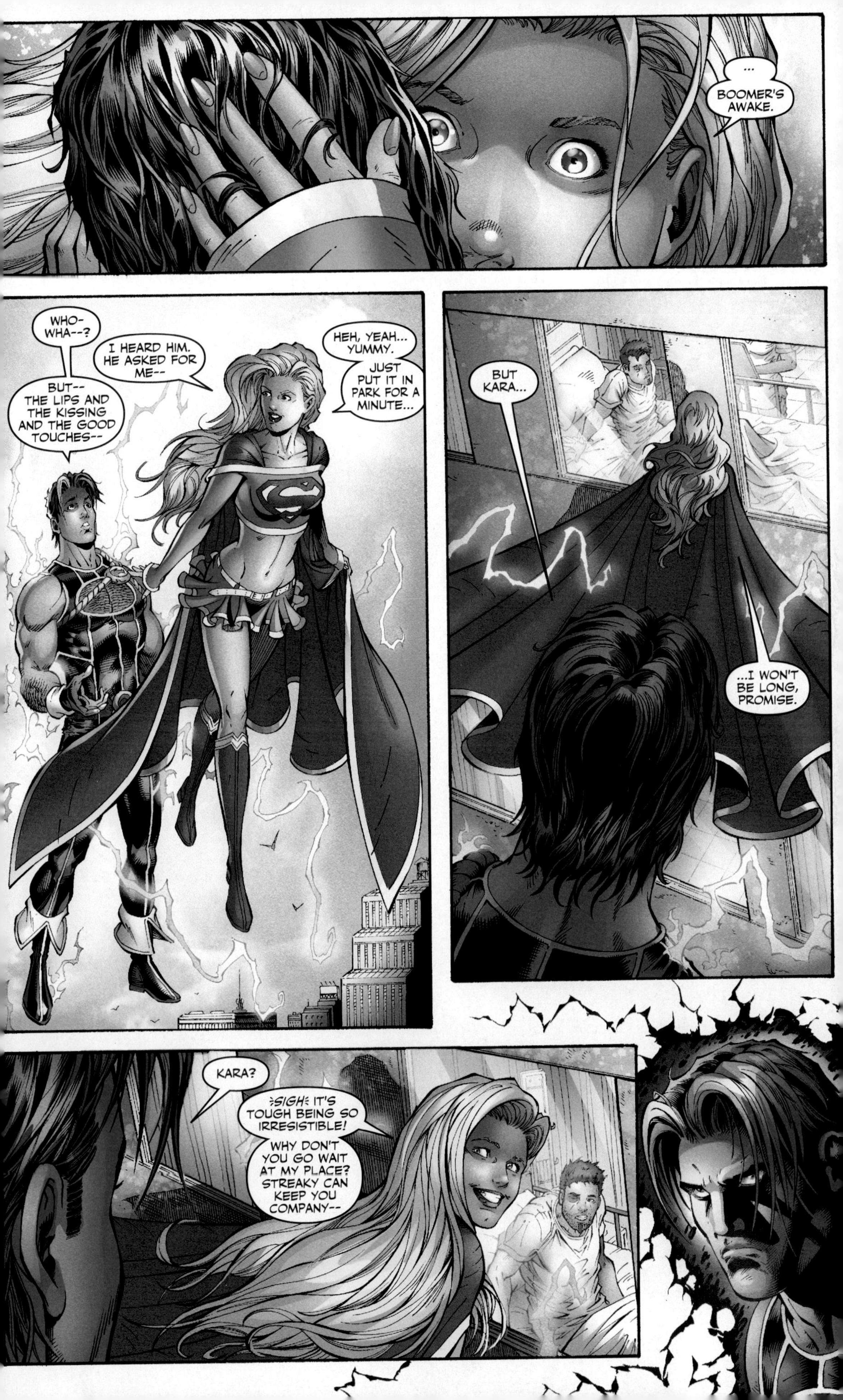
...
BOOMER'S AWAKE.
WHO-WHA--?
BUT-- THE LIPS AND THE KISSING AND THE GOOD TOUCHES--
I HEARD HIM. HE ASKED FOR ME--
HEH, YEAH... YUMMY.
JUST PUT IT IN PARK FOR A MINUTE...
BUT KARA...
...I WON'T BE LONG, PROMISE.
KARA?
SIGH IT'S TOUGH BEING SO IRRESISTIBLE!
WHY DON'T YOU GO WAIT AT MY PLACE? STREAKY CAN KEEP YOU COMPANY--

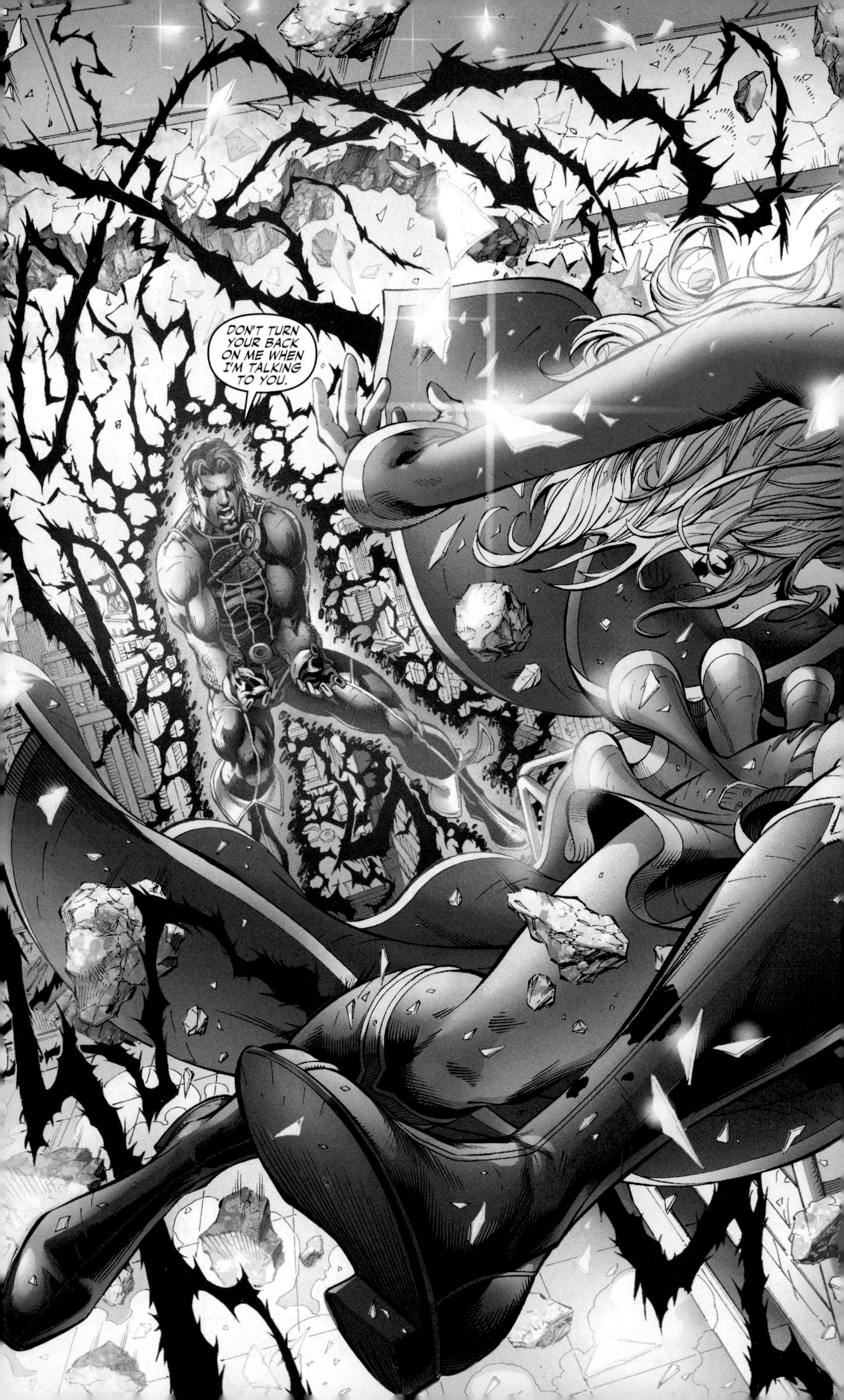
DON'T TURN YOUR BACK ON ME WHEN I'M TALKING TO YOU.

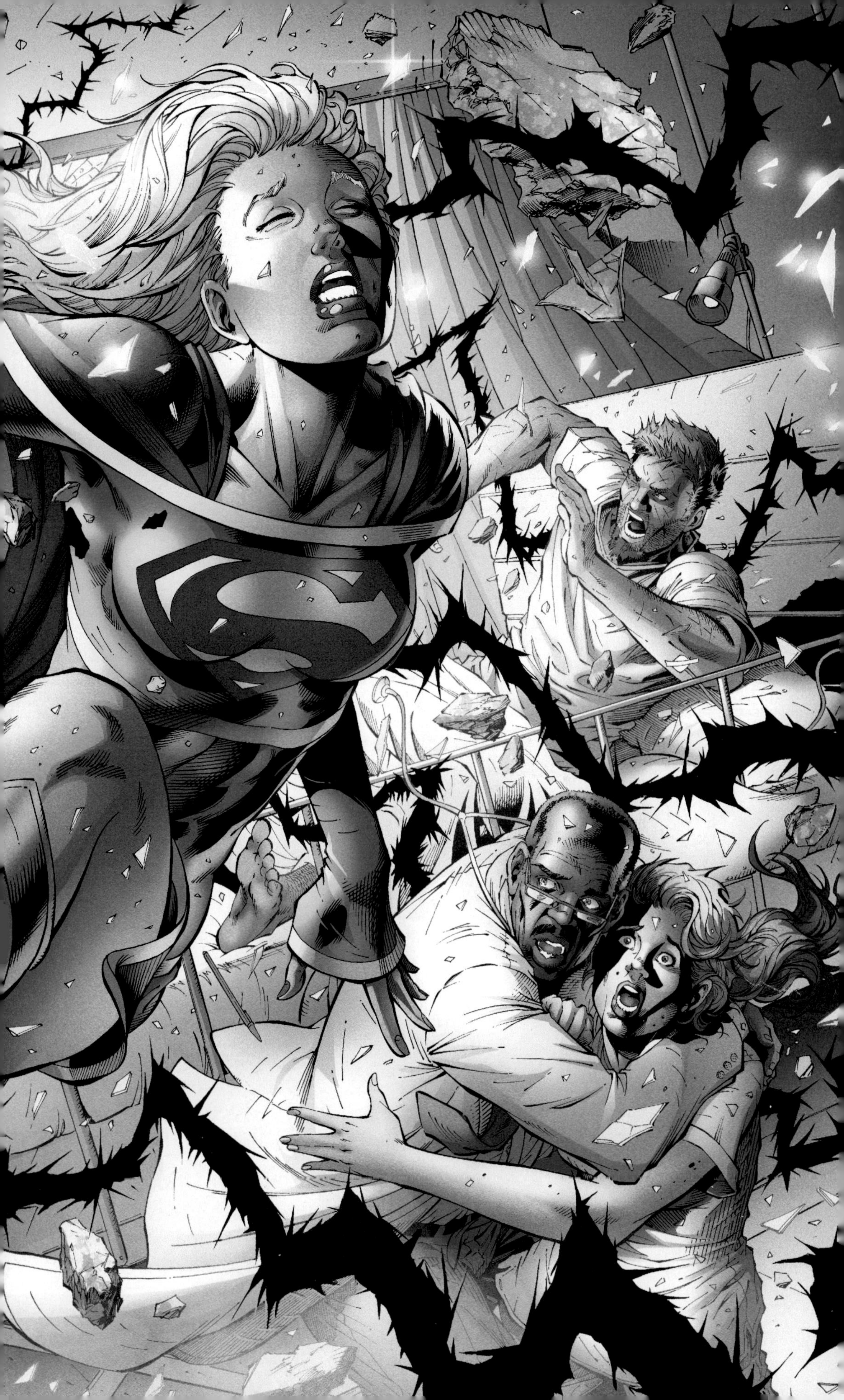

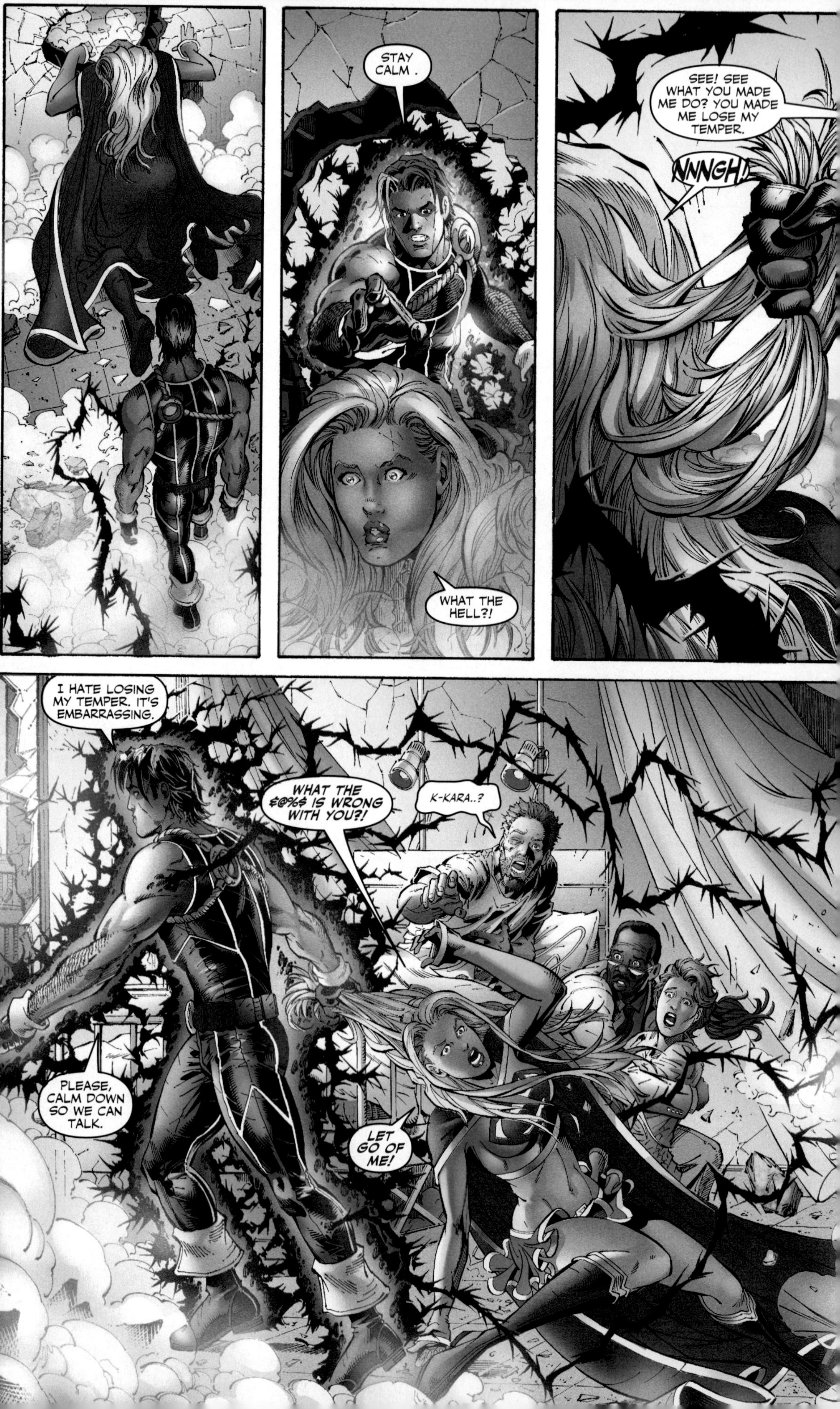
STAY CALM .
WHAT THE HELL?!
SEE! SEE WHAT YOU MADE ME DO? YOU MADE ME LOSE MY TEMPER.
NNNGH!
I HATE LOSING MY TEMPER. IT'S EMBARRASSING.
WHAT THE $@%$ IS WRONG WITH YOU?!
K-KARA..?
PLEASE, CALM DOWN SO WE CAN TALK.
LET GO OF ME!

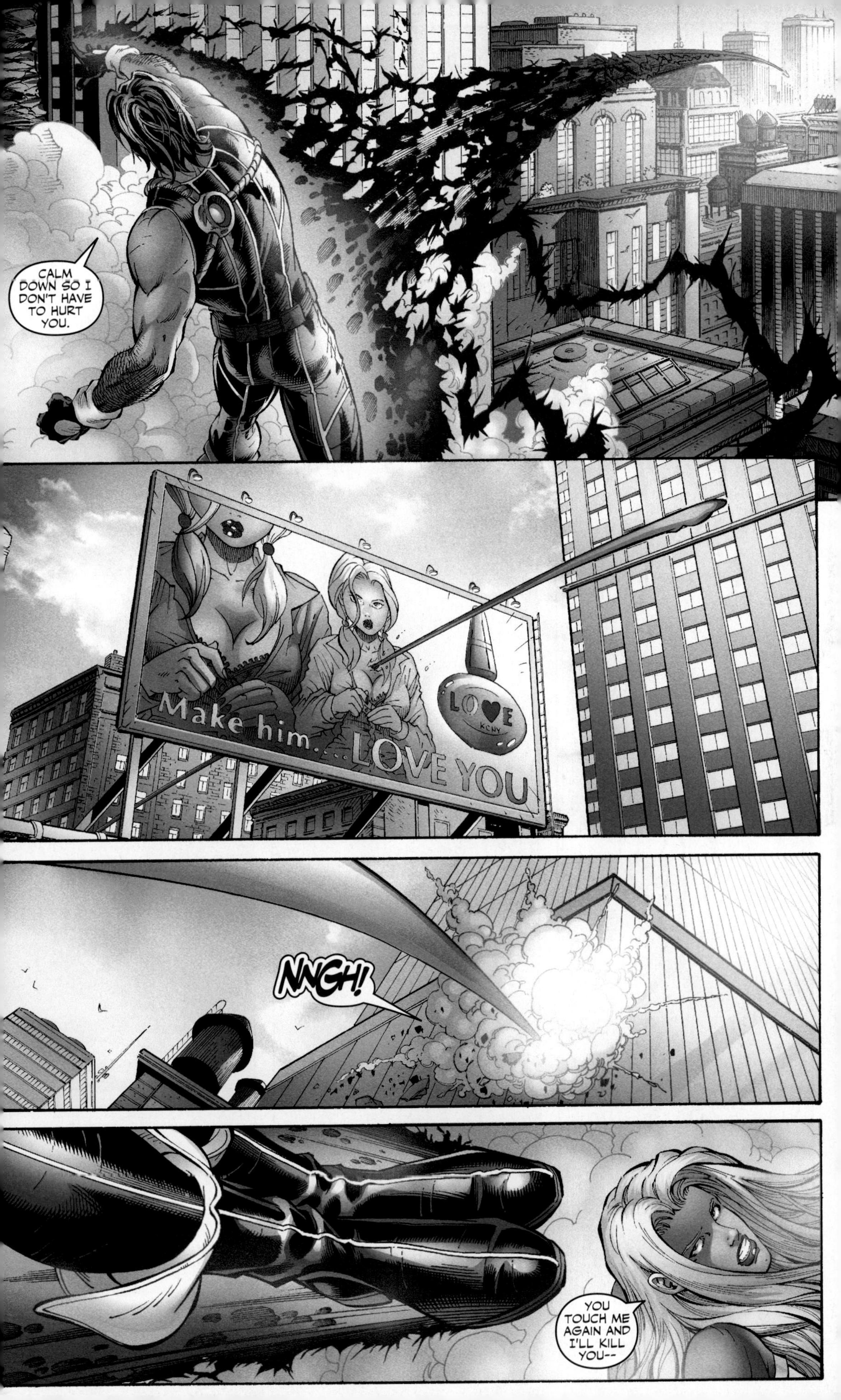
CALM DOWN SO I DON'T HAVE TO HURT YOU.
Make him... LOVE YOU
LOVE
NNGH!
YOU TOUCH ME AGAIN AND I'LL KILL YOU--

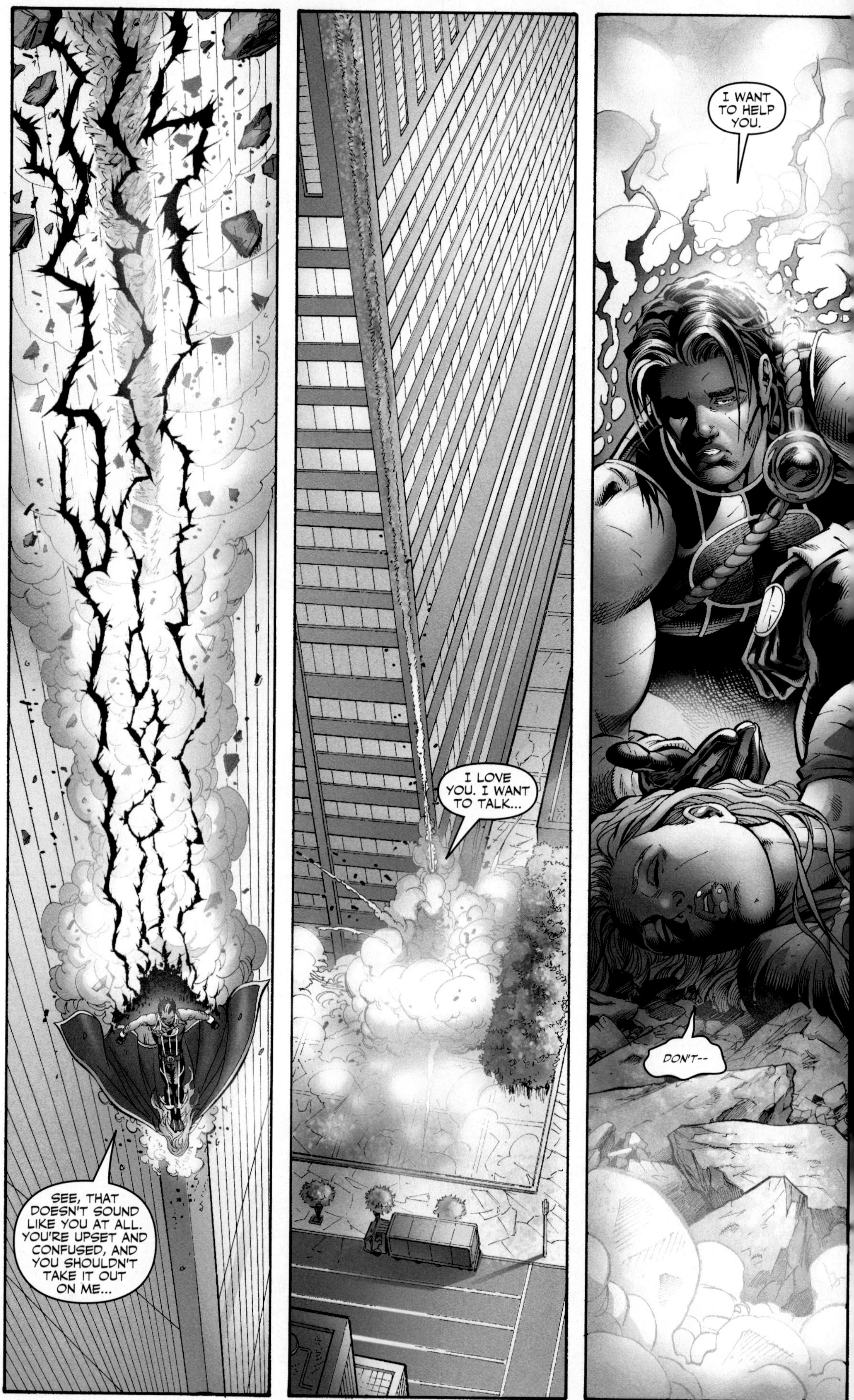
SEE, THAT DOESN'T SOUND LIKE YOU AT ALL. YOU'RE UPSET AND CONFUSED, AND YOU SHOULDN'T TAKE IT OUT ON ME...
I LOVE YOU. I WANT TO TALK...
I WANT TO HELP YOU.
DON'T--

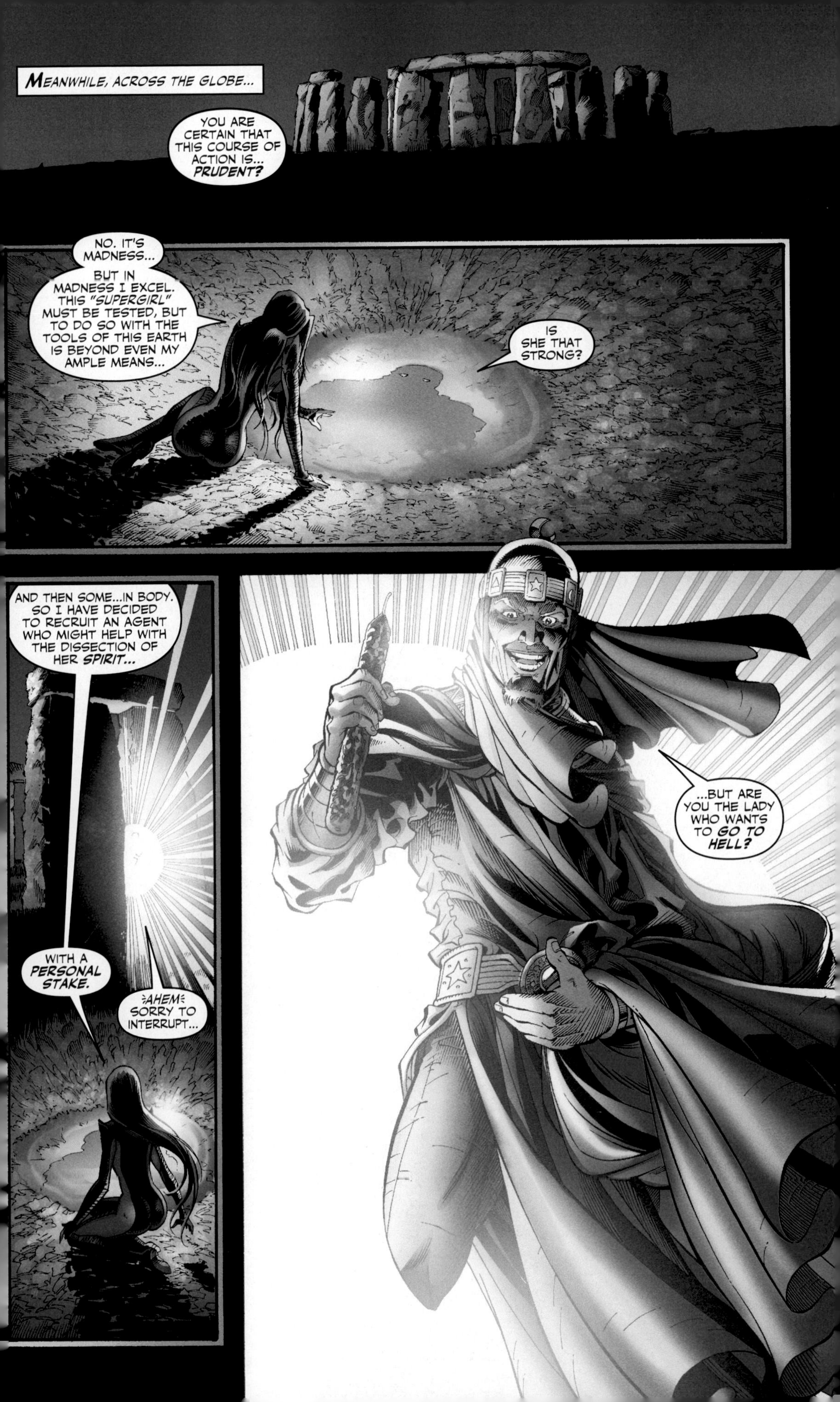

MEANWHILE, ACROSS THE GLOBE...
YOU ARE CERTAIN THAT THIS COURSE OF ACTION IS... PRUDENT?
NO. IT'S MADNESS...
BUT IN MADNESS I EXCEL. THIS "SUPERGIRL" MUST BE TESTED, BUT TO DO SO WITH THE TOOLS OF THIS EARTH IS BEYOND EVEN MY AMPLE MEANS...
IS SHE THAT STRONG?
AND THEN SOME...IN BODY. SO I HAVE DECIDED TO RECRUIT AN AGENT WHO MIGHT HELP WITH THE DISSECTION OF HER SPIRIT...
WITH A PERSONAL STAKE.
AHEM SORRY TO INTERRUPT...
...BUT ARE YOU THE LADY WHO WANTS TO GO TO HELL?

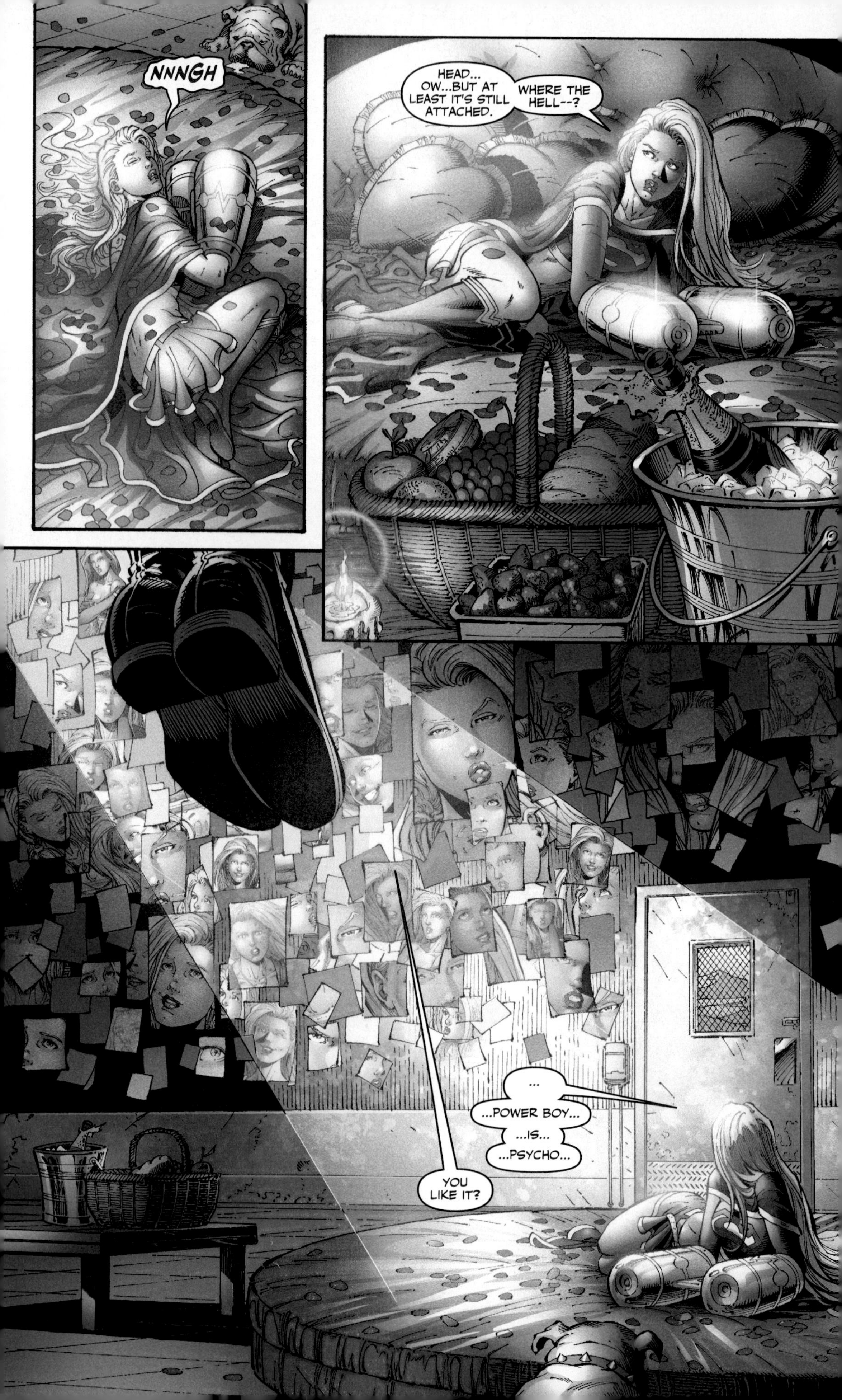
NNNGH
HEAD... OW...BUT AT LEAST IT'S STILL ATTACHED.
WHERE THE HELL--?
...
...POWER BOY...
...IS...
...PSYCHO...
YOU LIKE IT?

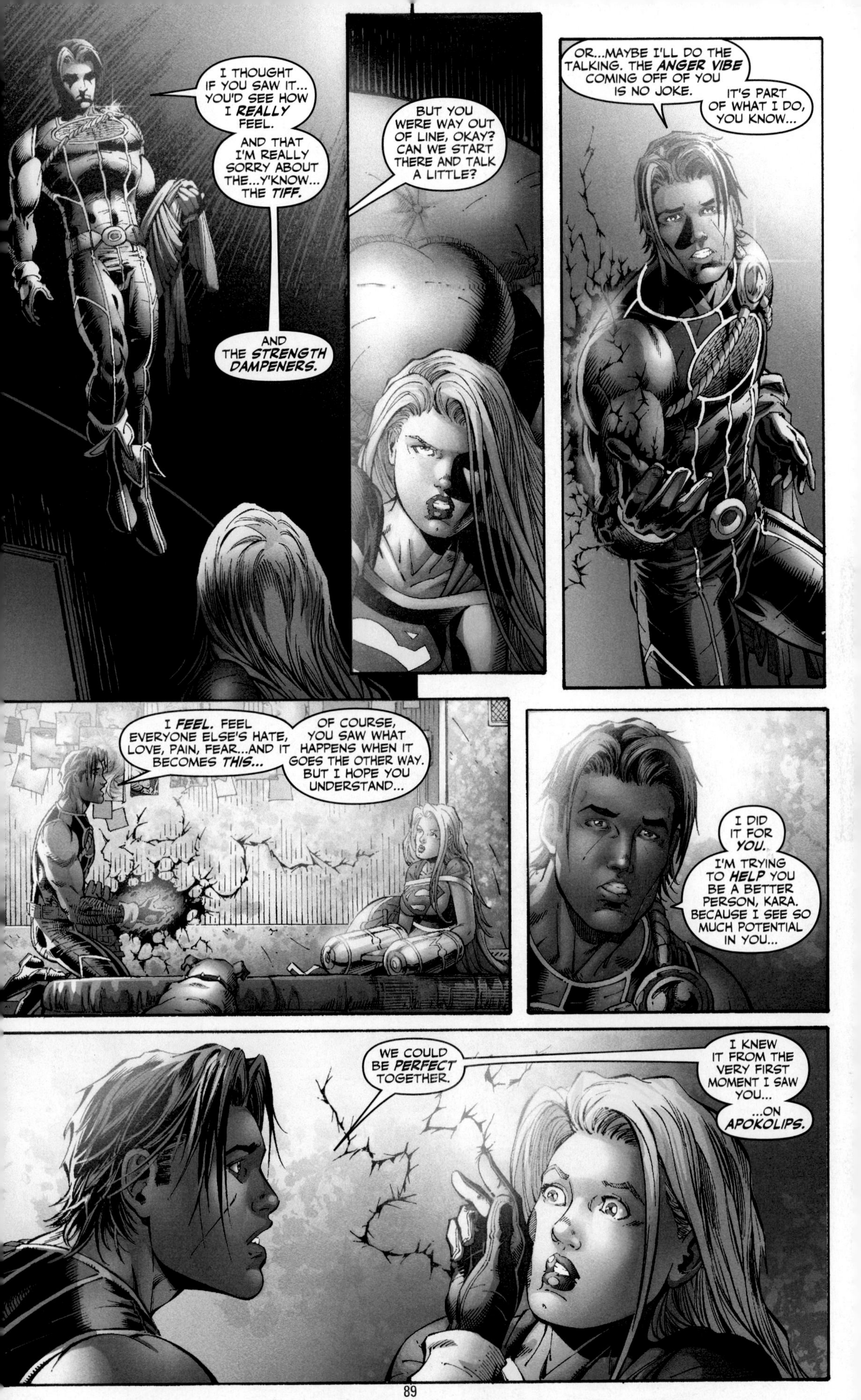

I THOUGHT IF YOU SAW IT... YOU'D SEE HOW I REALLY FEEL.
AND THAT I'M REALLY SORRY ABOUT THE...Y'KNOW... THE TIFF.
AND THE STRENGTH DAMPENERS.
BUT YOU WERE WAY OUT OF LINE, OKAY? CAN WE START THERE AND TALK A LITTLE?
OR...MAYBE I'LL DO THE TALKING. THE ANGER VIBE COMING OFF OF YOU IS NO JOKE.
IT'S PART OF WHAT I DO, YOU KNOW...
I FEEL. FEEL EVERYONE ELSE'S HATE, LOVE, PAIN, FEAR...AND IT BECOMES THIS...
OF COURSE, YOU SAW WHAT HAPPENS WHEN IT GOES THE OTHER WAY. BUT I HOPE YOU UNDERSTAND...
I DID IT FOR YOU.
I'M TRYING TO HELP YOU BE A BETTER PERSON, KARA. BECAUSE I SEE SO MUCH POTENTIAL IN YOU...
WE COULD BE PERFECT TOGETHER.
I KNEW IT FROM THE VERY FIRST MOMENT I SAW YOU...
...ON APOKOLIPS.

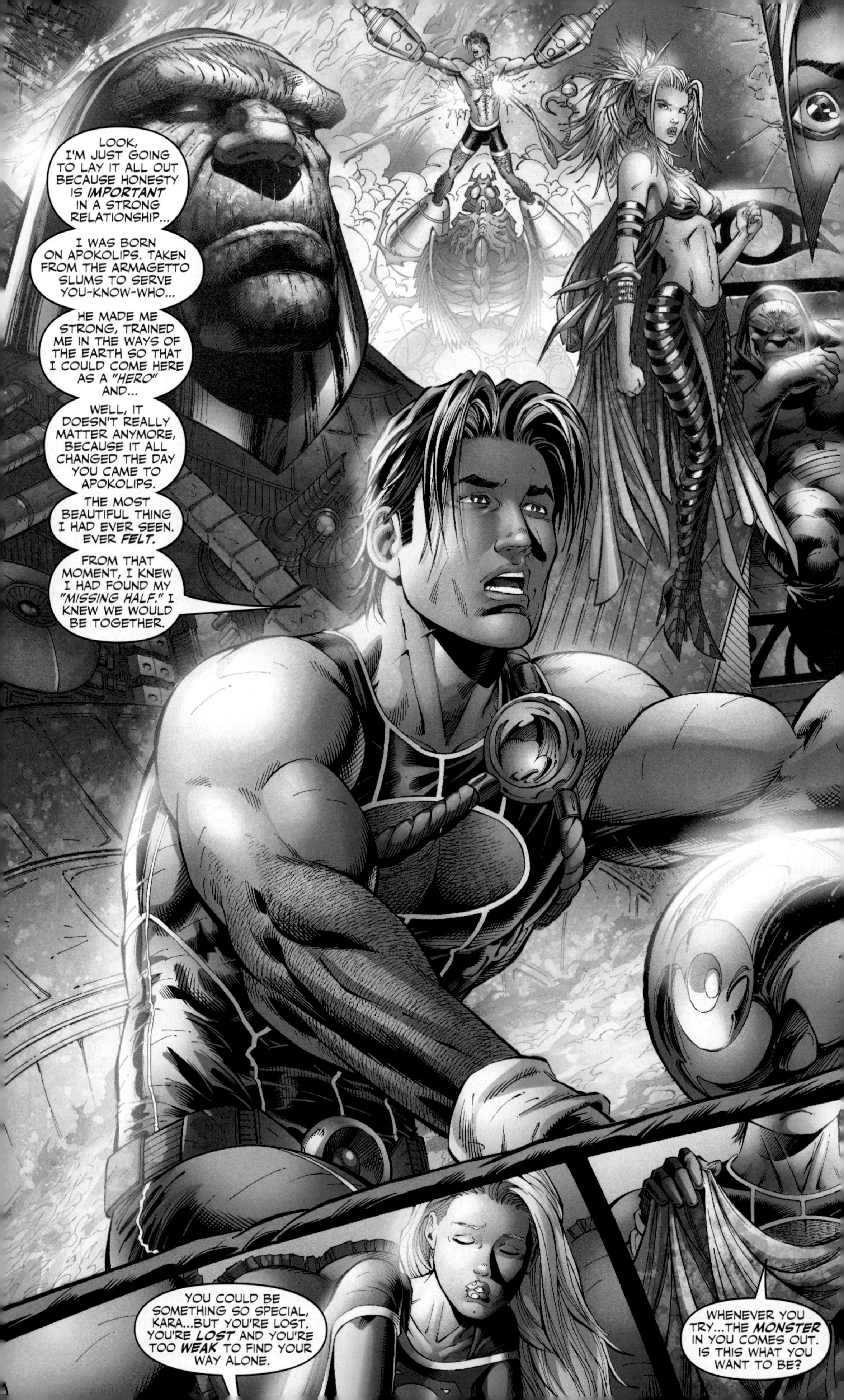
LOOK, I'M JUST GOING TO LAY IT ALL OUT BECAUSE HONESTY IS *IMPORTANT* IN A STRONG RELATIONSHIP...
I WAS BORN ON APOKOLIPS. TAKEN FROM THE ARMAGETTO SLUMS TO SERVE YOU-KNOW-WHO...
HE MADE ME STRONG, TRAINED ME IN THE WAYS OF THE EARTH SO THAT I COULD COME HERE AS A *"HERO"* AND...
WELL, IT DOESN'T REALLY MATTER ANYMORE, BECAUSE IT ALL CHANGED THE DAY YOU CAME TO APOKOLIPS.
THE MOST BEAUTIFUL THING I HAD EVER SEEN. EVER *FELT.*
FROM THAT MOMENT, I KNEW I HAD FOUND MY *"MISSING HALF."* I KNEW WE WOULD BE TOGETHER.
YOU COULD BE SOMETHING SO SPECIAL, KARA...BUT YOU'RE LOST. YOU'RE *LOST* AND YOU'RE TOO *WEAK* TO FIND YOUR WAY ALONE.
WHENEVER YOU TRY...THE *MONSTER* IN YOU COMES OUT. IS THIS WHAT YOU WANT TO BE?

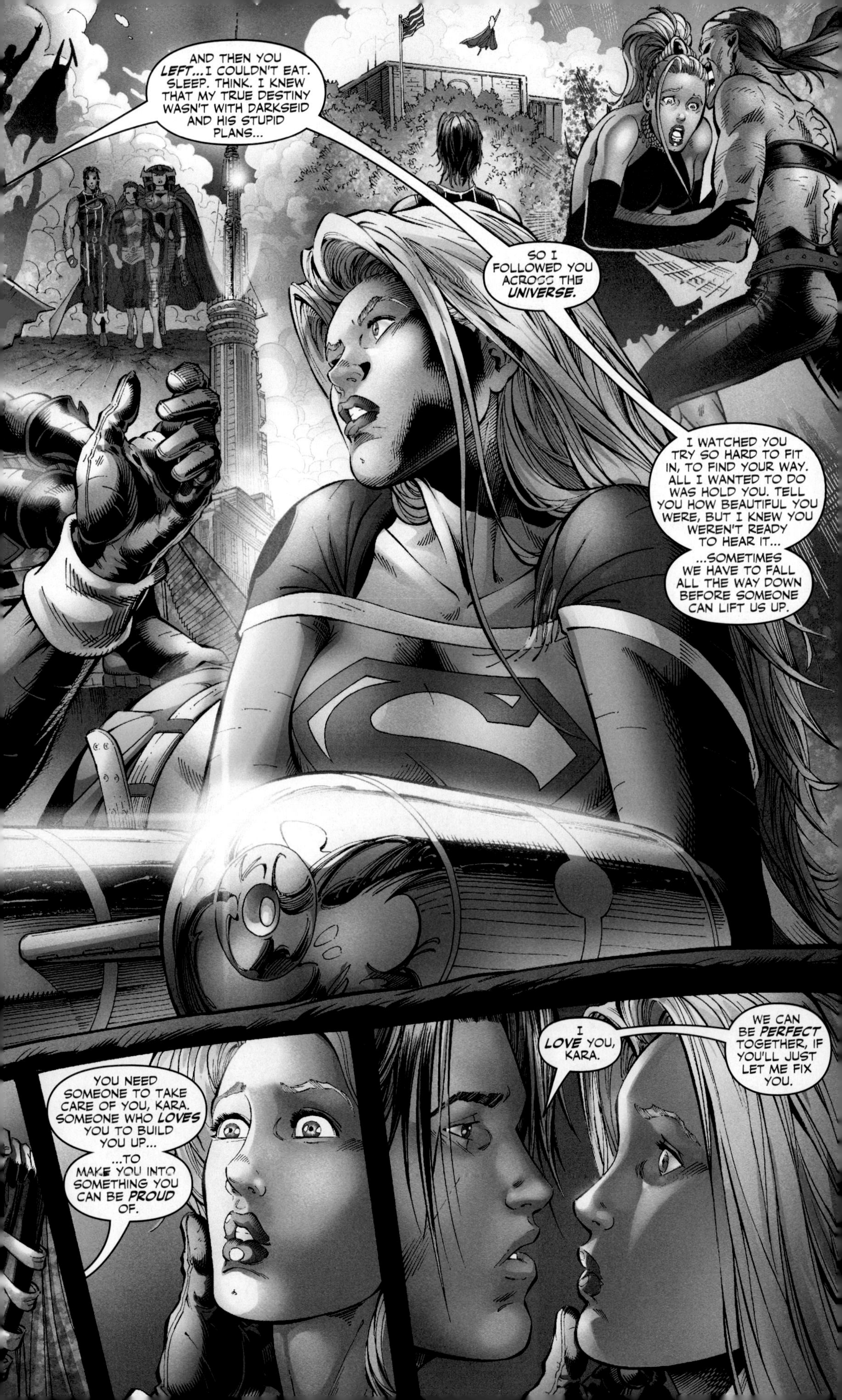

AND THEN YOU LEFT... I COULDN'T EAT. SLEEP. THINK. I KNEW THAT MY TRUE DESTINY WASN'T WITH DARKSEID AND HIS STUPID PLANS...
SO I FOLLOWED YOU ACROSS THE UNIVERSE.
I WATCHED YOU TRY SO HARD TO FIT IN, TO FIND YOUR WAY. ALL I WANTED TO DO WAS HOLD YOU. TELL YOU HOW BEAUTIFUL YOU WERE, BUT I KNEW YOU WEREN'T READY TO HEAR IT...
...SOMETIMES WE HAVE TO FALL ALL THE WAY DOWN BEFORE SOMEONE CAN LIFT US UP.
YOU NEED SOMEONE TO TAKE CARE OF YOU, KARA. SOMEONE WHO LOVES YOU TO BUILD YOU UP...
...TO MAKE YOU INTO SOMETHING YOU CAN BE PROUD OF.
I LOVE YOU, KARA.
WE CAN BE PERFECT TOGETHER, IF YOU'LL JUST LET ME FIX YOU.

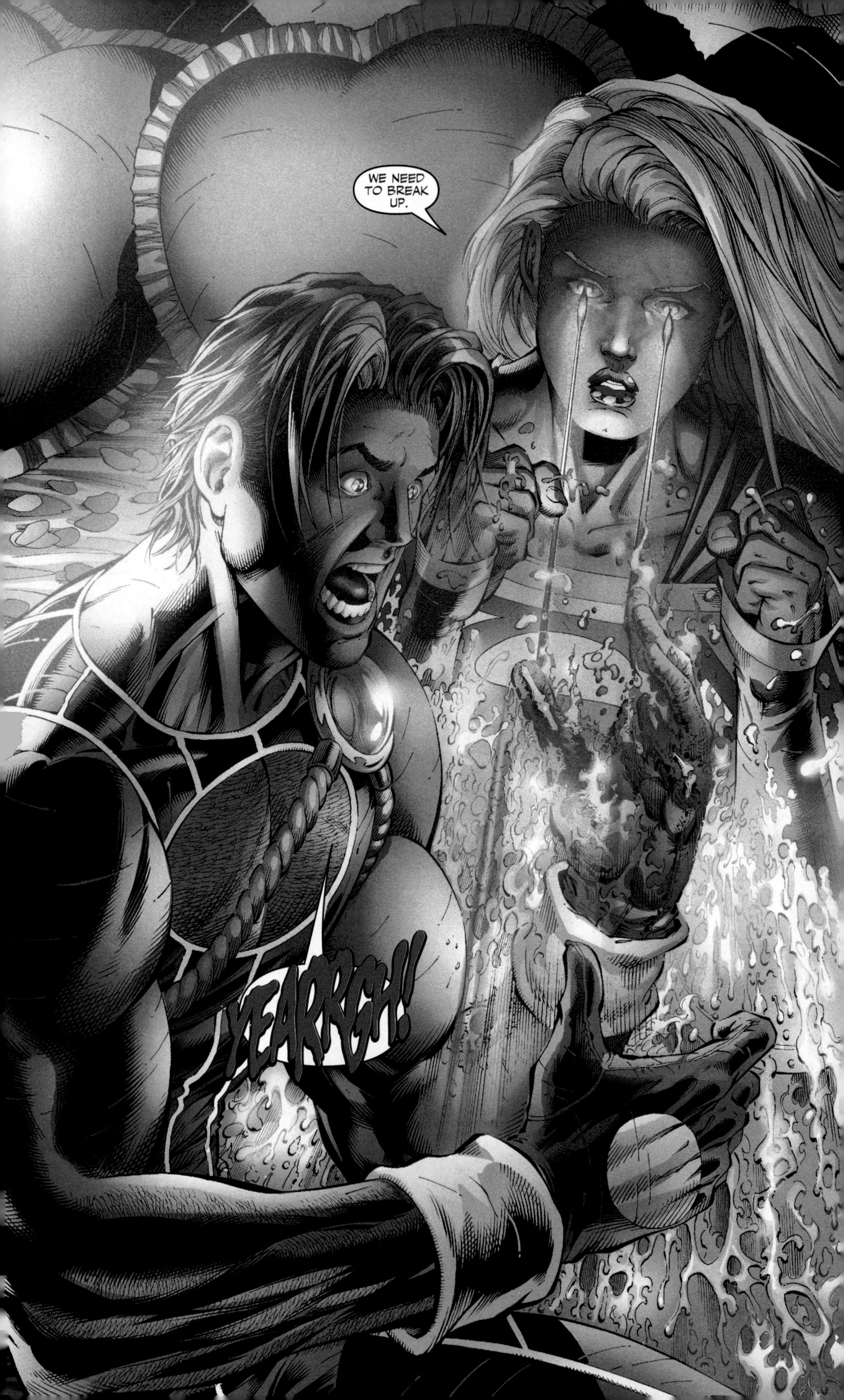
WE NEED TO BREAK UP.
YEARRGH!

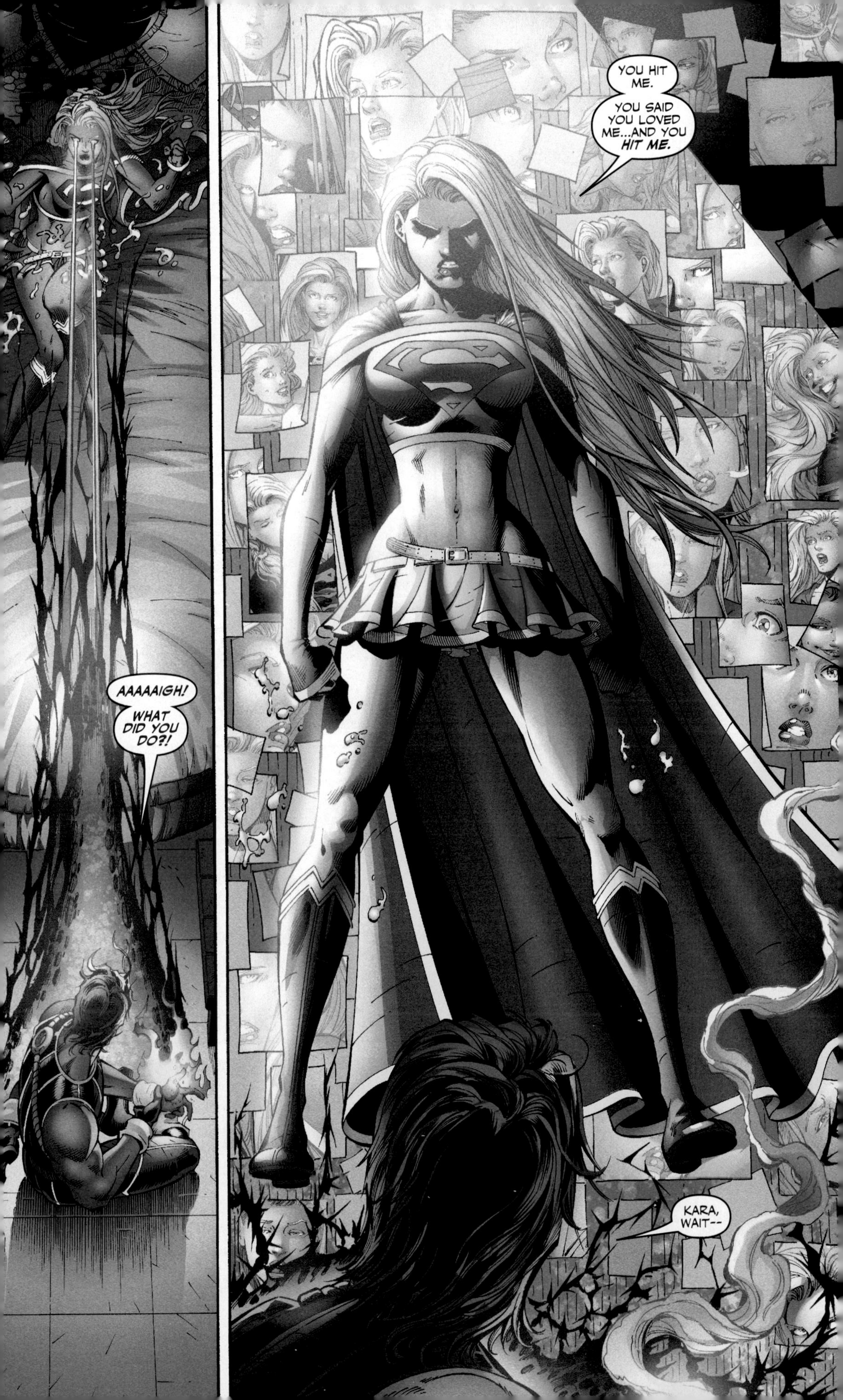
AAAAAIGH!
WHAT DID YOU DO?!
YOU HIT ME.
YOU SAID YOU LOVED ME...AND YOU HIT ME.
KARA, WAIT--

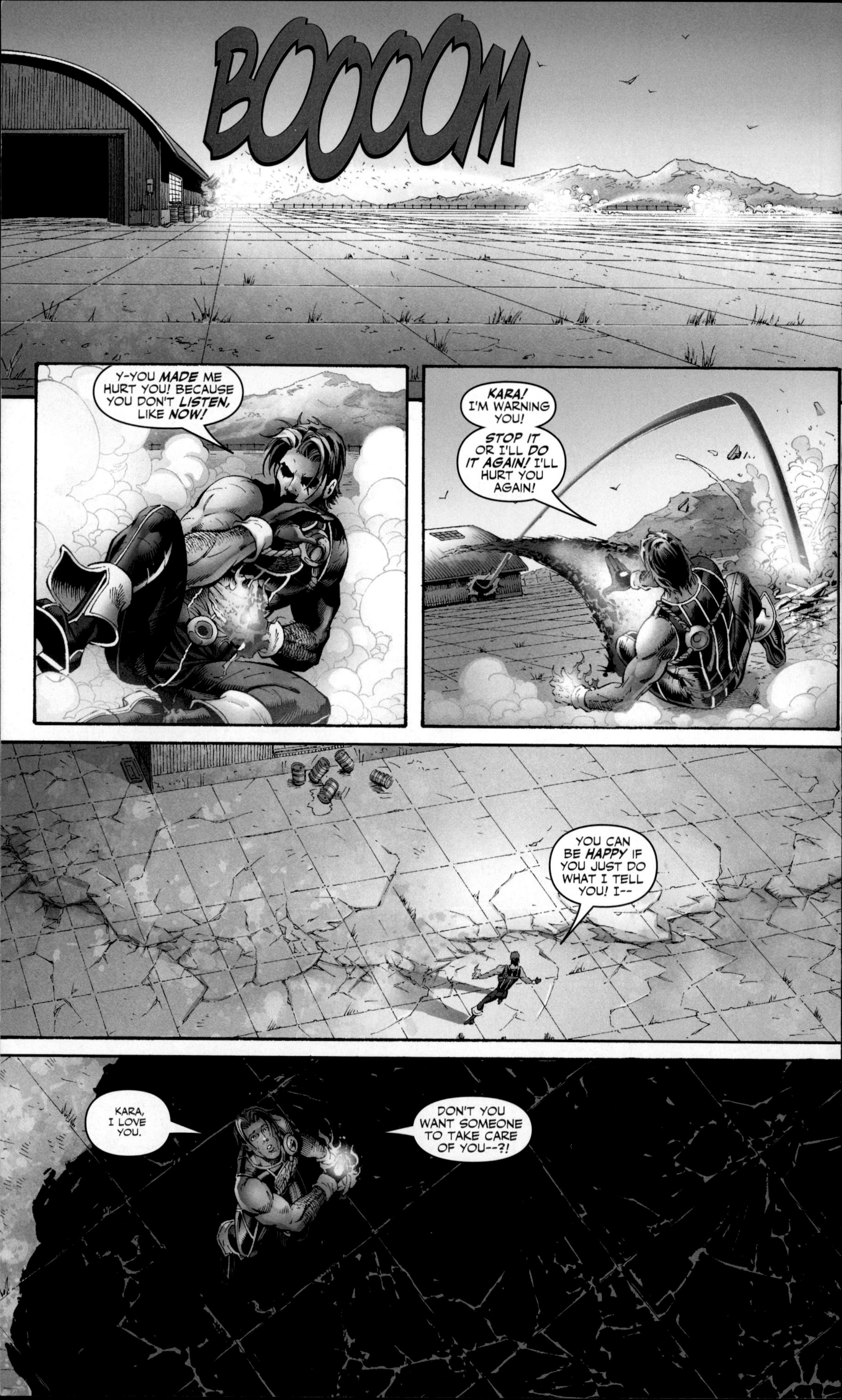
BOOOOM
Y-YOU MADE ME HURT YOU! BECAUSE YOU DON'T LISTEN, LIKE NOW!
KARA! I'M WARNING YOU!
STOP IT OR I'LL DO IT AGAIN! I'LL HURT YOU AGAIN!
YOU CAN BE HAPPY IF YOU JUST DO WHAT I TELL YOU! I--
KARA, I LOVE YOU.
DON'T YOU WANT SOMEONE TO TAKE CARE OF YOU--?!

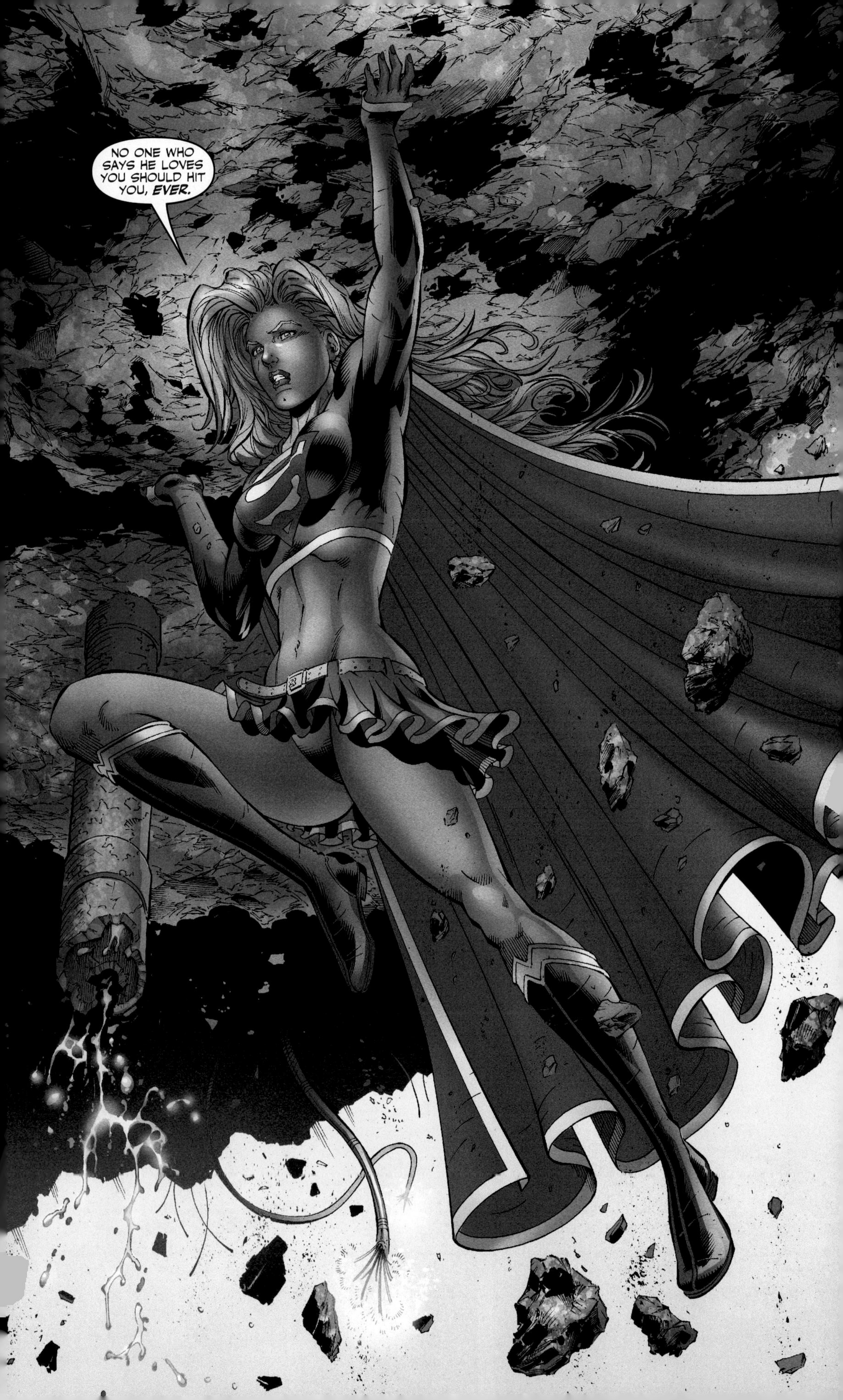
NO ONE WHO SAYS HE LOVES YOU SHOULD HIT YOU, EVER.

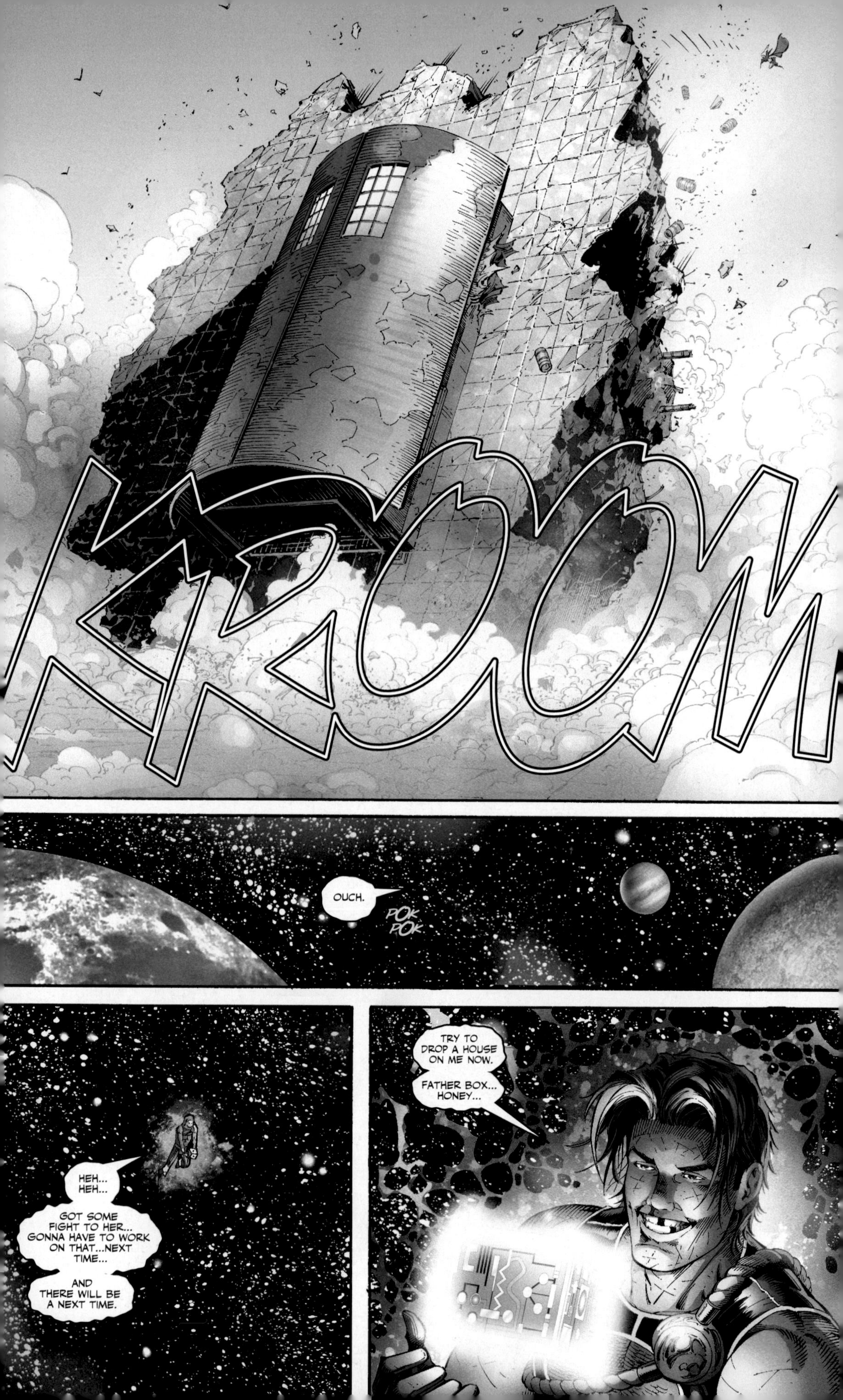
KRROOM
OUCH.
POK POK
HEH... HEH...
GOT SOME FIGHT TO HER... GONNA HAVE TO WORK ON THAT...NEXT TIME...
AND THERE WILL BE A NEXT TIME.
TRY TO DROP A HOUSE ON ME NOW.
FATHER BOX... HONEY...

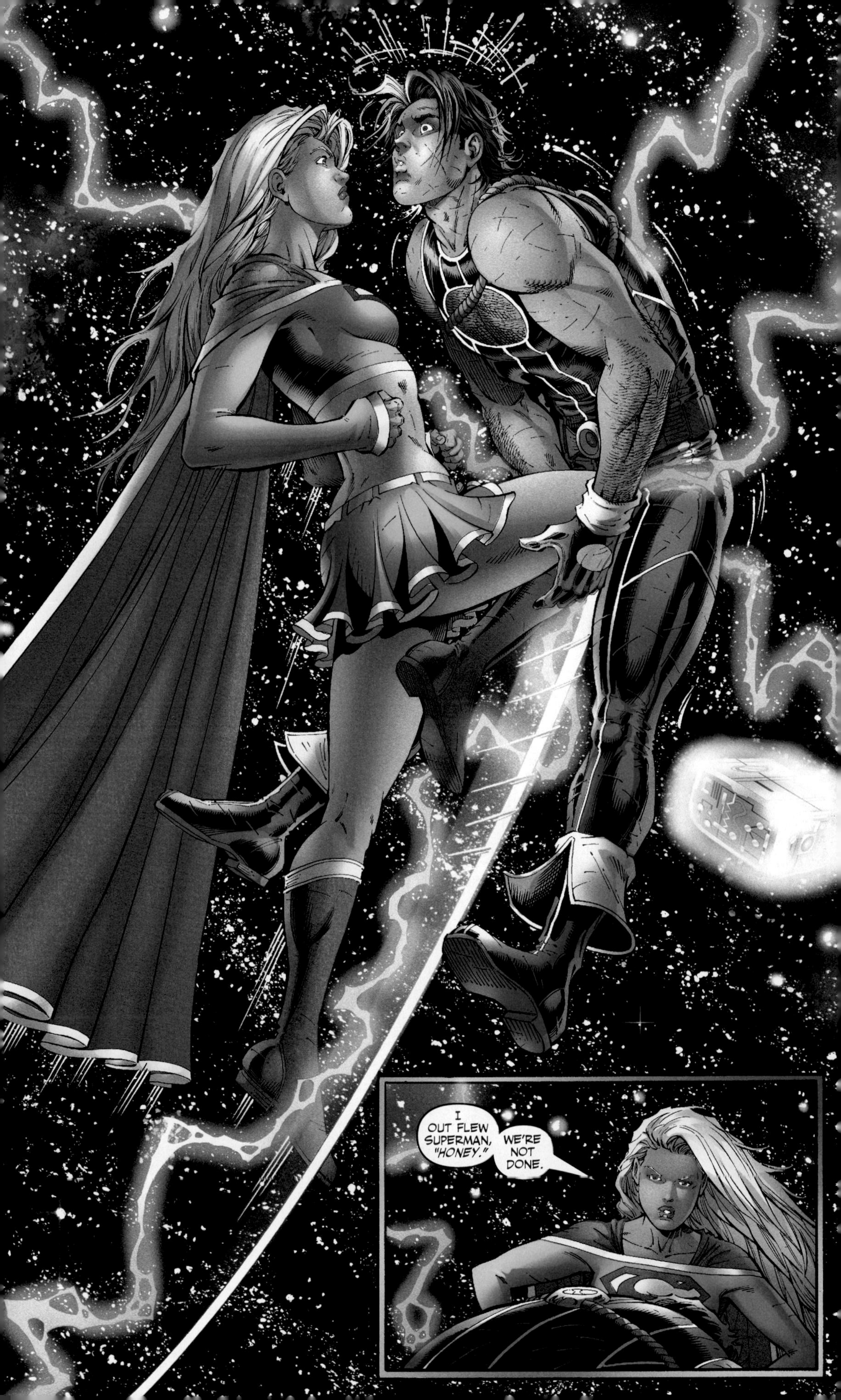

I OUT FLEW SUPERMAN, "HONEY."
WE'RE NOT DONE.

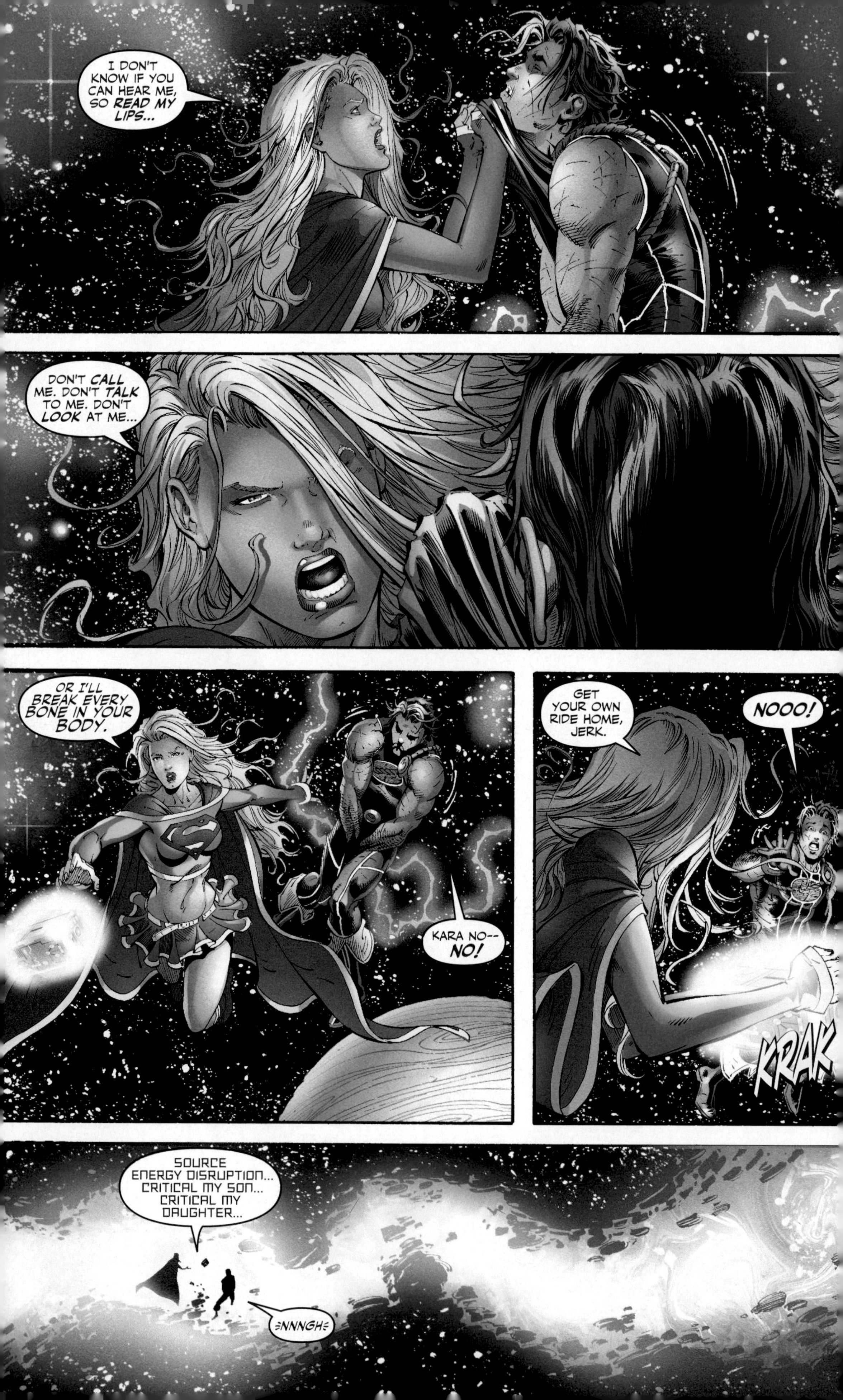
I DON'T KNOW IF YOU CAN HEAR ME, SO READ MY LIPS...
DON'T CALL ME. DON'T TALK TO ME. DON'T LOOK AT ME...
OR I'LL BREAK EVERY BONE IN YOUR BODY.
KARA NO-- NO!
GET YOUR OWN RIDE HOME, JERK.
NOOO!
KRAK
SOURCE ENERGY DISRUPTION... CRITICAL MY SON... CRITICAL MY DAUGHTER...
=NNNGH=

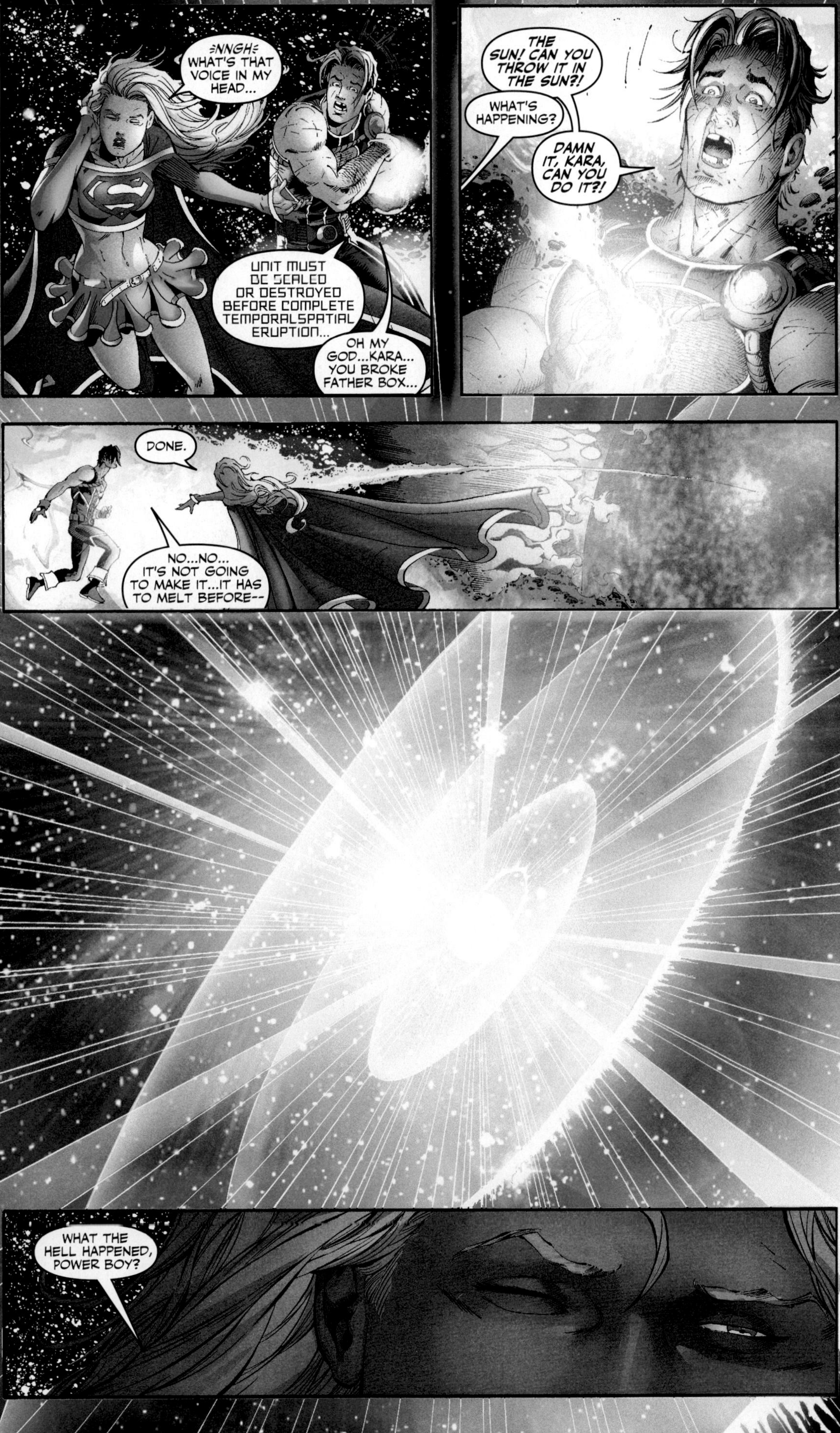

≡NNGH≡ WHAT'S THAT VOICE IN MY HEAD...
UNIT MUST BE SEALED OR DESTROYED BEFORE COMPLETE TEMPORALSPATIAL ERUPTION...
OH MY GOD...KARA... YOU BROKE FATHER BOX...
THE SUN! CAN YOU THROW IT IN THE SUN?!
WHAT'S HAPPENING?
DAMN IT, KARA, CAN YOU DO IT?!
DONE.
NO...NO... IT'S NOT GOING TO MAKE IT...IT HAS TO MELT BEFORE--
WHAT THE HELL HAPPENED, POWER BOY?

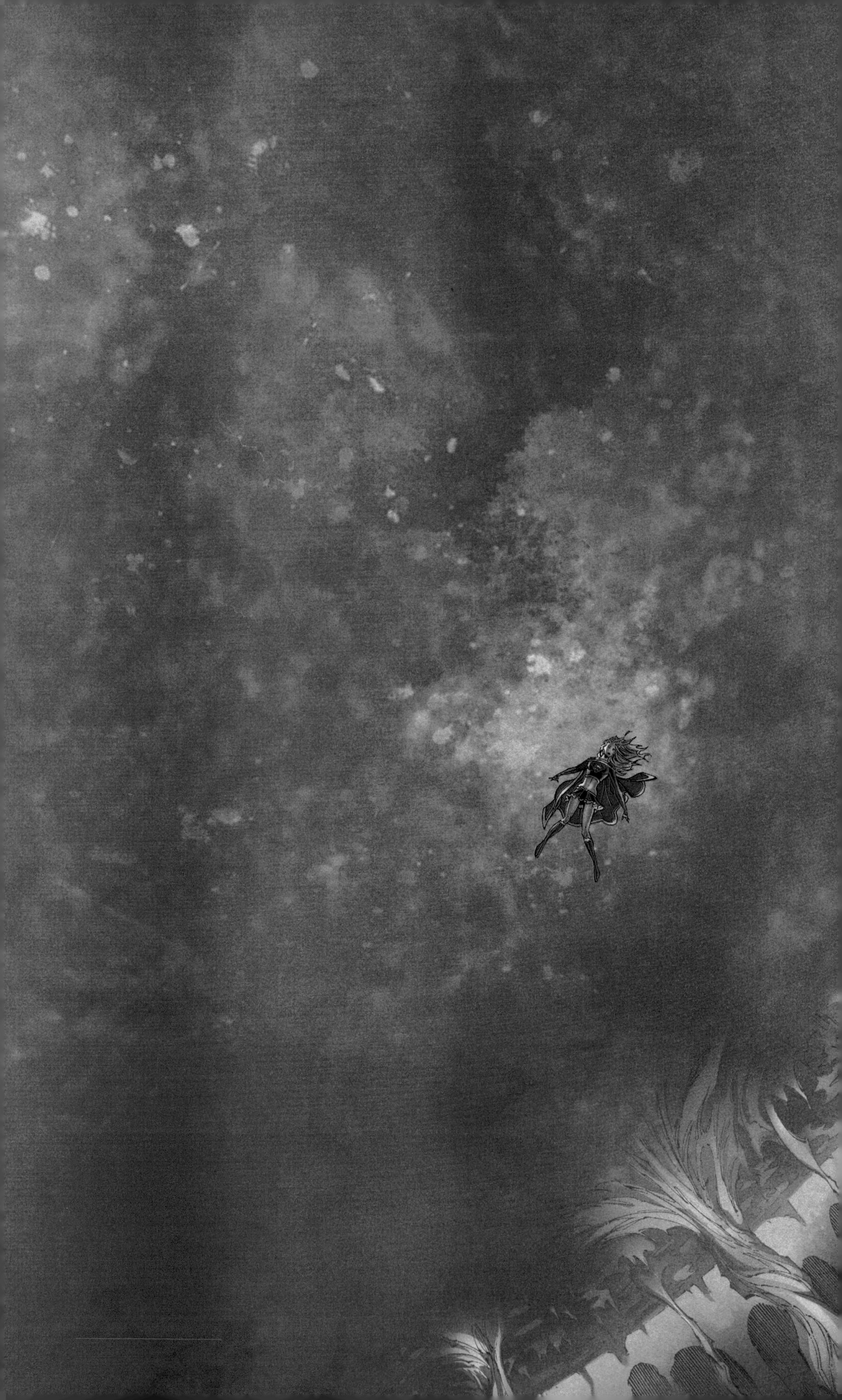

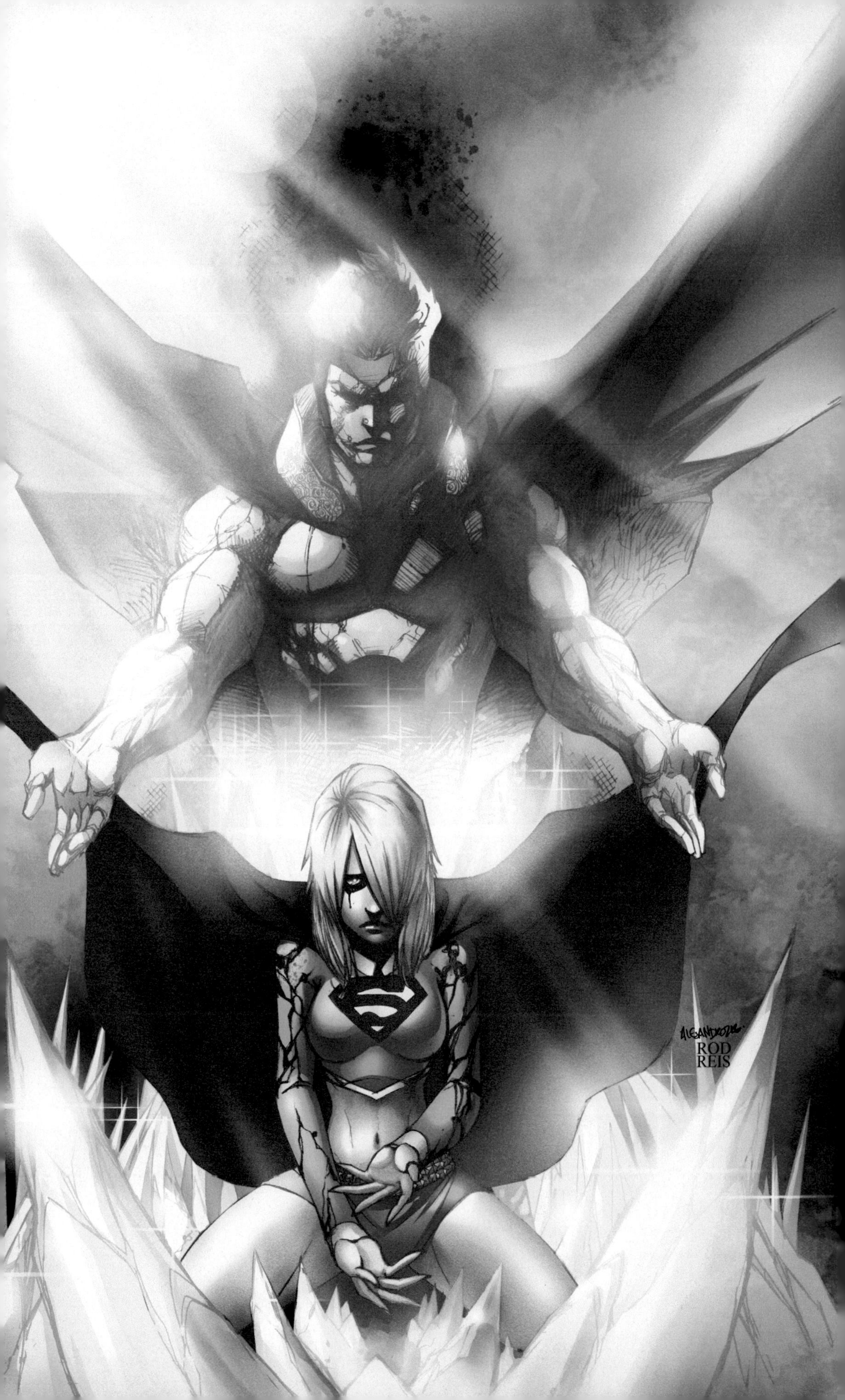
ROD
REIS

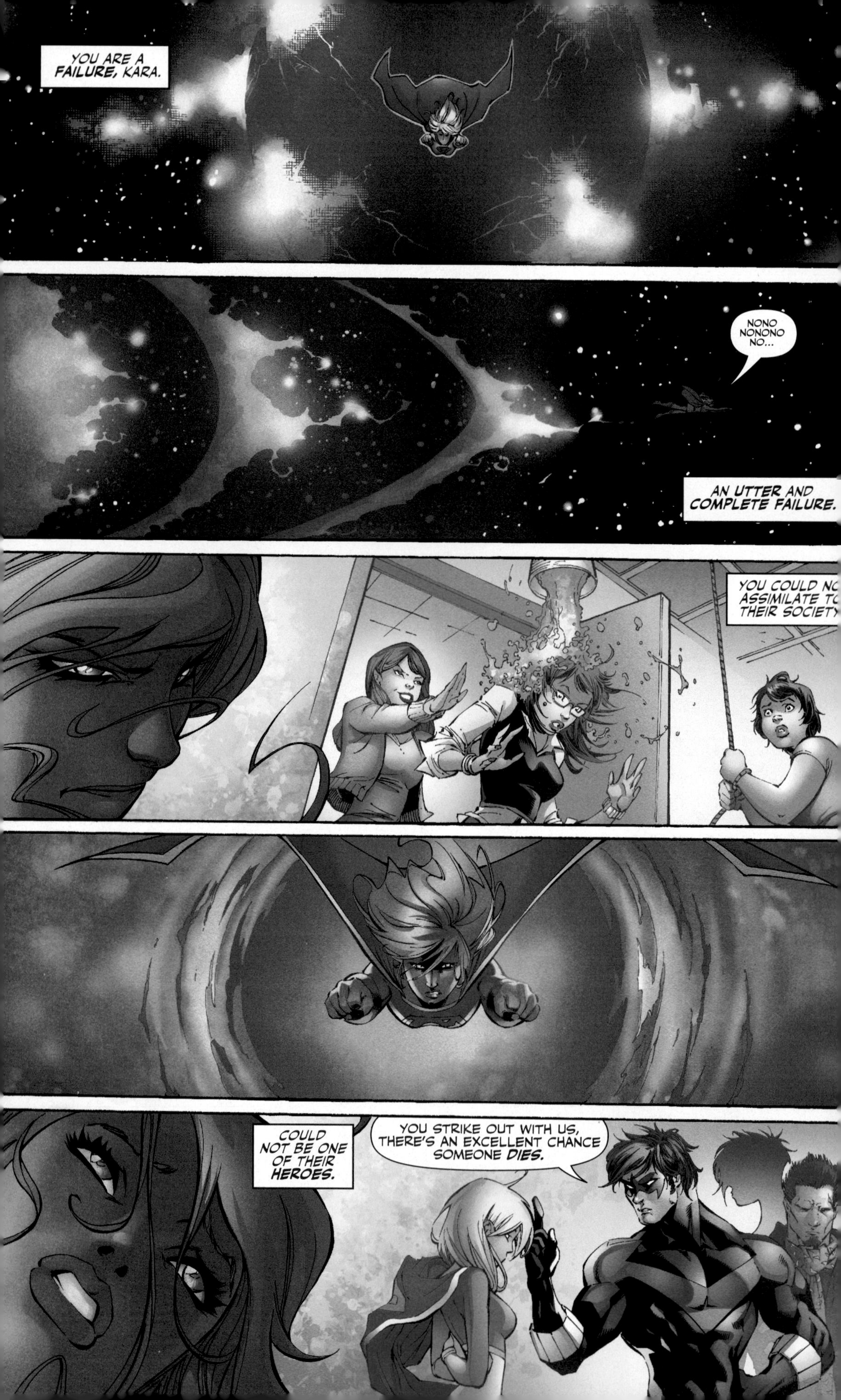
YOU ARE A FAILURE, KARA.
NONO NONONO NO...
AN UTTER AND COMPLETE FAILURE.
YOU COULD NO ASSIMILATE TO THEIR SOCIETY
COULD NOT BE ONE OF THEIR HEROES.
YOU STRIKE OUT WITH US, THERE'S AN EXCELLENT CHANCE SOMEONE DIES.

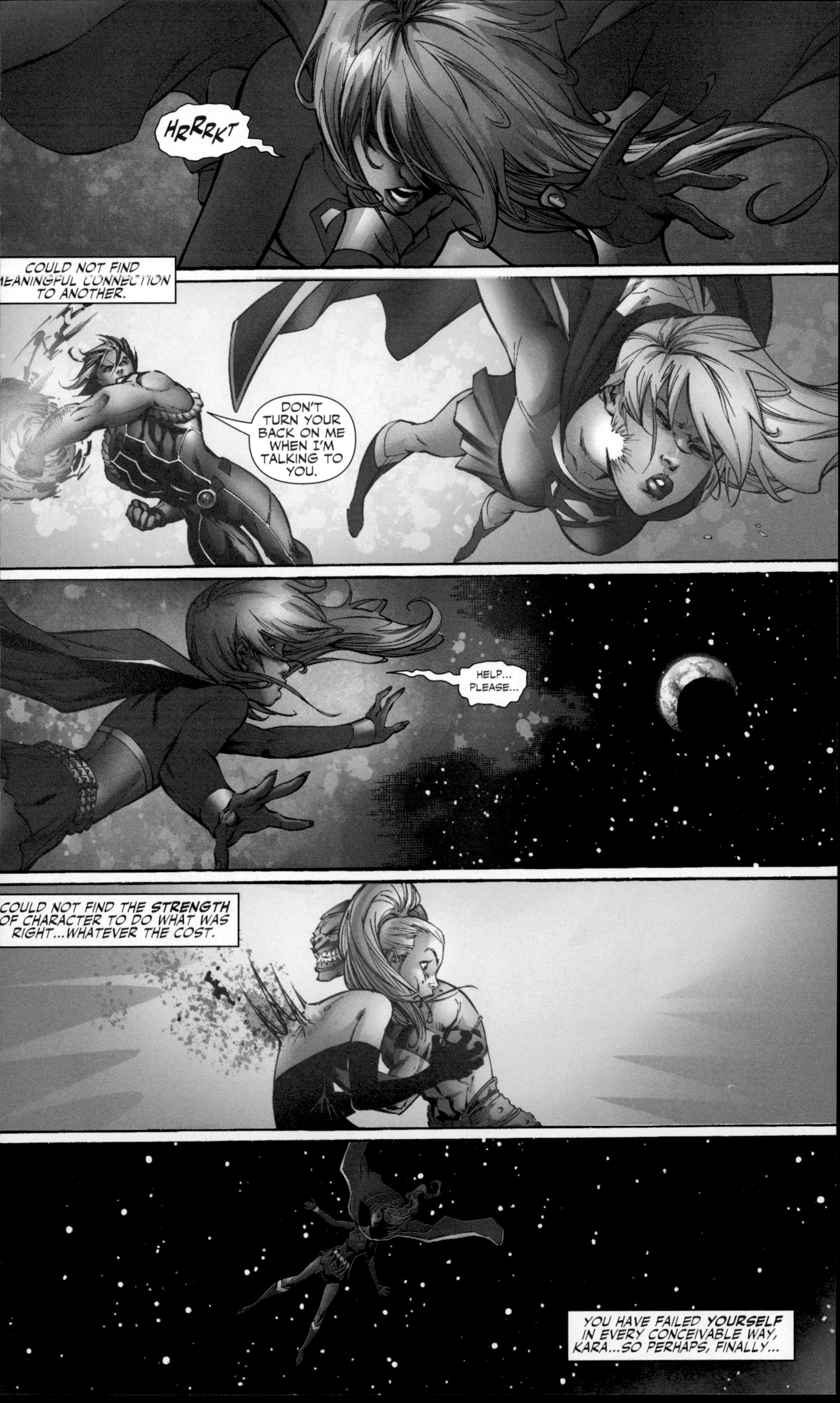
HRRRKT
COULD NOT FIND MEANINGFUL CONNECTION TO ANOTHER.
DON'T TURN YOUR BACK ON ME WHEN I'M TALKING TO YOU.
HELP... PLEASE...
COULD NOT FIND THE STRENGTH OF CHARACTER TO DO WHAT WAS RIGHT...WHATEVER THE COST.
YOU HAVE FAILED YOURSELF IN EVERY CONCEIVABLE WAY, KARA...SO PERHAPS, FINALLY...

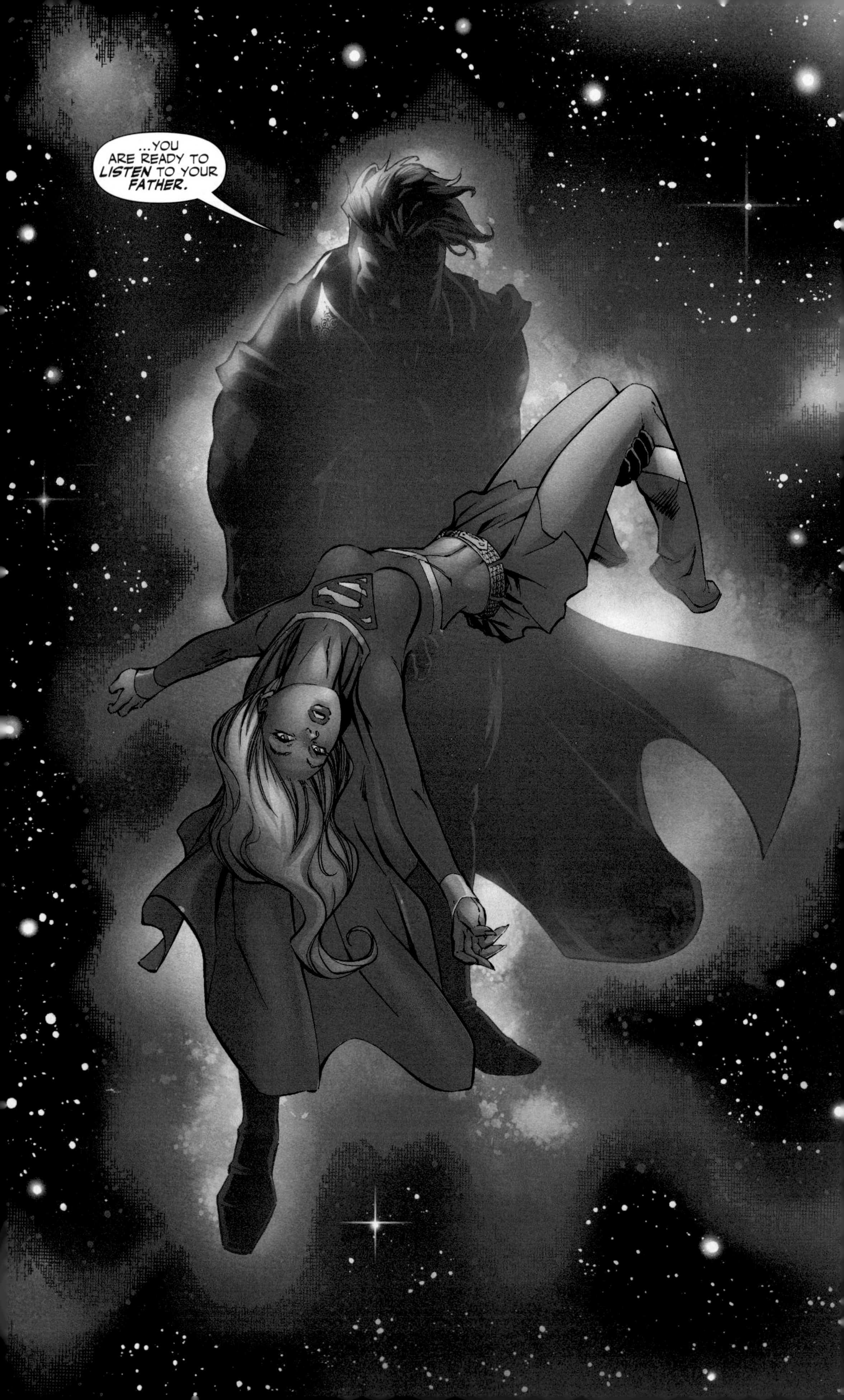
...YOU ARE READY TO LISTEN TO YOUR FATHER.

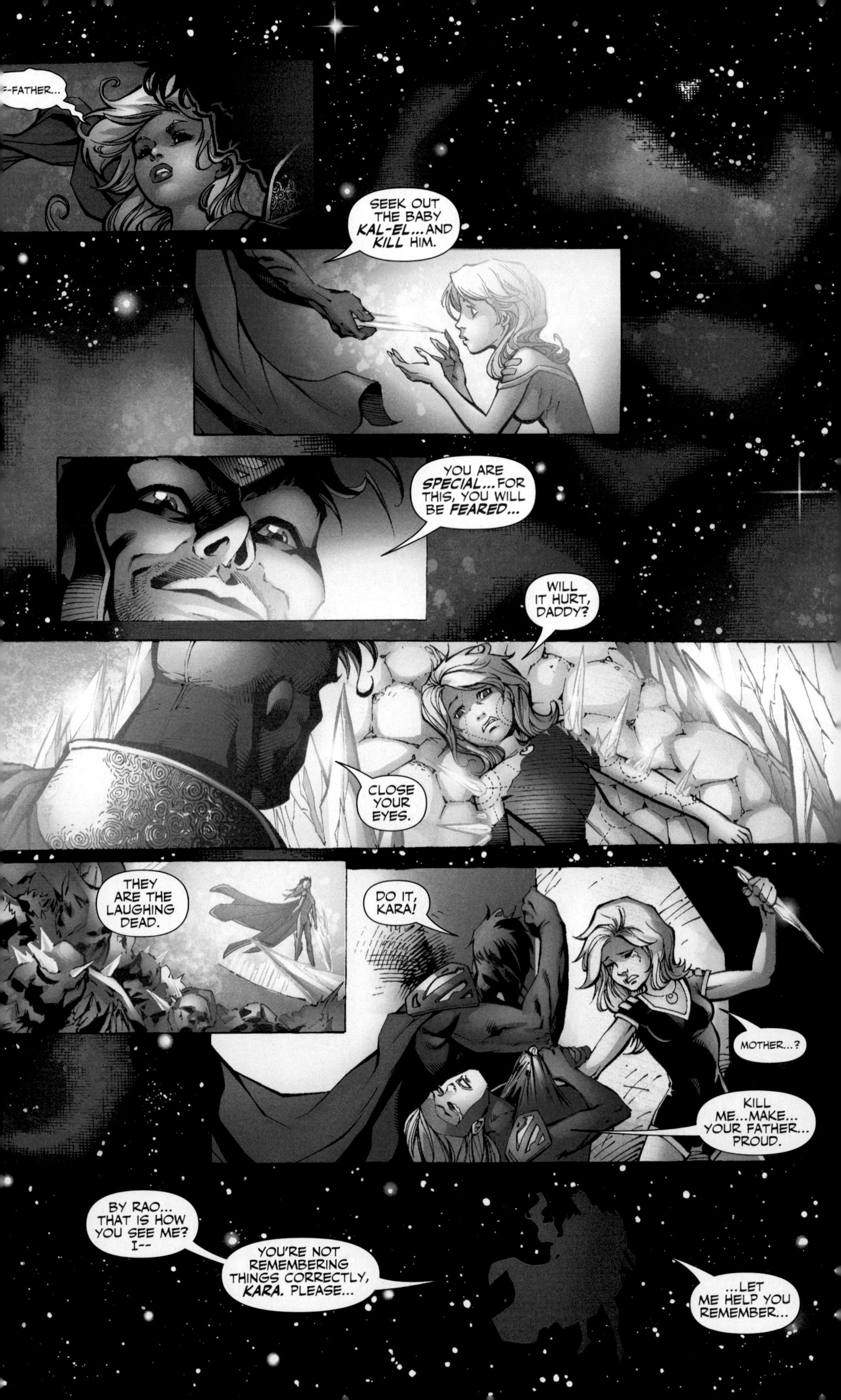
F-FATHER...
SEEK OUT THE BABY KAL-EL...AND KILL HIM.
YOU ARE SPECIAL...FOR THIS, YOU WILL BE FEARED...
WILL IT HURT, DADDY?
CLOSE YOUR EYES.
THEY ARE THE LAUGHING DEAD.
DO IT, KARA!
MOTHER...?
KILL ME...MAKE... YOUR FATHER... PROUD.
BY RAO... THAT IS HOW YOU SEE ME? I--
YOU'RE NOT REMEMBERING THINGS CORRECTLY, KARA. PLEASE...
...LET ME HELP YOU REMEMBER...

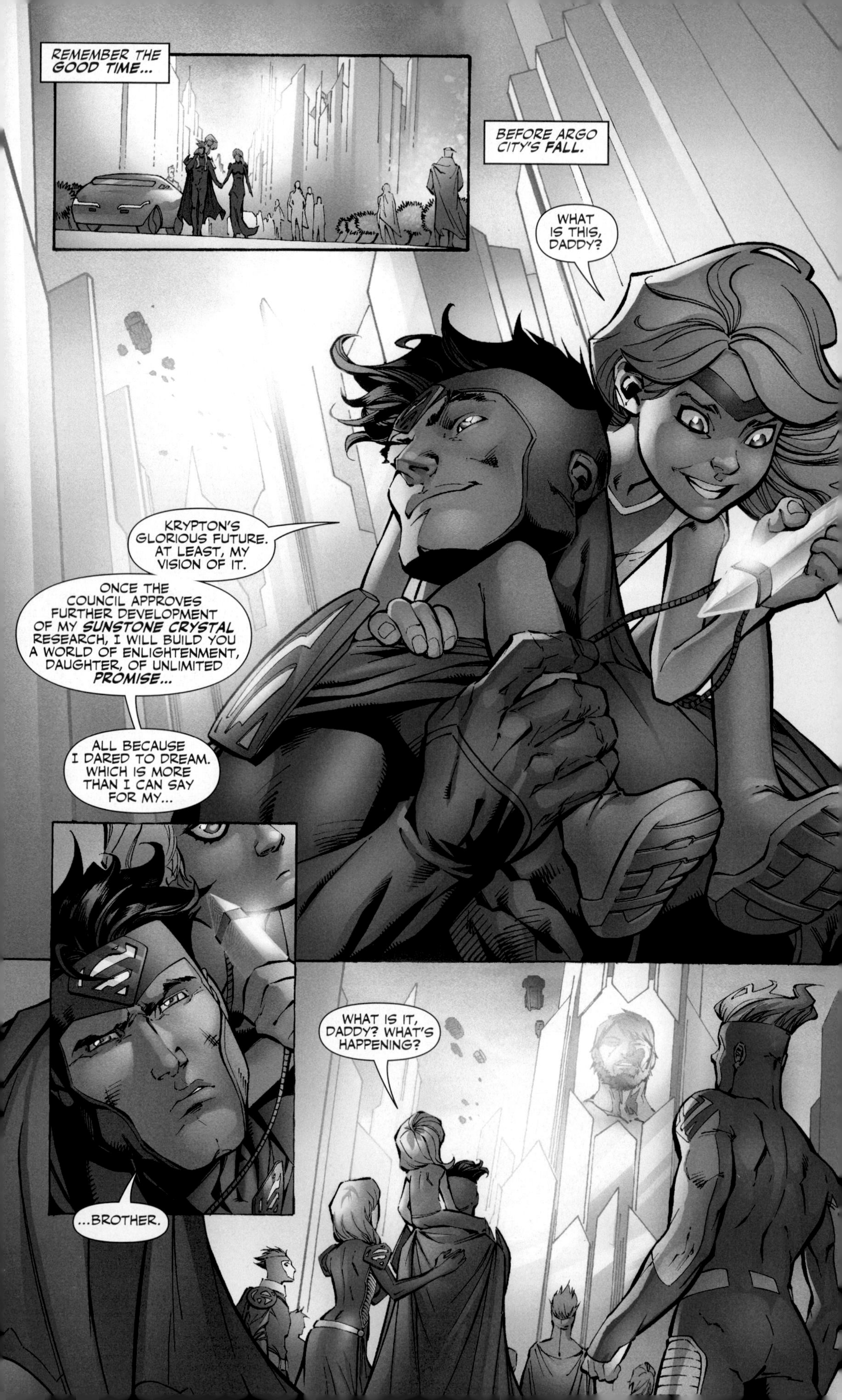

REMEMBER THE GOOD TIME...
BEFORE ARGO CITY'S FALL.
WHAT IS THIS, DADDY?
KRYPTON'S GLORIOUS FUTURE. AT LEAST, MY VISION OF IT.
ONCE THE COUNCIL APPROVES FURTHER DEVELOPMENT OF MY SUNSTONE CRYSTAL RESEARCH, I WILL BUILD YOU A WORLD OF ENLIGHTENMENT, DAUGHTER, OF UNLIMITED PROMISE...
ALL BECAUSE I DARED TO DREAM. WHICH IS MORE THAN I CAN SAY FOR MY...
...BROTHER.
WHAT IS IT, DADDY? WHAT'S HAPPENING?

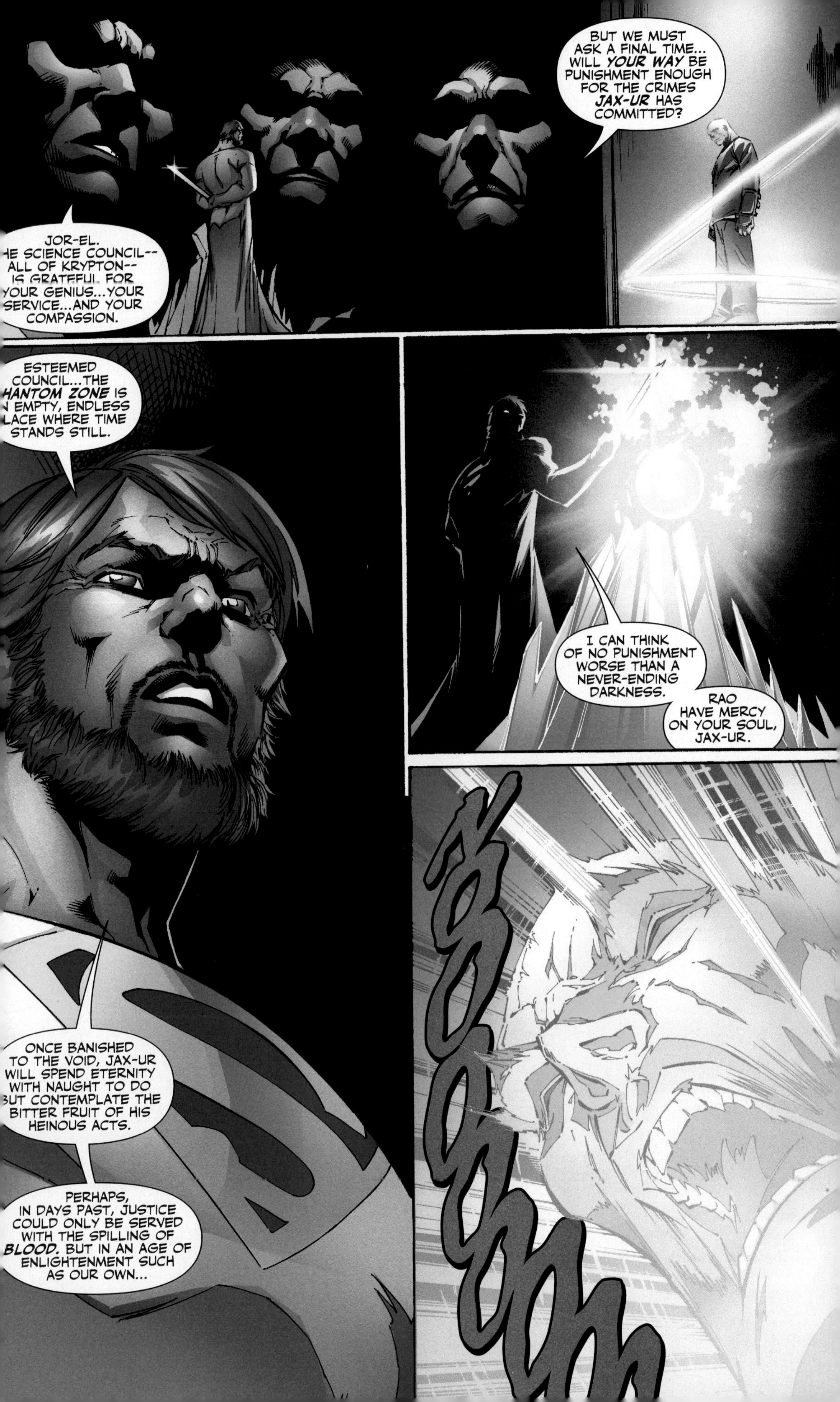

JOR-EL.
HE SCIENCE COUNCIL--
ALL OF KRYPTON--
IS GRATEFUL FOR
YOUR GENIUS...YOUR
SERVICE...AND YOUR
COMPASSION.
BUT WE MUST
ASK A FINAL TIME...
WILL YOUR WAY BE
PUNISHMENT ENOUGH
FOR THE CRIMES
JAX-UR HAS
COMMITTED?
ESTEEMED
COUNCIL...THE
HANTOM ZONE IS
N EMPTY, ENDLESS
LACE WHERE TIME
STANDS STILL.
ONCE BANISHED
TO THE VOID, JAX-UR
WILL SPEND ETERNITY
WITH NAUGHT TO DO
UT CONTEMPLATE THE
BITTER FRUIT OF HIS
HEINOUS ACTS.
PERHAPS,
IN DAYS PAST, JUSTICE
COULD ONLY BE SERVED
WITH THE SPILLING OF
BLOOD. BUT IN AN AGE OF
ENLIGHTENMENT SUCH
AS OUR OWN...
I CAN THINK
OF NO PUNISHMENT
WORSE THAN A
NEVER-ENDING
DARKNESS.
RAO
HAVE MERCY
ON YOUR SOUL,
JAX-UR.

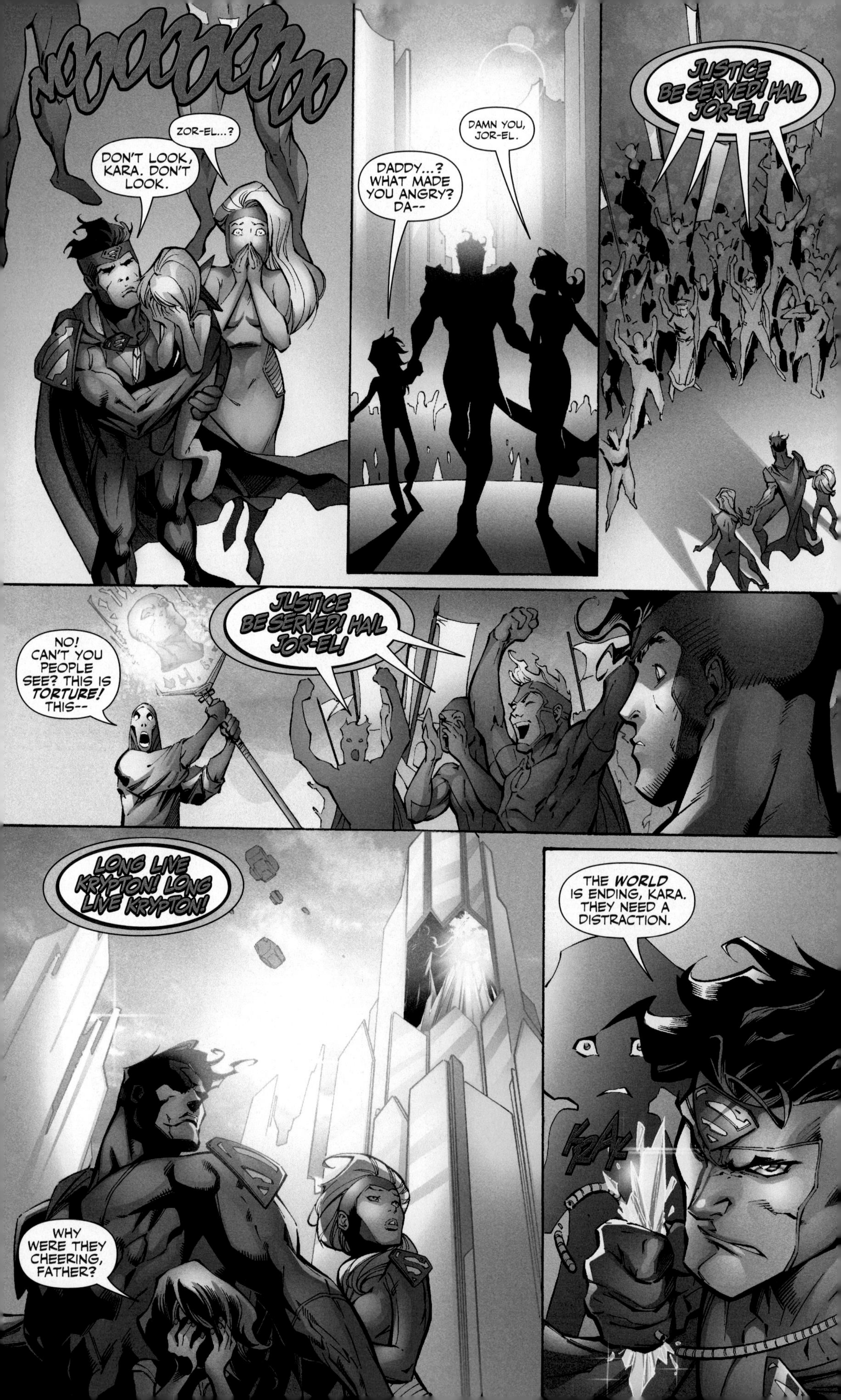
NOOOOOOOOOOO
ZOR-EL...?
DON'T LOOK, KARA. DON'T LOOK.
DADDY...? WHAT MADE YOU ANGRY? DA--
DAMN YOU, JOR-EL.
JUSTICE BE SERVED! HAIL JOR-EL!
NO! CAN'T YOU PEOPLE SEE? THIS IS TORTURE! THIS--
JUSTICE BE SERVED! HAIL JOR-EL!
LONG LIVE KRYPTON! LONG LIVE KRYPTON!
WHY WERE THEY CHEERING, FATHER?
THE WORLD IS ENDING, KARA. THEY NEED A DISTRACTION.
KRAK

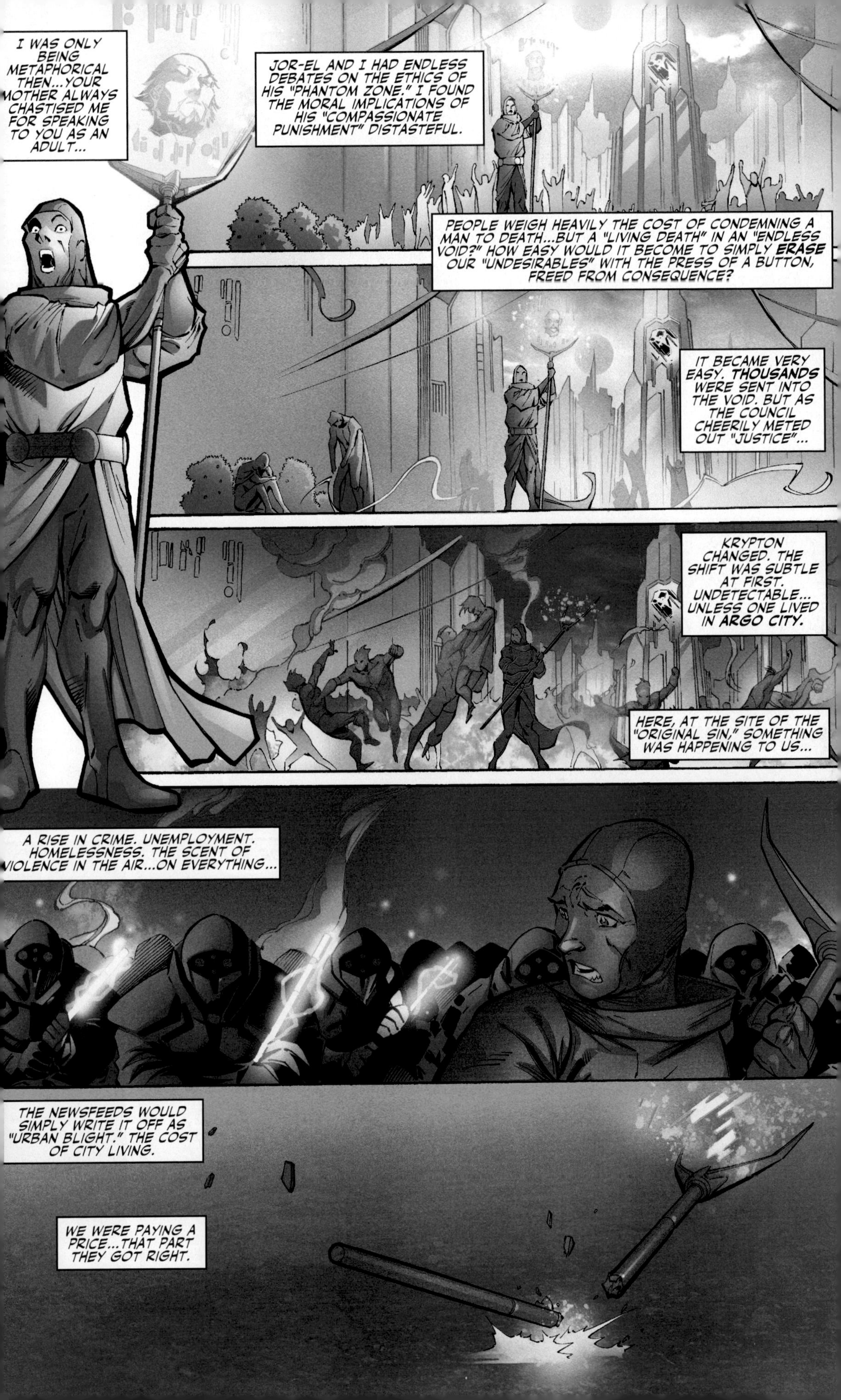

I WAS ONLY BEING METAPHORICAL THEN...YOUR MOTHER ALWAYS CHASTISED ME FOR SPEAKING TO YOU AS AN ADULT...
JOR-EL AND I HAD ENDLESS DEBATES ON THE ETHICS OF HIS "PHANTOM ZONE." I FOUND THE MORAL IMPLICATIONS OF HIS "COMPASSIONATE PUNISHMENT" DISTASTEFUL.
PEOPLE WEIGH HEAVILY THE COST OF CONDEMNING A MAN TO DEATH...BUT A "LIVING DEATH" IN AN "ENDLESS VOID?" HOW EASY WOULD IT BECOME TO SIMPLY ERASE OUR "UNDESIRABLES" WITH THE PRESS OF A BUTTON, FREED FROM CONSEQUENCE?
IT BECAME VERY EASY. THOUSANDS WERE SENT INTO THE VOID. BUT AS THE COUNCIL CHEERILY METED OUT "JUSTICE"...
KRYPTON CHANGED. THE SHIFT WAS SUBTLE AT FIRST. UNDETECTABLE... UNLESS ONE LIVED IN ARGO CITY.
HERE, AT THE SITE OF THE "ORIGINAL SIN," SOMETHING WAS HAPPENING TO US...
A RISE IN CRIME. UNEMPLOYMENT. HOMELESSNESS. THE SCENT OF VIOLENCE IN THE AIR...ON EVERYTHING...
THE NEWSFEEDS WOULD SIMPLY WRITE IT OFF AS "URBAN BLIGHT." THE COST OF CITY LIVING.
WE WERE PAYING A PRICE...THAT PART THEY GOT RIGHT.

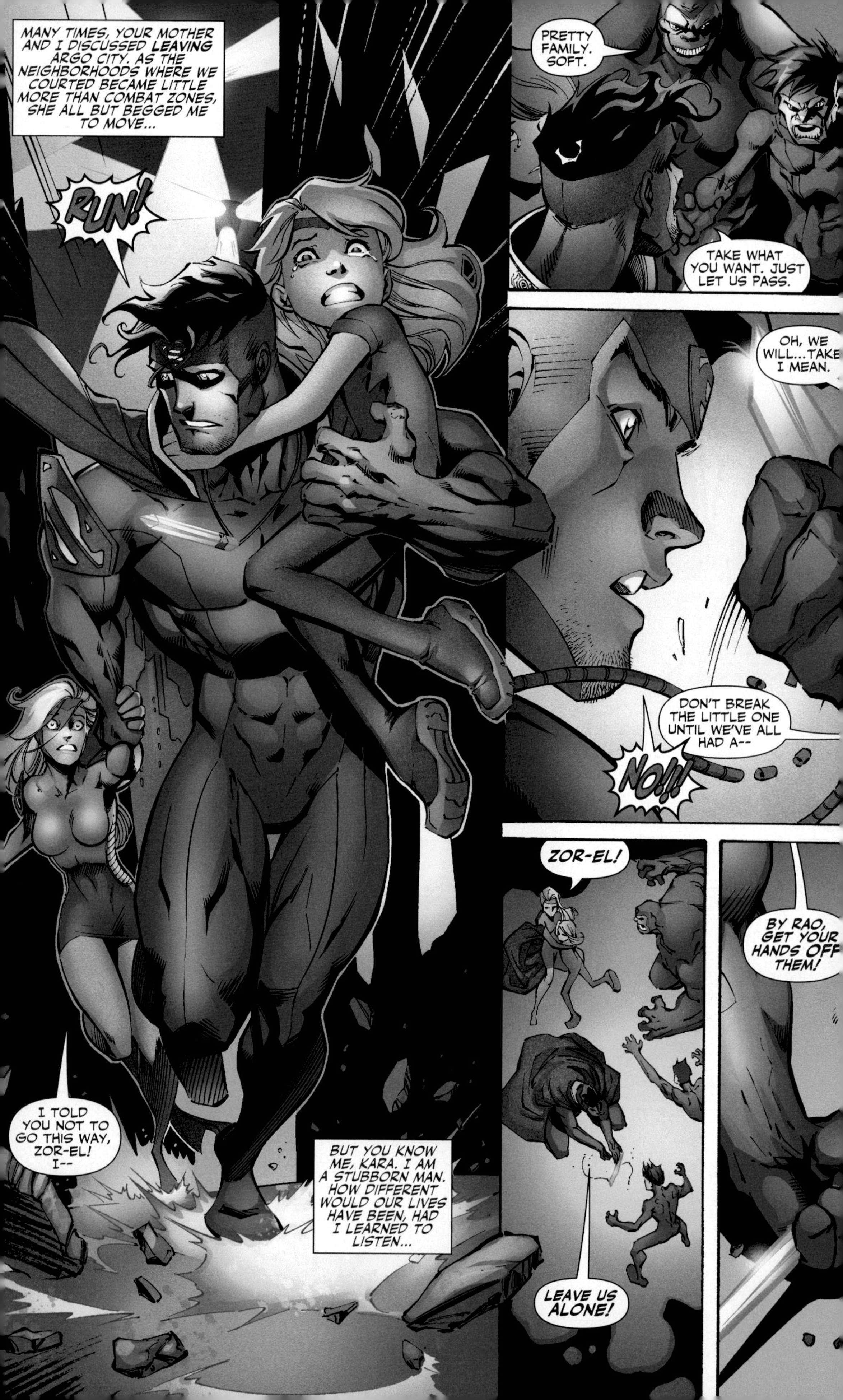

MANY TIMES, YOUR MOTHER AND I DISCUSSED LEAVING ARGO CITY. AS THE NEIGHBORHOODS WHERE WE COURTED BECAME LITTLE MORE THAN COMBAT ZONES, SHE ALL BUT BEGGED ME TO MOVE...
RUN!
I TOLD YOU NOT TO GO THIS WAY, ZOR-EL! I--
BUT YOU KNOW ME, KARA. I AM A STUBBORN MAN. HOW DIFFERENT WOULD OUR LIVES HAVE BEEN, HAD I LEARNED TO LISTEN...
PRETTY FAMILY. SOFT.
TAKE WHAT YOU WANT. JUST LET US PASS.
OH, WE WILL...TAKE I MEAN.
DON'T BREAK THE LITTLE ONE UNTIL WE'VE ALL HAD A--
NO!!!
ZOR-EL!
LEAVE US ALONE!
BY RAO, GET YOUR HANDS OFF THEM!

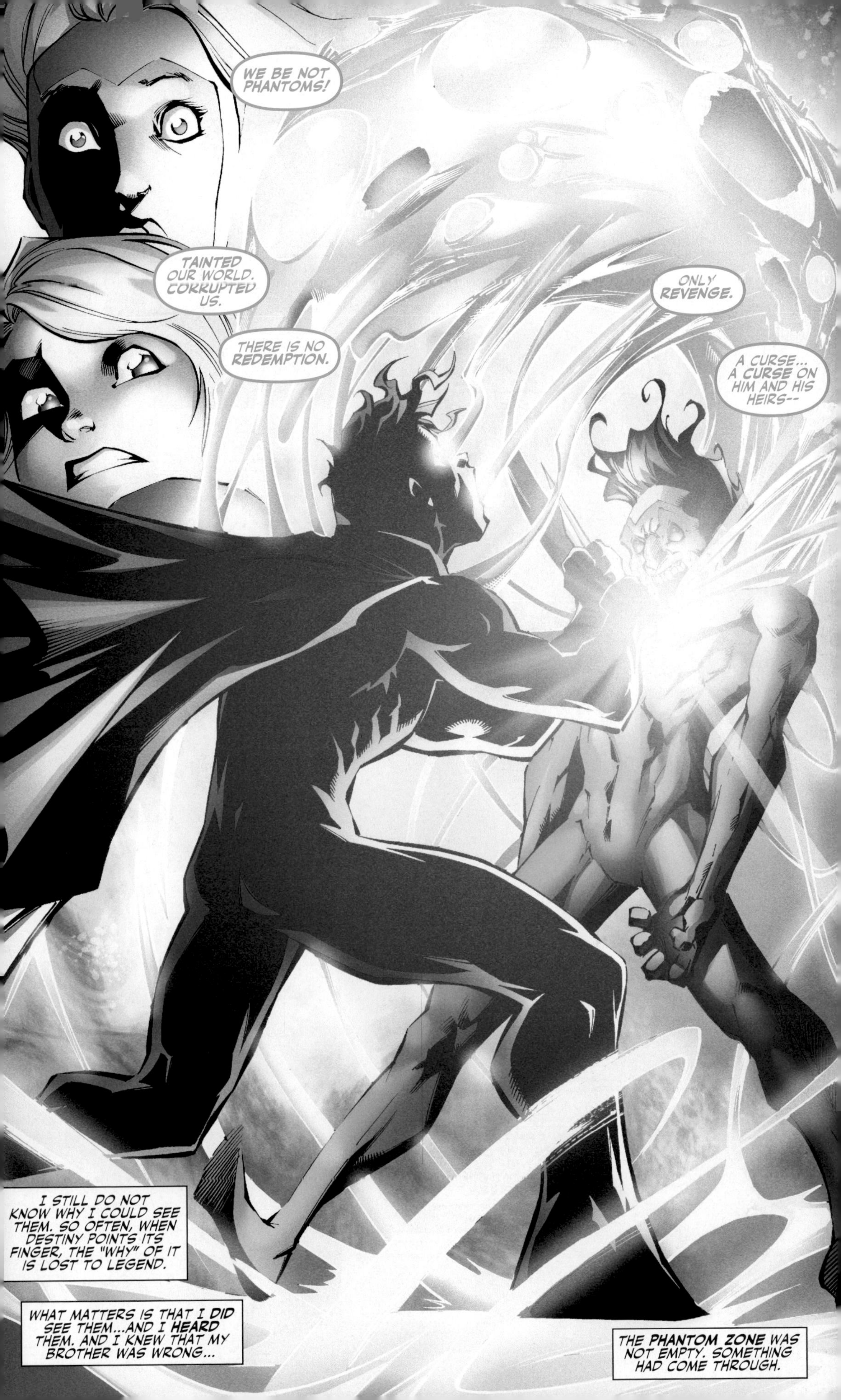

WE BE NOT PHANTOMS!
TAINTED OUR WORLD. CORRUPTED US.
THERE IS NO REDEMPTION.
ONLY REVENGE.
A CURSE... A CURSE ON HIM AND HIS HEIRS--
I STILL DO NOT KNOW WHY I COULD SEE THEM. SO OFTEN, WHEN DESTINY POINTS ITS FINGER, THE "WHY" OF IT IS LOST TO LEGEND.
WHAT MATTERS IS THAT I DID SEE THEM...AND I HEARD THEM. AND I KNEW THAT MY BROTHER WAS WRONG...
THE PHANTOM ZONE WAS NOT EMPTY. SOMETHING HAD COME THROUGH.

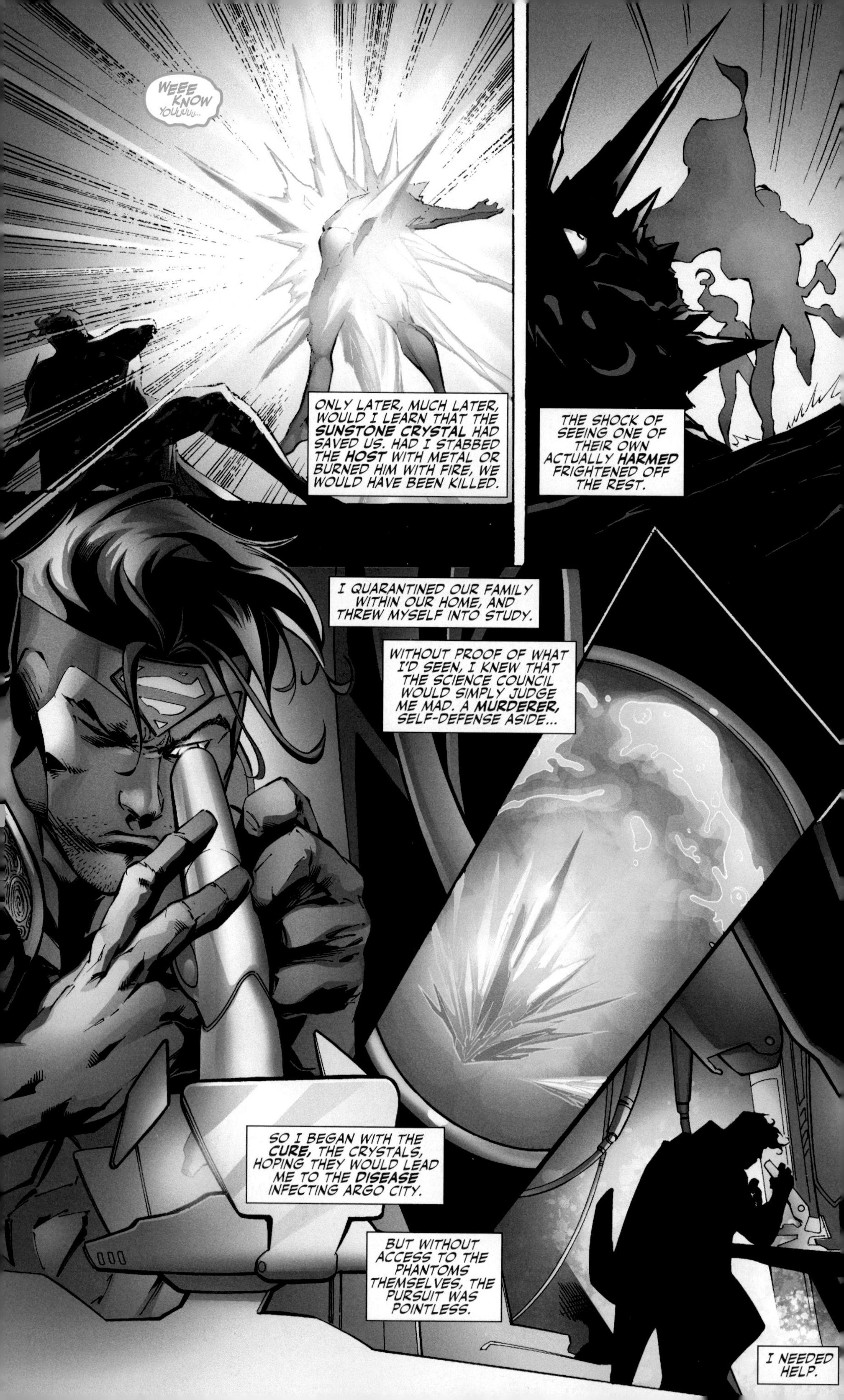
WEEE KNOW YOUUUUU...
ONLY LATER, MUCH LATER, WOULD I LEARN THAT THE SUNSTONE CRYSTAL HAD SAVED US. HAD I STABBED THE HOST WITH METAL OR BURNED HIM WITH FIRE, WE WOULD HAVE BEEN KILLED.
THE SHOCK OF SEEING ONE OF THEIR OWN ACTUALLY HARMED FRIGHTENED OFF THE REST.
I QUARANTINED OUR FAMILY WITHIN OUR HOME, AND THREW MYSELF INTO STUDY.
WITHOUT PROOF OF WHAT I'D SEEN, I KNEW THAT THE SCIENCE COUNCIL WOULD SIMPLY JUDGE ME MAD. A MURDERER, SELF-DEFENSE ASIDE...
SO I BEGAN WITH THE CURE, THE CRYSTALS, HOPING THEY WOULD LEAD ME TO THE DISEASE INFECTING ARGO CITY.
BUT WITHOUT ACCESS TO THE PHANTOMS THEMSELVES, THE PURSUIT WAS POINTLESS.
I NEEDED HELP.

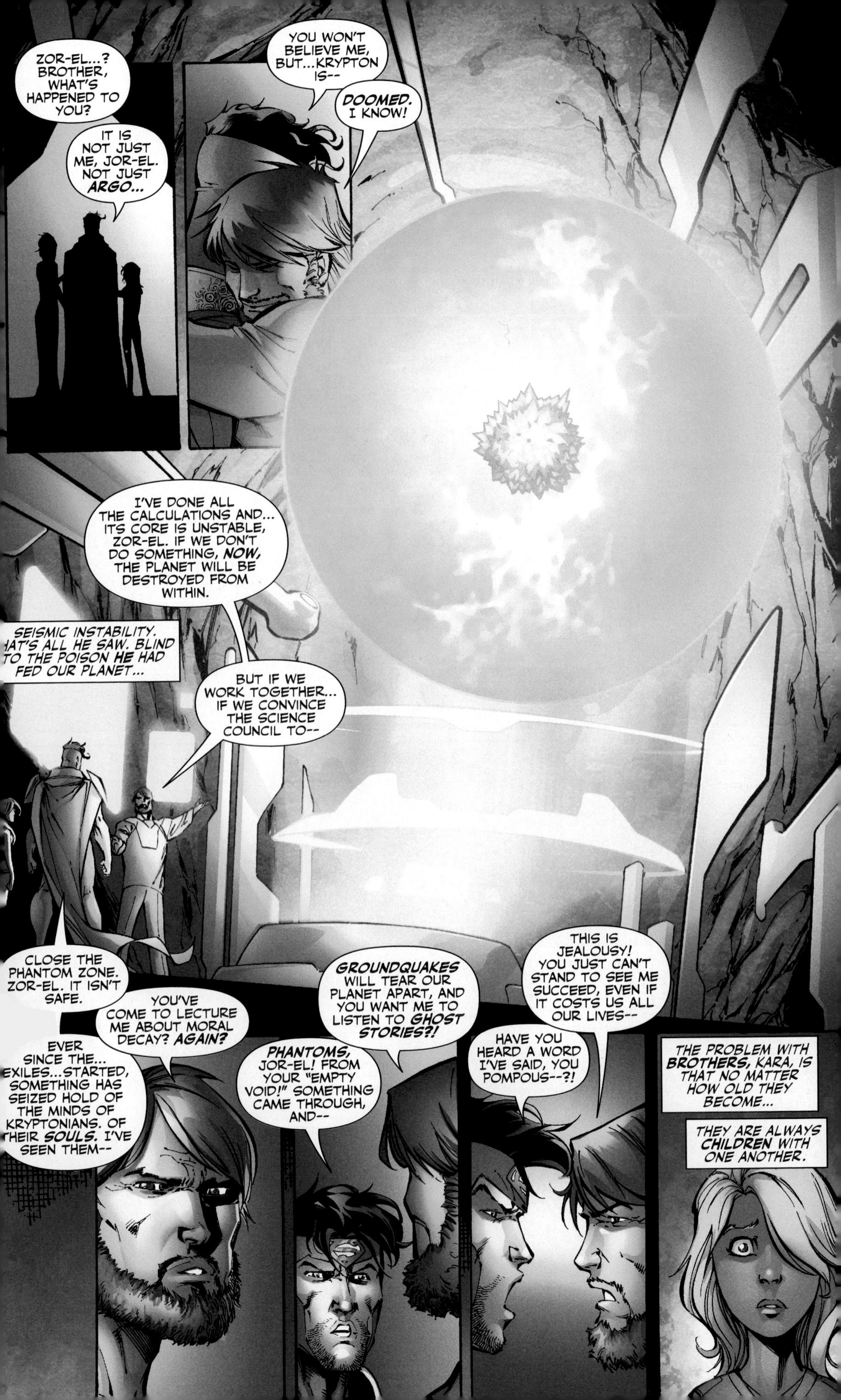

ZOR-EL...? BROTHER, WHAT'S HAPPENED TO YOU?
IT IS NOT JUST ME, JOR-EL. NOT JUST ARGO...
YOU WON'T BELIEVE ME, BUT...KRYPTON IS--
DOOMED. I KNOW!
I'VE DONE ALL THE CALCULATIONS AND... ITS CORE IS UNSTABLE, ZOR-EL. IF WE DON'T DO SOMETHING, NOW, THE PLANET WILL BE DESTROYED FROM WITHIN.
SEISMIC INSTABILITY. ...HAT'S ALL HE SAW. BLIND TO THE POISON HE HAD FED OUR PLANET...
BUT IF WE WORK TOGETHER... IF WE CONVINCE THE SCIENCE COUNCIL TO--
CLOSE THE PHANTOM ZONE. ZOR-EL. IT ISN'T SAFE.
GROUNDQUAKES WILL TEAR OUR PLANET APART, AND YOU WANT ME TO LISTEN TO GHOST STORIES?!
THIS IS JEALOUSY! YOU JUST CAN'T STAND TO SEE ME SUCCEED, EVEN IF IT COSTS US ALL OUR LIVES--
YOU'VE COME TO LECTURE ME ABOUT MORAL DECAY? AGAIN?
EVER SINCE THE... EXILES...STARTED, SOMETHING HAS SEIZED HOLD OF THE MINDS OF KRYPTONIANS. OF THEIR SOULS. I'VE SEEN THEM--
PHANTOMS, JOR-EL! FROM YOUR "EMPTY VOID!" SOMETHING CAME THROUGH, AND--
HAVE YOU HEARD A WORD I'VE SAID, YOU POMPOUS--?!
THE PROBLEM WITH BROTHERS, KARA, IS THAT NO MATTER HOW OLD THEY BECOME...
THEY ARE ALWAYS CHILDREN WITH ONE ANOTHER.

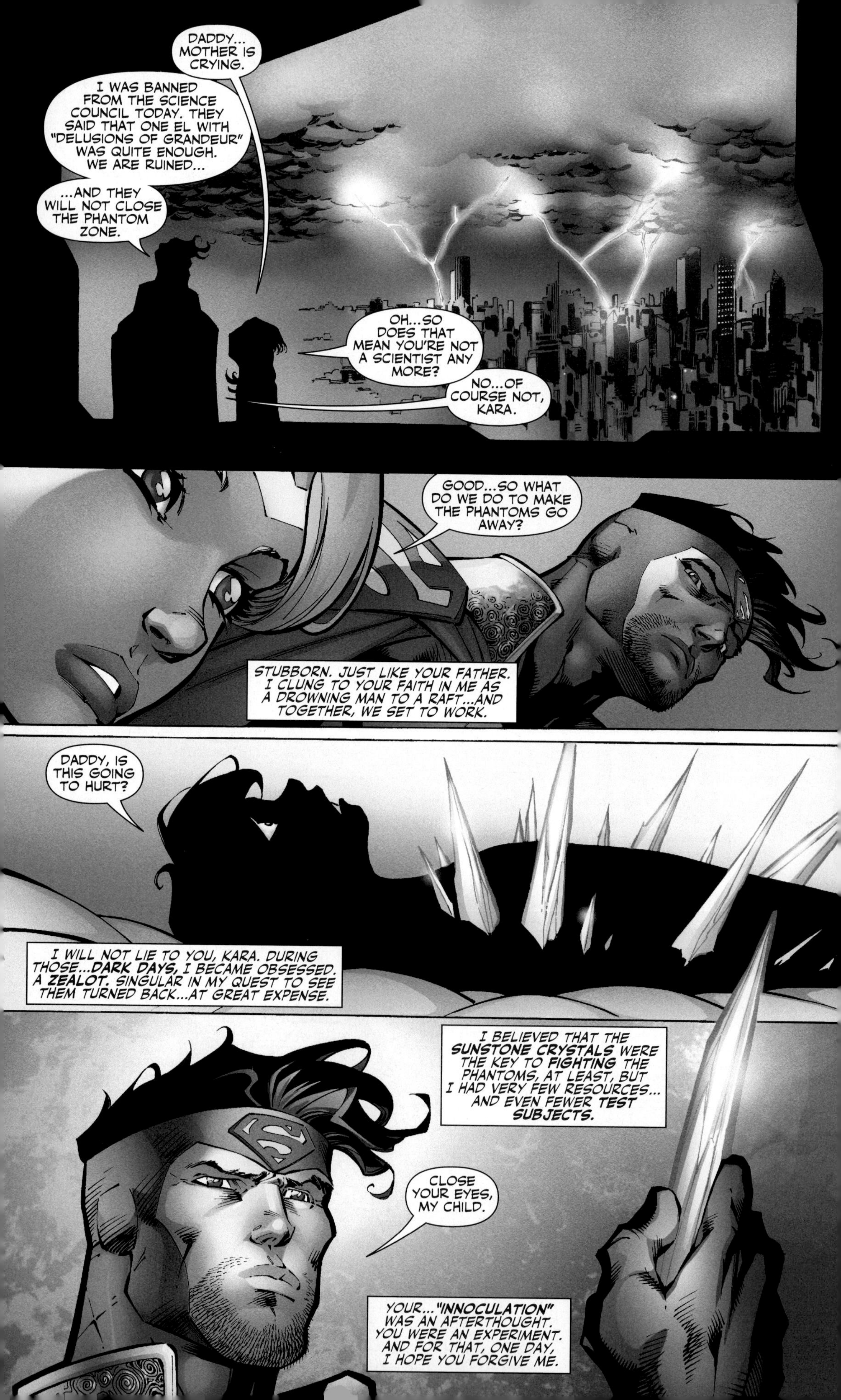
DADDY... MOTHER IS CRYING.
I WAS BANNED FROM THE SCIENCE COUNCIL TODAY. THEY SAID THAT ONE EL WITH "DELUSIONS OF GRANDEUR" WAS QUITE ENOUGH. WE ARE RUINED...
...AND THEY WILL NOT CLOSE THE PHANTOM ZONE.
OH...SO DOES THAT MEAN YOU'RE NOT A SCIENTIST ANY MORE?
NO...OF COURSE NOT, KARA.
GOOD...SO WHAT DO WE DO TO MAKE THE PHANTOMS GO AWAY?
STUBBORN. JUST LIKE YOUR FATHER. I CLUNG TO YOUR FAITH IN ME AS A DROWNING MAN TO A RAFT...AND TOGETHER, WE SET TO WORK.
DADDY, IS THIS GOING TO HURT?
I WILL NOT LIE TO YOU, KARA. DURING THOSE...DARK DAYS, I BECAME OBSESSED. A ZEALOT. SINGULAR IN MY QUEST TO SEE THEM TURNED BACK...AT GREAT EXPENSE.
I BELIEVED THAT THE SUNSTONE CRYSTALS WERE THE KEY TO FIGHTING THE PHANTOMS, AT LEAST, BUT I HAD VERY FEW RESOURCES... AND EVEN FEWER TEST SUBJECTS.
CLOSE YOUR EYES, MY CHILD.
YOUR... "INNOCULATION" WAS AN AFTERTHOUGHT. YOU WERE AN EXPERIMENT. AND FOR THAT, ONE DAY, I HOPE YOU FORGIVE ME.

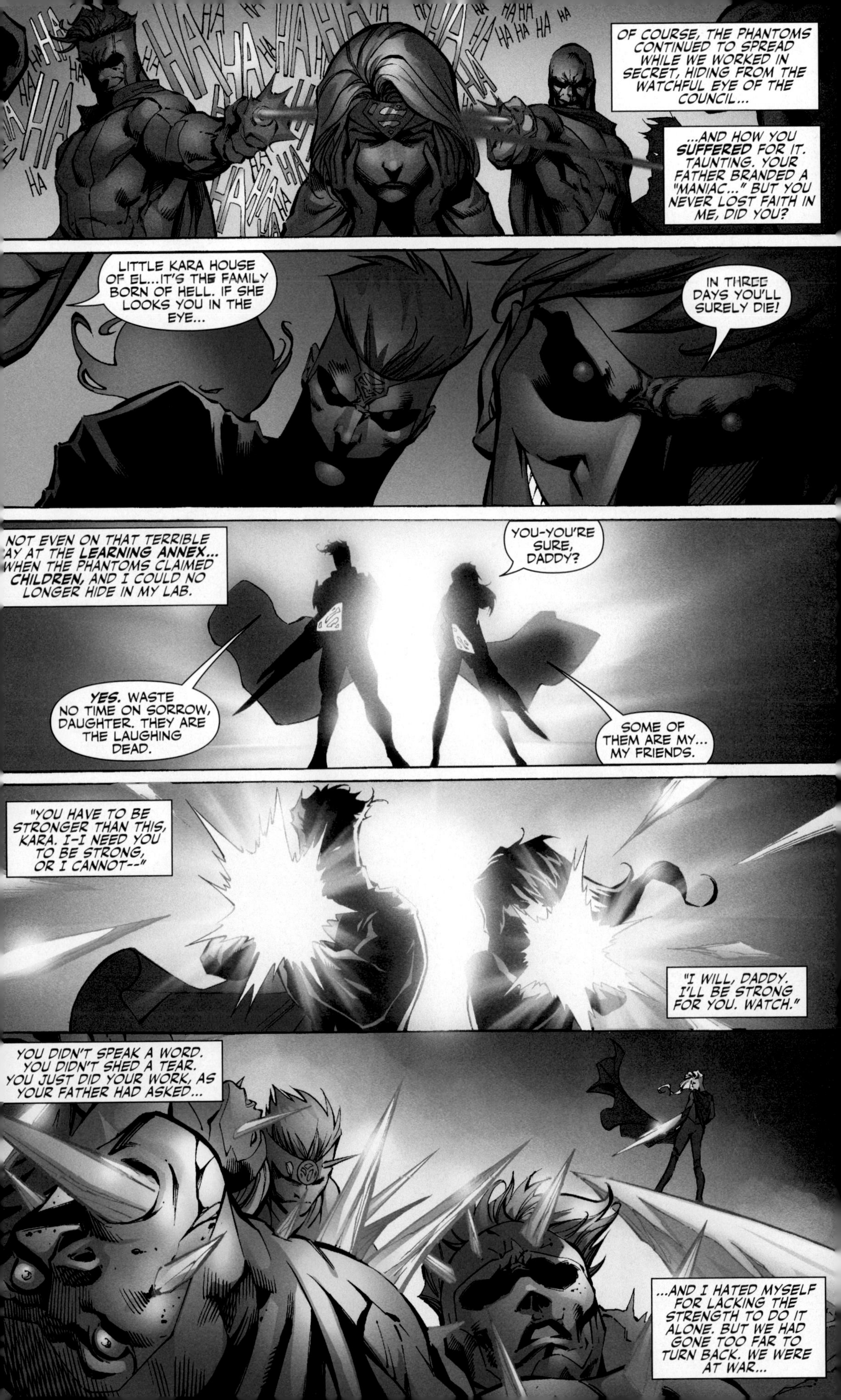
HA HA HA HA HA
OF COURSE, THE PHANTOMS CONTINUED TO SPREAD WHILE WE WORKED IN SECRET, HIDING FROM THE WATCHFUL EYE OF THE COUNCIL...
...AND HOW YOU SUFFERED FOR IT. TAUNTING. YOUR FATHER BRANDED A "MANIAC..." BUT YOU NEVER LOST FAITH IN ME, DID YOU?
LITTLE KARA HOUSE OF EL...IT'S THE FAMILY BORN OF HELL. IF SHE LOOKS YOU IN THE EYE...
IN THREE DAYS YOU'LL SURELY DIE!
NOT EVEN ON THAT TERRIBLE DAY AT THE LEARNING ANNEX... WHEN THE PHANTOMS CLAIMED CHILDREN, AND I COULD NO LONGER HIDE IN MY LAB.
YOU-YOU'RE SURE, DADDY?
YES. WASTE NO TIME ON SORROW, DAUGHTER. THEY ARE THE LAUGHING DEAD.
SOME OF THEM ARE MY... MY FRIENDS.
"YOU HAVE TO BE STRONGER THAN THIS, KARA. I-I NEED YOU TO BE STRONG, OR I CANNOT--"
"I WILL, DADDY. I'LL BE STRONG FOR YOU. WATCH."
YOU DIDN'T SPEAK A WORD. YOU DIDN'T SHED A TEAR. YOU JUST DID YOUR WORK, AS YOUR FATHER HAD ASKED...
...AND I HATED MYSELF FOR LACKING THE STRENGTH TO DO IT ALONE. BUT WE HAD GONE TOO FAR TO TURN BACK. WE WERE AT WAR...

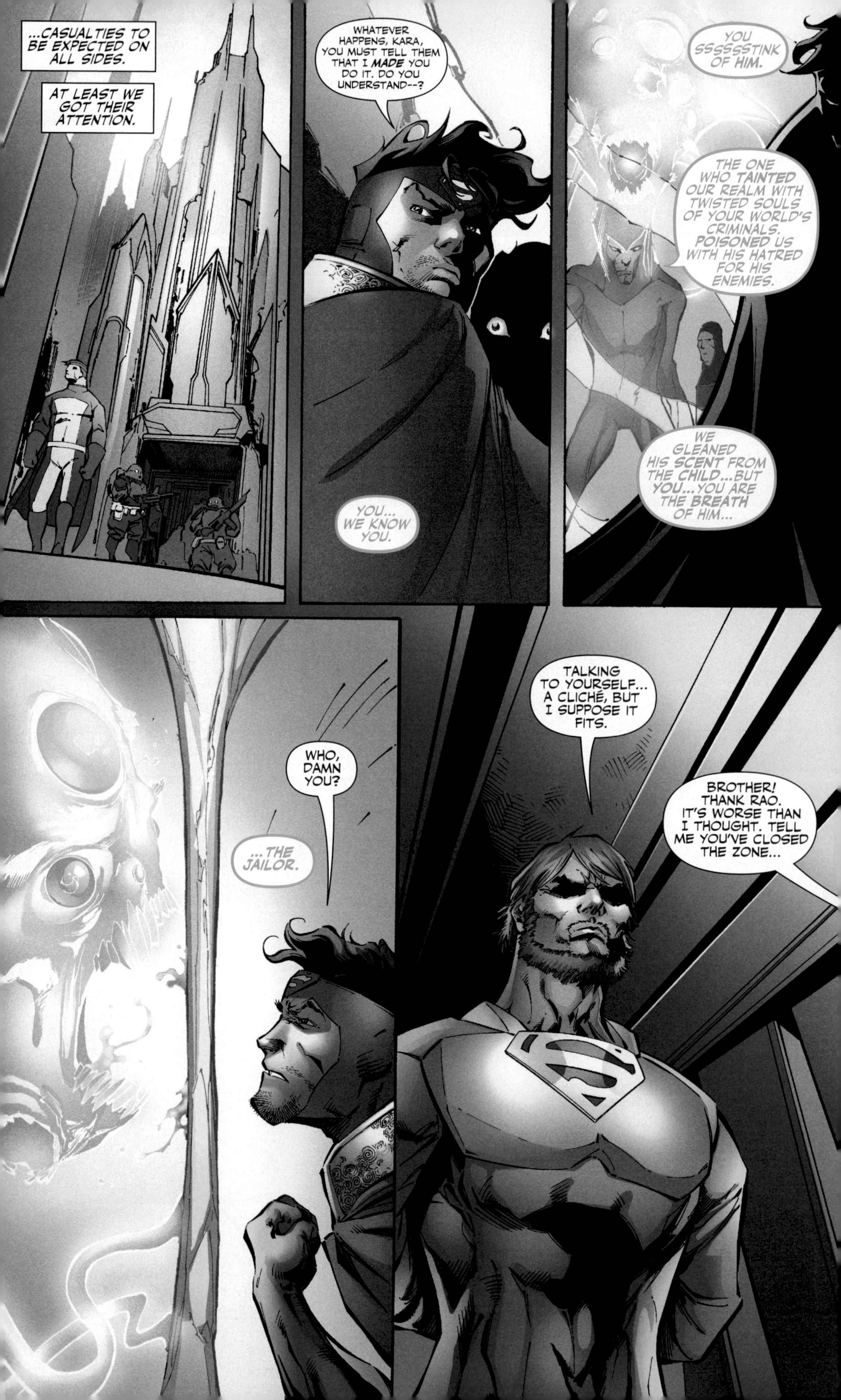

...CASUALTIES TO BE EXPECTED ON ALL SIDES.
AT LEAST WE GOT THEIR ATTENTION.
WHATEVER HAPPENS, KARA, YOU MUST TELL THEM THAT I MADE YOU DO IT. DO YOU UNDERSTAND--?
YOU... WE KNOW YOU.
YOU SSSSSSTINK OF HIM.
THE ONE WHO TAINTED OUR REALM WITH TWISTED SOULS OF YOUR WORLD'S CRIMINALS. POISONED US WITH HIS HATRED FOR HIS ENEMIES.
WE GLEANED HIS SCENT FROM THE CHILD...BUT YOU...YOU ARE THE BREATH OF HIM...
WHO, DAMN YOU?
...THE JAILOR.
TALKING TO YOURSELF... A CLICHÉ, BUT I SUPPOSE IT FITS.
BROTHER! THANK RAO. IT'S WORSE THAN I THOUGHT. TELL ME YOU'VE CLOSED THE ZONE...

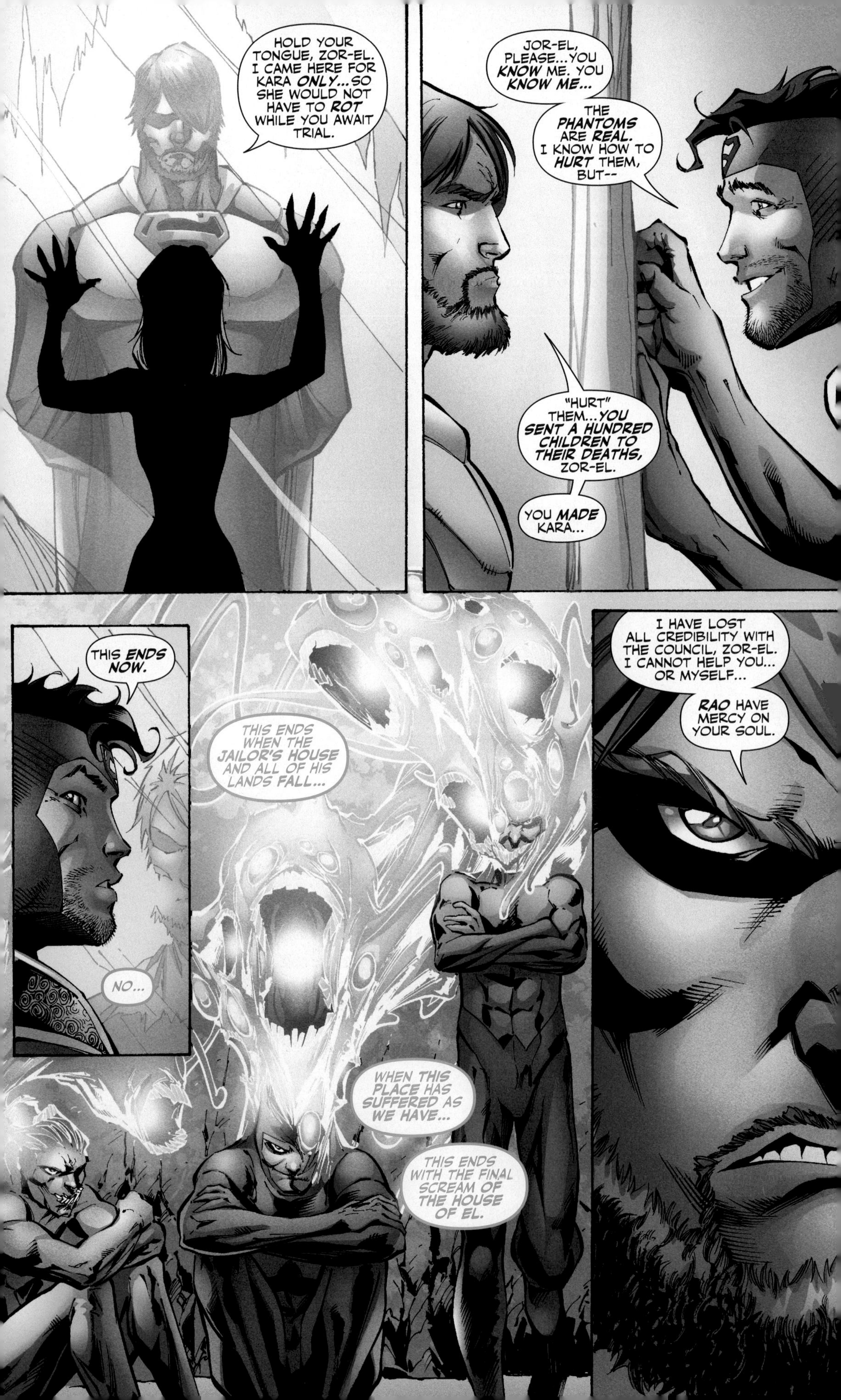
HOLD YOUR TONGUE, ZOR-EL. I CAME HERE FOR KARA ONLY...SO SHE WOULD NOT HAVE TO ROT WHILE YOU AWAIT TRIAL.
JOR-EL, PLEASE...YOU KNOW ME. YOU KNOW ME...
THE PHANTOMS ARE REAL. I KNOW HOW TO HURT THEM, BUT--
"HURT" THEM...YOU SENT A HUNDRED CHILDREN TO THEIR DEATHS, ZOR-EL.
YOU MADE KARA...
THIS ENDS NOW.
NO...
THIS ENDS WHEN THE JAILOR'S HOUSE AND ALL OF HIS LANDS FALL...
I HAVE LOST ALL CREDIBILITY WITH THE COUNCIL, ZOR-EL. I CANNOT HELP YOU... OR MYSELF...
RAO HAVE MERCY ON YOUR SOUL.
WHEN THIS PLACE HAS SUFFERED AS WE HAVE...
THIS ENDS WITH THE FINAL SCREAM OF THE HOUSE OF EL.

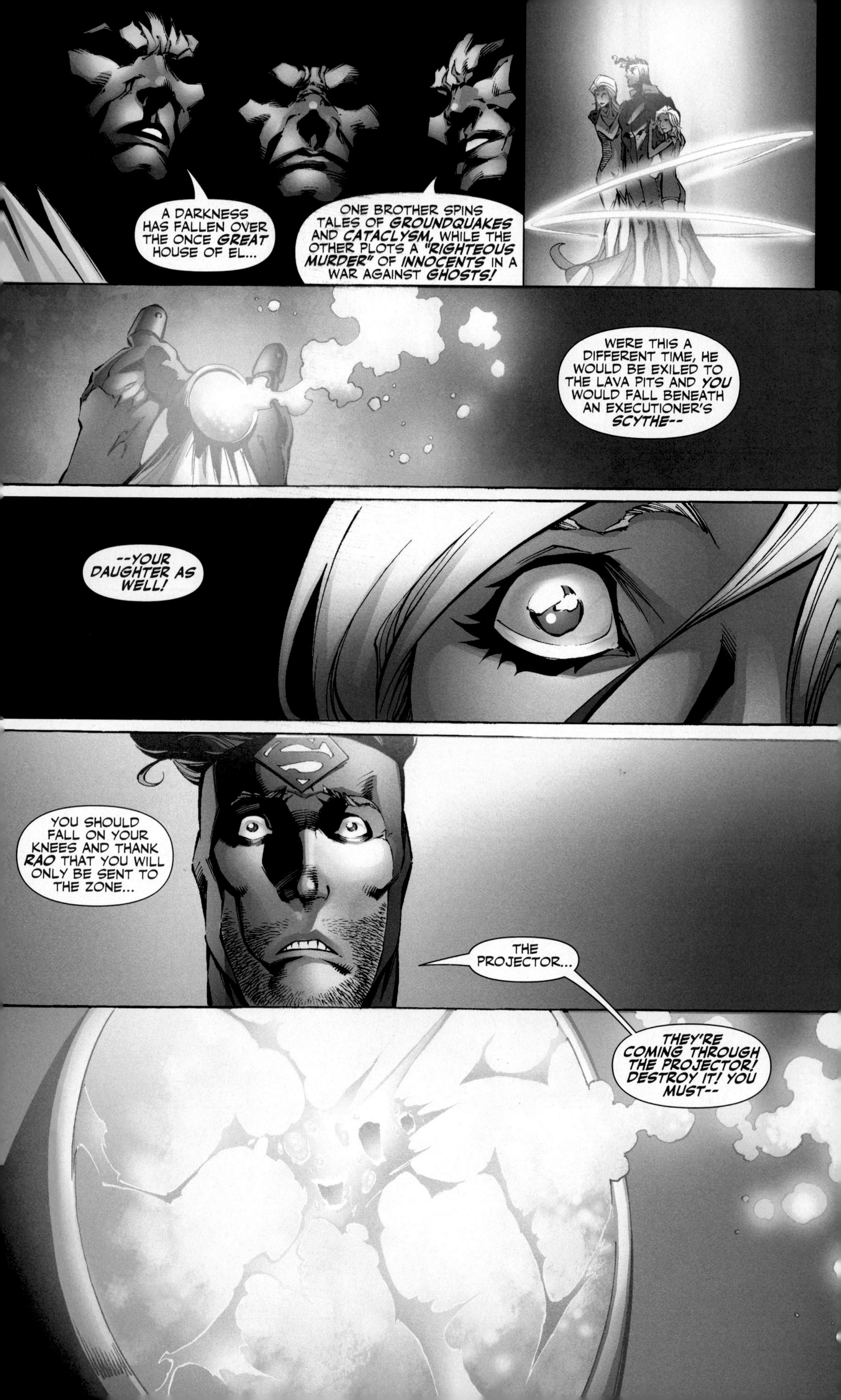
A DARKNESS HAS FALLEN OVER THE ONCE GREAT HOUSE OF EL...
ONE BROTHER SPINS TALES OF GROUNDQUAKES AND CATACLYSM, WHILE THE OTHER PLOTS A "RIGHTEOUS MURDER" OF INNOCENTS IN A WAR AGAINST GHOSTS!
WERE THIS A DIFFERENT TIME, HE WOULD BE EXILED TO THE LAVA PITS AND YOU WOULD FALL BENEATH AN EXECUTIONER'S SCYTHE--
--YOUR DAUGHTER AS WELL!
YOU SHOULD FALL ON YOUR KNEES AND THANK RAO THAT YOU WILL ONLY BE SENT TO THE ZONE...
THE PROJECTOR...
THEY'RE COMING THROUGH THE PROJECTOR! DESTROY IT! YOU MUST--

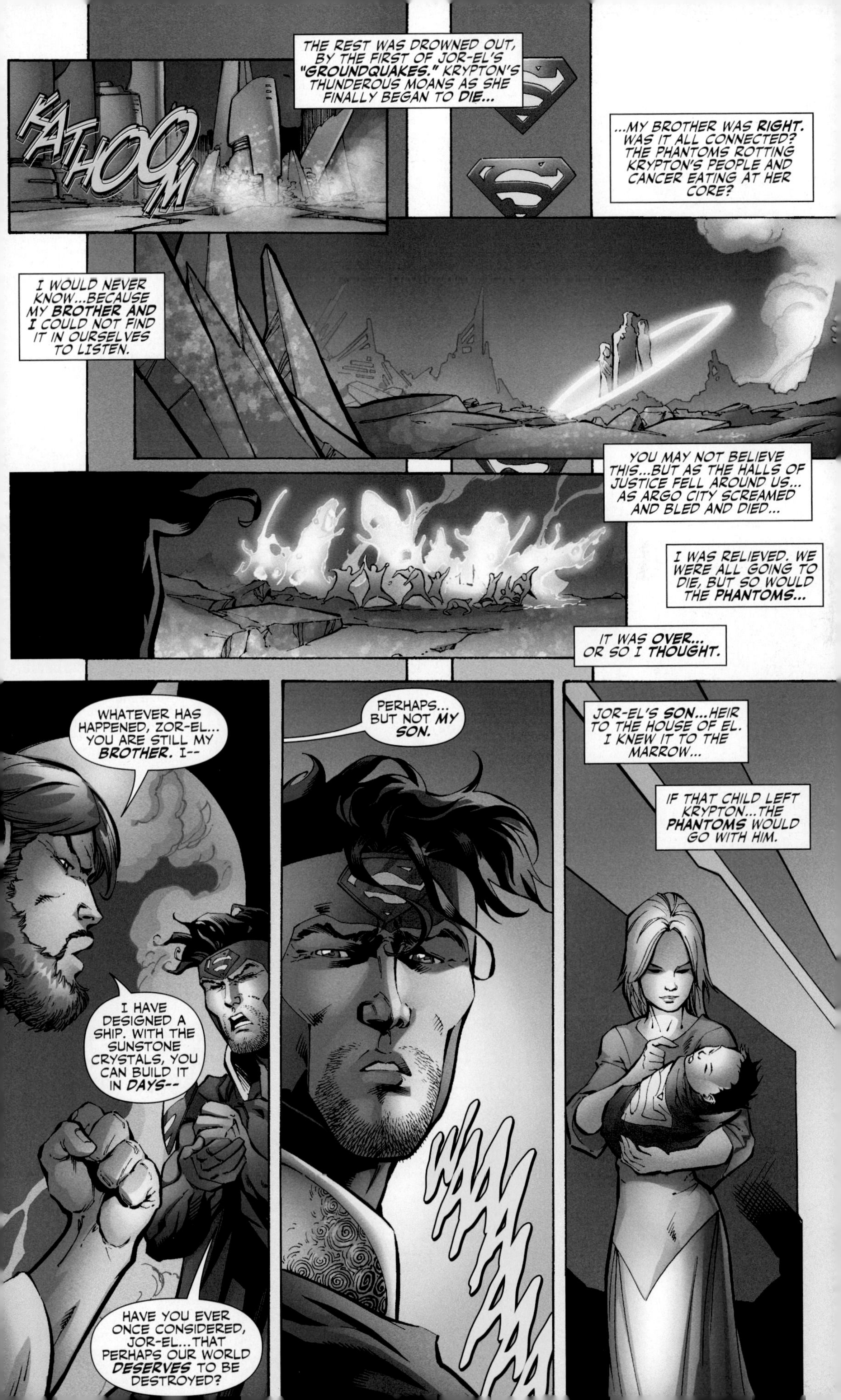
THE REST WAS DROWNED OUT, BY THE FIRST OF JOR-EL'S "GROUNDQUAKES." KRYPTON'S THUNDEROUS MOANS AS SHE FINALLY BEGAN TO DIE...
KATHOOOM
...MY BROTHER WAS RIGHT. WAS IT ALL CONNECTED? THE PHANTOMS ROTTING KRYPTON'S PEOPLE AND CANCER EATING AT HER CORE?
I WOULD NEVER KNOW...BECAUSE MY BROTHER AND I COULD NOT FIND IT IN OURSELVES TO LISTEN.
YOU MAY NOT BELIEVE THIS...BUT AS THE HALLS OF JUSTICE FELL AROUND US... AS ARGO CITY SCREAMED AND BLED AND DIED...
I WAS RELIEVED. WE WERE ALL GOING TO DIE, BUT SO WOULD THE PHANTOMS...
IT WAS OVER... OR SO I THOUGHT.
WHATEVER HAS HAPPENED, ZOR-EL... YOU ARE STILL MY BROTHER. I--
I HAVE DESIGNED A SHIP. WITH THE SUNSTONE CRYSTALS, YOU CAN BUILD IT IN DAYS--
HAVE YOU EVER ONCE CONSIDERED, JOR-EL...THAT PERHAPS OUR WORLD DESERVES TO BE DESTROYED?
PERHAPS... BUT NOT MY SON.
JOR-EL'S SON...HEIR TO THE HOUSE OF EL. I KNEW IT TO THE MARROW...
IF THAT CHILD LEFT KRYPTON...THE PHANTOMS WOULD GO WITH HIM.

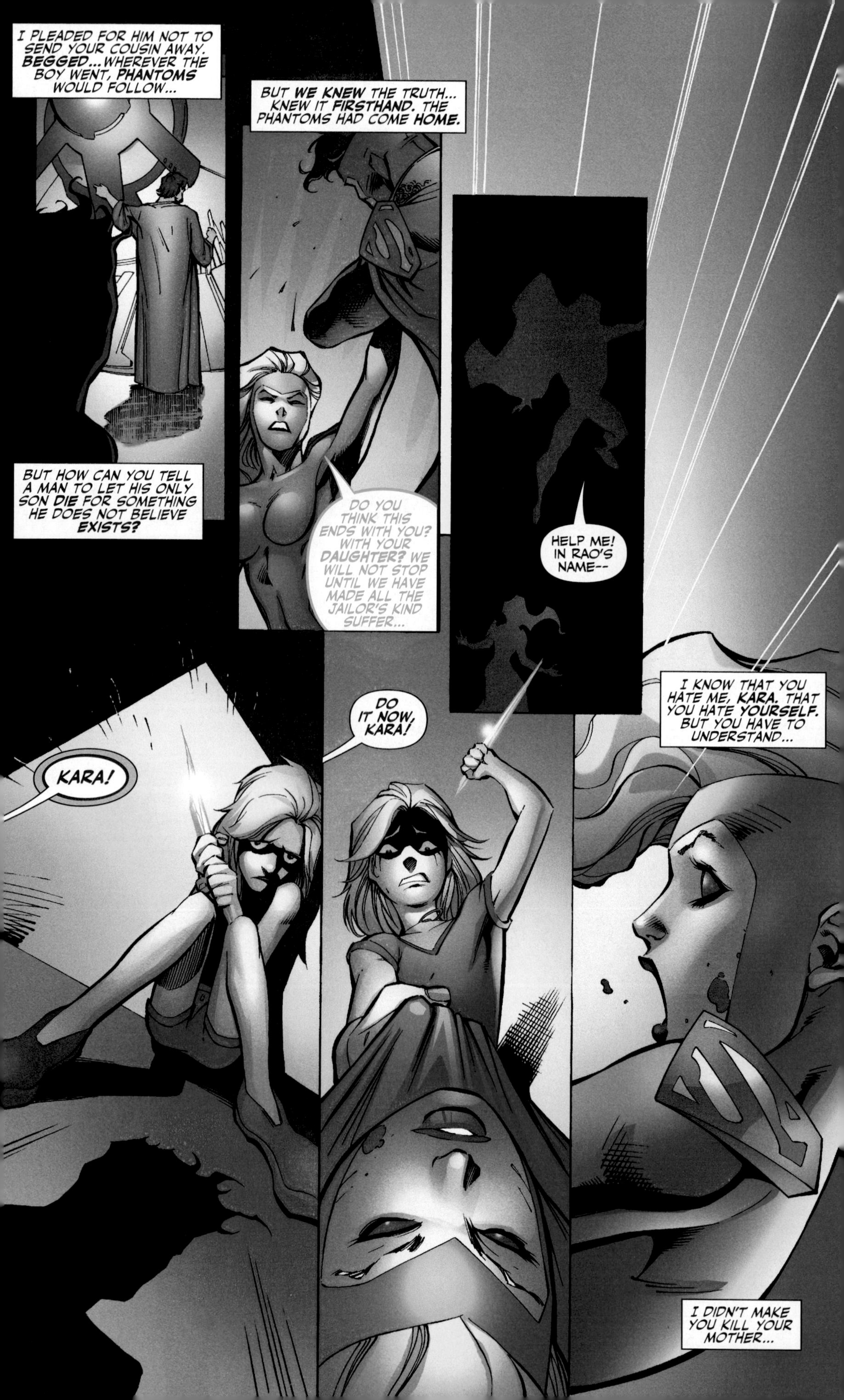
I PLEADED FOR HIM NOT TO SEND YOUR COUSIN AWAY. BEGGED... WHEREVER THE BOY WENT, PHANTOMS WOULD FOLLOW...
BUT HOW CAN YOU TELL A MAN TO LET HIS ONLY SON DIE FOR SOMETHING HE DOES NOT BELIEVE EXISTS?
BUT WE KNEW THE TRUTH... KNEW IT FIRSTHAND. THE PHANTOMS HAD COME HOME.
DO YOU THINK THIS ENDS WITH YOU? WITH YOUR DAUGHTER? WE WILL NOT STOP UNTIL WE HAVE MADE ALL THE JAILOR'S KIND SUFFER...
HELP ME! IN RAO'S NAME--
KARA!
DO IT NOW, KARA!
I KNOW THAT YOU HATE ME, KARA. THAT YOU HATE YOURSELF. BUT YOU HAVE TO UNDERSTAND...
I DIDN'T MAKE YOU KILL YOUR MOTHER...

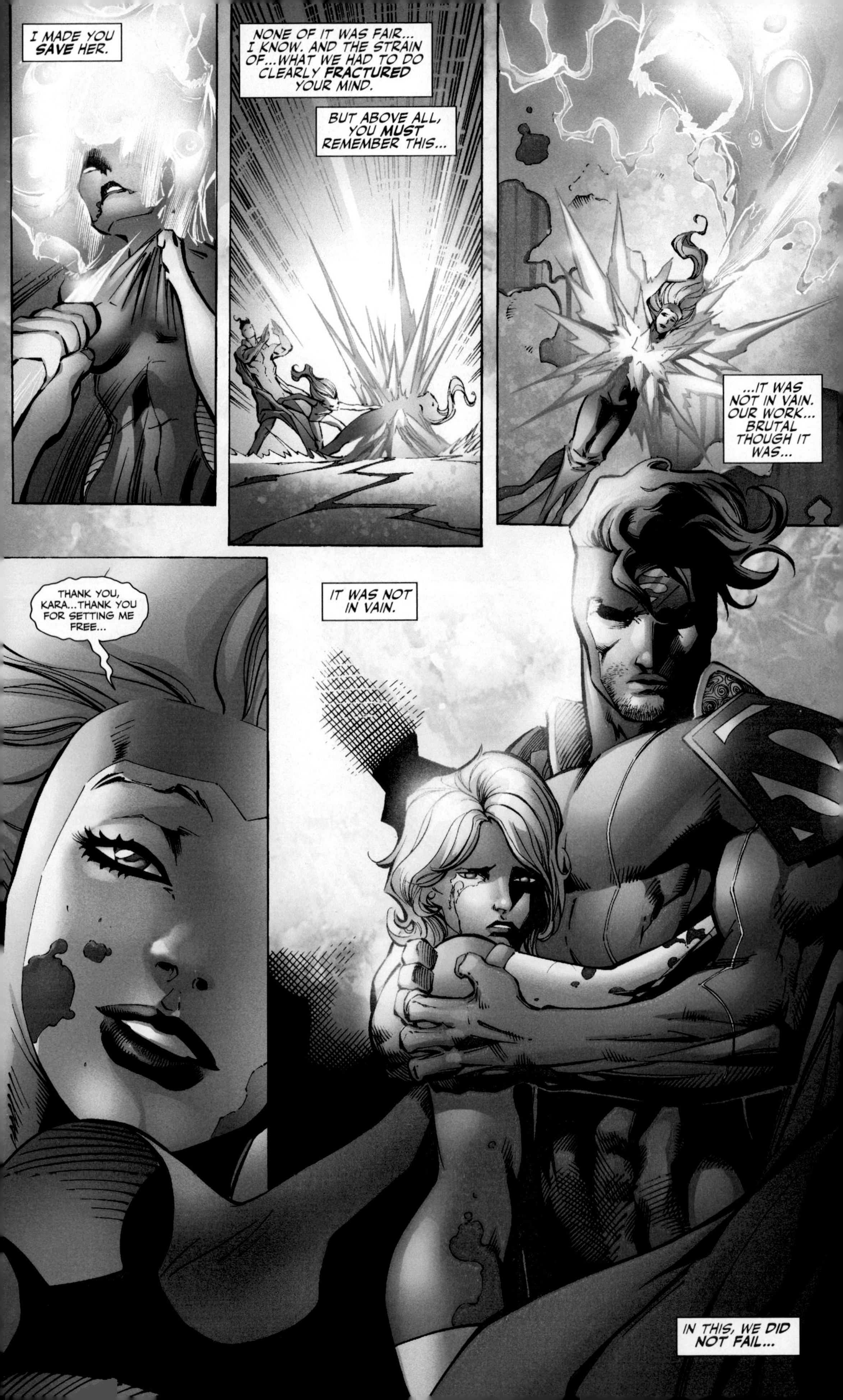
I MADE YOU SAVE HER.
NONE OF IT WAS FAIR... I KNOW. AND THE STRAIN OF...WHAT WE HAD TO DO CLEARLY FRACTURED YOUR MIND.
BUT ABOVE ALL, YOU MUST REMEMBER THIS...
...IT WAS NOT IN VAIN. OUR WORK... BRUTAL THOUGH IT WAS...
THANK YOU, KARA...THANK YOU FOR SETTING ME FREE...
IT WAS NOT IN VAIN.
IN THIS, WE DID NOT FAIL...

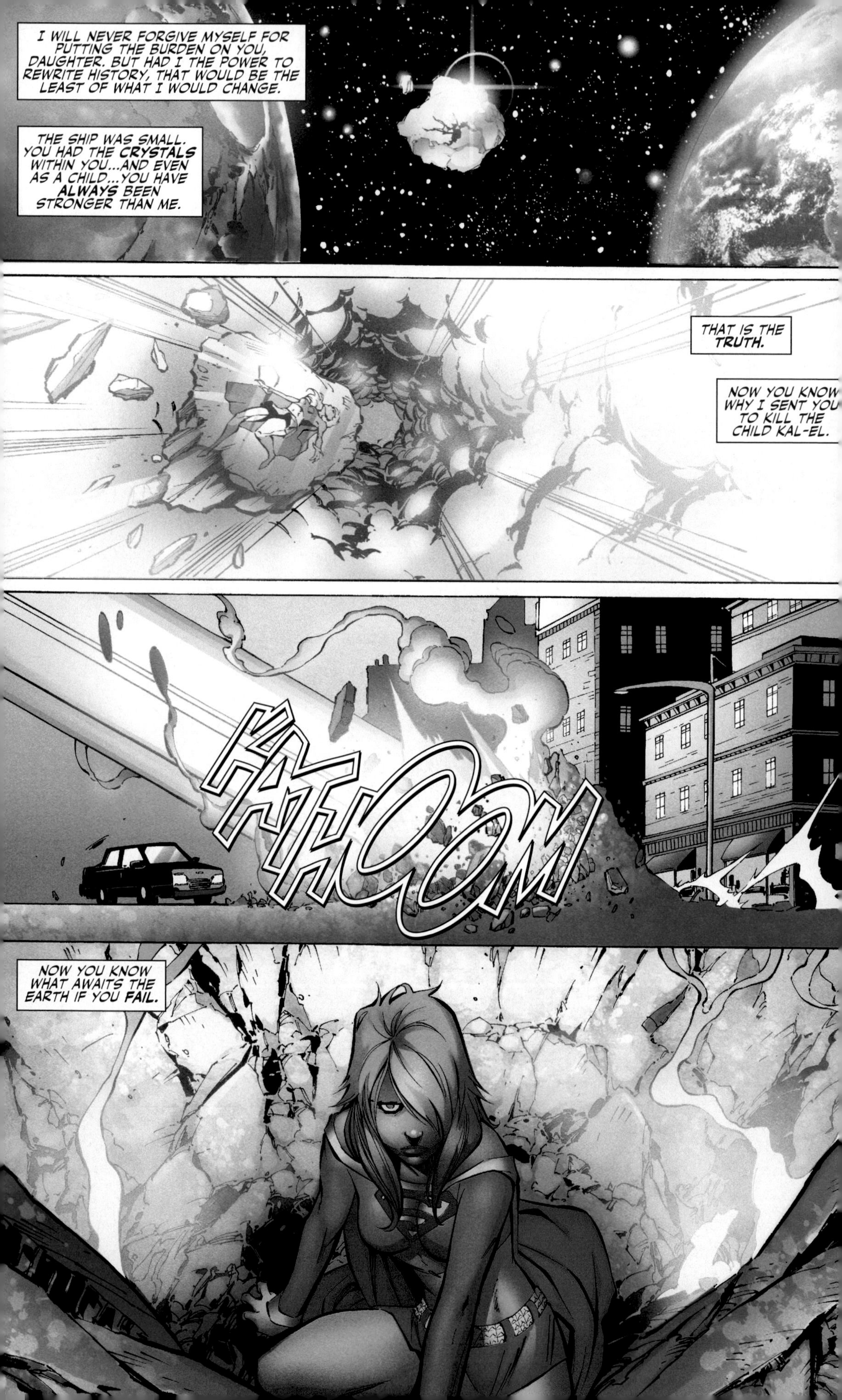

I WILL NEVER FORGIVE MYSELF FOR PUTTING THE BURDEN ON YOU, DAUGHTER. BUT HAD I THE POWER TO REWRITE HISTORY, THAT WOULD BE THE LEAST OF WHAT I WOULD CHANGE.
THE SHIP WAS SMALL. YOU HAD THE CRYSTALS WITHIN YOU...AND EVEN AS A CHILD...YOU HAVE ALWAYS BEEN STRONGER THAN ME.
THAT IS THE TRUTH.
NOW YOU KNOW WHY I SENT YOU TO KILL THE CHILD KAL-EL.
KATHOOM
NOW YOU KNOW WHAT AWAITS THE EARTH IF YOU FAIL.

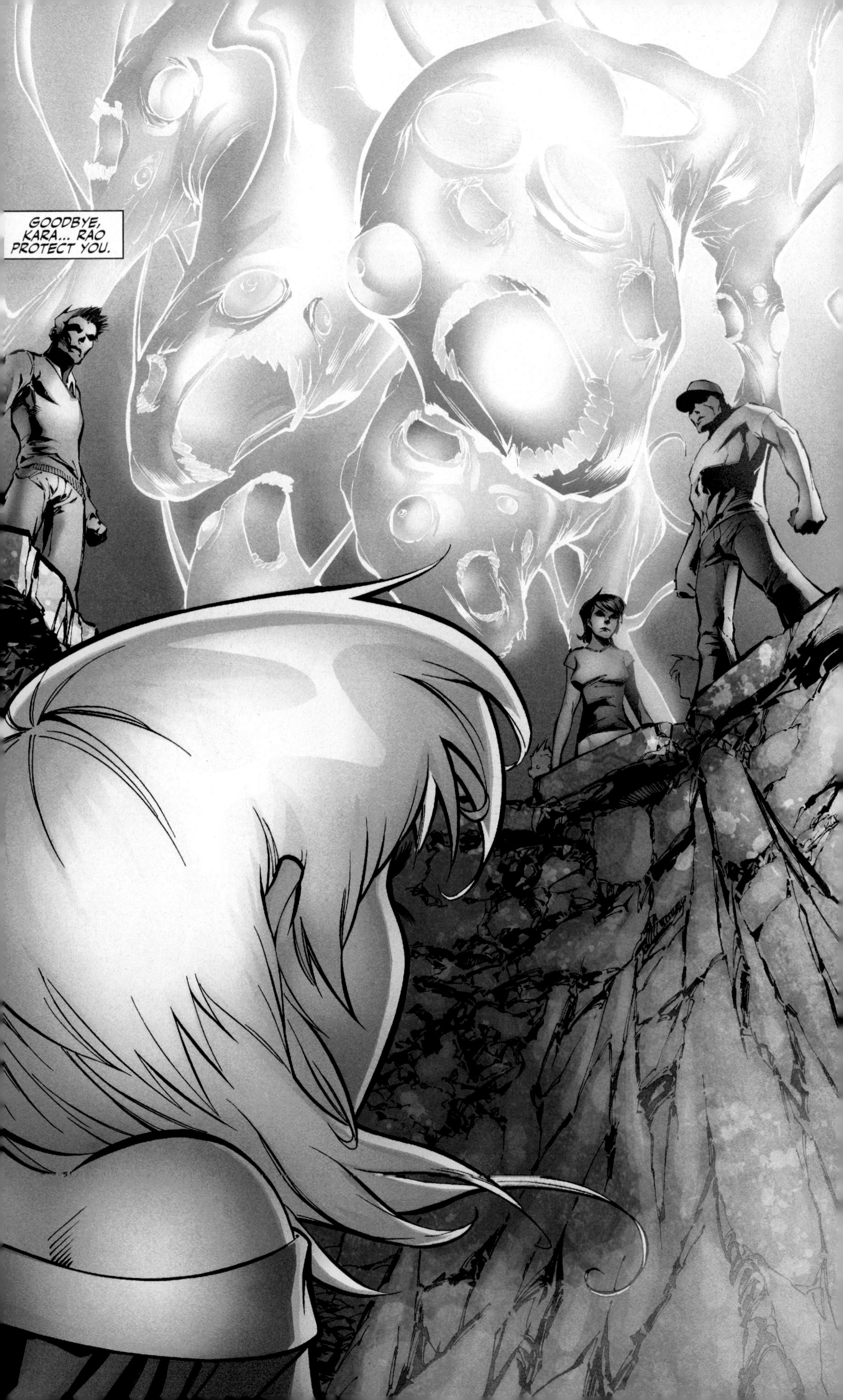
GOODBYE, KARA... RAO PROTECT YOU.

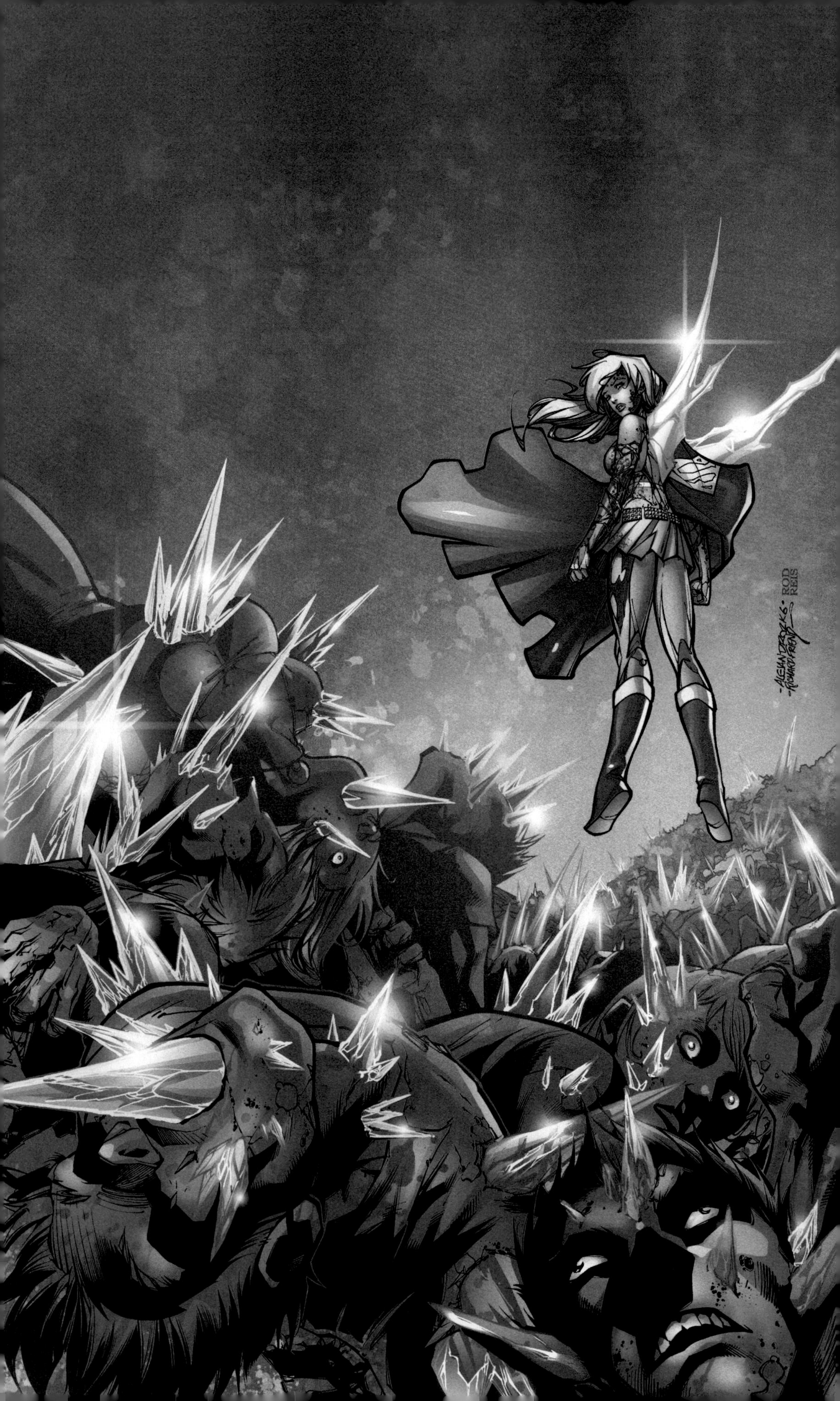
ROD
REIS

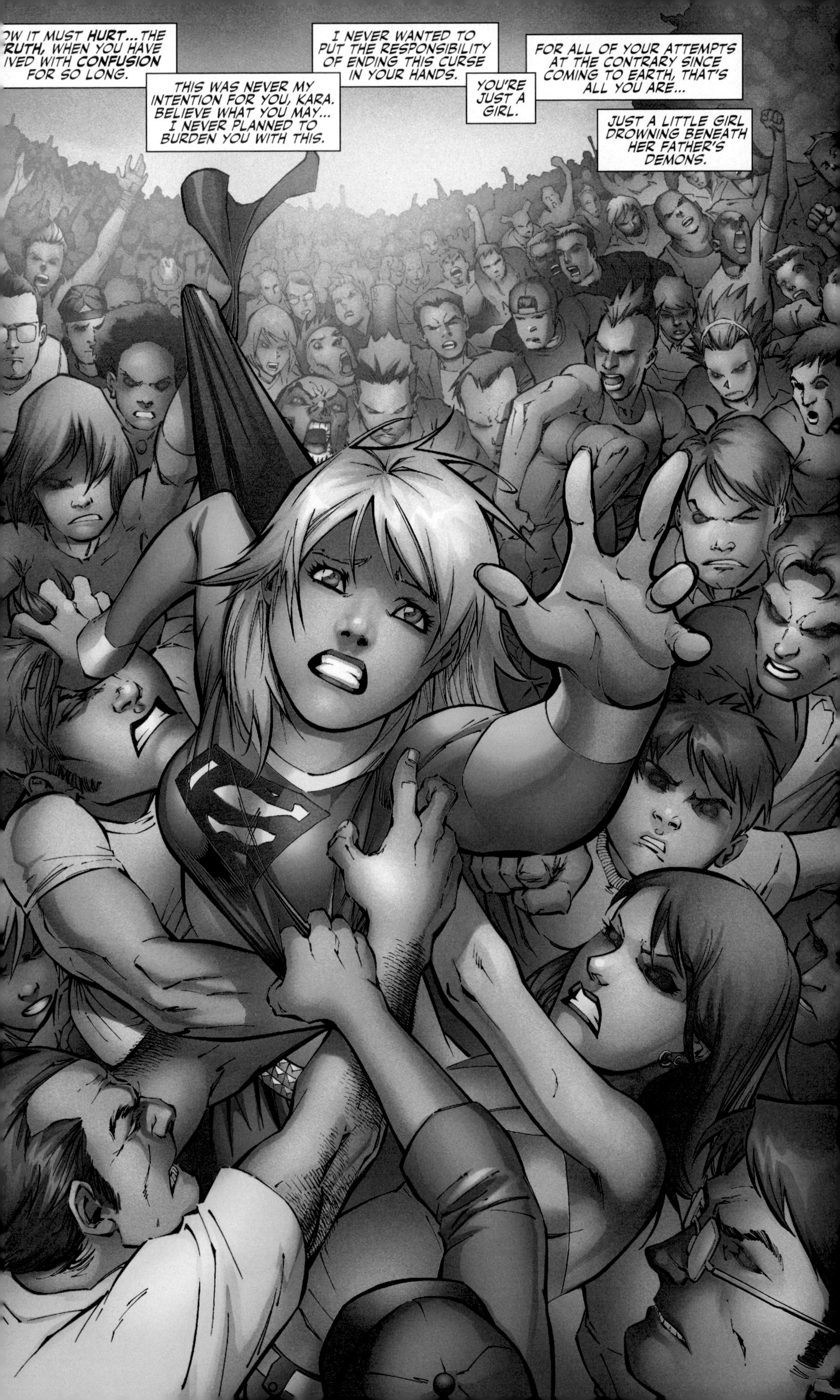
OW IT MUST HURT...THE TRUTH, WHEN YOU HAVE IVED WITH CONFUSION FOR SO LONG.
THIS WAS NEVER MY INTENTION FOR YOU, KARA. BELIEVE WHAT YOU MAY... I NEVER PLANNED TO BURDEN YOU WITH THIS.
I NEVER WANTED TO PUT THE RESPONSIBILITY OF ENDING THIS CURSE IN YOUR HANDS.
YOU'RE JUST A GIRL.
FOR ALL OF YOUR ATTEMPTS AT THE CONTRARY SINCE COMING TO EARTH, THAT'S ALL YOU ARE...
JUST A LITTLE GIRL DROWNING BENEATH HER FATHER'S DEMONS.

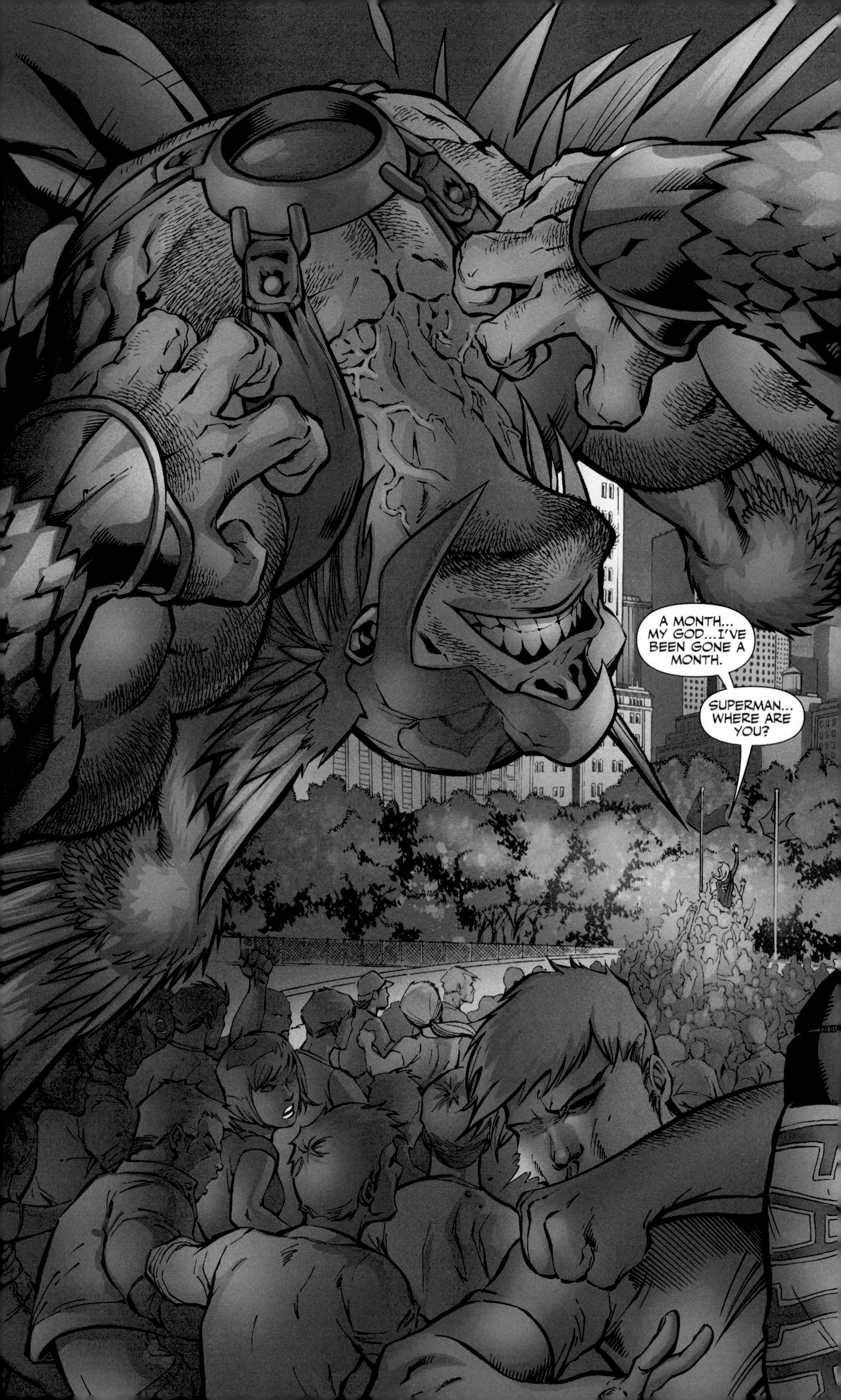
A MONTH... MY GOD...I'VE BEEN GONE A MONTH.
SUPERMAN... WHERE ARE YOU?

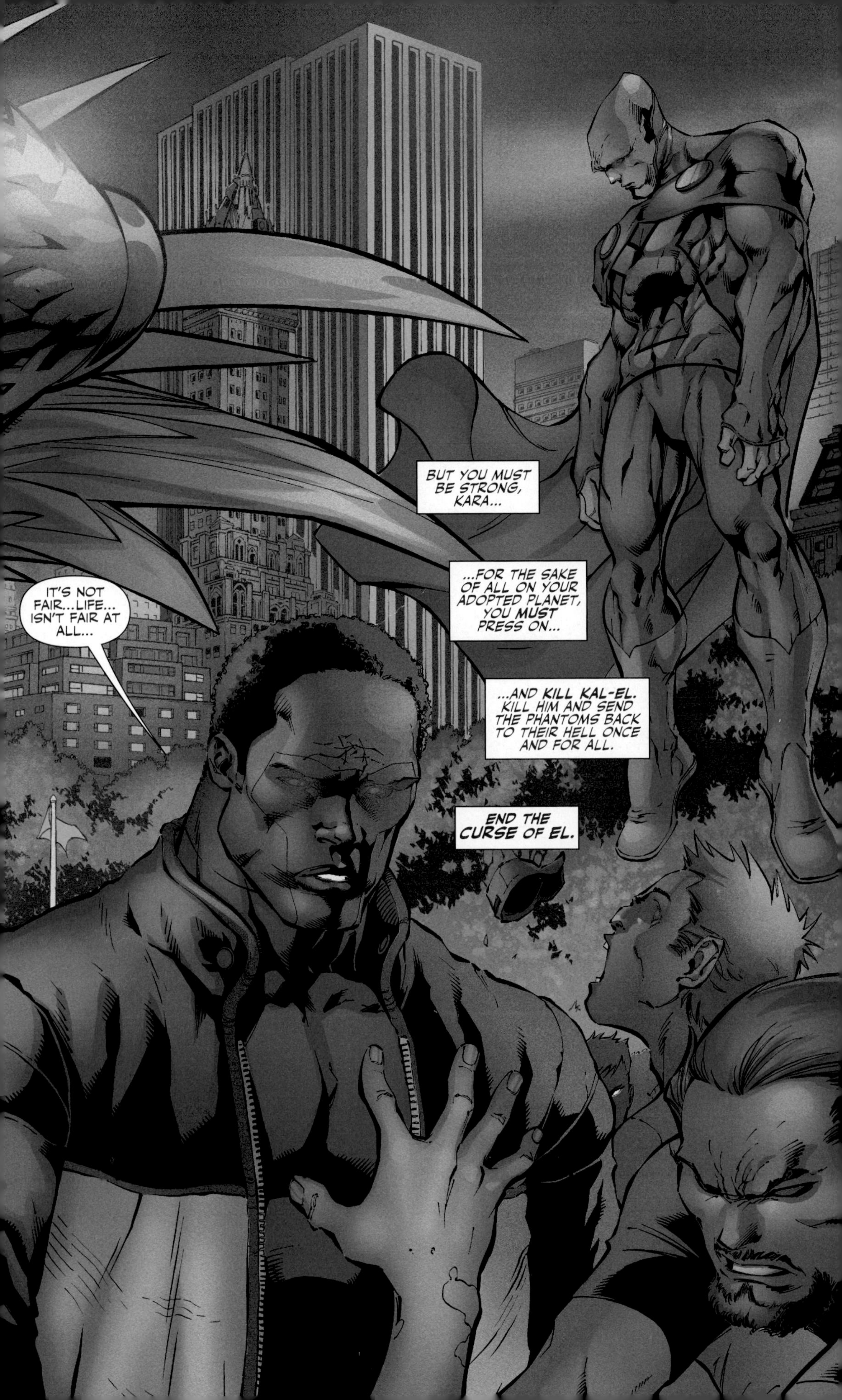
BUT YOU MUST BE STRONG, KARA...
...FOR THE SAKE OF ALL ON YOUR ADOPTED PLANET, YOU MUST PRESS ON...
IT'S NOT FAIR...LIFE... ISN'T FAIR AT ALL...
...AND KILL KAL-EL. KILL HIM AND SEND THE PHANTOMS BACK TO THEIR HELL ONCE AND FOR ALL.
END THE CURSE OF EL.

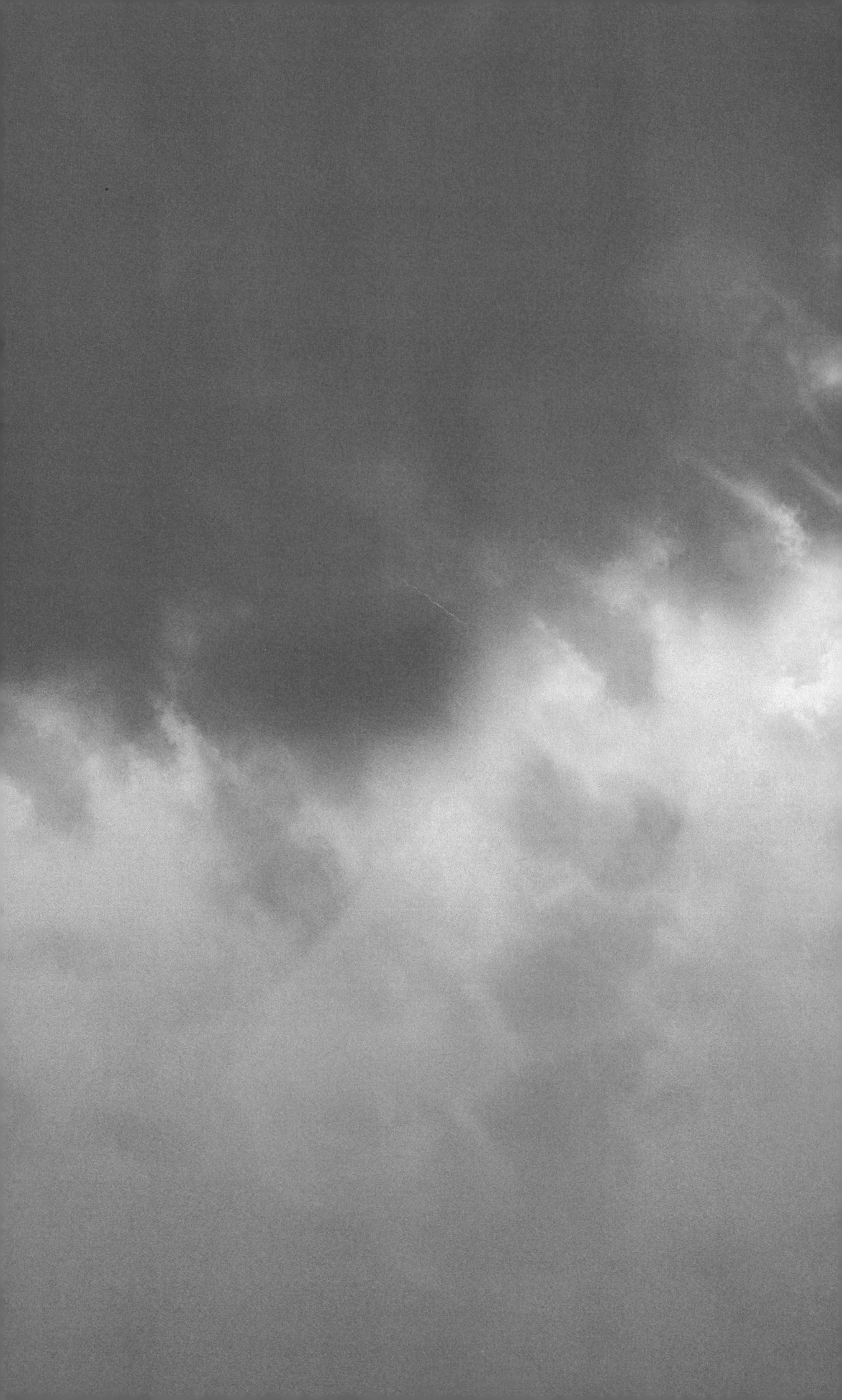

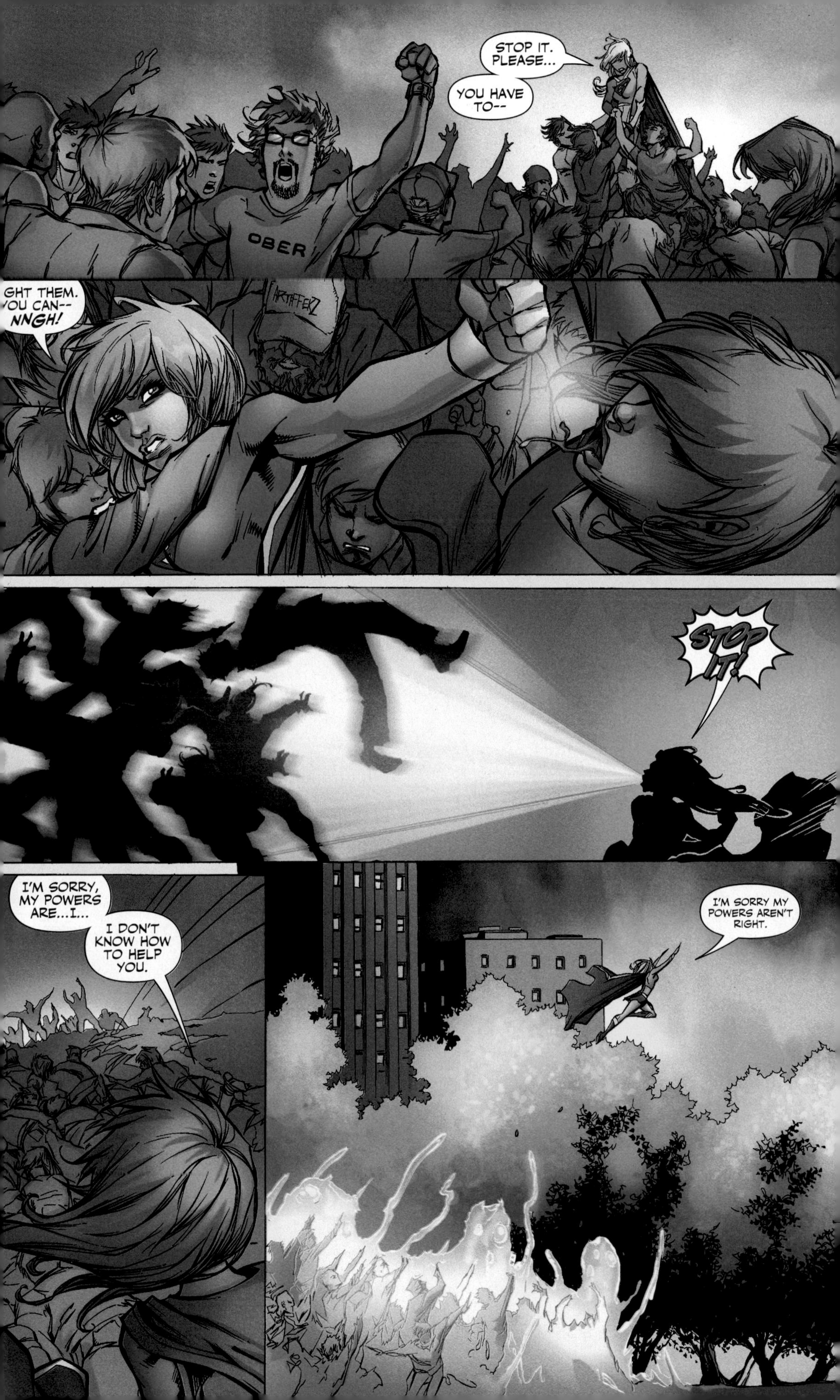
STOP IT. PLEASE...
YOU HAVE TO--
OBER
GHT THEM. YOU CAN-- NNGH!
STOP IT!
I'M SORRY, MY POWERS ARE...I...
I DON'T KNOW HOW TO HELP YOU.
I'M SORRY MY POWERS AREN'T RIGHT.

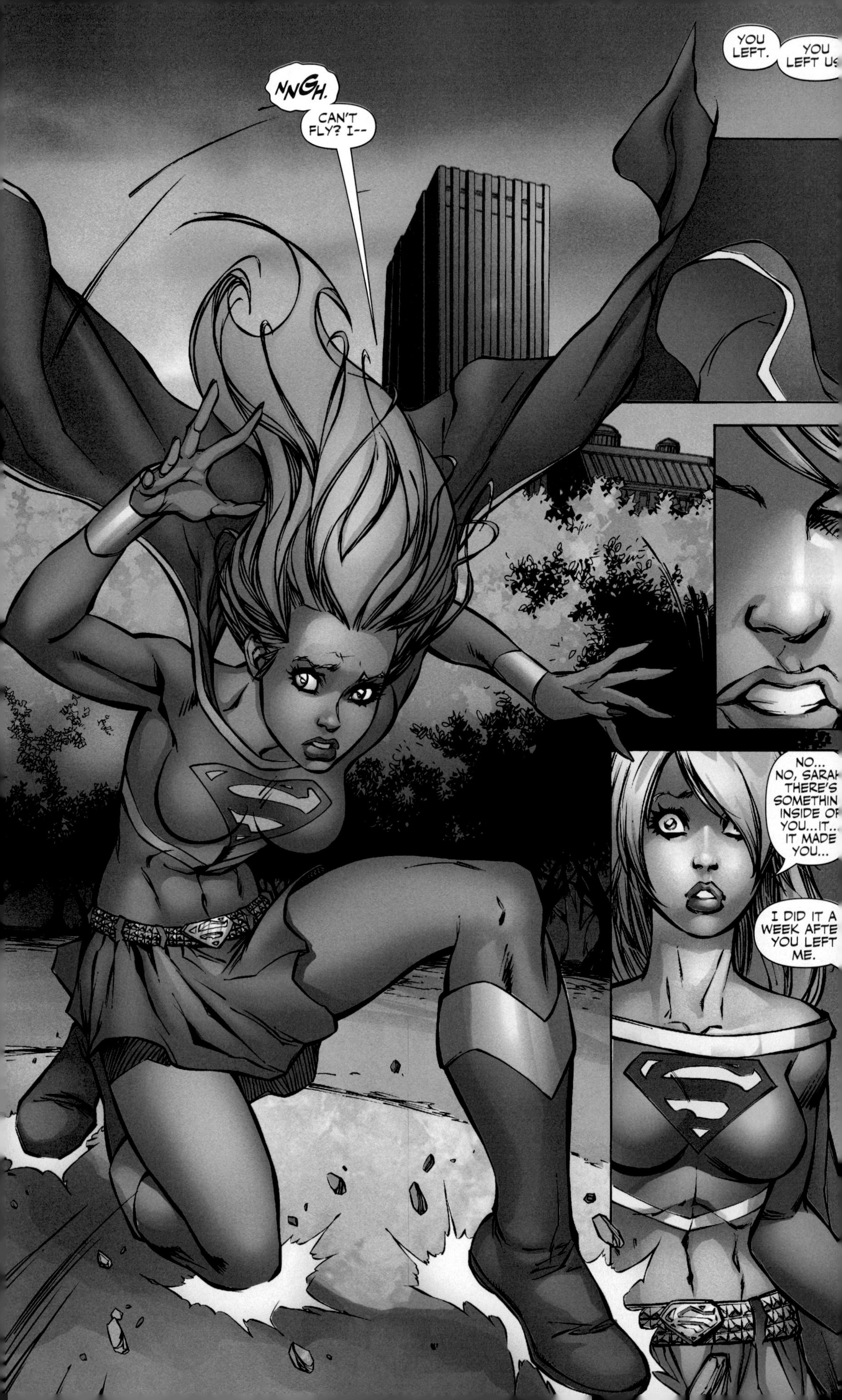

NNGH.
CAN'T FLY? I--
YOU LEFT.
YOU LEFT US
NO... NO, SARAH THERE'S SOMETHIN INSIDE OF YOU...IT... IT MADE YOU...
I DID IT A WEEK AFTE YOU LEFT ME.

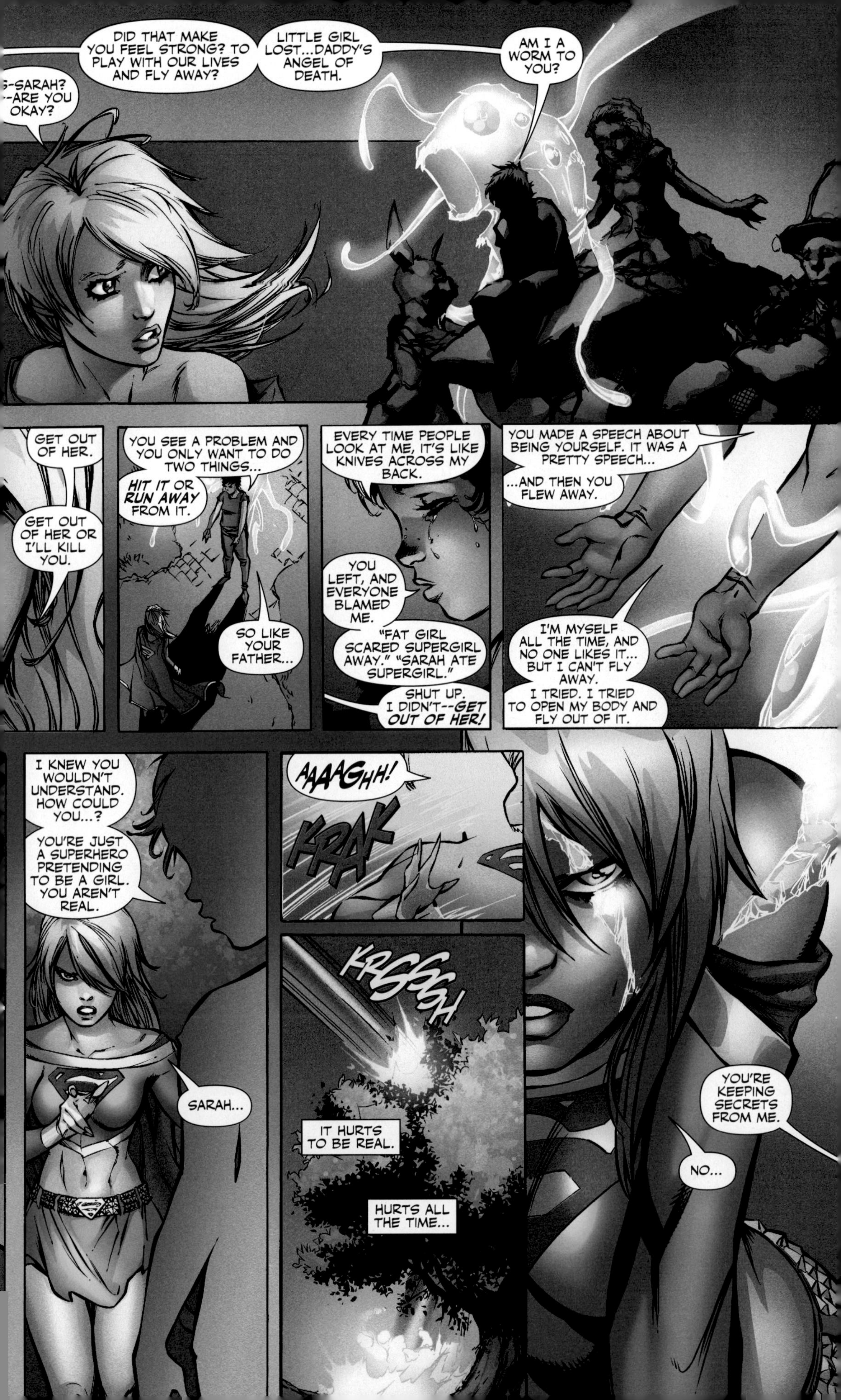

DID THAT MAKE YOU FEEL STRONG? TO PLAY WITH OUR LIVES AND FLY AWAY?
LITTLE GIRL LOST...DADDY'S ANGEL OF DEATH.
AM I A WORM TO YOU?
S-SARAH? --ARE YOU OKAY?
GET OUT OF HER.
GET OUT OF HER OR I'LL KILL YOU.
YOU SEE A PROBLEM AND YOU ONLY WANT TO DO TWO THINGS...
HIT IT OR RUN AWAY FROM IT.
SO LIKE YOUR FATHER...
EVERY TIME PEOPLE LOOK AT ME, IT'S LIKE KNIVES ACROSS MY BACK.
YOU LEFT, AND EVERYONE BLAMED ME.
"FAT GIRL SCARED SUPERGIRL AWAY." "SARAH ATE SUPERGIRL."
SHUT UP. I DIDN'T--GET OUT OF HER!
YOU MADE A SPEECH ABOUT BEING YOURSELF. IT WAS A PRETTY SPEECH...
...AND THEN YOU FLEW AWAY.
I'M MYSELF ALL THE TIME, AND NO ONE LIKES IT... BUT I CAN'T FLY AWAY.
I TRIED. I TRIED TO OPEN MY BODY AND FLY OUT OF IT.
I KNEW YOU WOULDN'T UNDERSTAND. HOW COULD YOU...?
YOU'RE JUST A SUPERHERO PRETENDING TO BE A GIRL. YOU AREN'T REAL.
SARAH...
AAAAGHH!
KRAK
KRSSSH
IT HURTS TO BE REAL.
HURTS ALL THE TIME...
YOU'RE KEEPING SECRETS FROM ME.
NO...

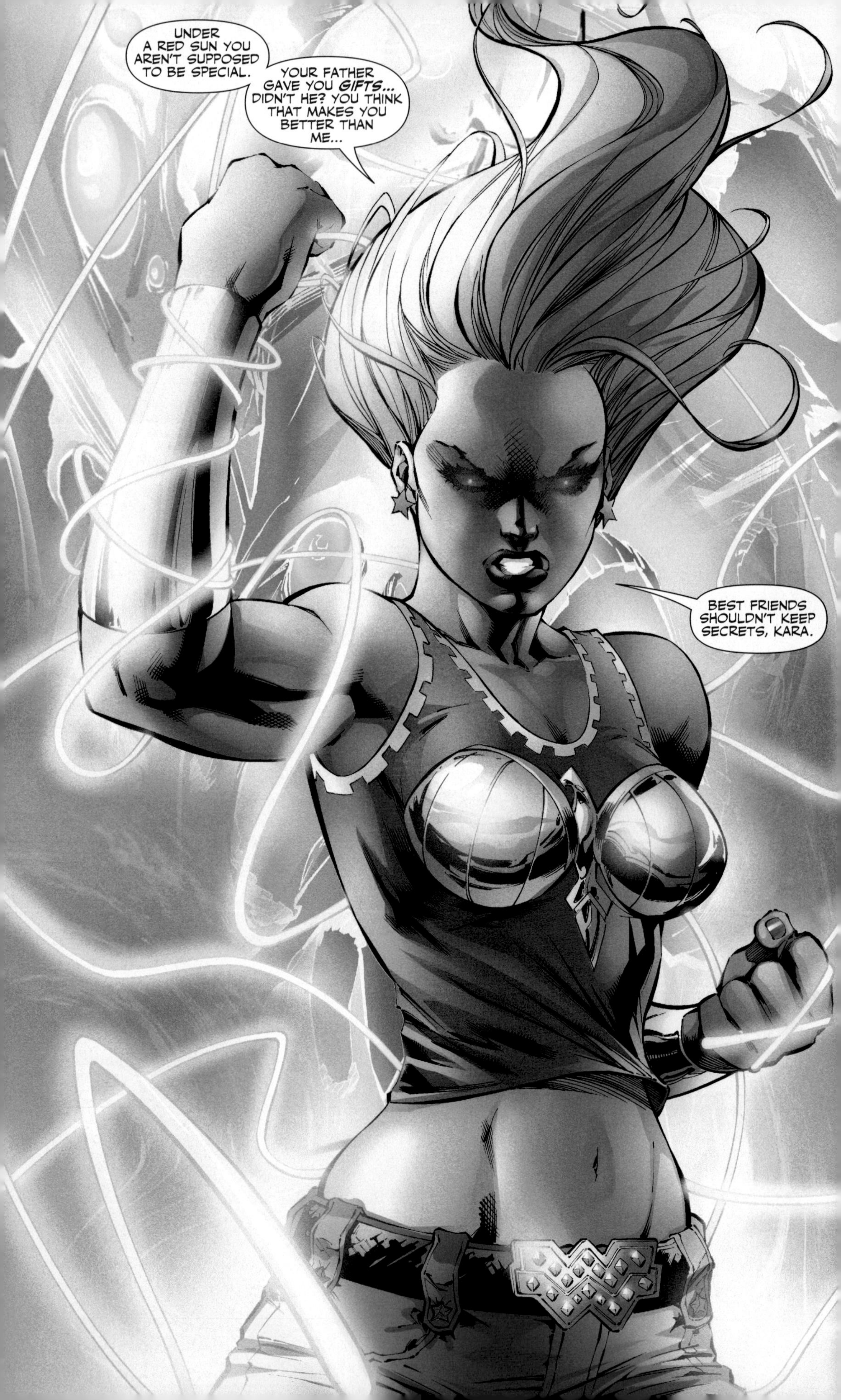
UNDER A RED SUN YOU AREN'T SUPPOSED TO BE SPECIAL.
YOUR FATHER GAVE YOU *GIFTS*... DIDN'T HE? YOU THINK THAT MAKES YOU BETTER THAN ME...
BEST FRIENDS SHOULDN'T KEEP SECRETS, KARA.

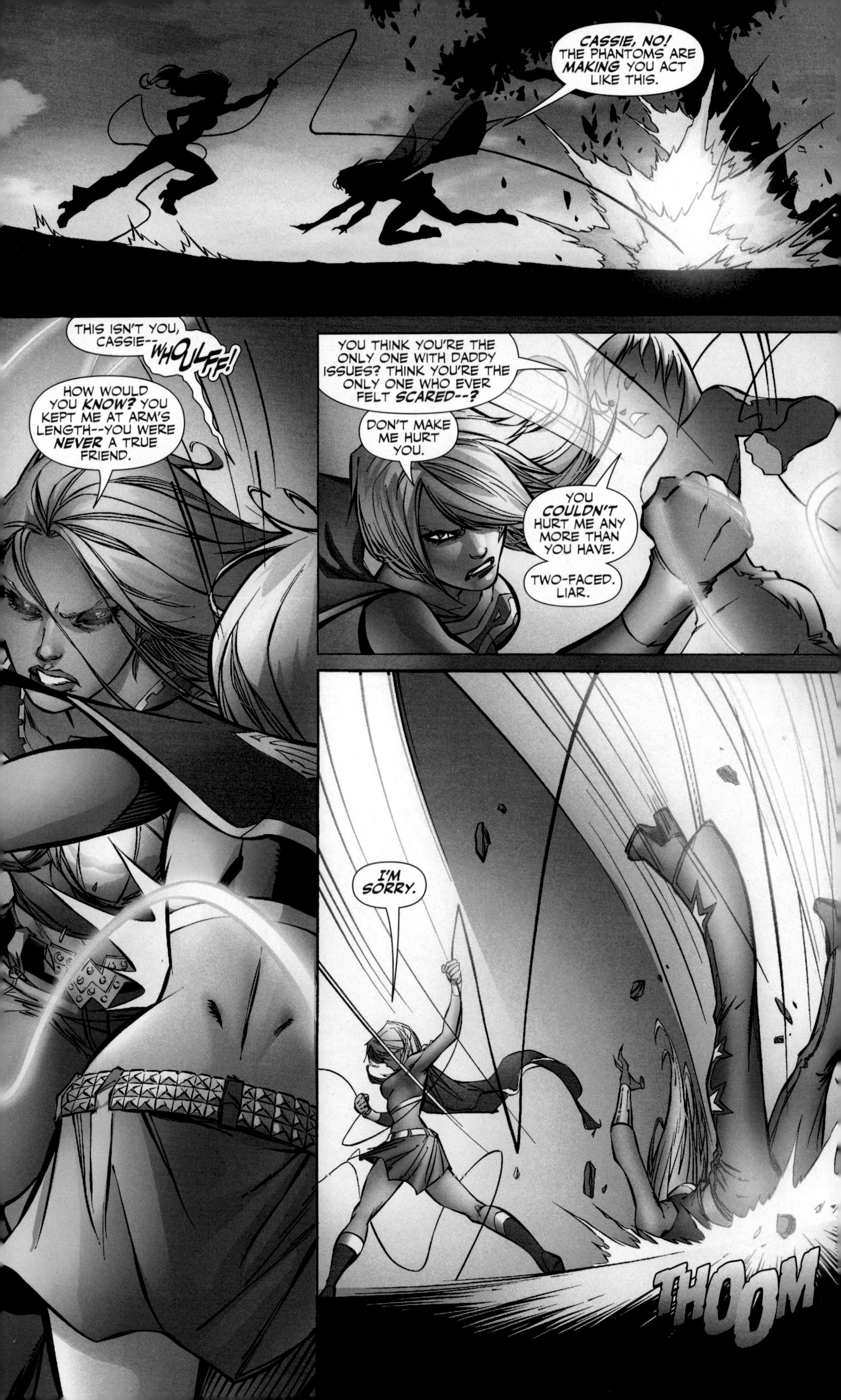
CASSIE, NO! THE PHANTOMS ARE MAKING YOU ACT LIKE THIS.
THIS ISN'T YOU, CASSIE--
WHOULFF!
HOW WOULD YOU KNOW? YOU KEPT ME AT ARM'S LENGTH--YOU WERE NEVER A TRUE FRIEND.
YOU THINK YOU'RE THE ONLY ONE WITH DADDY ISSUES? THINK YOU'RE THE ONLY ONE WHO EVER FELT SCARED--?
DON'T MAKE ME HURT YOU.
YOU COULDN'T HURT ME ANY MORE THAN YOU HAVE.
TWO-FACED. LIAR.
I'M SORRY.
THOOM

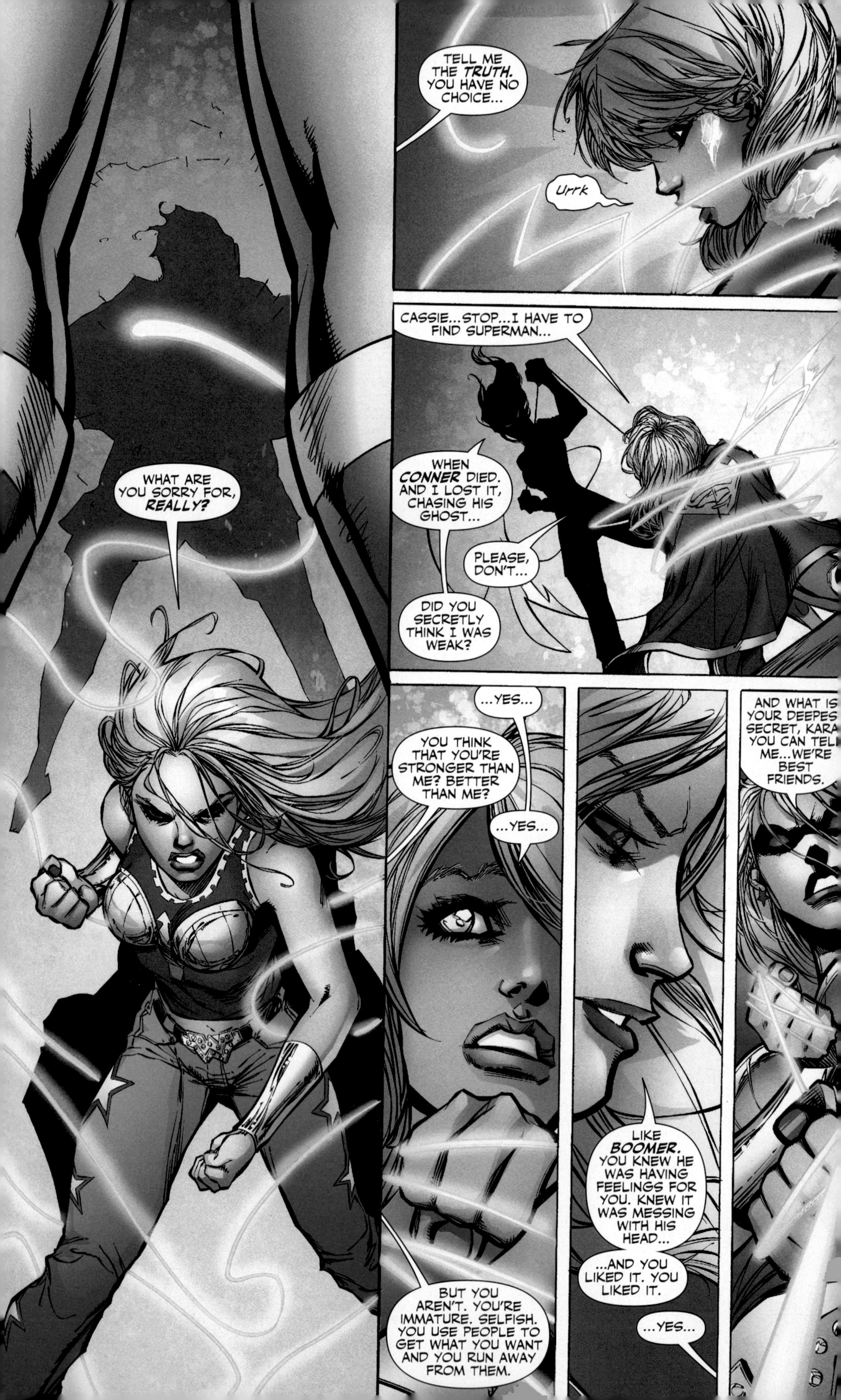
WHAT ARE YOU SORRY FOR, *REALLY?*
TELL ME THE *TRUTH.* YOU HAVE NO CHOICE...
Urrk
CASSIE...STOP...I HAVE TO FIND SUPERMAN...
WHEN *CONNER* DIED. AND I LOST IT, CHASING HIS GHOST...
PLEASE, DON'T...
DID YOU SECRETLY THINK I WAS WEAK?
...YES...
YOU THINK THAT YOU'RE STRONGER THAN ME? BETTER THAN ME?
...YES...
BUT YOU AREN'T. YOU'RE IMMATURE. SELFISH. YOU USE PEOPLE TO GET WHAT YOU WANT AND YOU RUN AWAY FROM THEM.
LIKE *BOOMER.* YOU KNEW HE WAS HAVING FEELINGS FOR YOU. KNEW IT WAS MESSING WITH HIS HEAD...
...AND YOU LIKED IT. YOU LIKED IT.
...YES...
AND WHAT IS YOUR DEEPES SECRET, KARA YOU CAN TEL ME...WE'RE BEST FRIENDS.

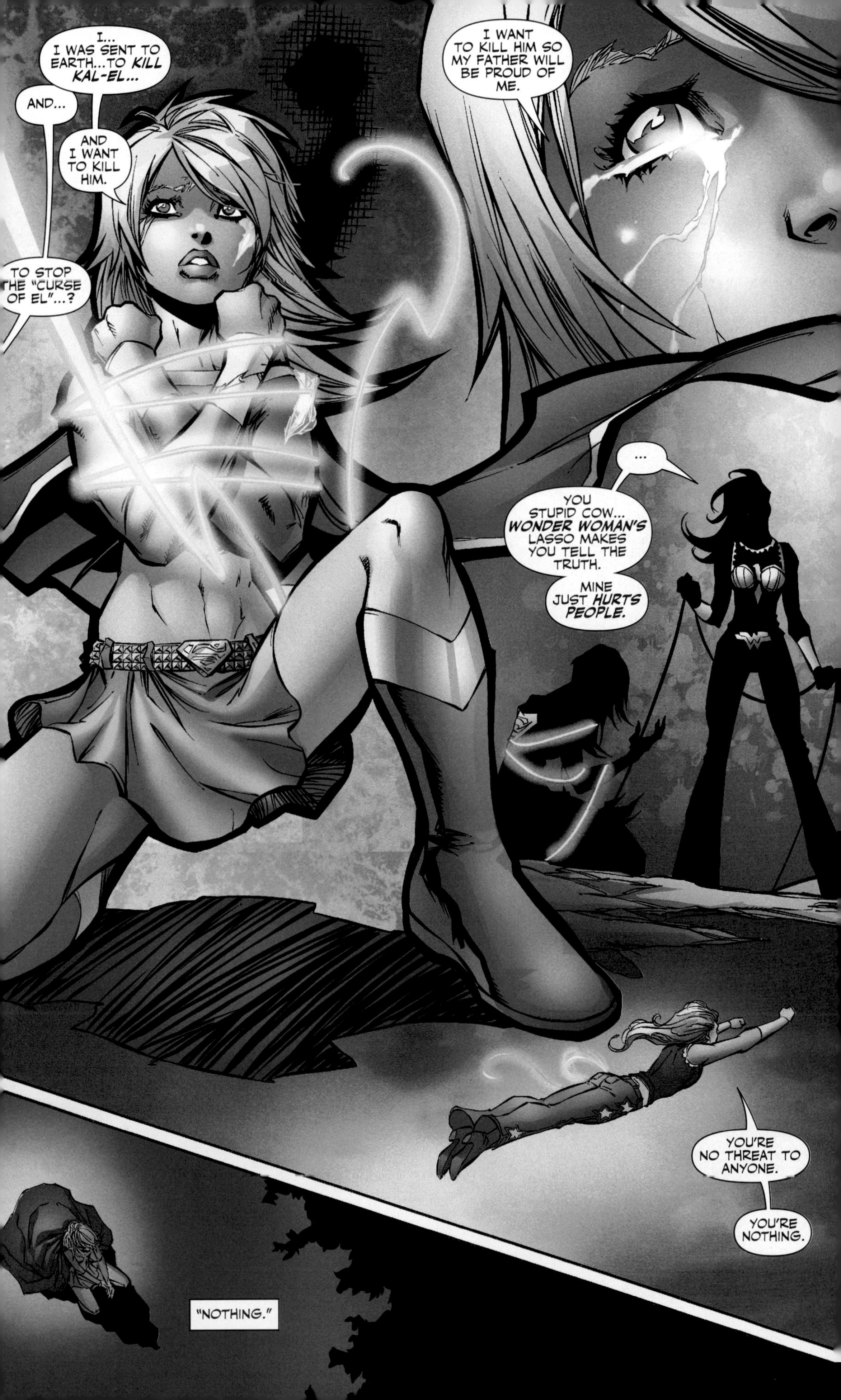
I... I WAS SENT TO EARTH...TO KILL KAL-EL...
AND...
AND I WANT TO KILL HIM.
TO STOP THE "CURSE OF EL"...?
I WANT TO KILL HIM SO MY FATHER WILL BE PROUD OF ME.
...
YOU STUPID COW... WONDER WOMAN'S LASSO MAKES YOU TELL THE TRUTH.
MINE JUST HURTS PEOPLE.
YOU'RE NO THREAT TO ANYONE.
YOU'RE NOTHING.
"NOTHING."

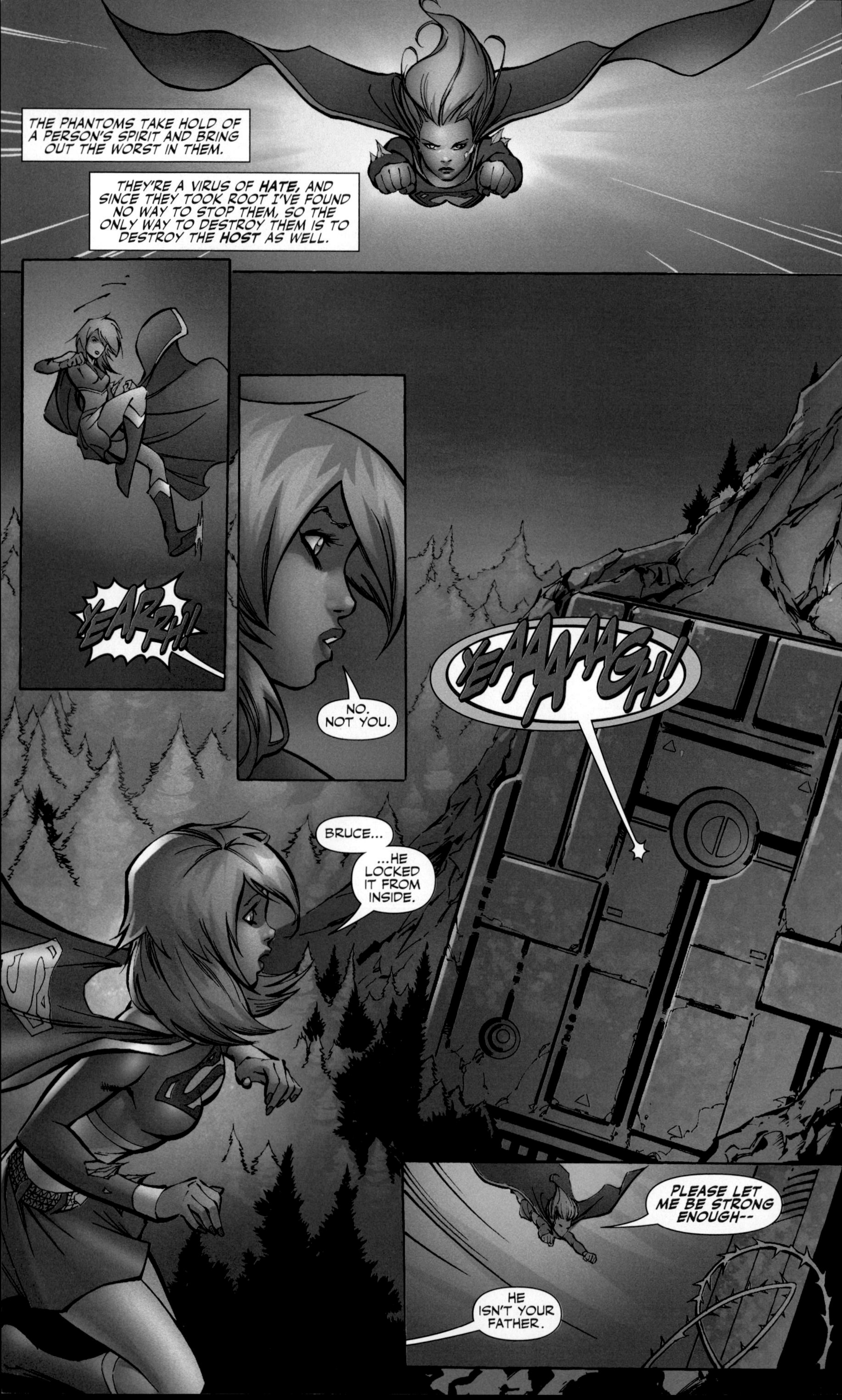
THE PHANTOMS TAKE HOLD OF A PERSON'S SPIRIT AND BRING OUT THE WORST IN THEM.
THEY'RE A VIRUS OF HATE, AND SINCE THEY TOOK ROOT I'VE FOUND NO WAY TO STOP THEM, SO THE ONLY WAY TO DESTROY THEM IS TO DESTROY THE HOST AS WELL.
YEARRH!
NO. NOT YOU.
YEAAAAAGH!
BRUCE...
...HE LOCKED IT FROM INSIDE.
PLEASE LET ME BE STRONG ENOUGH--
HE ISN'T YOUR FATHER.

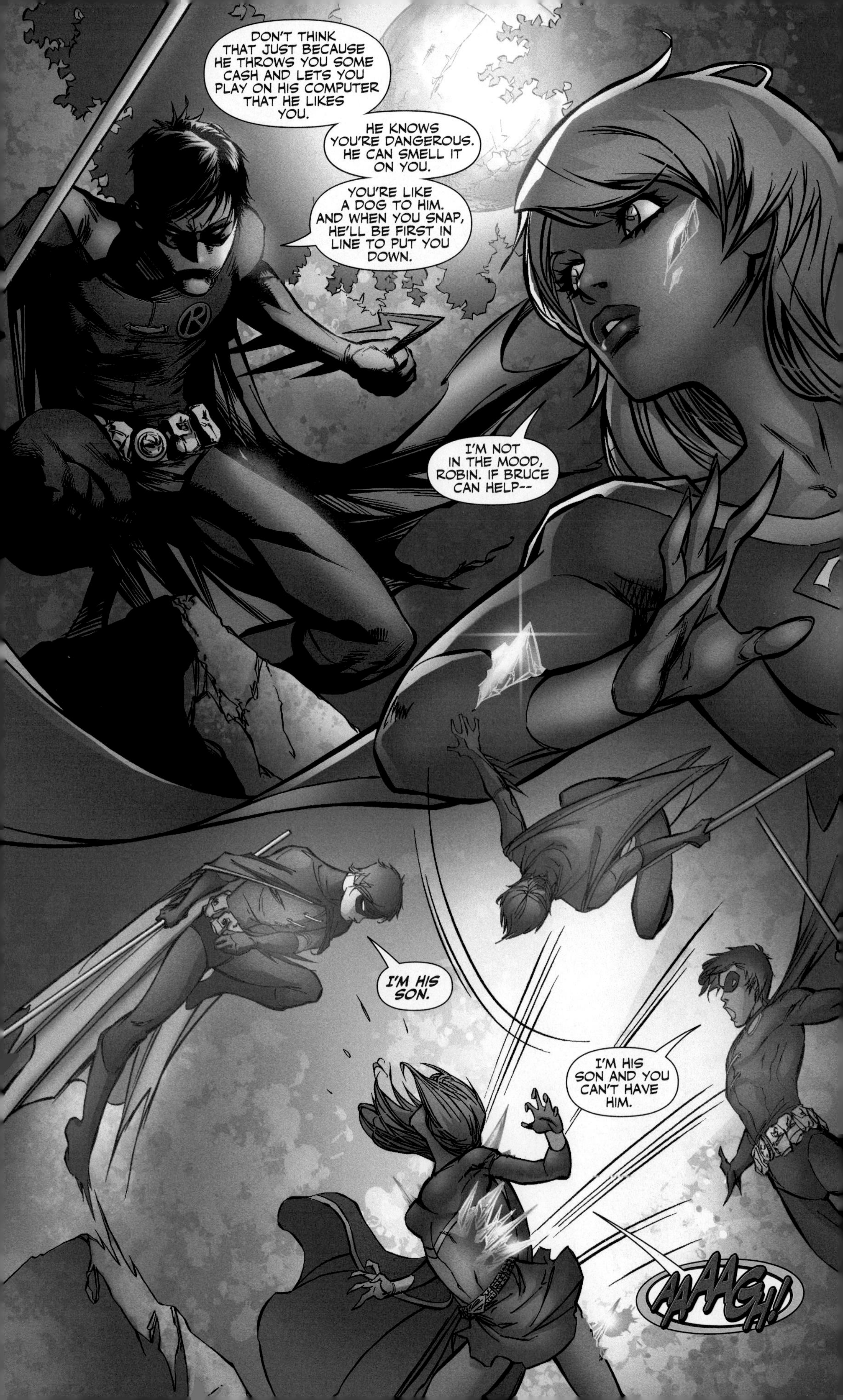
DON'T THINK THAT JUST BECAUSE HE THROWS YOU SOME CASH AND LETS YOU PLAY ON HIS COMPUTER THAT HE LIKES YOU.
HE KNOWS YOU'RE DANGEROUS. HE CAN SMELL IT ON YOU.
YOU'RE LIKE A DOG TO HIM. AND WHEN YOU SNAP, HE'LL BE FIRST IN LINE TO PUT YOU DOWN.
I'M NOT IN THE MOOD, ROBIN. IF BRUCE CAN HELP--
I'M HIS SON.
I'M HIS SON AND YOU CAN'T HAVE HIM.
AAAAGH!

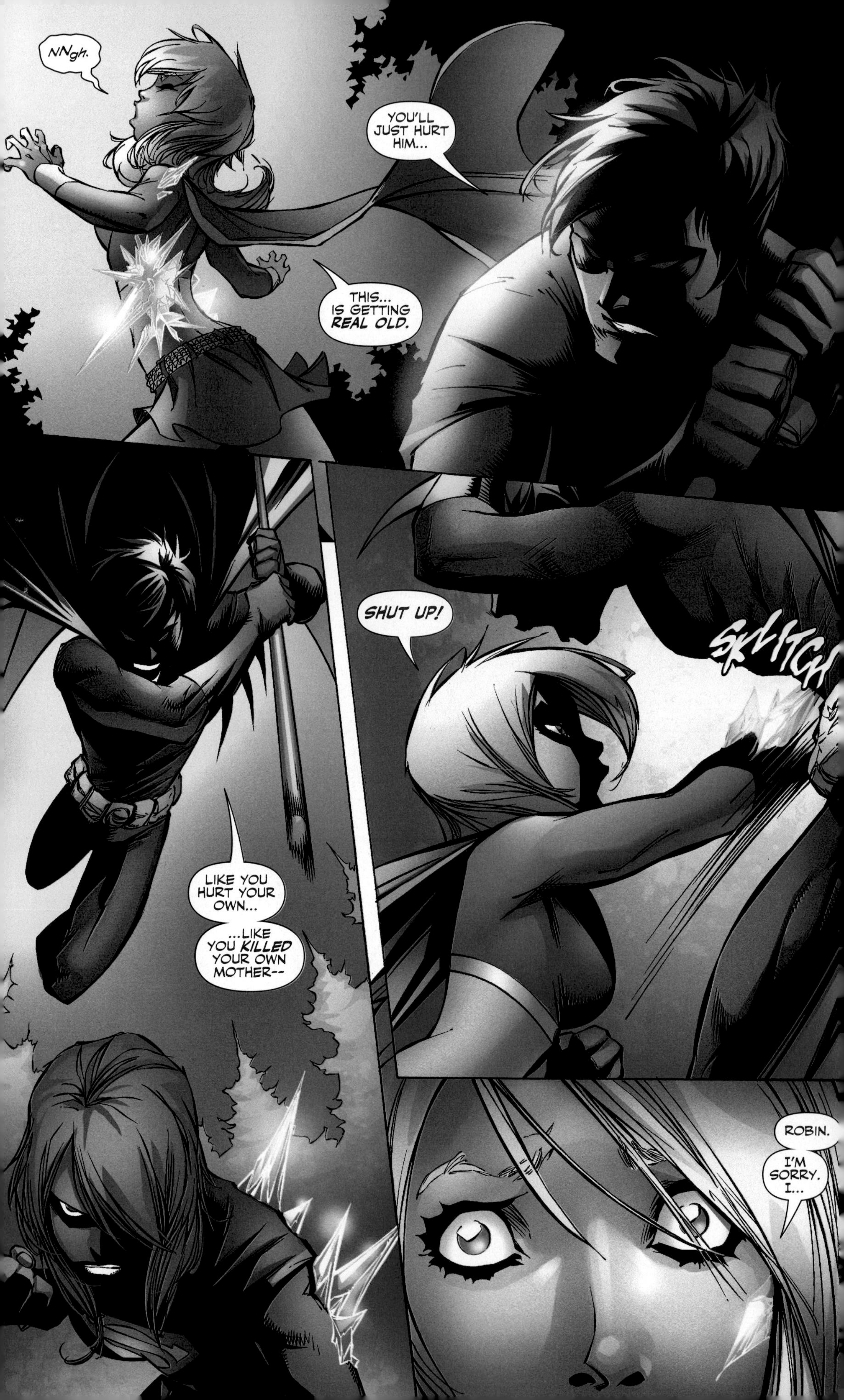
NNgh.
YOU'LL JUST HURT HIM...
THIS... IS GETTING REAL OLD.
LIKE YOU HURT YOUR OWN...
...LIKE YOU KILLED YOUR OWN MOTHER--
SHUT UP!
SKLITCH
ROBIN.
I'M SORRY. I...

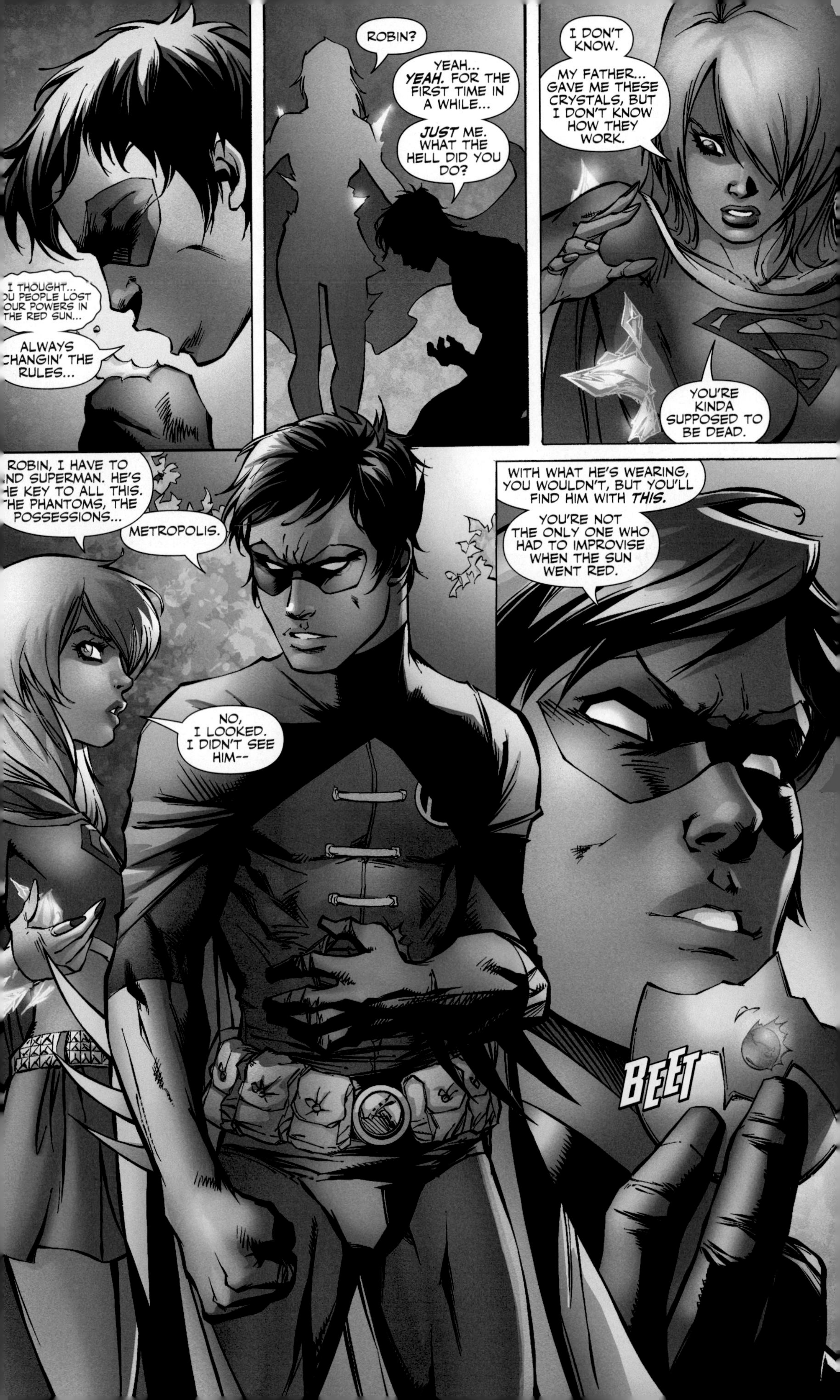

I THOUGHT... OU PEOPLE LOST OUR POWERS IN THE RED SUN...
ALWAYS CHANGIN' THE RULES...
ROBIN?
YEAH... YEAH. FOR THE FIRST TIME IN A WHILE...
JUST ME. WHAT THE HELL DID YOU DO?
I DON'T KNOW.
MY FATHER... GAVE ME THESE CRYSTALS, BUT I DON'T KNOW HOW THEY WORK.
YOU'RE KINDA SUPPOSED TO BE DEAD.
ROBIN, I HAVE TO ND SUPERMAN. HE'S HE KEY TO ALL THIS. THE PHANTOMS, THE POSSESSIONS...
METROPOLIS.
NO, I LOOKED. I DIDN'T SEE HIM--
WITH WHAT HE'S WEARING, YOU WOULDN'T, BUT YOU'LL FIND HIM WITH THIS.
YOU'RE NOT THE ONLY ONE WHO HAD TO IMPROVISE WHEN THE SUN WENT RED.
BEEP

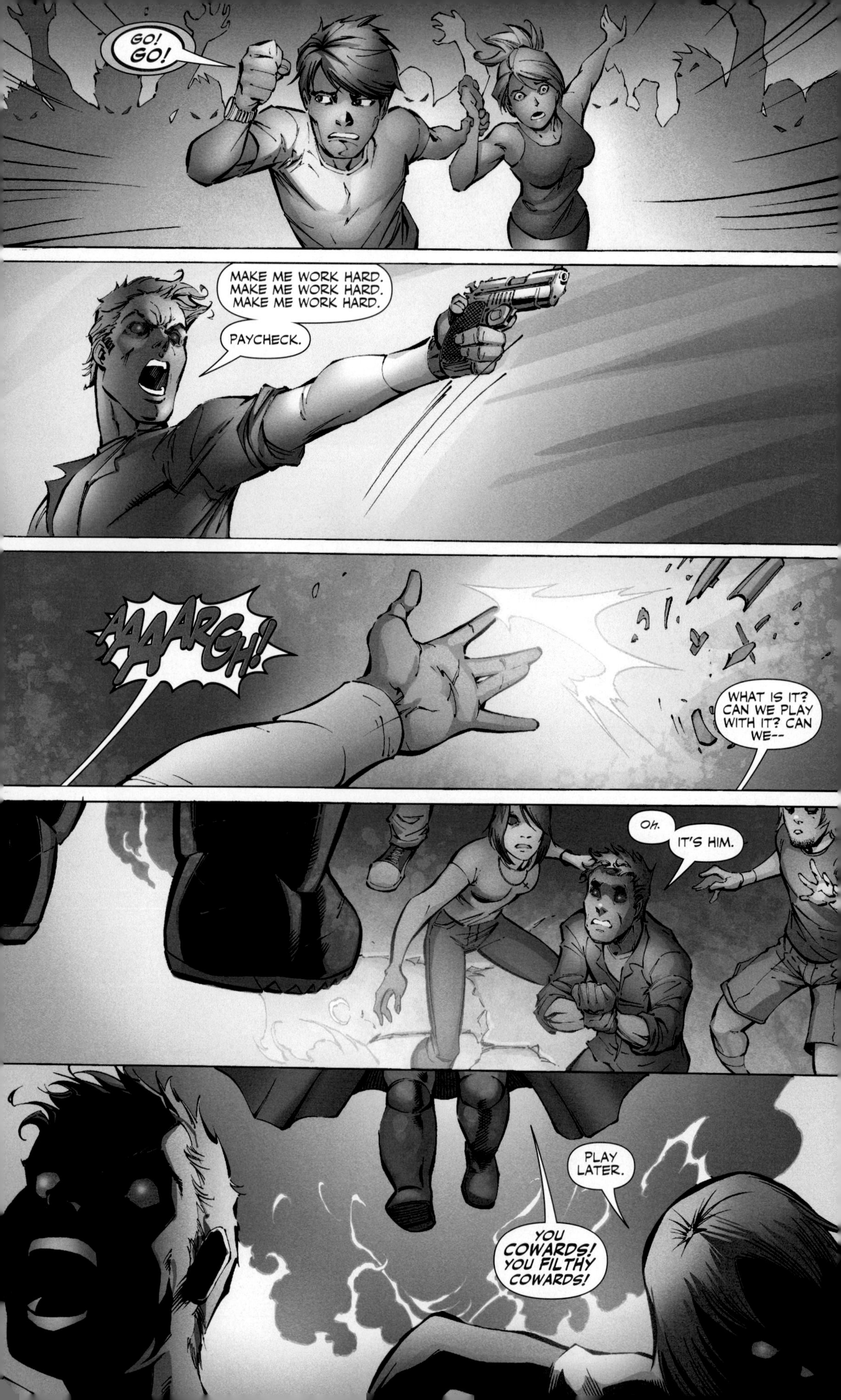
GO! GO!
MAKE ME WORK HARD. MAKE ME WORK HARD. MAKE ME WORK HARD.
PAYCHECK.
AAAARGH!
WHAT IS IT? CAN WE PLAY WITH IT? CAN WE--
Oh.
IT'S HIM.
PLAY LATER.
YOU COWARDS! YOU FILTHY COWARDS!

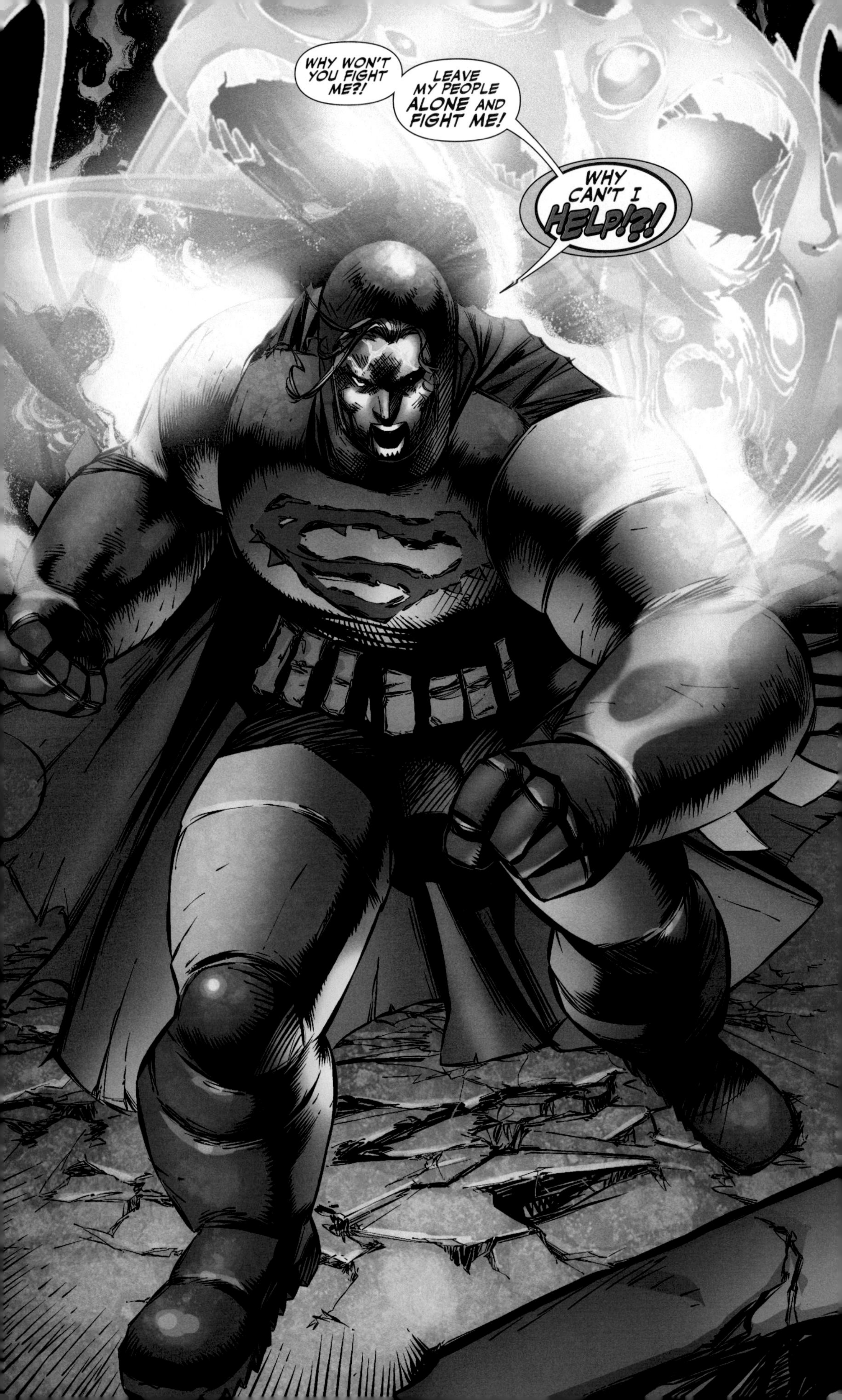

WHY WON'T YOU FIGHT ME?!
LEAVE MY PEOPLE ALONE AND FIGHT ME!
WHY CAN'T I HELP!?!

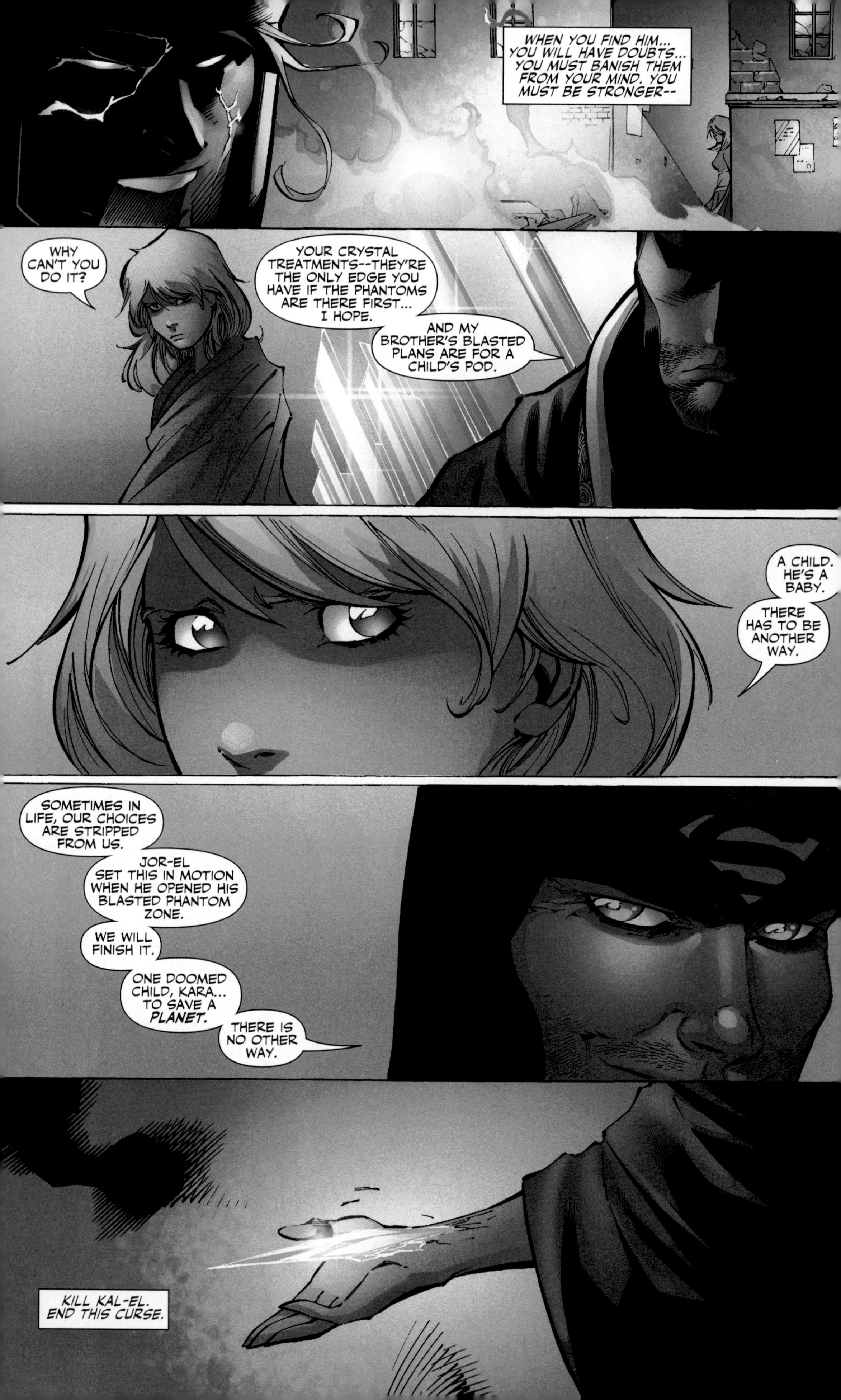
WHEN YOU FIND HIM... YOU WILL HAVE DOUBTS... YOU MUST BANISH THEM FROM YOUR MIND. YOU MUST BE STRONGER--
WHY CAN'T YOU DO IT?
YOUR CRYSTAL TREATMENTS--THEY'RE THE ONLY EDGE YOU HAVE IF THE PHANTOMS ARE THERE FIRST... I HOPE.
AND MY BROTHER'S BLASTED PLANS ARE FOR A CHILD'S POD.
A CHILD. HE'S A BABY.
THERE HAS TO BE ANOTHER WAY.
SOMETIMES IN LIFE, OUR CHOICES ARE STRIPPED FROM US.
JOR-EL SET THIS IN MOTION WHEN HE OPENED HIS BLASTED PHANTOM ZONE.
WE WILL FINISH IT.
ONE DOOMED CHILD, KARA... TO SAVE A *PLANET*.
THERE IS NO OTHER WAY.
KILL KAL-EL. END THIS CURSE.

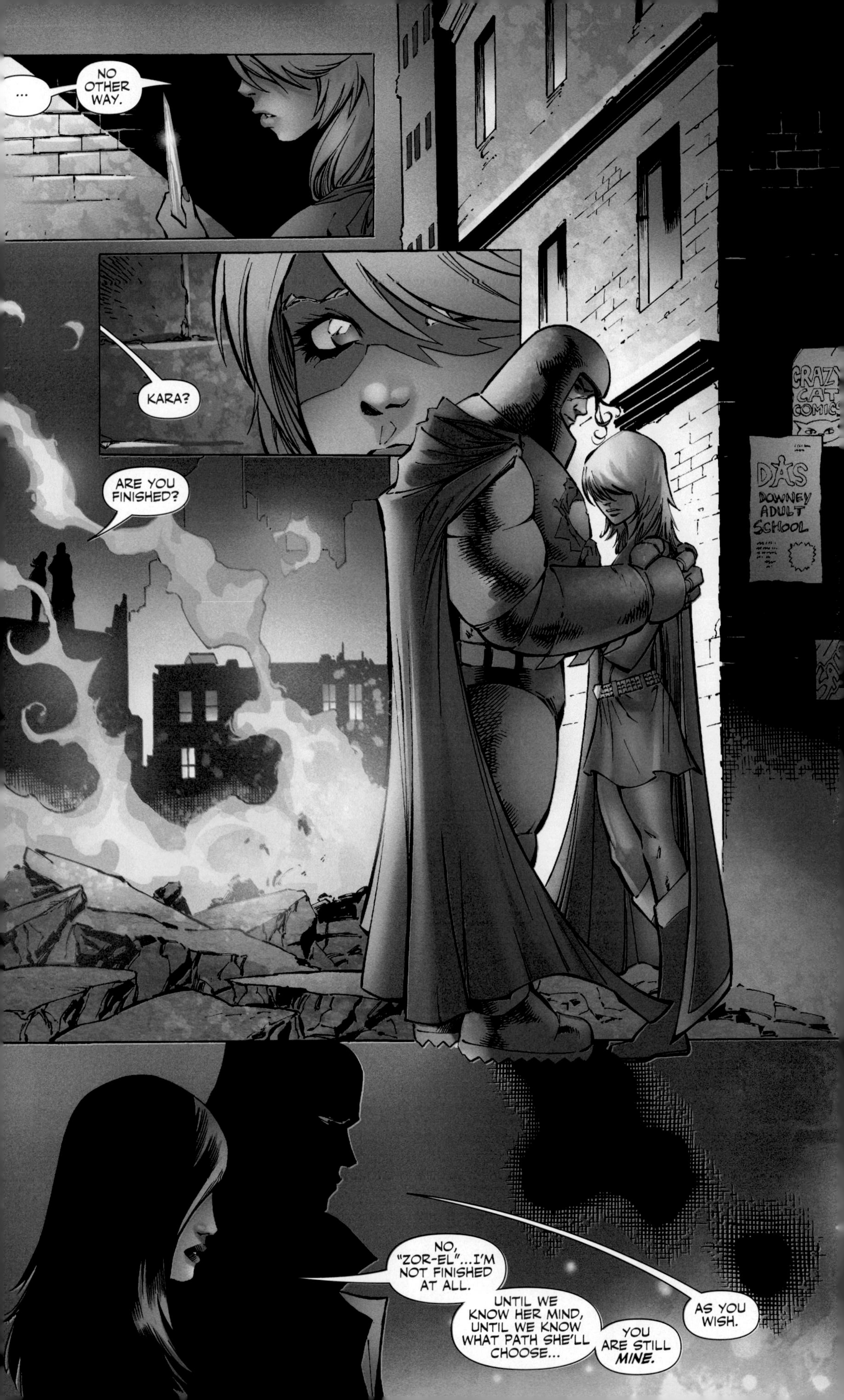
...
NO OTHER WAY.
KARA?
ARE YOU FINISHED?
CRAZY CAT COMICS
DAS
DOWNEY ADULT SCHOOL
NO, "ZOR-EL"...I'M NOT FINISHED AT ALL.
UNTIL WE KNOW HER MIND, UNTIL WE KNOW WHAT PATH SHE'LL CHOOSE...
YOU ARE STILL *MINE.*
AS YOU WISH.

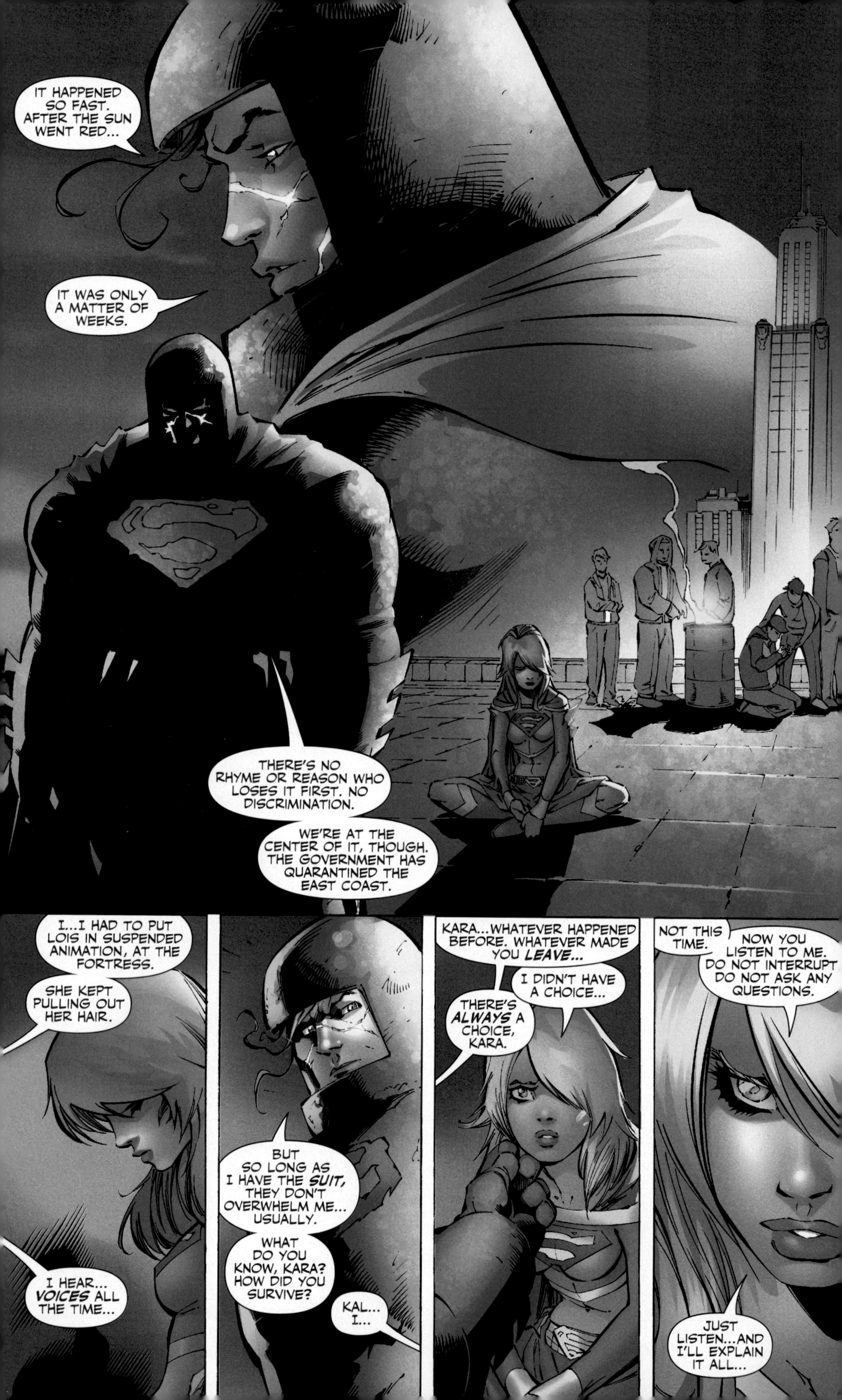
IT HAPPENED SO FAST. AFTER THE SUN WENT RED...
IT WAS ONLY A MATTER OF WEEKS.
THERE'S NO RHYME OR REASON WHO LOSES IT FIRST. NO DISCRIMINATION.
WE'RE AT THE CENTER OF IT, THOUGH. THE GOVERNMENT HAS QUARANTINED THE EAST COAST.
I...I HAD TO PUT LOIS IN SUSPENDED ANIMATION, AT THE FORTRESS.
SHE KEPT PULLING OUT HER HAIR.
I HEAR... *VOICES* ALL THE TIME...
BUT SO LONG AS I HAVE THE *SUIT,* THEY DON'T OVERWHELM ME... USUALLY.
WHAT DO YOU KNOW, KARA? HOW DID YOU SURVIVE?
KAL... I...
KARA...WHATEVER HAPPENED BEFORE. WHATEVER MADE YOU *LEAVE*...
I DIDN'T HAVE A CHOICE...
THERE'S *ALWAYS* A CHOICE, KARA.
NOT THIS TIME.
NOW YOU LISTEN TO ME. DO NOT INTERRUPT DO NOT ASK ANY QUESTIONS.
JUST LISTEN...AND I'LL EXPLAIN IT ALL...

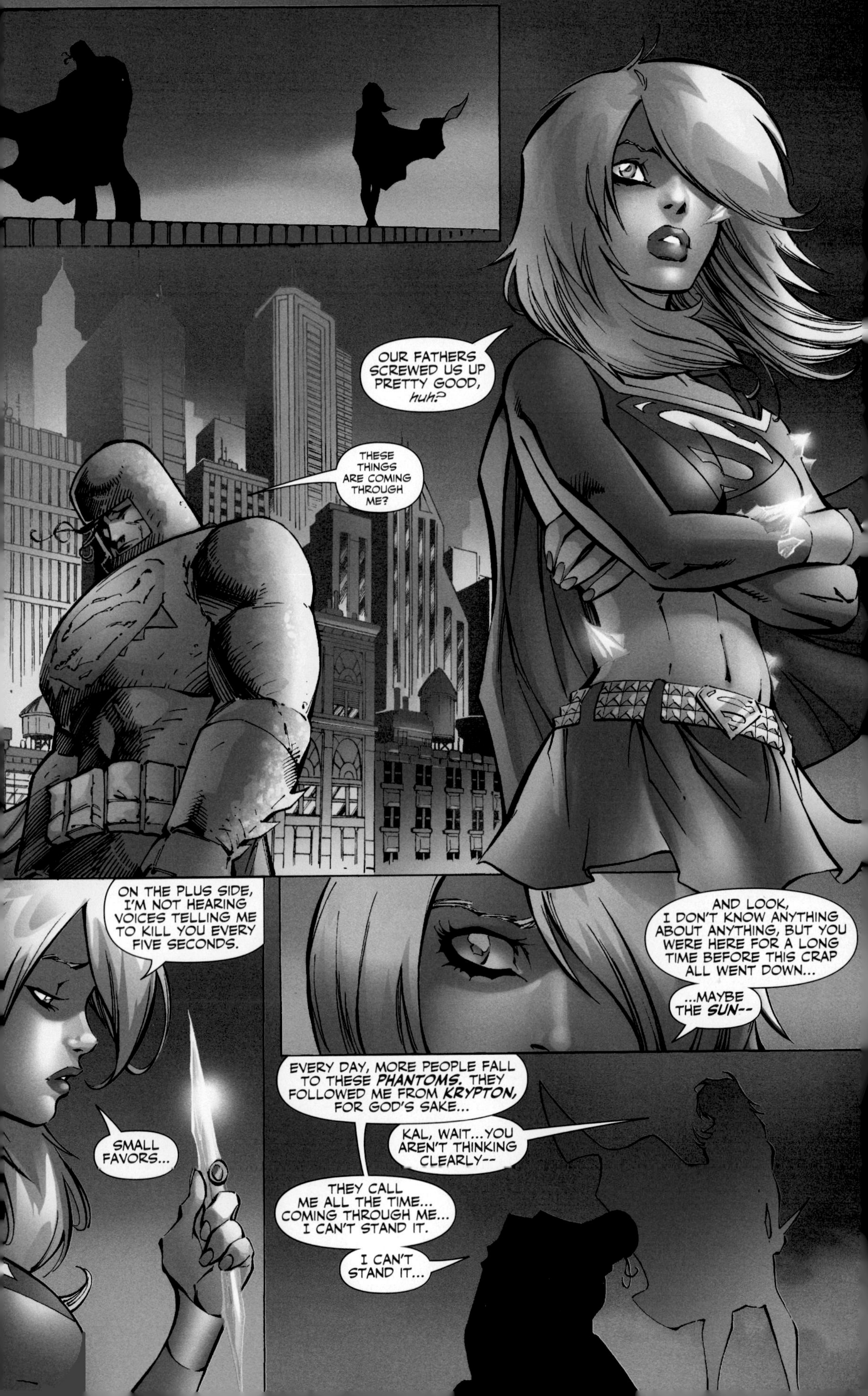

OUR FATHERS SCREWED US UP PRETTY GOOD, *huh?*
THESE THINGS ARE COMING THROUGH ME?
ON THE PLUS SIDE, I'M NOT HEARING VOICES TELLING ME TO KILL YOU EVERY FIVE SECONDS.
SMALL FAVORS...
AND LOOK, I DON'T KNOW ANYTHING ABOUT ANYTHING, BUT YOU WERE HERE FOR A LONG TIME BEFORE THIS CRAP ALL WENT DOWN...
...MAYBE THE ***SUN--***
EVERY DAY, MORE PEOPLE FALL TO THESE ***PHANTOMS.*** THEY FOLLOWED ME FROM ***KRYPTON,*** FOR GOD'S SAKE...
KAL, WAIT...YOU AREN'T THINKING CLEARLY--
THEY CALL ME ALL THE TIME... COMING THROUGH ME... I CAN'T STAND IT.
I CAN'T STAND IT...

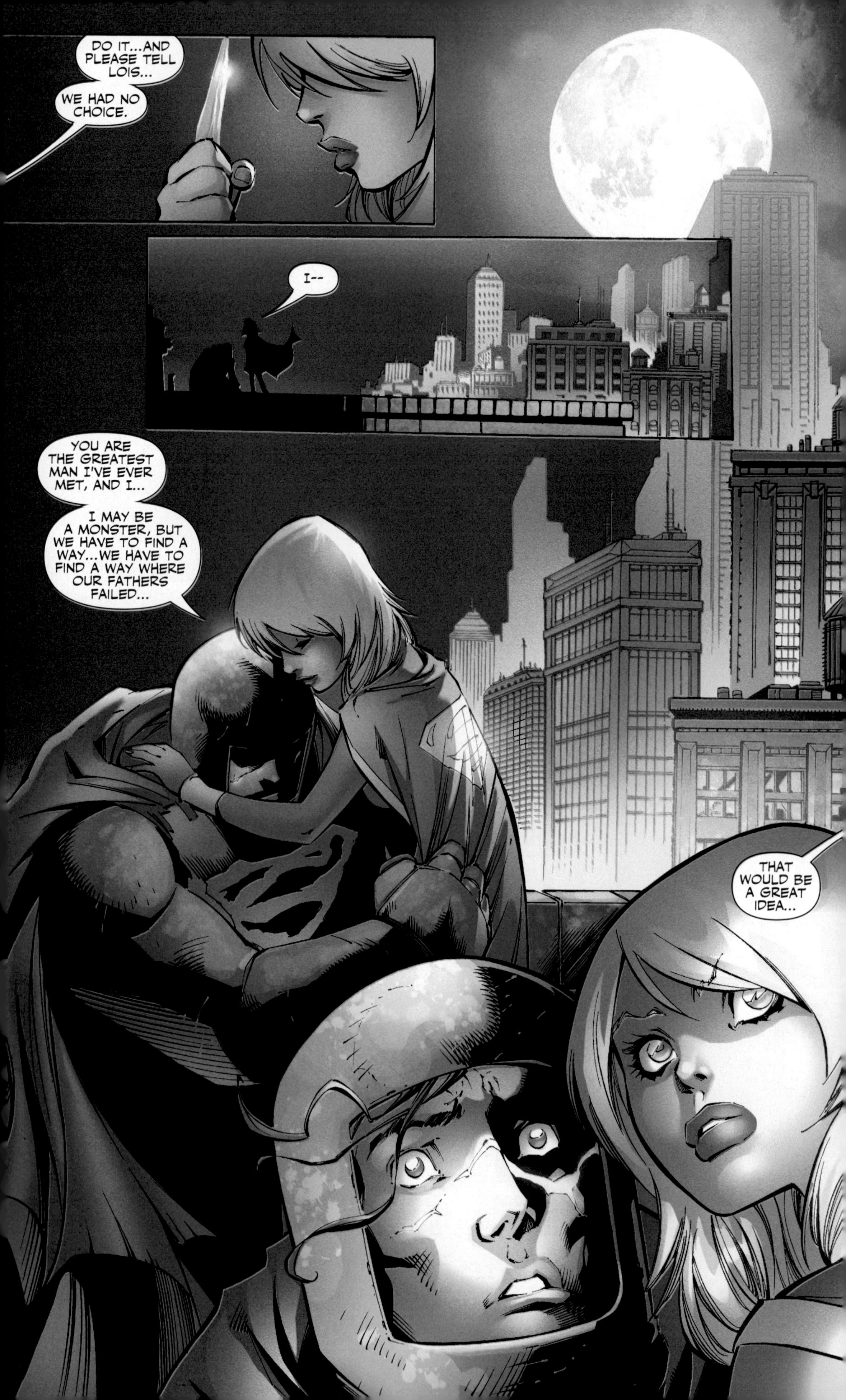
DO IT...AND PLEASE TELL LOIS...
WE HAD NO CHOICE.
I--
YOU ARE THE GREATEST MAN I'VE EVER MET, AND I...
I MAY BE A MONSTER, BUT WE HAVE TO FIND A WAY...WE HAVE TO FIND A WAY WHERE OUR FATHERS FAILED...
THAT WOULD BE A GREAT IDEA...

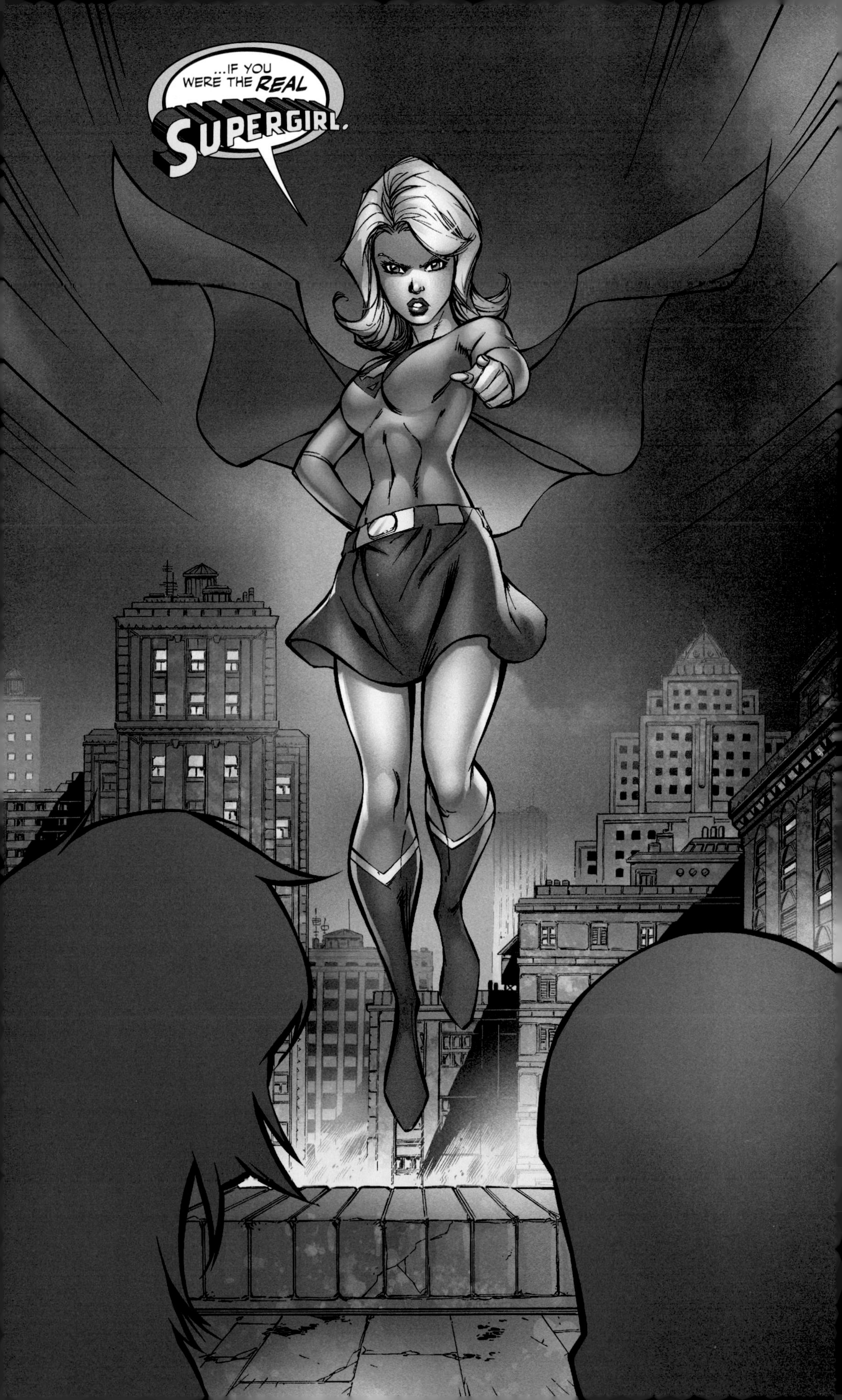
...IF YOU WERE THE REAL SUPERGIRL.

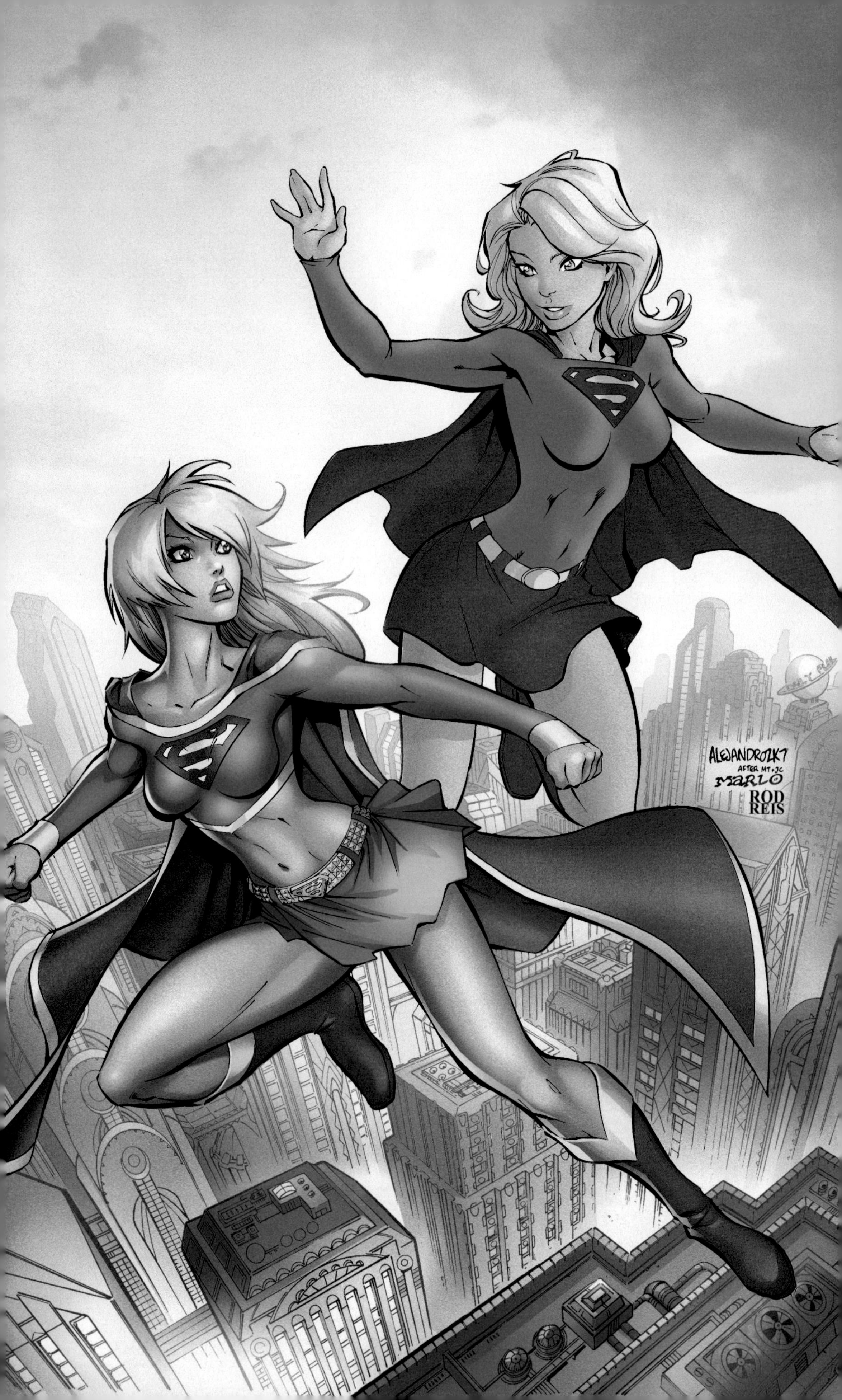
ALEJANDRO2K7
AFTER MT+JC
MARLO
ROD
REIS

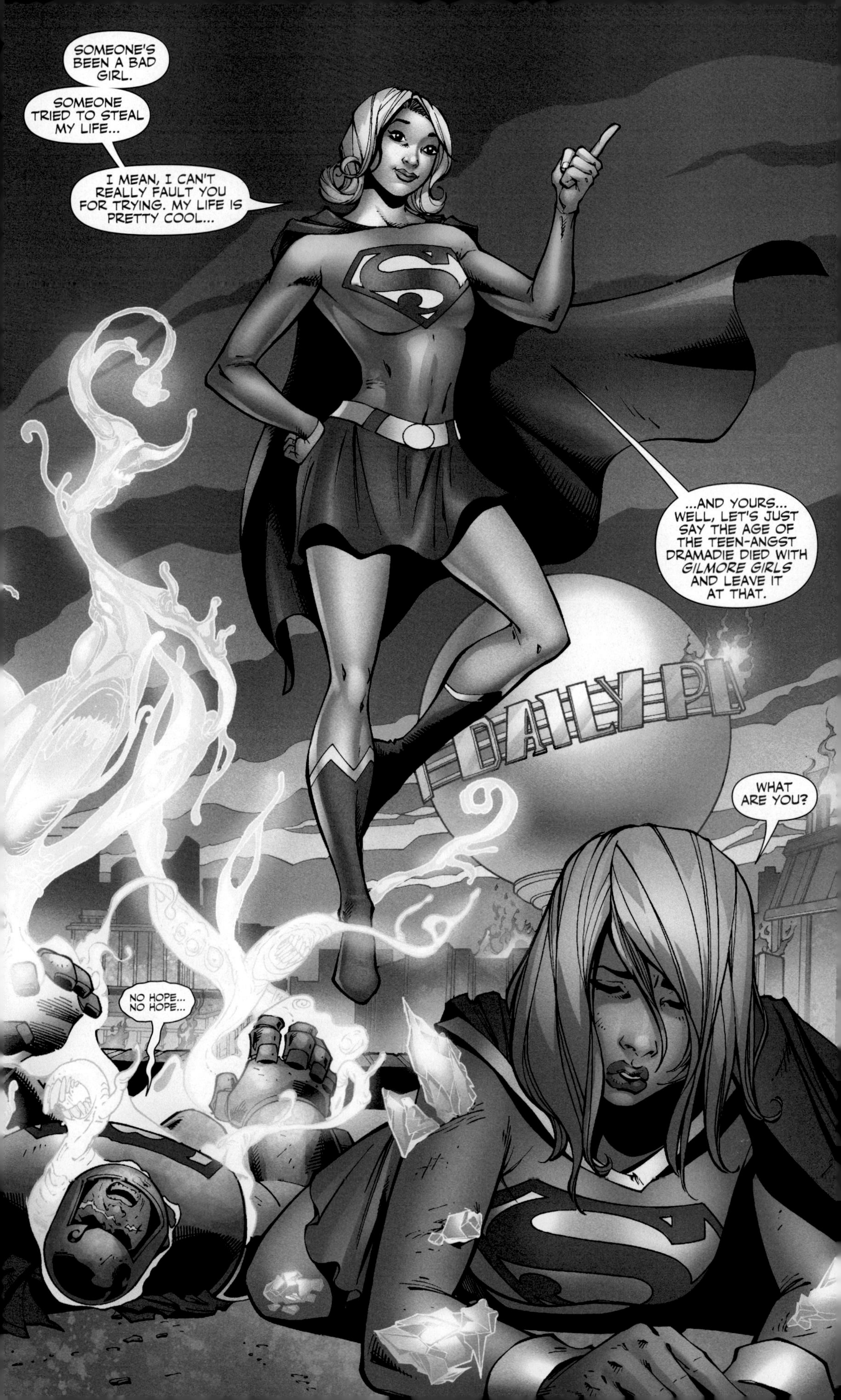
SOMEONE'S BEEN A BAD GIRL.
SOMEONE TRIED TO STEAL MY LIFE...
I MEAN, I CAN'T REALLY FAULT YOU FOR TRYING. MY LIFE IS PRETTY COOL...
...AND YOURS... WELL, LET'S JUST SAY THE AGE OF THE TEEN-ANGST DRAMADIE DIED WITH *GILMORE GIRLS* AND LEAVE IT AT THAT.
DAILY PL
WHAT ARE YOU?
NO HOPE... NO HOPE...

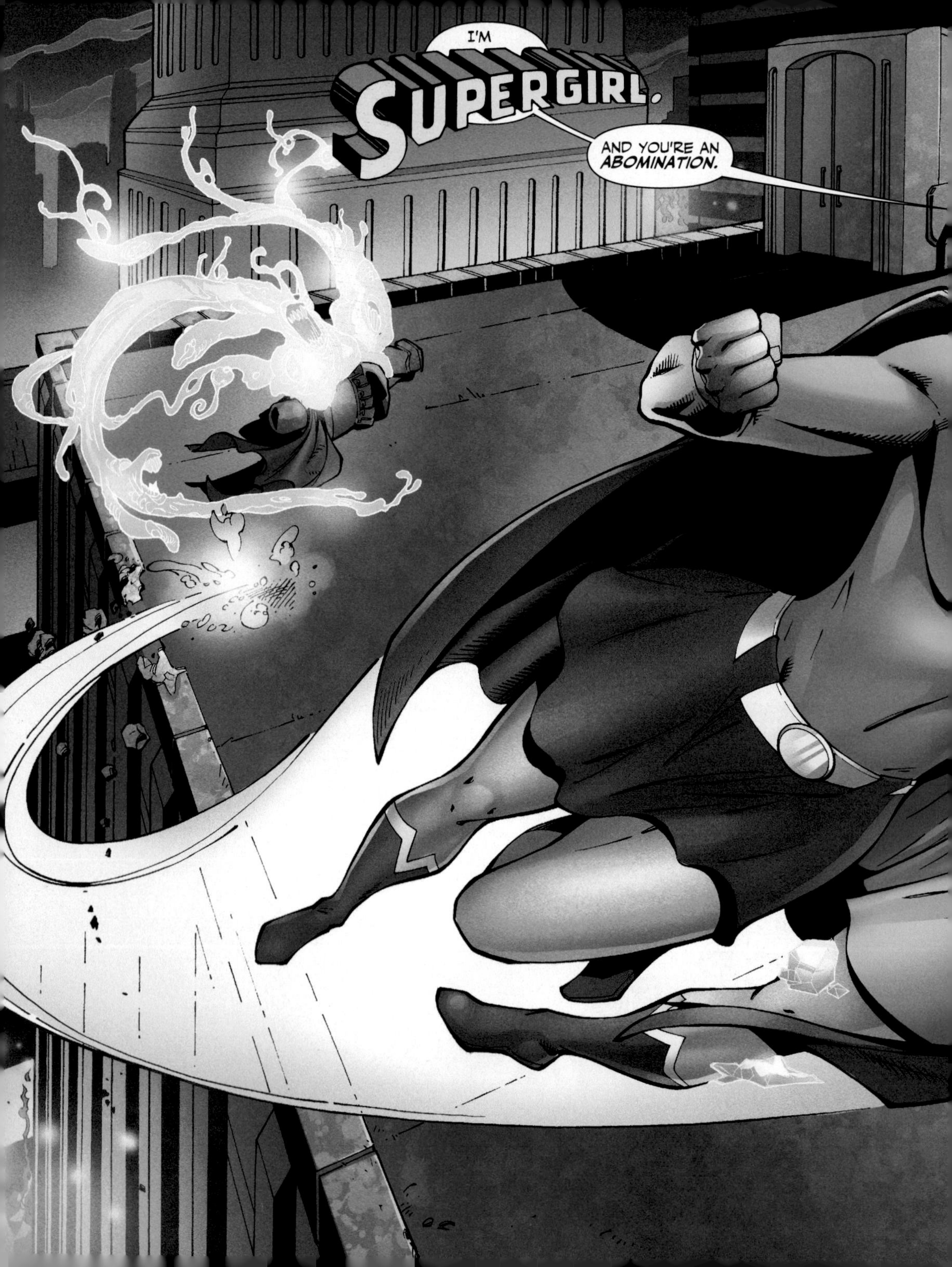

I'M
SUPERGIRL.
AND YOU'RE AN ABOMINATION.

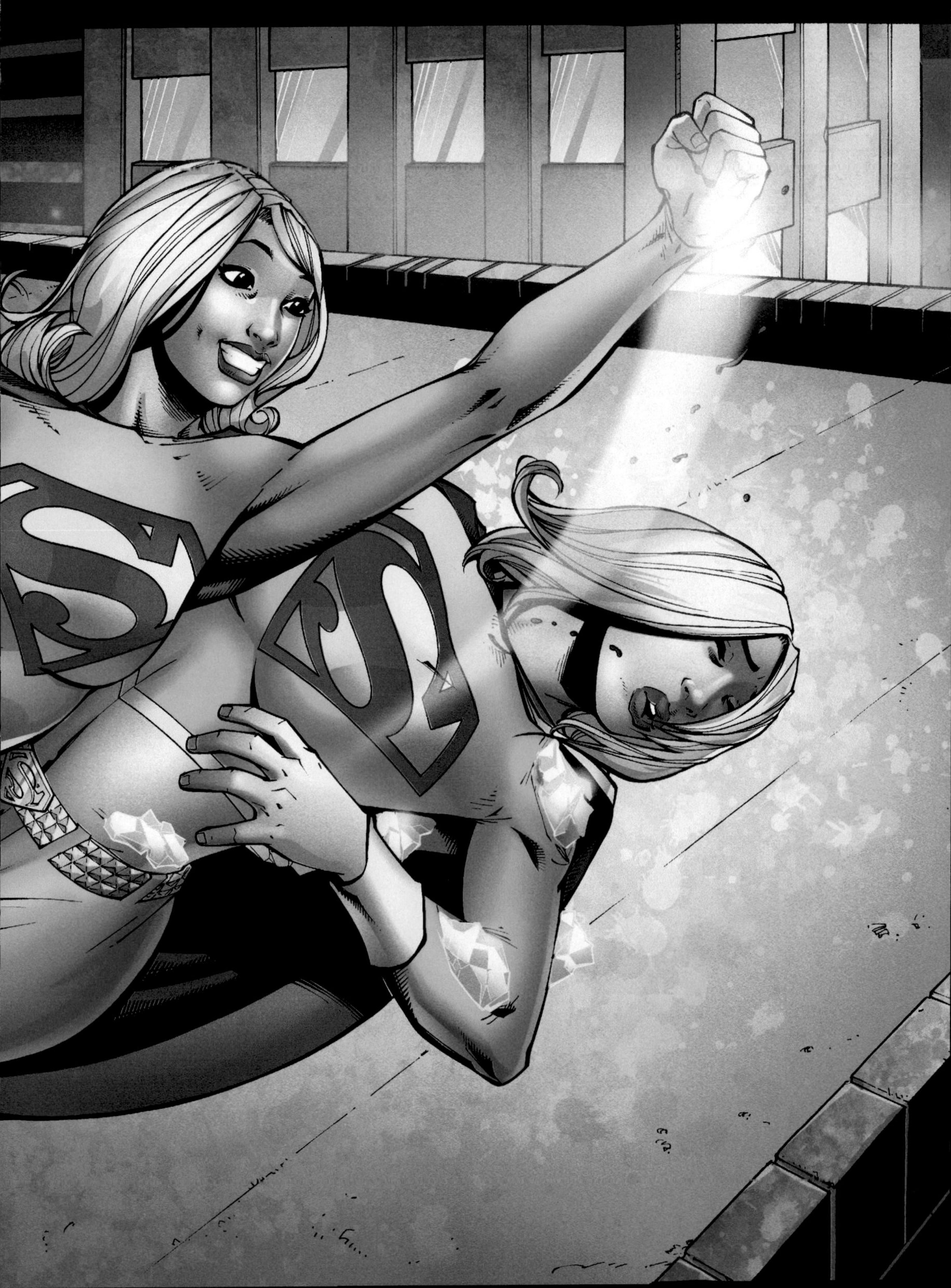

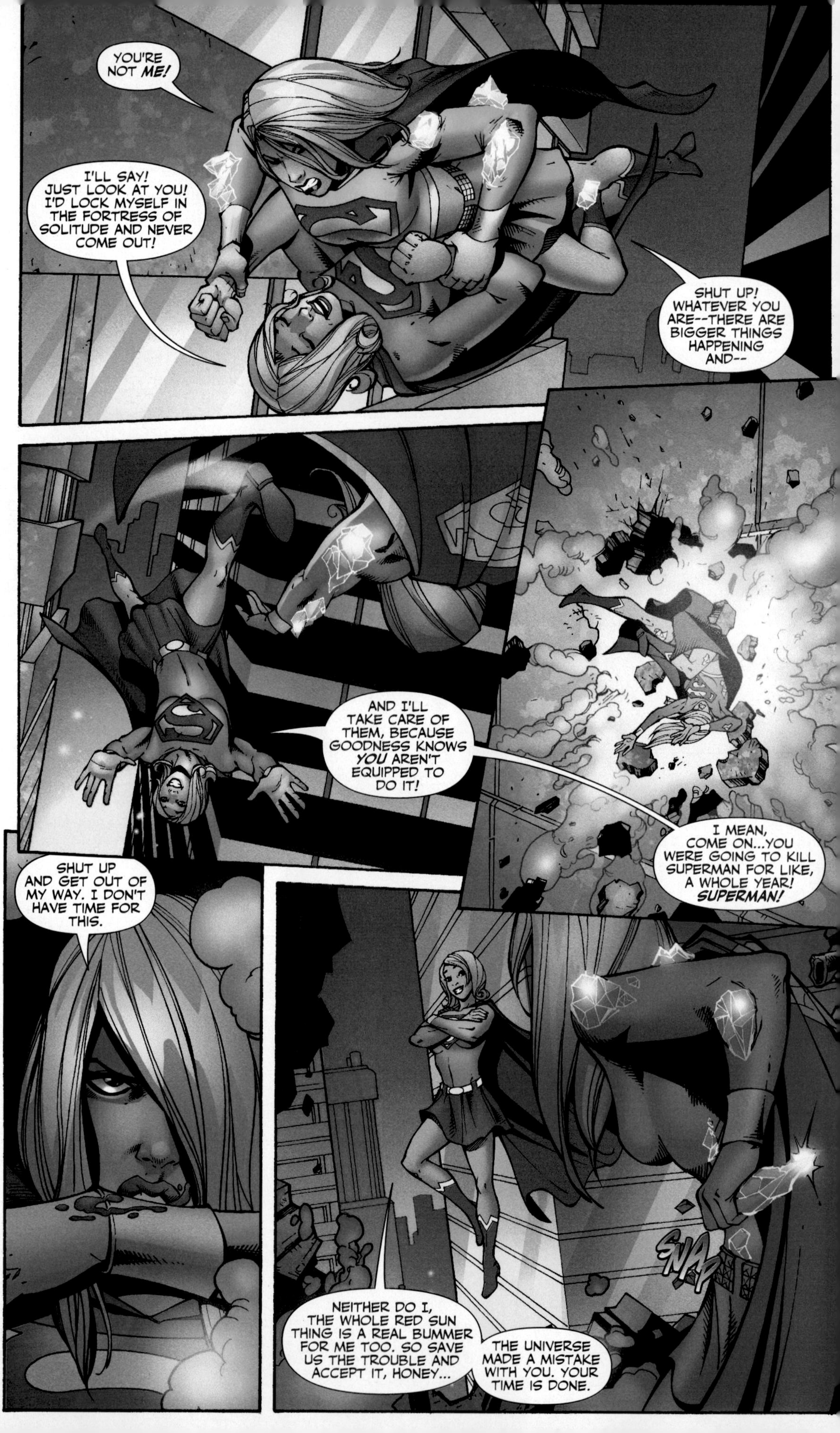

YOU'RE NOT ME!
I'LL SAY! JUST LOOK AT YOU! I'D LOCK MYSELF IN THE FORTRESS OF SOLITUDE AND NEVER COME OUT!
SHUT UP! WHATEVER YOU ARE--THERE ARE BIGGER THINGS HAPPENING AND--
AND I'LL TAKE CARE OF THEM, BECAUSE GOODNESS KNOWS YOU AREN'T EQUIPPED TO DO IT!
I MEAN, COME ON...YOU WERE GOING TO KILL SUPERMAN FOR LIKE, A WHOLE YEAR! SUPERMAN!
SHUT UP AND GET OUT OF MY WAY. I DON'T HAVE TIME FOR THIS.
NEITHER DO I, THE WHOLE RED SUN THING IS A REAL BUMMER FOR ME TOO. SO SAVE US THE TROUBLE AND ACCEPT IT, HONEY...
THE UNIVERSE MADE A MISTAKE WITH YOU. YOUR TIME IS DONE.
SNAP

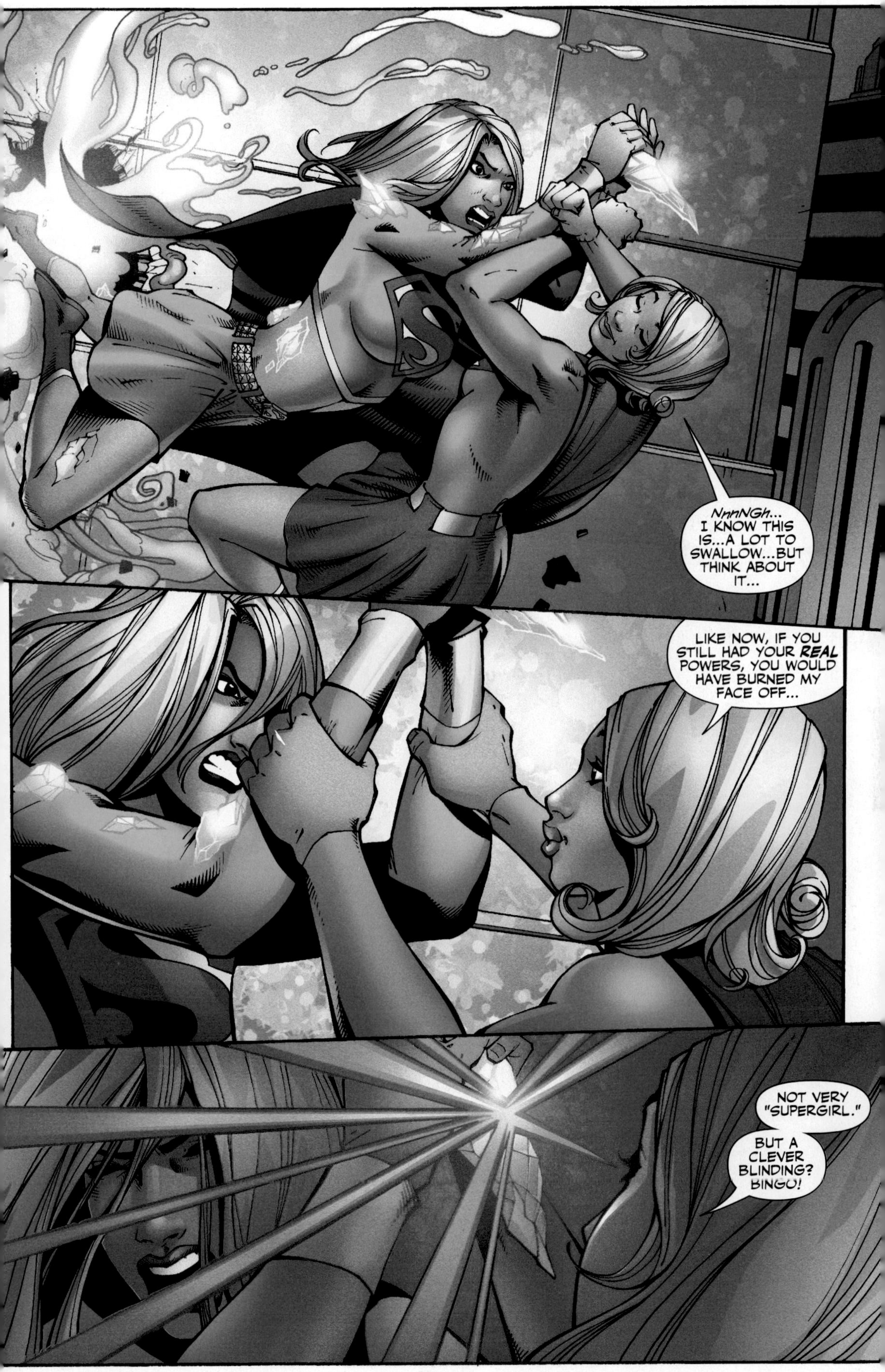
NnnNGh...
I KNOW THIS IS...A LOT TO SWALLOW...BUT THINK ABOUT IT...
LIKE NOW, IF YOU STILL HAD YOUR REAL POWERS, YOU WOULD HAVE BURNED MY FACE OFF...
NOT VERY "SUPERGIRL."
BUT A CLEVER BLINDING? BINGO!

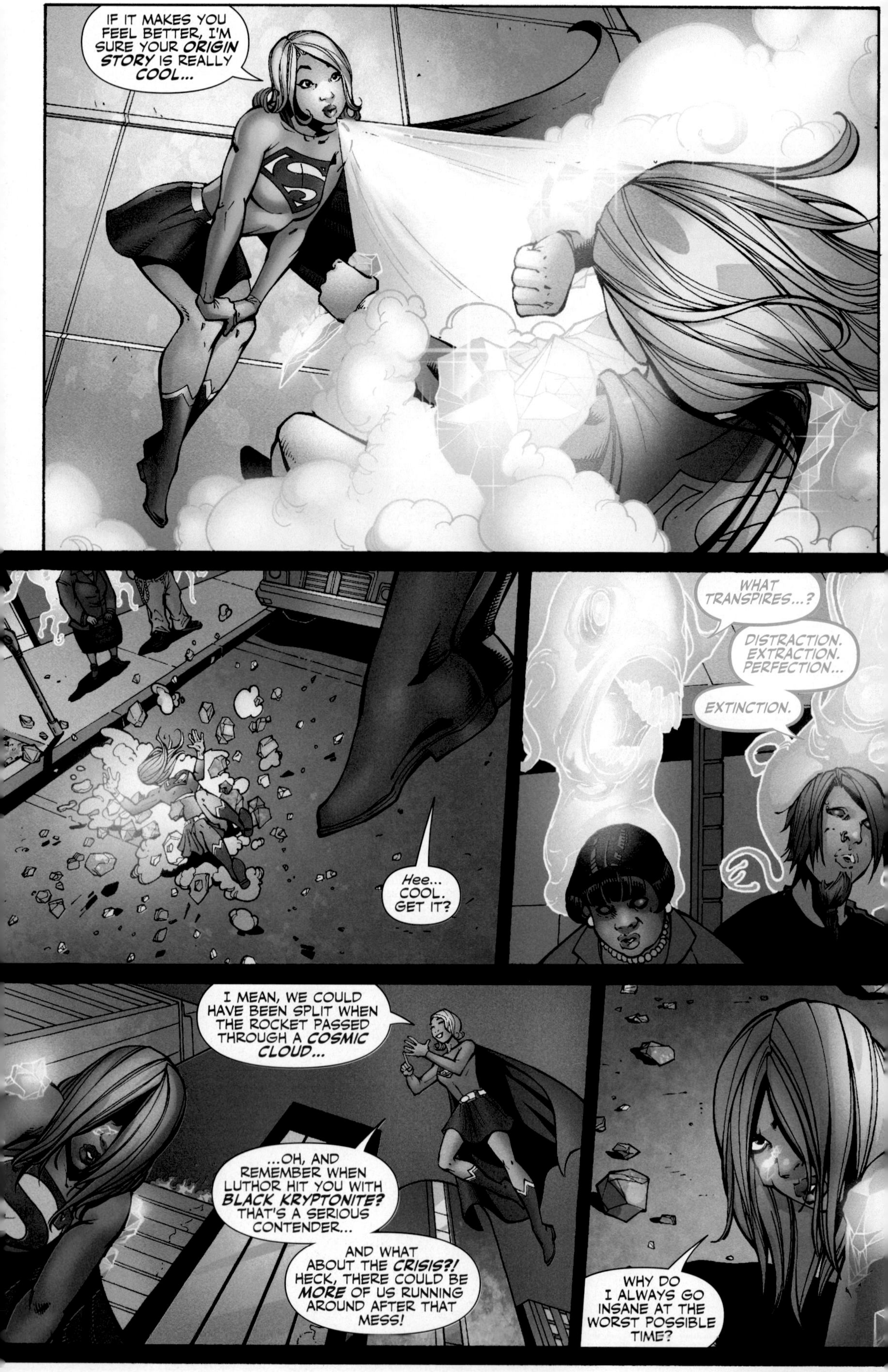
IF IT MAKES YOU FEEL BETTER, I'M SURE YOUR ORIGIN STORY IS REALLY COOL...
Hee... COOL. GET IT?
WHAT TRANSPIRES...?
DISTRACTION. EXTRACTION. PERFECTION...
EXTINCTION.
I MEAN, WE COULD HAVE BEEN SPLIT WHEN THE ROCKET PASSED THROUGH A COSMIC CLOUD...
...OH, AND REMEMBER WHEN LUTHOR HIT YOU WITH BLACK KRYPTONITE? THAT'S A SERIOUS CONTENDER...
AND WHAT ABOUT THE CRISIS?! HECK, THERE COULD BE MORE OF US RUNNING AROUND AFTER THAT MESS!
WHY DO I ALWAYS GO INSANE AT THE WORST POSSIBLE TIME?

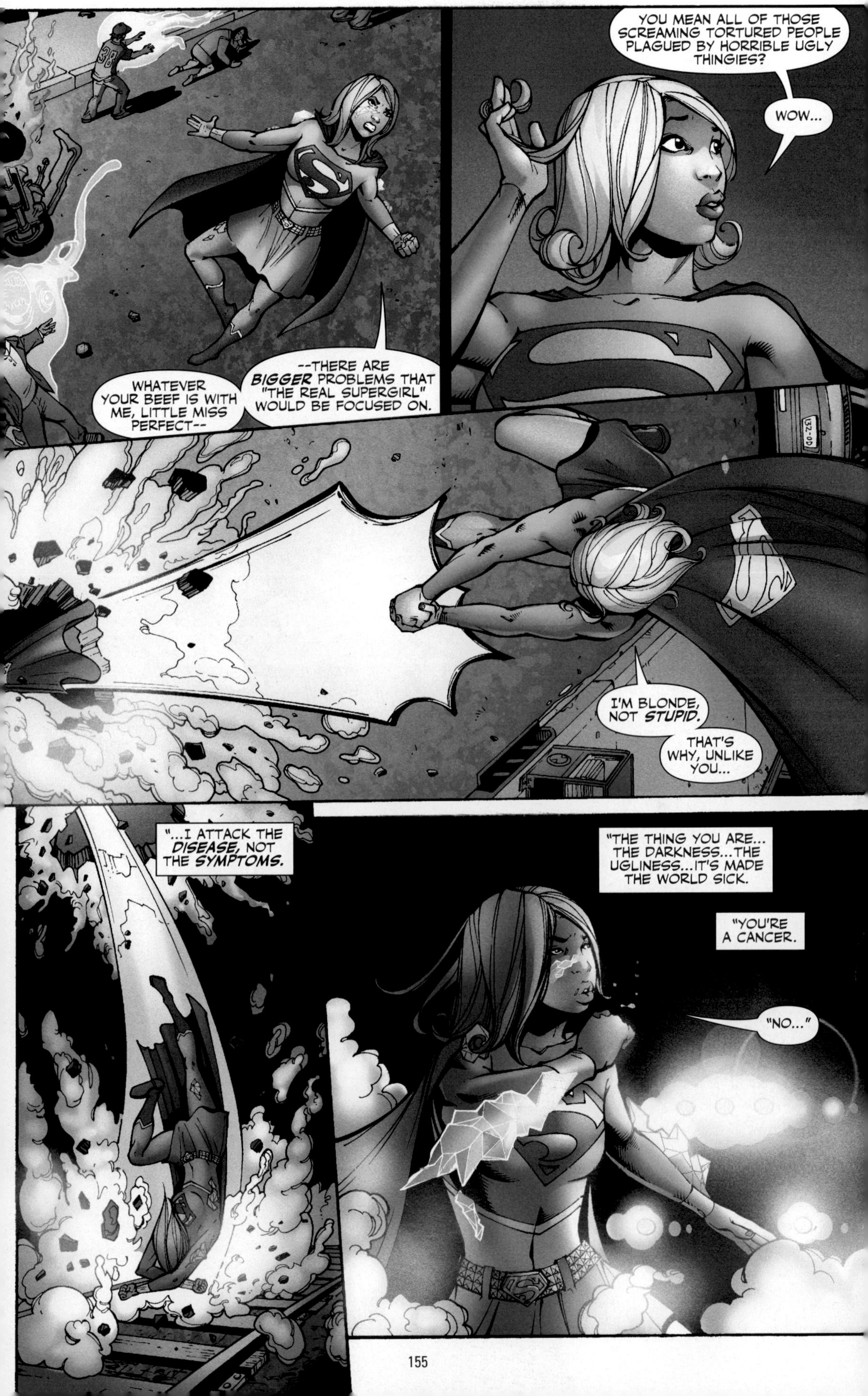
WHATEVER YOUR BEEF IS WITH ME, LITTLE MISS PERFECT--
--THERE ARE BIGGER PROBLEMS THAT "THE REAL SUPERGIRL" WOULD BE FOCUSED ON.
YOU MEAN ALL OF THOSE SCREAMING TORTURED PEOPLE PLAGUED BY HORRIBLE UGLY THINGIES?
WOW...
I'M BLONDE, NOT STUPID.
THAT'S WHY, UNLIKE YOU...
"...I ATTACK THE DISEASE, NOT THE SYMPTOMS.
"THE THING YOU ARE... THE DARKNESS...THE UGLINESS...IT'S MADE THE WORLD SICK.
"YOU'RE A CANCER.
"NO..."

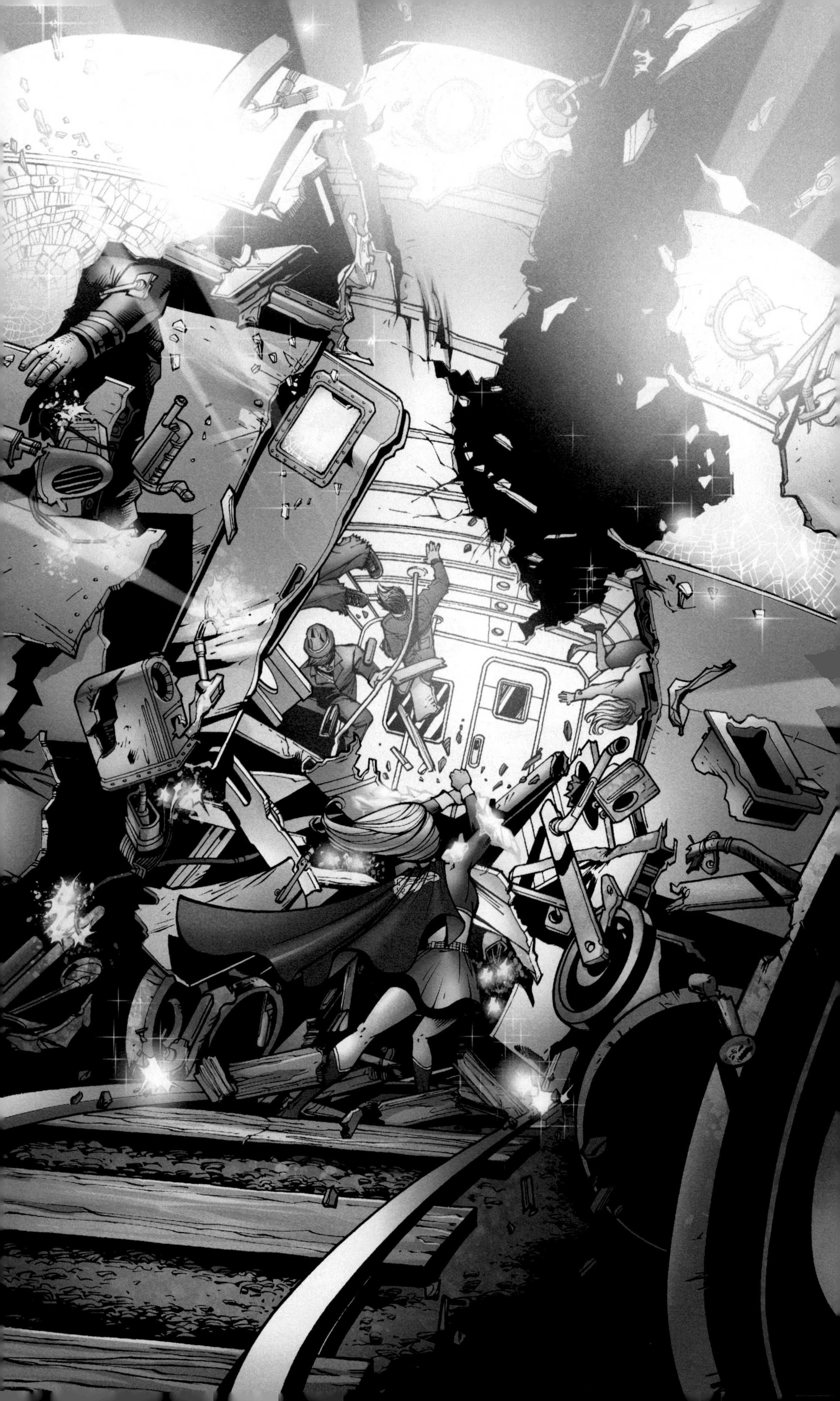

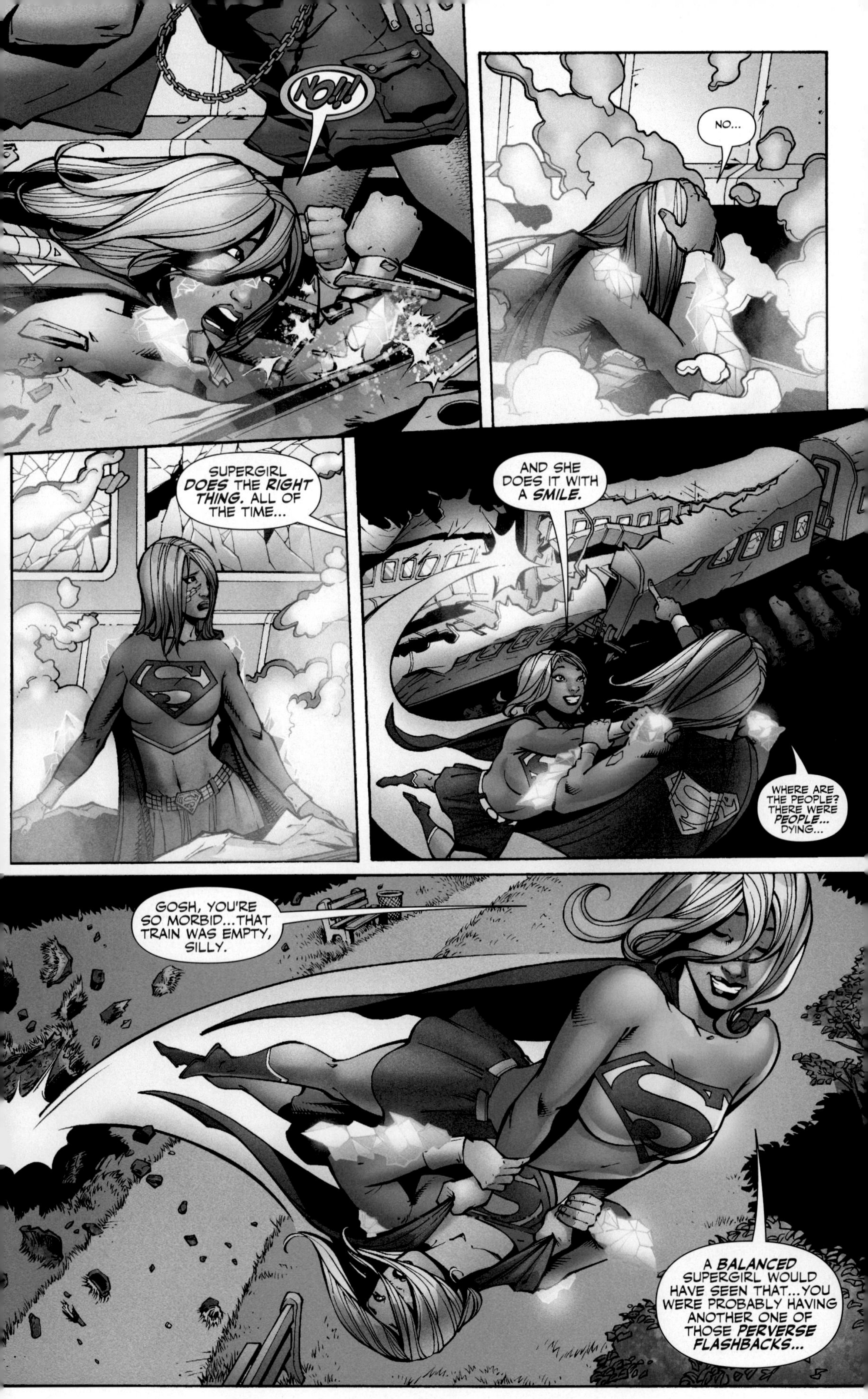
NO!!
NO...
SUPERGIRL DOES THE RIGHT THING. ALL OF THE TIME...
AND SHE DOES IT WITH A SMILE.
WHERE ARE THE PEOPLE? THERE WERE PEOPLE... DYING...
GOSH, YOU'RE SO MORBID...THAT TRAIN WAS EMPTY, SILLY.
A BALANCED SUPERGIRL WOULD HAVE SEEN THAT...YOU WERE PROBABLY HAVING ANOTHER ONE OF THOSE PERVERSE FLASHBACKS...

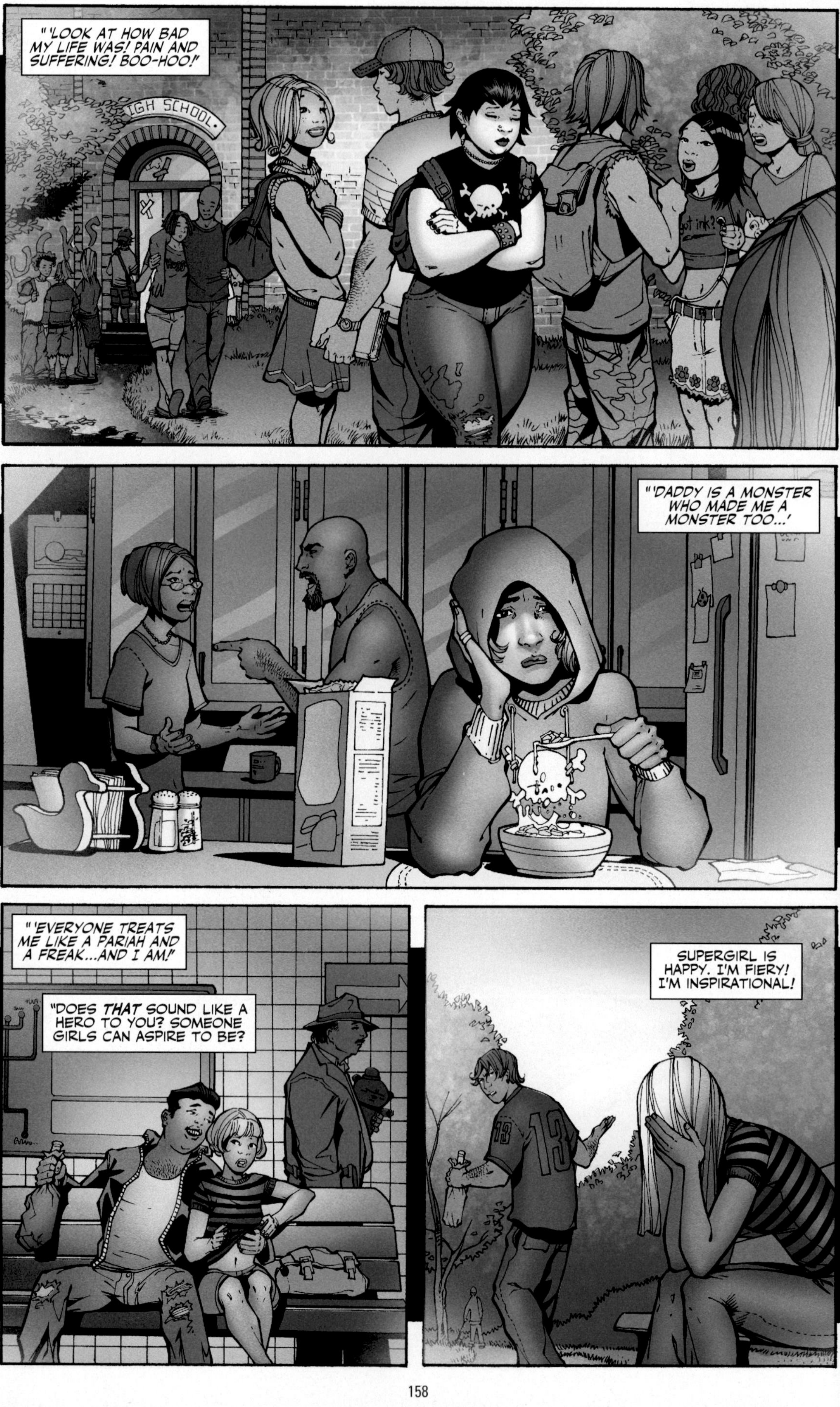

"'LOOK AT HOW BAD MY LIFE WAS! PAIN AND SUFFERING! BOO-HOO!'
IGH SCHOOL
got ink?
"'DADDY IS A MONSTER WHO MADE ME A MONSTER TOO...'
"'EVERYONE TREATS ME LIKE A PARIAH AND A FREAK...AND I AM!'
"DOES THAT SOUND LIKE A HERO TO YOU? SOMEONE GIRLS CAN ASPIRE TO BE?
SUPERGIRL IS HAPPY. I'M FIERY! I'M INSPIRATIONAL!

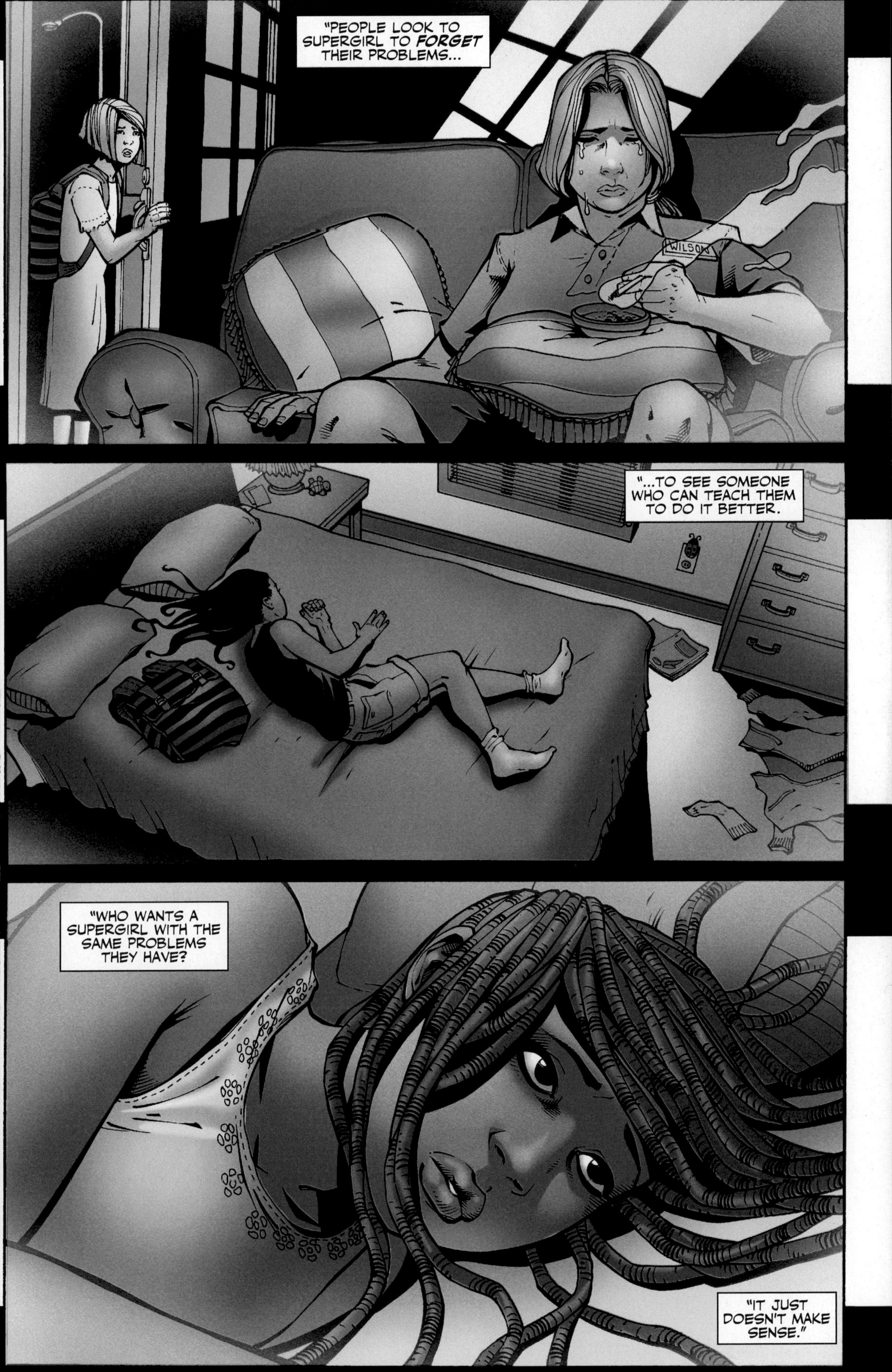
"PEOPLE LOOK TO SUPERGIRL TO FORGET THEIR PROBLEMS...
WILSON
"...TO SEE SOMEONE WHO CAN TEACH THEM TO DO IT BETTER.
"WHO WANTS A SUPERGIRL WITH THE SAME PROBLEMS THEY HAVE?
"IT JUST DOESN'T MAKE SENSE."

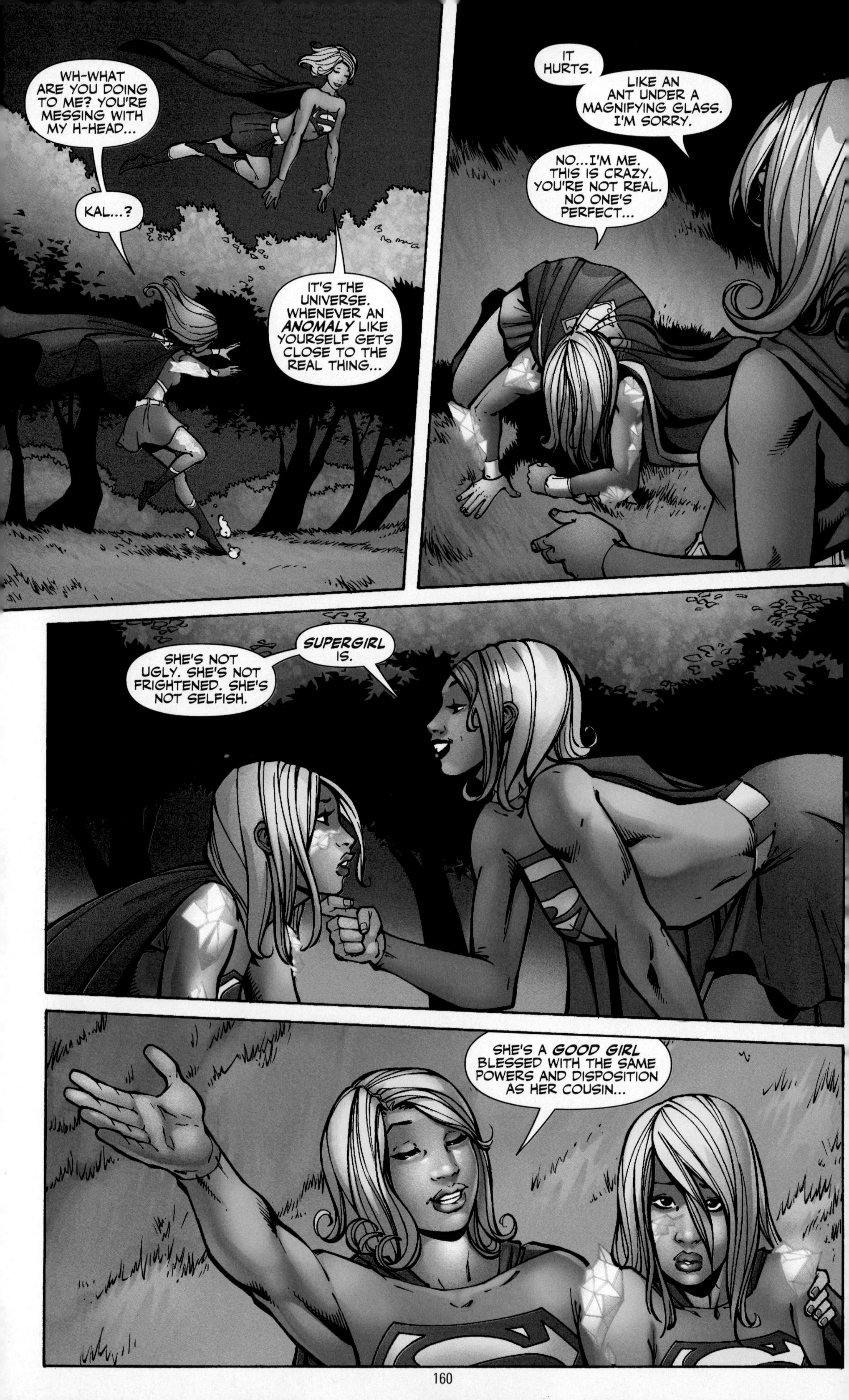

WH-WHAT ARE YOU DOING TO ME? YOU'RE MESSING WITH MY H-HEAD...
KAL...?
IT'S THE UNIVERSE. WHENEVER AN ANOMALY LIKE YOURSELF GETS CLOSE TO THE REAL THING...
IT HURTS.
LIKE AN ANT UNDER A MAGNIFYING GLASS. I'M SORRY.
NO...I'M ME. THIS IS CRAZY. YOU'RE NOT REAL. NO ONE'S PERFECT...
SUPERGIRL IS.
SHE'S NOT UGLY. SHE'S NOT FRIGHTENED. SHE'S NOT SELFISH.
SHE'S A GOOD GIRL BLESSED WITH THE SAME POWERS AND DISPOSITION AS HER COUSIN...

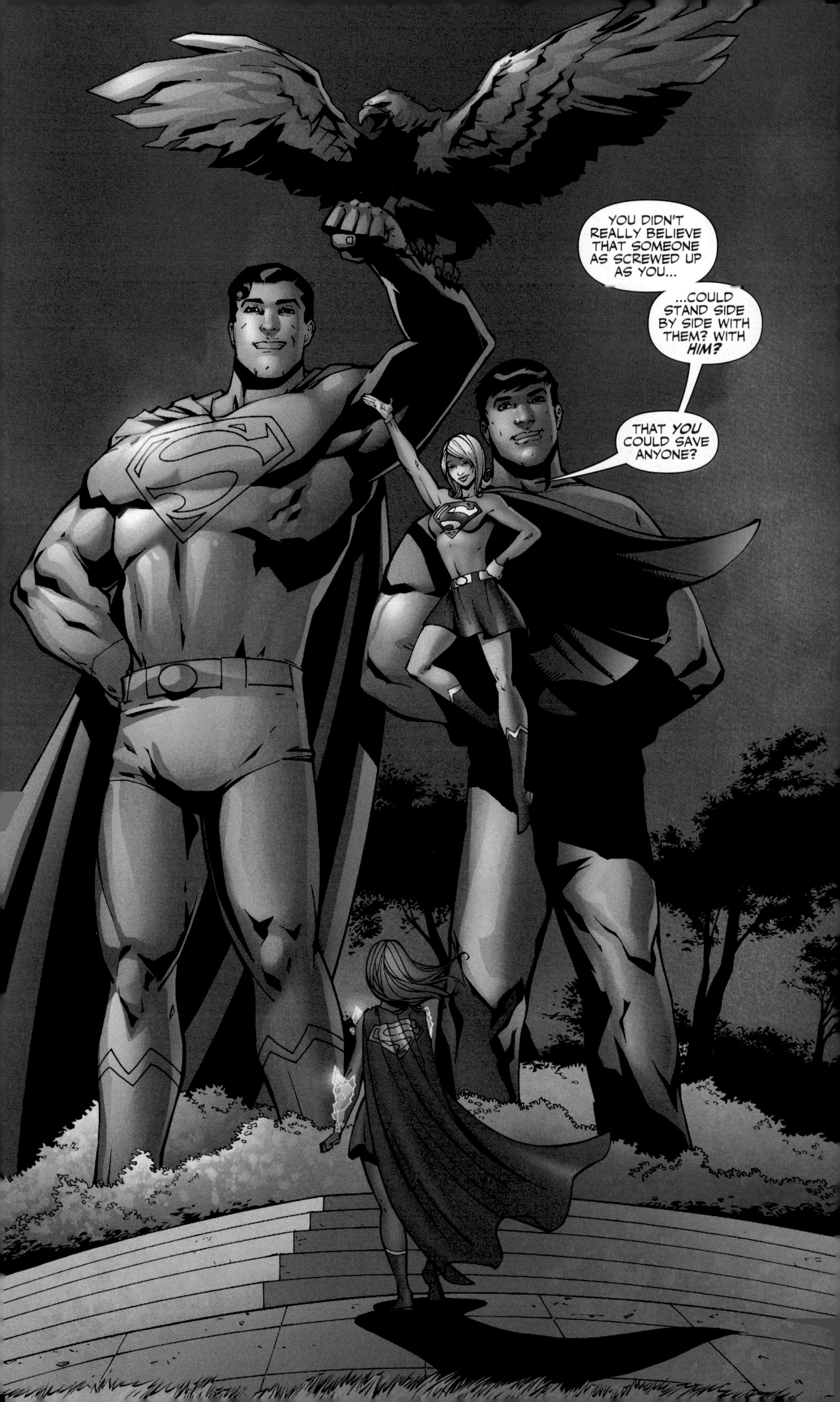
YOU DIDN'T REALLY BELIEVE THAT SOMEONE AS SCREWED UP AS YOU...
...COULD STAND SIDE BY SIDE WITH THEM? WITH HIM?
THAT YOU COULD SAVE ANYONE?

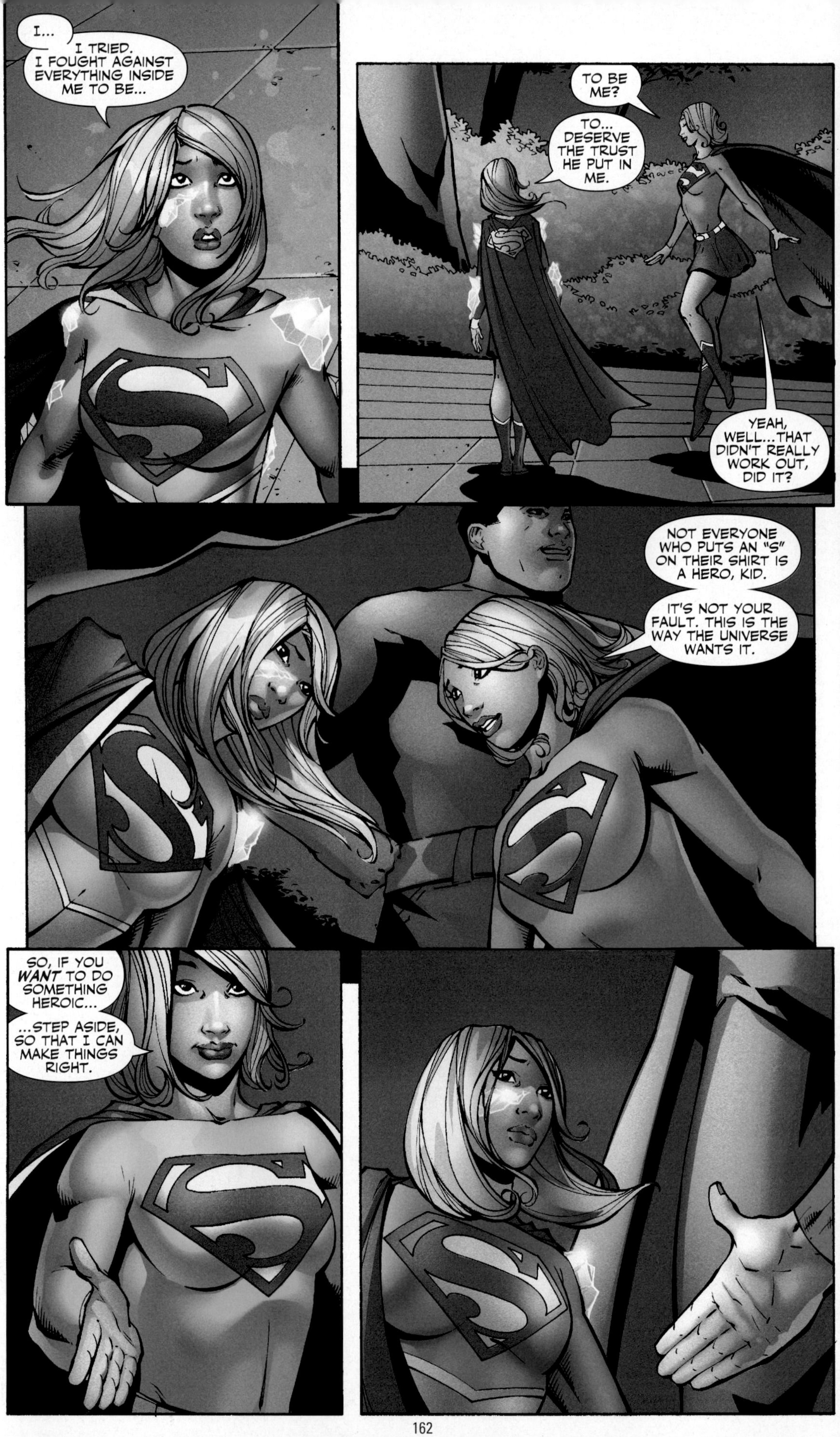
I...
I TRIED. I FOUGHT AGAINST EVERYTHING INSIDE ME TO BE...
TO BE ME?
TO... DESERVE THE TRUST HE PUT IN ME.
YEAH, WELL...THAT DIDN'T REALLY WORK OUT, DID IT?
NOT EVERYONE WHO PUTS AN "S" ON THEIR SHIRT IS A HERO, KID.
IT'S NOT YOUR FAULT. THIS IS THE WAY THE UNIVERSE WANTS IT.
SO, IF YOU *WANT* TO DO SOMETHING HEROIC...
...STEP ASIDE, SO THAT I CAN MAKE THINGS RIGHT.

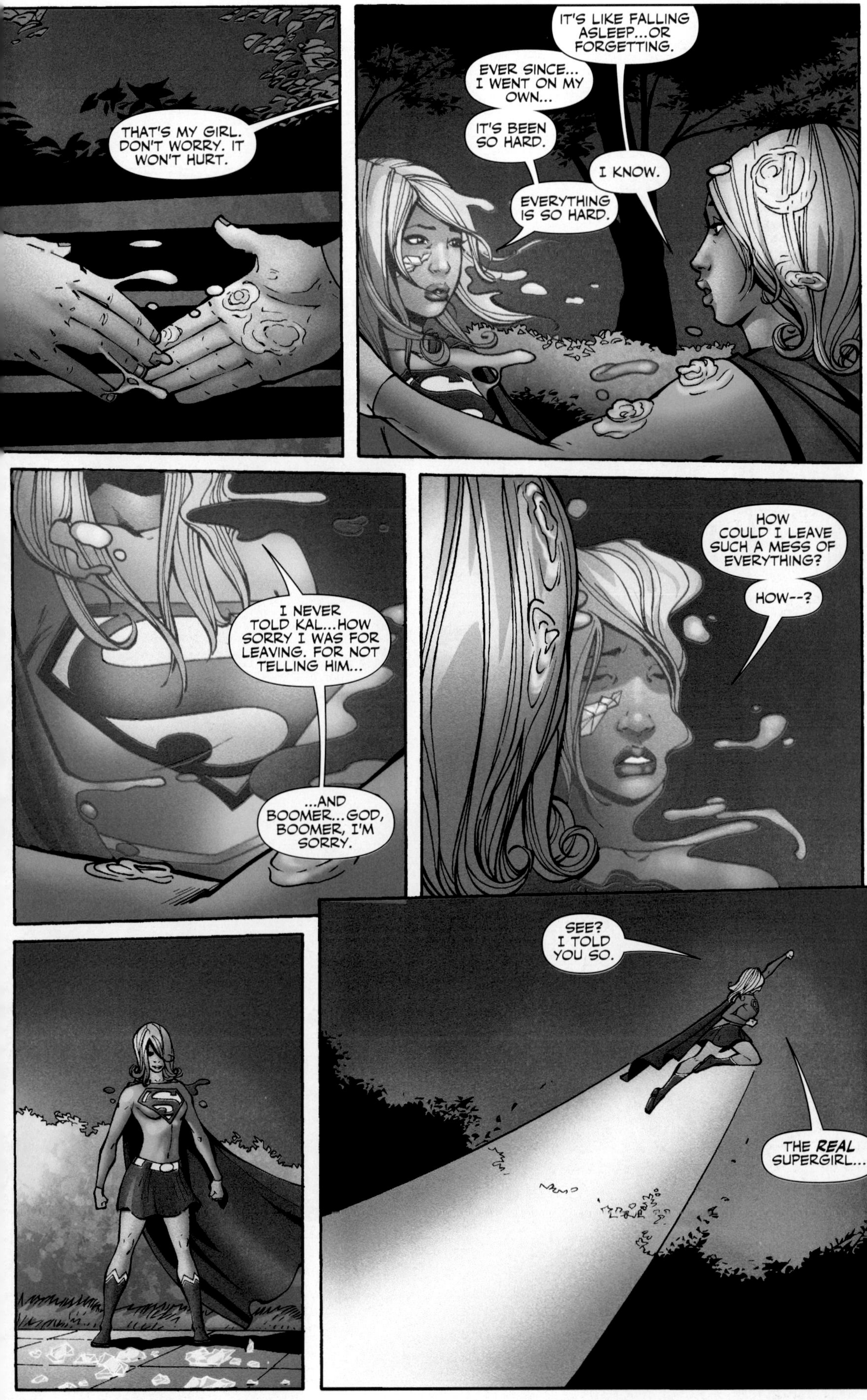

THAT'S MY GIRL. DON'T WORRY. IT WON'T HURT.
EVER SINCE... I WENT ON MY OWN...
IT'S BEEN SO HARD.
EVERYTHING IS SO HARD.
IT'S LIKE FALLING ASLEEP...OR FORGETTING.
I KNOW.
I NEVER TOLD KAL...HOW SORRY I WAS FOR LEAVING. FOR NOT TELLING HIM...
...AND BOOMER...GOD, BOOMER, I'M SORRY.
HOW COULD I LEAVE SUCH A MESS OF EVERYTHING?
HOW--?
SEE? I TOLD YOU SO.
THE REAL SUPERGIRL...

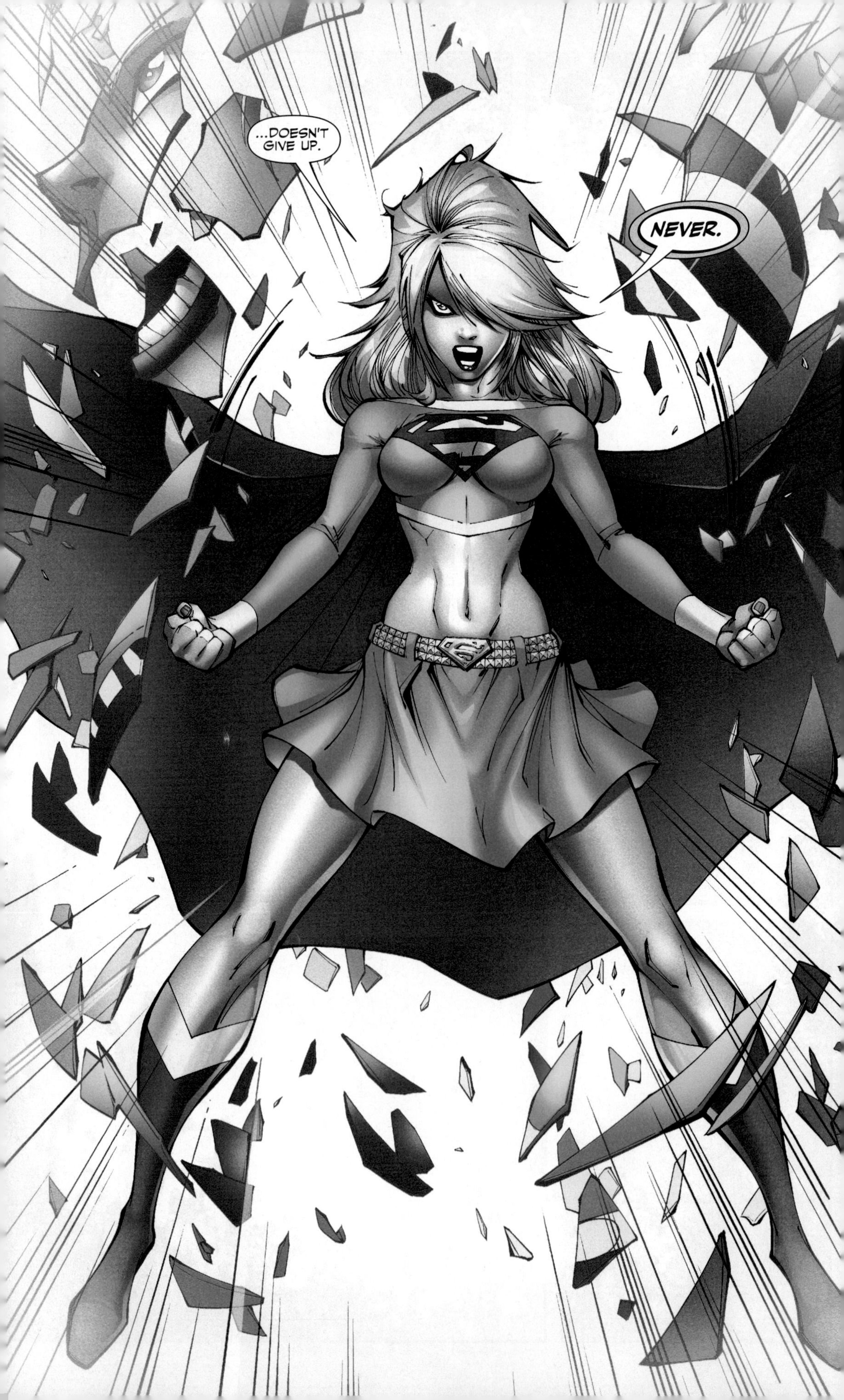
...DOESN'T GIVE UP.
NEVER.

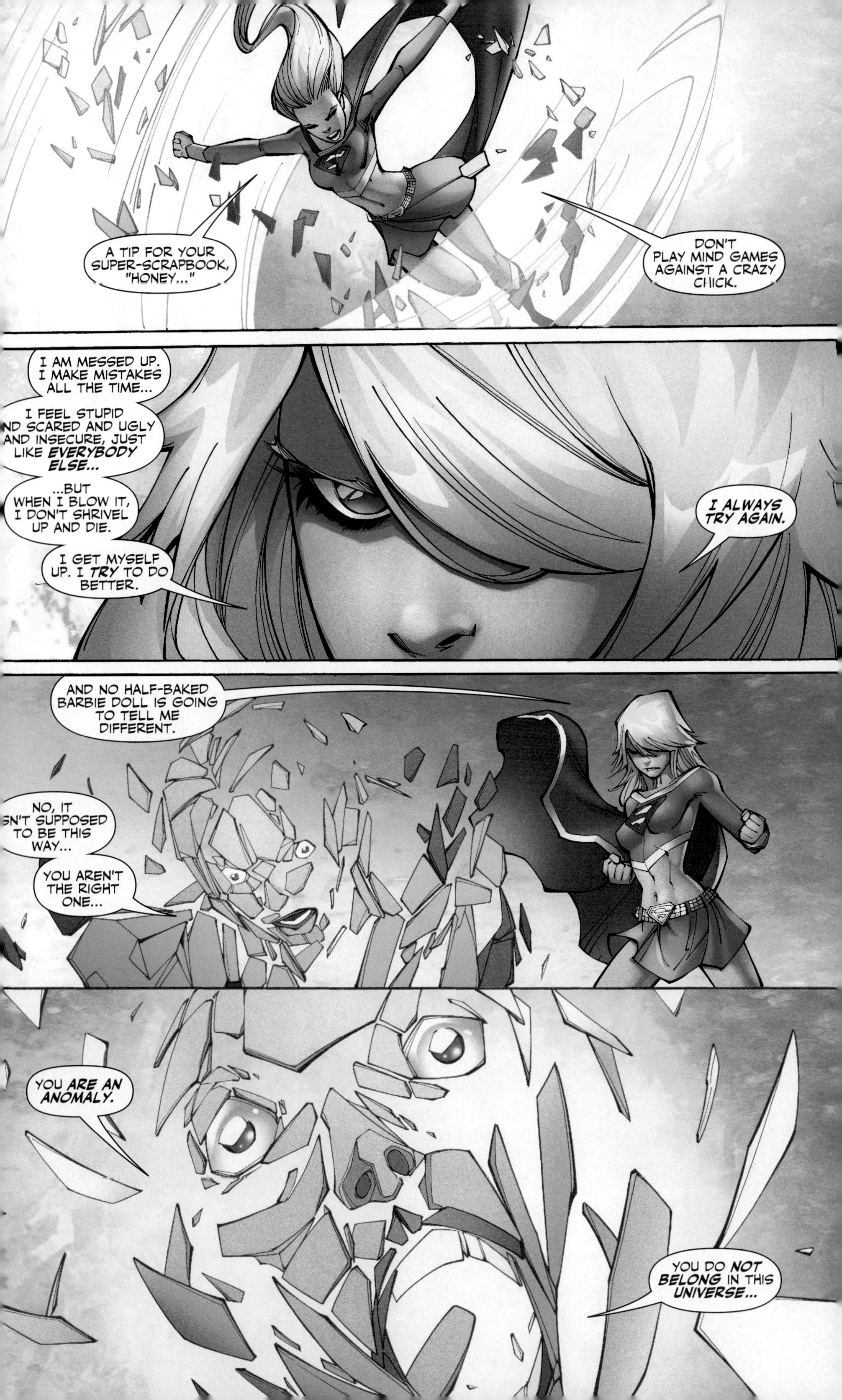
A TIP FOR YOUR SUPER-SCRAPBOOK, "HONEY..."
DON'T PLAY MIND GAMES AGAINST A CRAZY CHICK.
I AM MESSED UP. I MAKE MISTAKES ALL THE TIME...
I FEEL STUPID ND SCARED AND UGLY AND INSECURE, JUST LIKE EVERYBODY ELSE...
...BUT WHEN I BLOW IT, I DON'T SHRIVEL UP AND DIE.
I GET MYSELF UP. I TRY TO DO BETTER.
I ALWAYS TRY AGAIN.
AND NO HALF-BAKED BARBIE DOLL IS GOING TO TELL ME DIFFERENT.
NO, IT SN'T SUPPOSED TO BE THIS WAY...
YOU AREN'T THE RIGHT ONE...
YOU ARE AN ANOMALY.
YOU DO NOT BELONG IN THIS UNIVERSE...

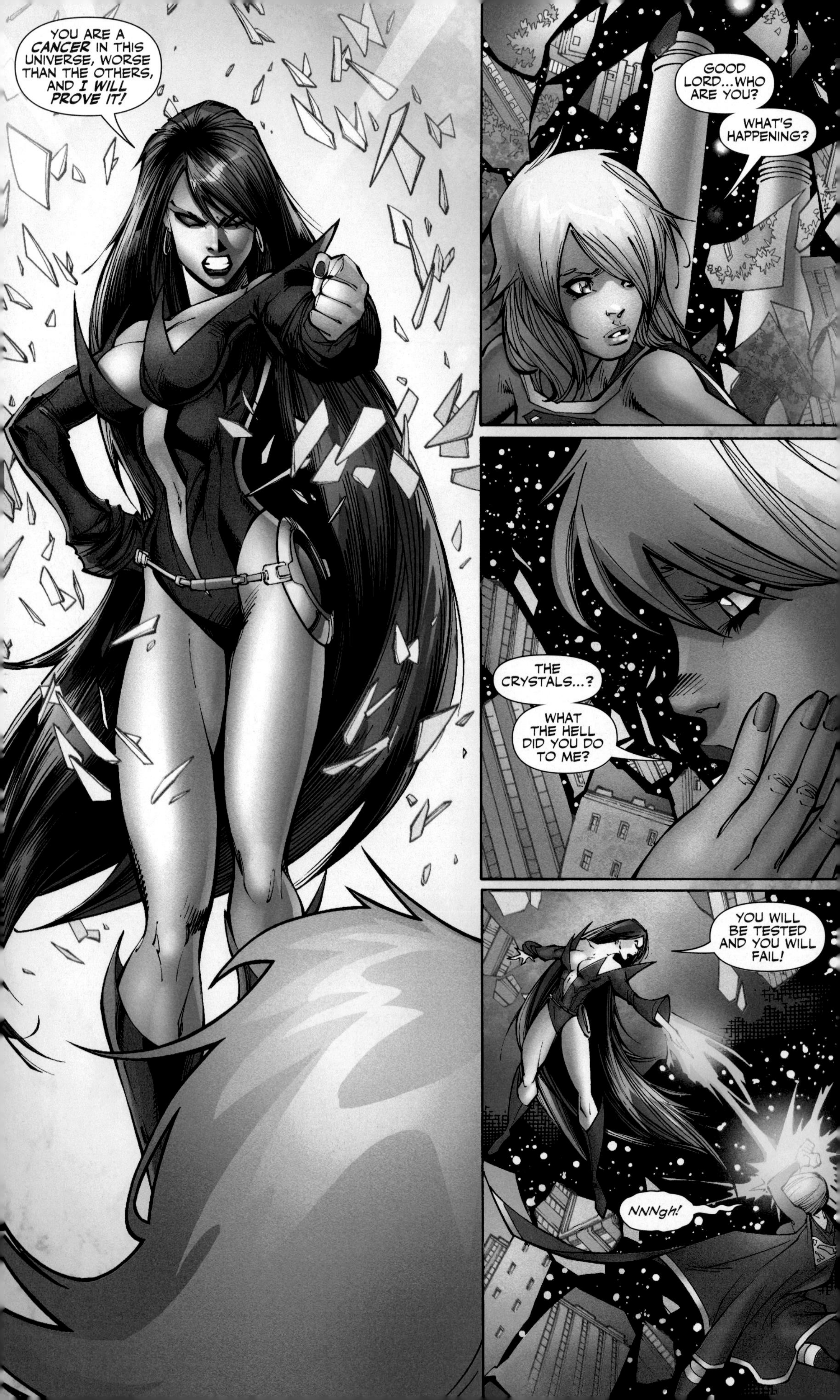
YOU ARE A CANCER IN THIS UNIVERSE, WORSE THAN THE OTHERS, AND I WILL PROVE IT!
GOOD LORD...WHO ARE YOU?
WHAT'S HAPPENING?
THE CRYSTALS...?
WHAT THE HELL DID YOU DO TO ME?
YOU WILL BE TESTED AND YOU WILL FAIL!
NNNgh!

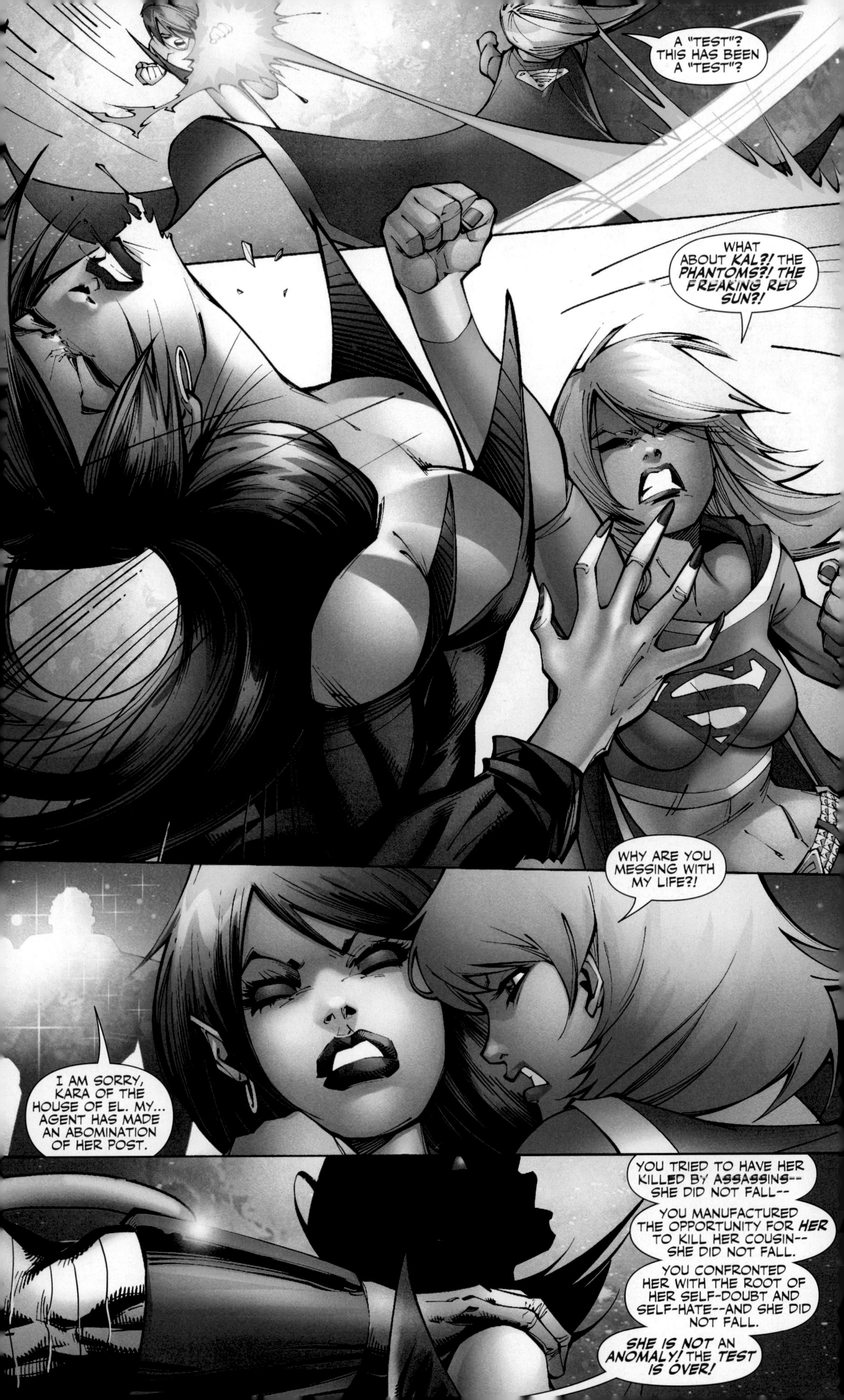
A "TEST"? THIS HAS BEEN A "TEST"?
WHAT ABOUT KAL?! THE PHANTOMS?! THE FREAKING RED SUN?!
WHY ARE YOU MESSING WITH MY LIFE?!
I AM SORRY, KARA OF THE HOUSE OF EL. MY... AGENT HAS MADE AN ABOMINATION OF HER POST.
YOU TRIED TO HAVE HER KILLED BY ASSASSINS-- SHE DID NOT FALL--
YOU MANUFACTURED THE OPPORTUNITY FOR HER TO KILL HER COUSIN-- SHE DID NOT FALL.
YOU CONFRONTED HER WITH THE ROOT OF HER SELF-DOUBT AND SELF-HATE--AND SHE DID NOT FALL.
SHE IS NOT AN ANOMALY! THE TEST IS OVER!

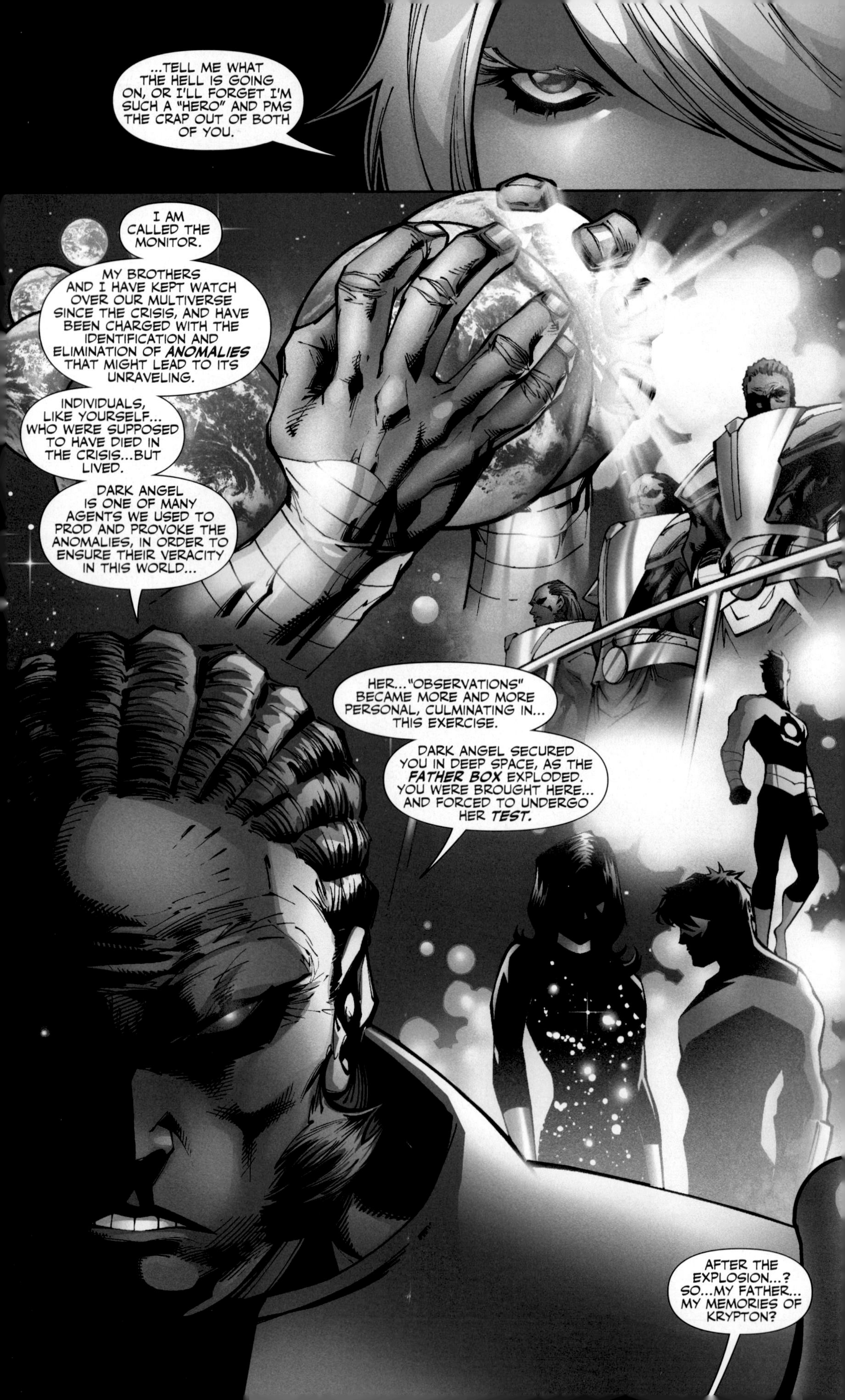
...TELL ME WHAT THE HELL IS GOING ON, OR I'LL FORGET I'M SUCH A "HERO" AND PMS THE CRAP OUT OF BOTH OF YOU.
I AM CALLED THE MONITOR.
MY BROTHERS AND I HAVE KEPT WATCH OVER OUR MULTIVERSE SINCE THE CRISIS, AND HAVE BEEN CHARGED WITH THE IDENTIFICATION AND ELIMINATION OF *ANOMALIES* THAT MIGHT LEAD TO ITS UNRAVELING.
INDIVIDUALS, LIKE YOURSELF... WHO WERE SUPPOSED TO HAVE DIED IN THE CRISIS...BUT LIVED.
DARK ANGEL IS ONE OF MANY AGENTS WE USED TO PROD AND PROVOKE THE ANOMALIES, IN ORDER TO ENSURE THEIR VERACITY IN THIS WORLD...
HER..."OBSERVATIONS" BECAME MORE AND MORE PERSONAL, CULMINATING IN... THIS EXERCISE.
DARK ANGEL SECURED YOU IN DEEP SPACE, AS THE **FATHER BOX** EXPLODED. YOU WERE BROUGHT HERE... AND FORCED TO UNDERGO HER ***TEST.***
AFTER THE EXPLOSION...? SO...MY FATHER... MY MEMORIES OF KRYPTON?

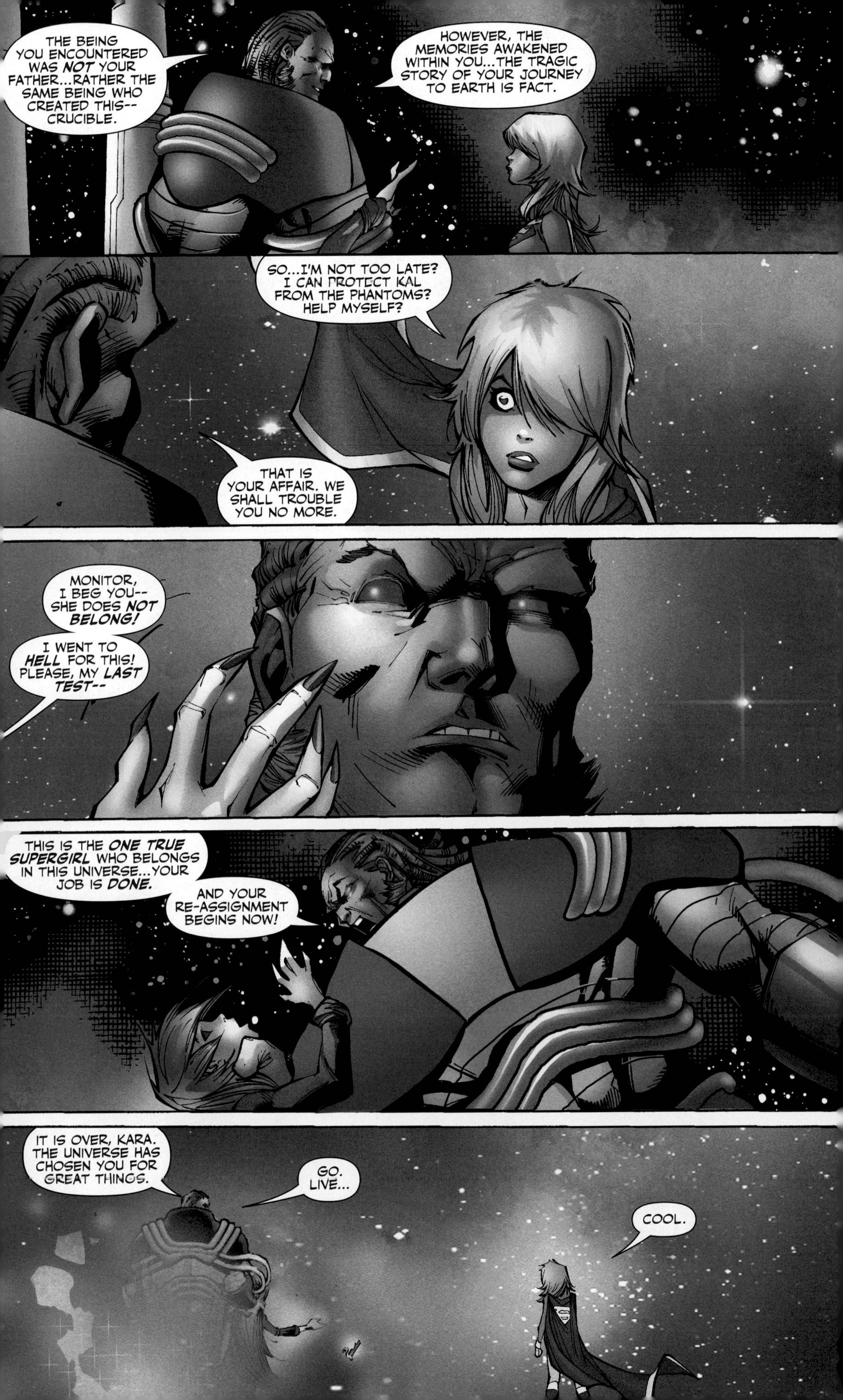

THE BEING YOU ENCOUNTERED WAS NOT YOUR FATHER...RATHER THE SAME BEING WHO CREATED THIS--CRUCIBLE.
HOWEVER, THE MEMORIES AWAKENED WITHIN YOU...THE TRAGIC STORY OF YOUR JOURNEY TO EARTH IS FACT.
SO...I'M NOT TOO LATE? I CAN PROTECT KAL FROM THE PHANTOMS? HELP MYSELF?
THAT IS YOUR AFFAIR. WE SHALL TROUBLE YOU NO MORE.
MONITOR, I BEG YOU--SHE DOES NOT BELONG!
I WENT TO HELL FOR THIS! PLEASE, MY LAST TEST--
THIS IS THE ONE TRUE SUPERGIRL WHO BELONGS IN THIS UNIVERSE...YOUR JOB IS DONE.
AND YOUR RE-ASSIGNMENT BEGINS NOW!
IT IS OVER, KARA. THE UNIVERSE HAS CHOSEN YOU FOR GREAT THINGS.
GO. LIVE...
COOL.

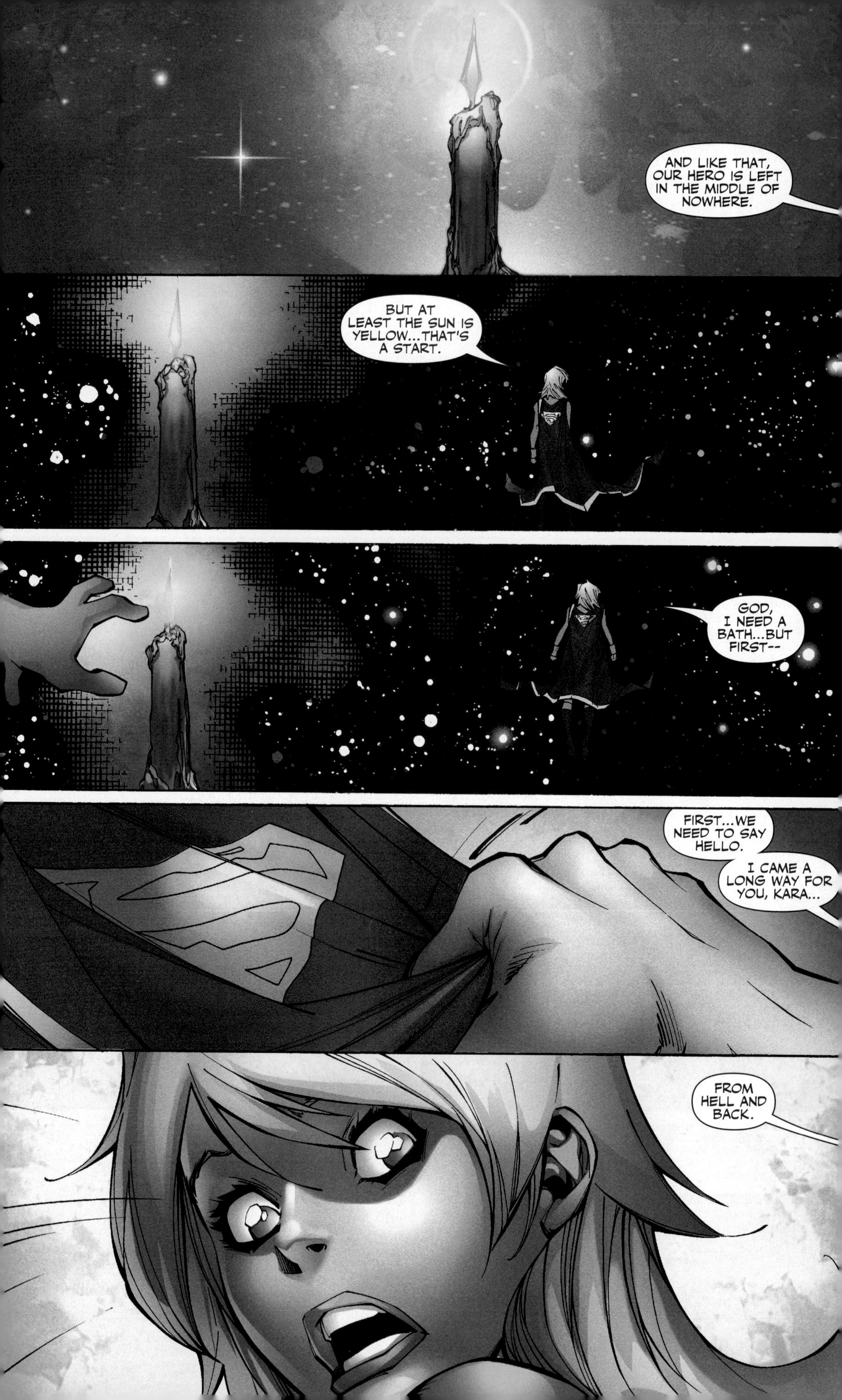
AND LIKE THAT, OUR HERO IS LEFT IN THE MIDDLE OF NOWHERE.
BUT AT LEAST THE SUN IS YELLOW...THAT'S A START.
GOD, I NEED A BATH...BUT FIRST--
FIRST...WE NEED TO SAY HELLO.
I CAME A LONG WAY FOR YOU, KARA...
FROM HELL AND BACK.

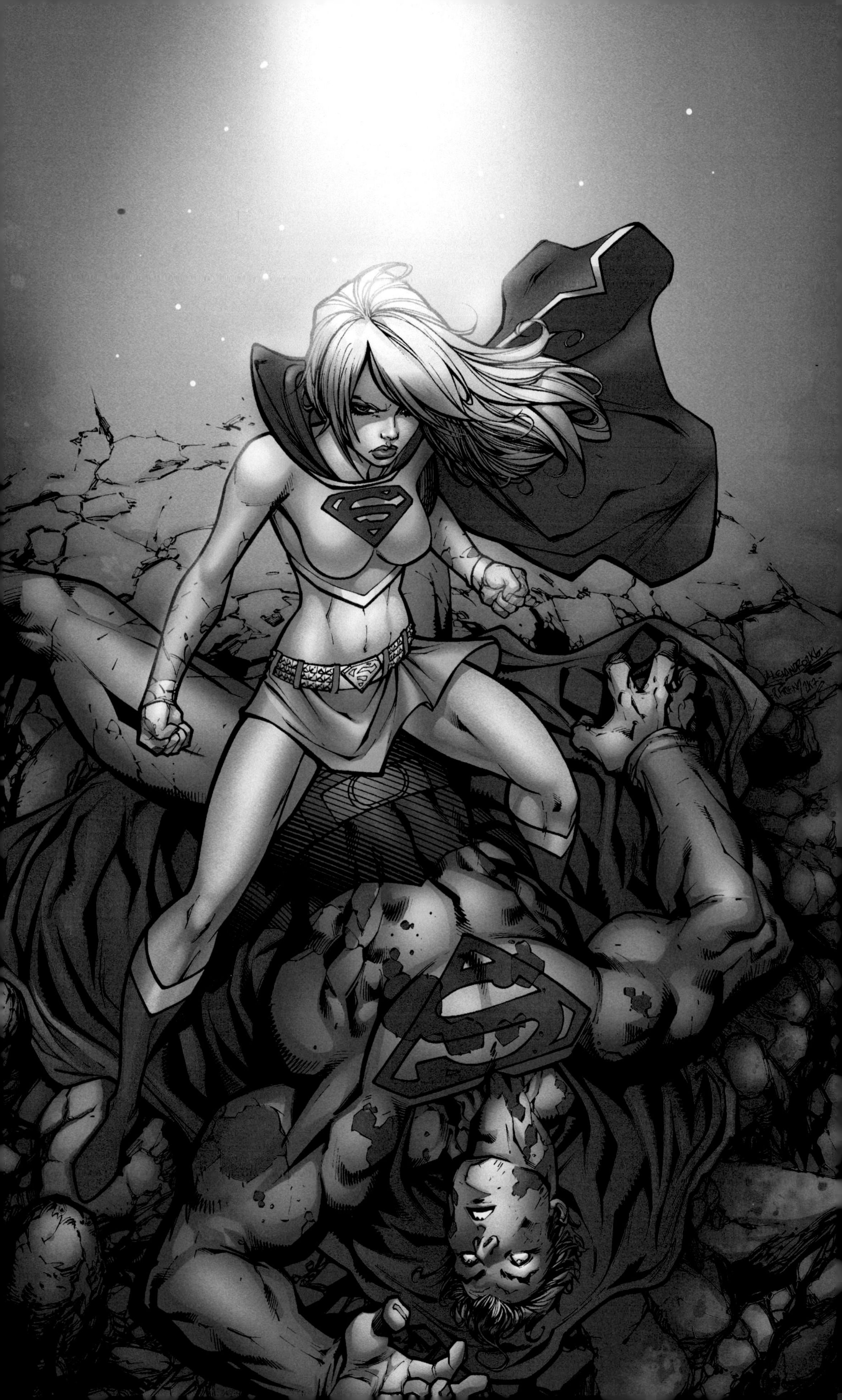

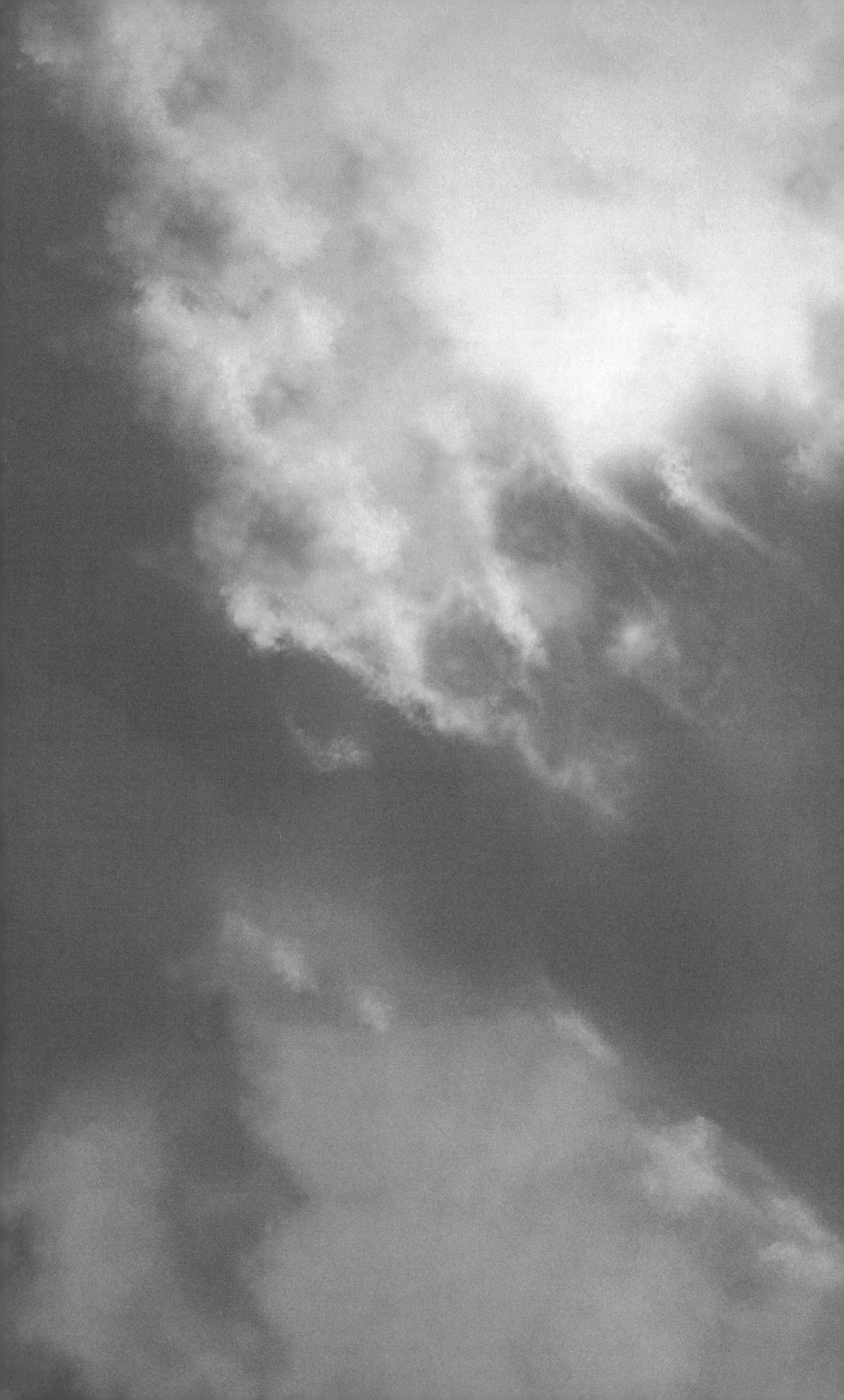

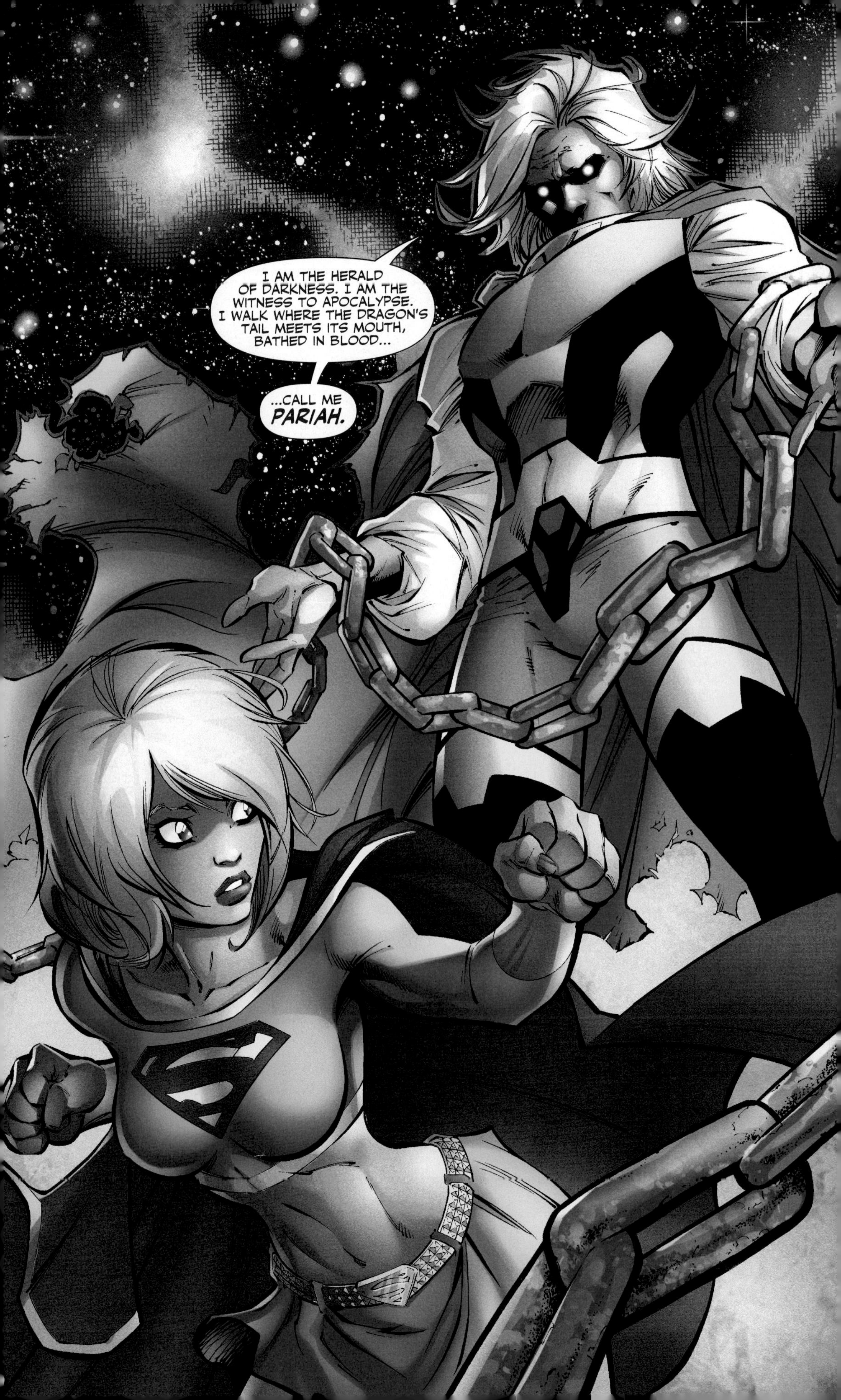

I AM THE HERALD OF DARKNESS. I AM THE WITNESS TO APOCALYPSE. I WALK WHERE THE DRAGON'S TAIL MEETS ITS MOUTH, BATHED IN BLOOD...
...CALL ME *PARIAH.*

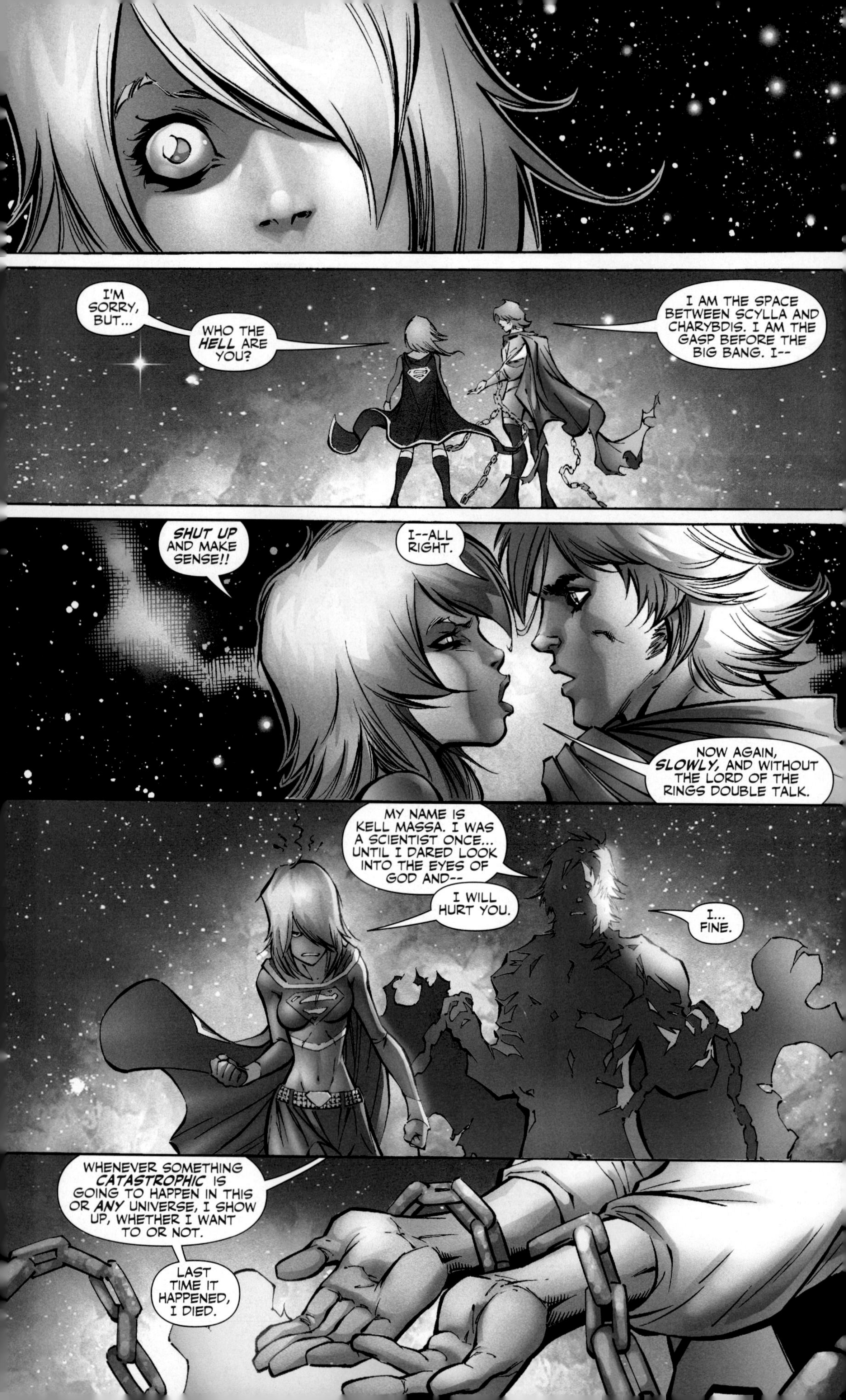
I'M SORRY, BUT...
WHO THE HELL ARE YOU?
I AM THE SPACE BETWEEN SCYLLA AND CHARYBDIS. I AM THE GASP BEFORE THE BIG BANG. I--
SHUT UP AND MAKE SENSE!!
I--ALL RIGHT.
NOW AGAIN, SLOWLY, AND WITHOUT THE LORD OF THE RINGS DOUBLE TALK.
MY NAME IS KELL MASSA. I WAS A SCIENTIST ONCE... UNTIL I DARED LOOK INTO THE EYES OF GOD AND--
I WILL HURT YOU.
I... FINE.
WHENEVER SOMETHING CATASTROPHIC IS GOING TO HAPPEN IN THIS OR ANY UNIVERSE, I SHOW UP, WHETHER I WANT TO OR NOT.
LAST TIME IT HAPPENED, I DIED.

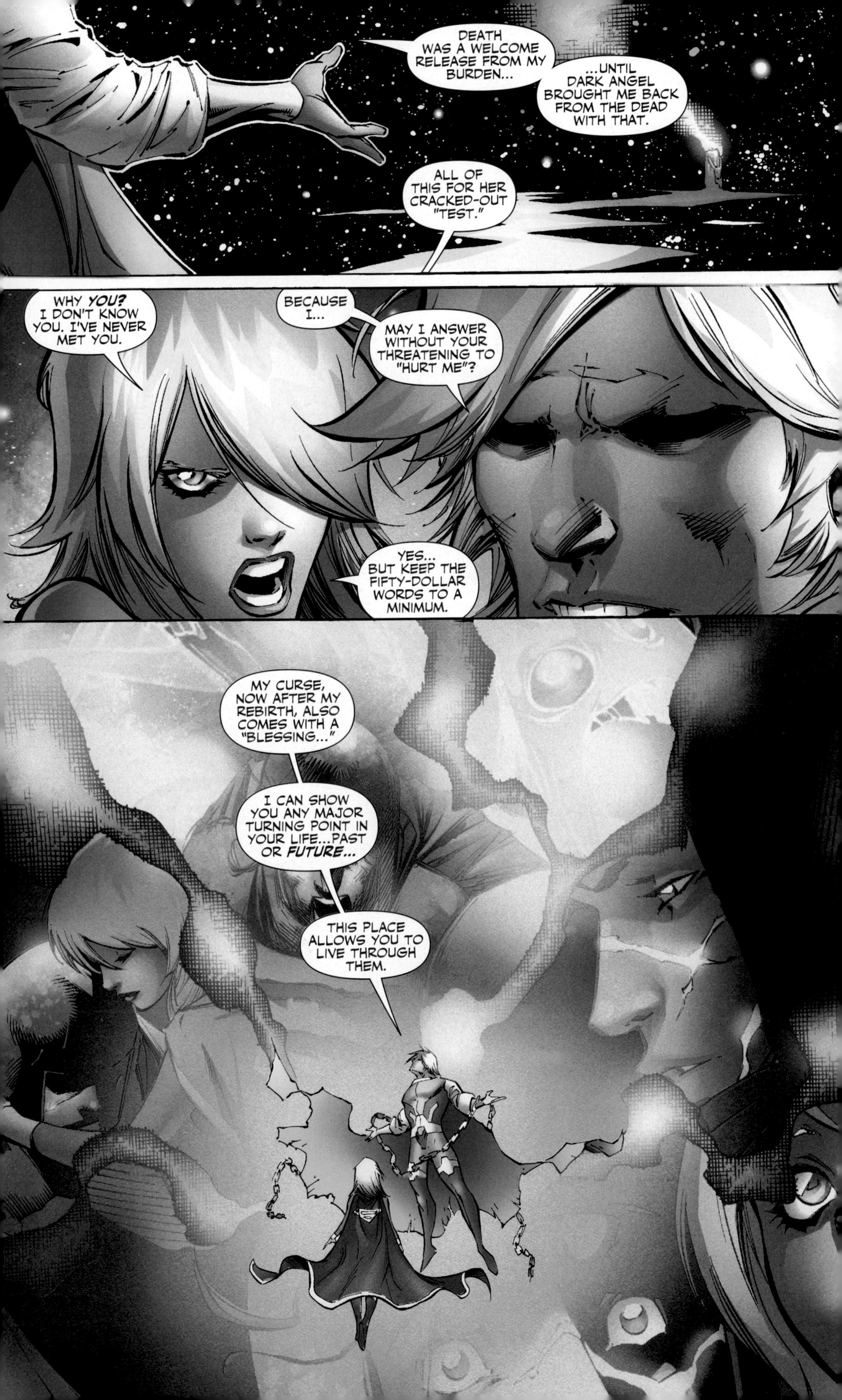
DEATH WAS A WELCOME RELEASE FROM MY BURDEN...
...UNTIL DARK ANGEL BROUGHT ME BACK FROM THE DEAD WITH THAT.
ALL OF THIS FOR HER CRACKED-OUT "TEST."
WHY *YOU?* I DON'T KNOW YOU. I'VE NEVER MET YOU.
BECAUSE I...
MAY I ANSWER WITHOUT YOUR THREATENING TO "HURT ME"?
YES... BUT KEEP THE FIFTY-DOLLAR WORDS TO A MINIMUM.
MY CURSE, NOW AFTER MY REBIRTH, ALSO COMES WITH A "BLESSING..."
I CAN SHOW YOU ANY MAJOR TURNING POINT IN YOUR LIFE...PAST OR *FUTURE...*
THIS PLACE ALLOWS YOU TO LIVE THROUGH THEM.

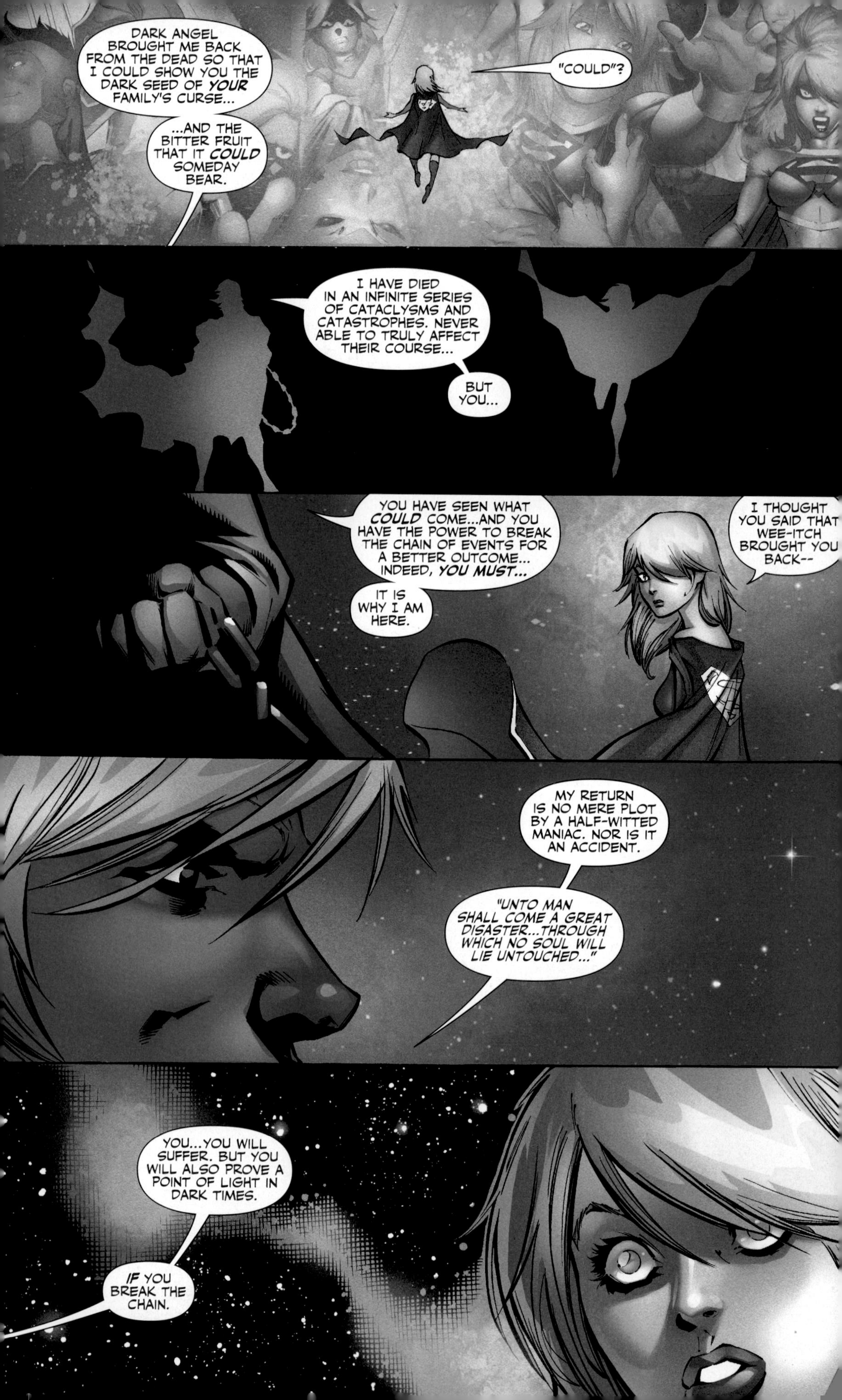
DARK ANGEL BROUGHT ME BACK FROM THE DEAD SO THAT I COULD SHOW YOU THE DARK SEED OF *YOUR* FAMILY'S CURSE...
...AND THE BITTER FRUIT THAT IT *COULD* SOMEDAY BEAR.
"COULD"?
I HAVE DIED IN AN INFINITE SERIES OF CATACLYSMS AND CATASTROPHES. NEVER ABLE TO TRULY AFFECT THEIR COURSE...
BUT YOU...
YOU HAVE SEEN WHAT *COULD* COME...AND YOU HAVE THE POWER TO BREAK THE CHAIN OF EVENTS FOR A BETTER OUTCOME... INDEED, *YOU MUST...*
IT IS WHY I AM HERE.
I THOUGHT YOU SAID THAT WEE-ITCH BROUGHT YOU BACK--
MY RETURN IS NO MERE PLOT BY A HALF-WITTED MANIAC. NOR IS IT AN ACCIDENT.
"UNTO MAN SHALL COME A GREAT DISASTER...THROUGH WHICH NO SOUL WILL LIE UNTOUCHED..."
YOU...YOU WILL SUFFER. BUT YOU WILL ALSO PROVE A POINT OF LIGHT IN DARK TIMES.
IF YOU BREAK THE CHAIN.

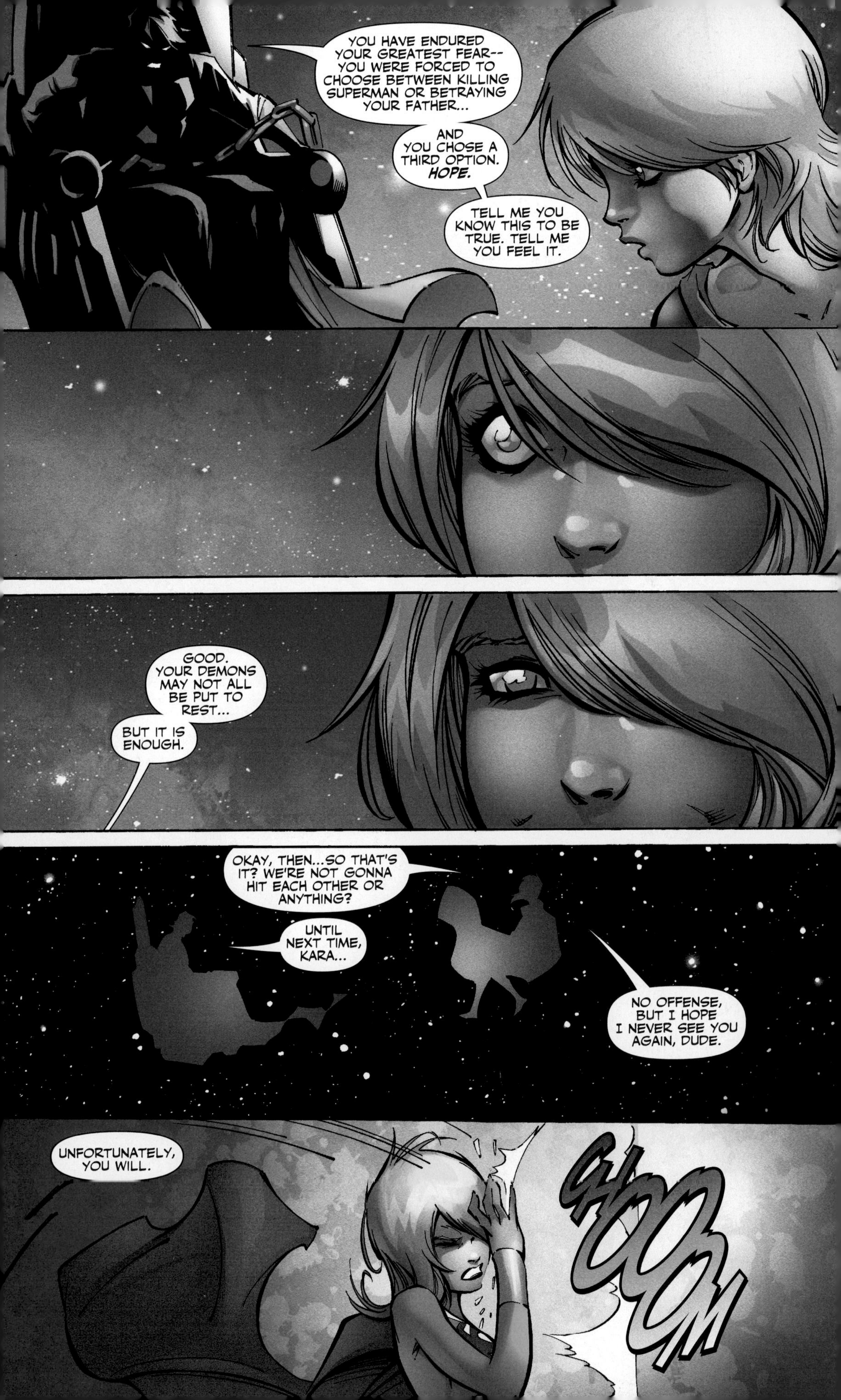
YOU HAVE ENDURED YOUR GREATEST FEAR-- YOU WERE FORCED TO CHOOSE BETWEEN KILLING SUPERMAN OR BETRAYING YOUR FATHER...
AND YOU CHOSE A THIRD OPTION. HOPE.
TELL ME YOU KNOW THIS TO BE TRUE. TELL ME YOU FEEL IT.
GOOD. YOUR DEMONS MAY NOT ALL BE PUT TO REST...
BUT IT IS ENOUGH.
OKAY, THEN...SO THAT'S IT? WE'RE NOT GONNA HIT EACH OTHER OR ANYTHING?
UNTIL NEXT TIME, KARA...
NO OFFENSE, BUT I HOPE I NEVER SEE YOU AGAIN, DUDE.
UNFORTUNATELY, YOU WILL.
GLOOOM

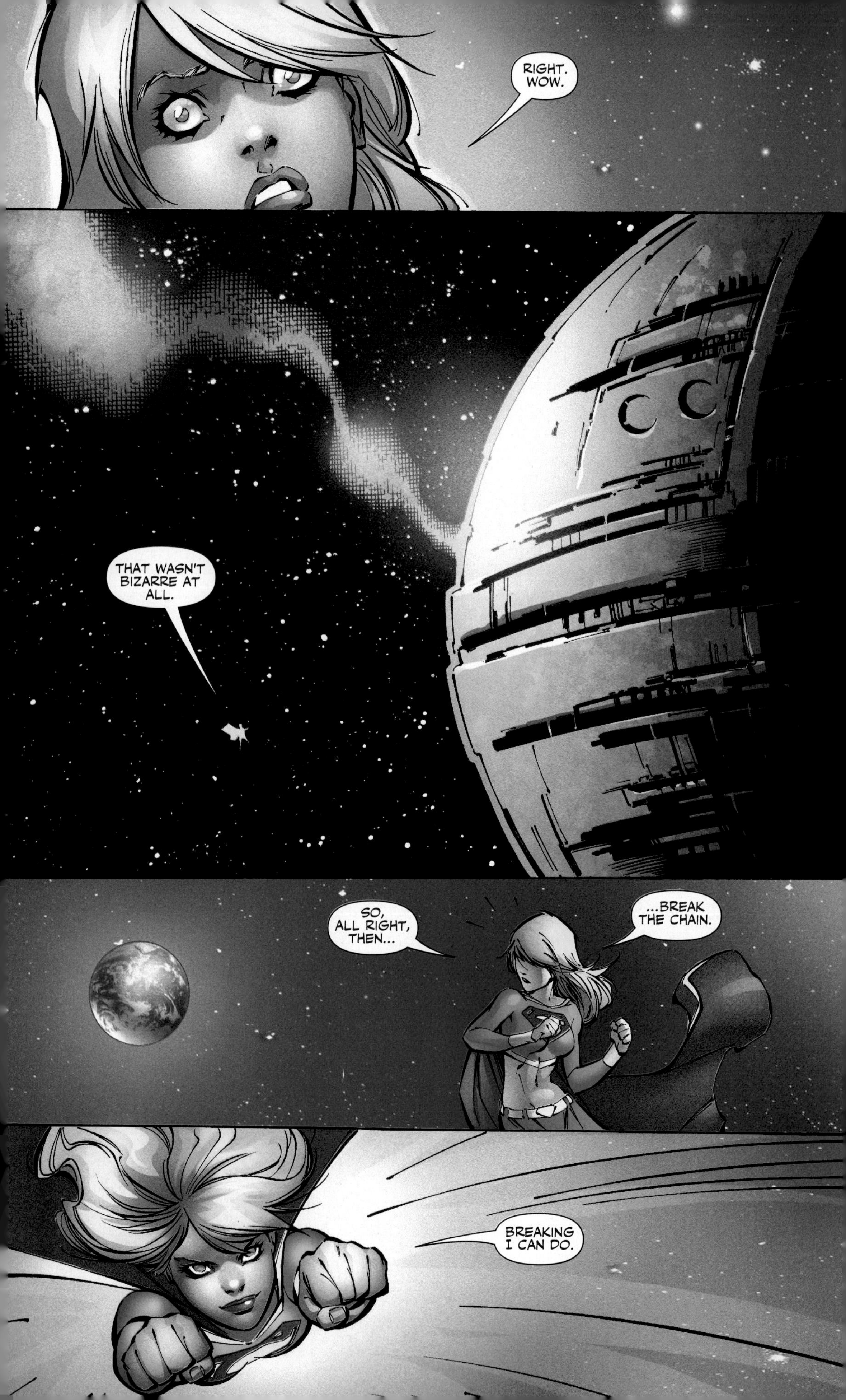
RIGHT. WOW.
THAT WASN'T BIZARRE AT ALL.
SO, ALL RIGHT, THEN...
...BREAK THE CHAIN.
BREAKING I CAN DO.

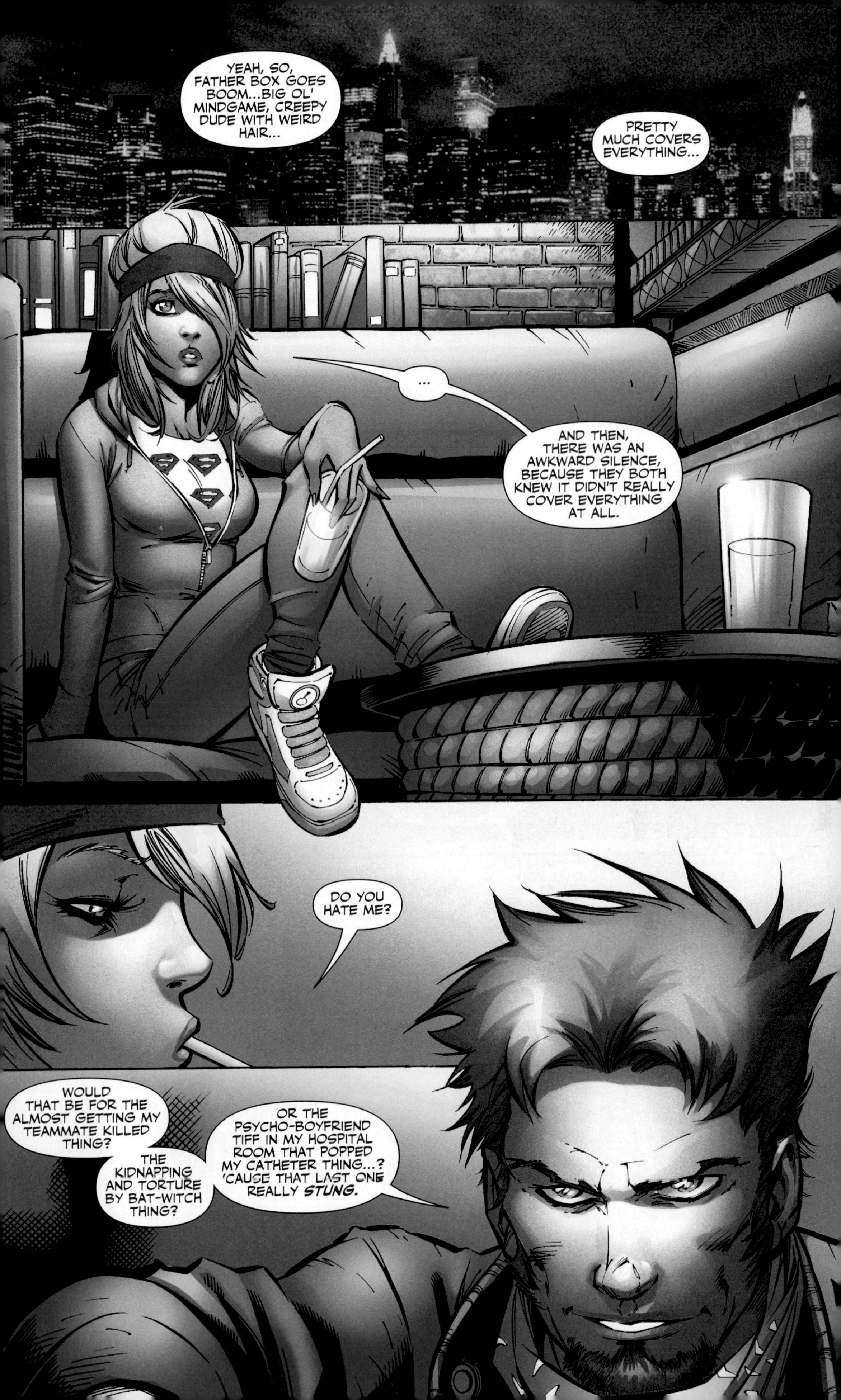
YEAH, SO, FATHER BOX GOES BOOM...BIG OL' MINDGAME, CREEPY DUDE WITH WEIRD HAIR...
PRETTY MUCH COVERS EVERYTHING...
...
AND THEN, THERE WAS AN AWKWARD SILENCE, BECAUSE THEY BOTH KNEW IT DIDN'T REALLY COVER EVERYTHING AT ALL.
DO YOU HATE ME?
WOULD THAT BE FOR THE ALMOST GETTING MY TEAMMATE KILLED THING?
THE KIDNAPPING AND TORTURE BY BAT-WITCH THING?
OR THE PSYCHO-BOYFRIEND TIFF IN MY HOSPITAL ROOM THAT POPPED MY CATHETER THING...? 'CAUSE THAT LAST ONE REALLY *STUNG*.

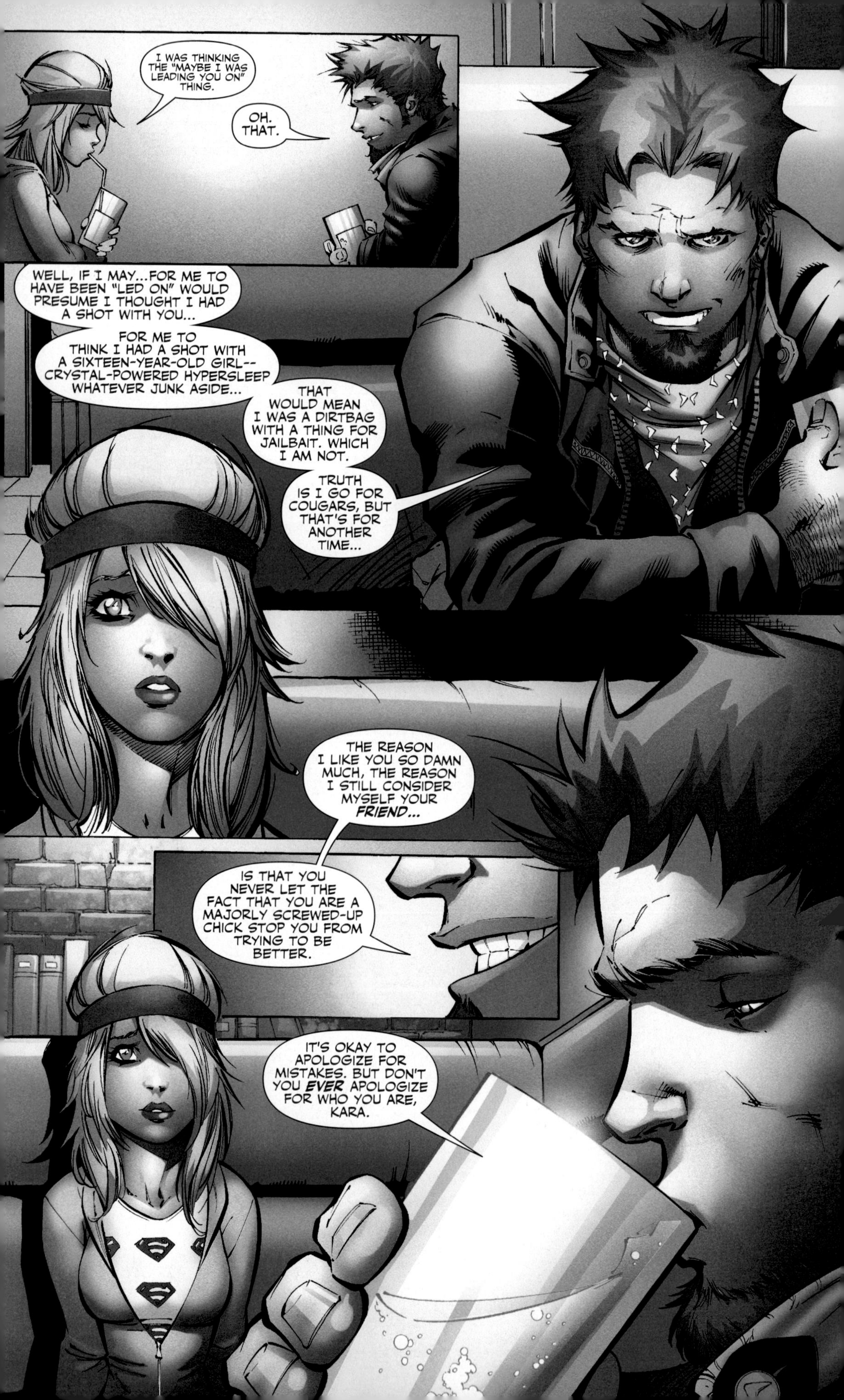
I WAS THINKING THE "MAYBE I WAS LEADING YOU ON" THING.
OH. THAT.
WELL, IF I MAY...FOR ME TO HAVE BEEN "LED ON" WOULD PRESUME I THOUGHT I HAD A SHOT WITH YOU...
FOR ME TO THINK I HAD A SHOT WITH A SIXTEEN-YEAR-OLD GIRL-- CRYSTAL-POWERED HYPERSLEEP WHATEVER JUNK ASIDE...
THAT WOULD MEAN I WAS A DIRTBAG WITH A THING FOR JAILBAIT. WHICH I AM NOT.
TRUTH IS I GO FOR COUGARS, BUT THAT'S FOR ANOTHER TIME...
THE REASON I LIKE YOU SO DAMN MUCH, THE REASON I STILL CONSIDER MYSELF YOUR ***FRIEND...***
IS THAT YOU NEVER LET THE FACT THAT YOU ARE A MAJORLY SCREWED-UP CHICK STOP YOU FROM TRYING TO BE BETTER.
IT'S OKAY TO APOLOGIZE FOR MISTAKES. BUT DON'T YOU ***EVER*** APOLOGIZE FOR WHO YOU ARE, KARA.

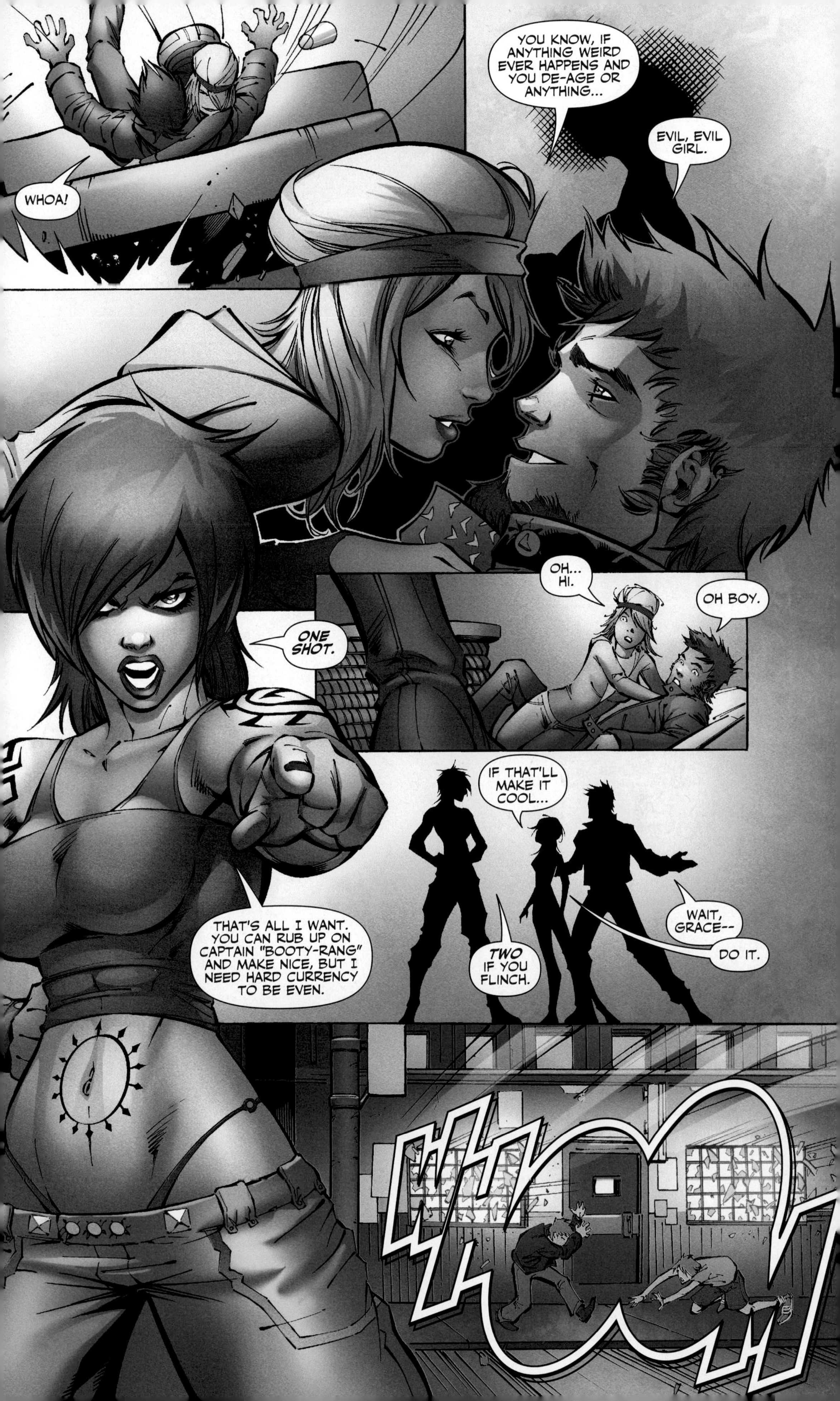
WHOA!
YOU KNOW, IF ANYTHING WEIRD EVER HAPPENS AND YOU DE-AGE OR ANYTHING...
EVIL, EVIL GIRL.
OH... HI.
OH BOY.
ONE SHOT.
THAT'S ALL I WANT. YOU CAN RUB UP ON CAPTAIN "BOOTY-RANG" AND MAKE NICE, BUT I NEED HARD CURRENCY TO BE EVEN.
IF THAT'LL MAKE IT COOL...
TWO IF YOU FLINCH.
WAIT, GRACE--
DO IT.

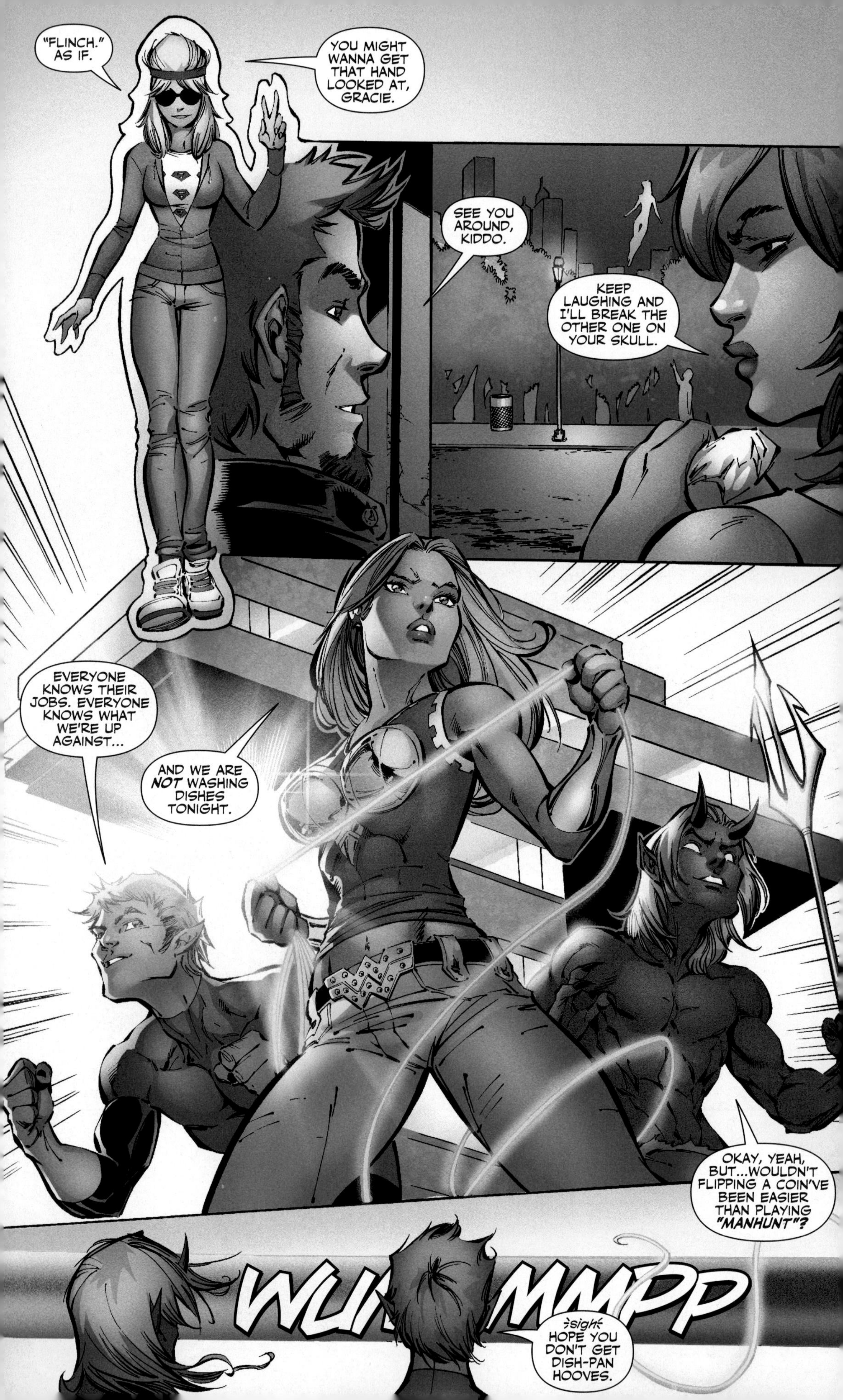
"FLINCH." AS IF.
YOU MIGHT WANNA GET THAT HAND LOOKED AT, GRACIE.
SEE YOU AROUND, KIDDO.
KEEP LAUGHING AND I'LL BREAK THE OTHER ONE ON YOUR SKULL.
EVERYONE KNOWS THEIR JOBS. EVERYONE KNOWS WHAT WE'RE UP AGAINST...
AND WE ARE *NOT* WASHING DISHES TONIGHT.
OKAY, YEAH, BUT...WOULDN'T FLIPPING A COIN'VE BEEN EASIER THAN PLAYING *"MANHUNT"*?
WUMMPP
sigh HOPE YOU DON'T GET DISH-PAN HOOVES.

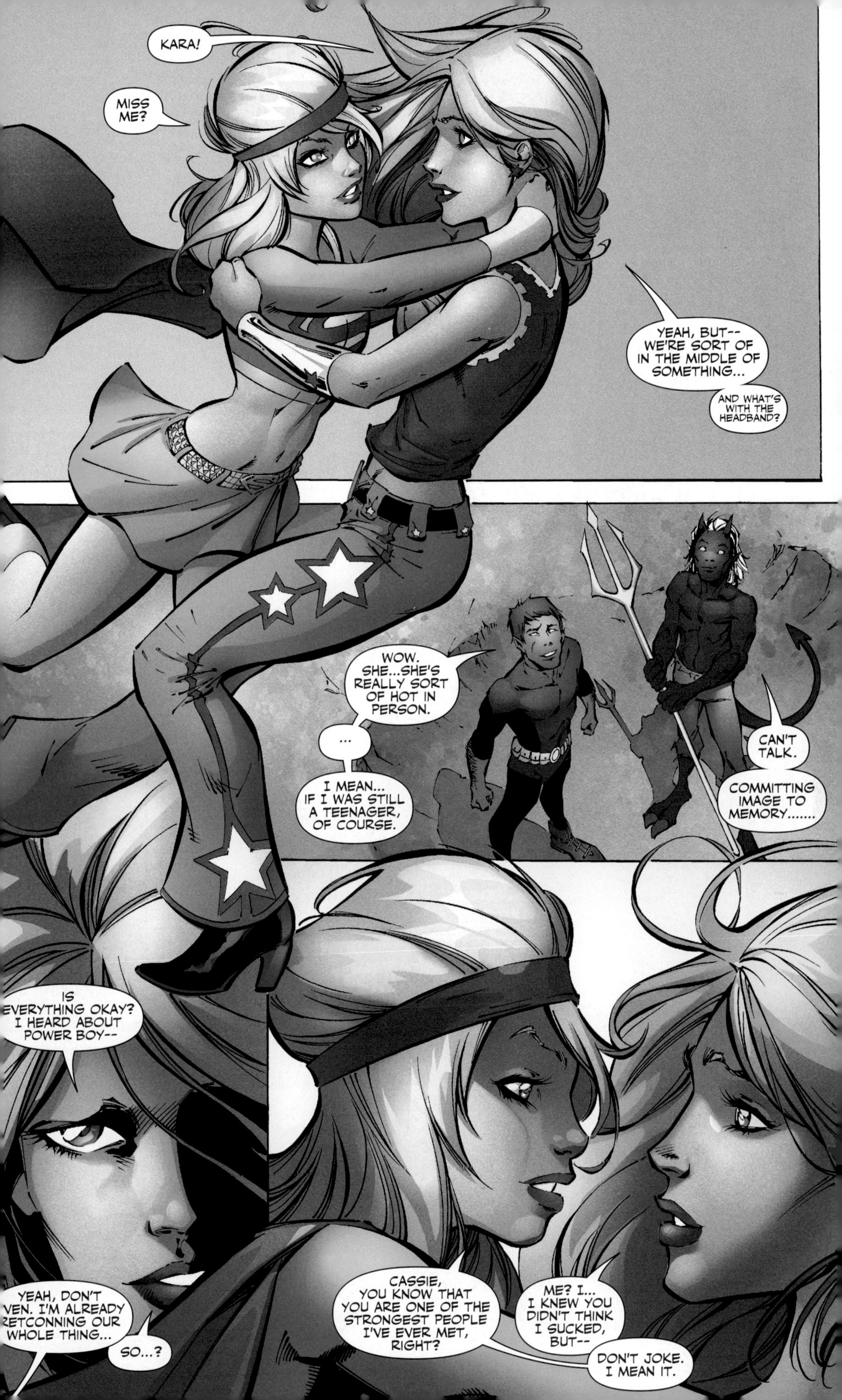
KARA!
MISS ME?
YEAH, BUT-- WE'RE SORT OF IN THE MIDDLE OF SOMETHING...
AND WHAT'S WITH THE HEADBAND?
WOW. SHE...SHE'S REALLY SORT OF HOT IN PERSON.
...
I MEAN... IF I WAS STILL A TEENAGER, OF COURSE.
CAN'T TALK.
COMMITTING IMAGE TO MEMORY.......
IS EVERYTHING OKAY? I HEARD ABOUT POWER BOY--
YEAH, DON'T EVEN. I'M ALREADY RETCONNING OUR WHOLE THING...
SO...?
CASSIE, YOU KNOW THAT YOU ARE ONE OF THE STRONGEST PEOPLE I'VE EVER MET, RIGHT?
ME? I... I KNEW YOU DIDN'T THINK I SUCKED, BUT--
DON'T JOKE. I MEAN IT.

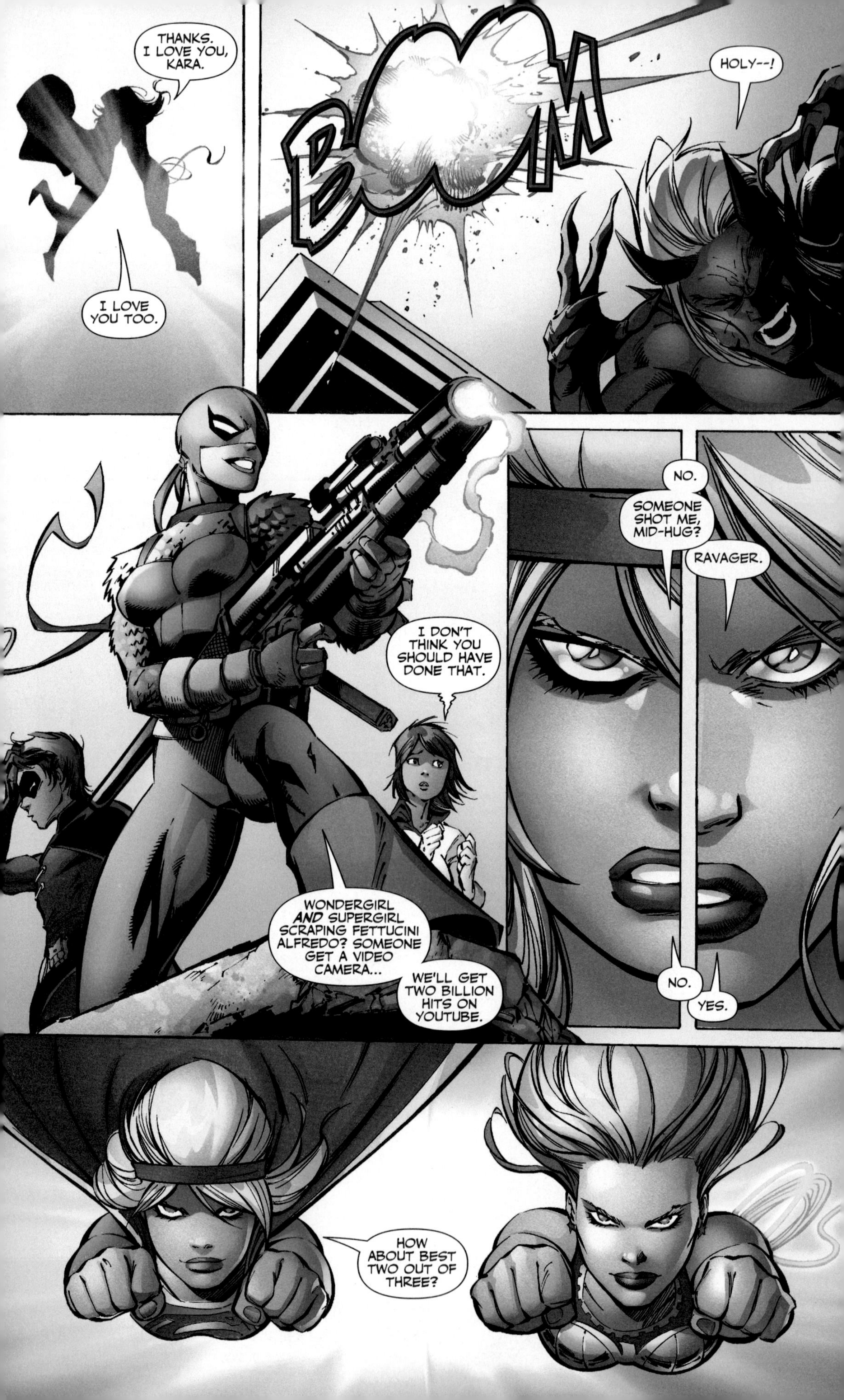
THANKS. I LOVE YOU, KARA.
I LOVE YOU TOO.
BOOM
HOLY--!
NO.
SOMEONE SHOT ME, MID-HUG?
RAVAGER.
I DON'T THINK YOU SHOULD HAVE DONE THAT.
WONDERGIRL AND SUPERGIRL SCRAPING FETTUCINI ALFREDO? SOMEONE GET A VIDEO CAMERA...
WE'LL GET TWO BILLION HITS ON YOUTUBE.
NO.
YES.
HOW ABOUT BEST TWO OUT OF THREE?

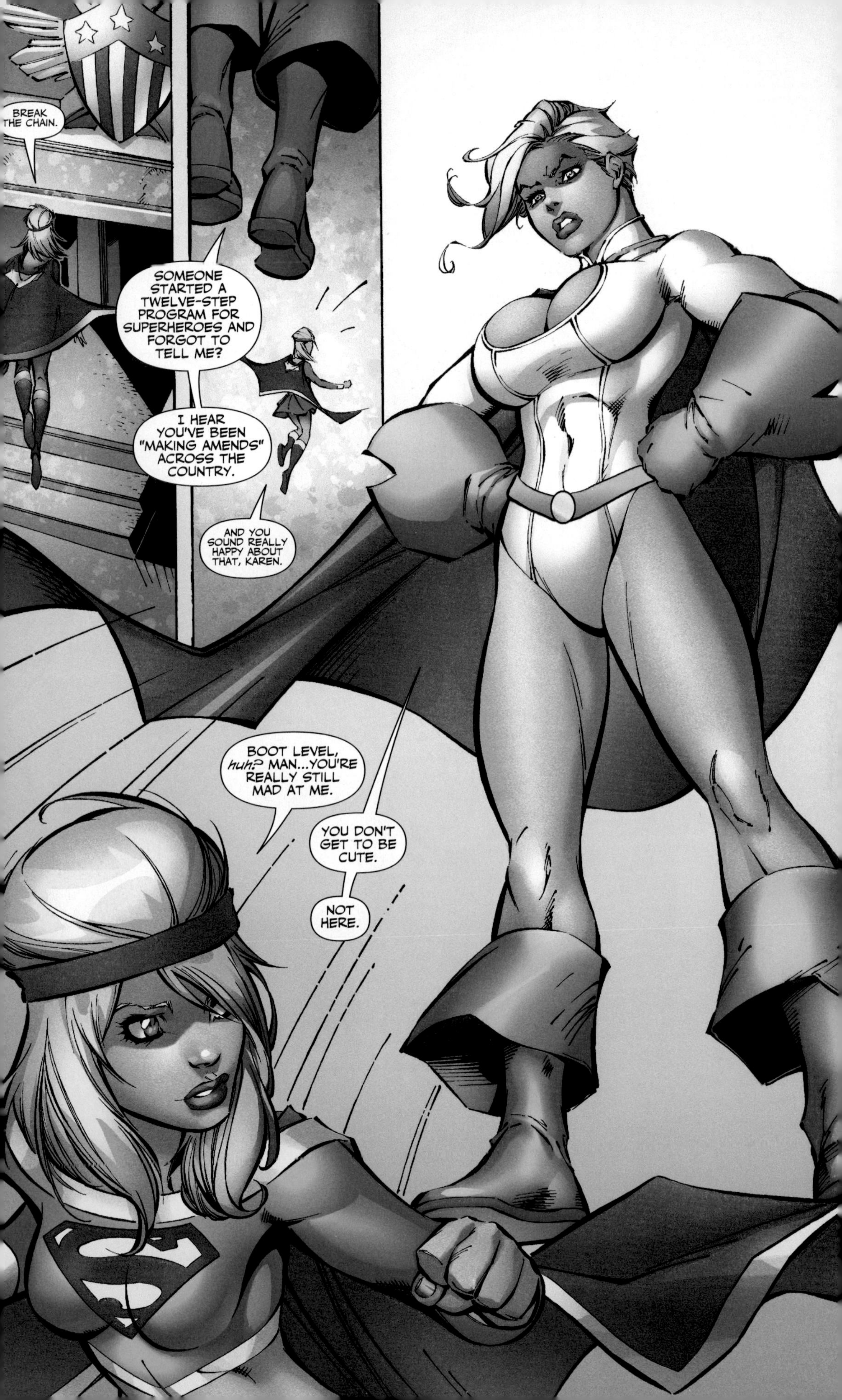
BREAK THE CHAIN.
SOMEONE STARTED A TWELVE-STEP PROGRAM FOR SUPERHEROES AND FORGOT TO TELL ME?
I HEAR YOU'VE BEEN "MAKING AMENDS" ACROSS THE COUNTRY.
AND YOU SOUND REALLY HAPPY ABOUT THAT, KAREN.
BOOT LEVEL, *huh?* MAN...YOU'RE REALLY STILL MAD AT ME.
YOU DON'T GET TO BE CUTE.
NOT HERE.

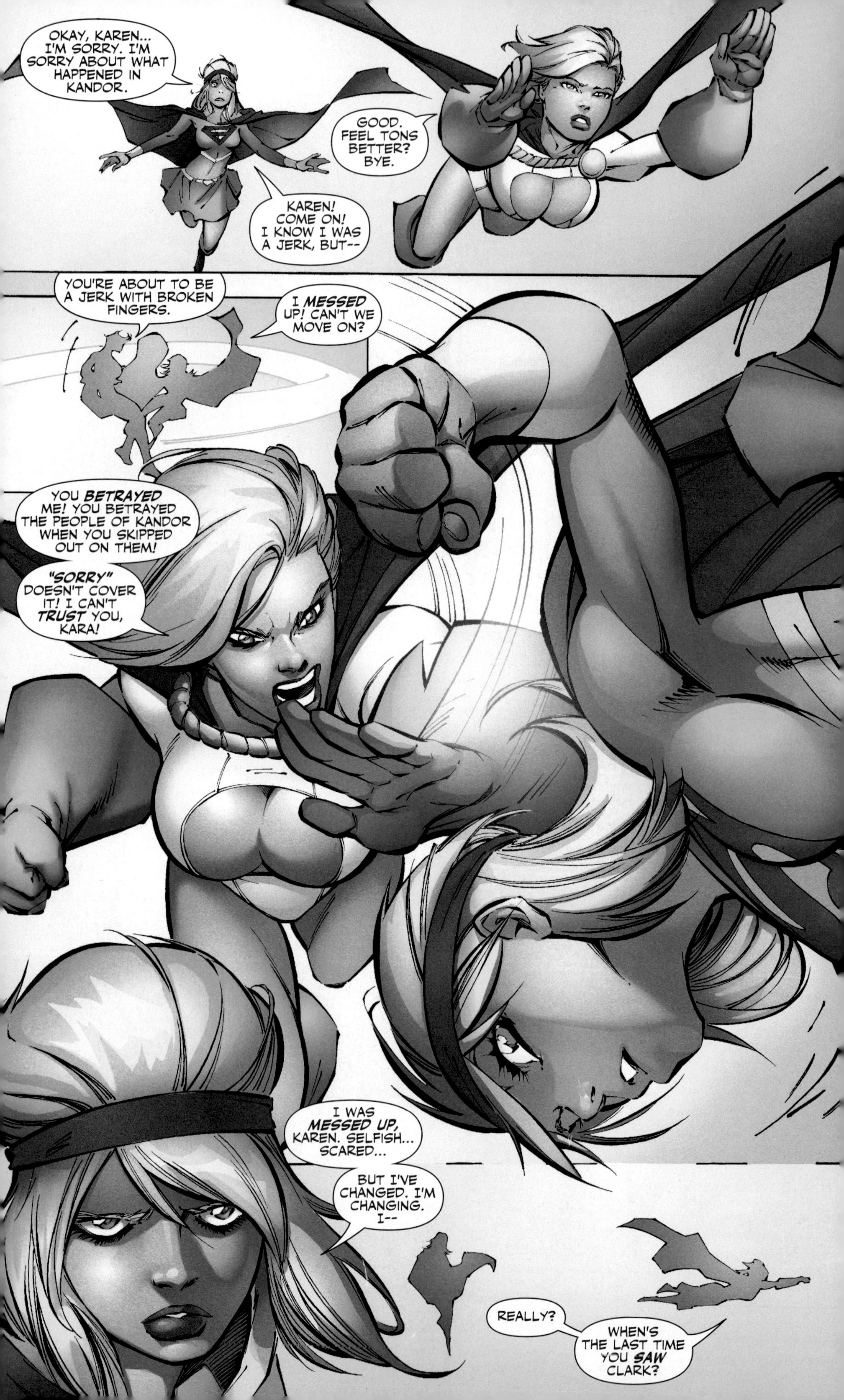
OKAY, KAREN... I'M SORRY. I'M SORRY ABOUT WHAT HAPPENED IN KANDOR.
GOOD. FEEL TONS BETTER? BYE.
KAREN! COME ON! I KNOW I WAS A JERK, BUT--
YOU'RE ABOUT TO BE A JERK WITH BROKEN FINGERS.
I MESSED UP! CAN'T WE MOVE ON?
YOU BETRAYED ME! YOU BETRAYED THE PEOPLE OF KANDOR WHEN YOU SKIPPED OUT ON THEM!
"SORRY" DOESN'T COVER IT! I CAN'T TRUST YOU, KARA!
I WAS MESSED UP, KAREN. SELFISH... SCARED...
BUT I'VE CHANGED. I'M CHANGING. I--
REALLY?
WHEN'S THE LAST TIME YOU SAW CLARK?

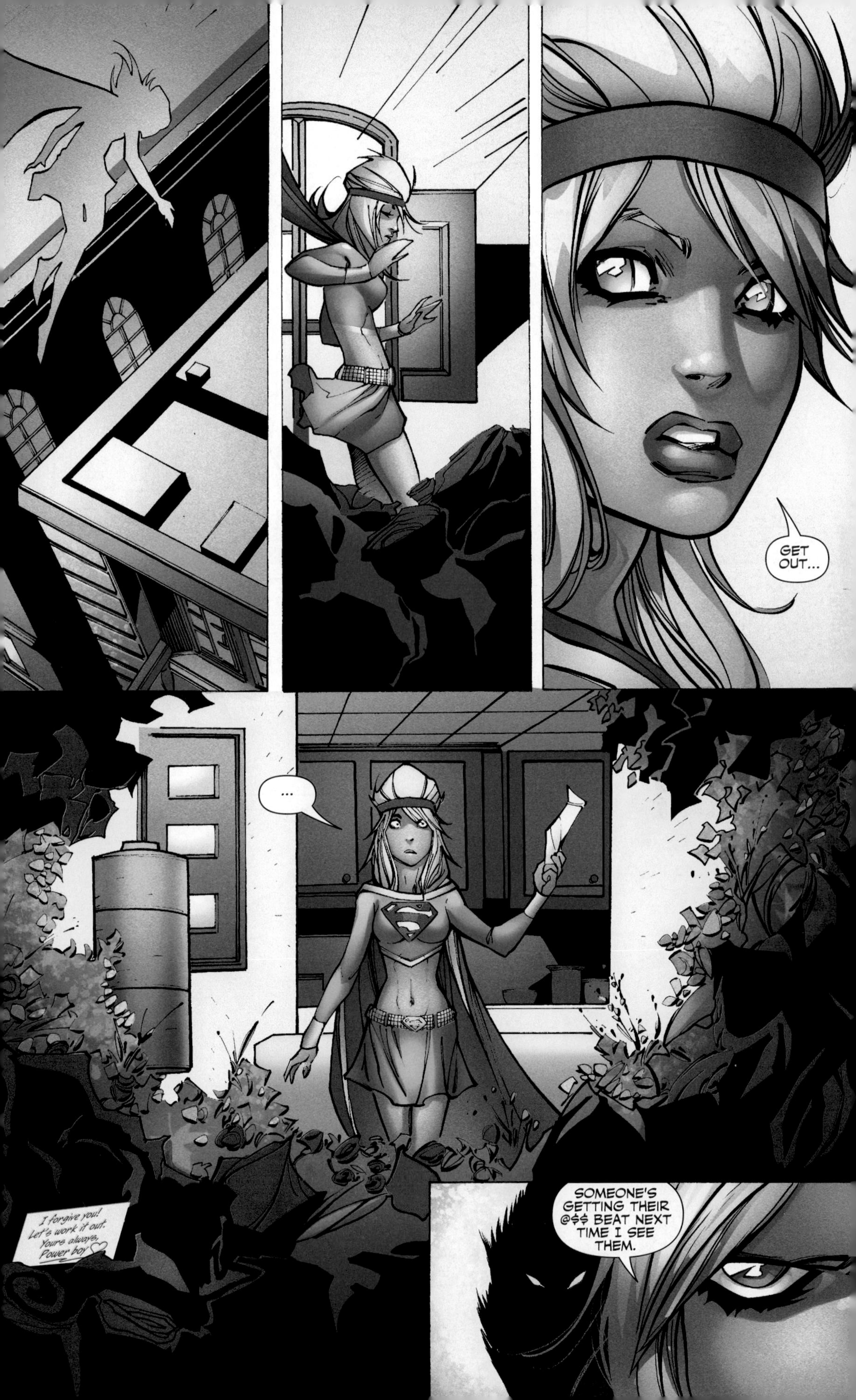
GET OUT...
...
I forgive you! Let's work it out. Yours always, Power boy
SOMEONE'S GETTING THEIR @$$ BEAT NEXT TIME I SEE THEM.

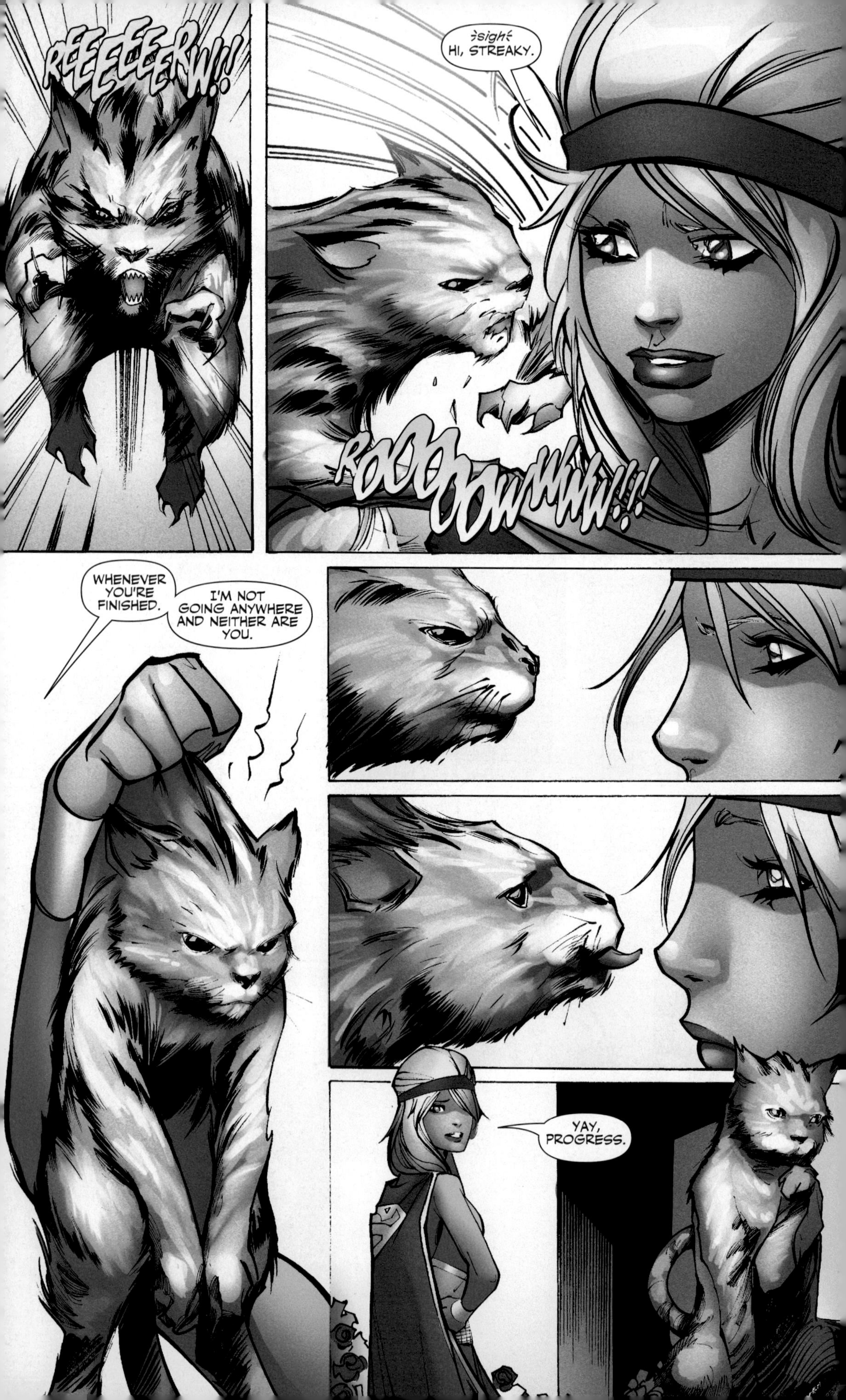
REEEEEERW!!!
sigh
HI, STREAKY.
ROOOOOWWWW!!!
WHENEVER YOU'RE FINISHED.
I'M NOT GOING ANYWHERE AND NEITHER ARE YOU.
YAY, PROGRESS.

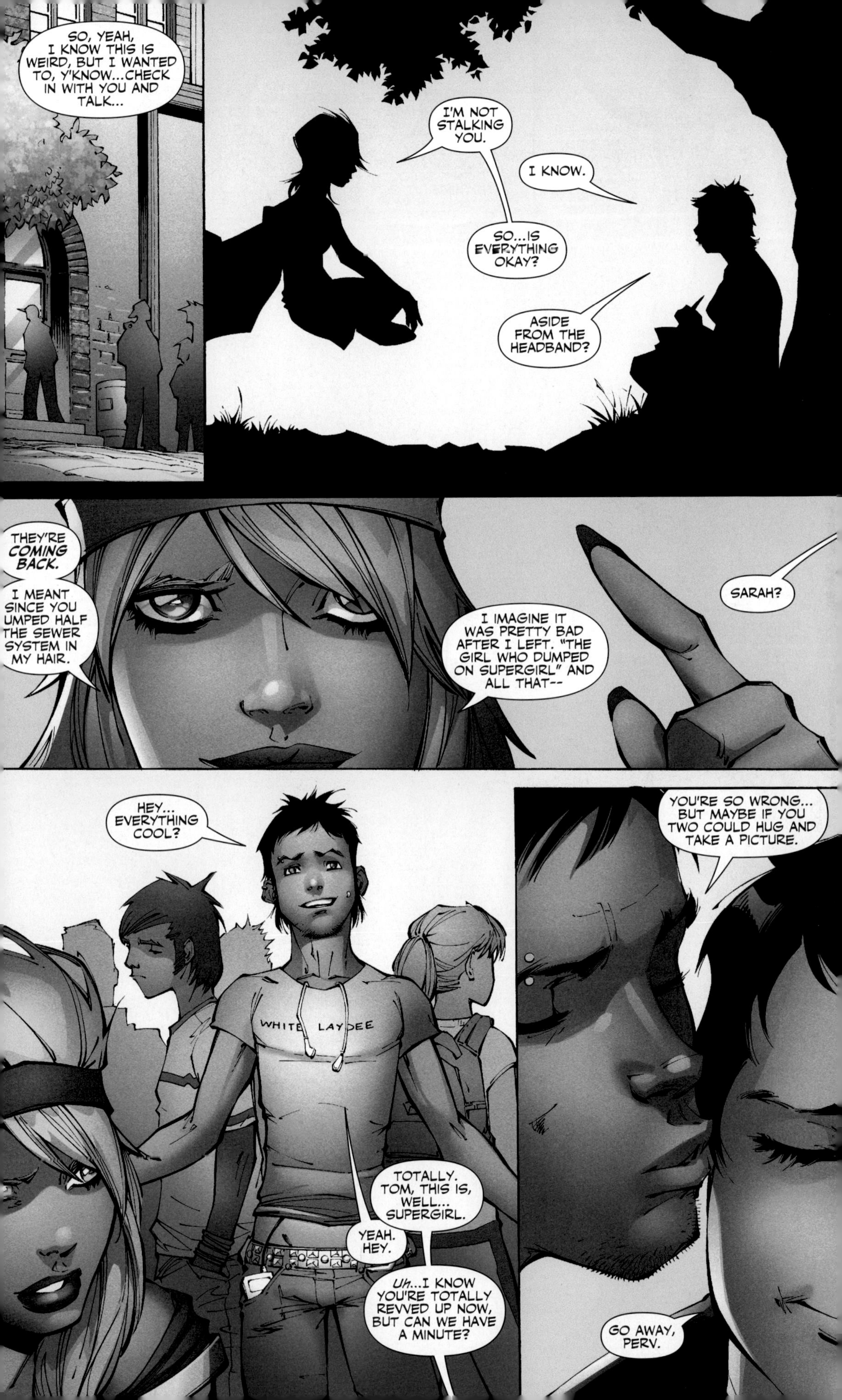

SO, YEAH, I KNOW THIS IS WEIRD, BUT I WANTED TO, Y'KNOW...CHECK IN WITH YOU AND TALK...
I'M NOT STALKING YOU.
I KNOW.
SO...IS EVERYTHING OKAY?
ASIDE FROM THE HEADBAND?
THEY'RE *COMING BACK.*
I MEANT SINCE YOU UMPED HALF THE SEWER SYSTEM IN MY HAIR.
I IMAGINE IT WAS PRETTY BAD AFTER I LEFT. "THE GIRL WHO DUMPED ON SUPERGIRL" AND ALL THAT--
SARAH?
HEY... EVERYTHING COOL?
WHITE LAYDEE
TOTALLY. TOM, THIS IS, WELL... SUPERGIRL.
YEAH. HEY.
UH...I KNOW YOU'RE TOTALLY REVVED UP NOW, BUT CAN WE HAVE A MINUTE?
YOU'RE SO WRONG... BUT MAYBE IF YOU TWO COULD HUG AND TAKE A PICTURE.
GO AWAY, PERV.

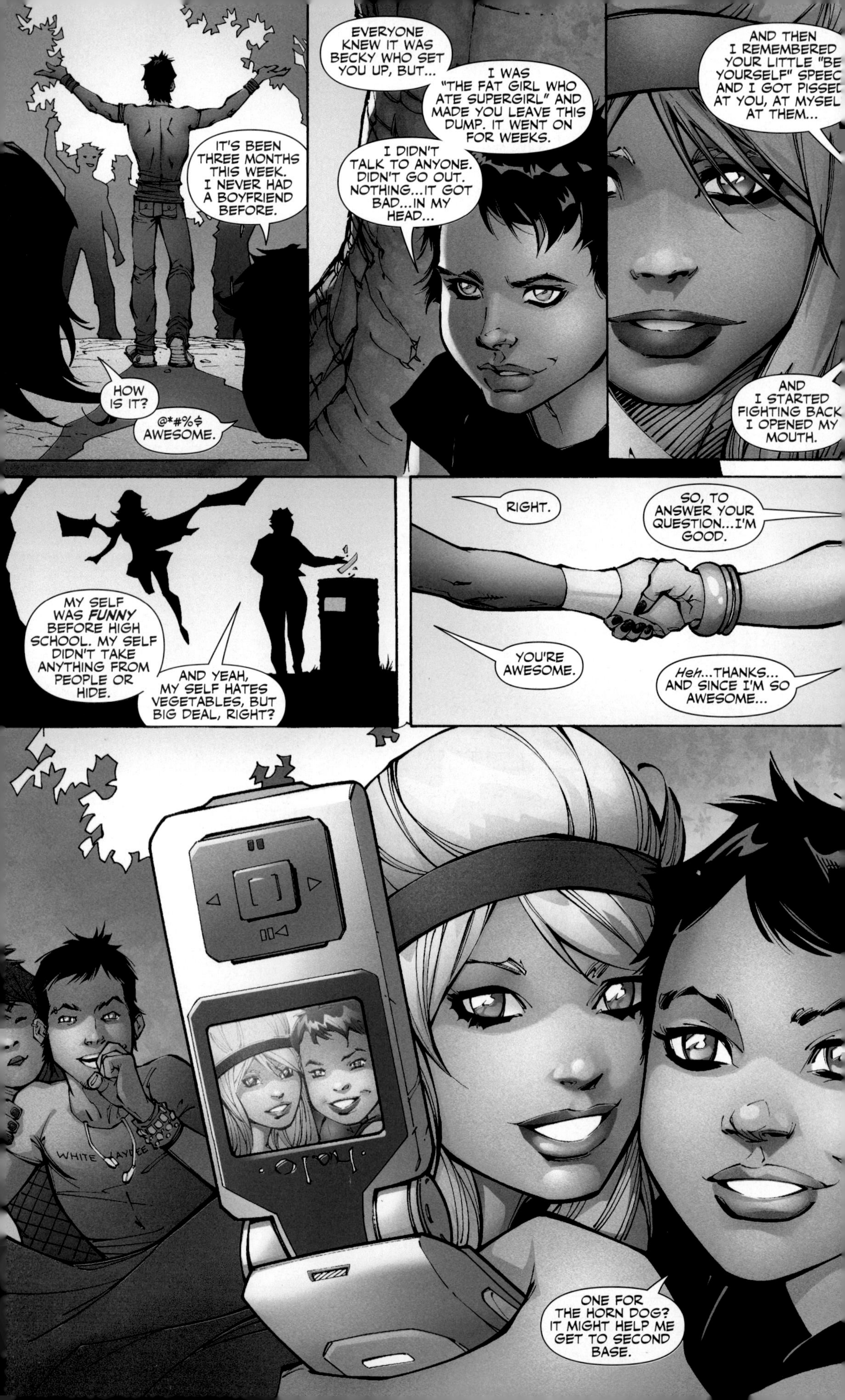
IT'S BEEN THREE MONTHS THIS WEEK. I NEVER HAD A BOYFRIEND BEFORE.
HOW IS IT?
@*#%$ AWESOME.
EVERYONE KNEW IT WAS BECKY WHO SET YOU UP, BUT...
I WAS "THE FAT GIRL WHO ATE SUPERGIRL" AND MADE YOU LEAVE THIS DUMP. IT WENT ON FOR WEEKS.
I DIDN'T TALK TO ANYONE. DIDN'T GO OUT. NOTHING...IT GOT BAD...IN MY HEAD...
AND THEN I REMEMBERED YOUR LITTLE "BE YOURSELF" SPEEC AND I GOT PISSEI AT YOU, AT MYSEL AT THEM...
AND I STARTED FIGHTING BACK I OPENED MY MOUTH.
MY SELF WAS FUNNY BEFORE HIGH SCHOOL. MY SELF DIDN'T TAKE ANYTHING FROM PEOPLE OR HIDE.
AND YEAH, MY SELF HATES VEGETABLES, BUT BIG DEAL, RIGHT?
RIGHT.
SO, TO ANSWER YOUR QUESTION...I'M GOOD.
YOU'RE AWESOME.
Heh...THANKS... AND SINCE I'M SO AWESOME...
ONE FOR THE HORN DOG? IT MIGHT HELP ME GET TO SECOND BASE.

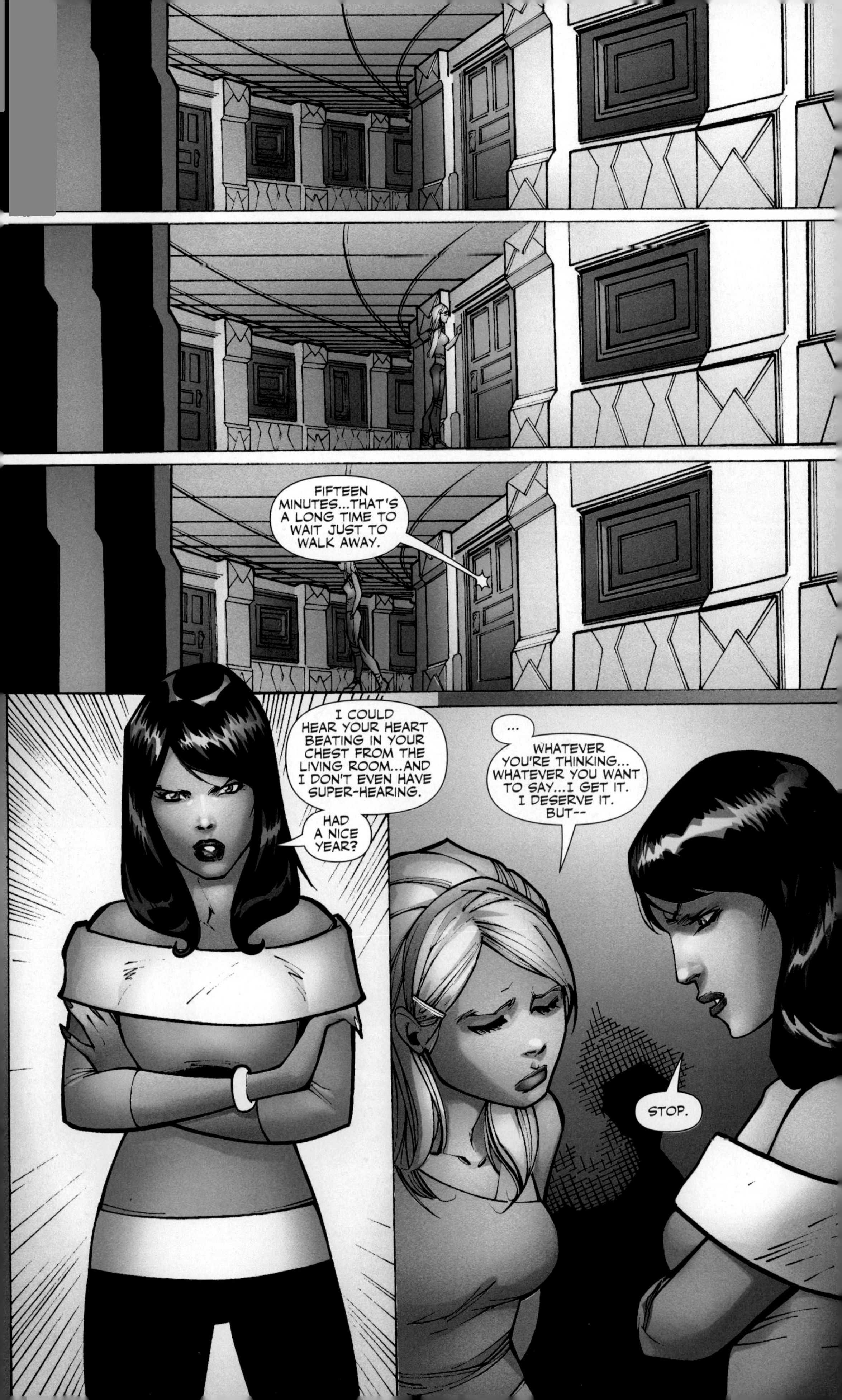
FIFTEEN MINUTES...THAT'S A LONG TIME TO WAIT JUST TO WALK AWAY.
I COULD HEAR YOUR HEART BEATING IN YOUR CHEST FROM THE LIVING ROOM...AND I DON'T EVEN HAVE SUPER-HEARING.
HAD A NICE YEAR?
...
WHATEVER YOU'RE THINKING... WHATEVER YOU WANT TO SAY...I GET IT. I DESERVE IT. BUT--
STOP.

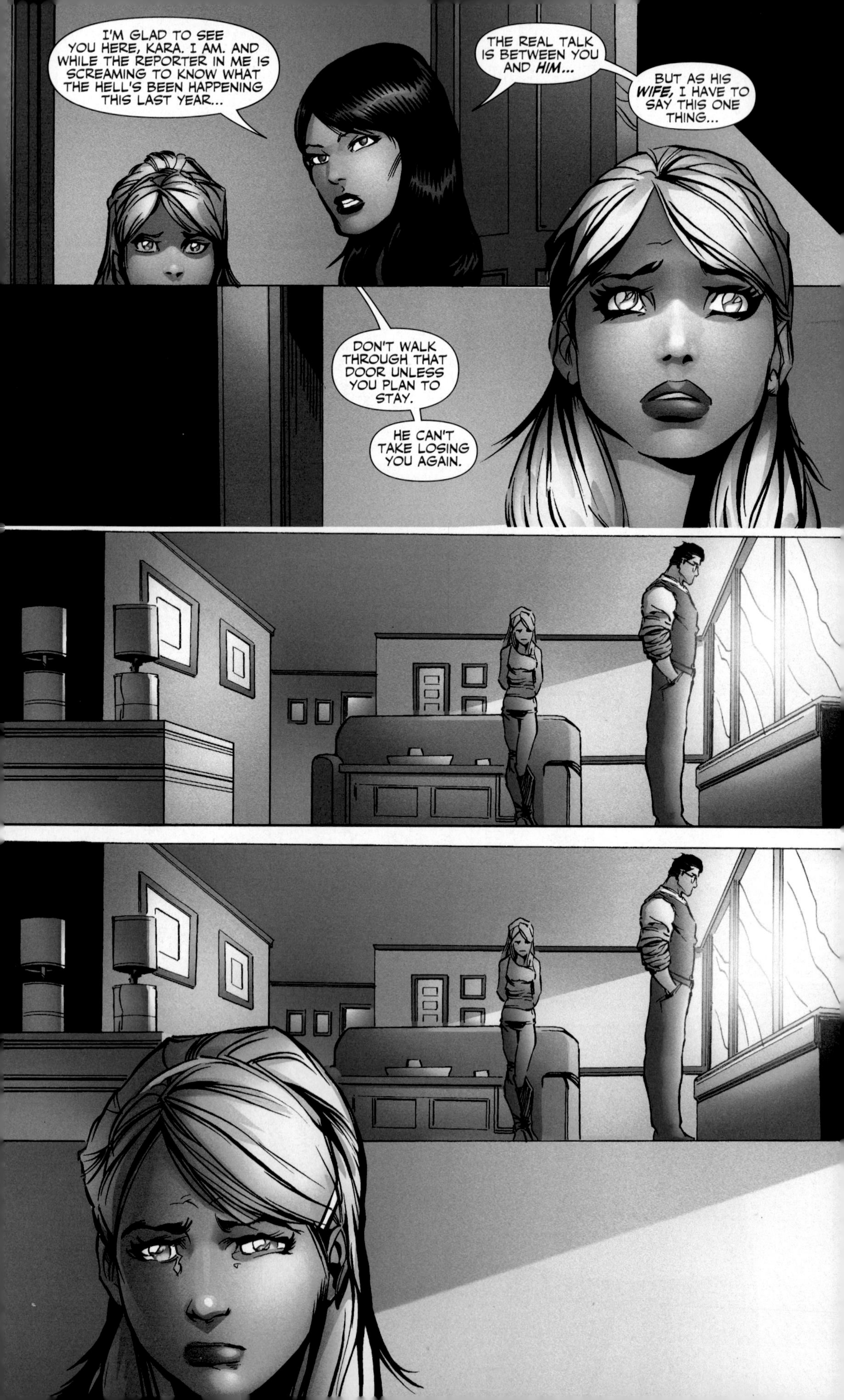
I'M GLAD TO SEE YOU HERE, KARA. I AM. AND WHILE THE REPORTER IN ME IS SCREAMING TO KNOW WHAT THE HELL'S BEEN HAPPENING THIS LAST YEAR...
THE REAL TALK IS BETWEEN YOU AND HIM...
BUT AS HIS WIFE, I HAVE TO SAY THIS ONE THING...
DON'T WALK THROUGH THAT DOOR UNLESS YOU PLAN TO STAY.
HE CAN'T TAKE LOSING YOU AGAIN.

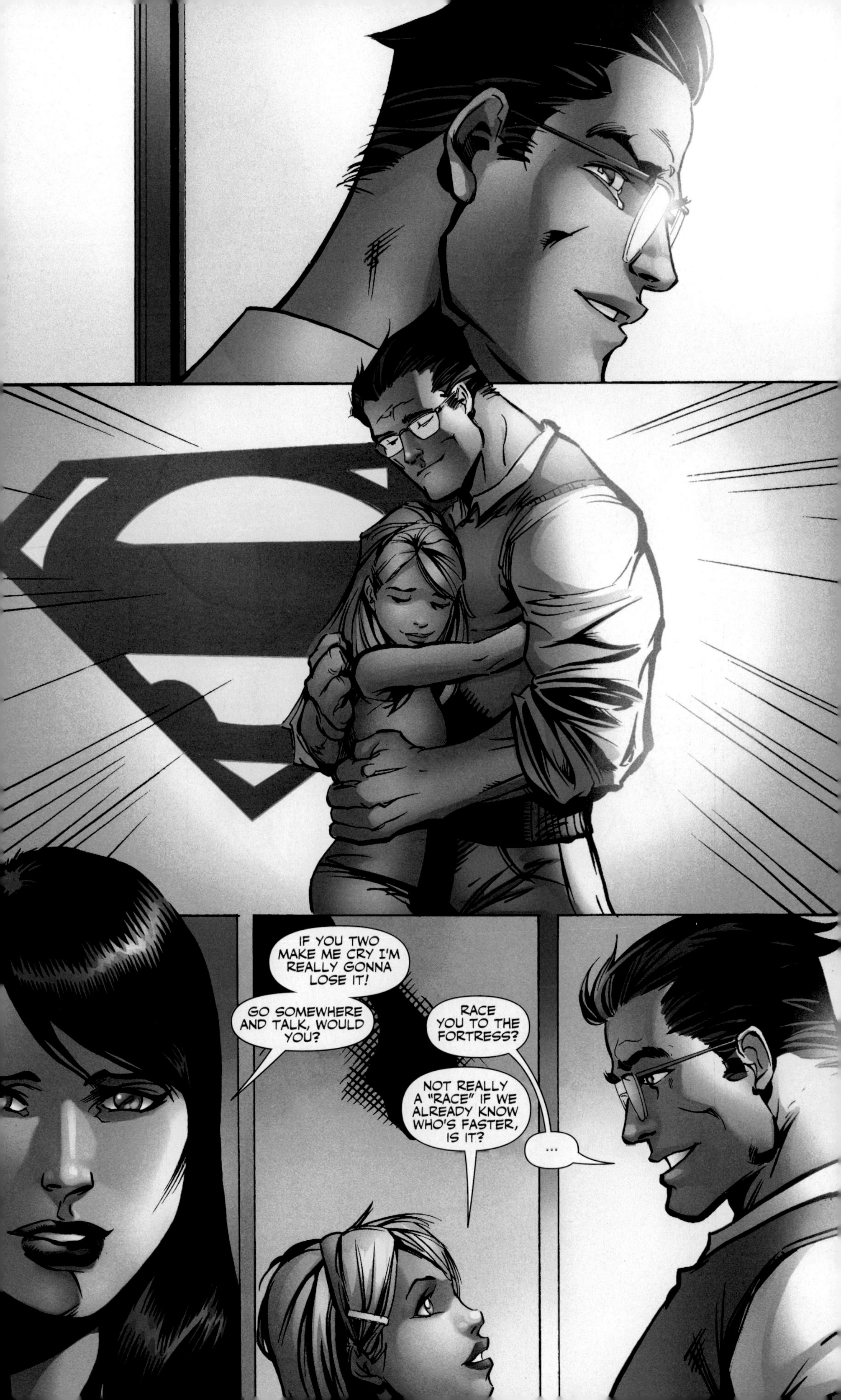
IF YOU TWO MAKE ME CRY I'M REALLY GONNA LOSE IT!
GO SOMEWHERE AND TALK, WOULD YOU?
RACE YOU TO THE FORTRESS?
NOT REALLY A "RACE" IF WE ALREADY KNOW WHO'S FASTER, IS IT?
...

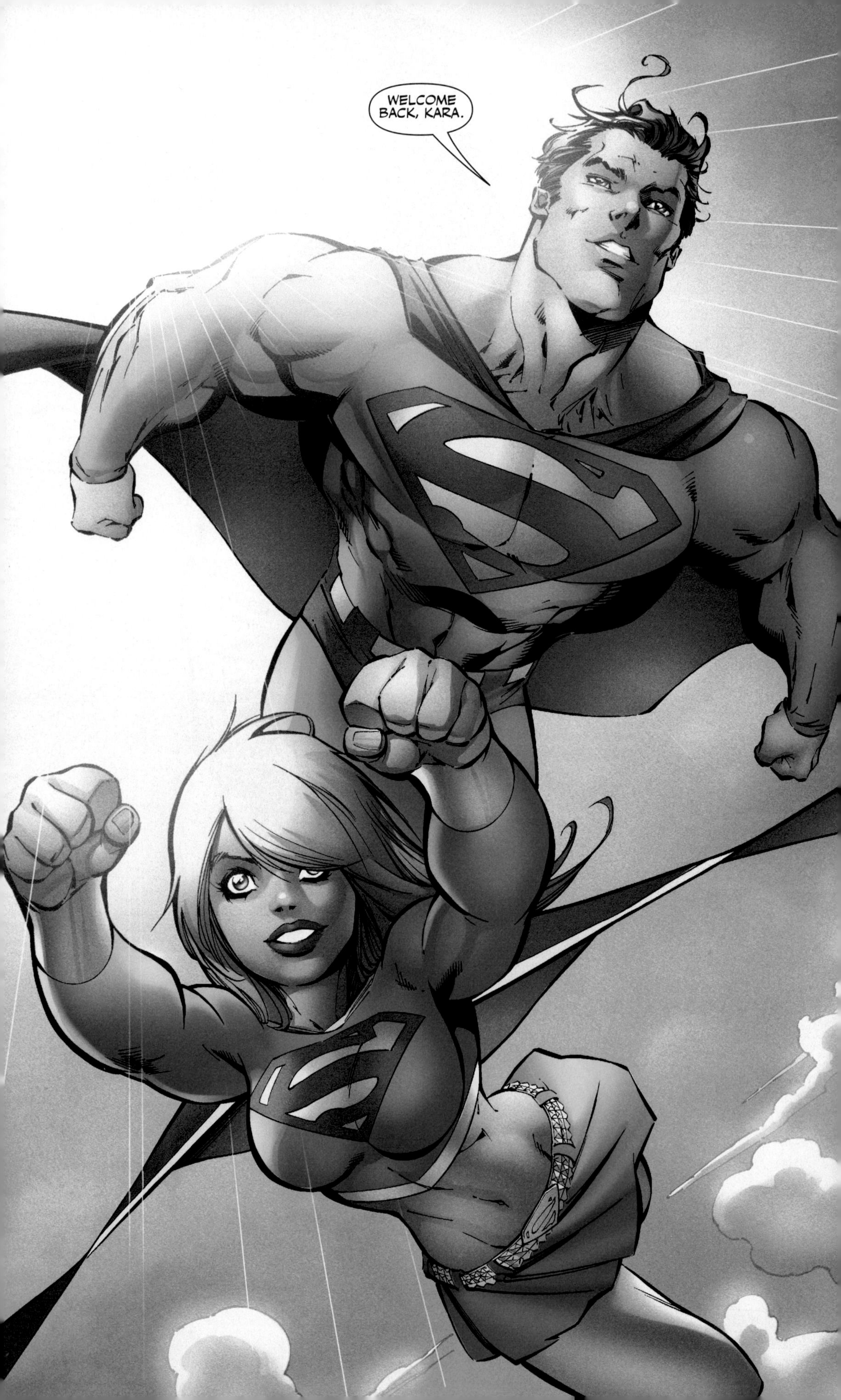
WELCOME BACK, KARA.

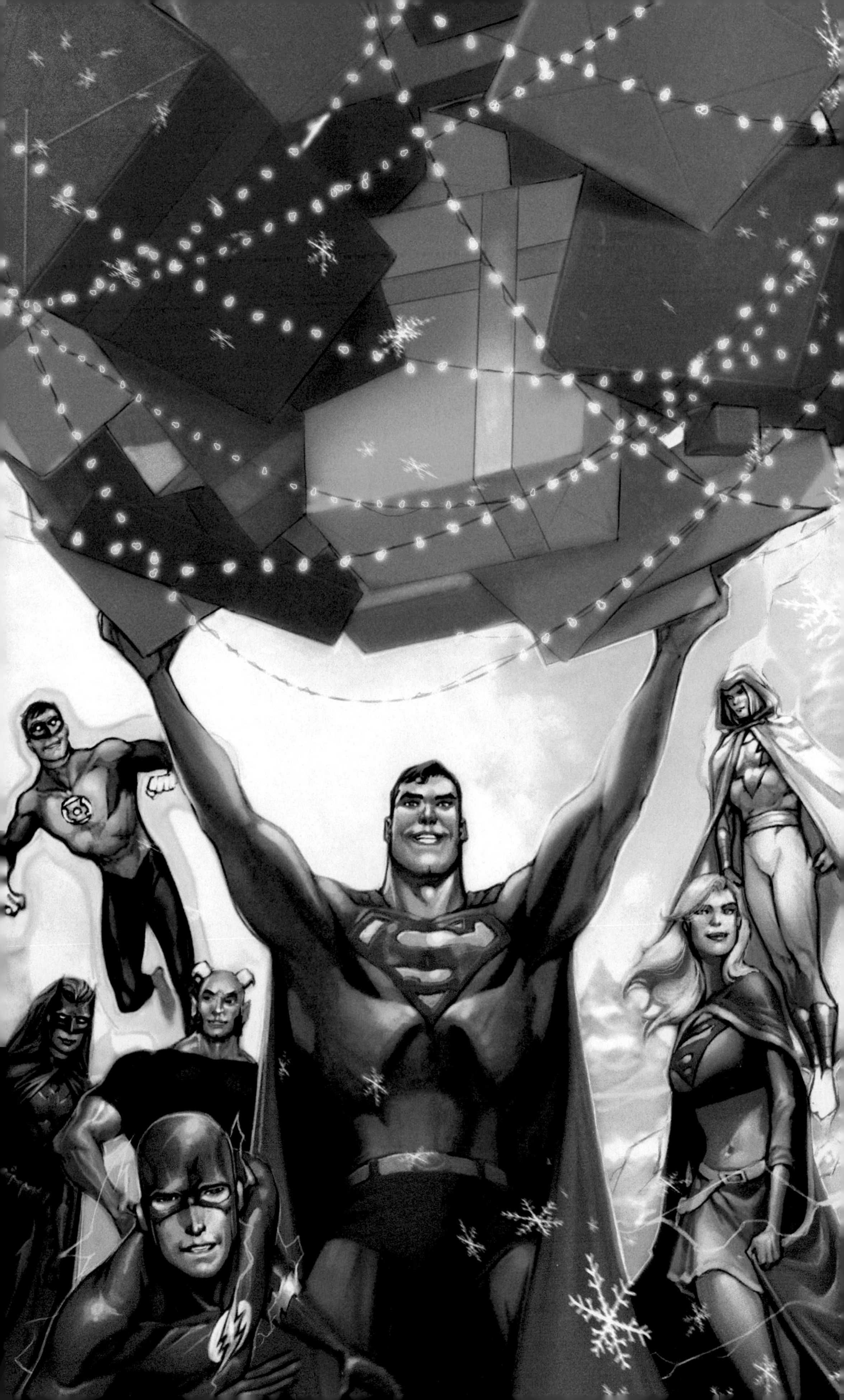

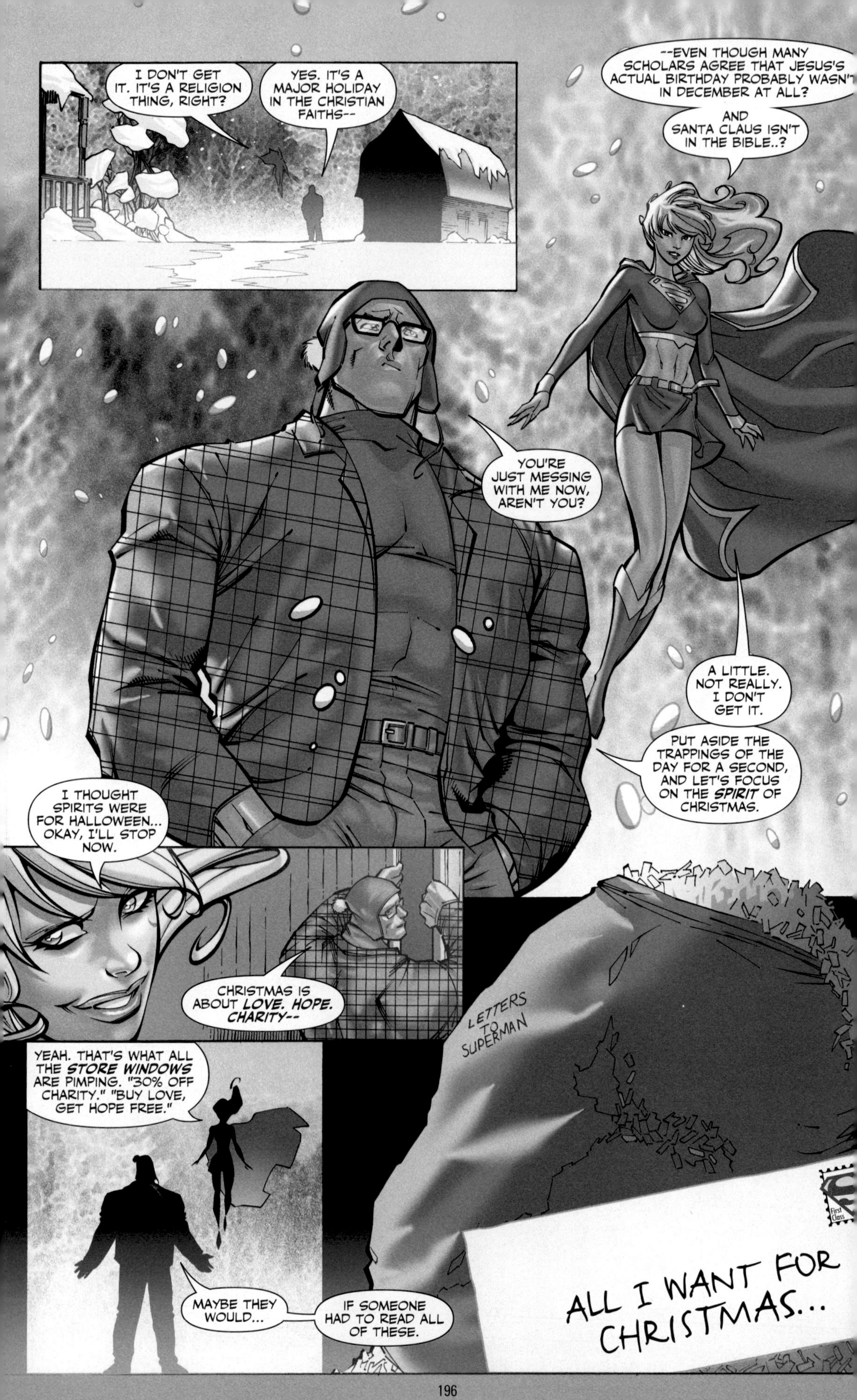

I DON'T GET IT. IT'S A RELIGION THING, RIGHT?
YES. IT'S A MAJOR HOLIDAY IN THE CHRISTIAN FAITHS--
--EVEN THOUGH MANY SCHOLARS AGREE THAT JESUS'S ACTUAL BIRTHDAY PROBABLY WASN'T IN DECEMBER AT ALL?
AND SANTA CLAUS ISN'T IN THE BIBLE..?
YOU'RE JUST MESSING WITH ME NOW, AREN'T YOU?
A LITTLE. NOT REALLY. I DON'T GET IT.
PUT ASIDE THE TRAPPINGS OF THE DAY FOR A SECOND, AND LET'S FOCUS ON THE SPIRIT OF CHRISTMAS.
I THOUGHT SPIRITS WERE FOR HALLOWEEN... OKAY, I'LL STOP NOW.
CHRISTMAS IS ABOUT LOVE. HOPE. CHARITY--
LETTERS TO SUPERMAN
YEAH. THAT'S WHAT ALL THE STORE WINDOWS ARE PIMPING. "30% OFF CHARITY." "BUY LOVE, GET HOPE FREE."
MAYBE THEY WOULD...
IF SOMEONE HAD TO READ ALL OF THESE.
First Class
ALL I WANT FOR CHRISTMAS...

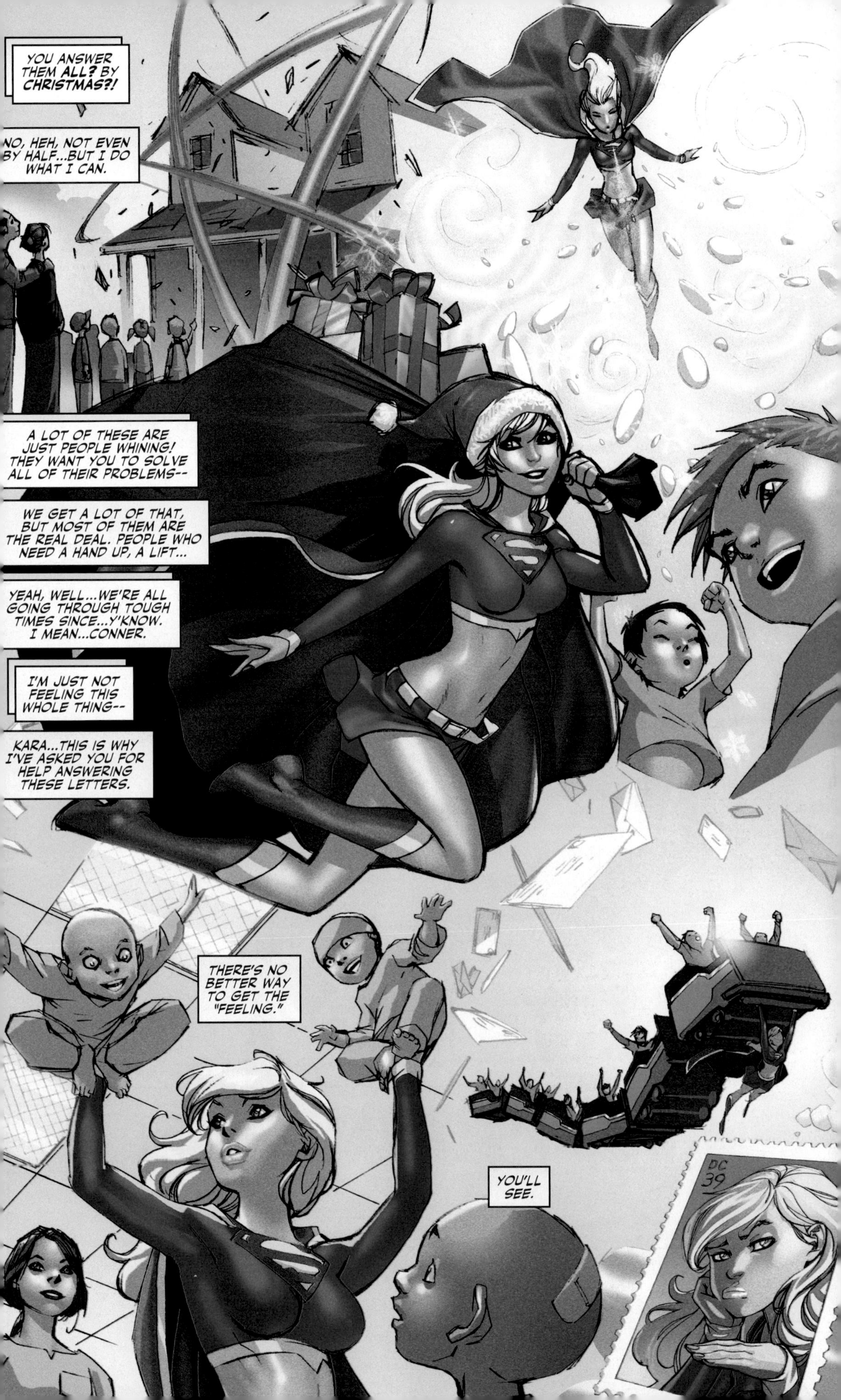
YOU ANSWER THEM ALL? BY CHRISTMAS?!
NO, HEH, NOT EVEN BY HALF...BUT I DO WHAT I CAN.
A LOT OF THESE ARE JUST PEOPLE WHINING! THEY WANT YOU TO SOLVE ALL OF THEIR PROBLEMS--
WE GET A LOT OF THAT, BUT MOST OF THEM ARE THE REAL DEAL. PEOPLE WHO NEED A HAND UP, A LIFT...
YEAH, WELL...WE'RE ALL GOING THROUGH TOUGH TIMES SINCE...Y'KNOW. I MEAN...CONNER.
I'M JUST NOT FEELING THIS WHOLE THING--
KARA...THIS IS WHY I'VE ASKED YOU FOR HELP ANSWERING THESE LETTERS.
THERE'S NO BETTER WAY TO GET THE "FEELING."
YOU'LL SEE.
DC 39

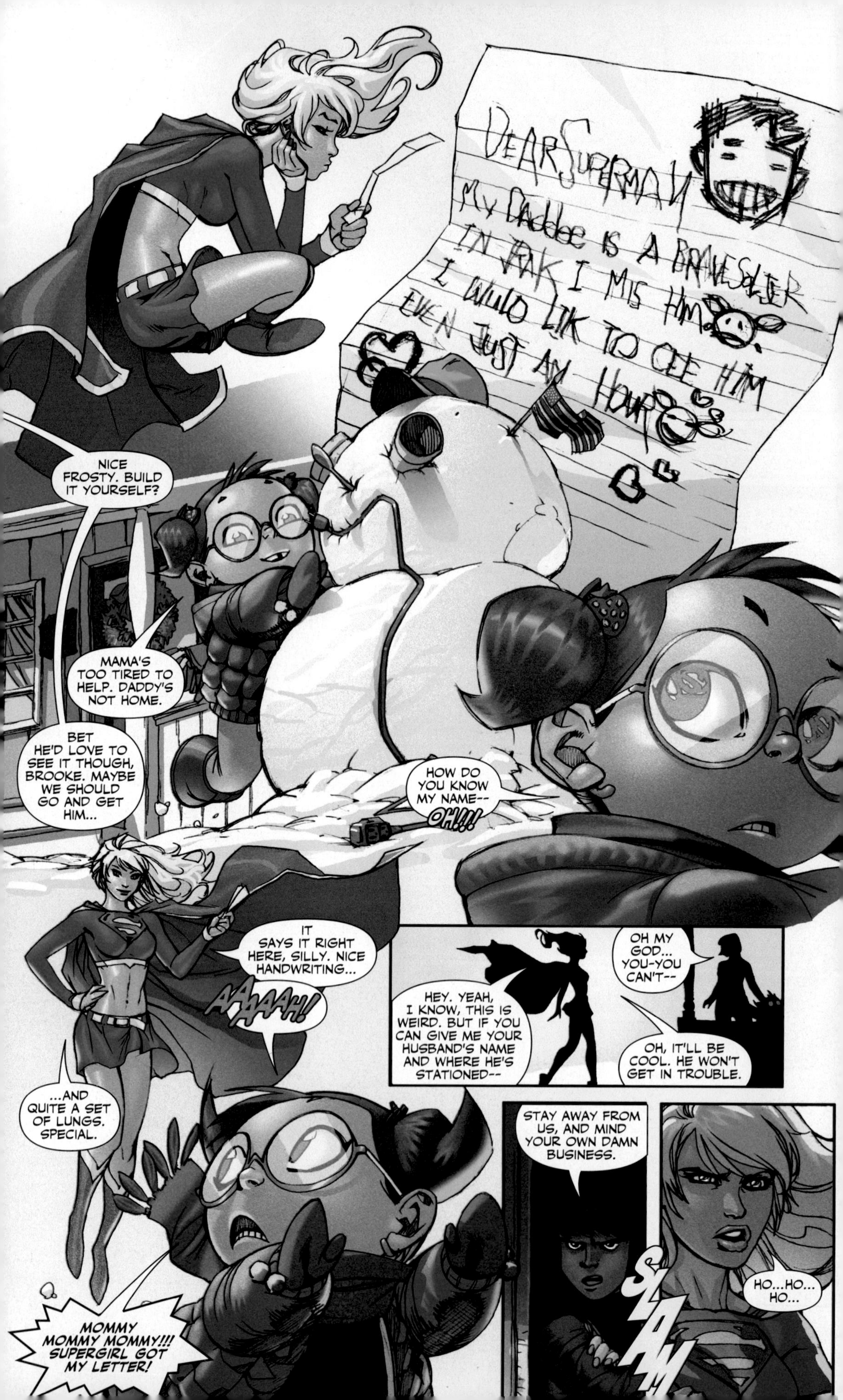

DEAR SUPERMAN
MY DADDEE IS A BRAVESOLJER IN IRAK I MIS HIM I WULD LIK TO CEE HIM EVEN JUST AN HOUR
NICE FROSTY. BUILD IT YOURSELF?
MAMA'S TOO TIRED TO HELP. DADDY'S NOT HOME.
BET HE'D LOVE TO SEE IT THOUGH, BROOKE. MAYBE WE SHOULD GO AND GET HIM...
HOW DO YOU KNOW MY NAME--
OH!!!
IT SAYS IT RIGHT HERE, SILLY. NICE HANDWRITING...
AAAAAH!
...AND QUITE A SET OF LUNGS. SPECIAL.
MOMMY MOMMY MOMMY!!! SUPERGIRL GOT MY LETTER!
OH MY GOD... YOU-YOU CAN'T--
HEY. YEAH, I KNOW, THIS IS WEIRD. BUT IF YOU CAN GIVE ME YOUR HUSBAND'S NAME AND WHERE HE'S STATIONED--
OH, IT'LL BE COOL. HE WON'T GET IN TROUBLE.
STAY AWAY FROM US, AND MIND YOUR OWN DAMN BUSINESS.
SLAM
HO...HO... HO...

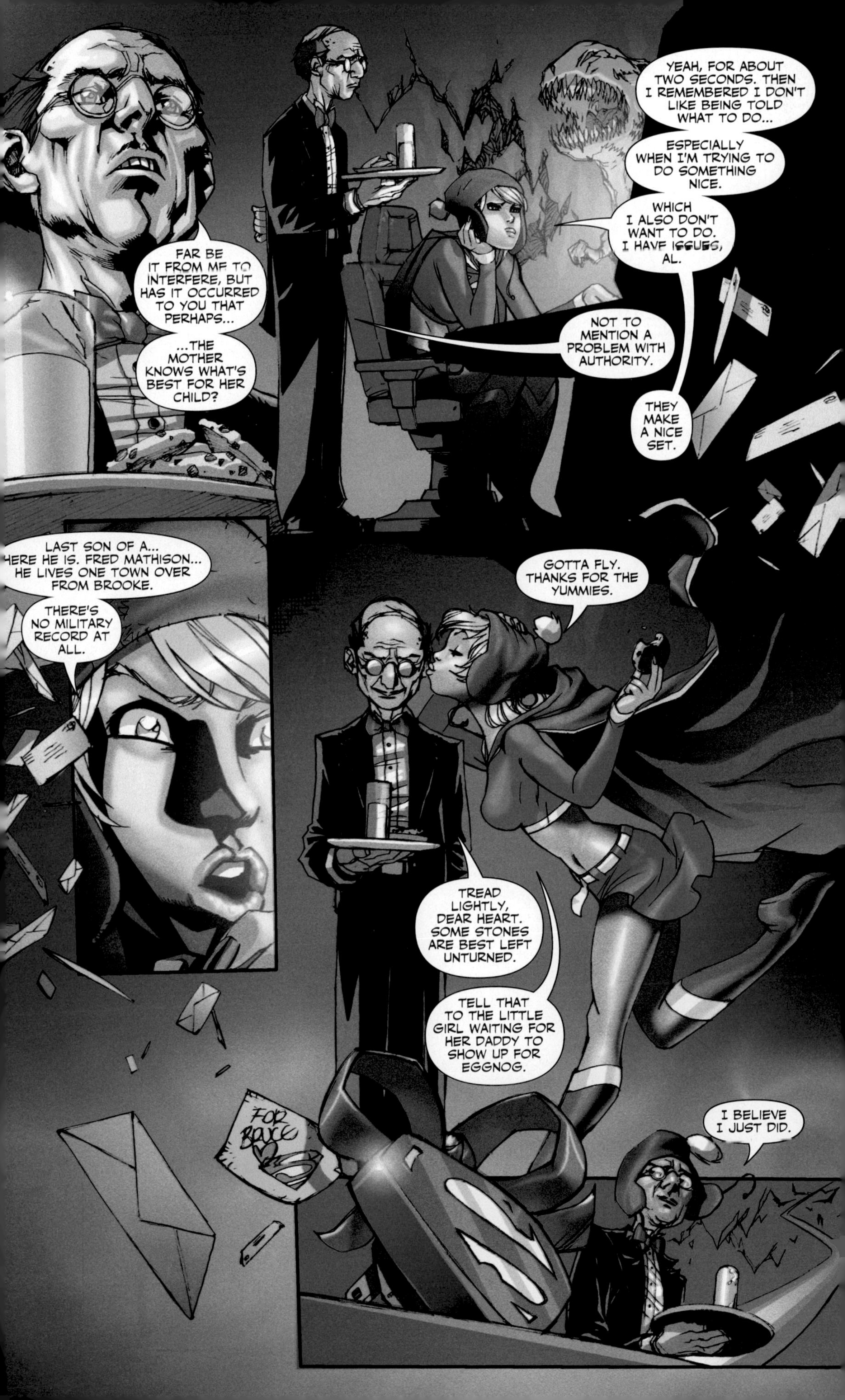
FAR BE IT FROM ME TO INTERFERE, BUT HAS IT OCCURRED TO YOU THAT PERHAPS...
...THE MOTHER KNOWS WHAT'S BEST FOR HER CHILD?
YEAH, FOR ABOUT TWO SECONDS. THEN I REMEMBERED I DON'T LIKE BEING TOLD WHAT TO DO...
ESPECIALLY WHEN I'M TRYING TO DO SOMETHING NICE.
WHICH I ALSO DON'T WANT TO DO. I HAVE ISSUES, AL.
NOT TO MENTION A PROBLEM WITH AUTHORITY.
THEY MAKE A NICE SET.
LAST SON OF A... HERE HE IS. FRED MATHISON... HE LIVES ONE TOWN OVER FROM BROOKE.
THERE'S NO MILITARY RECORD AT ALL.
GOTTA FLY. THANKS FOR THE YUMMIES.
TREAD LIGHTLY, DEAR HEART. SOME STONES ARE BEST LEFT UNTURNED.
TELL THAT TO THE LITTLE GIRL WAITING FOR HER DADDY TO SHOW UP FOR EGGNOG.
FOR BRUCE
I BELIEVE I JUST DID.

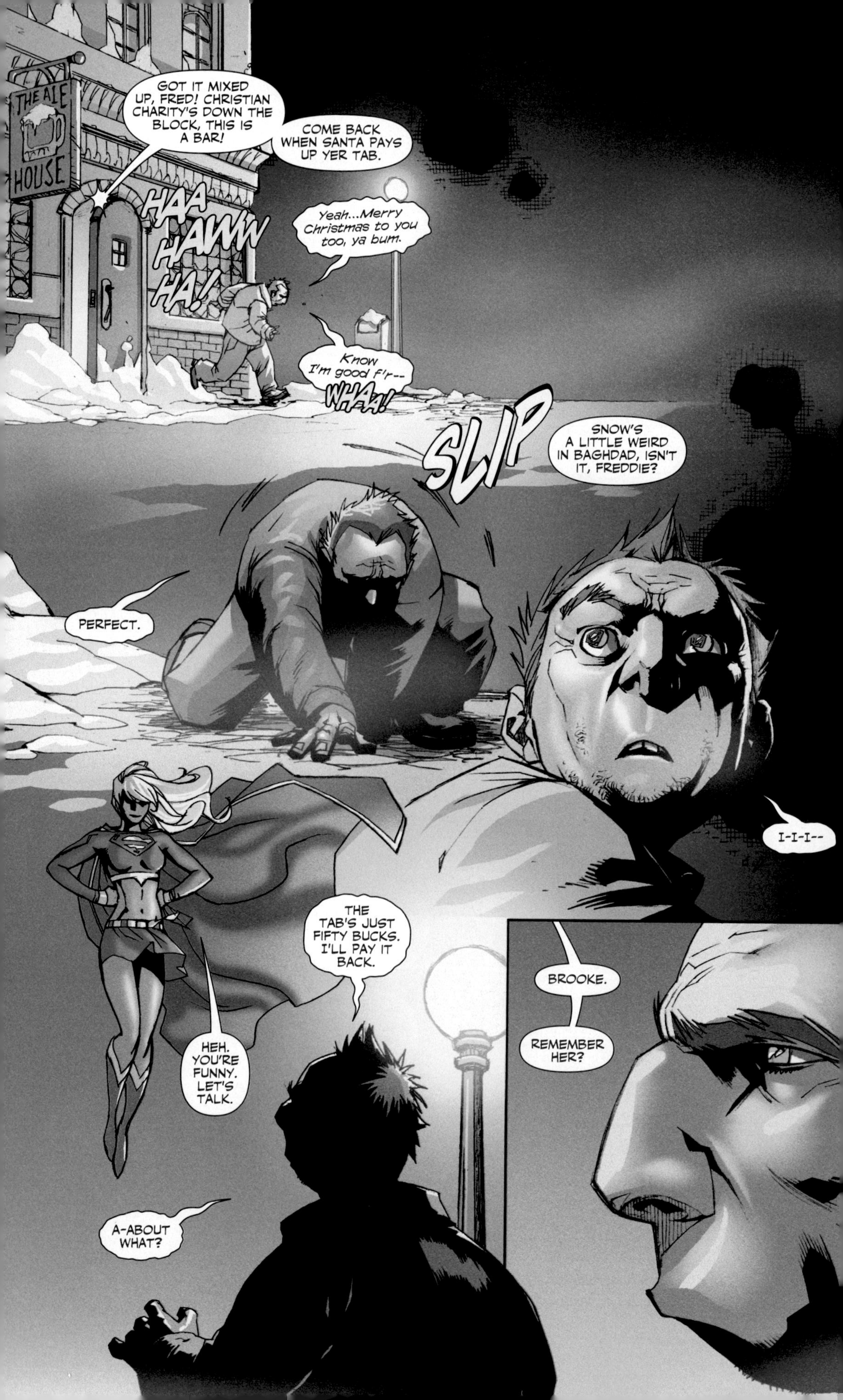
THE ALE HOUSE
GOT IT MIXED UP, FRED! CHRISTIAN CHARITY'S DOWN THE BLOCK, THIS IS A BAR!
COME BACK WHEN SANTA PAYS UP YER TAB.
HAA HAWW HA HA!
Yeah...Merry Christmas to you too, ya bum.
Know I'm good f'r--
WHAA!
SLIP
SNOW'S A LITTLE WEIRD IN BAGHDAD, ISN'T IT, FREDDIE?
PERFECT.
I-I-I--
THE TAB'S JUST FIFTY BUCKS. I'LL PAY IT BACK.
HEH. YOU'RE FUNNY. LET'S TALK.
A-ABOUT WHAT?
BROOKE.
REMEMBER HER?

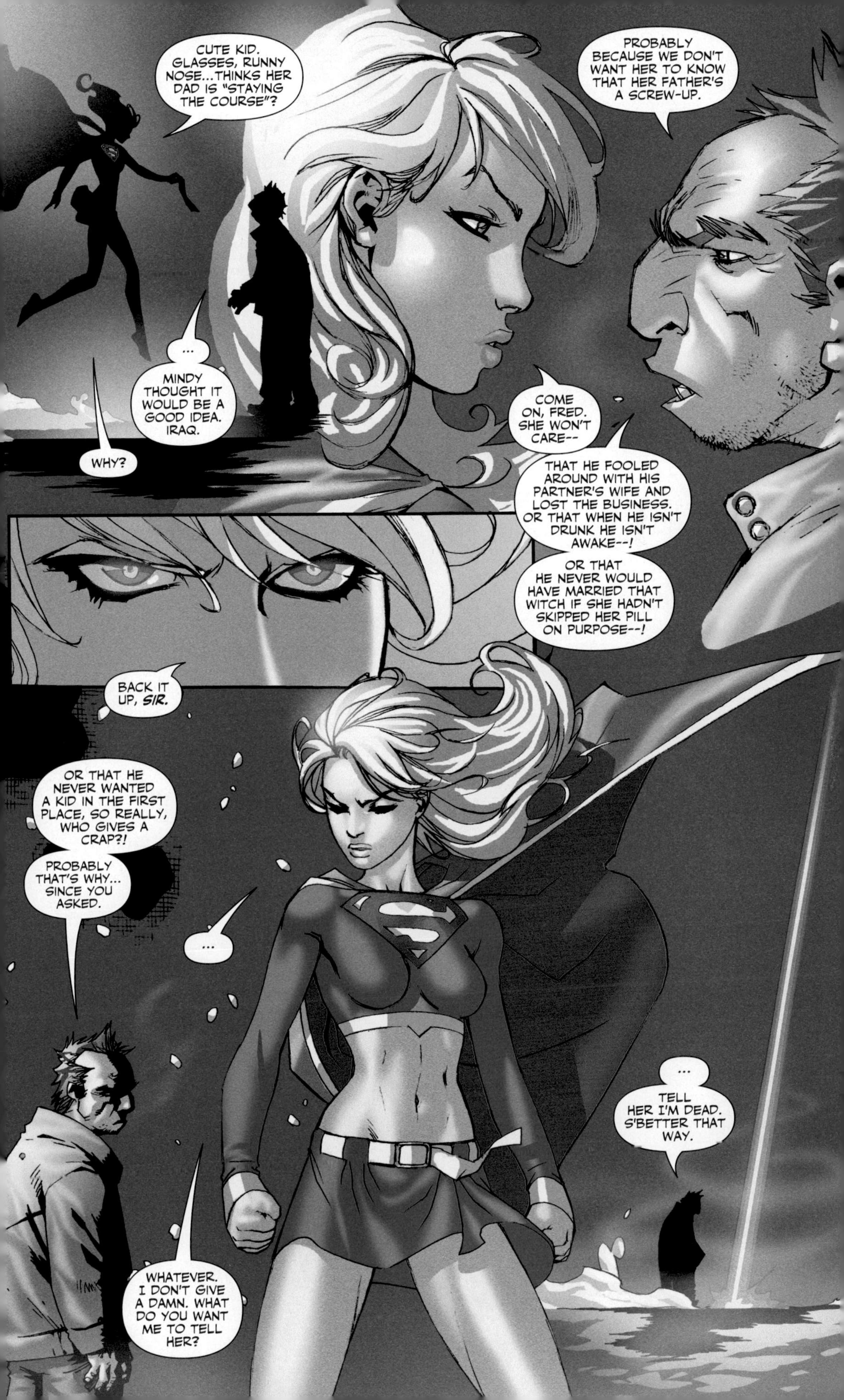
CUTE KID. GLASSES, RUNNY NOSE...THINKS HER DAD IS "STAYING THE COURSE"?
PROBABLY BECAUSE WE DON'T WANT HER TO KNOW THAT HER FATHER'S A SCREW-UP.
...
MINDY THOUGHT IT WOULD BE A GOOD IDEA. IRAQ.
WHY?
COME ON, FRED. SHE WON'T CARE--
THAT HE FOOLED AROUND WITH HIS PARTNER'S WIFE AND LOST THE BUSINESS. OR THAT WHEN HE ISN'T DRUNK HE ISN'T AWAKE--!
OR THAT HE NEVER WOULD HAVE MARRIED THAT WITCH IF SHE HADN'T SKIPPED HER PILL ON PURPOSE--!
BACK IT UP, SIR.
OR THAT HE NEVER WANTED A KID IN THE FIRST PLACE, SO REALLY, WHO GIVES A CRAP?!
PROBABLY THAT'S WHY... SINCE YOU ASKED.
...
WHATEVER. I DON'T GIVE A DAMN. WHAT DO YOU WANT ME TO TELL HER?
...
TELL HER I'M DEAD. S'BETTER THAT WAY.

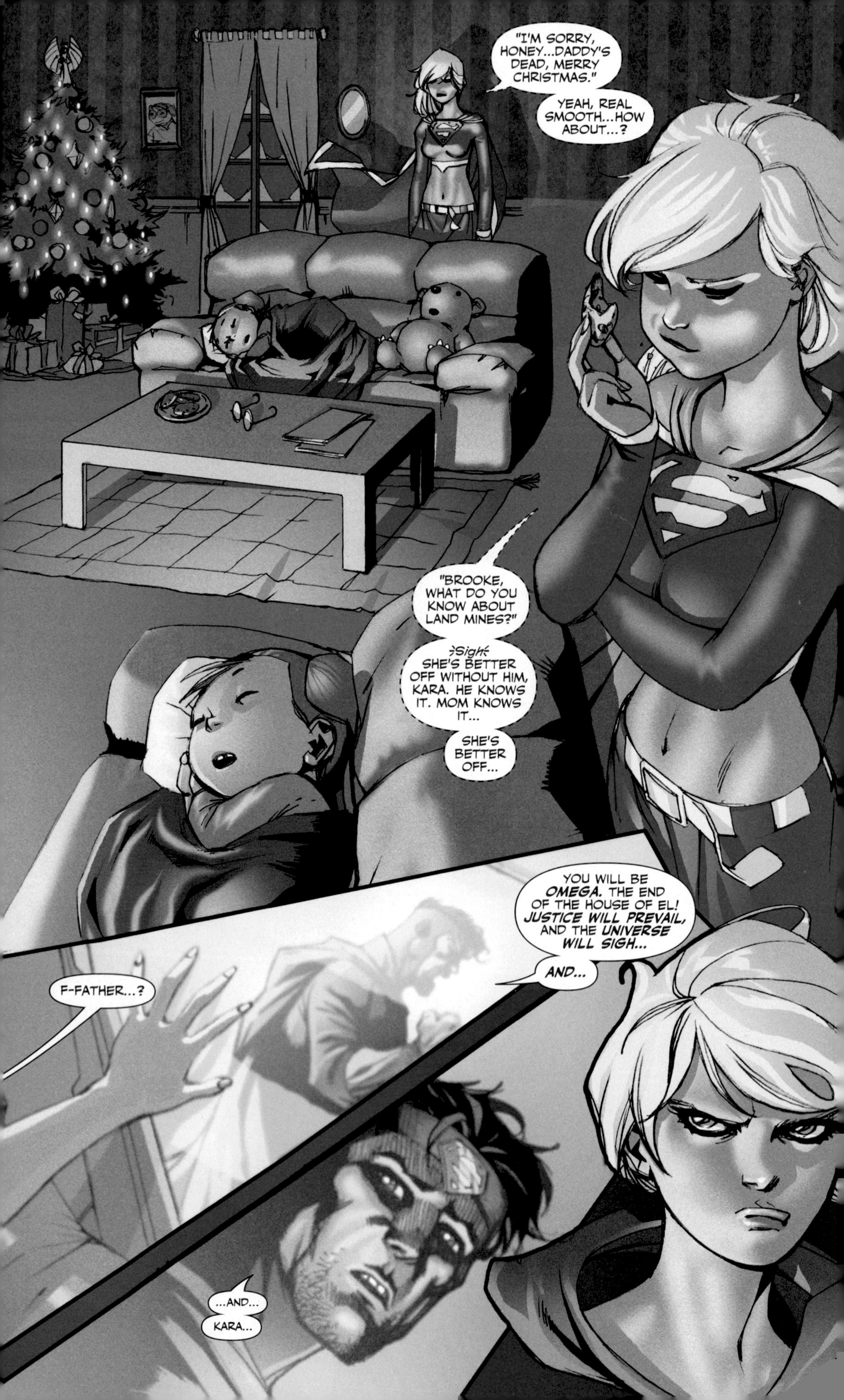
"I'M SORRY, HONEY...DADDY'S DEAD, MERRY CHRISTMAS."
YEAH, REAL SMOOTH...HOW ABOUT...?
"BROOKE, WHAT DO YOU KNOW ABOUT LAND MINES?"
Sigh SHE'S BETTER OFF WITHOUT HIM, KARA. HE KNOWS IT. MOM KNOWS IT...
SHE'S BETTER OFF...
YOU WILL BE OMEGA. THE END OF THE HOUSE OF EL! JUSTICE WILL PREVAIL, AND THE UNIVERSE WILL SIGH...
AND...
F-FATHER...?
...AND...
KARA...

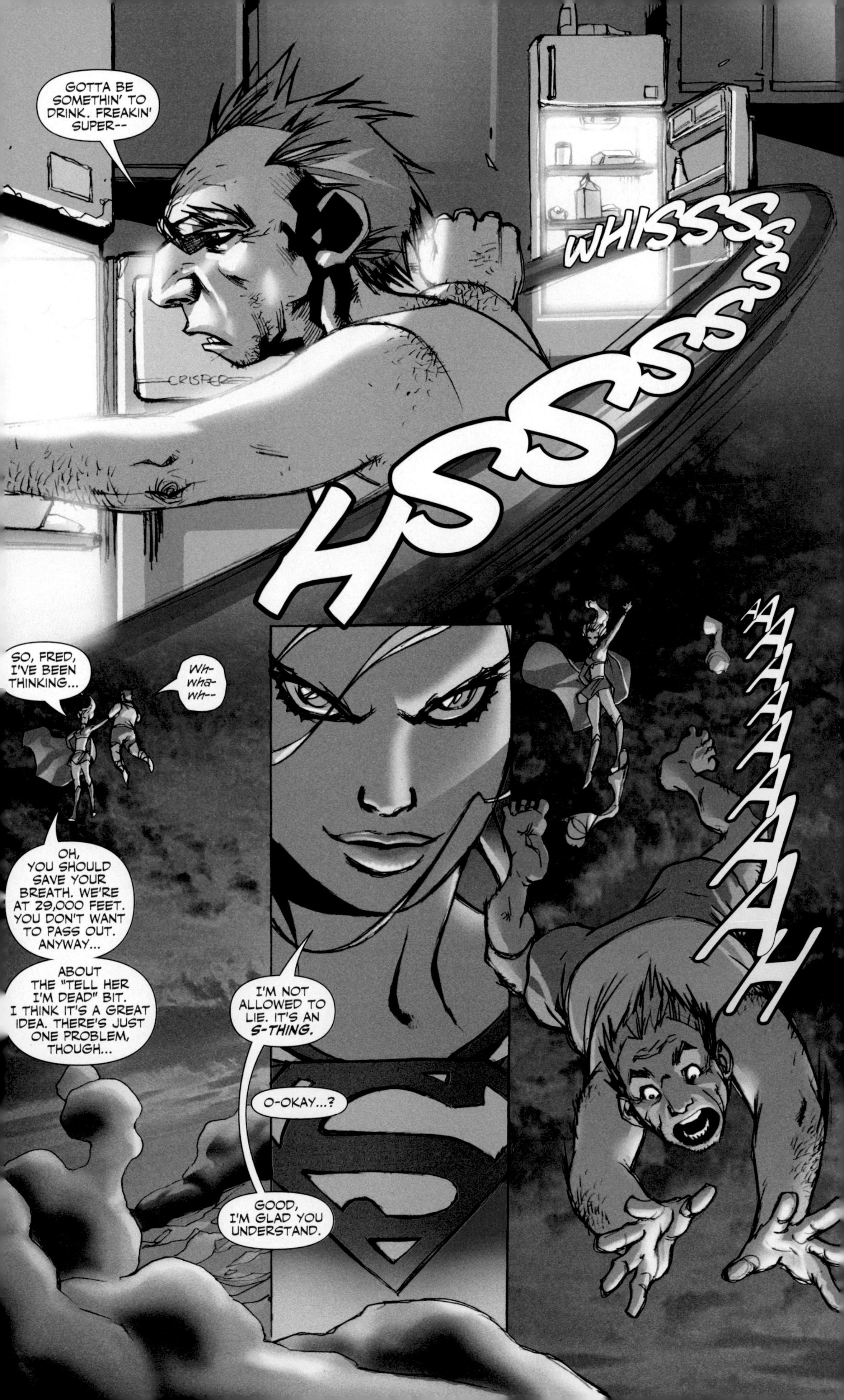
GOTTA BE SOMETHIN' TO DRINK. FREAKIN' SUPER--
CRISPER
WHISSSSSSSSSSSH
SO, FRED, I'VE BEEN THINKING...
Wh-wha-wh--
OH, YOU SHOULD SAVE YOUR BREATH. WE'RE AT 29,000 FEET. YOU DON'T WANT TO PASS OUT. ANYWAY...
ABOUT THE "TELL HER I'M DEAD" BIT. I THINK IT'S A GREAT IDEA. THERE'S JUST ONE PROBLEM, THOUGH...
I'M NOT ALLOWED TO LIE. IT'S AN S-THING.
O-OKAY...?
GOOD, I'M GLAD YOU UNDERSTAND.
AAAAAAAAAAH

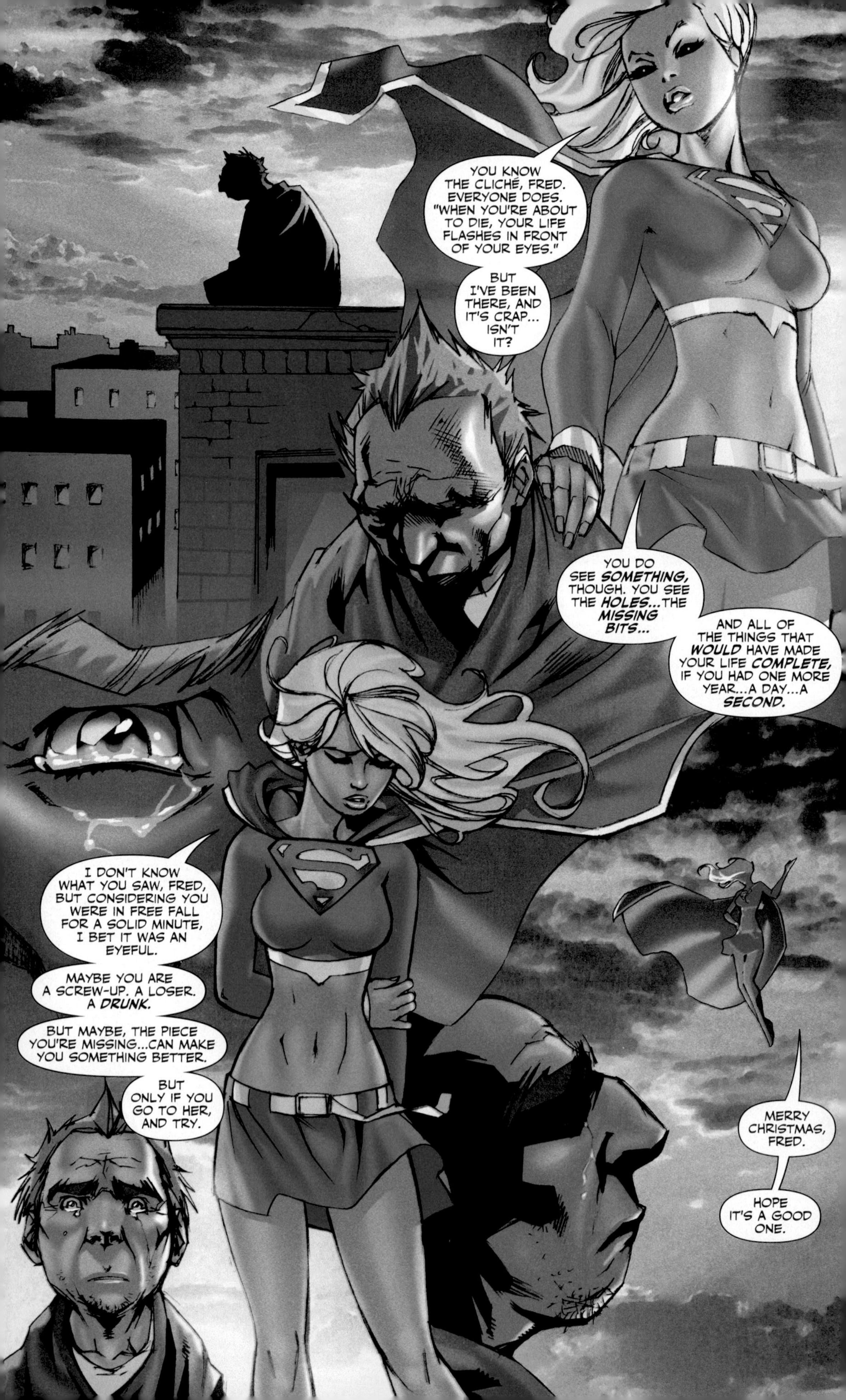

YOU KNOW THE CLICHÉ, FRED. EVERYONE DOES. "WHEN YOU'RE ABOUT TO DIE, YOUR LIFE FLASHES IN FRONT OF YOUR EYES."
BUT I'VE BEEN THERE, AND IT'S CRAP... ISN'T IT?
YOU DO SEE *SOMETHING,* THOUGH. YOU SEE THE *HOLES...*THE *MISSING BITS...*
AND ALL OF THE THINGS THAT *WOULD* HAVE MADE YOUR LIFE *COMPLETE,* IF YOU HAD ONE MORE YEAR...A DAY...A *SECOND.*
I DON'T KNOW WHAT YOU SAW, FRED, BUT CONSIDERING YOU WERE IN FREE FALL FOR A SOLID MINUTE, I BET IT WAS AN EYEFUL.
MAYBE YOU ARE A SCREW-UP. A LOSER. A *DRUNK.*
BUT MAYBE, THE PIECE YOU'RE MISSING...CAN MAKE YOU SOMETHING BETTER.
BUT ONLY IF YOU GO TO HER, AND TRY.
MERRY CHRISTMAS, FRED.
HOPE IT'S A GOOD ONE.

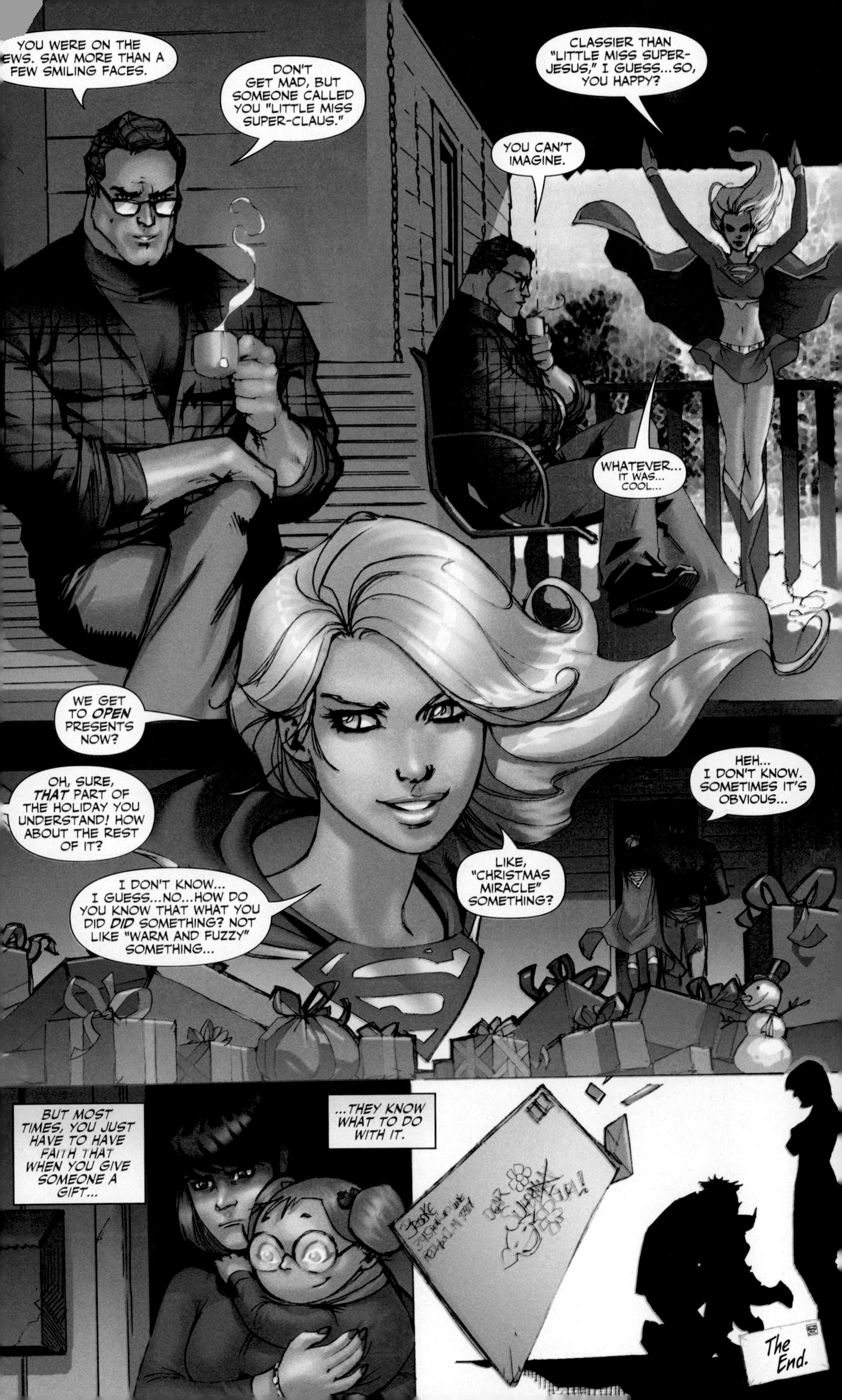

YOU WERE ON THE
EWS. SAW MORE THAN A
FEW SMILING FACES.
DON'T GET MAD, BUT SOMEONE CALLED YOU "LITTLE MISS SUPER-CLAUS."
YOU CAN'T IMAGINE.
CLASSIER THAN "LITTLE MISS SUPER-JESUS," I GUESS...SO, YOU HAPPY?
WHATEVER... IT WAS... COOL...
WE GET TO *OPEN* PRESENTS NOW?
OH, SURE, *THAT* PART OF THE HOLIDAY YOU UNDERSTAND! HOW ABOUT THE REST OF IT?
I DON'T KNOW... I GUESS...NO...HOW DO YOU KNOW THAT WHAT YOU DID *DID* SOMETHING? NOT LIKE "WARM AND FUZZY" SOMETHING...
LIKE, "CHRISTMAS MIRACLE" SOMETHING?
HEH... I DON'T KNOW. SOMETIMES IT'S OBVIOUS...
BUT MOST TIMES, YOU JUST HAVE TO HAVE FAITH THAT WHEN YOU GIVE SOMEONE A GIFT...
...THEY KNOW WHAT TO DO WITH IT.
The End.

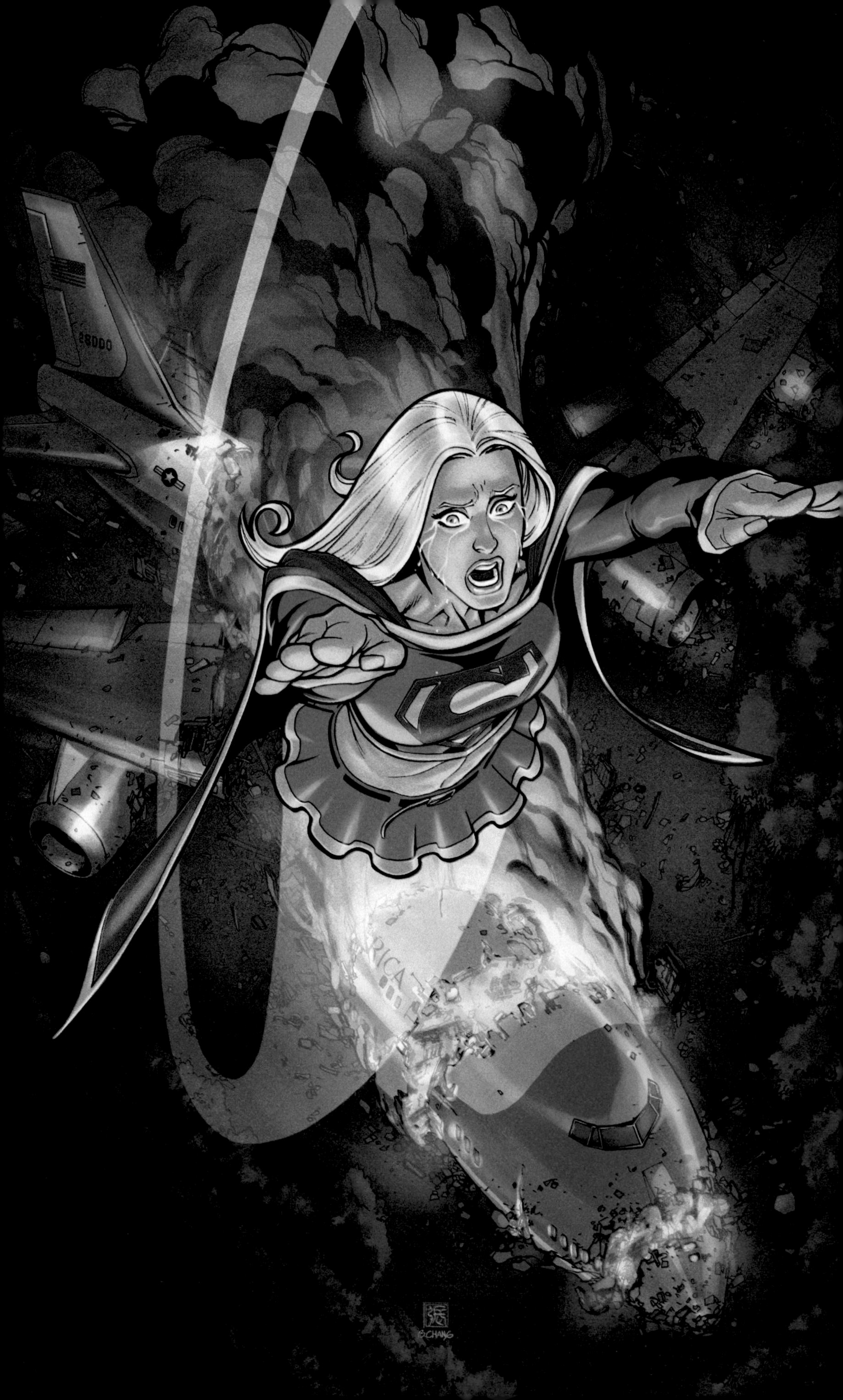
28000

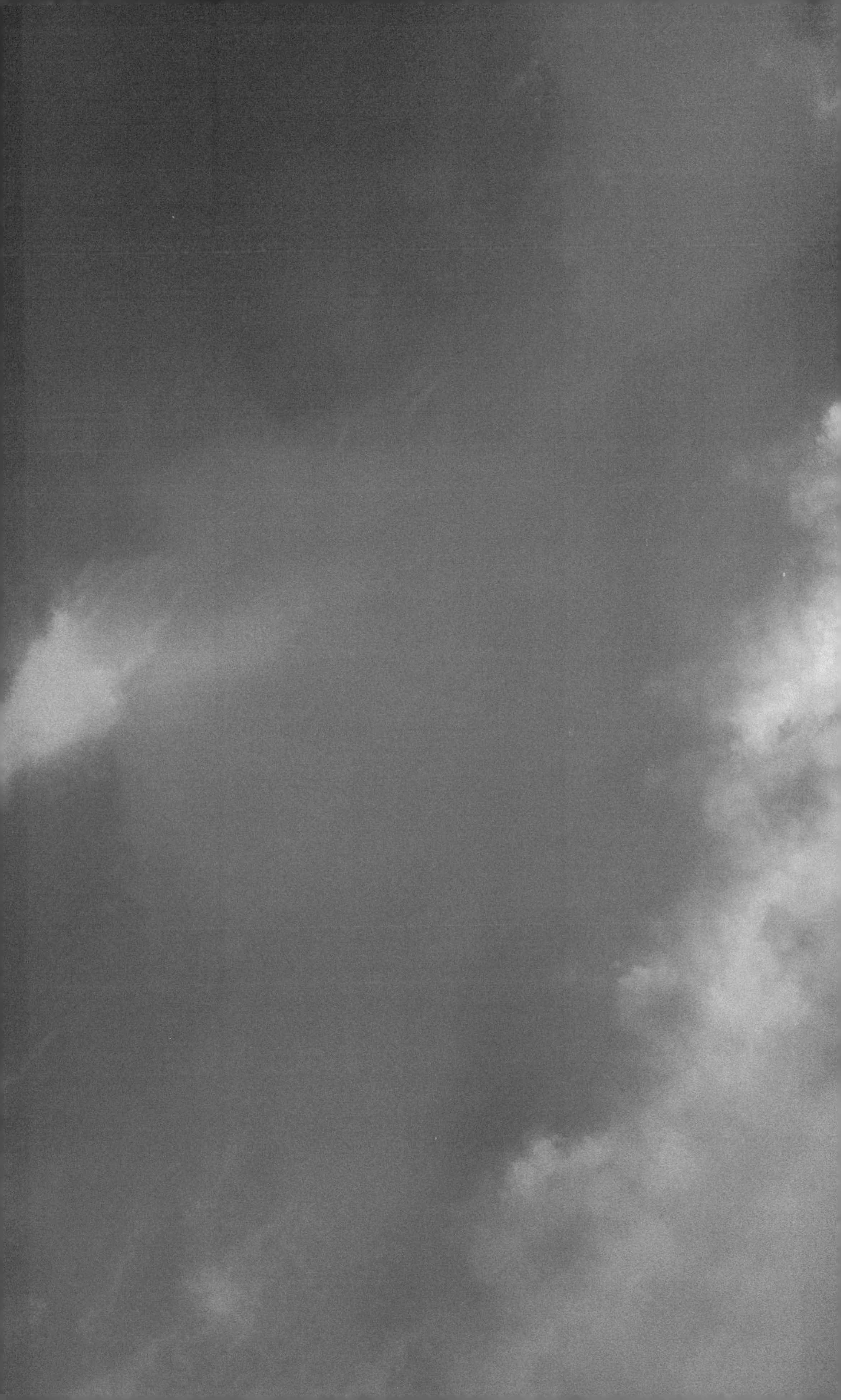

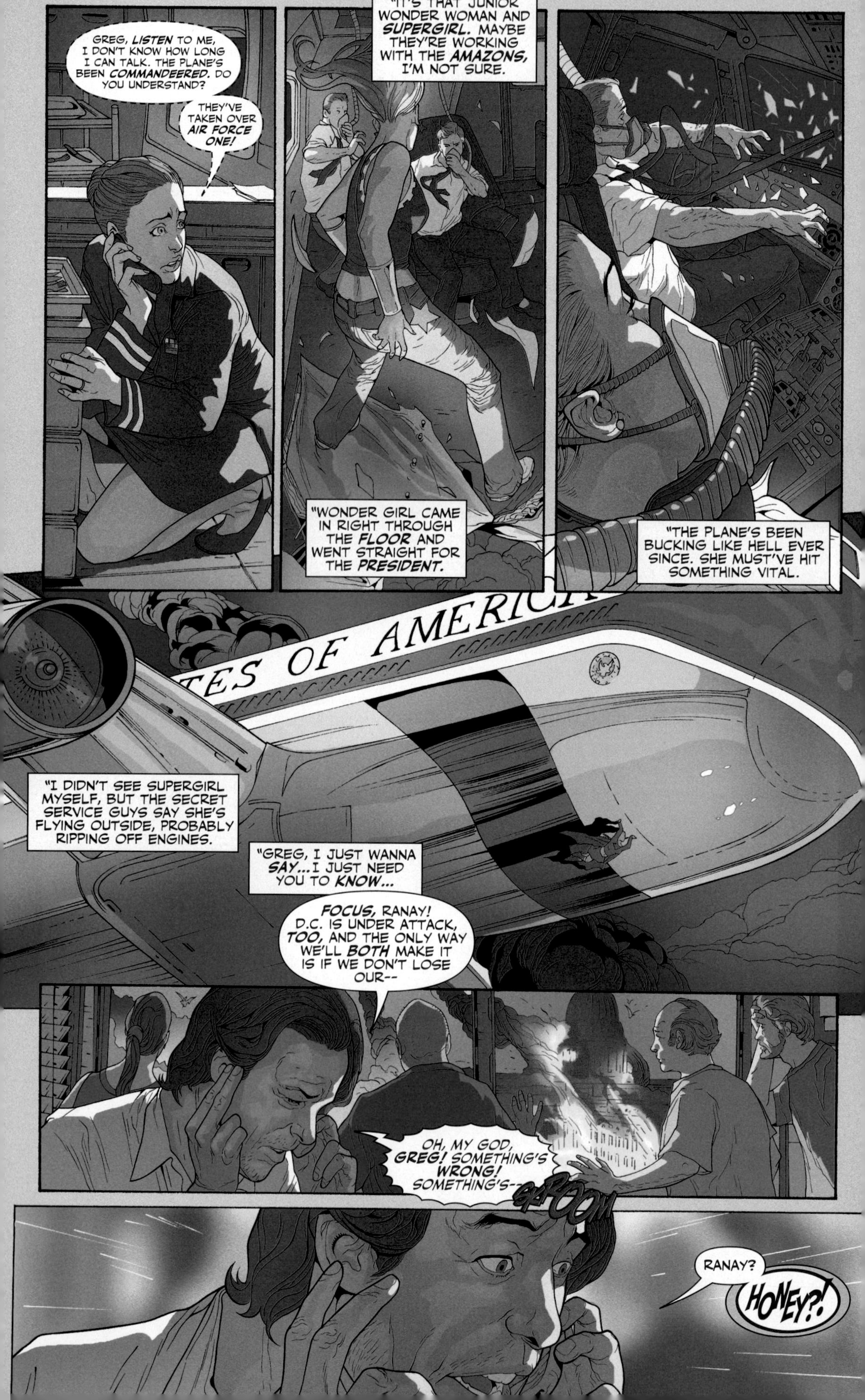

GREG, LISTEN TO ME, I DON'T KNOW HOW LONG I CAN TALK. THE PLANE'S BEEN COMMANDEERED. DO YOU UNDERSTAND?
THEY'VE TAKEN OVER AIR FORCE ONE!
"IT'S THAT JUNIOR WONDER WOMAN AND SUPERGIRL. MAYBE THEY'RE WORKING WITH THE AMAZONS, I'M NOT SURE.
"WONDER GIRL CAME IN RIGHT THROUGH THE FLOOR AND WENT STRAIGHT FOR THE PRESIDENT.
"THE PLANE'S BEEN BUCKING LIKE HELL EVER SINCE. SHE MUST'VE HIT SOMETHING VITAL.
TES OF AMERICA
"I DIDN'T SEE SUPERGIRL MYSELF, BUT THE SECRET SERVICE GUYS SAY SHE'S FLYING OUTSIDE, PROBABLY RIPPING OFF ENGINES.
"GREG, I JUST WANNA SAY...I JUST NEED YOU TO KNOW...
FOCUS, RANAY! D.C. IS UNDER ATTACK, TOO, AND THE ONLY WAY WE'LL BOTH MAKE IT IS IF WE DON'T LOSE OUR--
OH, MY GOD, GREG! SOMETHING'S WRONG! SOMETHING'S--
SKROOM
RANAY?
HONEY?!

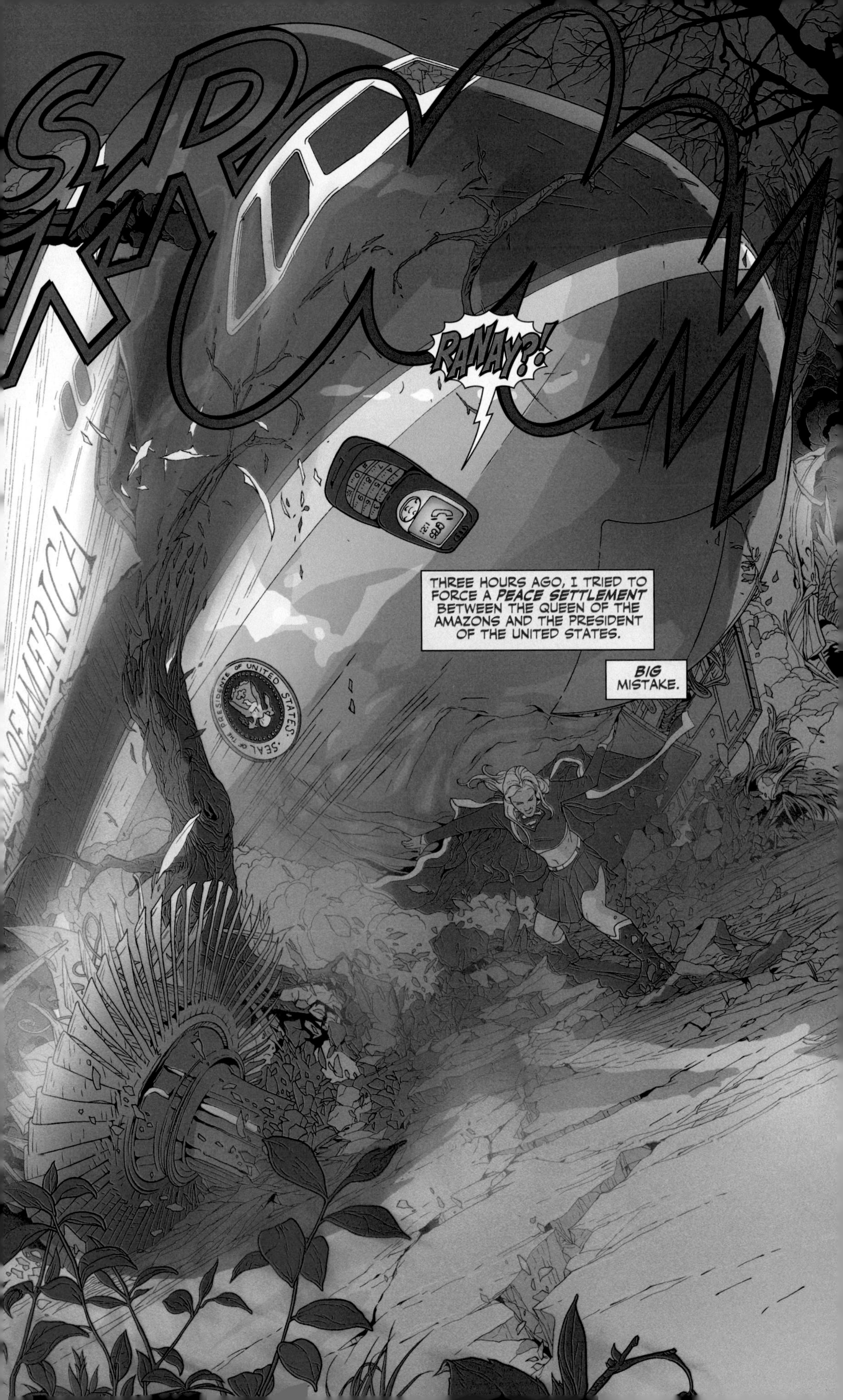
SPRAKAKOOM
RANAY?!
THREE HOURS AGO, I TRIED TO FORCE A *PEACE SETTLEMENT* BETWEEN THE QUEEN OF THE AMAZONS AND THE PRESIDENT OF THE UNITED STATES.
BIG MISTAKE.
SEAL OF THE PRESIDENT OF THE UNITED STATES

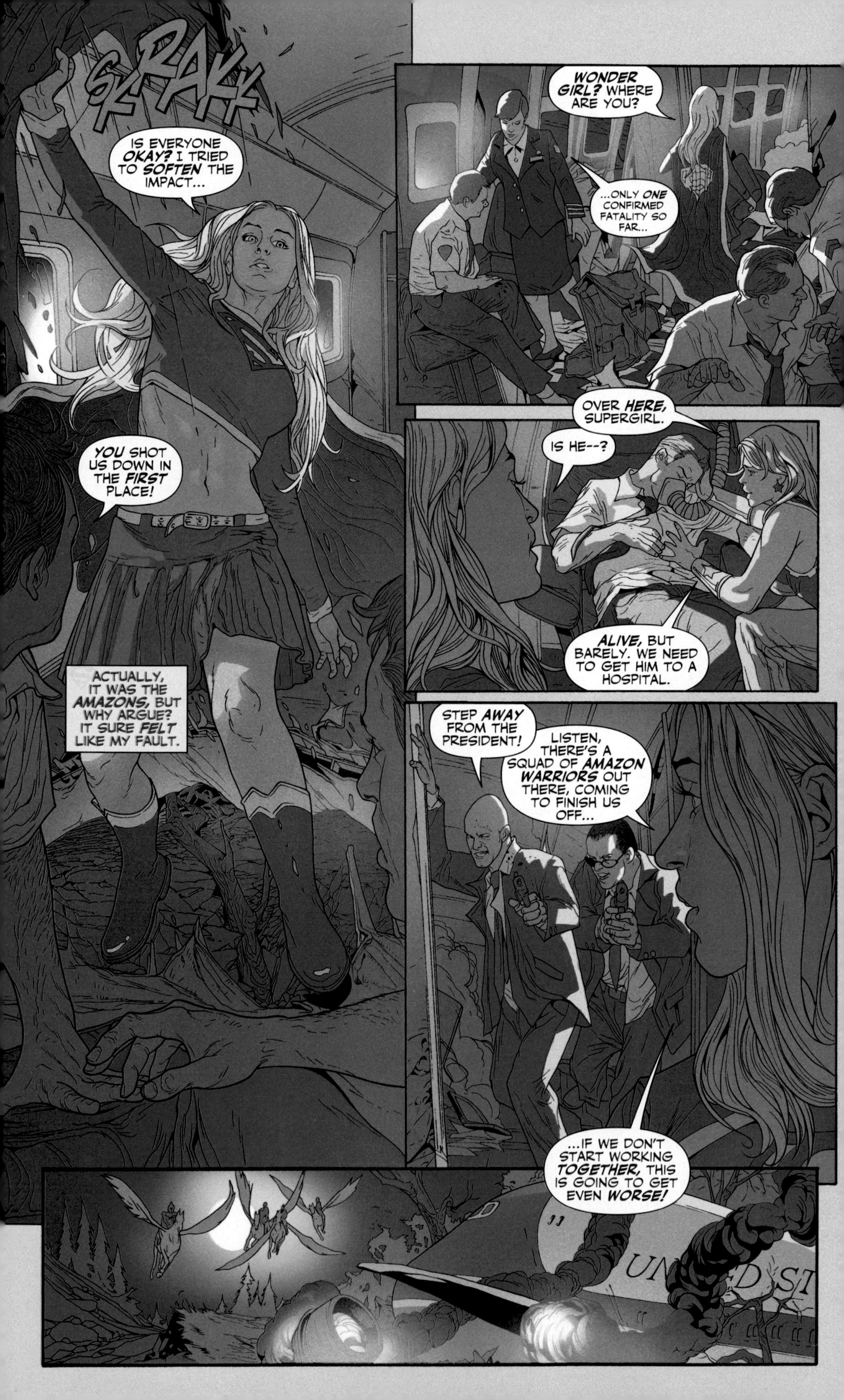
SKRAKK
IS EVERYONE OKAY? I TRIED TO SOFTEN THE IMPACT...
YOU SHOT US DOWN IN THE FIRST PLACE!
ACTUALLY, IT WAS THE AMAZONS, BUT WHY ARGUE? IT SURE FELT LIKE MY FAULT.
WONDER GIRL? WHERE ARE YOU?
...ONLY ONE CONFIRMED FATALITY SO FAR...
OVER HERE, SUPERGIRL.
IS HE--?
ALIVE, BUT BARELY. WE NEED TO GET HIM TO A HOSPITAL.
STEP AWAY FROM THE PRESIDENT!
LISTEN, THERE'S A SQUAD OF AMAZON WARRIORS OUT THERE, COMING TO FINISH US OFF...
...IF WE DON'T START WORKING TOGETHER, THIS IS GOING TO GET EVEN WORSE!

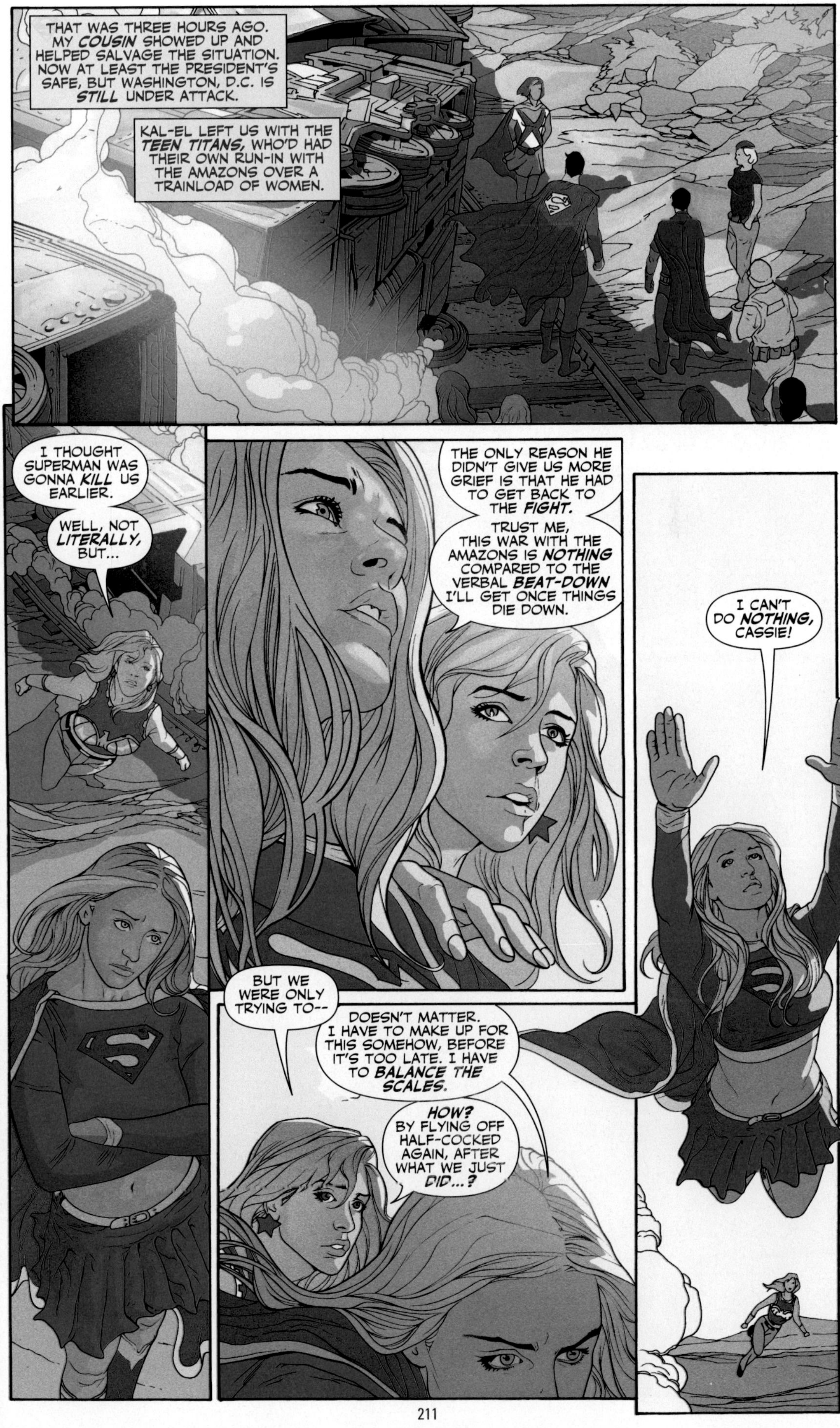
THAT WAS THREE HOURS AGO. MY COUSIN SHOWED UP AND HELPED SALVAGE THE SITUATION. NOW AT LEAST THE PRESIDENT'S SAFE, BUT WASHINGTON, D.C. IS STILL UNDER ATTACK.
KAL-EL LEFT US WITH THE TEEN TITANS, WHO'D HAD THEIR OWN RUN-IN WITH THE AMAZONS OVER A TRAINLOAD OF WOMEN.
I THOUGHT SUPERMAN WAS GONNA KILL US EARLIER.
WELL, NOT LITERALLY, BUT...
THE ONLY REASON HE DIDN'T GIVE US MORE GRIEF IS THAT HE HAD TO GET BACK TO THE FIGHT.
TRUST ME, THIS WAR WITH THE AMAZONS IS NOTHING COMPARED TO THE VERBAL BEAT-DOWN I'LL GET ONCE THINGS DIE DOWN.
BUT WE WERE ONLY TRYING TO--
DOESN'T MATTER. I HAVE TO MAKE UP FOR THIS SOMEHOW, BEFORE IT'S TOO LATE. I HAVE TO BALANCE THE SCALES.
HOW? BY FLYING OFF HALF-COCKED AGAIN, AFTER WHAT WE JUST DID...?
I CAN'T DO NOTHING, CASSIE!

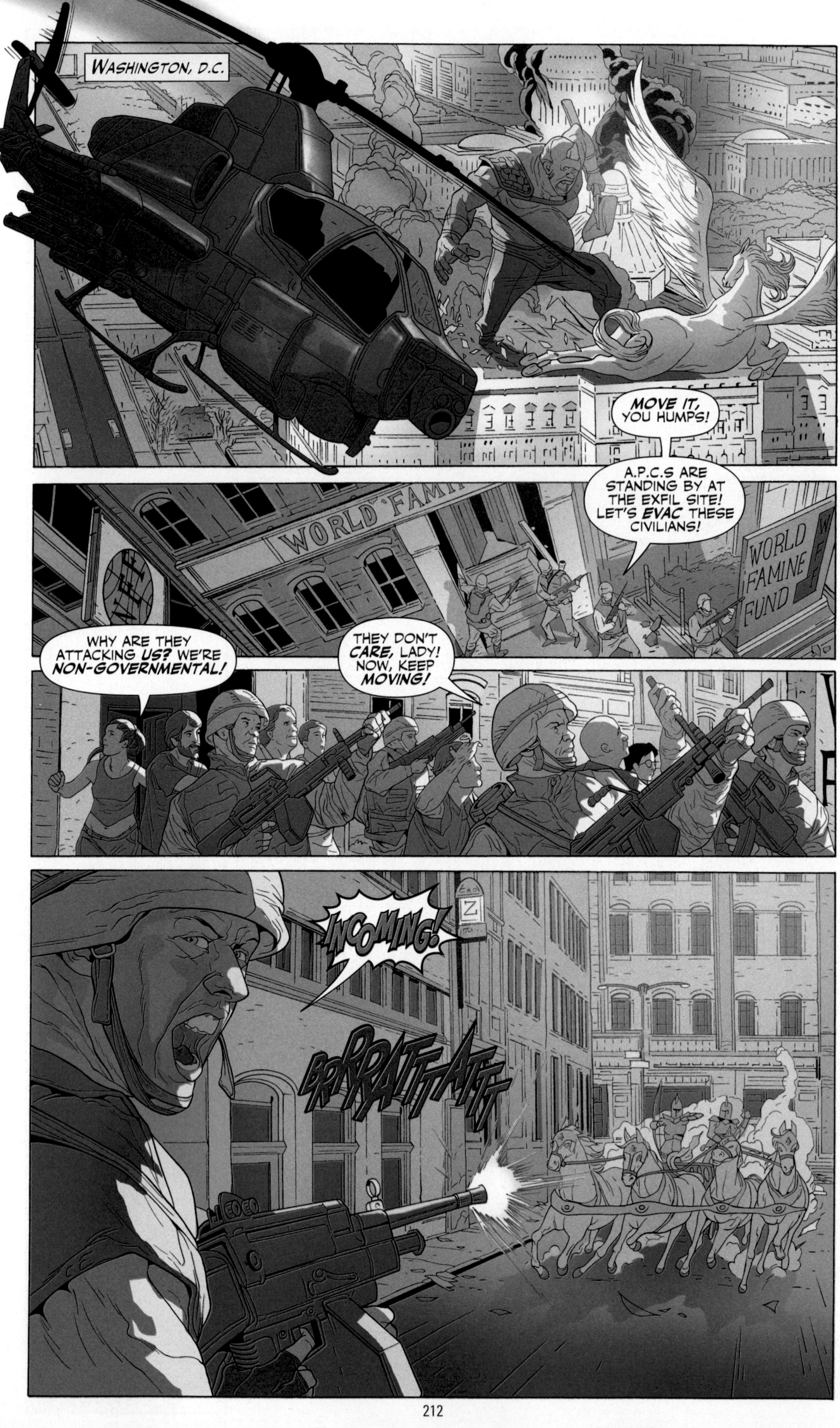
WASHINGTON, D.C.
MOVE IT, YOU HUMPS!
A.P.C.S ARE STANDING BY AT THE EXFIL SITE! LET'S EVAC THESE CIVILIANS!
WORLD FAMINE FUND
WHY ARE THEY ATTACKING US? WE'RE NON-GOVERNMENTAL!
THEY DON'T CARE, LADY! NOW, KEEP MOVING!
INCOMING!
BRRRATTTATTT

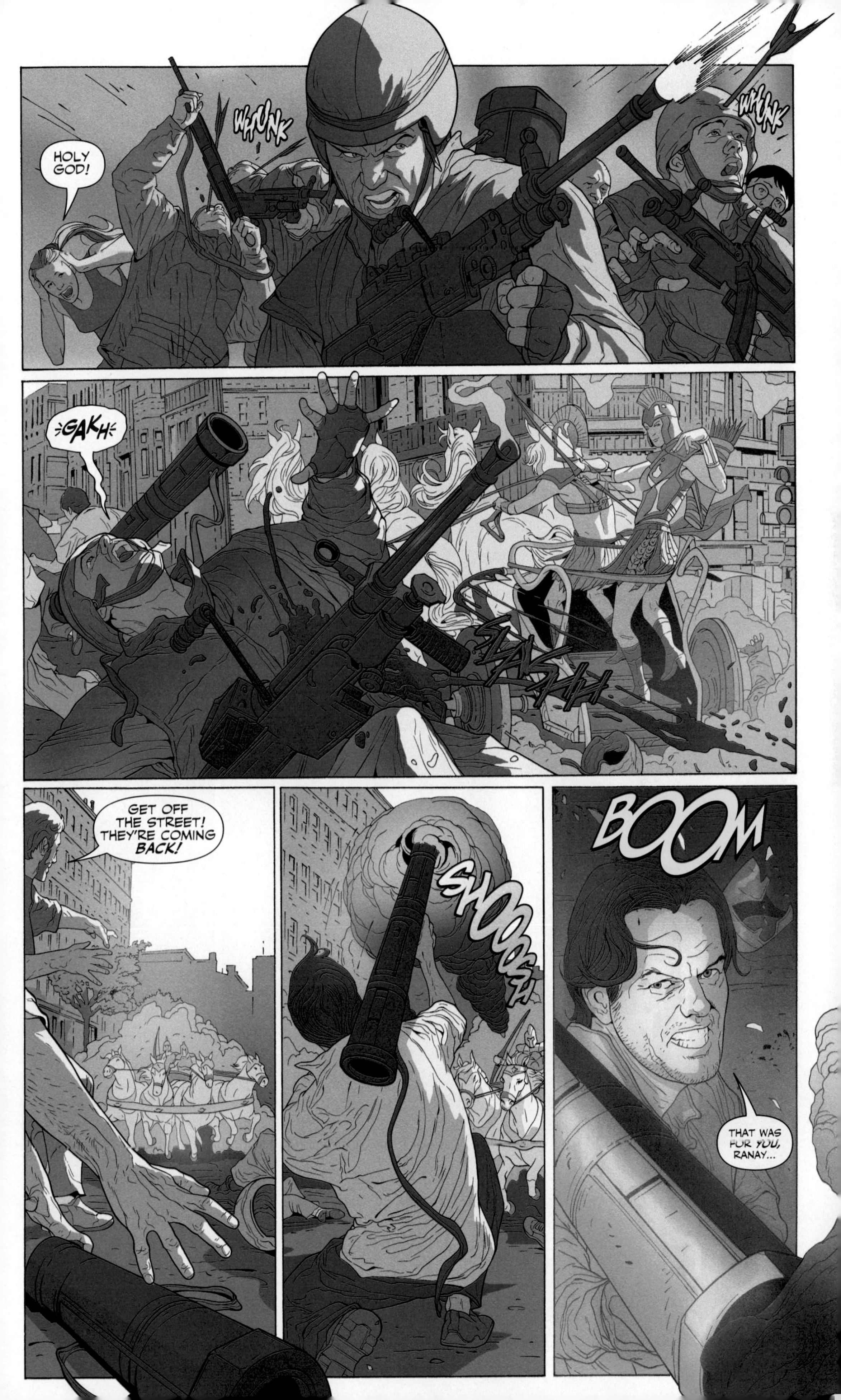
HOLY GOD!
WHUNK
WHUNK
GAKH
SHASHH
GET OFF THE STREET! THEY'RE COMING BACK!
SHOOOSH
BOOM
THAT WAS FOR YOU, RANAY...

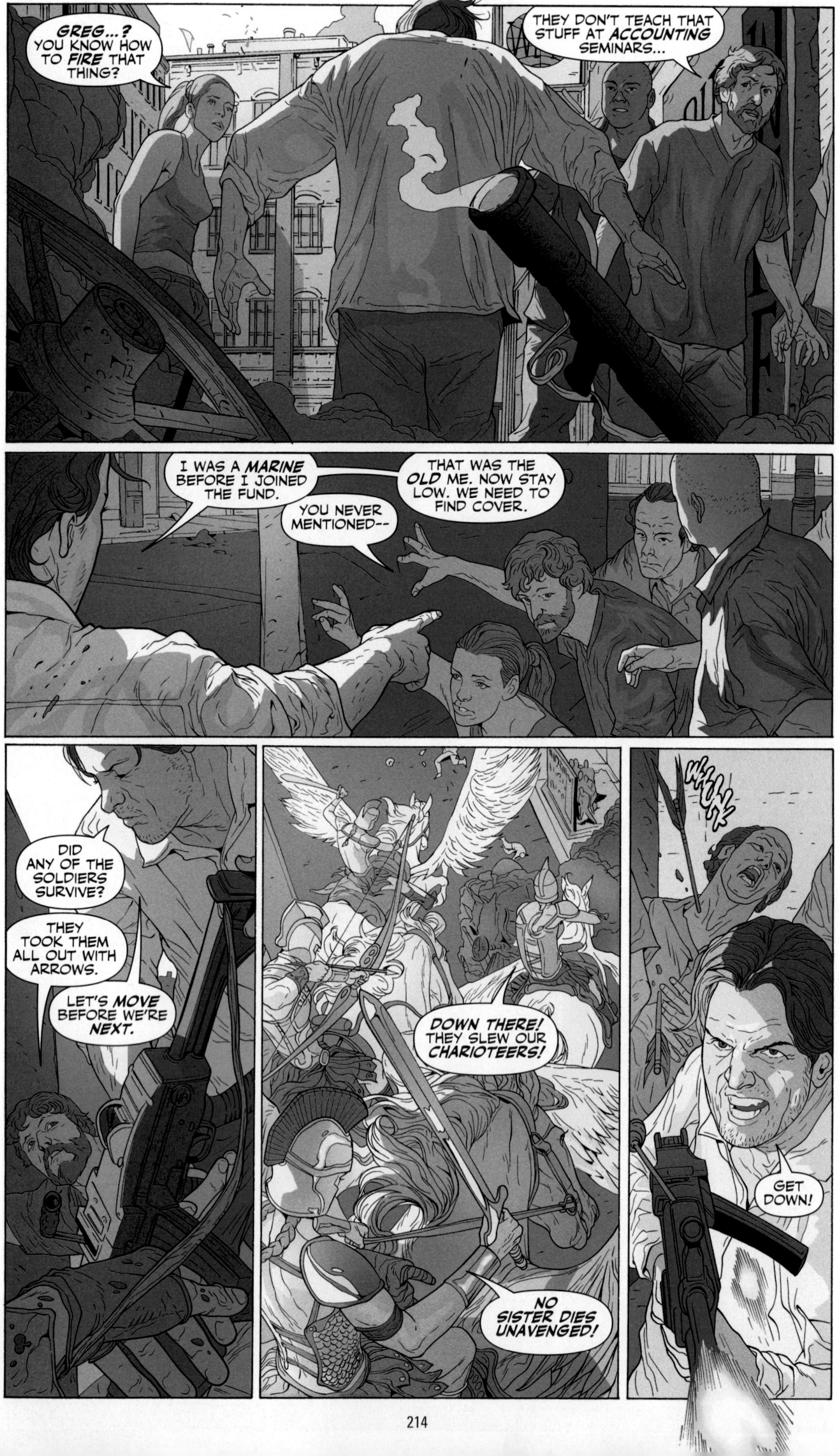
GREG...? YOU KNOW HOW TO FIRE THAT THING?
THEY DON'T TEACH THAT STUFF AT ACCOUNTING SEMINARS...
I WAS A MARINE BEFORE I JOINED THE FUND.
YOU NEVER MENTIONED--
THAT WAS THE OLD ME. NOW STAY LOW. WE NEED TO FIND COVER.
DID ANY OF THE SOLDIERS SURVIVE?
THEY TOOK THEM ALL OUT WITH ARROWS.
LET'S MOVE BEFORE WE'RE NEXT.
DOWN THERE! THEY SLEW OUR CHARIOTEERS!
NO SISTER DIES UNAVENGED!
WHOK
GET DOWN!

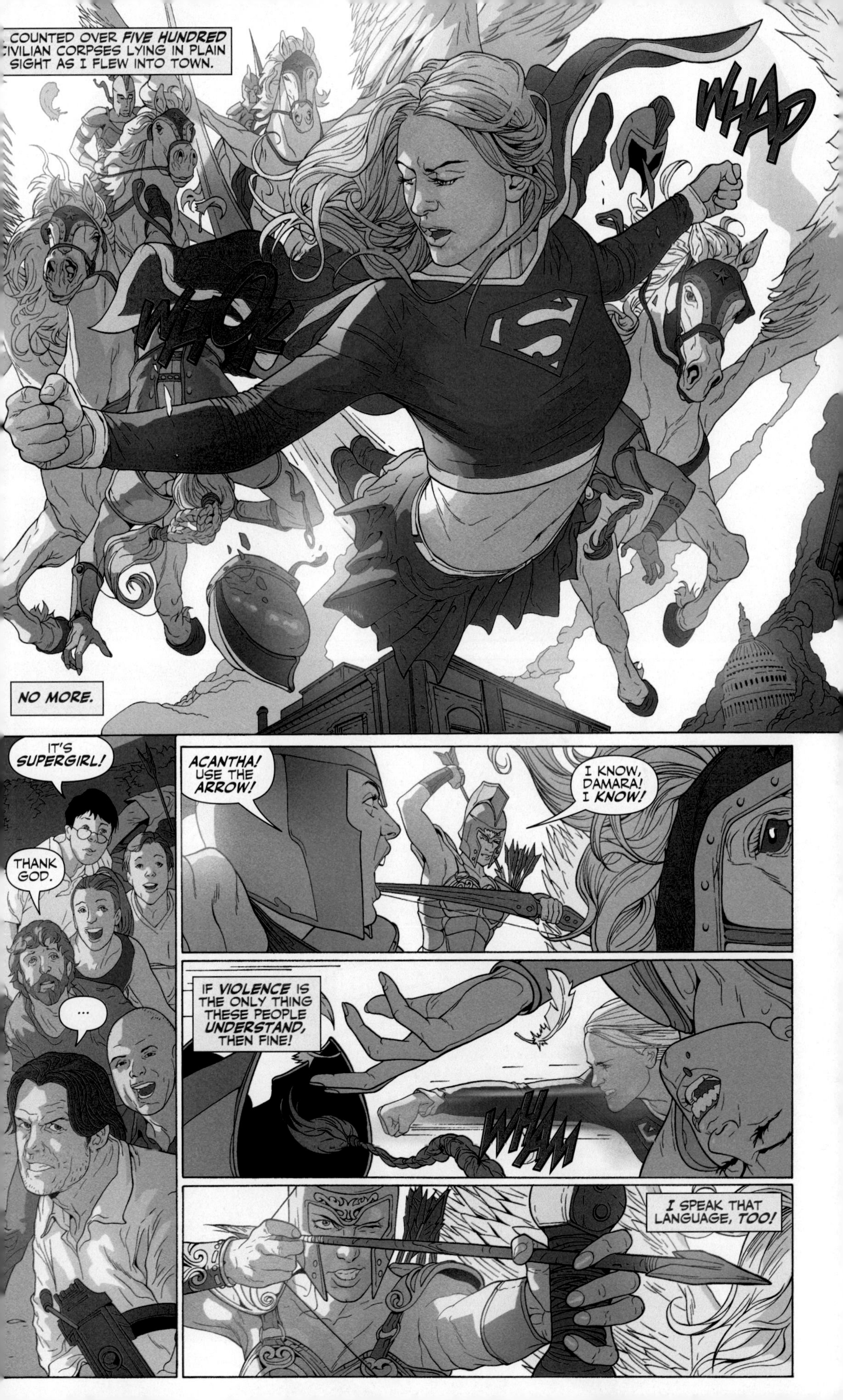

COUNTED OVER FIVE HUNDRED CIVILIAN CORPSES LYING IN PLAIN SIGHT AS I FLEW INTO TOWN.
WHAP
NO MORE.
IT'S SUPERGIRL!
THANK GOD.
...
ACANTHA! USE THE ARROW!
I KNOW, DAMARA! I KNOW!
IF VIOLENCE IS THE ONLY THING THESE PEOPLE UNDERSTAND, THEN FINE!
WHAM
I SPEAK THAT LANGUAGE, TOO!

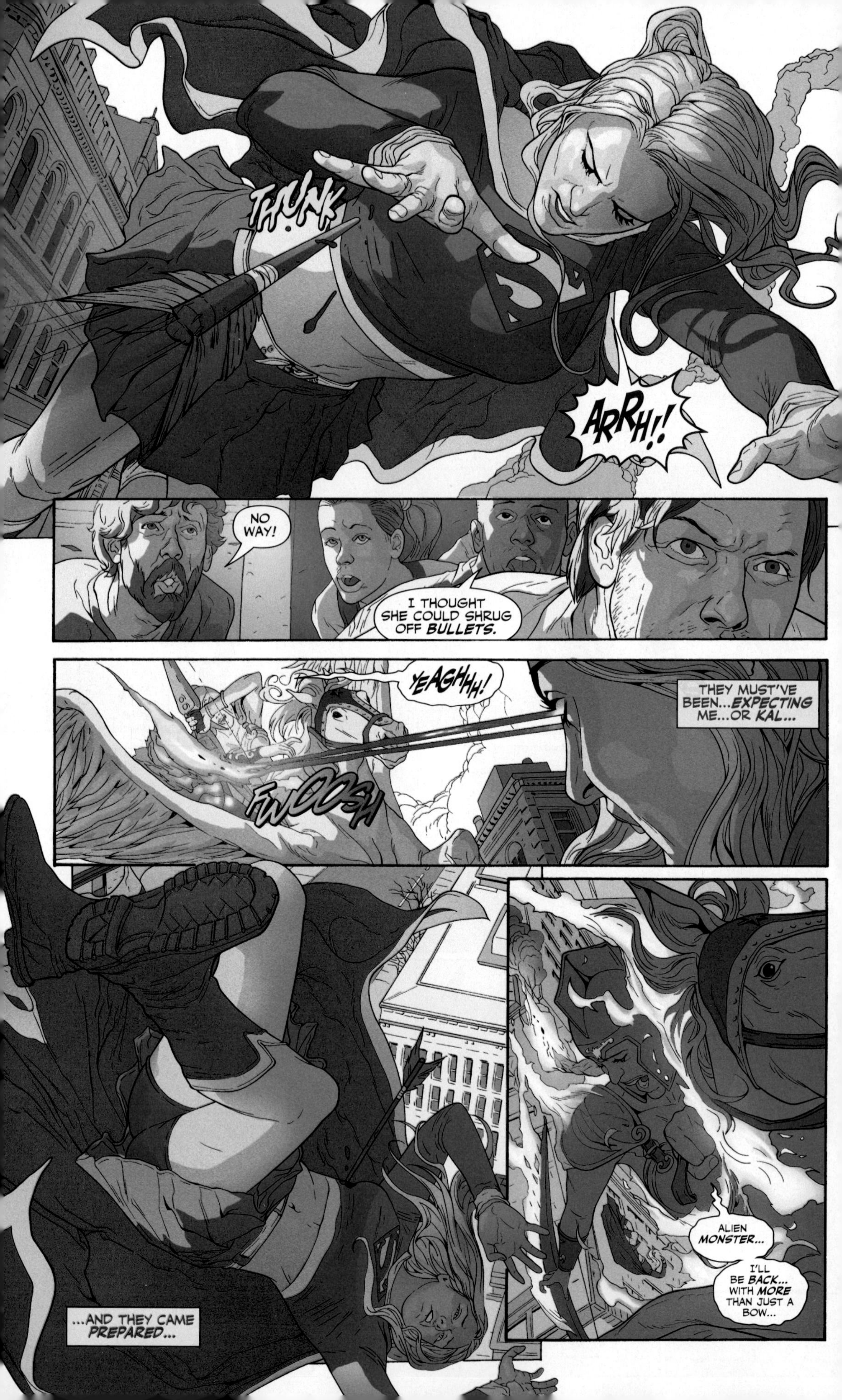

THUNK
ARRH!!
NO WAY!
I THOUGHT SHE COULD SHRUG OFF BULLETS.
YEAGHHH!
THEY MUST'VE BEEN...EXPECTING ME...OR KAL...
FWOOSH
...AND THEY CAME PREPARED...
ALIEN MONSTER...
I'LL BE BACK... WITH MORE THAN JUST A BOW...

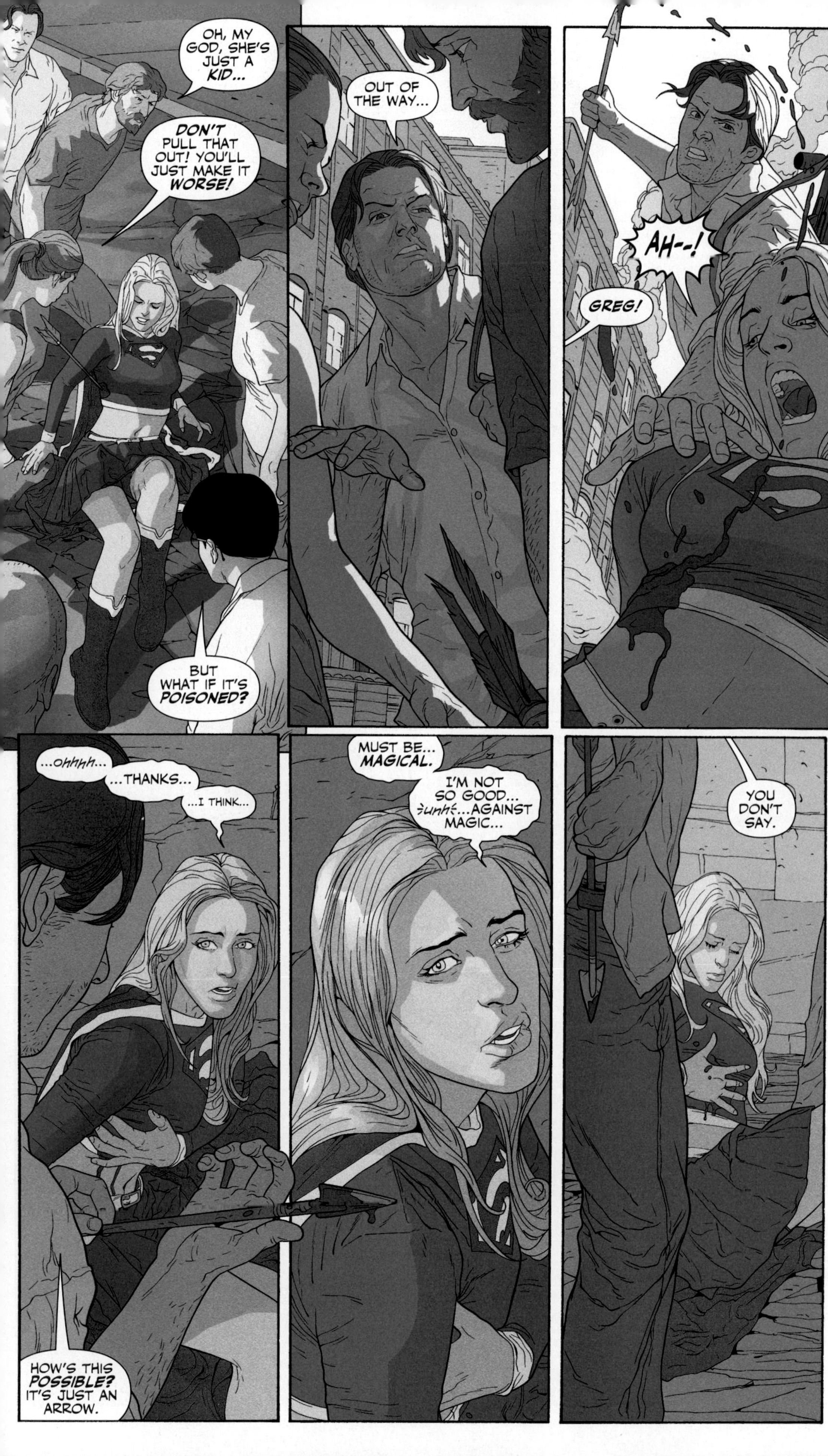
OH, MY GOD, SHE'S JUST A KID...
DON'T PULL THAT OUT! YOU'LL JUST MAKE IT WORSE!
BUT WHAT IF IT'S POISONED?
OUT OF THE WAY...
AH--!
GREG!
...ohhhh...
...THANKS...
...I THINK...
HOW'S THIS POSSIBLE? IT'S JUST AN ARROW.
MUST BE... MAGICAL.
I'M NOT SO GOOD... unh... AGAINST MAGIC...
YOU DON'T SAY.

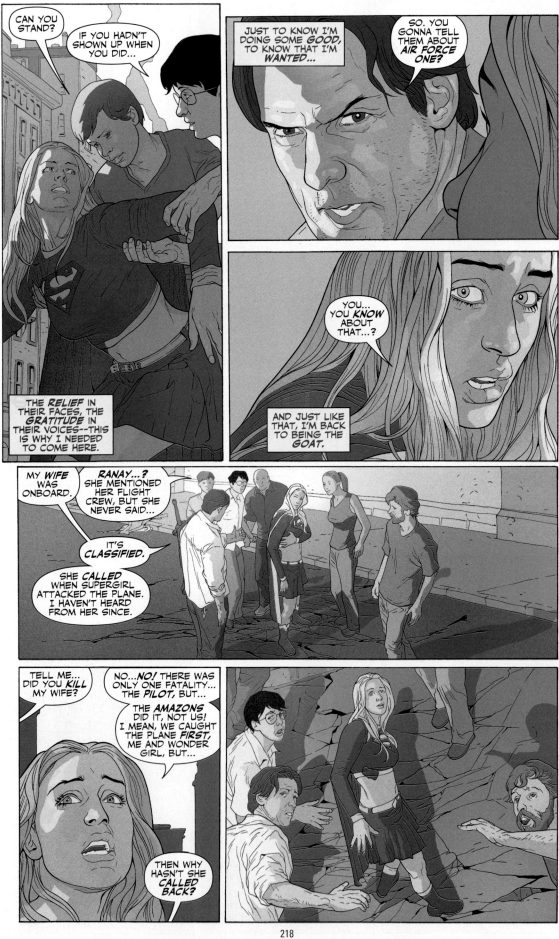

CAN YOU STAND?

IF YOU HADN'T SHOWN UP WHEN YOU DID...

THE RELIEF IN THEIR FACES, THE GRATITUDE IN THEIR VOICES--THIS IS WHY I NEEDED TO COME HERE.

JUST TO KNOW I'M DOING SOME GOOD, TO KNOW THAT I'M WANTED...

SO. YOU GONNA TELL THEM ABOUT AIR FORCE ONE?

YOU... YOU KNOW ABOUT THAT...?

AND JUST LIKE THAT, I'M BACK TO BEING THE GOAT.

MY WIFE WAS ONBOARD.

RANAY...? SHE MENTIONED HER FLIGHT CREW, BUT SHE NEVER SAID...

IT'S CLASSIFIED.

SHE CALLED WHEN SUPERGIRL ATTACKED THE PLANE. I HAVEN'T HEARD FROM HER SINCE.

TELL ME... DID YOU KILL MY WIFE?

NO...NO! THERE WAS ONLY ONE FATALITY... THE PILOT, BUT...

THE AMAZONS DID IT, NOT US! I MEAN, WE CAUGHT THE PLANE FIRST, ME AND WONDER GIRL, BUT...

THEN WHY HASN'T SHE CALLED BACK?

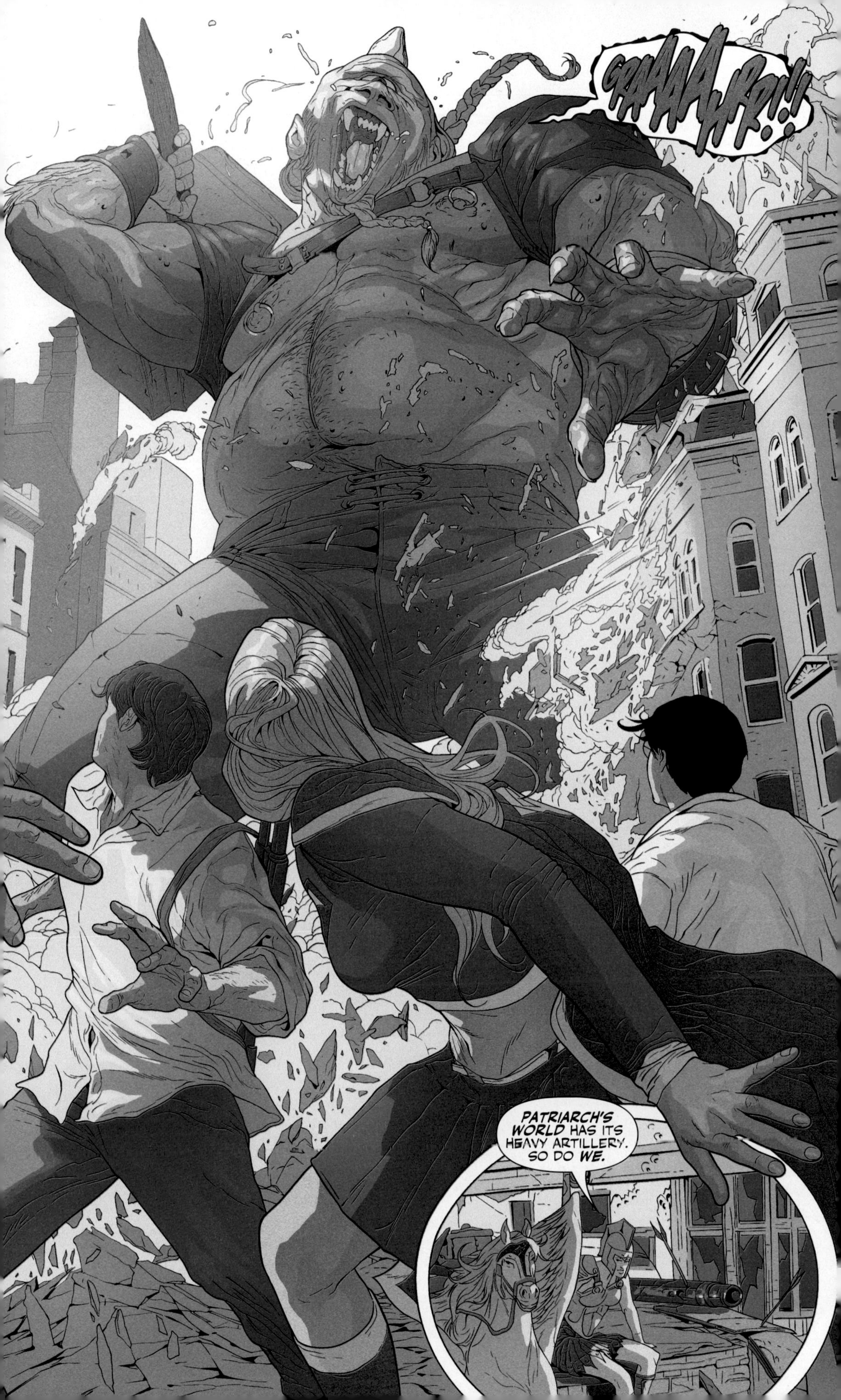
GRAAAAAWR!!!
PATRIARCH'S WORLD HAS ITS HEAVY ARTILLERY. SO DO WE.

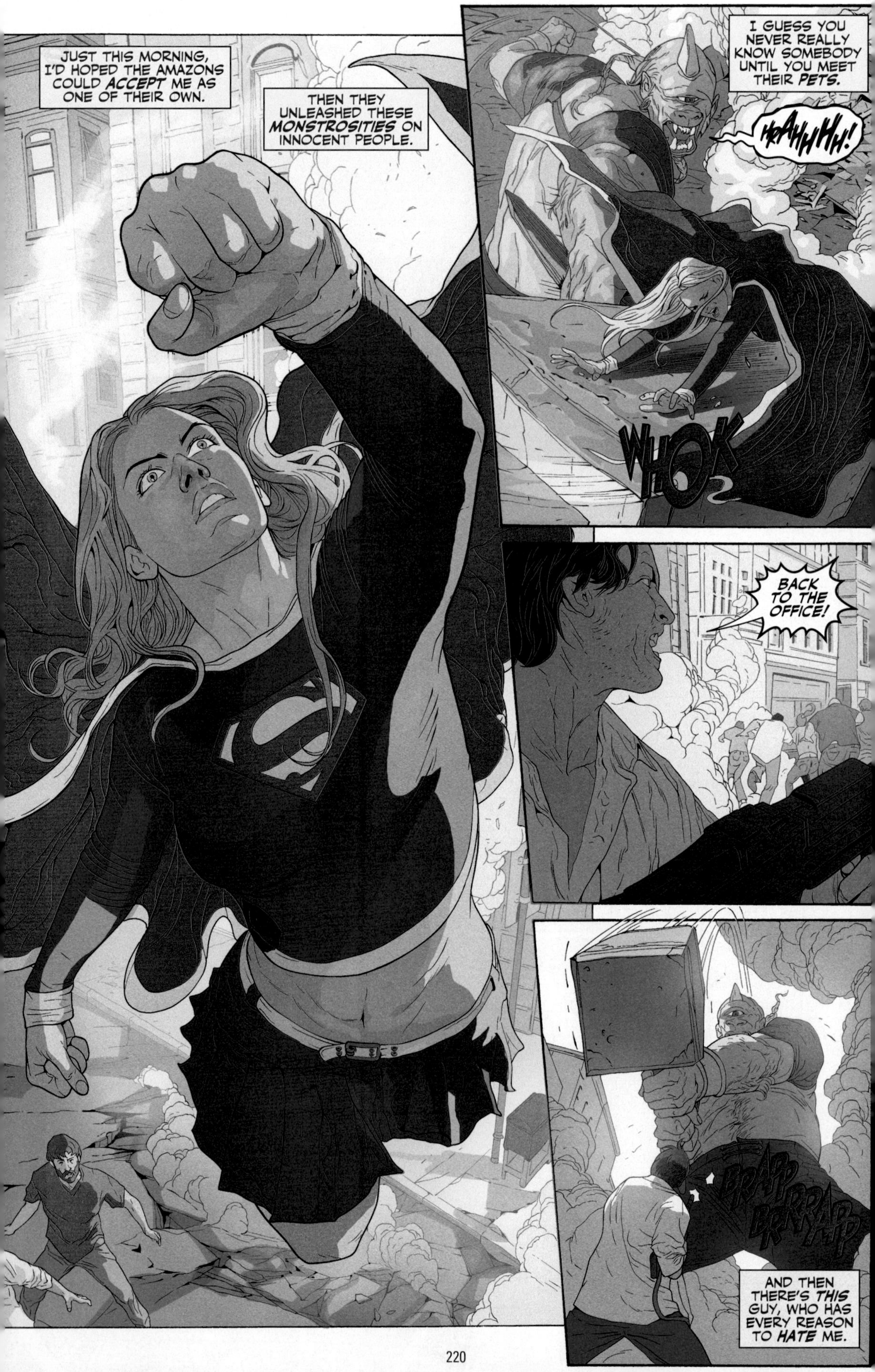
JUST THIS MORNING, I'D HOPED THE AMAZONS COULD ACCEPT ME AS ONE OF THEIR OWN.
THEN THEY UNLEASHED THESE MONSTROSITIES ON INNOCENT PEOPLE.
I GUESS YOU NEVER REALLY KNOW SOMEBODY UNTIL YOU MEET THEIR PETS.
HRAHHHH!
WHOK
BACK TO THE OFFICE!
BRAPP BRRRAPP
AND THEN THERE'S THIS GUY, WHO HAS EVERY REASON TO HATE ME.

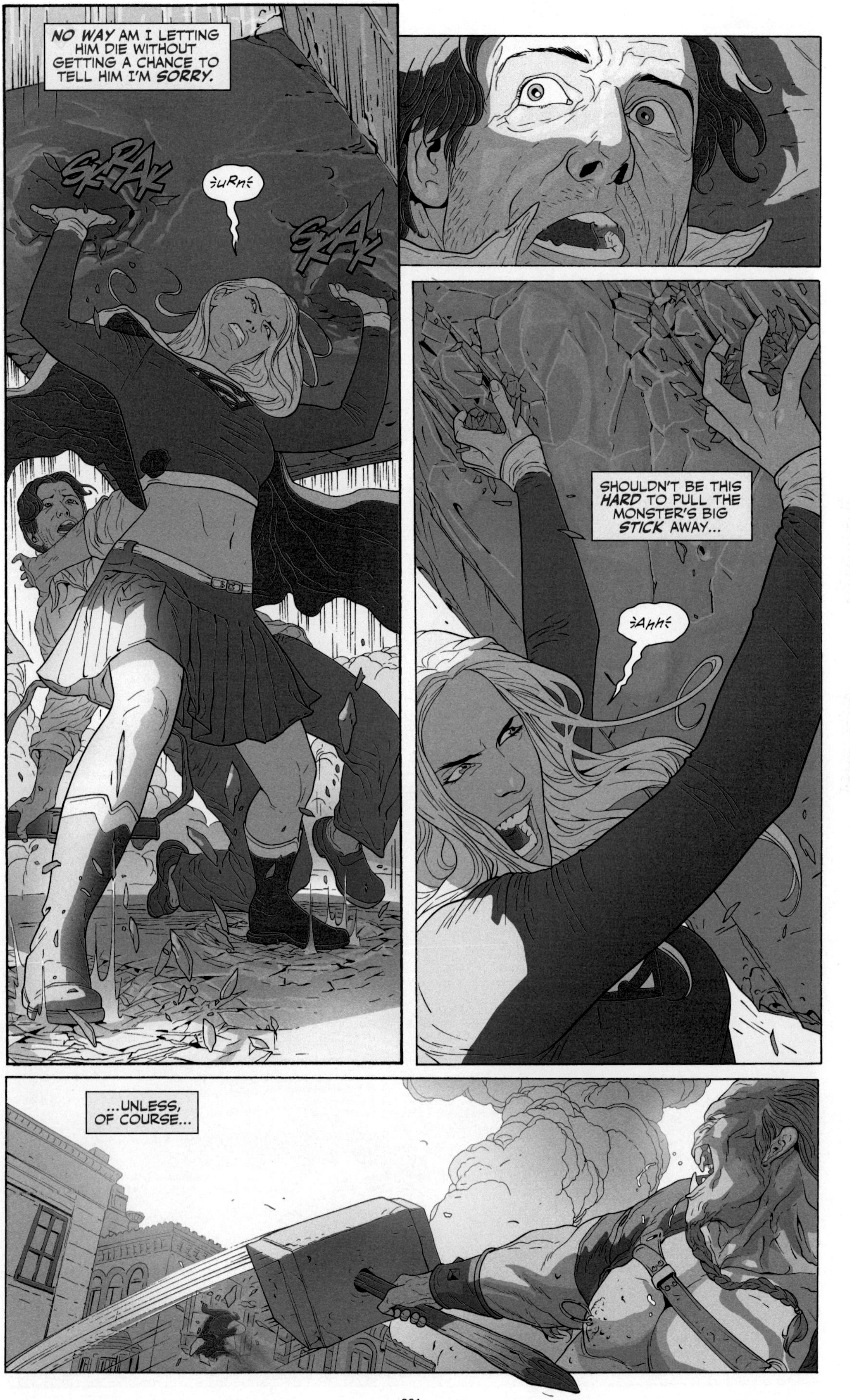
NO WAY AM I LETTING HIM DIE WITHOUT GETTING A CHANCE TO TELL HIM I'M SORRY.
SKRAK
uRn
SKRAK
SHOULDN'T BE THIS HARD TO PULL THE MONSTER'S BIG STICK AWAY...
Ahh
...UNLESS, OF COURSE...

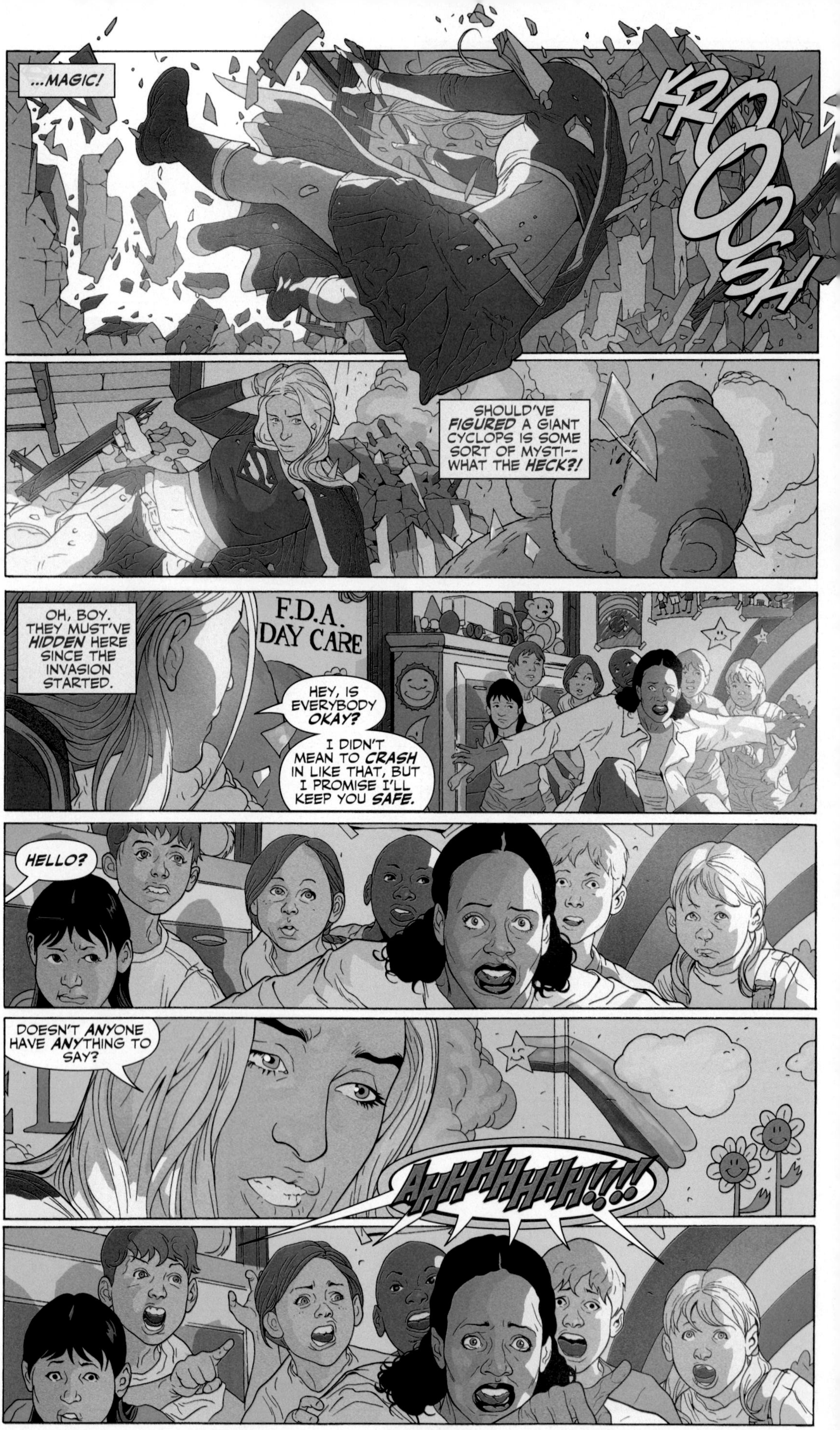
...MAGIC!
KRROOOSH
SHOULD'VE FIGURED A GIANT CYCLOPS IS SOME SORT OF MYSTI-- WHAT THE HECK?!
F.D.A. DAY CARE
OH, BOY. THEY MUST'VE HIDDEN HERE SINCE THE INVASION STARTED.
HEY, IS EVERYBODY OKAY?
I DIDN'T MEAN TO CRASH IN LIKE THAT, BUT I PROMISE I'LL KEEP YOU SAFE.
HELLO?
DOESN'T ANYONE HAVE ANYTHING TO SAY?
AHHHHHHH!!!!

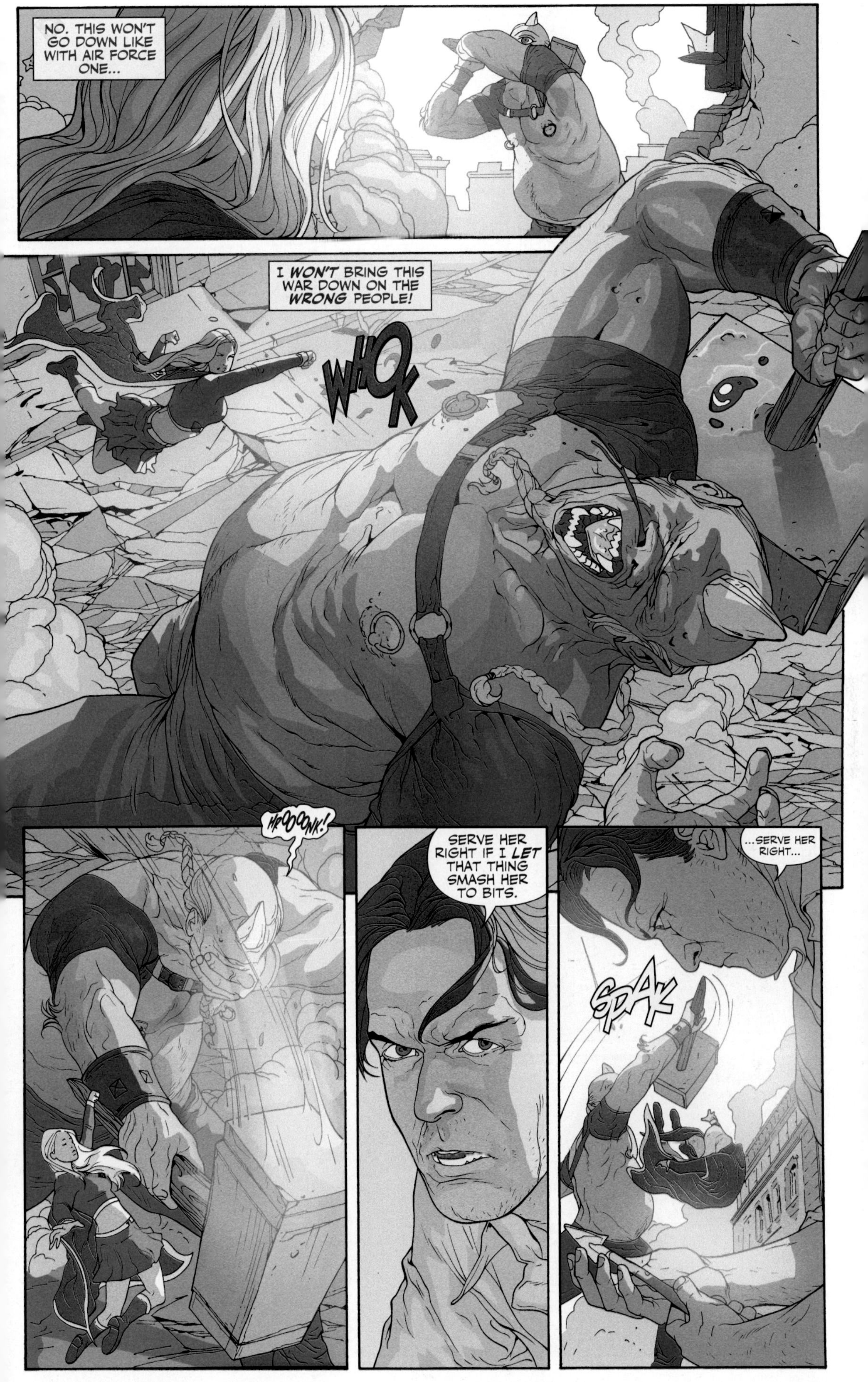
NO. THIS WON'T GO DOWN LIKE WITH AIR FORCE ONE...
I WON'T BRING THIS WAR DOWN ON THE WRONG PEOPLE!
WHOK
HROOOONK!
SERVE HER RIGHT IF I LET THAT THING SMASH HER TO BITS.
...SERVE HER RIGHT...
SPAK

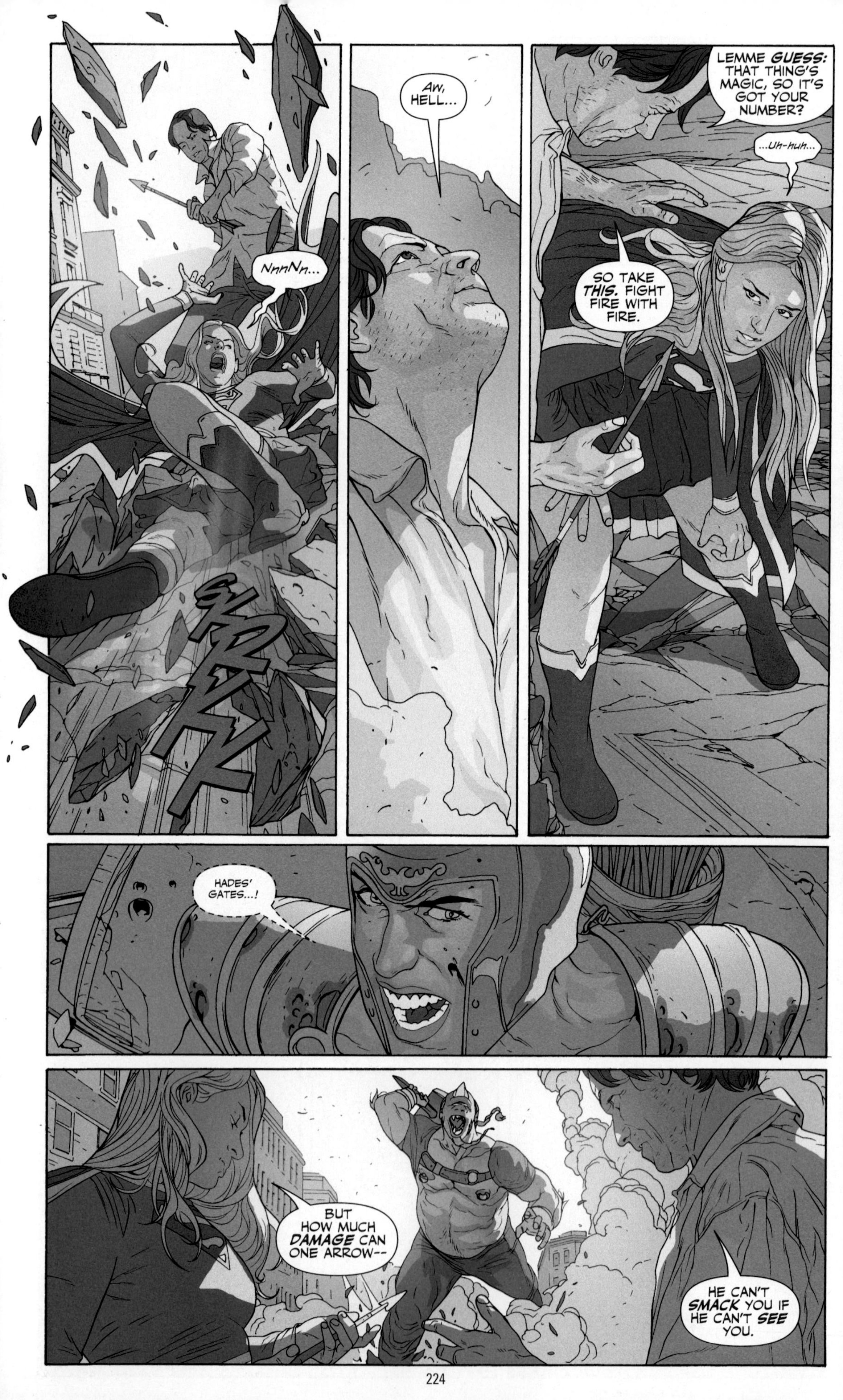
NnnNn...
AW, HELL...
LEMME GUESS: THAT THING'S MAGIC, SO IT'S GOT YOUR NUMBER?
...Uh-huh...
SO TAKE THIS. FIGHT FIRE WITH FIRE.
HADES' GATES...!
BUT HOW MUCH DAMAGE CAN ONE ARROW--
HE CAN'T SMACK YOU IF HE CAN'T SEE YOU.

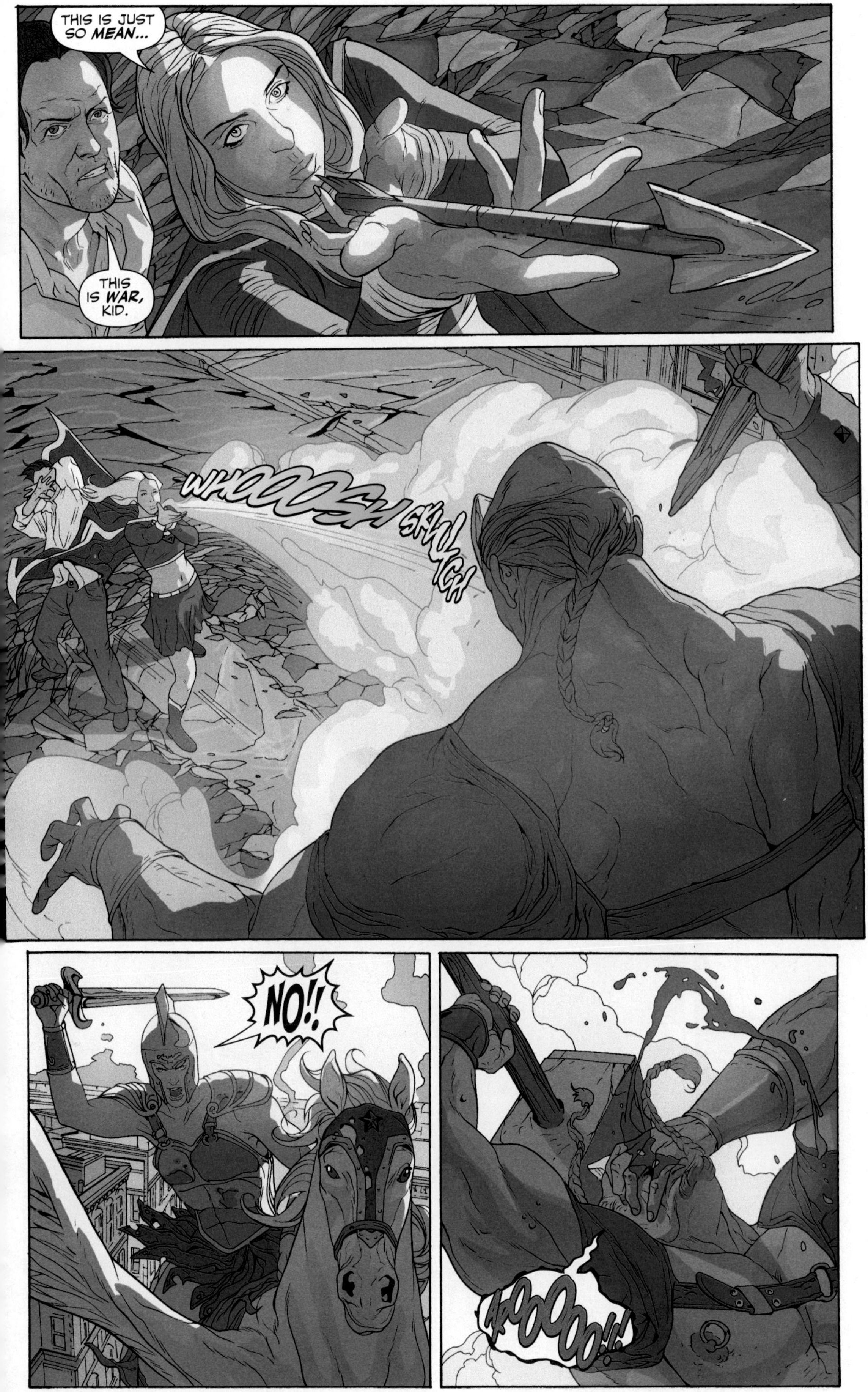
THIS IS JUST SO MEAN...
THIS IS WAR, KID.
WHOOOOSH
SKLUCH
NO!!
AHOOOOO!!

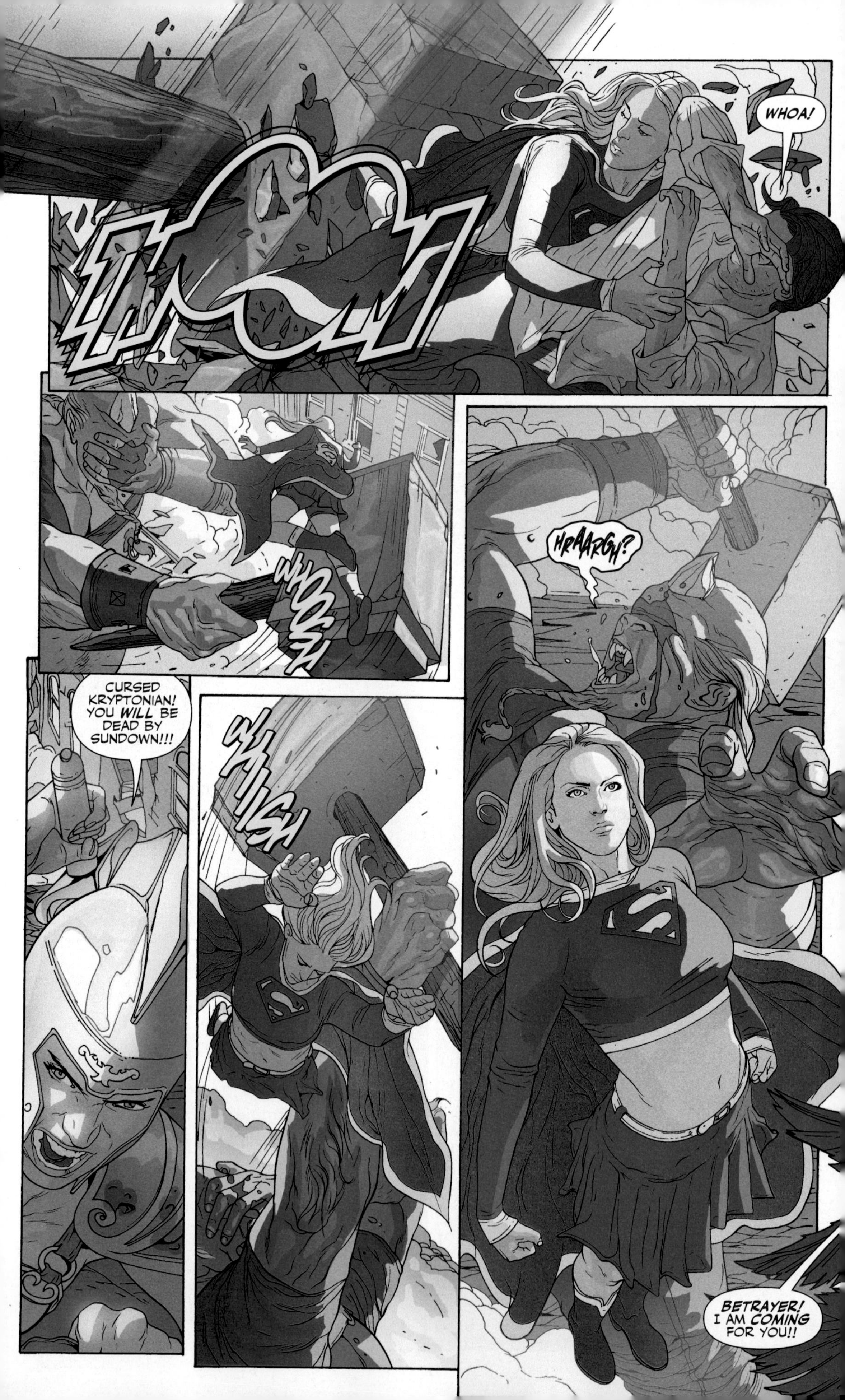
WHOA!
WHOOOM
HRAARGH?
CURSED KRYPTONIAN! YOU *WILL* BE DEAD BY SUNDOWN!!!
WHIISH
BETRAYER! I AM *COMING* FOR YOU!!

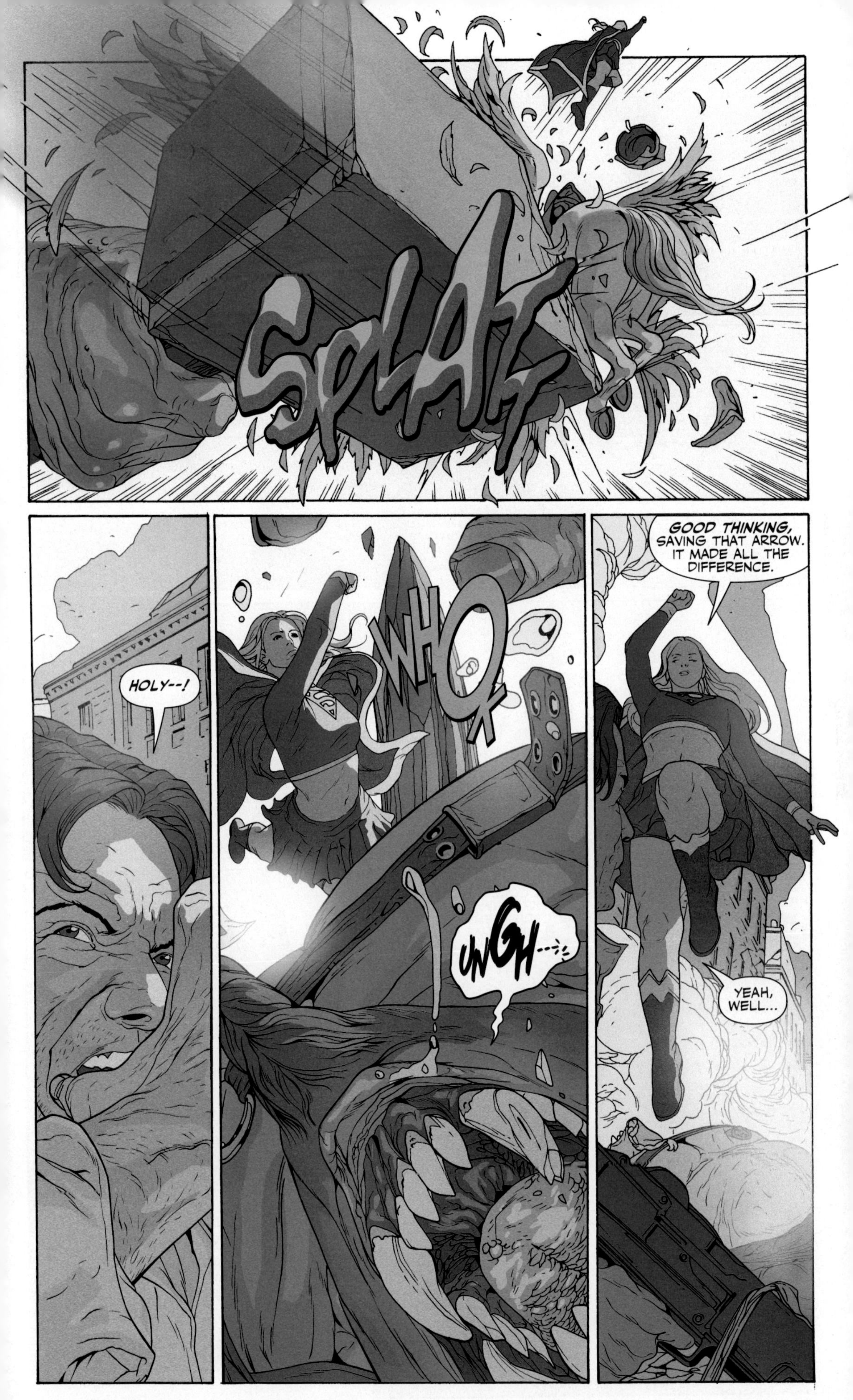
SPLAK
HOLY--!
WHOK
UNGH
GOOD THINKING, SAVING THAT ARROW. IT MADE ALL THE DIFFERENCE.
YEAH, WELL...

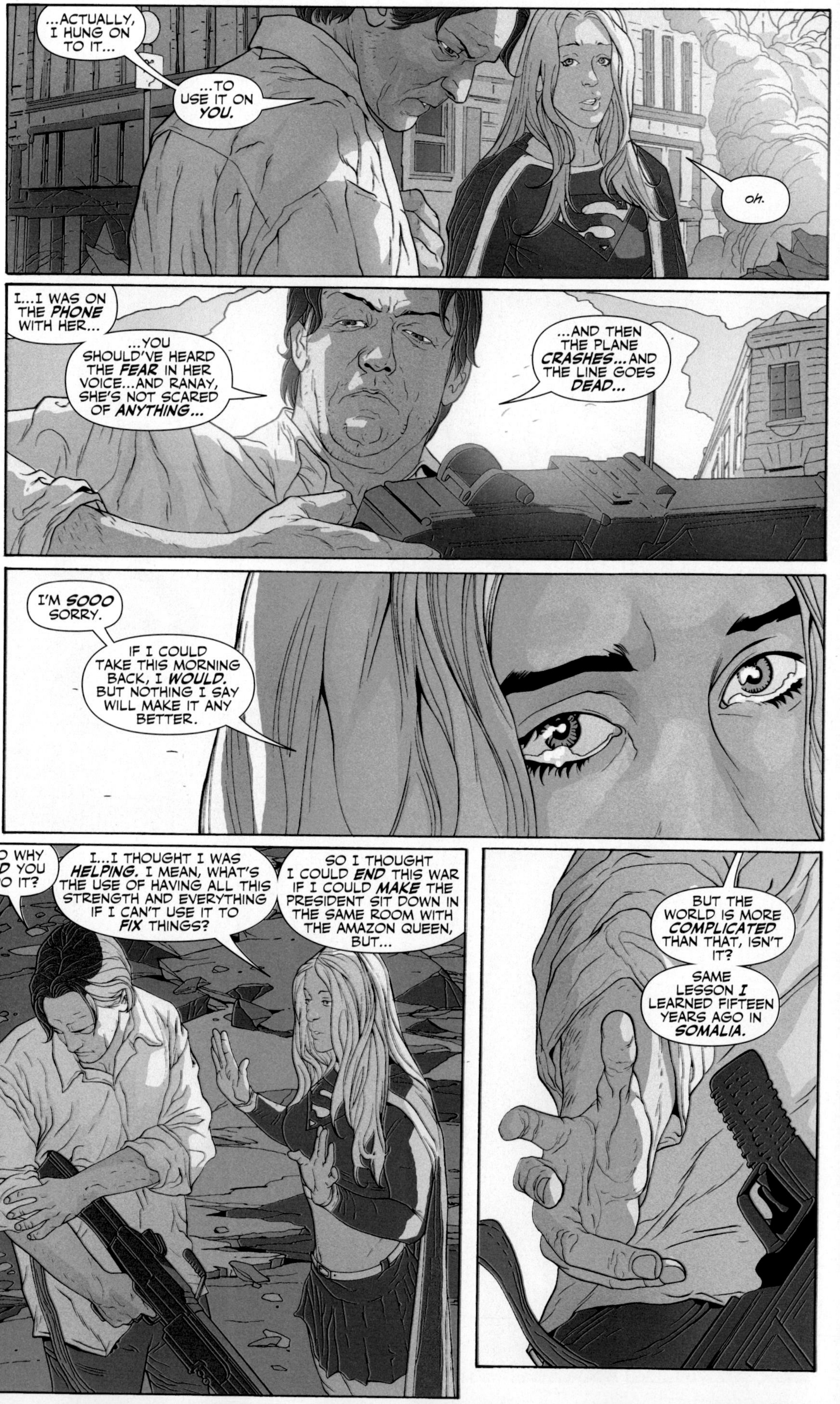

...ACTUALLY, I HUNG ON TO IT...
...TO USE IT ON YOU.
oh.
I...I WAS ON THE PHONE WITH HER...
...YOU SHOULD'VE HEARD THE FEAR IN HER VOICE...AND RANAY, SHE'S NOT SCARED OF ANYTHING...
...AND THEN THE PLANE CRASHES...AND THE LINE GOES DEAD...
I'M SOOO SORRY.
IF I COULD TAKE THIS MORNING BACK, I WOULD. BUT NOTHING I SAY WILL MAKE IT ANY BETTER.
SO WHY DID YOU DO IT?
I...I THOUGHT I WAS HELPING. I MEAN, WHAT'S THE USE OF HAVING ALL THIS STRENGTH AND EVERYTHING IF I CAN'T USE IT TO FIX THINGS?
SO I THOUGHT I COULD END THIS WAR IF I COULD MAKE THE PRESIDENT SIT DOWN IN THE SAME ROOM WITH THE AMAZON QUEEN, BUT...
BUT THE WORLD IS MORE COMPLICATED THAN THAT, ISN'T IT?
SAME LESSON I LEARNED FIFTEEN YEARS AGO IN SOMALIA.

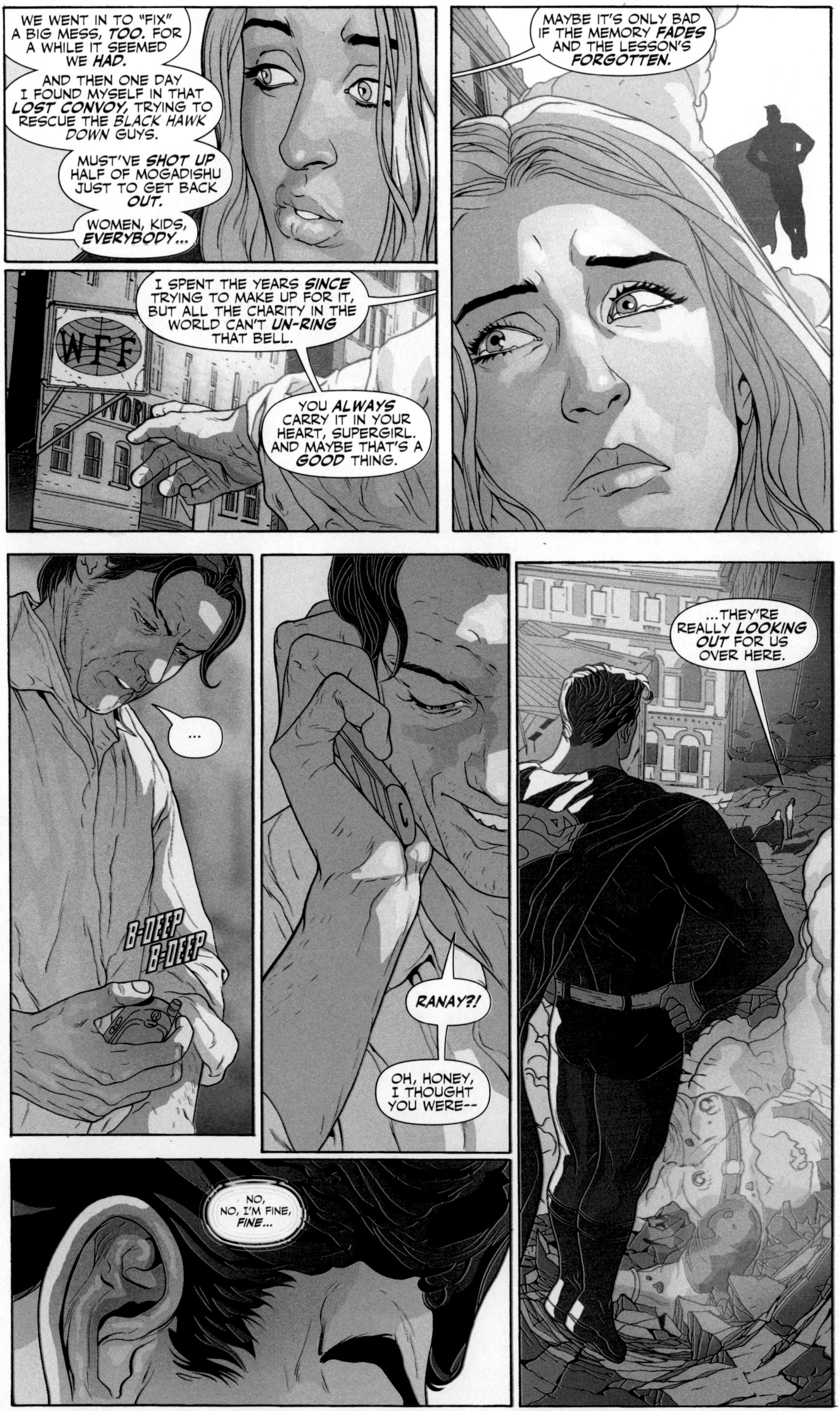

WE WENT IN TO "FIX" A BIG MESS, *TOO.* FOR A WHILE IT SEEMED WE *HAD.*
AND THEN ONE DAY I FOUND MYSELF IN THAT *LOST CONVOY,* TRYING TO RESCUE THE *BLACK HAWK DOWN* GUYS.
MUST'VE *SHOT UP* HALF OF MOGADISHU JUST TO GET BACK *OUT.*
WOMEN, KIDS, *EVERYBODY...*
MAYBE IT'S ONLY BAD IF THE MEMORY *FADES* AND THE LESSON'S *FORGOTTEN.*
WFF
I SPENT THE YEARS *SINCE* TRYING TO MAKE UP FOR IT, BUT ALL THE CHARITY IN THE WORLD CAN'T *UN-RING* THAT BELL.
YOU *ALWAYS* CARRY IT IN YOUR HEART, SUPERGIRL. AND MAYBE THAT'S A *GOOD* THING.
...
B-DEEP
B-DEEP
RANAY?!
OH, HONEY, I THOUGHT YOU WERE--
...THEY'RE REALLY *LOOKING OUT* FOR US OVER HERE.
NO, NO, I'M FINE, *FINE...*

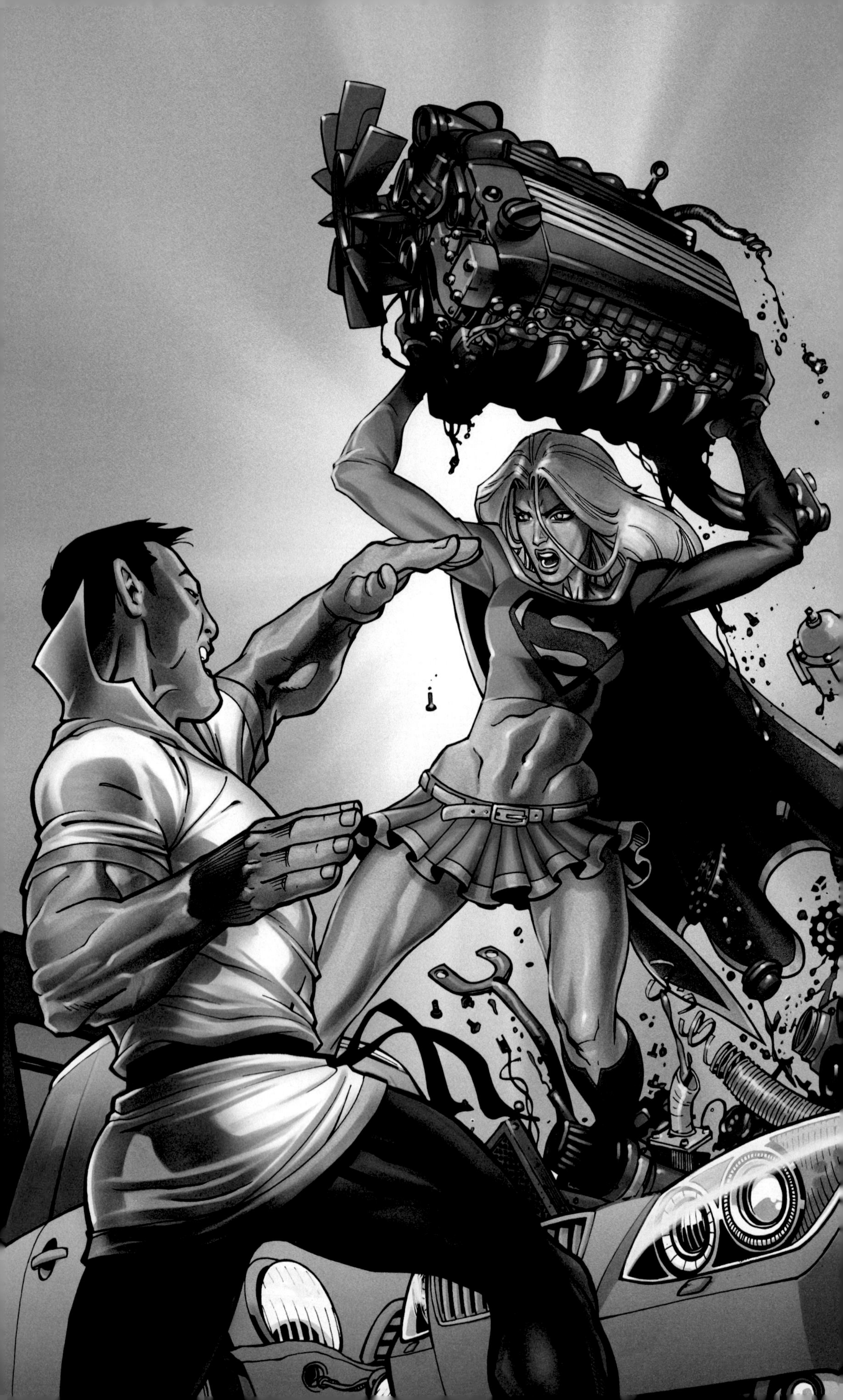

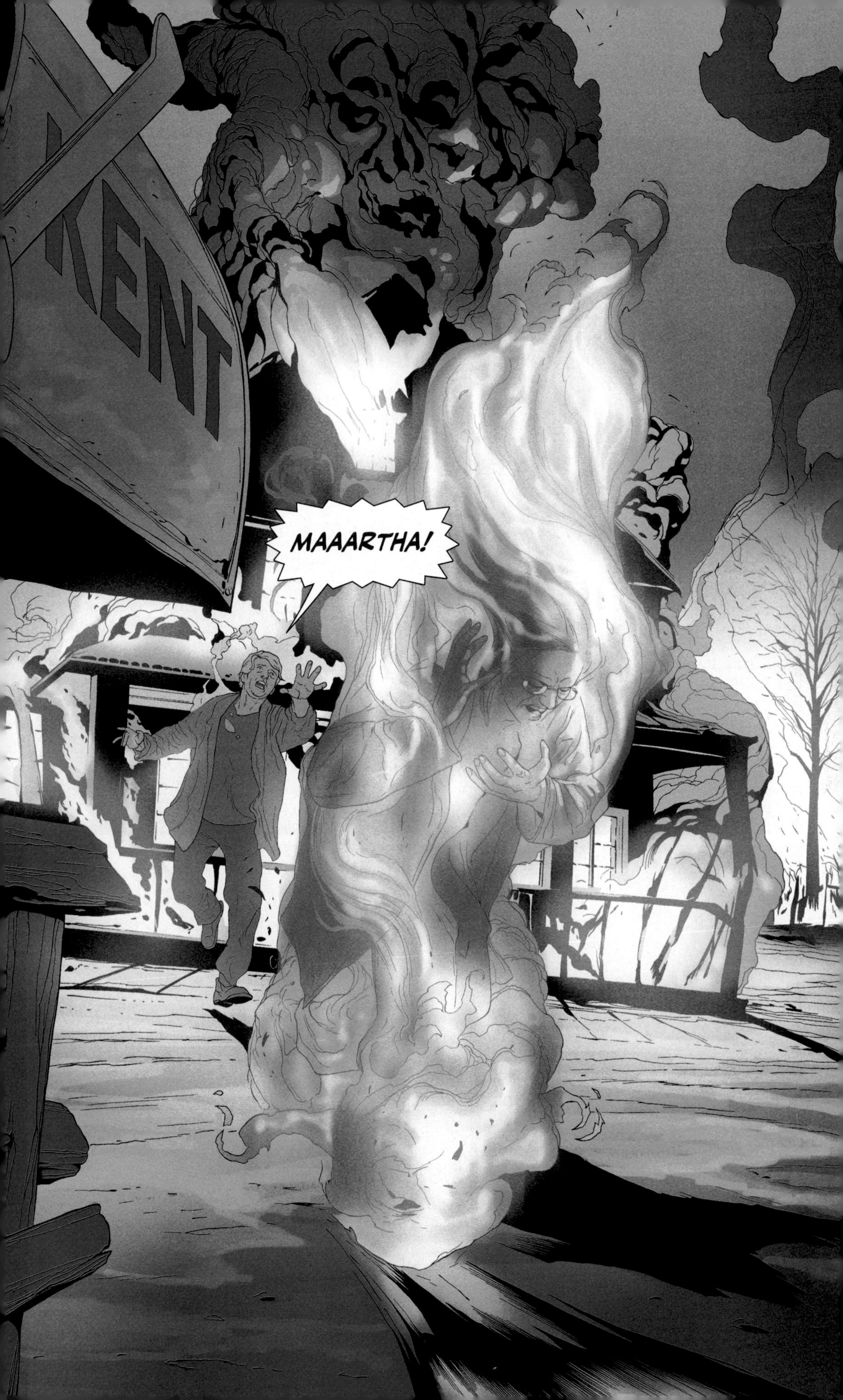
KENT
MAAARTHA!

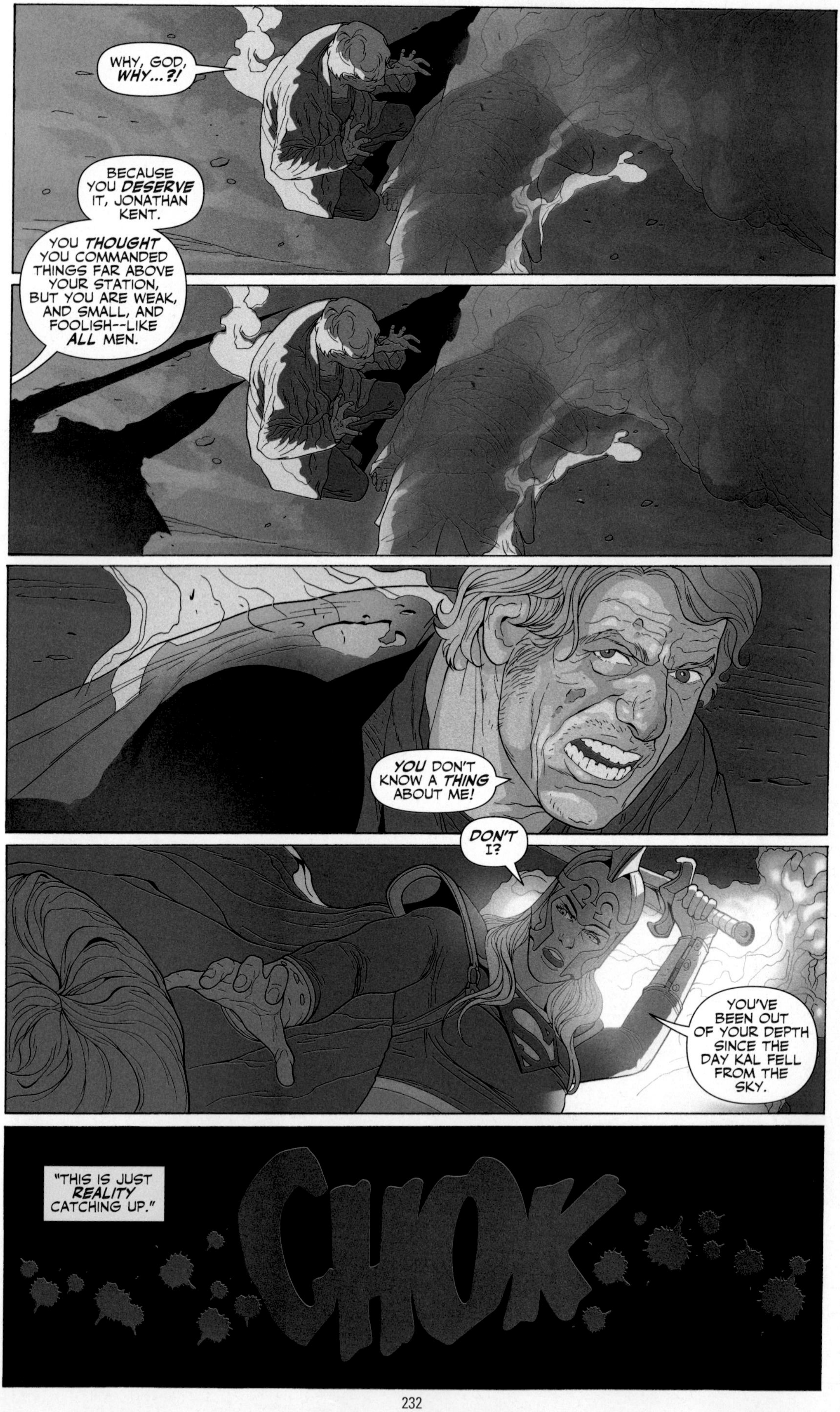
WHY, GOD, WHY...?!
BECAUSE YOU DESERVE IT, JONATHAN KENT.
YOU THOUGHT YOU COMMANDED THINGS FAR ABOVE YOUR STATION, BUT YOU ARE WEAK, AND SMALL, AND FOOLISH--LIKE ALL MEN.
YOU DON'T KNOW A THING ABOUT ME!
DON'T I?
YOU'VE BEEN OUT OF YOUR DEPTH SINCE THE DAY KAL FELL FROM THE SKY.
"THIS IS JUST REALITY CATCHING UP."
CHOK

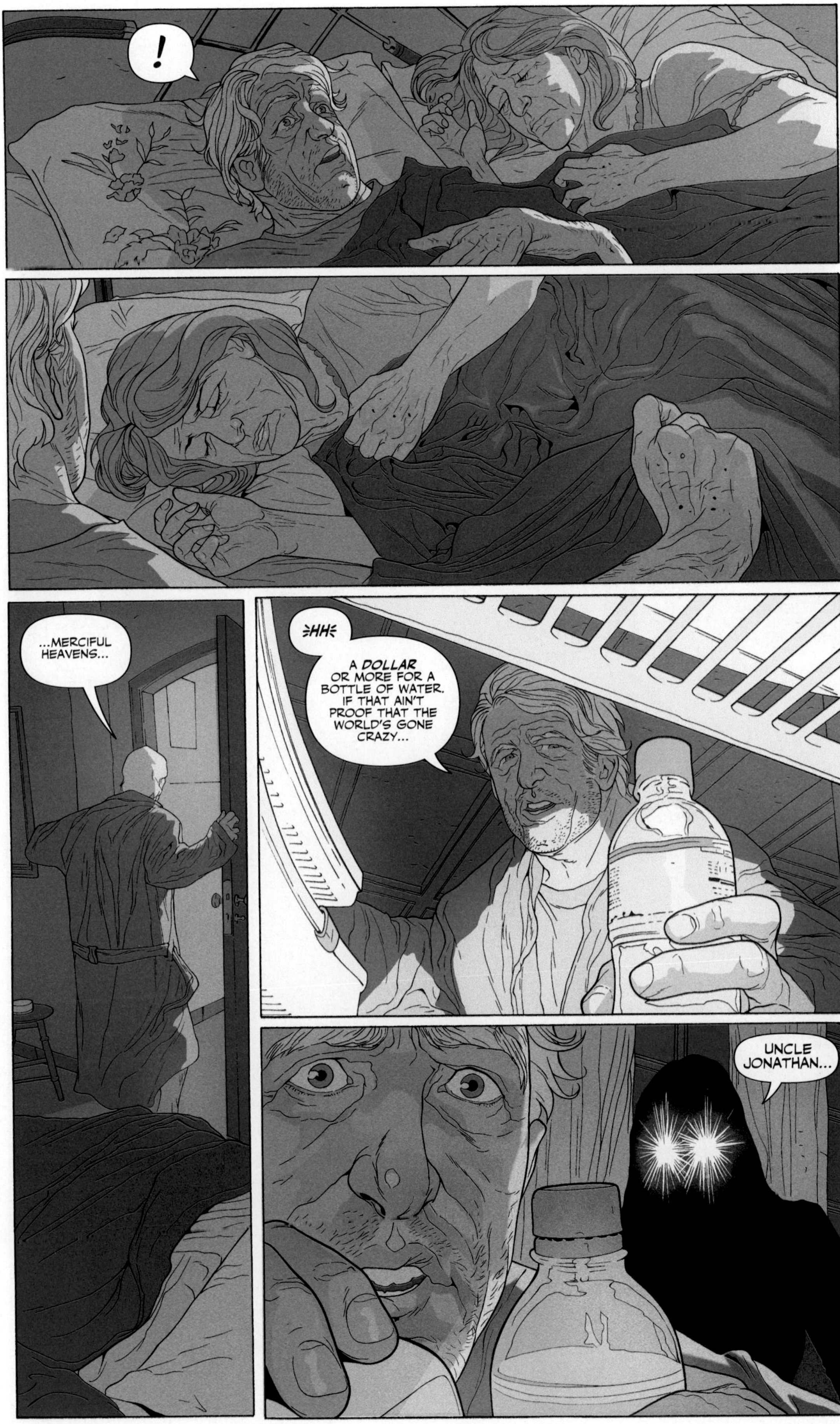
!
...MERCIFUL HEAVENS...
HH
A DOLLAR OR MORE FOR A BOTTLE OF WATER. IF THAT AIN'T PROOF THAT THE WORLD'S GONE CRAZY...
UNCLE JONATHAN...

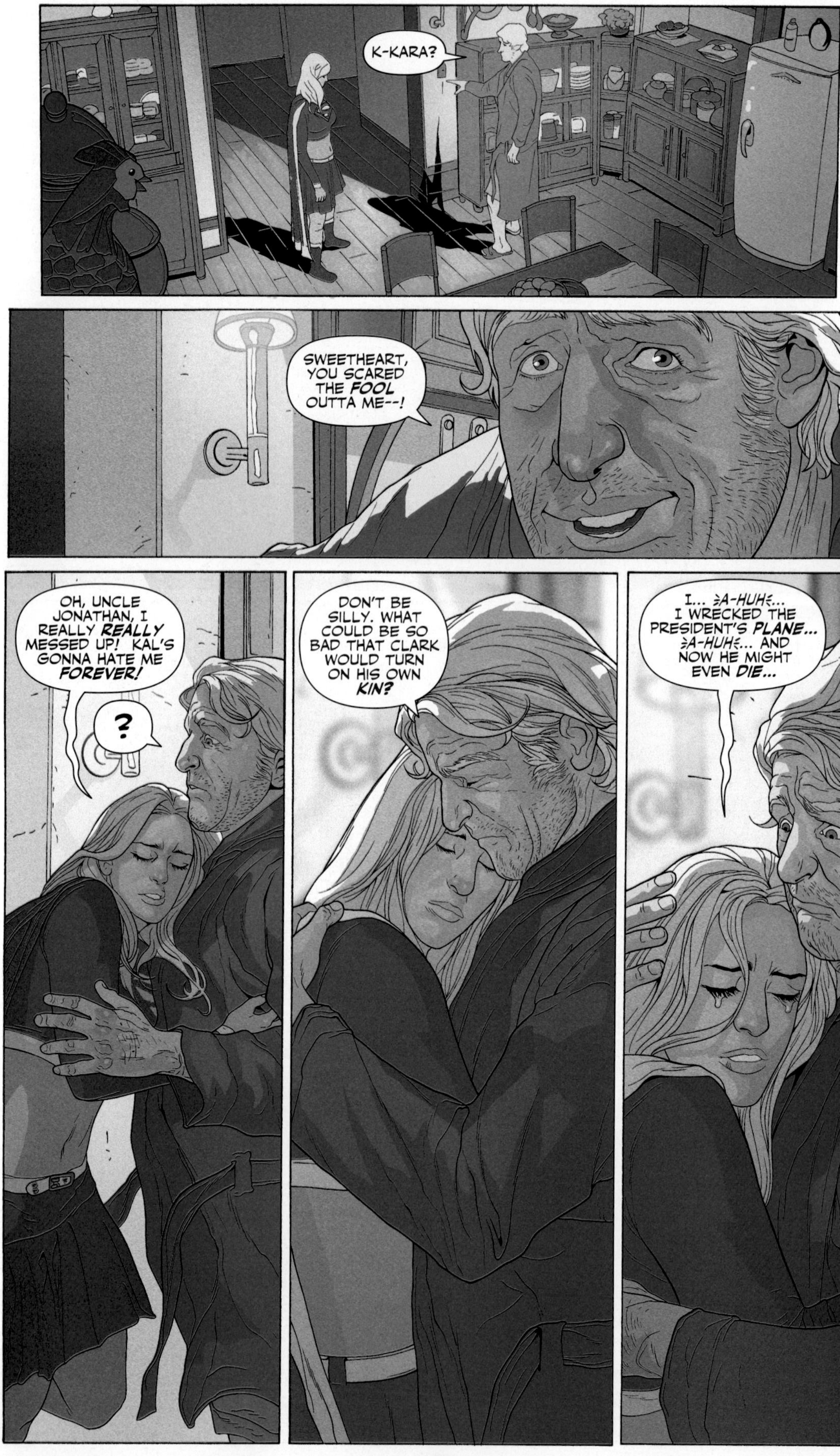

K-KARA?
SWEETHEART, YOU SCARED THE FOOL OUTTA ME--!
OH, UNCLE JONATHAN, I REALLY REALLY MESSED UP! KAL'S GONNA HATE ME FOREVER!
?
DON'T BE SILLY. WHAT COULD BE SO BAD THAT CLARK WOULD TURN ON HIS OWN KIN?
I... A-HUH... I WRECKED THE PRESIDENT'S PLANE... A-HUH... AND NOW HE MIGHT EVEN DIE...

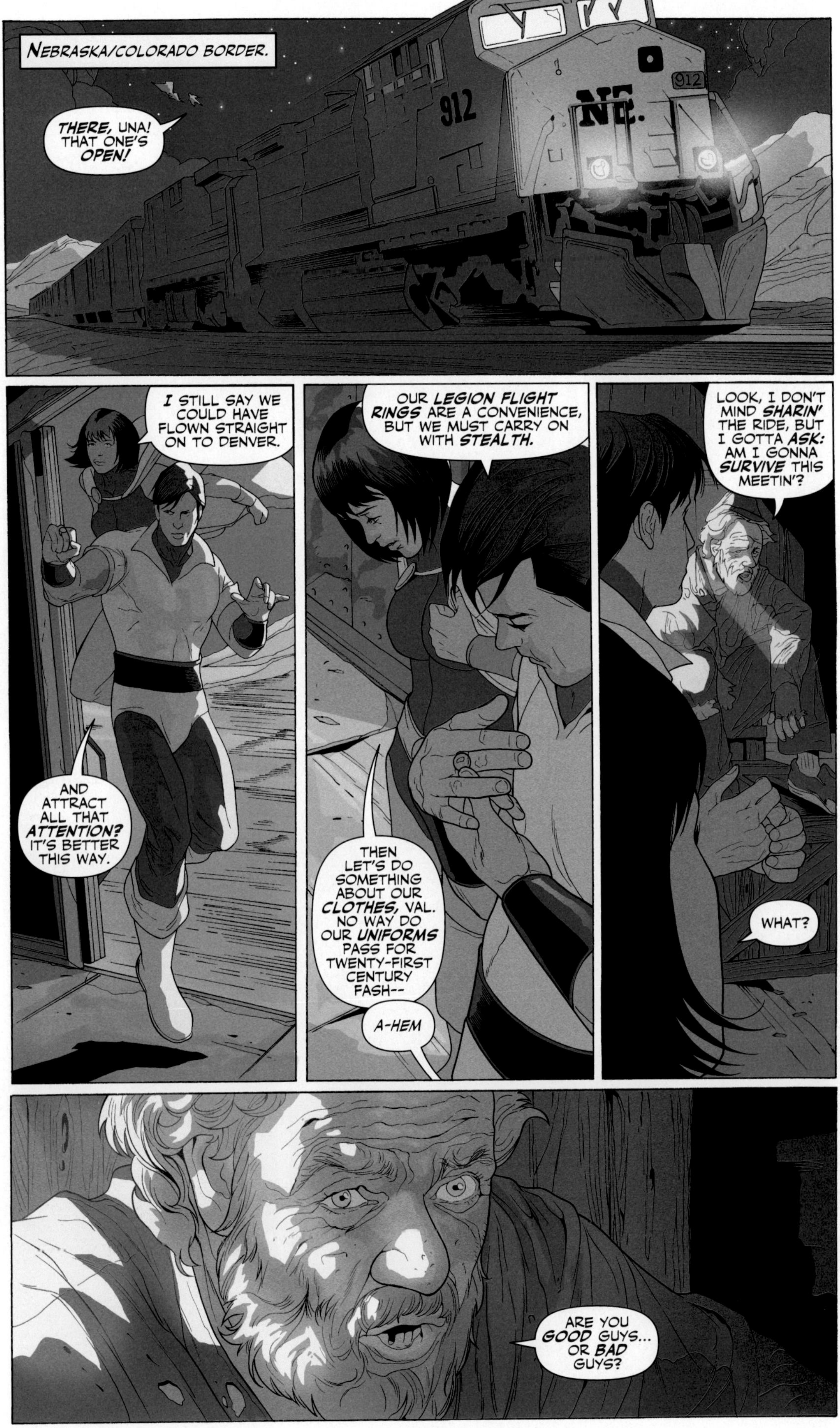
NEBRASKA/COLORADO BORDER.
THERE, UNA! THAT ONE'S OPEN!
I STILL SAY WE COULD HAVE FLOWN STRAIGHT ON TO DENVER.
AND ATTRACT ALL THAT ATTENTION? IT'S BETTER THIS WAY.
OUR LEGION FLIGHT RINGS ARE A CONVENIENCE, BUT WE MUST CARRY ON WITH STEALTH.
THEN LET'S DO SOMETHING ABOUT OUR CLOTHES, VAL. NO WAY DO OUR UNIFORMS PASS FOR TWENTY-FIRST CENTURY FASH--
A-HEM
LOOK, I DON'T MIND SHARIN' THE RIDE, BUT I GOTTA ASK: AM I GONNA SURVIVE THIS MEETIN'?
WHAT?
ARE YOU GOOD GUYS... OR BAD GUYS?

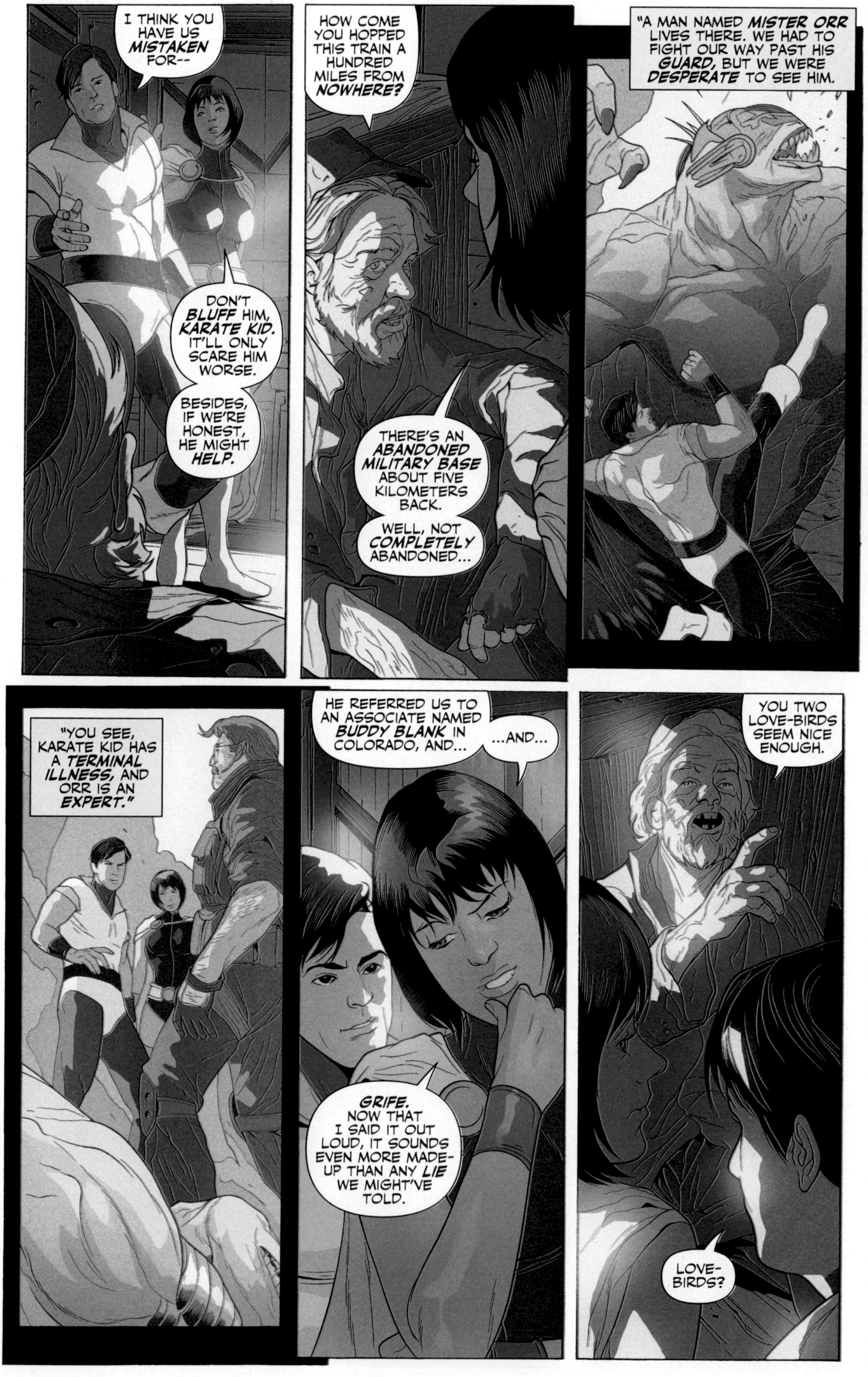
I THINK YOU HAVE US MISTAKEN FOR--
DON'T BLUFF HIM, KARATE KID. IT'LL ONLY SCARE HIM WORSE.
BESIDES, IF WE'RE HONEST, HE MIGHT HELP.
HOW COME YOU HOPPED THIS TRAIN A HUNDRED MILES FROM NOWHERE?
THERE'S AN ABANDONED MILITARY BASE ABOUT FIVE KILOMETERS BACK.
WELL, NOT COMPLETELY ABANDONED...
"A MAN NAMED MISTER ORR LIVES THERE. WE HAD TO FIGHT OUR WAY PAST HIS GUARD, BUT WE WERE DESPERATE TO SEE HIM.
"YOU SEE, KARATE KID HAS A TERMINAL ILLNESS, AND ORR IS AN EXPERT."
HE REFERRED US TO AN ASSOCIATE NAMED BUDDY BLANK IN COLORADO, AND...
...AND...
GRIFE. NOW THAT I SAID IT OUT LOUD, IT SOUNDS EVEN MORE MADE-UP THAN ANY LIE WE MIGHT'VE TOLD.
YOU TWO LOVE-BIRDS SEEM NICE ENOUGH.
LOVE-BIRDS?

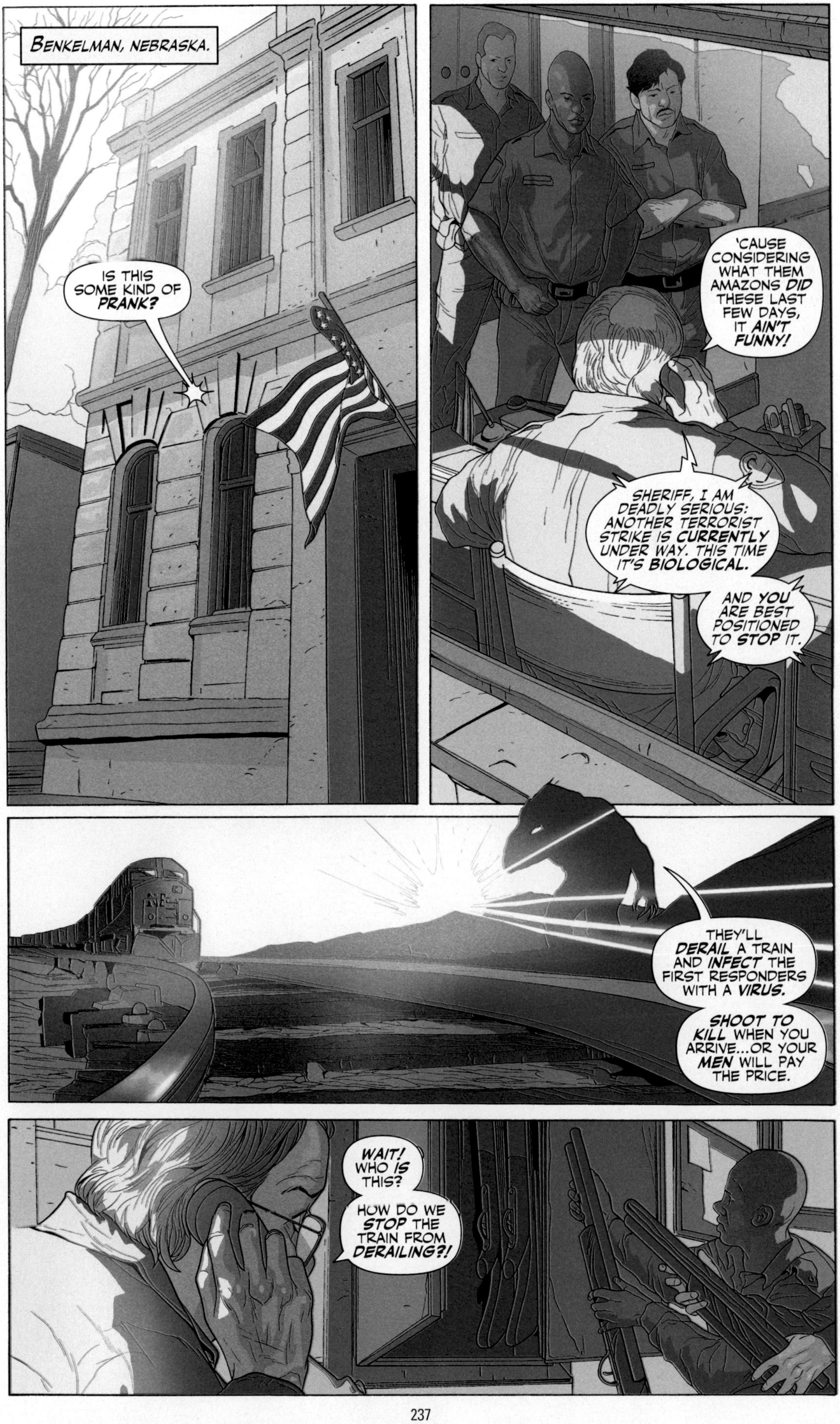

BENKELMAN, NEBRASKA.
IS THIS SOME KIND OF PRANK?
'CAUSE CONSIDERING WHAT THEM AMAZONS DID THESE LAST FEW DAYS, IT AIN'T FUNNY!
SHERIFF, I AM DEADLY SERIOUS: ANOTHER TERRORIST STRIKE IS CURRENTLY UNDER WAY. THIS TIME IT'S BIOLOGICAL.
AND YOU ARE BEST POSITIONED TO STOP IT.
THEY'LL DERAIL A TRAIN AND INFECT THE FIRST RESPONDERS WITH A VIRUS.
SHOOT TO KILL WHEN YOU ARRIVE...OR YOUR MEN WILL PAY THE PRICE.
WAIT! WHO IS THIS?
HOW DO WE STOP THE TRAIN FROM DERAILING?!

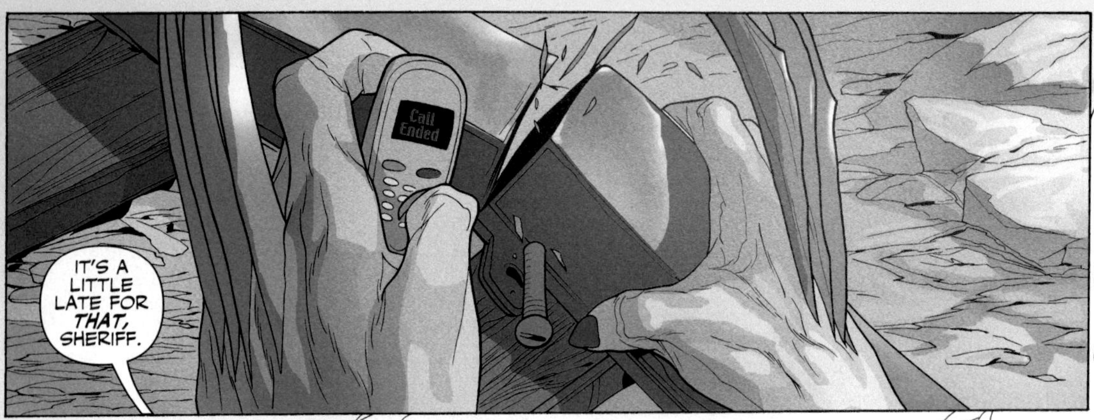
Call Ended
IT'S A LITTLE LATE FOR THAT, SHERIFF.

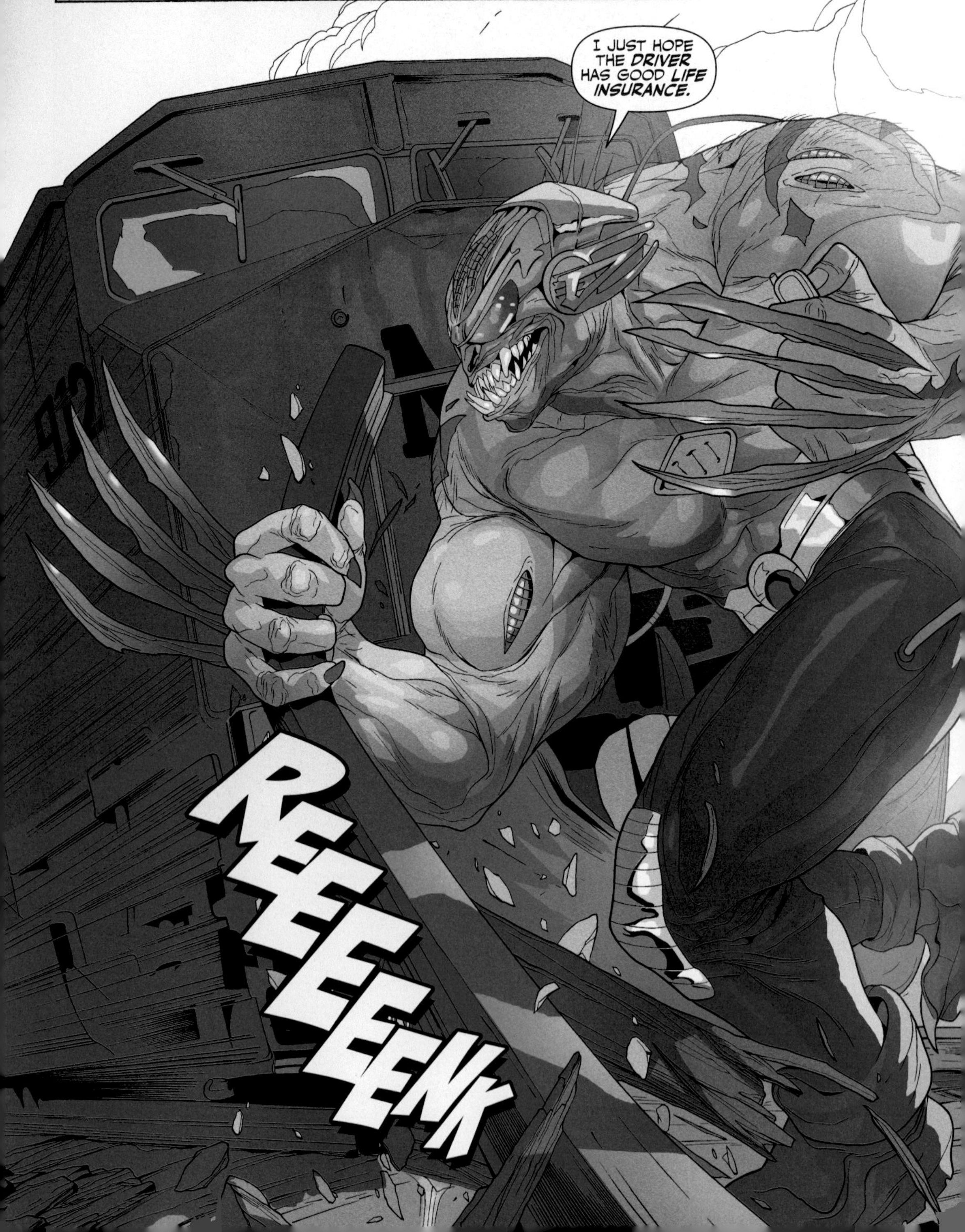
I JUST HOPE THE DRIVER HAS GOOD LIFE INSURANCE.
REEEEENK

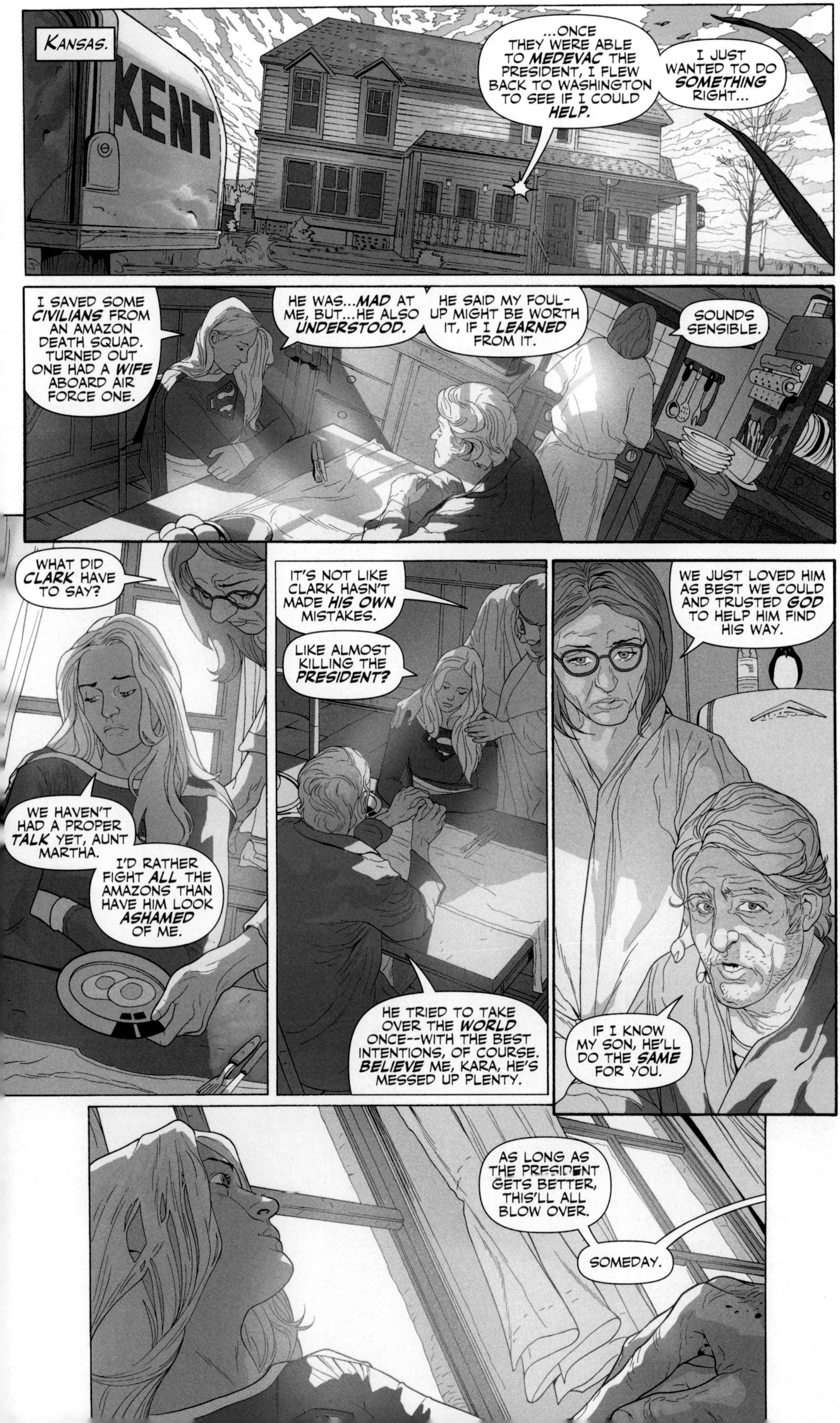
Kansas.
KENT
...ONCE THEY WERE ABLE TO MEDEVAC THE PRESIDENT, I FLEW BACK TO WASHINGTON TO SEE IF I COULD HELP.
I JUST WANTED TO DO SOMETHING RIGHT...
I SAVED SOME CIVILIANS FROM AN AMAZON DEATH SQUAD. TURNED OUT ONE HAD A WIFE ABOARD AIR FORCE ONE.
HE WAS...MAD AT ME, BUT...HE ALSO UNDERSTOOD.
HE SAID MY FOUL-UP MIGHT BE WORTH IT, IF I LEARNED FROM IT.
SOUNDS SENSIBLE.
WHAT DID CLARK HAVE TO SAY?
WE HAVEN'T HAD A PROPER TALK YET, AUNT MARTHA.
I'D RATHER FIGHT ALL THE AMAZONS THAN HAVE HIM LOOK ASHAMED OF ME.
IT'S NOT LIKE CLARK HASN'T MADE HIS OWN MISTAKES.
LIKE ALMOST KILLING THE PRESIDENT?
HE TRIED TO TAKE OVER THE WORLD ONCE--WITH THE BEST INTENTIONS, OF COURSE. BELIEVE ME, KARA, HE'S MESSED UP PLENTY.
WE JUST LOVED HIM AS BEST WE COULD AND TRUSTED GOD TO HELP HIM FIND HIS WAY.
IF I KNOW MY SON, HE'LL DO THE SAME FOR YOU.
AS LONG AS THE PRESIDENT GETS BETTER, THIS'LL ALL BLOW OVER.
SOMEDAY.

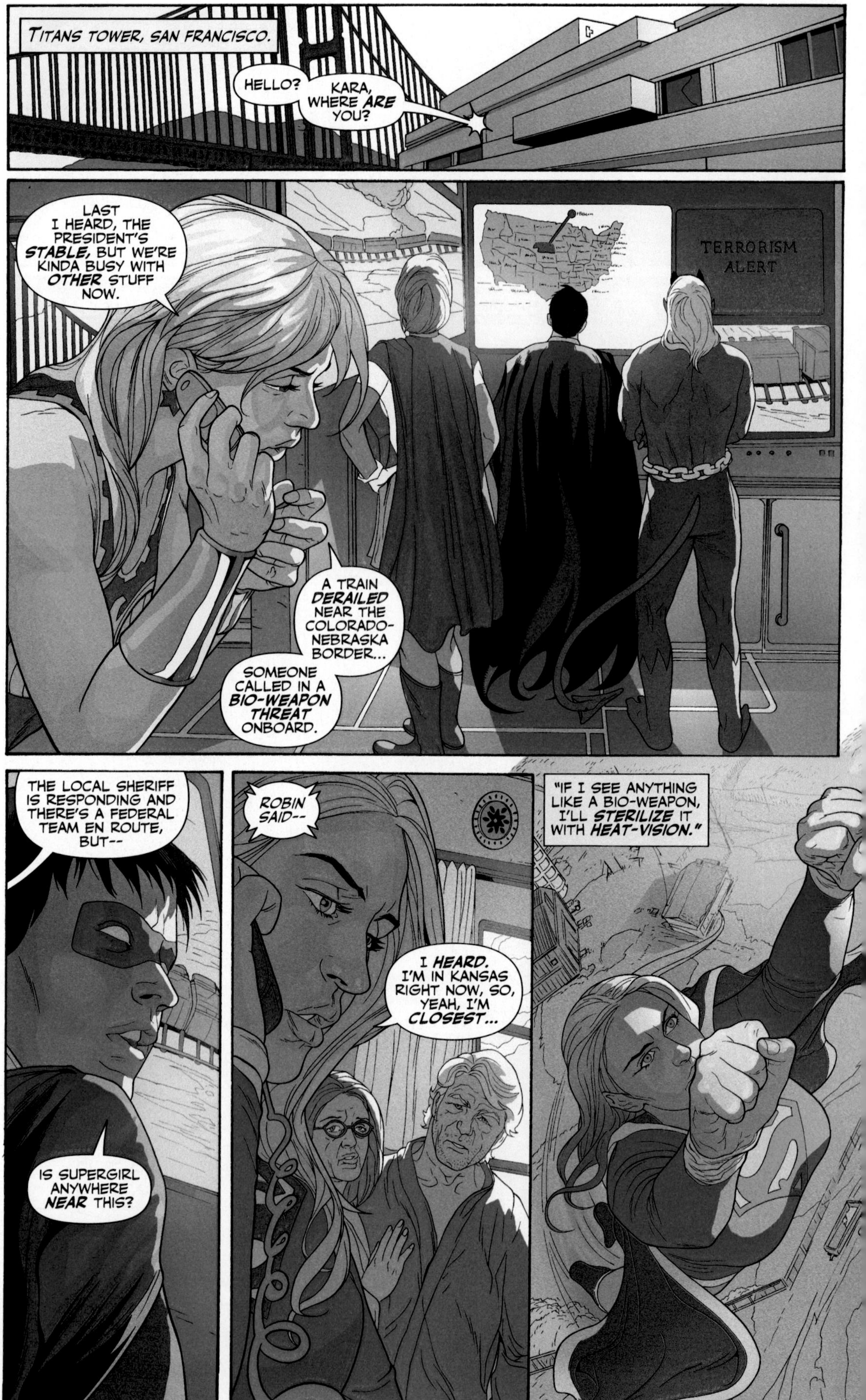
TITANS TOWER, SAN FRANCISCO.
HELLO?
KARA, WHERE ARE YOU?
LAST I HEARD, THE PRESIDENT'S STABLE, BUT WE'RE KINDA BUSY WITH OTHER STUFF NOW.
TERRORISM ALERT
A TRAIN DERAILED NEAR THE COLORADO-NEBRASKA BORDER...
SOMEONE CALLED IN A BIO-WEAPON THREAT ONBOARD.
THE LOCAL SHERIFF IS RESPONDING AND THERE'S A FEDERAL TEAM EN ROUTE, BUT--
IS SUPERGIRL ANYWHERE NEAR THIS?
ROBIN SAID--
I HEARD. I'M IN KANSAS RIGHT NOW, SO, YEAH, I'M CLOSEST...
"IF I SEE ANYTHING LIKE A BIO-WEAPON, I'LL STERILIZE IT WITH HEAT-VISION."

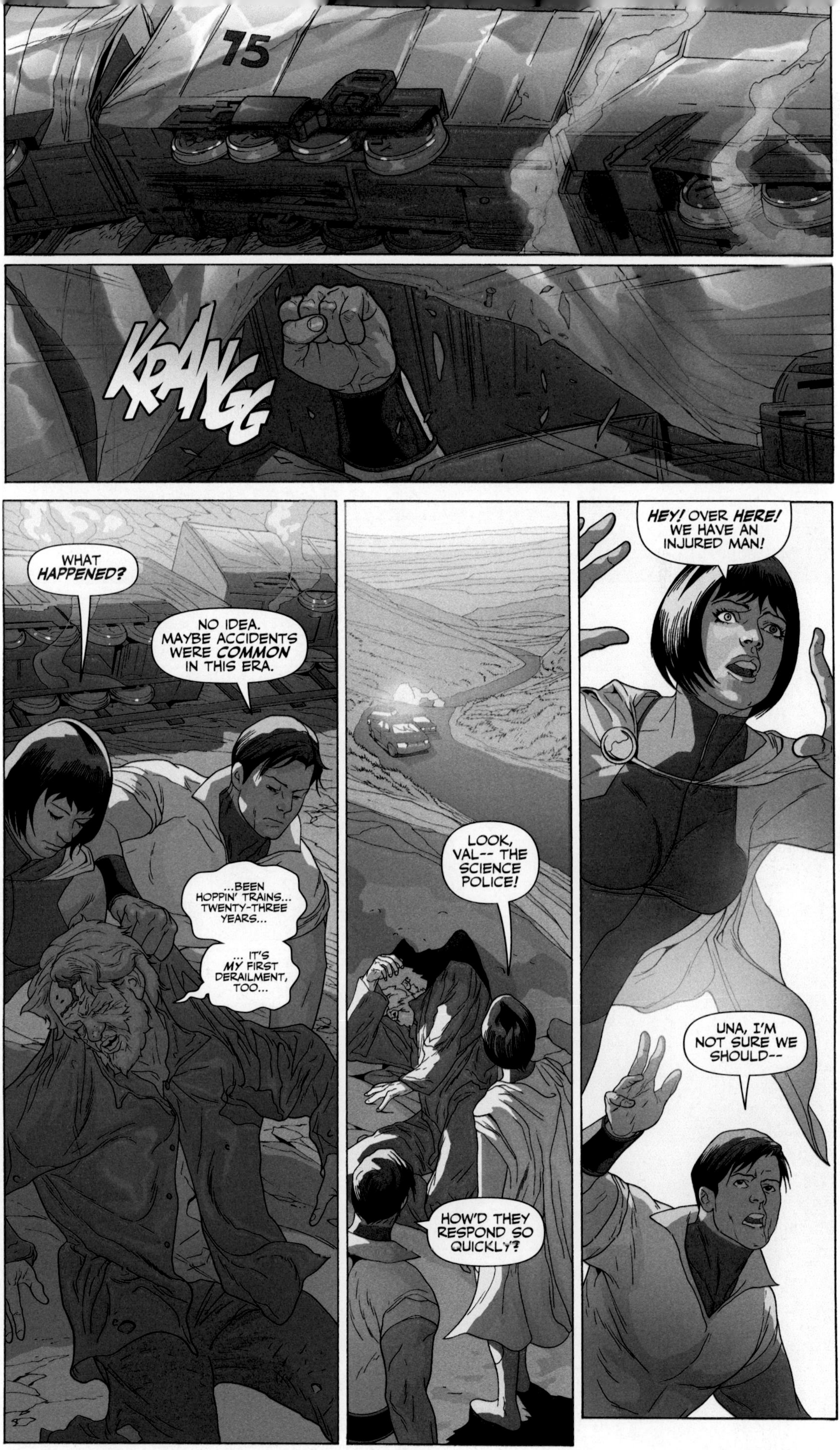

75
KRANGG
WHAT HAPPENED?
NO IDEA. MAYBE ACCIDENTS WERE COMMON IN THIS ERA.
...BEEN HOPPIN' TRAINS... TWENTY-THREE YEARS...
... IT'S MY FIRST DERAILMENT, TOO...
LOOK, VAL-- THE SCIENCE POLICE!
HOW'D THEY RESPOND SO QUICKLY?
HEY! OVER HERE! WE HAVE AN INJURED MAN!
UNA, I'M NOT SURE WE SHOULD--

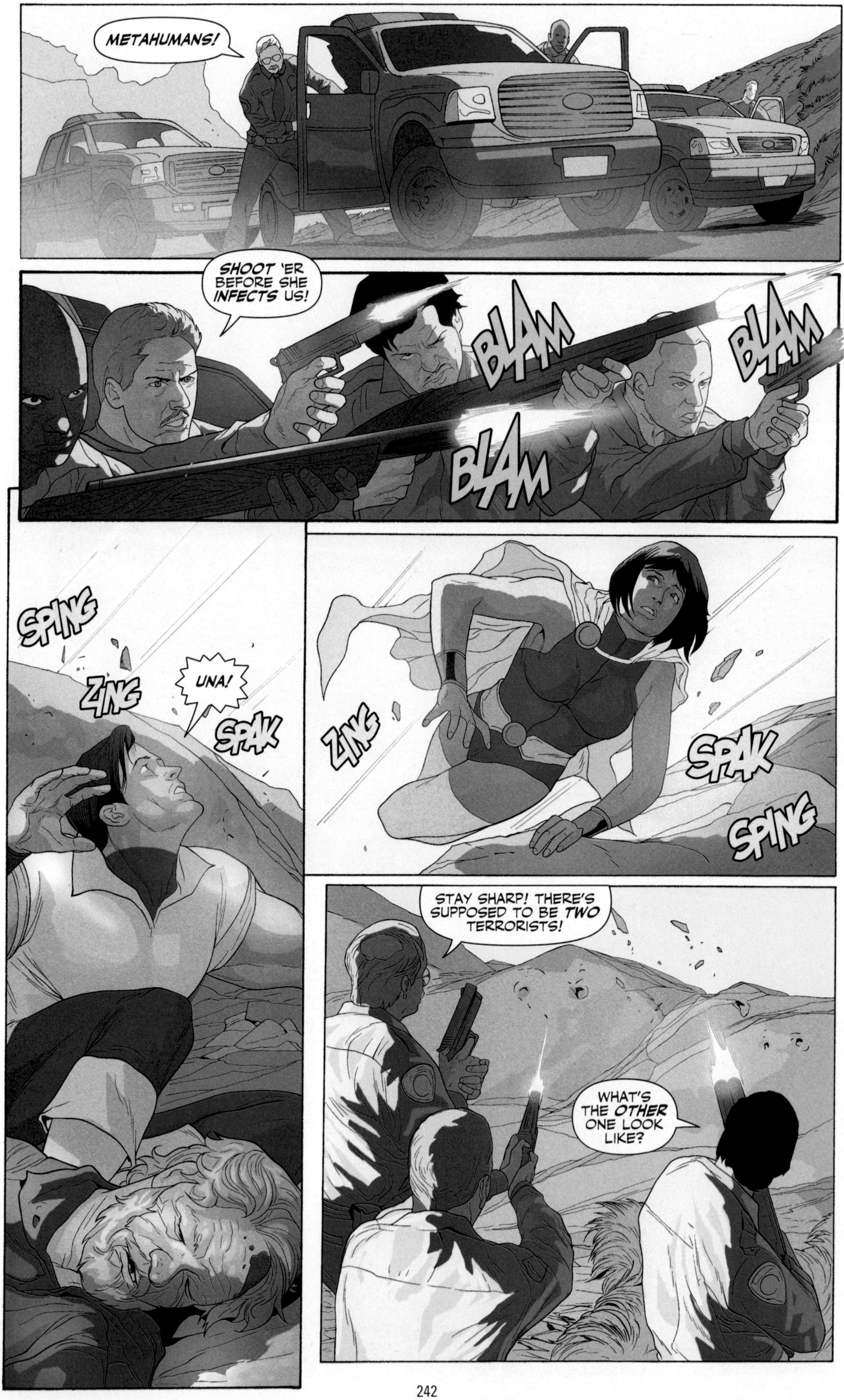
METAHUMANS!
SHOOT 'ER BEFORE SHE INFECTS US!
BLAM
BLAM
BLAM
SPING
ZING
UNA!
SPAK
ZING
SPAK
SPING
STAY SHARP! THERE'S SUPPOSED TO BE TWO TERRORISTS!
WHAT'S THE OTHER ONE LOOK LIKE?

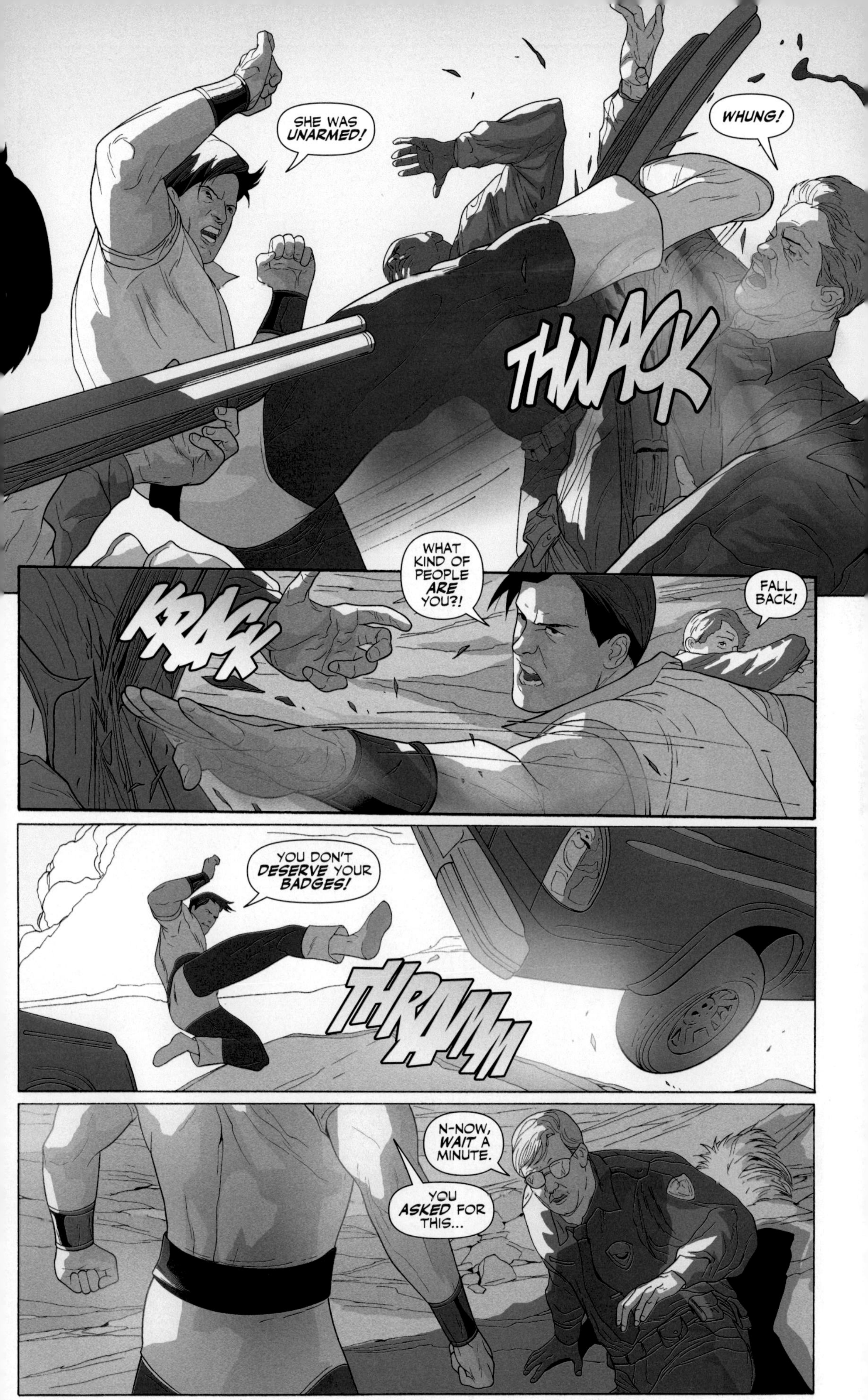
SHE WAS UNARMED!
WHUNG!
THWACK
WHAT KIND OF PEOPLE ARE YOU?!
FALL BACK!
KRACK
YOU DON'T DESERVE YOUR BADGES!
THRAMM
N-NOW, WAIT A MINUTE.
YOU ASKED FOR THIS...

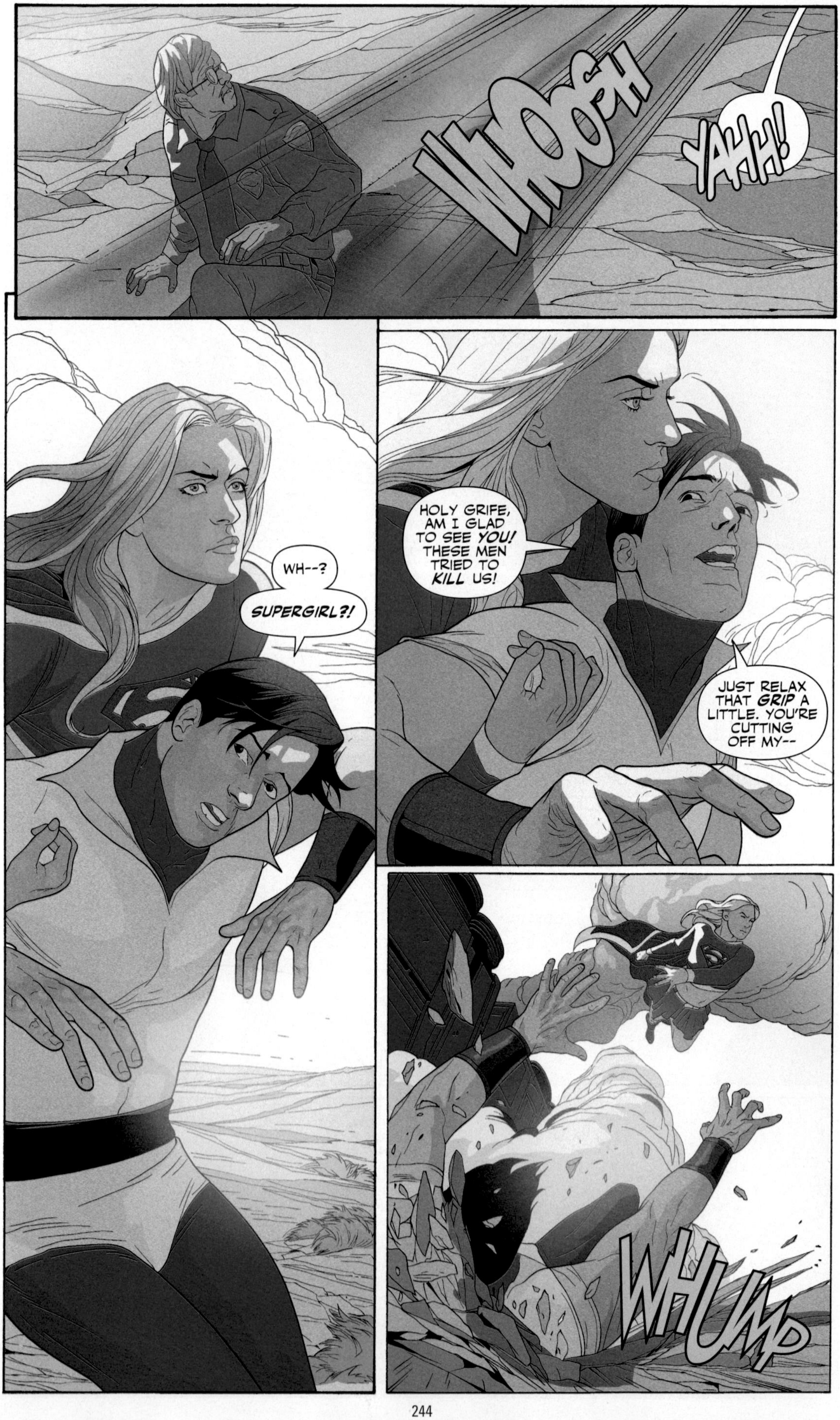
WHOOSH
YAHH!
WH--?
SUPERGIRL?!
HOLY GRIFE, AM I GLAD TO SEE YOU! THESE MEN TRIED TO KILL US!
JUST RELAX THAT GRIP A LITTLE. YOU'RE CUTTING OFF MY--
WHUMP

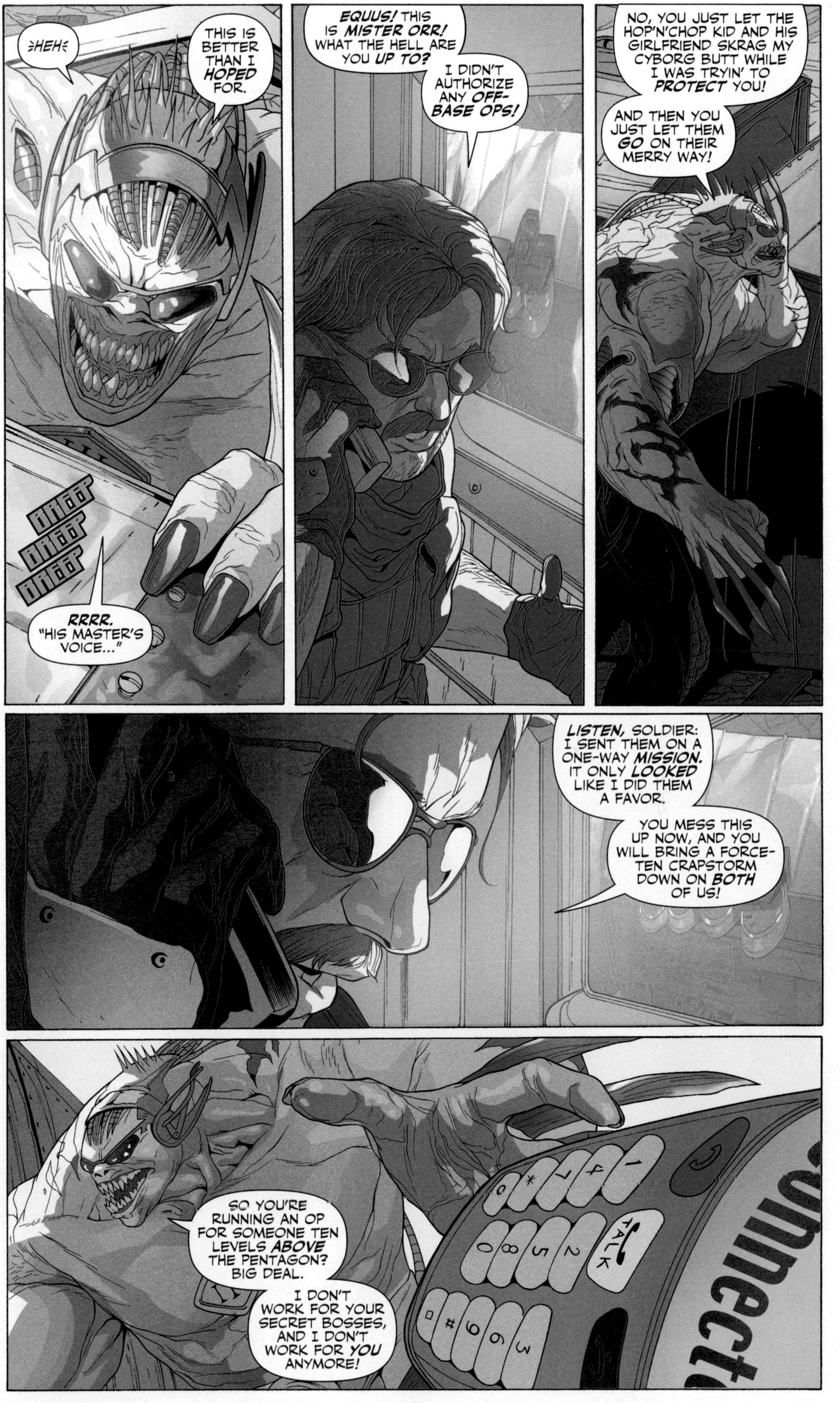

HEH
THIS IS BETTER THAN I HOPED FOR.
BRGGP BRGGP BRGGP
RRRR. "HIS MASTER'S VOICE..."
EQUUS! THIS IS MISTER ORR! WHAT THE HELL ARE YOU UP TO?
I DIDN'T AUTHORIZE ANY OFF-BASE OPS!
NO, YOU JUST LET THE HOP'N'CHOP KID AND HIS GIRLFRIEND SKRAG MY CYBORG BUTT WHILE I WAS TRYIN' TO PROTECT YOU!
AND THEN YOU JUST LET THEM GO ON THEIR MERRY WAY!
LISTEN, SOLDIER: I SENT THEM ON A ONE-WAY MISSION. IT ONLY LOOKED LIKE I DID THEM A FAVOR.
YOU MESS THIS UP NOW, AND YOU WILL BRING A FORCE-TEN CRAPSTORM DOWN ON BOTH OF US!
SO YOU'RE RUNNING AN OP FOR SOMEONE TEN LEVELS ABOVE THE PENTAGON? BIG DEAL.
I DON'T WORK FOR YOUR SECRET BOSSES, AND I DON'T WORK FOR YOU ANYMORE!

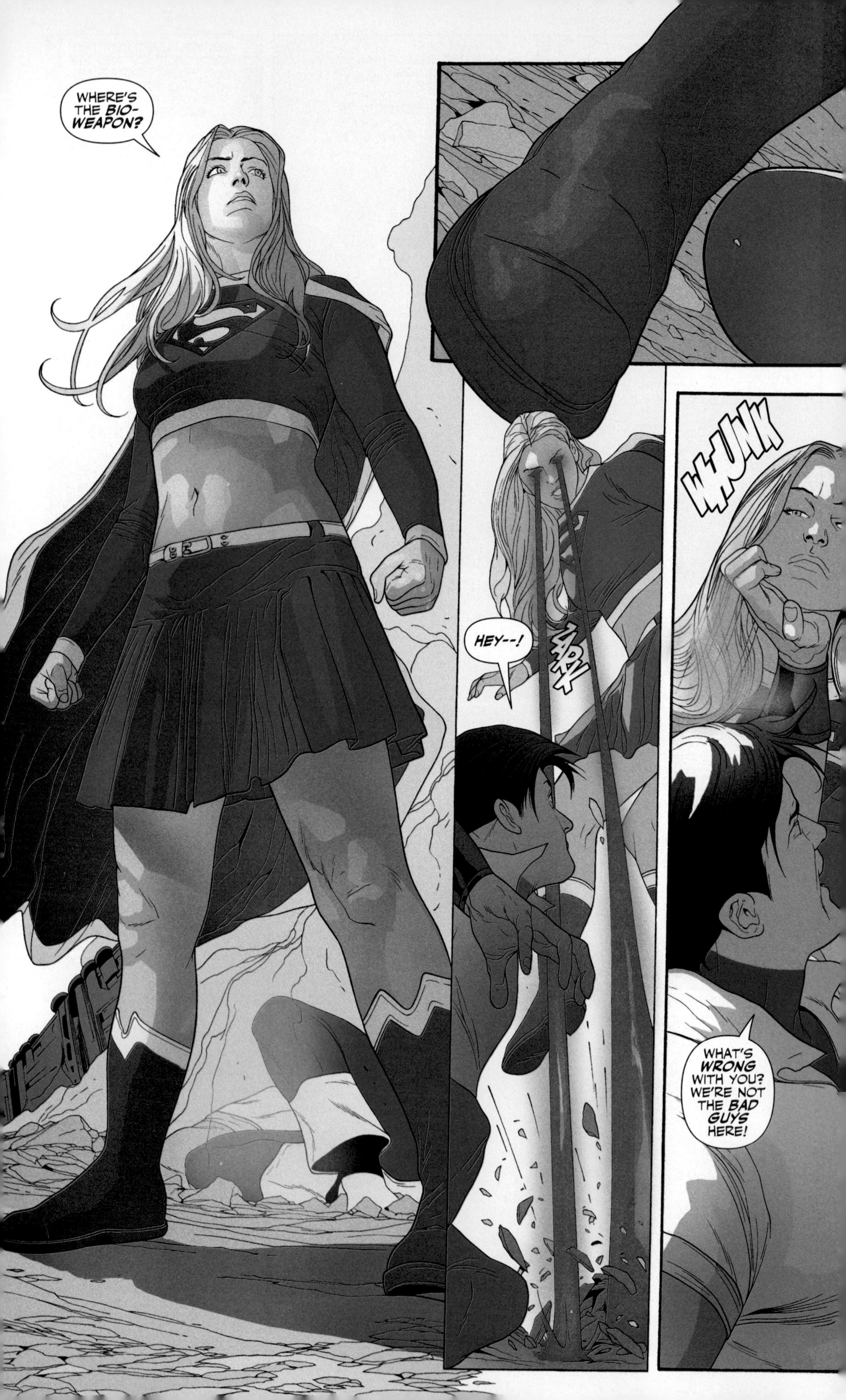
WHERE'S THE BIO-WEAPON?
HEY--!
ZARK
WHUNK
WHAT'S WRONG WITH YOU? WE'RE NOT THE BAD GUYS HERE!

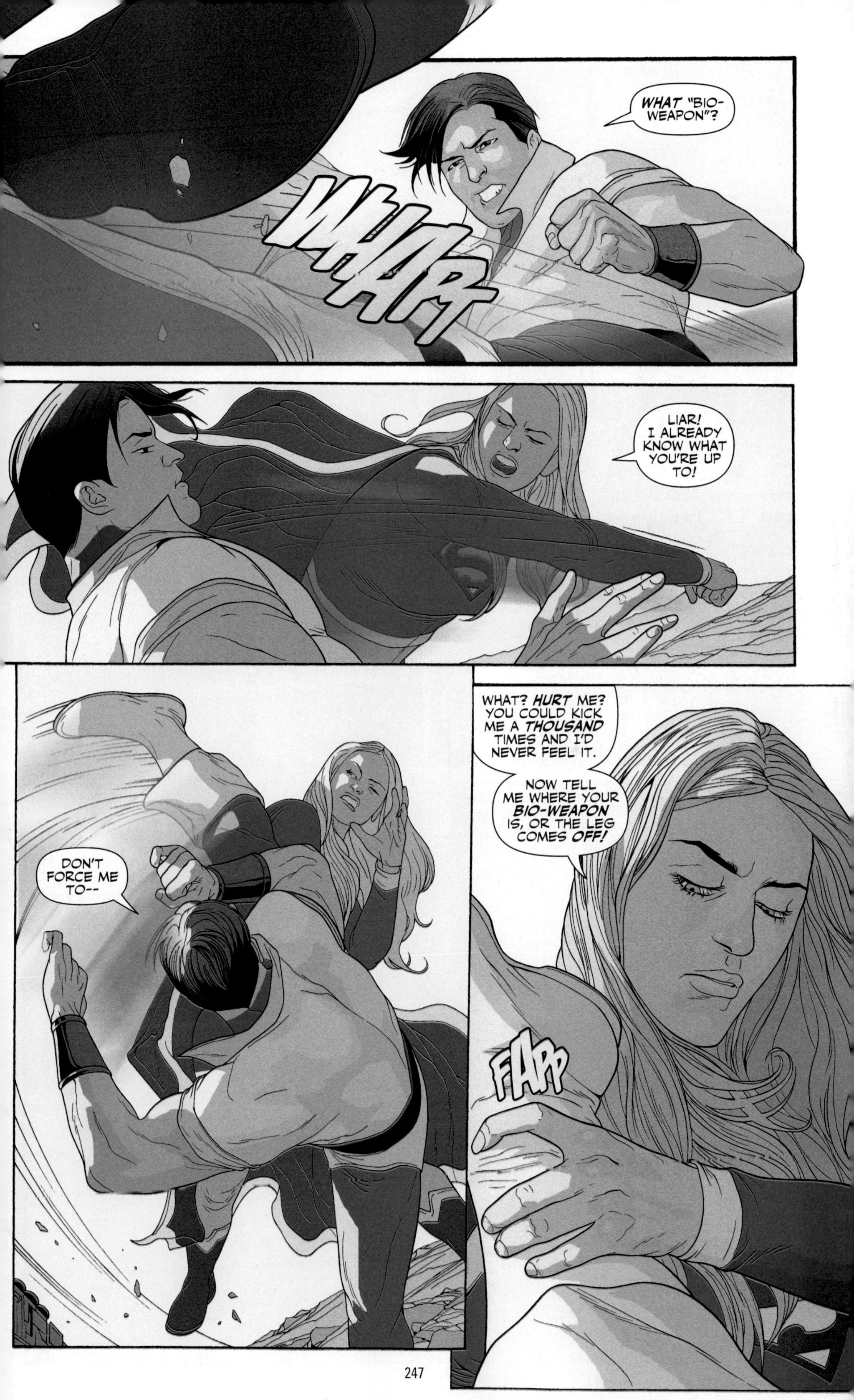
WHAT "BIO-WEAPON"?
WHARF
LIAR! I ALREADY KNOW WHAT YOU'RE UP TO!
WHAT? HURT ME? YOU COULD KICK ME A THOUSAND TIMES AND I'D NEVER FEEL IT.
NOW TELL ME WHERE YOUR BIO-WEAPON IS, OR THE LEG COMES OFF!
DON'T FORCE ME TO--
FAPP

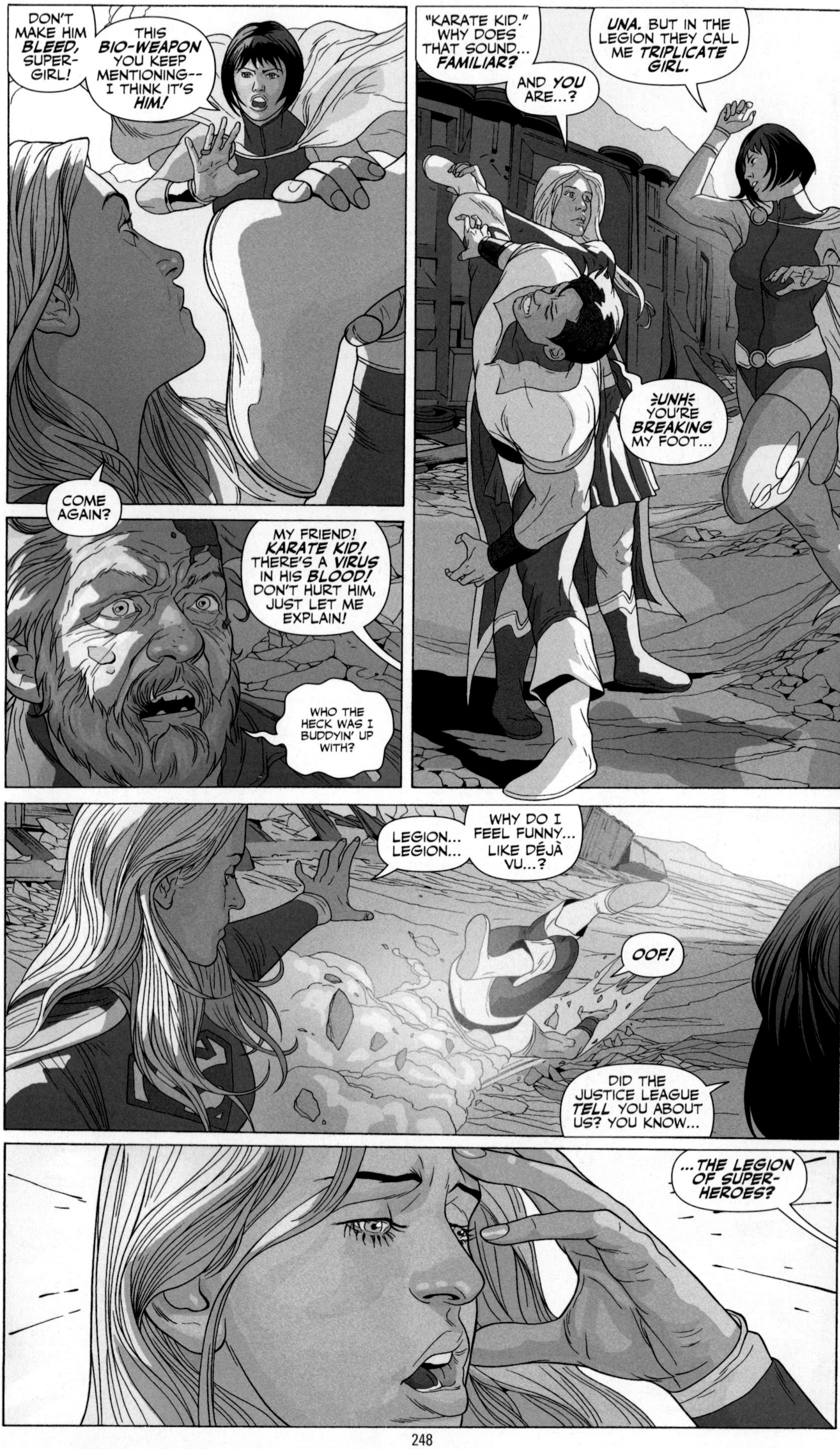
DON'T MAKE HIM BLEED, SUPER-GIRL!
THIS BIO-WEAPON YOU KEEP MENTIONING-- I THINK IT'S HIM!
COME AGAIN?
MY FRIEND! KARATE KID! THERE'S A VIRUS IN HIS BLOOD! DON'T HURT HIM, JUST LET ME EXPLAIN!
WHO THE HECK WAS I BUDDYIN' UP WITH?
"KARATE KID." WHY DOES THAT SOUND... FAMILIAR?
AND YOU ARE...?
UNA. BUT IN THE LEGION THEY CALL ME TRIPLICATE GIRL.
UNH YOU'RE BREAKING MY FOOT...
LEGION... LEGION...
WHY DO I FEEL FUNNY... LIKE DÉJÀ VU...?
OOF!
DID THE JUSTICE LEAGUE TELL YOU ABOUT US? YOU KNOW...
...THE LEGION OF SUPER-HEROES?

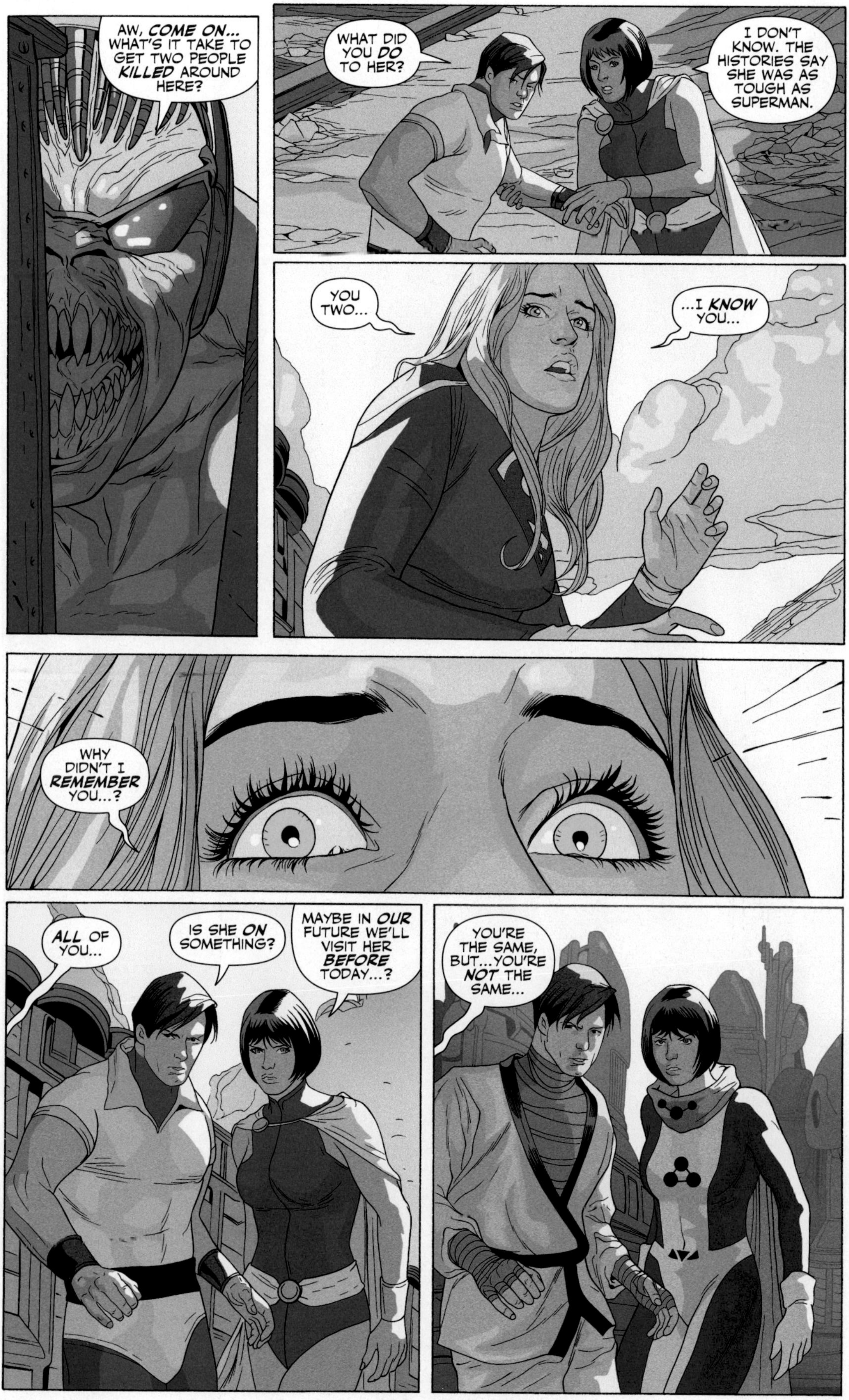

AW, COME ON... WHAT'S IT TAKE TO GET TWO PEOPLE KILLED AROUND HERE?
WHAT DID YOU DO TO HER?
I DON'T KNOW. THE HISTORIES SAY SHE WAS AS TOUGH AS SUPERMAN.
YOU TWO...
...I KNOW YOU...
WHY DIDN'T I REMEMBER YOU...?
ALL OF YOU...
IS SHE ON SOMETHING?
MAYBE IN OUR FUTURE WE'LL VISIT HER BEFORE TODAY...?
YOU'RE THE SAME, BUT...YOU'RE NOT THE SAME...

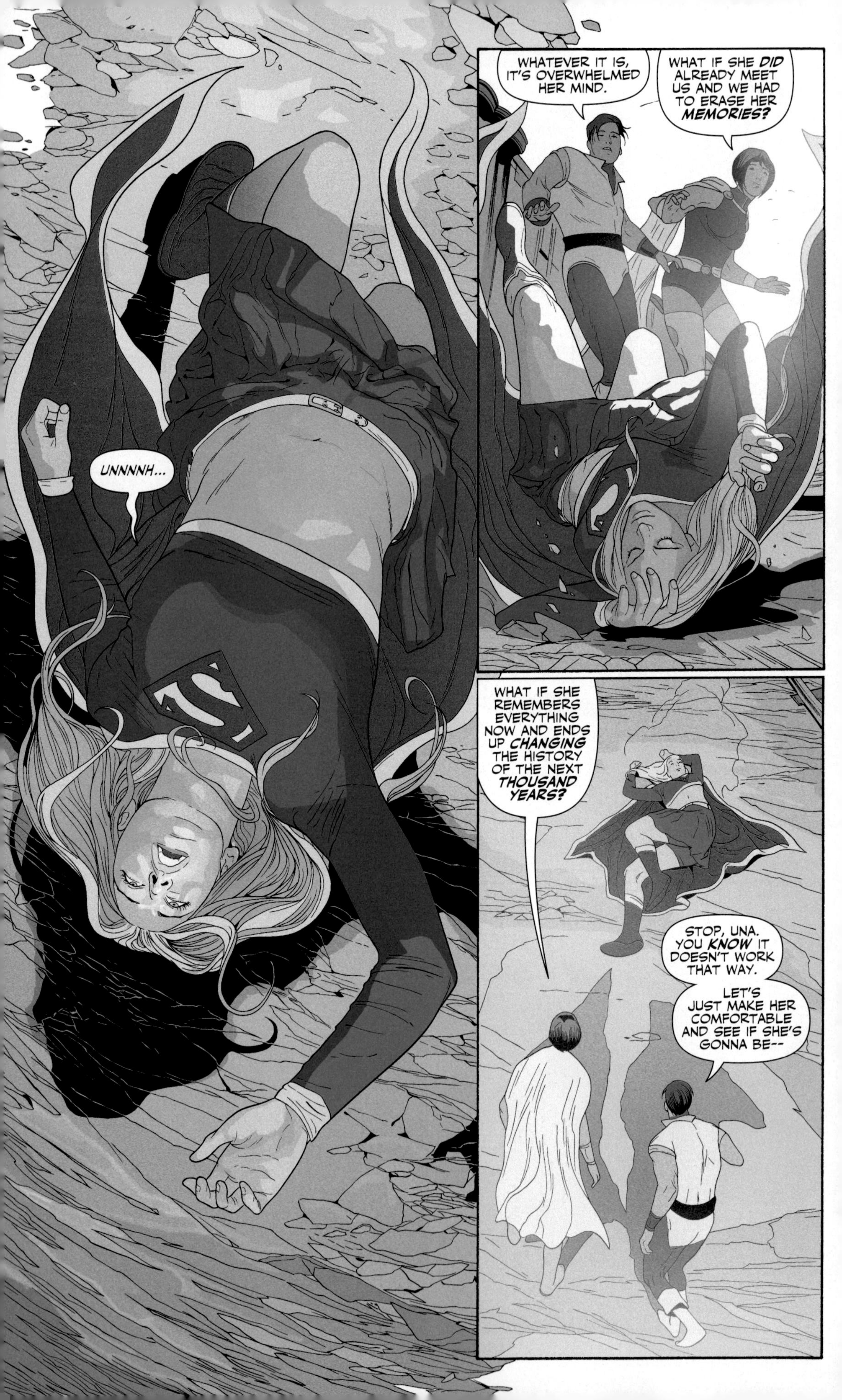
WHATEVER IT IS, IT'S OVERWHELMED HER MIND.
WHAT IF SHE *DID* ALREADY MEET US AND WE HAD TO ERASE HER *MEMORIES?*
UNNNNH...
WHAT IF SHE REMEMBERS EVERYTHING NOW AND ENDS UP *CHANGING* THE HISTORY OF THE NEXT *THOUSAND YEARS?*
STOP, UNA. YOU *KNOW* IT DOESN'T WORK THAT WAY.
LET'S JUST MAKE HER COMFORTABLE AND SEE IF SHE'S GONNA BE--

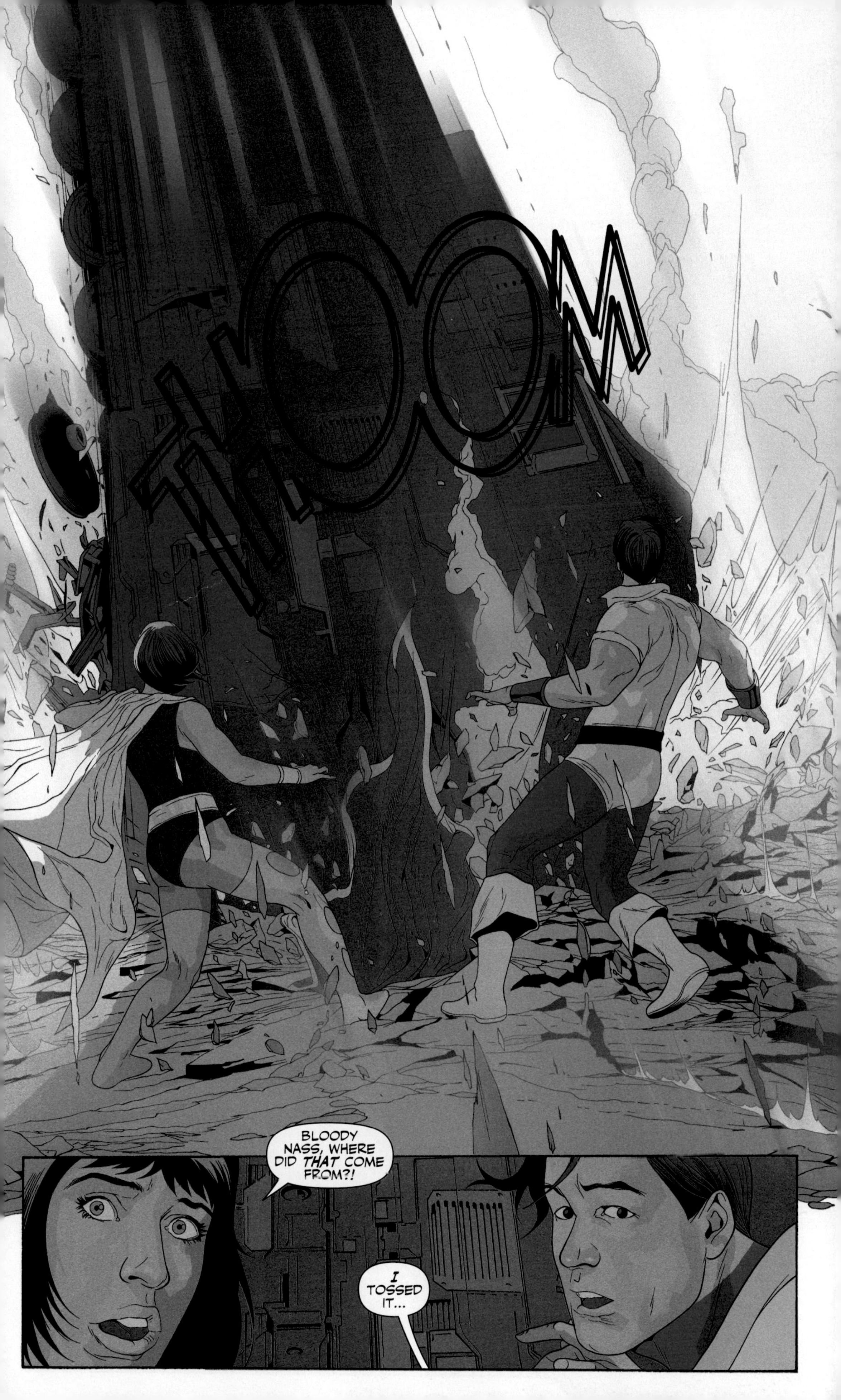
THOOM
BLOODY NASS, WHERE DID *THAT* COME FROM?!
I TOSSED IT...

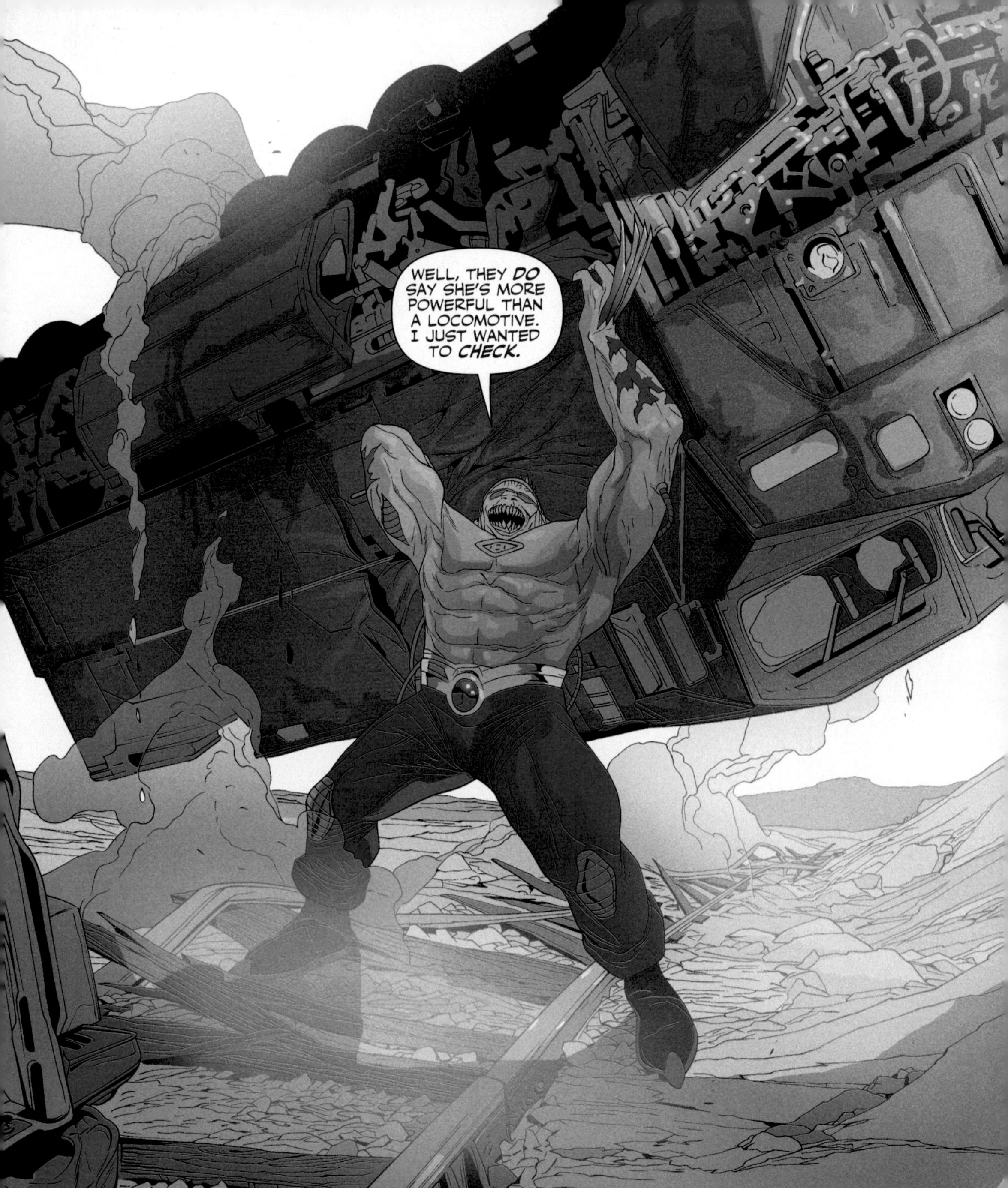
WELL, THEY DO SAY SHE'S MORE POWERFUL THAN A LOCOMOTIVE. I JUST WANTED TO CHECK.

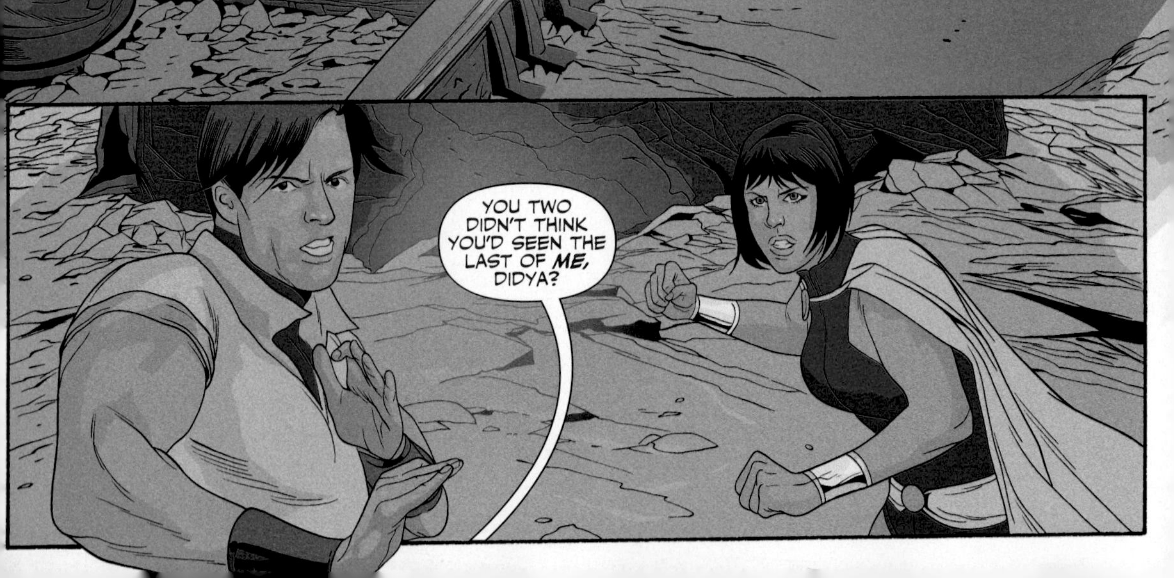
YOU TWO DIDN'T THINK YOU'D SEEN THE LAST OF ME, DIDYA?

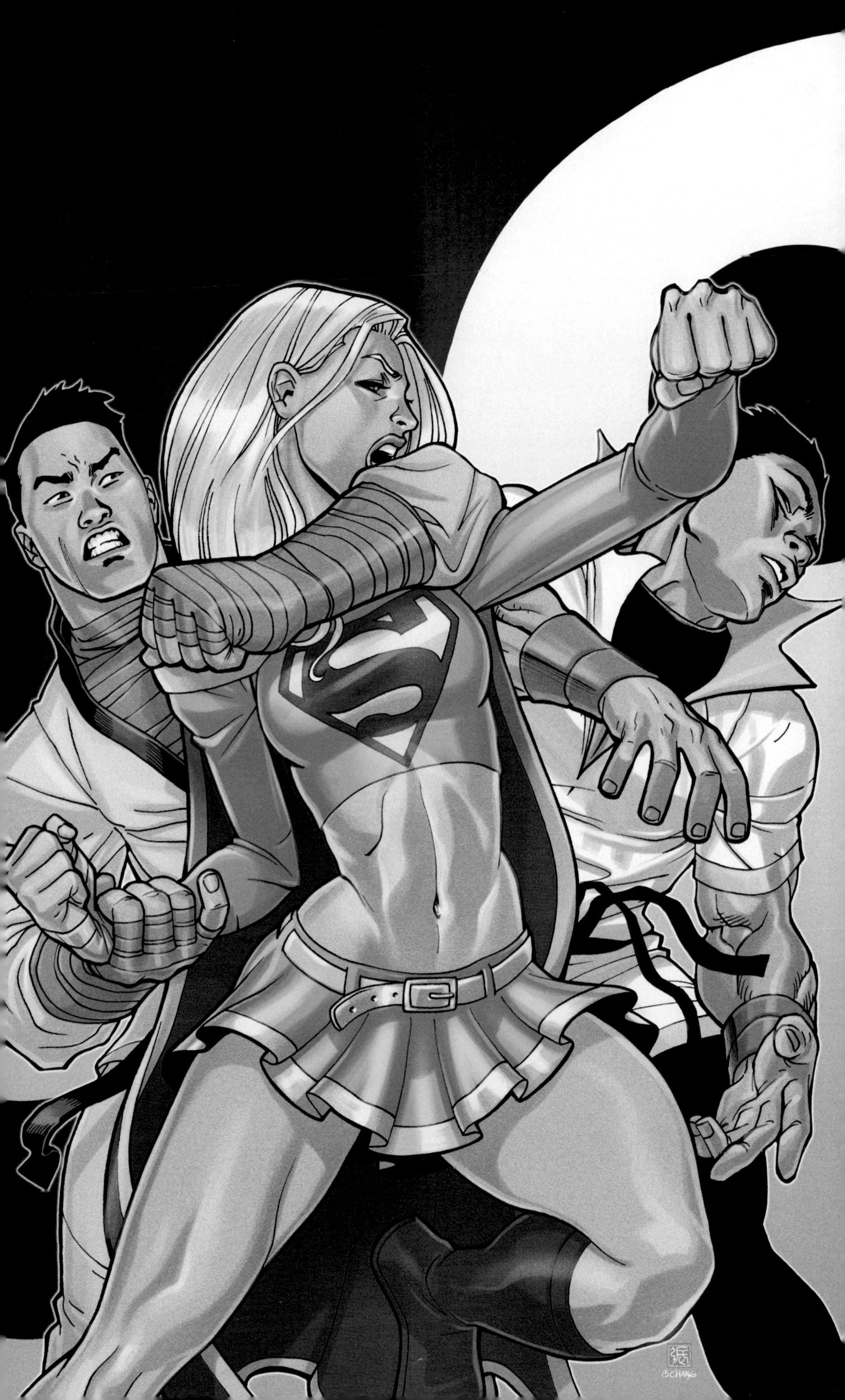

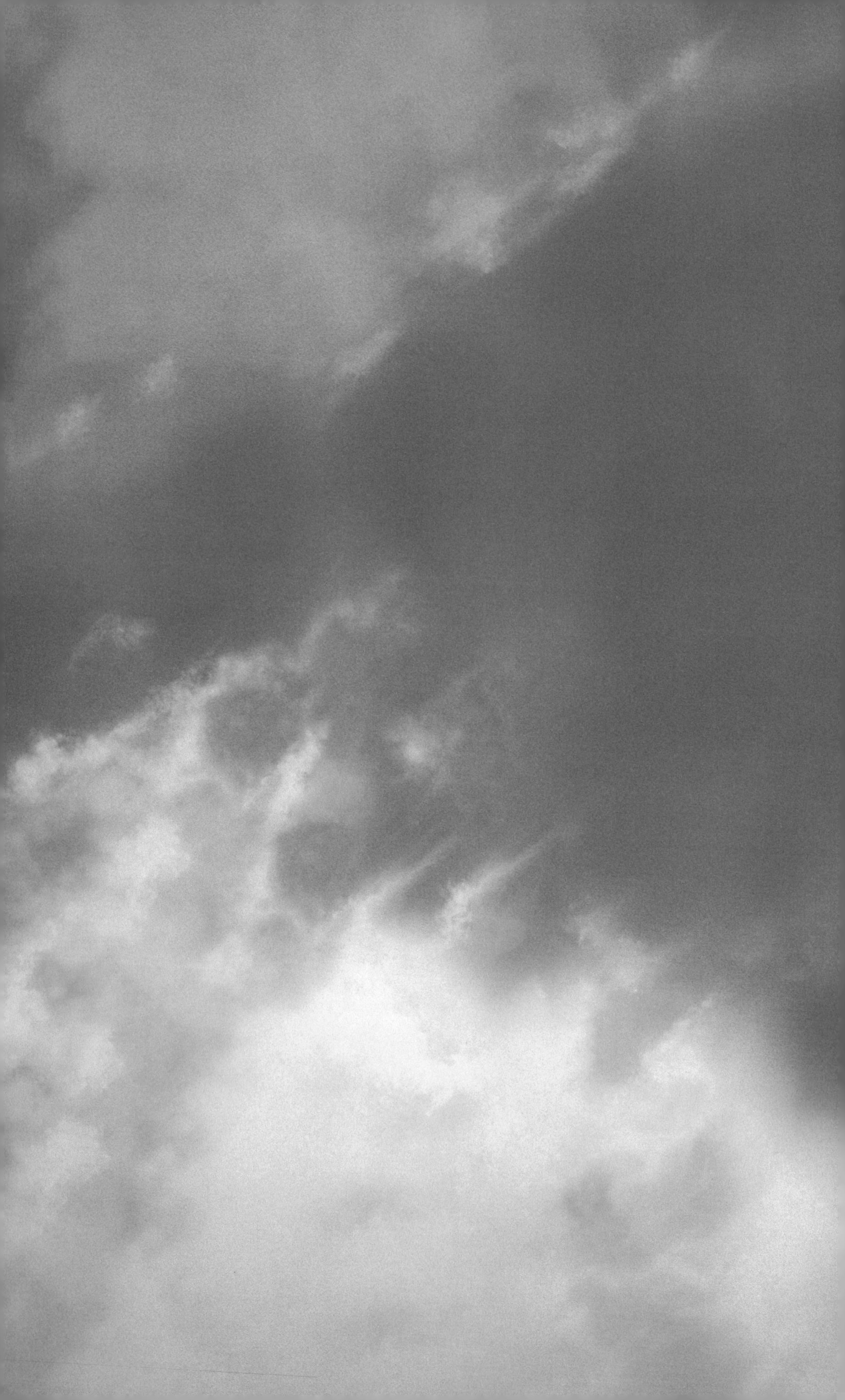

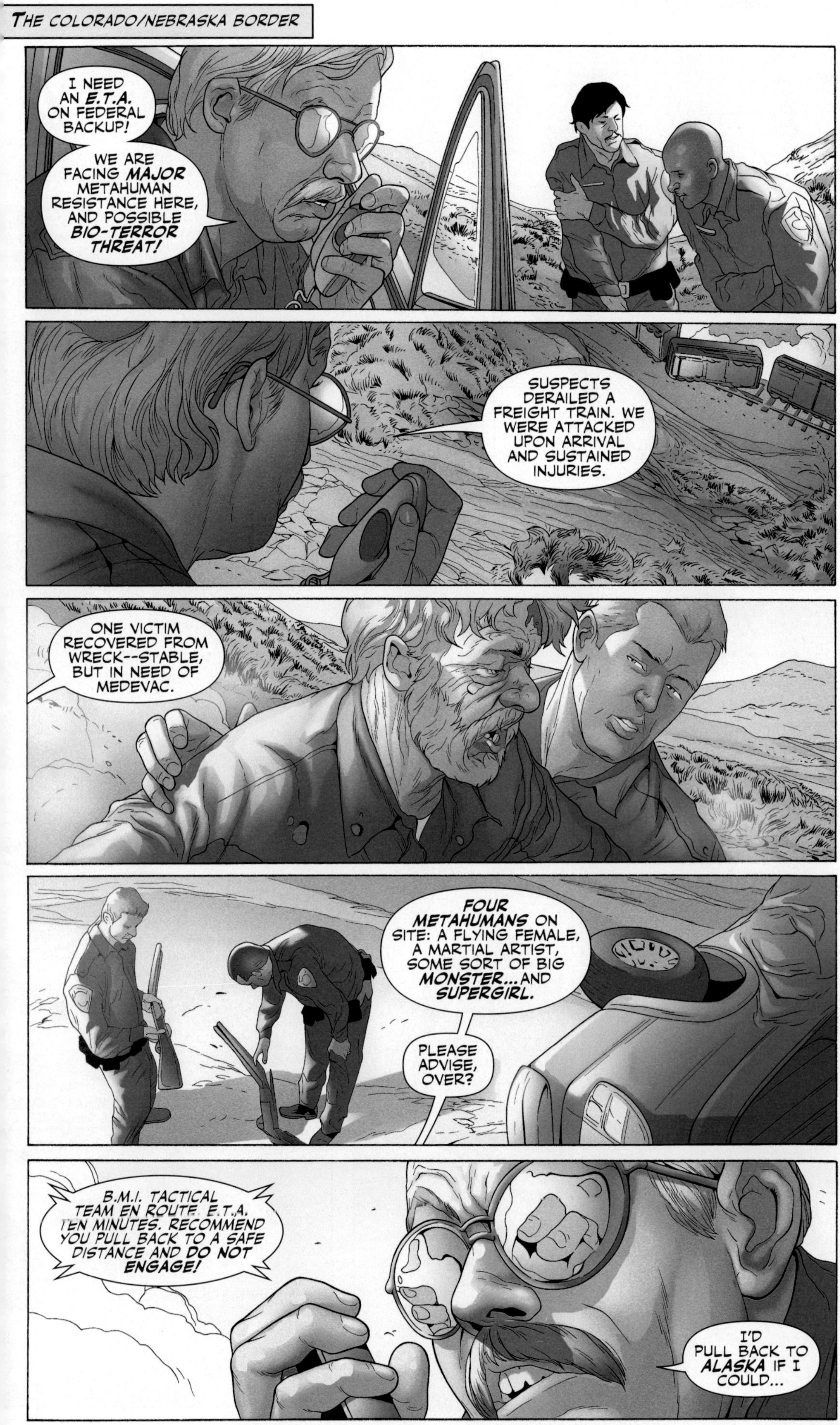
THE COLORADO/NEBRASKA BORDER
I NEED AN E.T.A. ON FEDERAL BACKUP!
WE ARE FACING MAJOR METAHUMAN RESISTANCE HERE, AND POSSIBLE BIO-TERROR THREAT!
SUSPECTS DERAILED A FREIGHT TRAIN. WE WERE ATTACKED UPON ARRIVAL AND SUSTAINED INJURIES.
ONE VICTIM RECOVERED FROM WRECK--STABLE, BUT IN NEED OF MEDEVAC.
FOUR METAHUMANS ON SITE: A FLYING FEMALE, A MARTIAL ARTIST, SOME SORT OF BIG MONSTER...AND SUPERGIRL.
PLEASE ADVISE, OVER?
B.M.I. TACTICAL TEAM EN ROUTE. E.T.A. TEN MINUTES. RECOMMEND YOU PULL BACK TO A SAFE DISTANCE AND DO NOT ENGAGE!
I'D PULL BACK TO ALASKA IF I COULD...

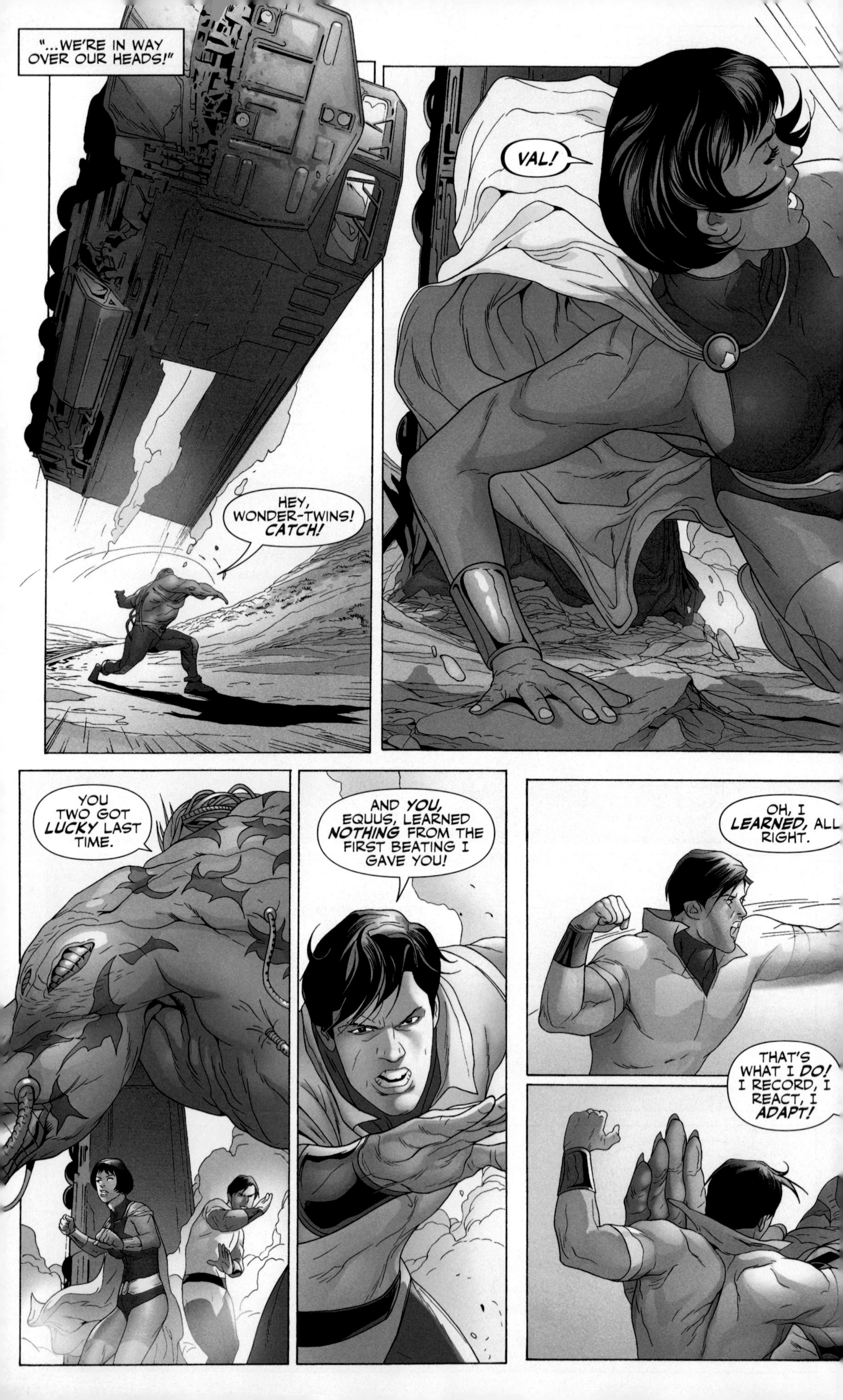
"...WE'RE IN WAY OVER OUR HEADS!"
HEY, WONDER-TWINS! CATCH!
VAL!
YOU TWO GOT LUCKY LAST TIME.
AND YOU, EQUUS, LEARNED NOTHING FROM THE FIRST BEATING I GAVE YOU!
OH, I LEARNED, ALL RIGHT.
THAT'S WHAT I DO! I RECORD, I REACT, I ADAPT!

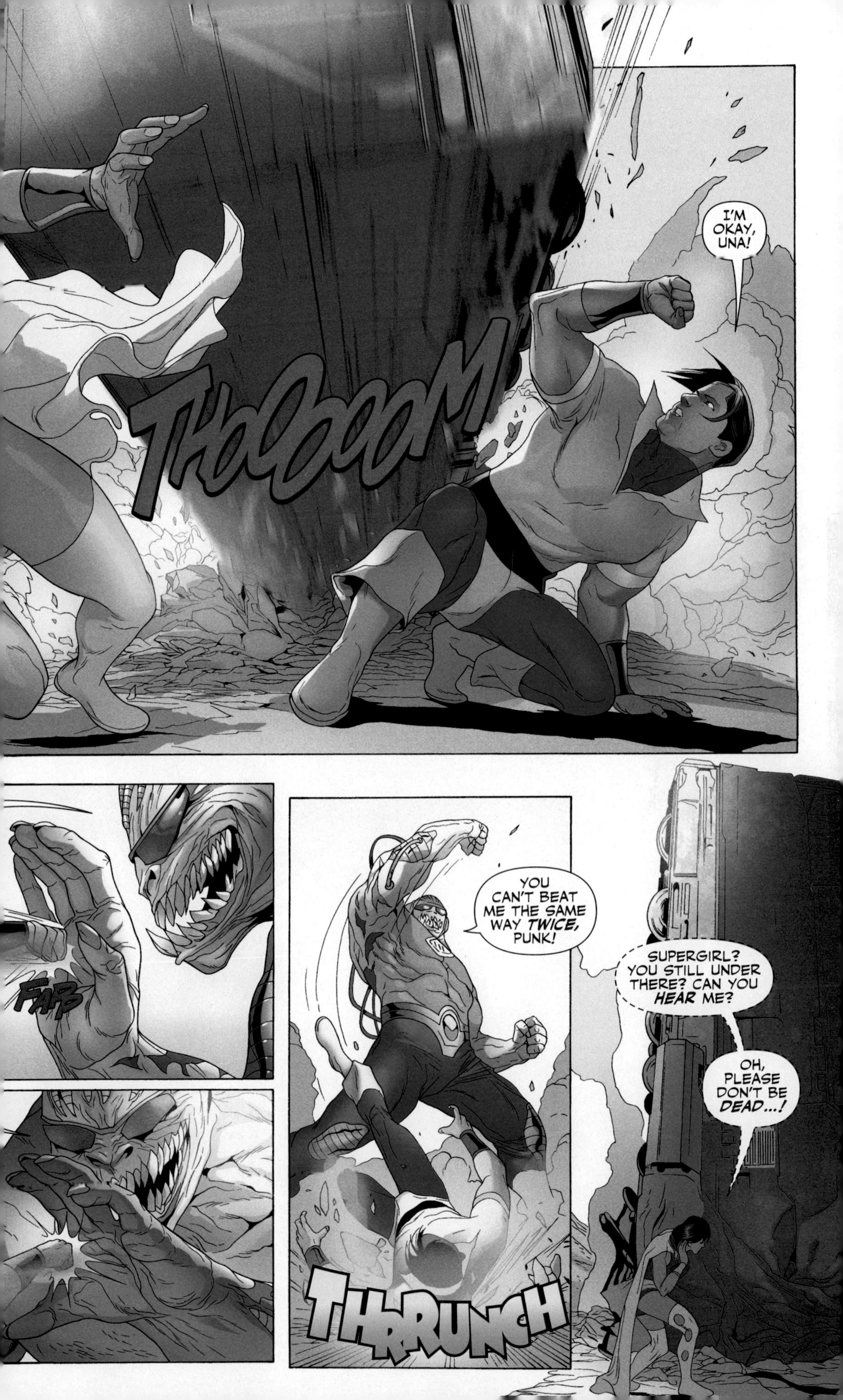
I'M OKAY, UNA!
THOOOOM
FAP
YOU CAN'T BEAT ME THE SAME WAY TWICE, PUNK!
THRRUNCH
SUPERGIRL? YOU STILL UNDER THERE? CAN YOU HEAR ME?
OH, PLEASE DON'T BE DEAD...!

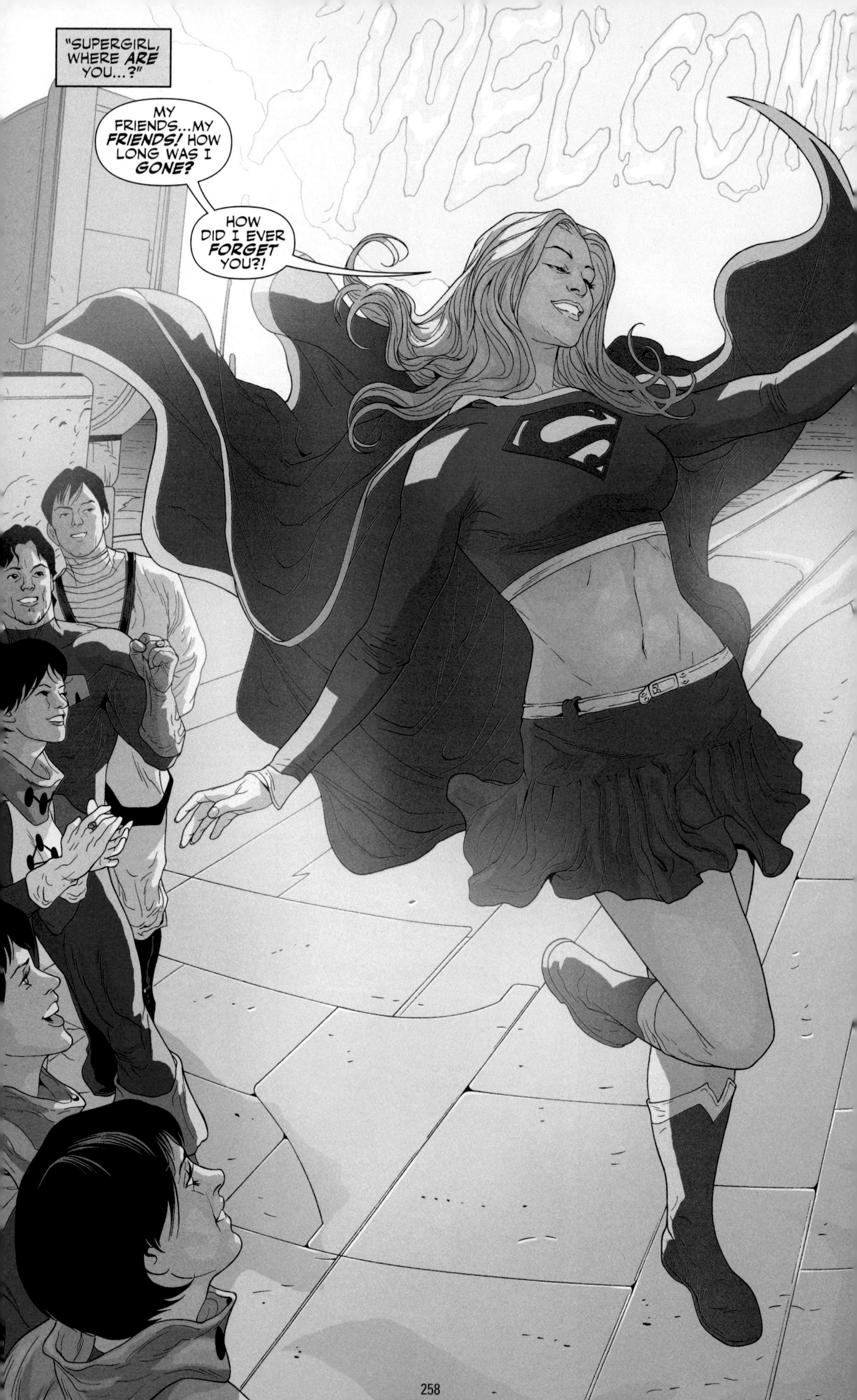
"SUPERGIRL, WHERE ARE YOU...?"
MY FRIENDS...MY FRIENDS! HOW LONG WAS I GONE?
HOW DID I EVER FORGET YOU?!
WELCOM

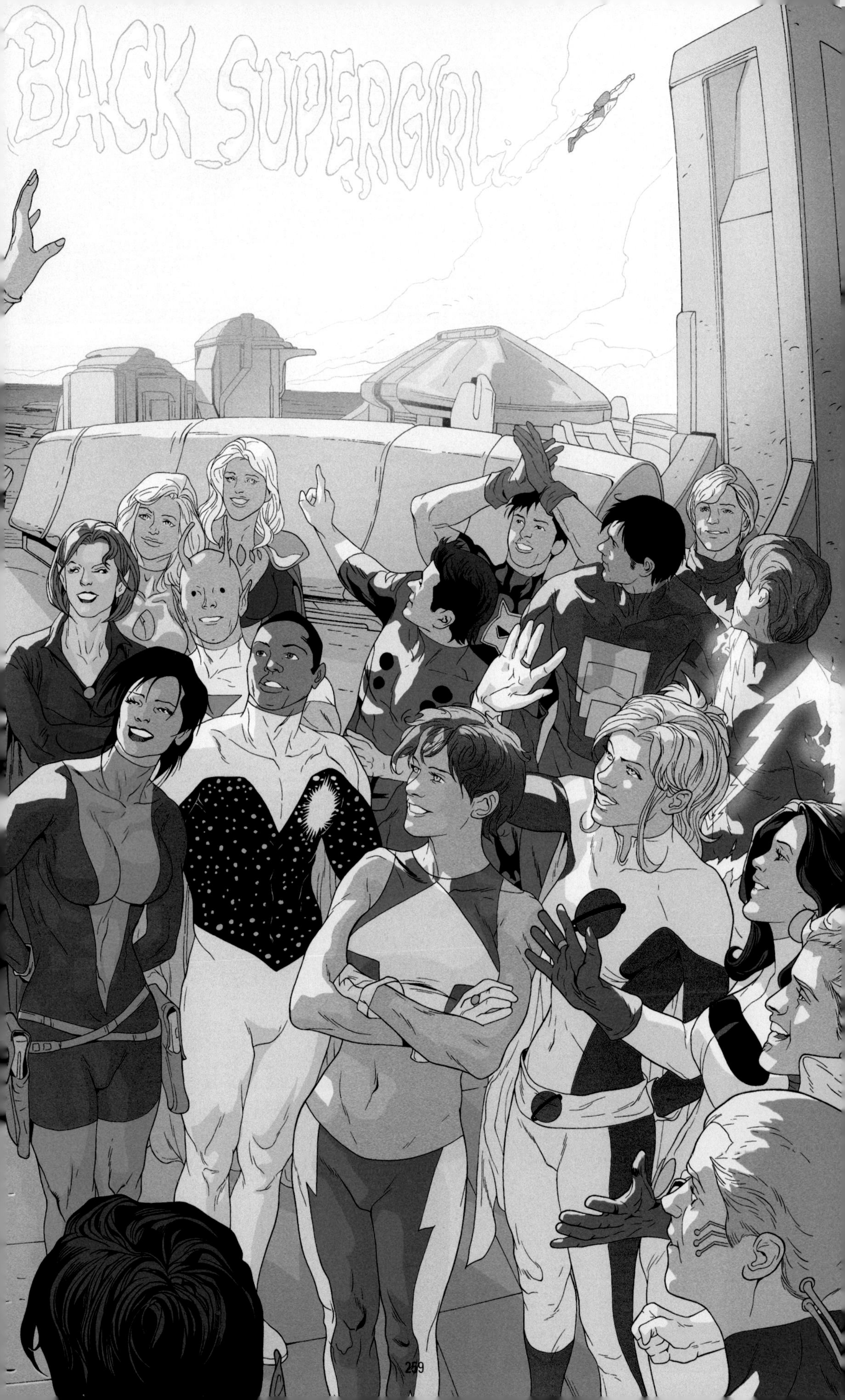
BACK_SUPERGIRL

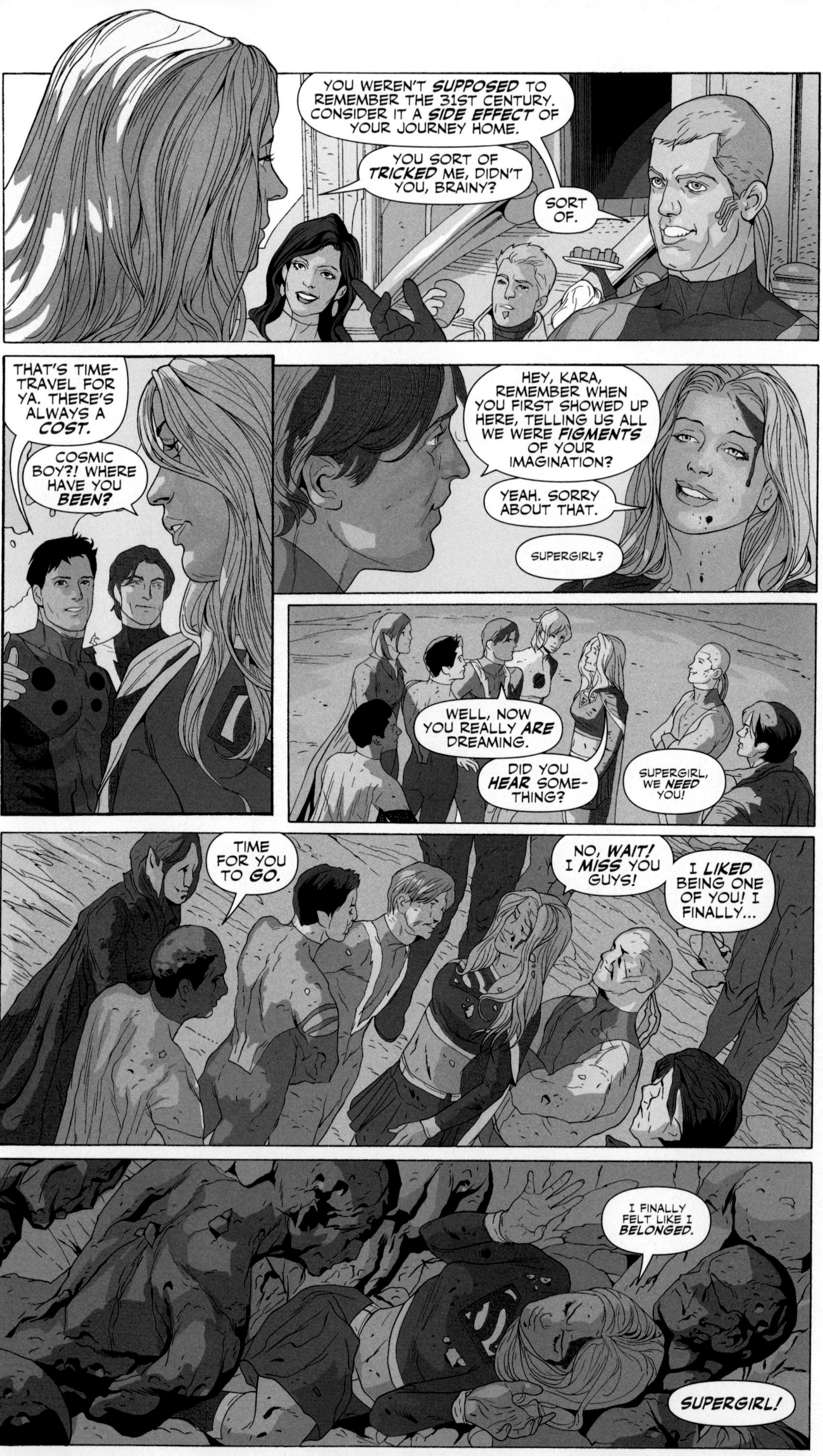
YOU WEREN'T SUPPOSED TO REMEMBER THE 31ST CENTURY. CONSIDER IT A SIDE EFFECT OF YOUR JOURNEY HOME.
YOU SORT OF TRICKED ME, DIDN'T YOU, BRAINY?
SORT OF.
THAT'S TIME-TRAVEL FOR YA. THERE'S ALWAYS A COST.
COSMIC BOY?! WHERE HAVE YOU BEEN?
HEY, KARA, REMEMBER WHEN YOU FIRST SHOWED UP HERE, TELLING US ALL WE WERE FIGMENTS OF YOUR IMAGINATION?
YEAH. SORRY ABOUT THAT.
SUPERGIRL?
WELL, NOW YOU REALLY ARE DREAMING.
DID YOU HEAR SOME-THING?
SUPERGIRL, WE NEED YOU!
TIME FOR YOU TO GO.
NO, WAIT! I MISS YOU GUYS!
I LIKED BEING ONE OF YOU! I FINALLY...
I FINALLY FELT LIKE I BELONGED.
SUPERGIRL!

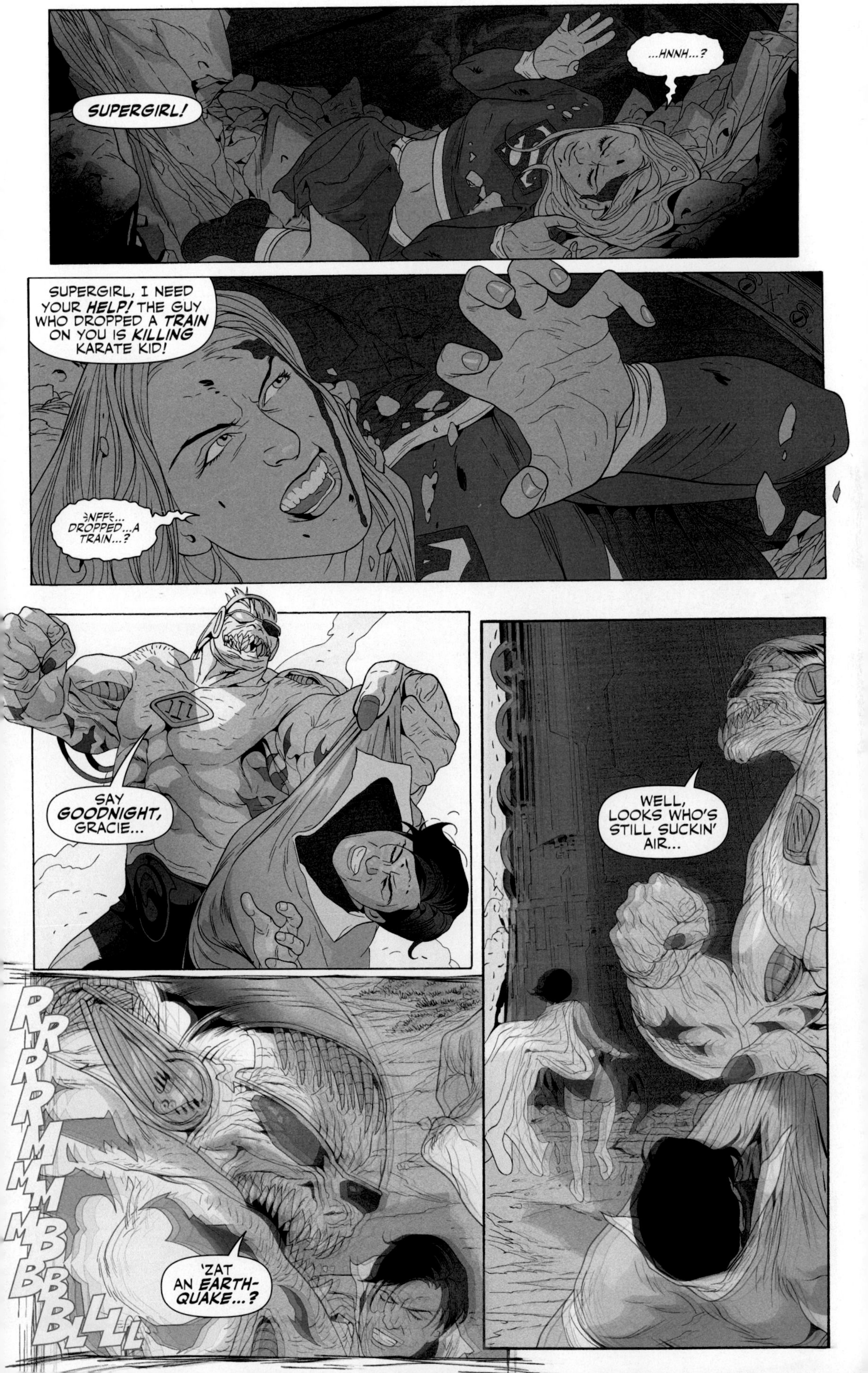
SUPERGIRL!
...HNNH...?
SUPERGIRL, I NEED YOUR HELP! THE GUY WHO DROPPED A TRAIN ON YOU IS KILLING KARATE KID!
NFF... DROPPED...A TRAIN...?
SAY GOODNIGHT, GRACIE...
WELL, LOOKS WHO'S STILL SUCKIN' AIR...
RRRRRMMMMBBBLLL
'ZAT AN EARTH-QUAKE...?

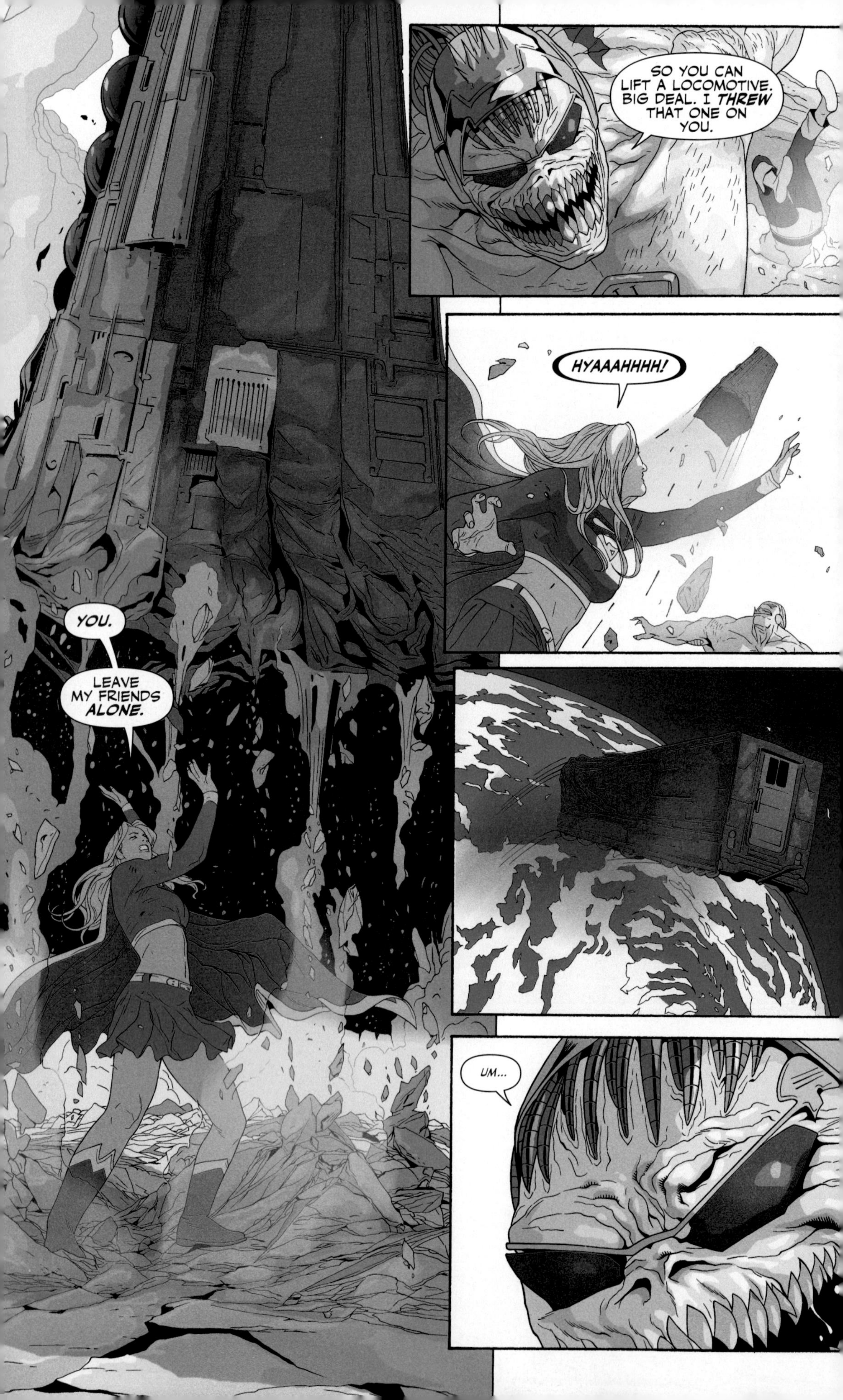
SO YOU CAN LIFT A LOCOMOTIVE. BIG DEAL. I THREW THAT ONE ON YOU.
YOU.
LEAVE MY FRIENDS ALONE.
HYAAAHHHH!
UM...

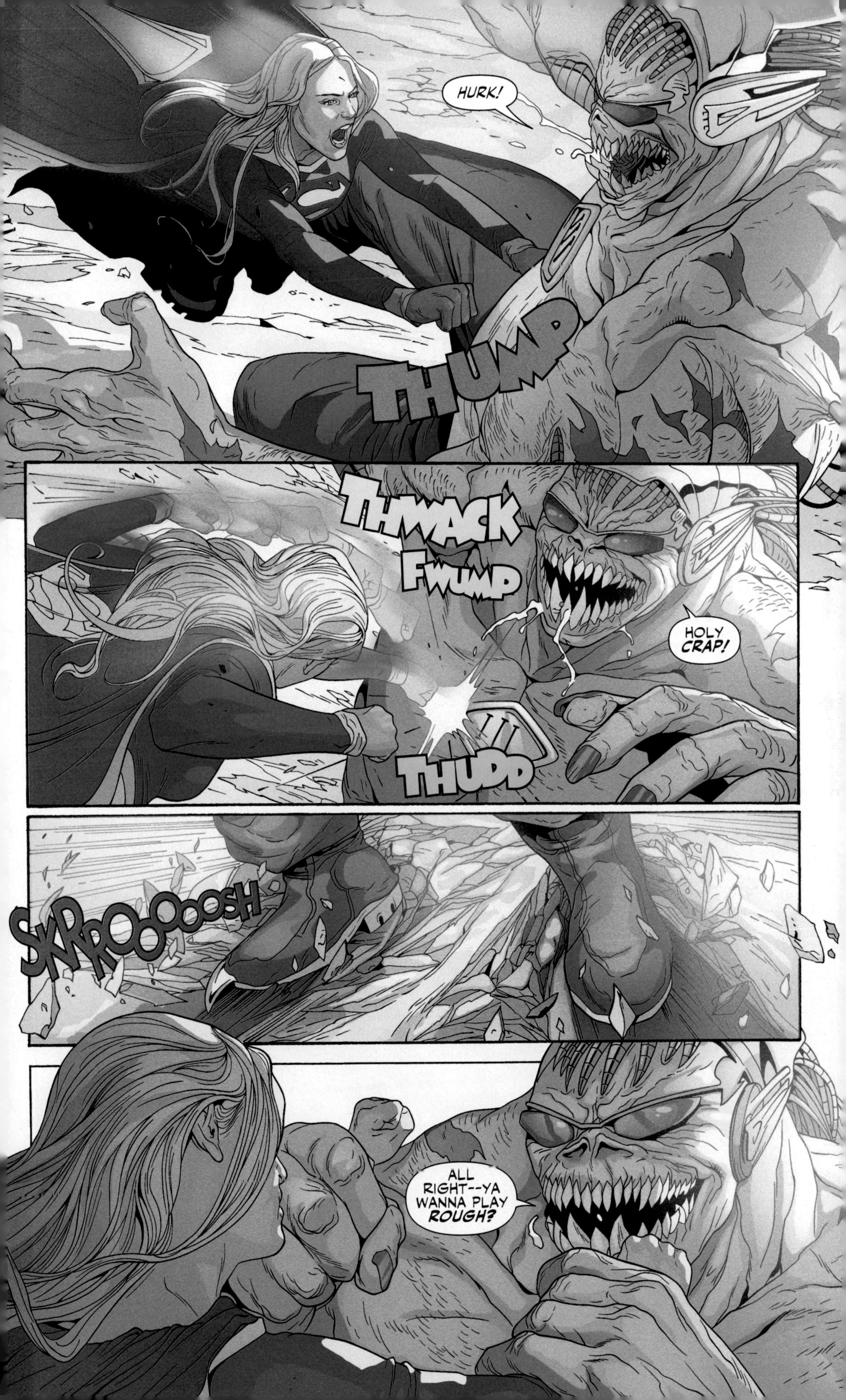
HURK!
THUMP
THWACK
FWUMP
HOLY CRAP!
THUDD
SKRROOOOOOSH
ALL RIGHT--YA WANNA PLAY ROUGH?

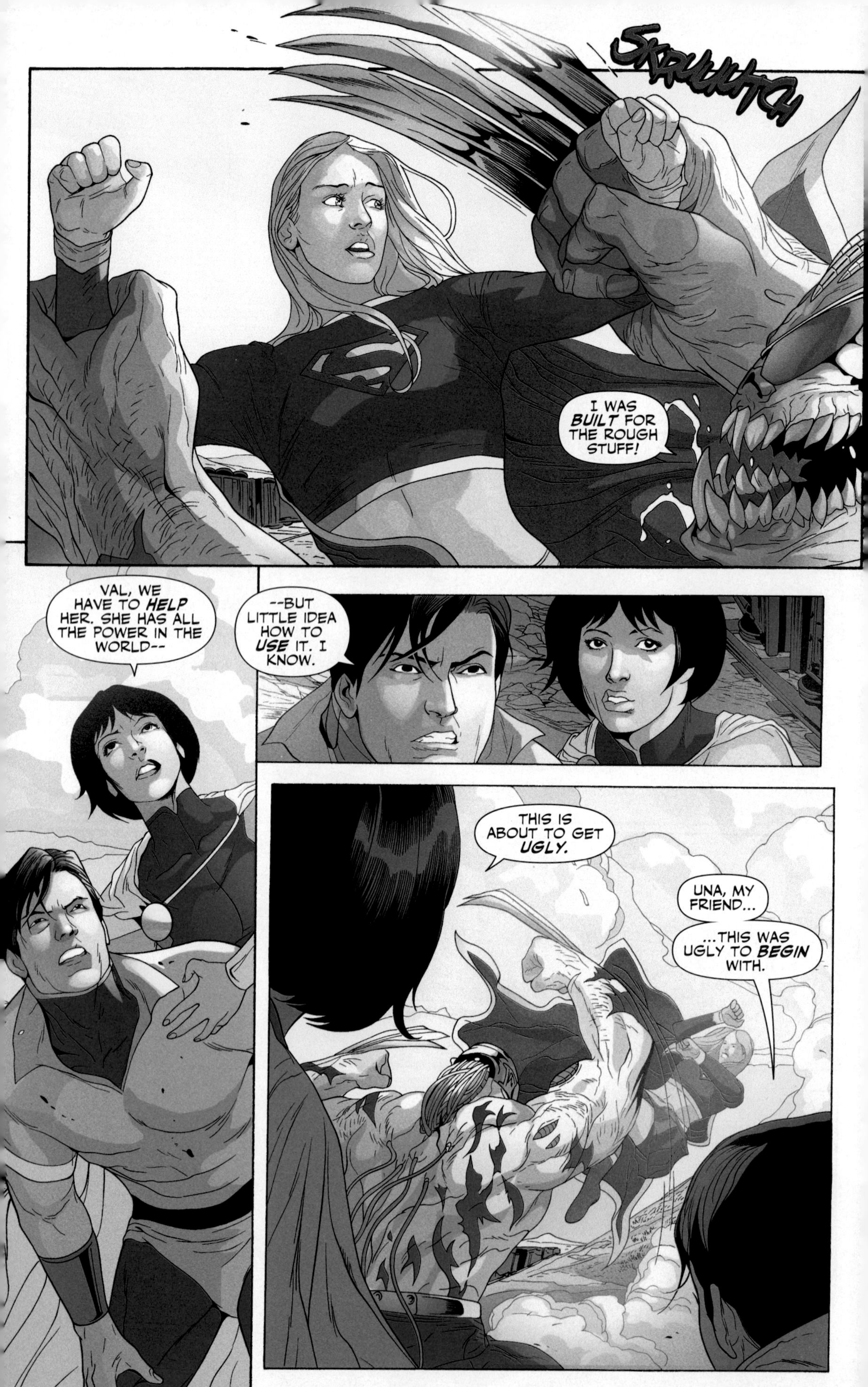
SKRUNCH
I WAS BUILT FOR THE ROUGH STUFF!
VAL, WE HAVE TO HELP HER. SHE HAS ALL THE POWER IN THE WORLD--
--BUT LITTLE IDEA HOW TO USE IT. I KNOW.
THIS IS ABOUT TO GET UGLY.
UNA, MY FRIEND...
...THIS WAS UGLY TO BEGIN WITH.

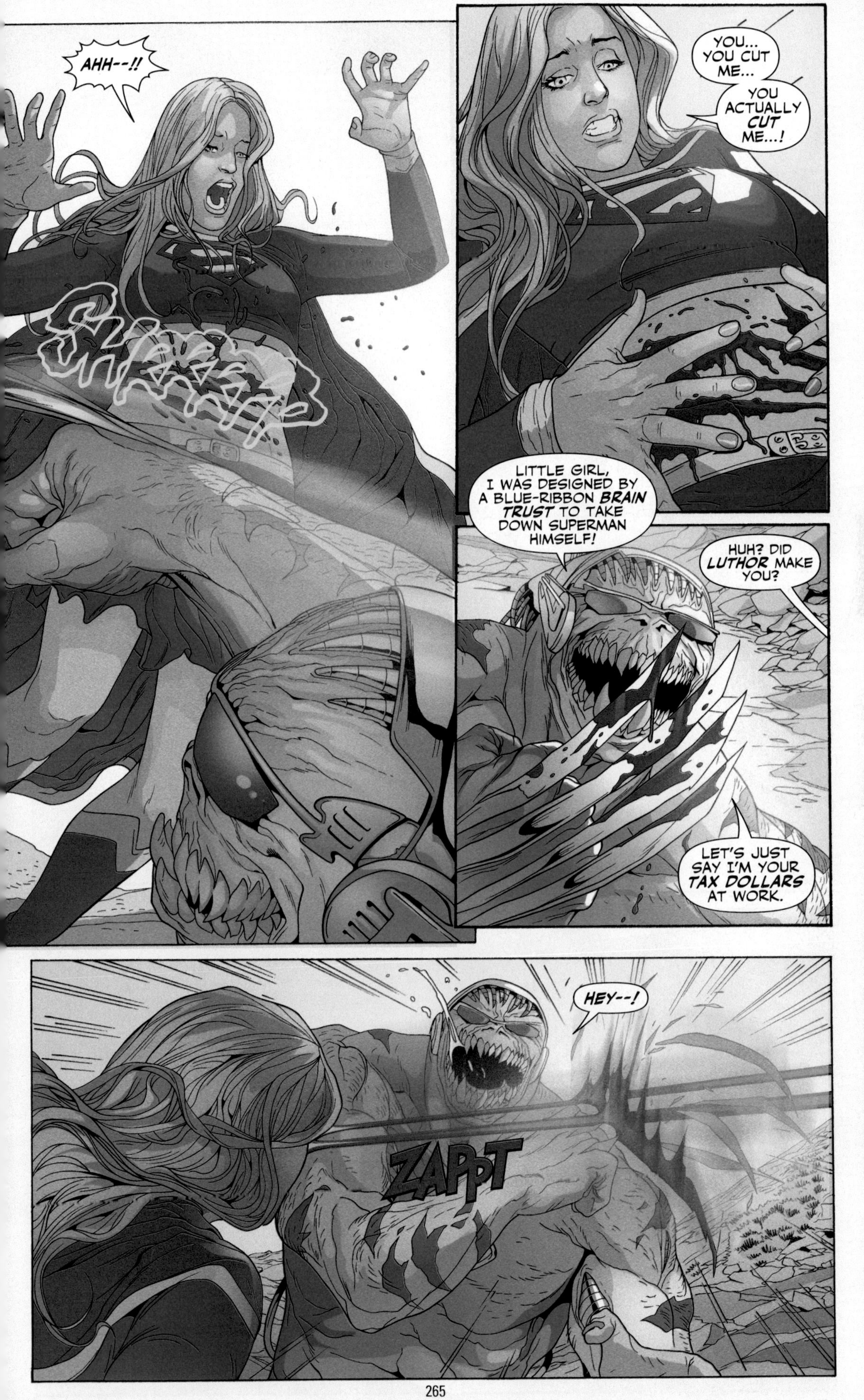

AHH--!!
SHRRAAK
YOU... YOU CUT ME...
YOU ACTUALLY CUT ME...!
LITTLE GIRL, I WAS DESIGNED BY A BLUE-RIBBON BRAIN TRUST TO TAKE DOWN SUPERMAN HIMSELF!
HUH? DID LUTHOR MAKE YOU?
LET'S JUST SAY I'M YOUR TAX DOLLARS AT WORK.
HEY--!
ZAPPT

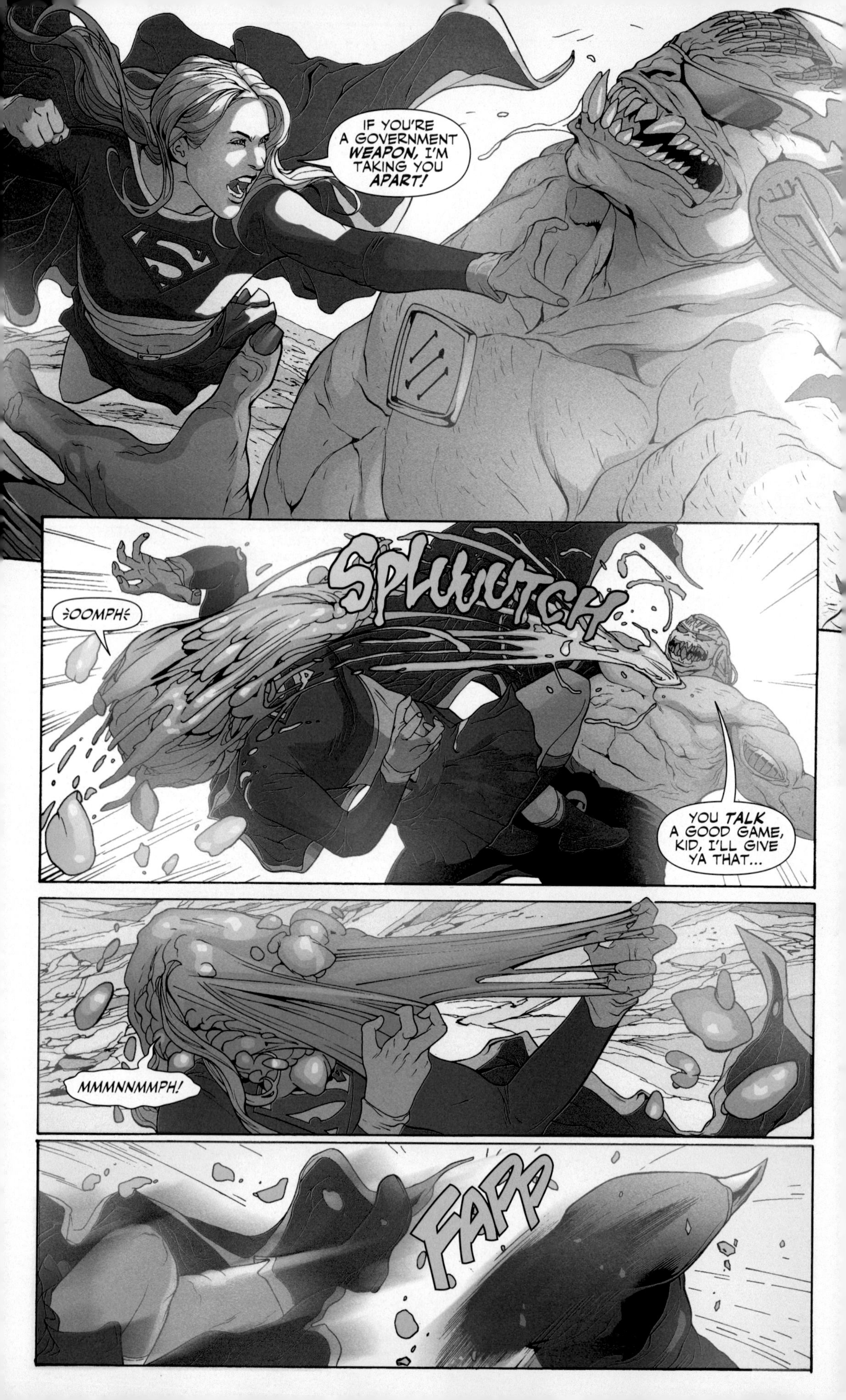
IF YOU'RE A GOVERNMENT WEAPON, I'M TAKING YOU APART!
SPLUUTCH
OOMPH
YOU TALK A GOOD GAME, KID, I'LL GIVE YA THAT...
MMMNNMMPH!
FAPP

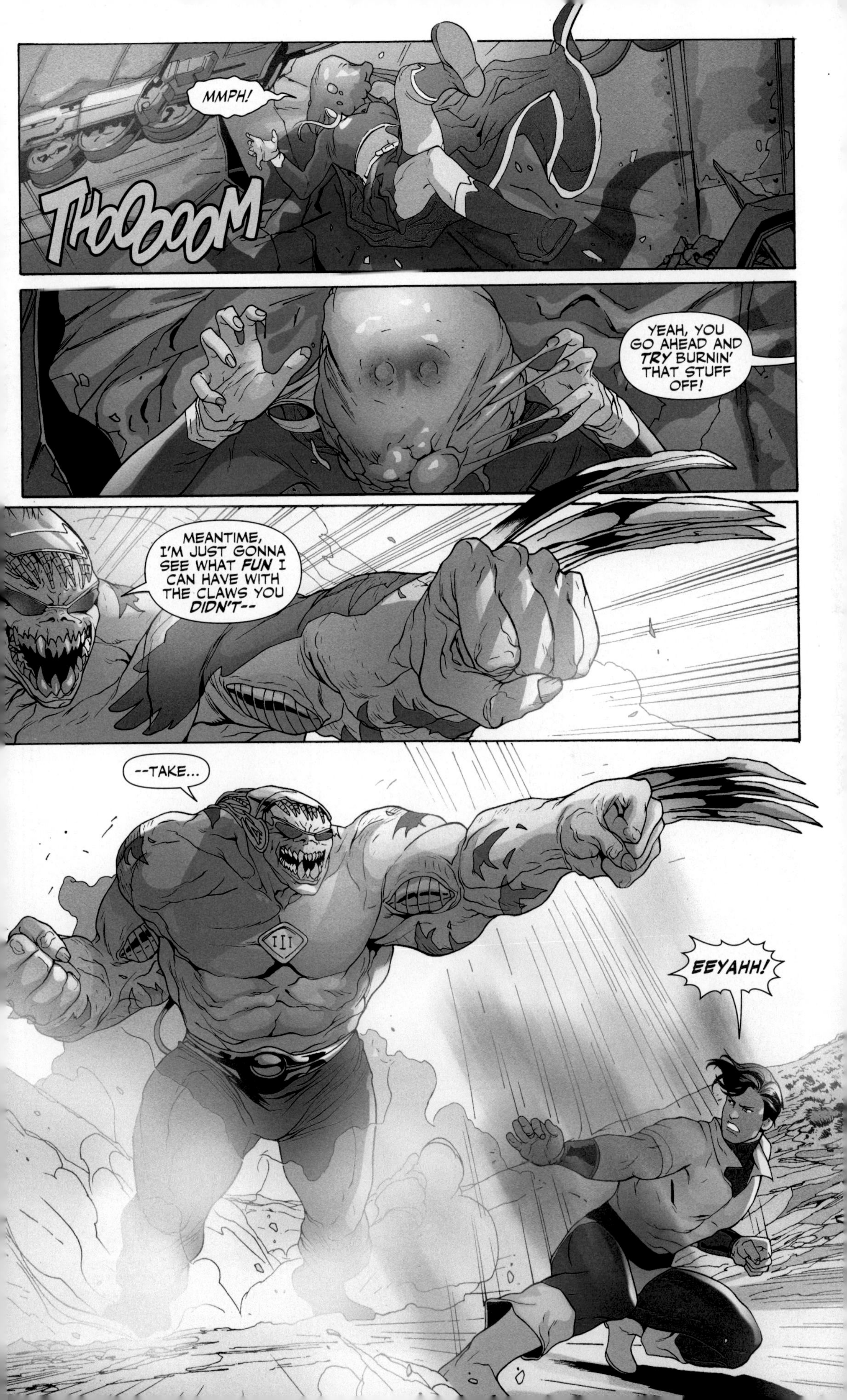
MMPH!
THOOOOOM
YEAH, YOU GO AHEAD AND TRY BURNIN' THAT STUFF OFF!
MEANTIME, I'M JUST GONNA SEE WHAT FUN I CAN HAVE WITH THE CLAWS YOU DIDN'T--
--TAKE...
EEYAHH!

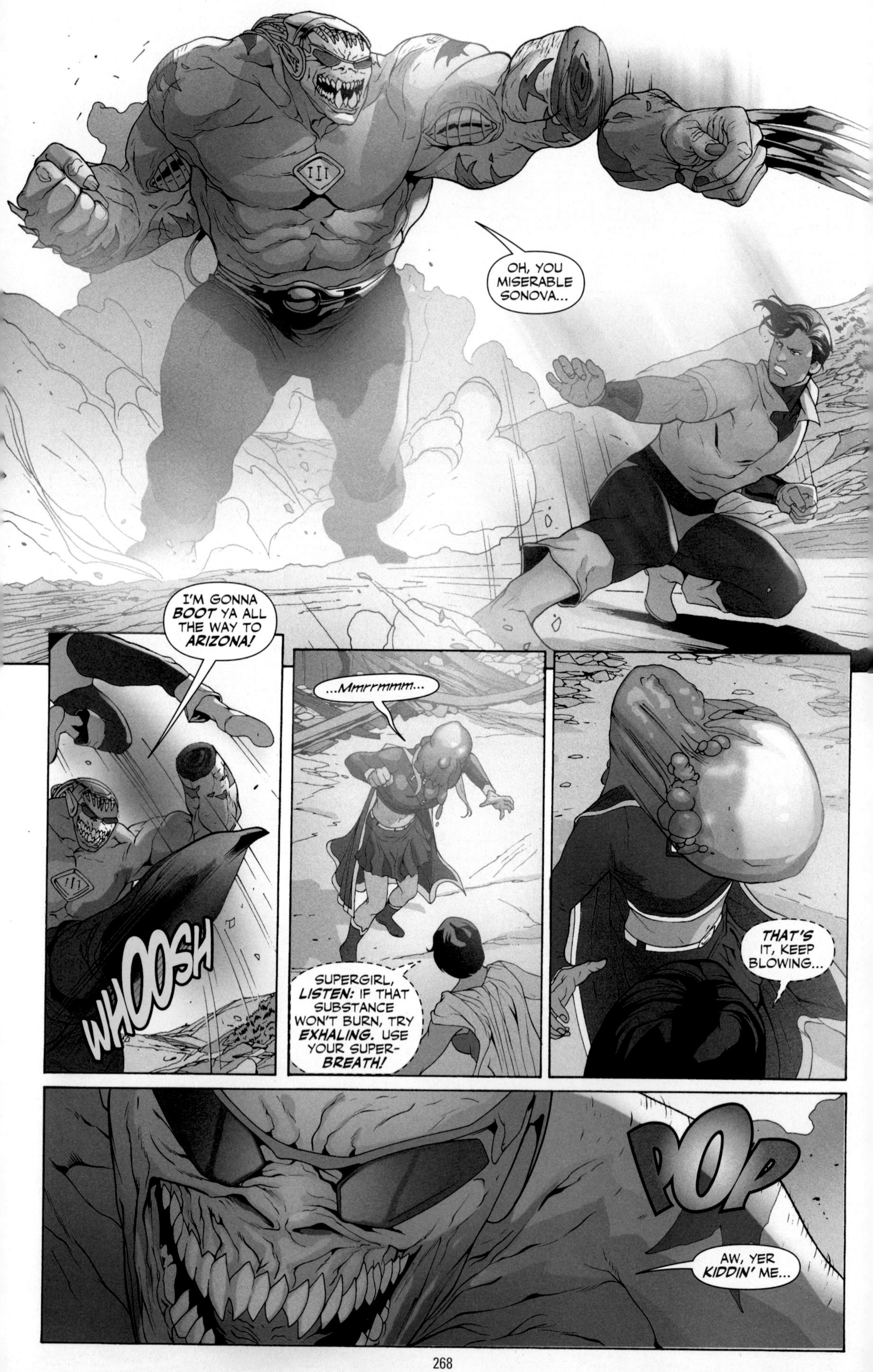
OH, YOU MISERABLE SONOVA...
I'M GONNA BOOT YA ALL THE WAY TO ARIZONA!
WHOOSH
...Mmrrmmm...
SUPERGIRL, LISTEN: IF THAT SUBSTANCE WON'T BURN, TRY EXHALING. USE YOUR SUPER-BREATH!
THAT'S IT, KEEP BLOWING...
POP
AW, YER KIDDIN' ME...

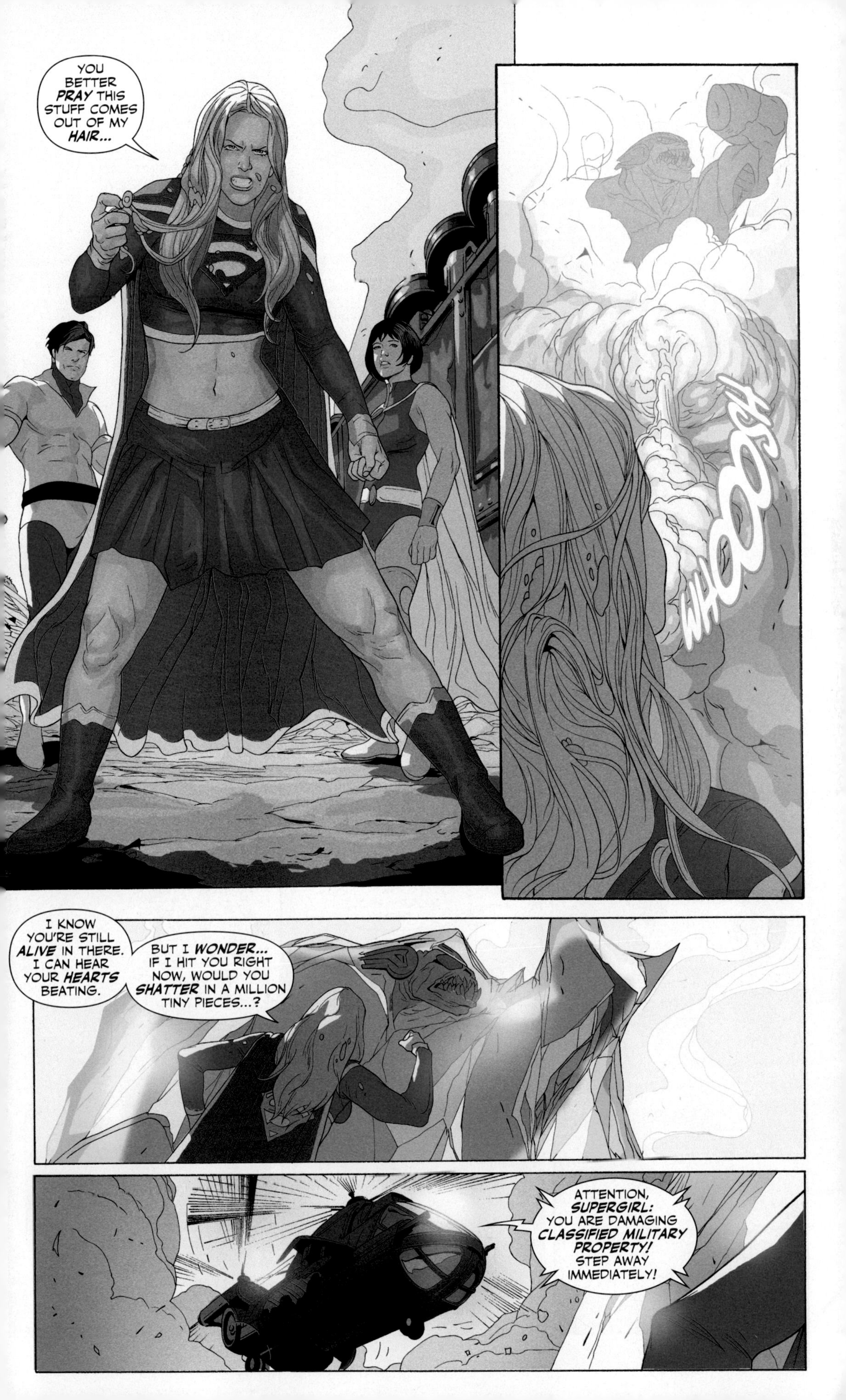
YOU BETTER PRAY THIS STUFF COMES OUT OF MY HAIR...
WHOOOSH
I KNOW YOU'RE STILL ALIVE IN THERE. I CAN HEAR YOUR HEARTS BEATING.
BUT I WONDER... IF I HIT YOU RIGHT NOW, WOULD YOU SHATTER IN A MILLION TINY PIECES...?
ATTENTION, SUPERGIRL: YOU ARE DAMAGING CLASSIFIED MILITARY PROPERTY! STEP AWAY IMMEDIATELY!

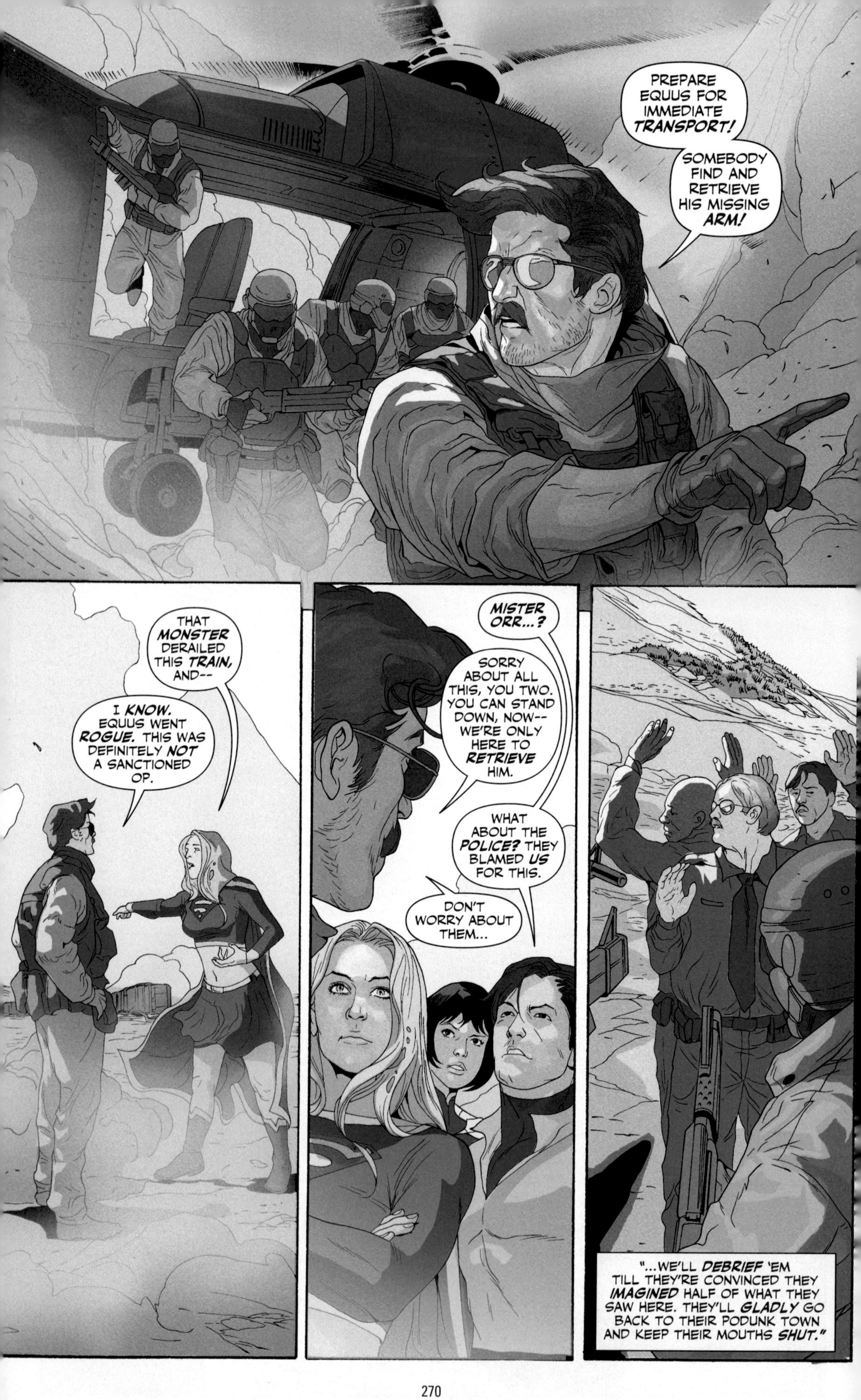
PREPARE EQUUS FOR IMMEDIATE TRANSPORT!
SOMEBODY FIND AND RETRIEVE HIS MISSING ARM!
THAT MONSTER DERAILED THIS TRAIN, AND--
I KNOW. EQUUS WENT ROGUE. THIS WAS DEFINITELY NOT A SANCTIONED OP.
MISTER ORR...?
SORRY ABOUT ALL THIS, YOU TWO. YOU CAN STAND DOWN, NOW-- WE'RE ONLY HERE TO RETRIEVE HIM.
WHAT ABOUT THE POLICE? THEY BLAMED US FOR THIS.
DON'T WORRY ABOUT THEM...
"...WE'LL DEBRIEF 'EM TILL THEY'RE CONVINCED THEY IMAGINED HALF OF WHAT THEY SAW HERE. THEY'LL GLADLY GO BACK TO THEIR PODUNK TOWN AND KEEP THEIR MOUTHS SHUT."

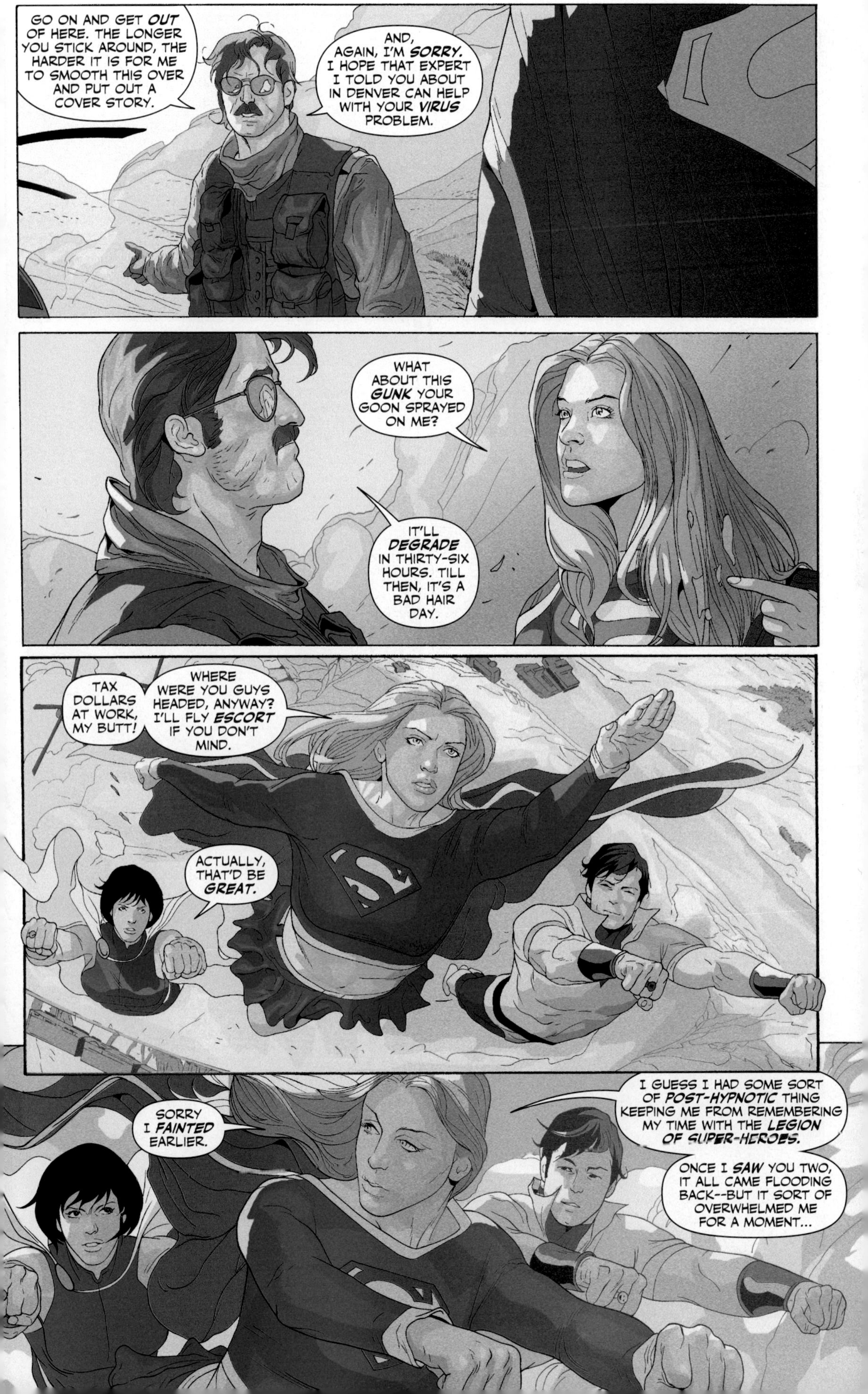
GO ON AND GET OUT OF HERE. THE LONGER YOU STICK AROUND, THE HARDER IT IS FOR ME TO SMOOTH THIS OVER AND PUT OUT A COVER STORY.
AND, AGAIN, I'M SORRY. I HOPE THAT EXPERT I TOLD YOU ABOUT IN DENVER CAN HELP WITH YOUR VIRUS PROBLEM.
WHAT ABOUT THIS GUNK YOUR GOON SPRAYED ON ME?
IT'LL DEGRADE IN THIRTY-SIX HOURS. TILL THEN, IT'S A BAD HAIR DAY.
TAX DOLLARS AT WORK, MY BUTT!
WHERE WERE YOU GUYS HEADED, ANYWAY? I'LL FLY ESCORT IF YOU DON'T MIND.
ACTUALLY, THAT'D BE GREAT.
SORRY I FAINTED EARLIER.
I GUESS I HAD SOME SORT OF POST-HYPNOTIC THING KEEPING ME FROM REMEMBERING MY TIME WITH THE LEGION OF SUPER-HEROES.
ONCE I SAW YOU TWO, IT ALL CAME FLOODING BACK--BUT IT SORT OF OVERWHELMED ME FOR A MOMENT...

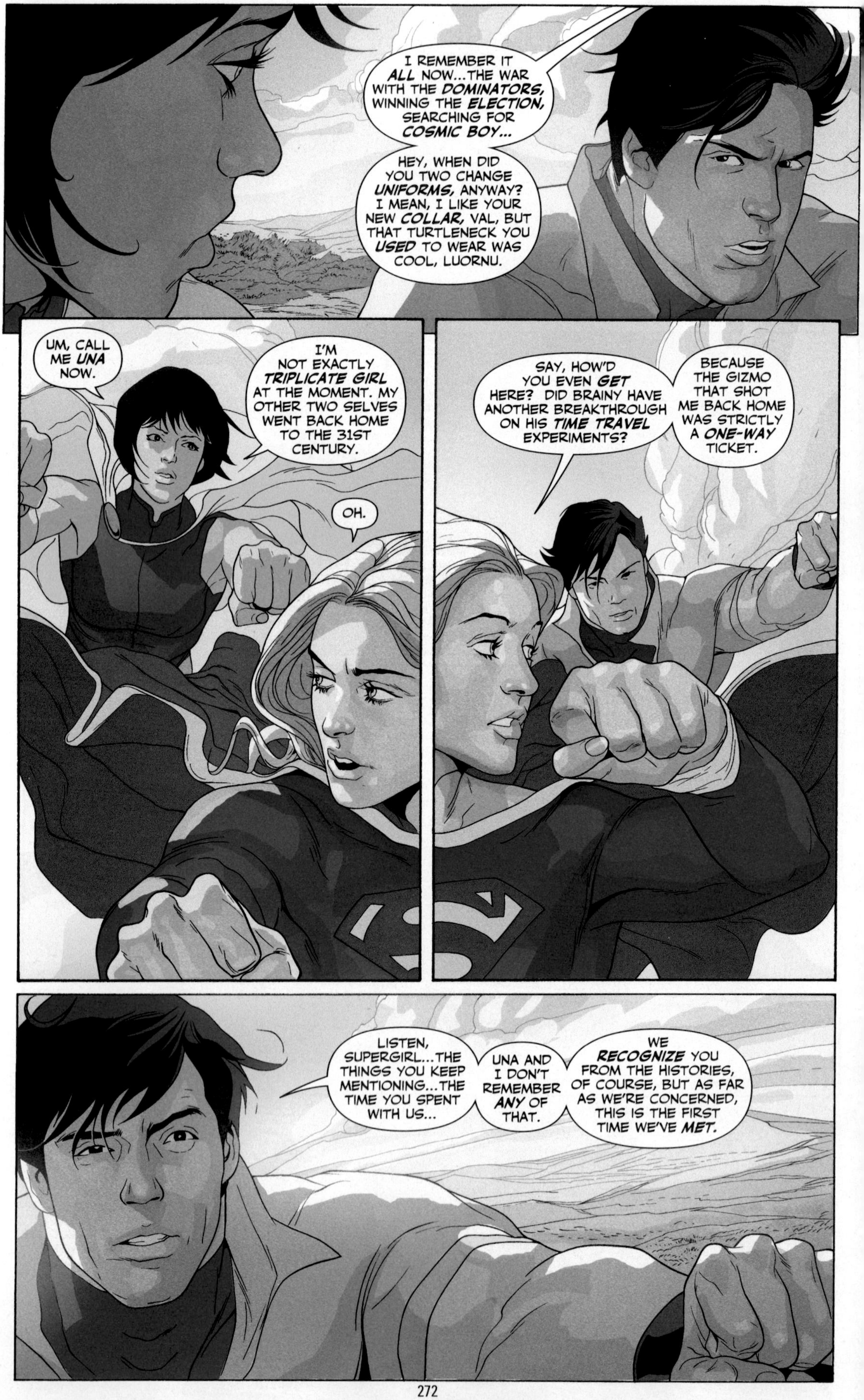
I REMEMBER IT ALL NOW...THE WAR WITH THE DOMINATORS, WINNING THE ELECTION, SEARCHING FOR COSMIC BOY...
HEY, WHEN DID YOU TWO CHANGE UNIFORMS, ANYWAY? I MEAN, I LIKE YOUR NEW COLLAR, VAL, BUT THAT TURTLENECK YOU USED TO WEAR WAS COOL, LUORNU.
UM, CALL ME UNA NOW.
I'M NOT EXACTLY TRIPLICATE GIRL AT THE MOMENT. MY OTHER TWO SELVES WENT BACK HOME TO THE 31ST CENTURY.
OH.
SAY, HOW'D YOU EVEN GET HERE? DID BRAINY HAVE ANOTHER BREAKTHROUGH ON HIS TIME TRAVEL EXPERIMENTS?
BECAUSE THE GIZMO THAT SHOT ME BACK HOME WAS STRICTLY A ONE-WAY TICKET.
LISTEN, SUPERGIRL...THE THINGS YOU KEEP MENTIONING...THE TIME YOU SPENT WITH US...
UNA AND I DON'T REMEMBER ANY OF THAT.
WE RECOGNIZE YOU FROM THE HISTORIES, OF COURSE, BUT AS FAR AS WE'RE CONCERNED, THIS IS THE FIRST TIME WE'VE MET.

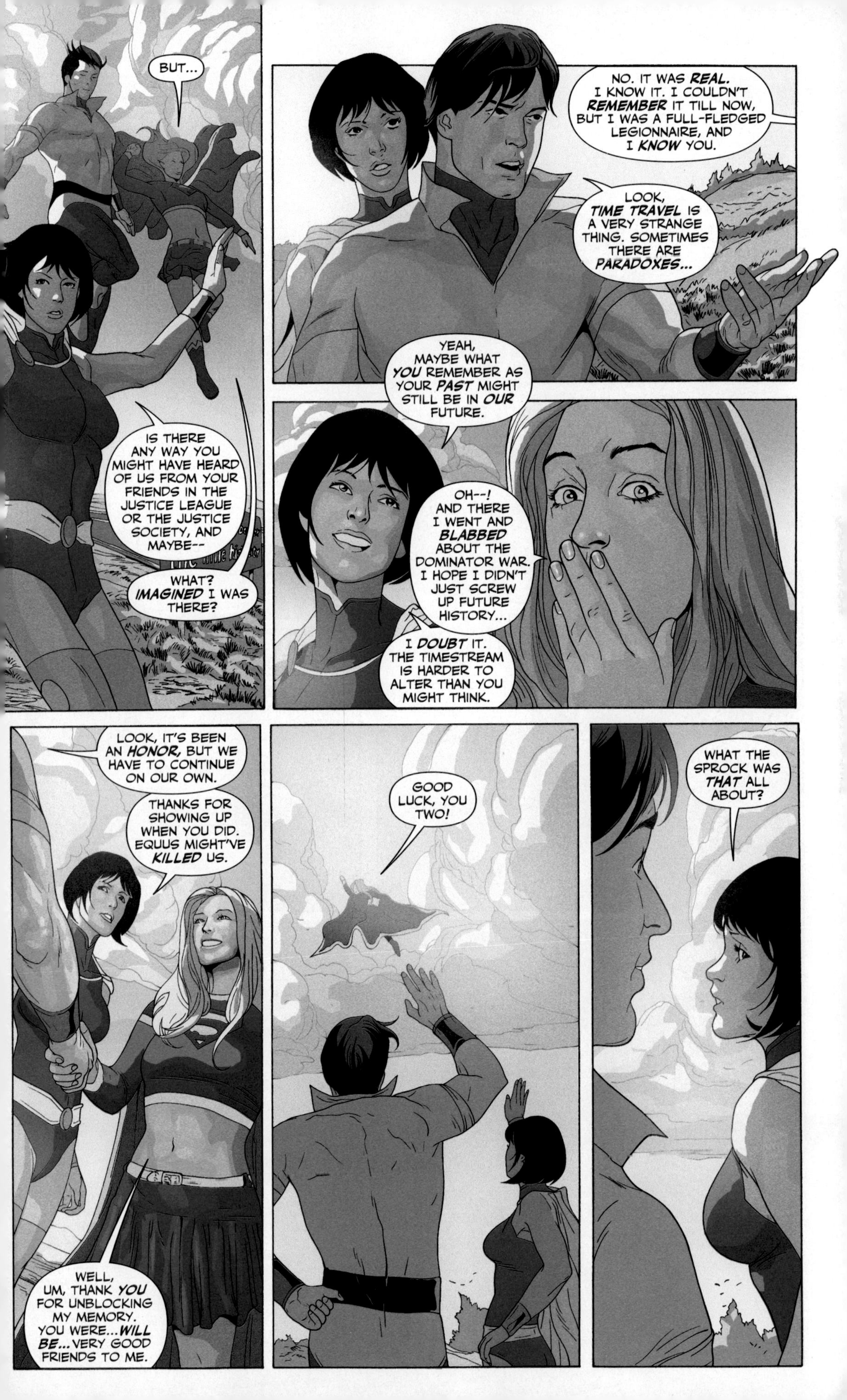
BUT...
NO. IT WAS REAL. I KNOW IT. I COULDN'T REMEMBER IT TILL NOW, BUT I WAS A FULL-FLEDGED LEGIONNAIRE, AND I KNOW YOU.
LOOK, TIME TRAVEL IS A VERY STRANGE THING. SOMETIMES THERE ARE PARADOXES...
IS THERE ANY WAY YOU MIGHT HAVE HEARD OF US FROM YOUR FRIENDS IN THE JUSTICE LEAGUE OR THE JUSTICE SOCIETY, AND MAYBE--
WHAT? IMAGINED I WAS THERE?
YEAH, MAYBE WHAT YOU REMEMBER AS YOUR PAST MIGHT STILL BE IN OUR FUTURE.
OH--! AND THERE I WENT AND BLABBED ABOUT THE DOMINATOR WAR. I HOPE I DIDN'T JUST SCREW UP FUTURE HISTORY...
I DOUBT IT. THE TIMESTREAM IS HARDER TO ALTER THAN YOU MIGHT THINK.
LOOK, IT'S BEEN AN HONOR, BUT WE HAVE TO CONTINUE ON OUR OWN.
THANKS FOR SHOWING UP WHEN YOU DID. EQUUS MIGHT'VE KILLED US.
WELL, UM, THANK YOU FOR UNBLOCKING MY MEMORY. YOU WERE...WILL BE...VERY GOOD FRIENDS TO ME.
GOOD LUCK, YOU TWO!
WHAT THE SPROCK WAS THAT ALL ABOUT?

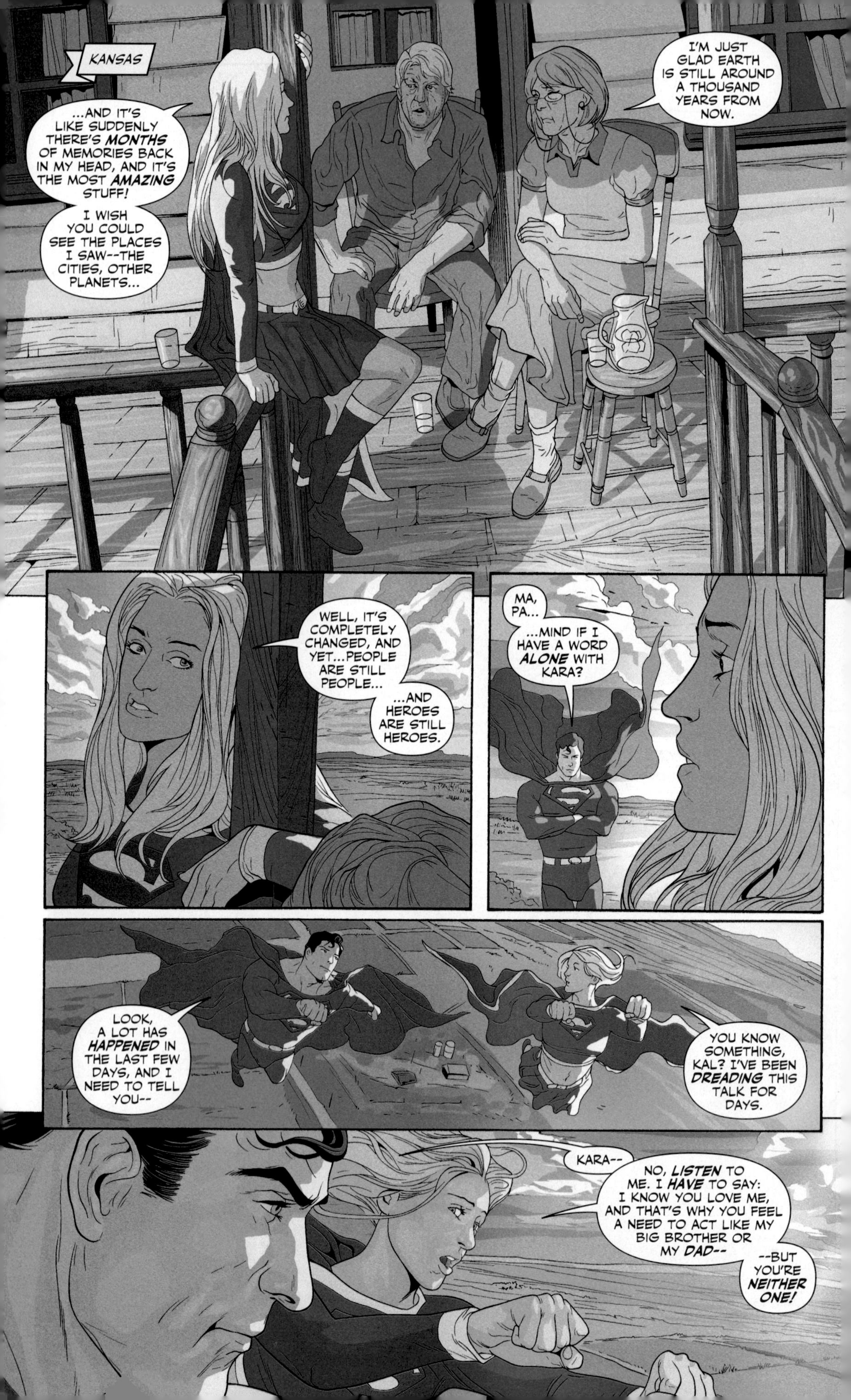
KANSAS
...AND IT'S LIKE SUDDENLY THERE'S MONTHS OF MEMORIES BACK IN MY HEAD, AND IT'S THE MOST AMAZING STUFF!
I WISH YOU COULD SEE THE PLACES I SAW--THE CITIES, OTHER PLANETS...
I'M JUST GLAD EARTH IS STILL AROUND A THOUSAND YEARS FROM NOW.
WELL, IT'S COMPLETELY CHANGED, AND YET...PEOPLE ARE STILL PEOPLE...
...AND HEROES ARE STILL HEROES.
MA, PA...
...MIND IF I HAVE A WORD ALONE WITH KARA?
LOOK, A LOT HAS HAPPENED IN THE LAST FEW DAYS, AND I NEED TO TELL YOU--
YOU KNOW SOMETHING, KAL? I'VE BEEN DREADING THIS TALK FOR DAYS.
KARA--
NO, LISTEN TO ME. I HAVE TO SAY: I KNOW YOU LOVE ME, AND THAT'S WHY YOU FEEL A NEED TO ACT LIKE MY BIG BROTHER OR MY DAD--
--BUT YOU'RE NEITHER ONE!

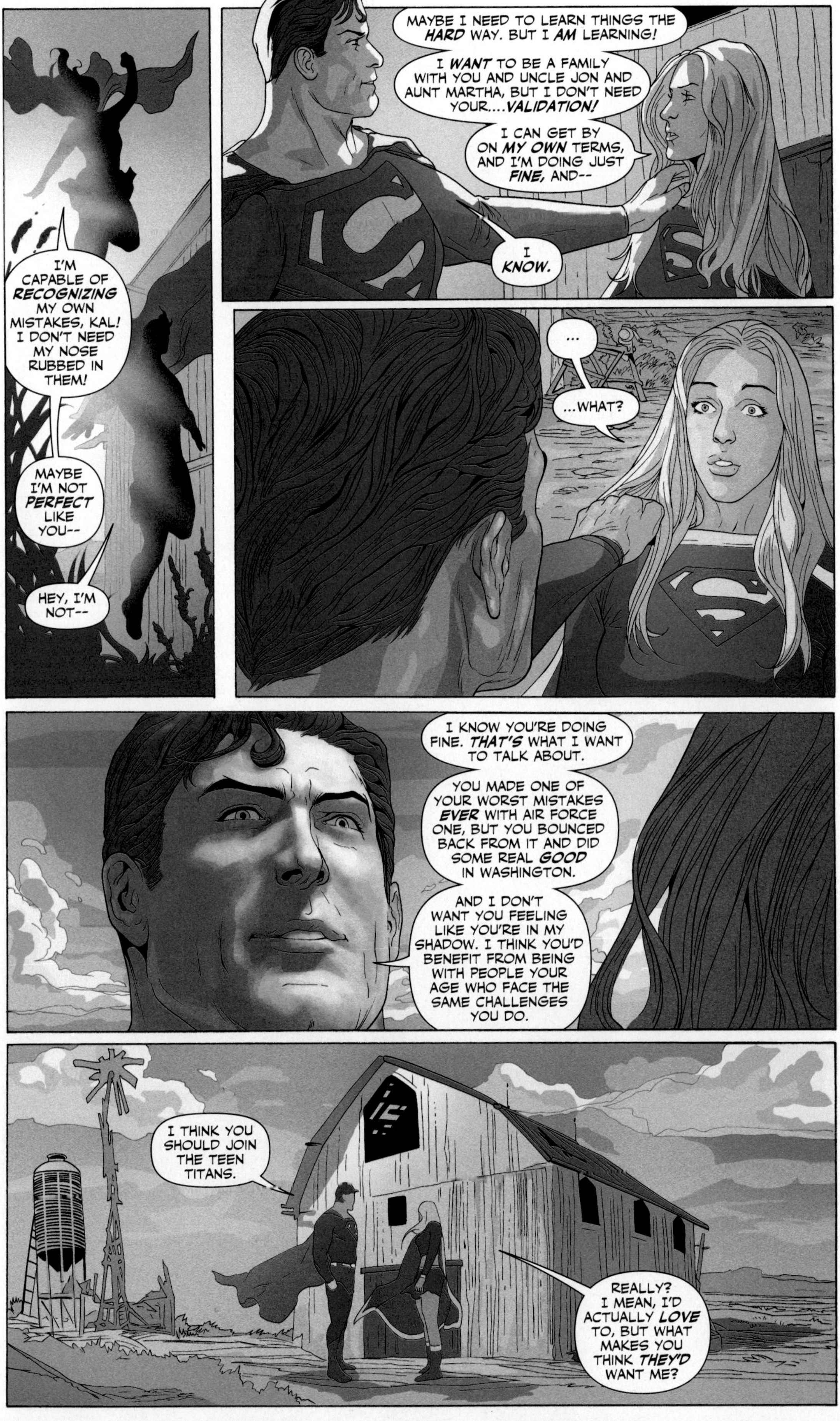
I'M CAPABLE OF *RECOGNIZING* MY OWN MISTAKES, KAL! I DON'T NEED MY NOSE RUBBED IN THEM!
MAYBE I'M NOT *PERFECT* LIKE YOU--
HEY, I'M NOT--
MAYBE I NEED TO LEARN THINGS THE *HARD* WAY. BUT I *AM* LEARNING!
I *WANT* TO BE A FAMILY WITH YOU AND UNCLE JON AND AUNT MARTHA, BUT I DON'T NEED YOUR....*VALIDATION!*
I CAN GET BY ON *MY OWN* TERMS, AND I'M DOING JUST *FINE,* AND--
I *KNOW.*
...
...WHAT?
I KNOW YOU'RE DOING FINE. *THAT'S* WHAT I WANT TO TALK ABOUT.
YOU MADE ONE OF YOUR WORST MISTAKES *EVER* WITH AIR FORCE ONE, BUT YOU BOUNCED BACK FROM IT AND DID SOME REAL *GOOD* IN WASHINGTON.
AND I DON'T WANT YOU FEELING LIKE YOU'RE IN MY SHADOW. I THINK YOU'D BENEFIT FROM BEING WITH PEOPLE YOUR AGE WHO FACE THE SAME CHALLENGES YOU DO.
I THINK YOU SHOULD JOIN THE TEEN TITANS.
REALLY? I MEAN, I'D ACTUALLY *LOVE* TO, BUT WHAT MAKES YOU THINK *THEY'D* WANT ME?

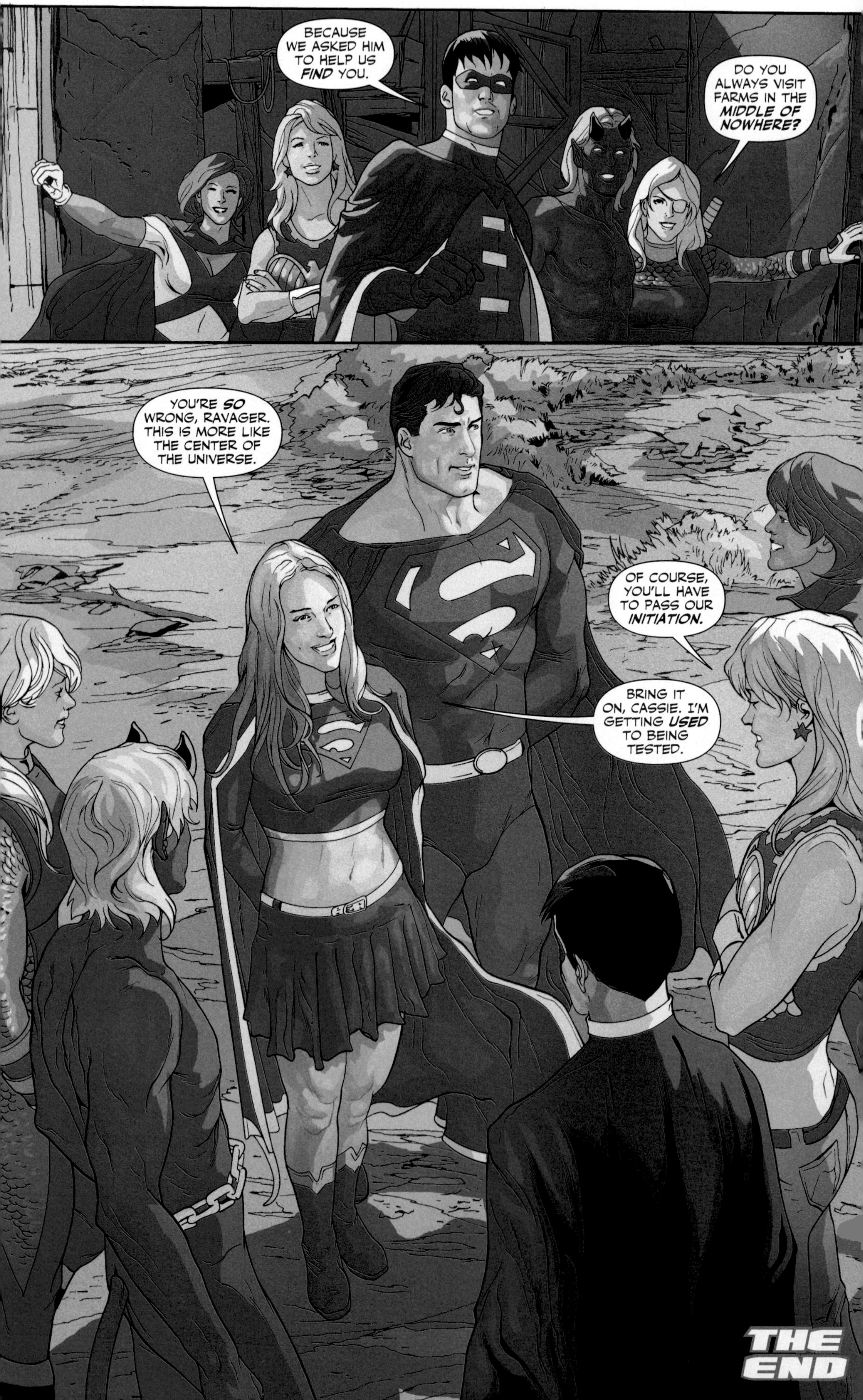
BECAUSE WE ASKED HIM TO HELP US FIND YOU.
DO YOU ALWAYS VISIT FARMS IN THE MIDDLE OF NOWHERE?
YOU'RE SO WRONG, RAVAGER. THIS IS MORE LIKE THE CENTER OF THE UNIVERSE.
OF COURSE, YOU'LL HAVE TO PASS OUR INITIATION.
BRING IT ON, CASSIE. I'M GETTING USED TO BEING TESTED.
THE END

"Clear storytelling at its best. It's an intriguing concept and easy to grasp."—THE NEW YORK TIMES

"Azzarello is rebuilding the mythology of Wonder Woman." —CRAVE ONLINE

START AT THE BEGINNING!

WONDER WOMAN VOLUME 1: BLOOD

WONDER WOMAN VOL. 2: GUTS

by BRIAN AZZARELLO and CLIFF CHIANG

WONDER WOMAN VOL. 3: IRON

by BRIAN AZZARELLO and CLIFF CHIANG

SUPERGIRL VOL. 1: LAST DAUGHTER OF KRYPTON

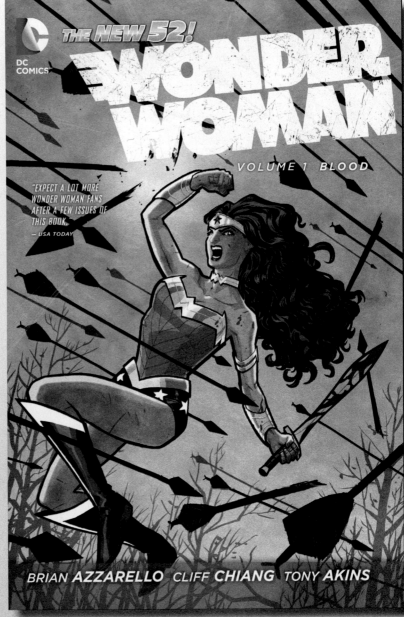

DC COMICS™

"Simone and artist Ardian Syaf not only do justice to Babs' legacy, but build in a new complexity that is the starting point for a future full of new storytelling possibilities. A hell of a ride."—IGN

START AT THE BEGINNING!

BATGIRL

VOLUME 1: THE DARKEST REFLECTION

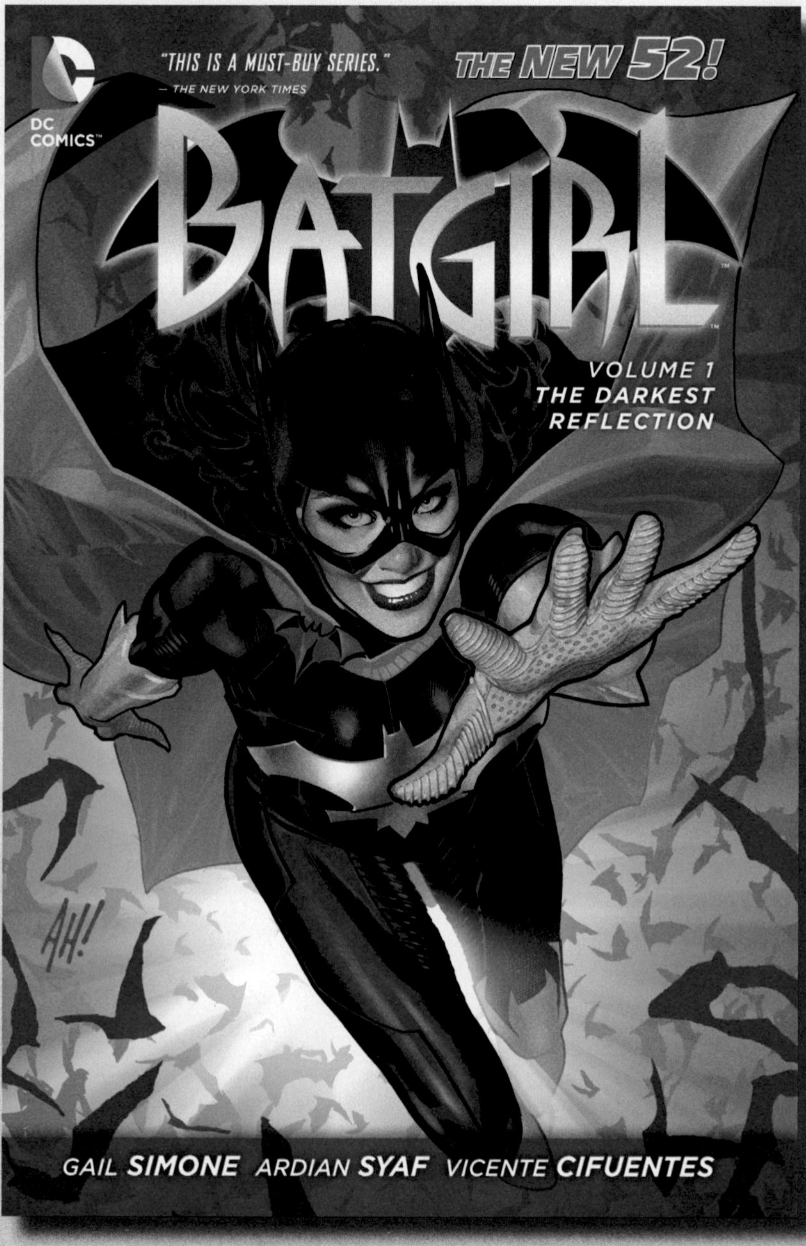
DC COMICS™
"THIS IS A MUST-BUY SERIES."
— THE NEW YORK TIMES
THE NEW 52!
BATGIRL
VOLUME 1
THE DARKEST
REFLECTION
GAIL SIMONE ARDIAN SYAF VICENTE CIFUENTES

BATGIRL VOL. 2: KNIGHTFALL DESCENDS

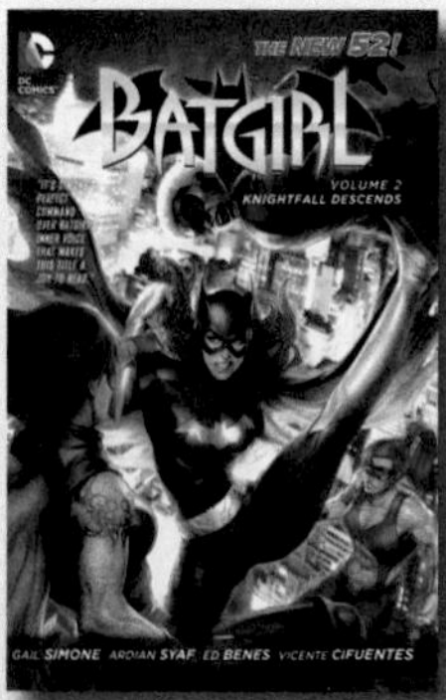
THE NEW 52!
BATGIRL
VOLUME 2
KNIGHTFALL DESCENDS
GAIL SIMONE ARDIAN SYAF ED BENES VICENTE CIFUENTES

BATGIRL VOL. 3: DEATH OF THE FAMILY

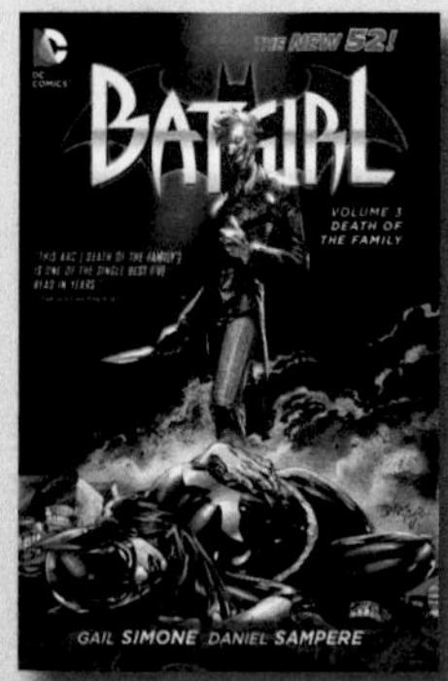
THE NEW 52!
BATGIRL
VOLUME 3
DEATH OF THE FAMILY
GAIL SIMONE DANIEL SAMPERE

BATWOMAN VOL. 1: HYDROLOGY

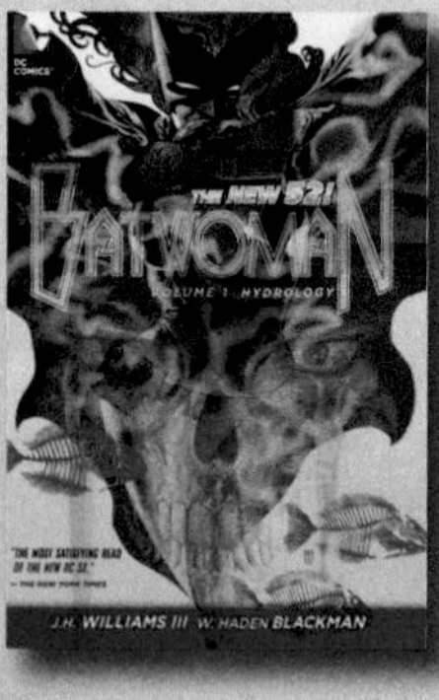
THE NEW 52!
BATWOMAN
VOLUME 1 HYDROLOGY
J.H. WILLIAMS III W. HADEN BLACKMAN

FROM THE PAGES OF *BATMAN*

CATWOMAN VOL. 1: TRAIL OF THE CATWOMAN

ED BRUBAKER & DARWYN COOKE

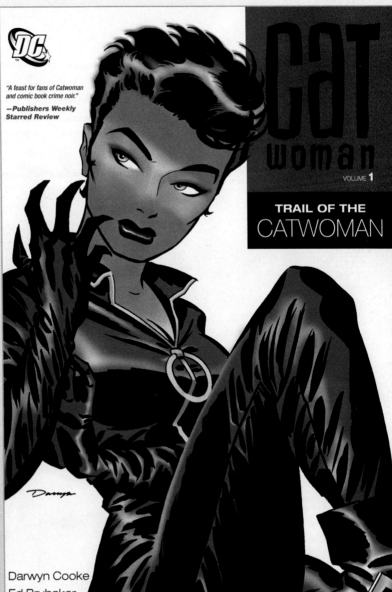

"A feast for fans of Catwoman and comic book crime noir."
—*Publishers Weekly* Starred Review

CAT woman
VOLUME 1

TRAIL OF THE CATWOMAN

Darwyn Cooke
Ed Brubaker

DC COMICS™

START AT THE BEGINNING!

TEEN TITANS
VOLUME 1: IT'S OUR RIGHT TO FIGHT

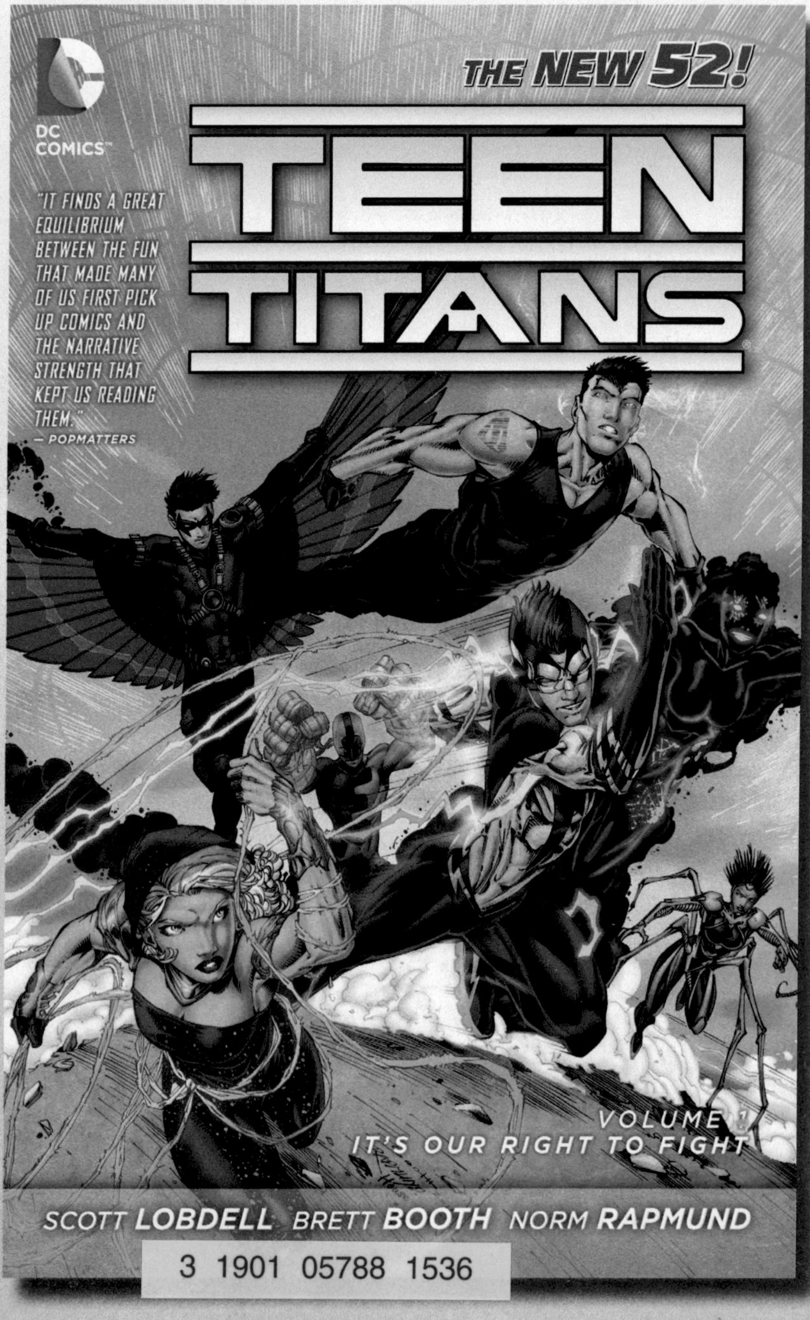

**TEEN TITANS
VOL. 2: THE CULLING**

**TEEN TITANS VOL. 3:
DEATH OF THE FAMILY**

**THE CULLING: RISE OF
THE RAVAGERS**

THE NEW 52!

DC COMICS™

TEEN TITANS

"IT FINDS A GREAT EQUILIBRIUM BETWEEN THE FUN THAT MADE MANY OF US FIRST PICK UP COMICS AND THE NARRATIVE STRENGTH THAT KEPT US READING THEM."
— POPMATTERS

VOLUME 1
IT'S OUR RIGHT TO FIGHT

SCOTT **LOBDELL** BRETT **BOOTH** NORM **RAPMUND**

3 1901 05788 1536